1989

A Resource Book
for Remediating
Common Behavior and
Learning Problems

A Resource Book for Remediating Common Behavior and Learning Problems

Thomas McIntyre

Allyn and Bacon
Boston London Sydney Toronto

Copyright © 1989 by Allyn and Bacon
A Division of Simon & Schuster
160 Gould Street
Needham Heights, Massachusetts 02194

Library of Congress Cataloging-in-Publication Data

McIntyre, Thomas, 1952–
    A resource book for remediating common behavior and learning
    problems / Thomas McIntyre.
        p.   cm.
    Bibliography: p.
    ISBN 0–205–11707–4
        1. Problem children—Education—United States—Handbooks, manuals,
etc. 2. Learning disabled children—Education—United States—
—Handbooks, manuals, etc. 3. Behavior modification—United States—
—Handbooks, manuals, etc. I. Title.
LC4802.M36 1989
371.93—dc19   88–15527
                                                                            CIP

Printed in the United States of America
10 9 8 7 6 5 4 3 2 1 92 91 90 89 88

To America's teachers,
who, under great constraints,
continue to educate and enlighten our youth

Contents

Preface

"That kid is driving me crazy. What do I do with him?" That's a question one teacher often asks another. Perhaps you've felt this way about specific irritating, disruptive, or dangerous behaviors displayed by your students. You may have implemented one or more of the comprehensive and systematic behavior management approaches that are presented in the companion edition to this book, *The Behavior Management Handbook: Setting Up Effective Behavior Management Systems.* However, while those comprehensive plans of action are effective in helping you establish and maintain a smoother running, more disciplined classroom, they may not address specific problem behaviors possessed by certain students. You know that someone else must have dealt with this behavior before, but who? You know that something must be written somewhere that addresses this behavior, but where? Where can you find practical, workable ideas? This book was developed to provide the answers. It lists between 10 and 100 effective interventions for each of 350 different behavior and learning problems. It is designed to be a resource guide for those who work with students displaying learning/behav-

ior disabilities. It can also be a valuable tool for administrators, parents, consultants, psychologists, social workers, and other school support personnel. School libraries might retain a copy of this book for reference by teachers.

This volume contains an immense amount of useful ideas based on research and practice. You will find it to be useful in the remediation of learning and behavior problems.

For ease in reading, and due to the overwhelming prevalence of males exhibiting emotional/behavioral difficulties, we have chosen to refer to the student as being male. Sometimes, however, we refer to a female student when conditions that pertain predominantly to females are discussed.

Acknowledgments

My sincerest thanks are extended to my former students who contributed to this volume by researching the available literature and providing their ideas and those of practicing teachers. Thanks also to Karol Cowell and Dr. Richard Schwab for their support and critique of this book.

SECTION ONE

Introduction

1

How to Use This Book

A Resource Book for Remediating Common Behavior and Learning Problems is a collection of ideas intended to provide you with strategies that are effective in dealing with any of 350 different behaviors often exhibited by students with behavior problems or learning difficulties. These behaviors were chosen from various behavior checklists which are used to assist in the identification of pupils with behavioral/emotional difficulties. The purpose of this introduction is to extend the usefulness of the published checklists by providing you with interventions for the behaviors of concern. For each listed behavior, there are between 10 and 100 ideas for intervention that were gleaned from relevant research and the experiences of teachers and education majors. The source for each intervention strategy is listed following that idea. If you wish to obtain more information regarding the strategies, the research references are listed in the Appendix. Those without an indicated source are the ideas of the author.

The ideas presented for each behavior are *not* listed in a hierarchical or preferential order. Due to variances in student skills, needs, and characteristics, teacher abilities and philoso-

phy, the available resources of the school, and the input and cooperativeness of the parents, what is preferred in one setting may be inappropriate in another milieu. There is no one correct intervention for remediating an undesired behavior.

As you survey the various ideas, it is important to keep in mind certain precautions. Some remedial practices are not appropriate for use by teachers. However, you are certainly within your rights to request that other specialists consider the use of a certain technique. For those techniques that do apply to teachers, be sure to use the least punitive and least restrictive interventions before attempting those that are more severe in nature. Be sure that less intensive measures have been used in a consistent manner before implementing unusual procedures. And last, weigh moral, legal, and ethical considerations and, if necessary, gain parental or administrative permission before implementing an approach.

As you read through this book, consider the use of variations of these ideas. Perhaps an idea that at first appears as if it might be ineffective with your student could become a useful procedure with a few modifications. Additionally, remember to consider the ideas listed in *The Behavior Management Handbook: Setting Up Effective Behavior Management Systems* (Allyn and Bacon, 1989) as they are effective in reducing a wide variety of aberrant behaviors.

Steps in How to Use This Book

1. Find the behavior of concern in the Main Index. If you have identified various misbehaviors through the use of one of the published behavior checklists, you will find cross references for sixteen of these following the Main Index.
2. Turn to the strategy sheet listed in front of the behavior of concern. If you used a published behavior checklist, turn to the cross reference for that checklist, find the number that you marked on that checklist, and turn to the strategy sheet listed after that number.
3. Review the ideas on the strategy sheet. Think of variations of these ideas that might also be useful.
4. Choose an idea for implementation with the student. Consider moral, ethical, and legal issues before implementation. Obtain any necessary permission from the parents or administration.
5. Implement the strategy and monitor its effectiveness.
6. Repeat steps three through five if the chosen idea appears to be ineffective or counterproductive.

SECTION TWO

Index of Behaviors

2

Main Index

Physical Health Concerns

Self-Abuse

Self-Care

Self-Concept

Sexual Behavior

SECTION THREE

Cross-References

3

Published Behavior Checklists

AAMD Adaptive Behavior Scale (School Edition)

Item	Strategy Sheets
1.	296
2.	296
3.	296
4.	296
5.	296, 302
6.	300
7.	300
8.	291, 300, 295, 298
9.	N/A
10.	301
11.	298
12.	301
13.	301
14.	168
15.	N/A
16.	N/A
17.	N/A

Item	Strategy Sheets
18.	N/A
19.	N/A
20.	218
21.	218, 219
22.	220, 221, 222
23.	222
24.	N/A
25.	N/A
26.	N/A
27.	N/A
28.	200, 201
29.	*See* Oral Expression
30.	255, 260
31.	258
32.	N/A
33.	189, 190, 191, 192
34.	170, 168
35.	N/A
36.	N/A
37.	176, 177, 178, 179
38.	205

Item	Strategy Sheets
39.	204, 205
40.	N/A
41.	1, 2, 4, 71, 65, 69
42.	84, 138, 78, 79, 66, 67, 94
43.	62, 63
44.	128, 136, 137, 138
45.	N/A
46.	57, 58
47.	N/A
48.	292
49.	129, 133
50.	159, 163
51.	108, 109, 163, 166
52.	181
53.	344
54.	344, 162
55.	123, 126
56.	323, 112
57.	107, 89, *see also* Aggressive Behavior
58.	49, 292
59.	10, 49, 96, 86
60.	96, 87, 86
61.	142
62.	135, 9, 13, 14, 337
63.	8, 9, 11, 108
64.	*See* Disruption of Classroom Routine
65.	103, 105, 166
66.	133, 127
67.	83, 48, 18
68.	*See* Authority Conflicts
69.	333, *see also* Authority Conflicts
70.	*See* Authority Conflicts
71.	75, 84, 70, 78, 94, 113
72.	70
73.	78, *see also* Disruption of Classroom Routine
74.	93
75.	135, 337
76.	6, 348

Item	Strategy Sheets
77.	286, *see also* Withdrawn or Overinhibited Behavior
78.	346
79.	336, 335, 290
80.	326
81.	166, 323, 128
82.	101, 103, 105, 106, 332, 253
83.	338
84.	236, 16, 297
85.	N/A
86.	288, 317, 335, 244
87.	5, 103, 88
88.	306, 328
89.	36, 33
90.	33, 58, 142, 143, 127, 123
91.	121, 122, 131, 134, 138
92.	242, 303, 125, 126
93.	272, 277
94.	238, 144, 115, 266, 98
95.	95

Behavior Problem Checklist (Peterson and Quay, 1979)

Item	Strategy Sheets
1.	338
2.	5
3.	80, 100
4.	*See* Immaturity
5.	154
6.	139
7.	348
8.	157, *see also* Disruption of Classroom Routine
9.	303, 307, 308
10.	88, 93
11.	27, 71, 80, 100, 101, 103
12.	36, 144, 145
13.	22, 23, 239, 333
14.	*See* Withdrawn or Overinhibited Behavior

Item	Strategy Sheets
15.	*See* Withdrawn or Overinhibited Behavior
16.	211, 213–216
17.	122, 125, 126, 130, 134, 140, 142, 145
18.	85, 88, 91
19.	261
20.	19, 20, 24
21.	305, 307
22.	22
23.	57, 58, 63, *see also* Learning Difficulties: Confusion/Disorganization
24.	255, 259, 260
25.	11, 12, 13
26.	85, 88, 91
27.	142
28.	*See* Withdrawn or Overinhibited Behavior
29.	94
30.	36, 110
31.	6, *see also* Motivation
32.	*See* Neuroticism
33.	127, 133
34.	22, 72
35.	317
36.	85, 88, 91
37.	231
38.	*See* Authority Conflicts
39.	97, 140
40.	73, 100, 110, 103, 104, 105, 106, 159, 229, 329, 344, *see also* Immaturity; Impulse Control
41.	156
42.	161
43.	*See* Movement
44.	5
45.	19, 20, 24
46.	49, 207
47.	32, *see also* Authority Conflicts
48.	32, *see also* Authority Conflicts
49.	6
50.	6

Item	Strategy Sheets
51.	48, 83
52.	20, 147
53.	58, 88
54.	270, 302
55.	266, 268, 272, 277

Bower-Lambert Behavior Ratings of Pupils (Bower and Lambert, 1962)

Item	Strategy Sheets
A	11
B	14, 344, 350
C	*See* Learning Difficulties
D	18, *see also* Immaturity
E	51, 225, 243, 251
F	71
G	97, 144
H	233, 266, 272

Burk's Behavior Rating Scales (Burks, 1968)

Item	Strategy Sheets
1.	169, 338
2.	235, 246
3.	30, 135, 145
4.	73
5.	48, 58
6.	221
7.	23
8.	20
9.	126
10.	218, 219, 220, 222
11.	60
12.	110
13.	19
14.	2
15.	55, 349
16.	140, 143, 162

Item	Strategy Sheets	Item	Strategy Sheets
17.	243	57.	5, 146, 147, 148, 152
18.	19, 20	58.	94
19.	1, 198	59.	226
20.	*See* Memory	60.	26, 58
21.	135, 143	61.	167, 325
22.	209	62.	30, 42
23.	303	63.	312
24.	20, 54, 149	64.	273
25.	304	65.	33, 36
26.	220, 222	66.	26
27.	175	67.	319
28.	244	68.	340
29.	337	69.	6
30.	191	70.	310
31.	147	71.	127, 135
32.	255, 259	72.	58
33.	30, 214, 215	73.	158
34.	201	74.	324
35.	135	75.	30, 42
36.	5	76.	226
37.	22, 72	77.	319, 322
38.	231	78.	58
39.	92, 127, 133, 164	79.	14
40.	58, 330	80.	6
41.	224	81.	163
42.	252	82.	12
43.	248	83.	310, 315, 323
44.	170, 172, 182, 187	84.	167, 325
45.	332	85.	140
46.	28–32, 40, 42	86.	343
47.	124	87.	305
48.	336	88.	109
49.	2, 220	89.	128, 136
50.	84	90.	9, 13, 14
51.	146, 148	91.	97, 140
52.	341	92.	108, 109, 127, 143, 164, 166, 348
53.	85, 91, 92, 164	93.	35
54.	231	94.	65, 208
55.	22	95.	43
56.	53, 61	96.	344, 350

Item	Strategy Sheets
97.	232
98.	8
99.	161
100.	346
101.	43
102.	15, 100
103.	57
104.	348
105.	131
106.	9, 13
107.	121
108.	45, 66, 67, 128, 137
109.	36, 307
110.	305, 307
111.	136
112.	164
113.	50
114.	97, 140
115.	138
116.	100

Devereux Adolescent Behavior Rating Scale (Spivak, Spotts, and Haimes, 1967)

Item	Strategy Sheets
1.	245
2.	321
3.	348
4.	135
5.	324
6.	122, 134, 136, 138
7.	38
8.	110, 304
9.	101, 102, 103, 105
10.	46, 47
11.	253
12.	22, 24, 72, 286
13.	253

Item	Strategy Sheets
14.	297
15.	110, 304
16.	20
17.	*See* Learning Difficulties: Confusion/ Disorganization
18.	28, 29, 31, 32, 39, 40, 42
19.	289, 290, 335, 336
20.	128, 134, 136
21.	8, 9, 13, 14
22.	7, 11, 12, 15, 16, 17, 18, 125, 140, 142, 144, 145, 166, 330
23.	80, 102, 103, 105, 106, 152
24.	336
25.	253, 255, 256, 259
26.	26, 330
27.	*See* Sexual Behavior
28.	80
29.	19, 22, 23, 329, 350
30.	161, 239, 339
31.	5, 78
32.	328, 339
33.	97
34.	262
35.	258, 262
36.	8, 9, 13
37.	326, 331
38.	26, 28, 32, 40, 42
39.	122, 134, 137, 138
40.	30
41.	93
42.	328, 337, 339
43.	260
44.	258
45.	258, 259
46.	*See* Impulse Control
47.	5
48.	123, 125, 131, 143
49.	97, 303, 307
50.	128, 134, 136, 137
51.	30

Item	Strategy Sheets
52.	326
53.	22, 23, 72, 286
54.	242, 249
55.	242, 249
56.	227, 239
57.	268, 272, 277
58.	226
59.	234, 335, 338
60.	239, 242, 245, 246, 339
61.	148
62.	348, 350
63.	226, 232
64.	346, 350
65.	246
66.	310
67.	160
68.	280
69.	238
70.	280, 283
71.	82, 164
72.	161, 345
73.	165
74.	6, 283
75.	342, 343
76.	330
77.	306, 291
78.	20, 24, 149
79.	156, 158, 344, 346, 350
80.	*See* Withdrawn or Overinhibited Behavior
81.	8, 9, 11, 13, 14
82.	101–104, 106
83.	21, 147
84.	90, 310, 315, 317, 320, 323

Devereux Child Behavior Rating Scale (Spivak and Spotts, 1966)

Item	Strategy Sheets
1.	112
2.	276, 326, 327
3.	*See* Authority Conflicts
4.	327
5.	128, 136, 137
6.	142
7.	125, 303
8.	348
9.	279
10.	268, 272, 277
11.	122, 130, 134, 136, 138
12.	278
13.	260
14.	7, 11, 12, 13, 14, 16, 17, 58
15.	12, 58
16.	6
17.	328, 337, 339
18.	326
19.	136, 323
20.	58, 330, *see also* Aggressive Behavior; Authority Conflicts
21.	135
22.	274
23.	8, 9, 13
24.	25, 38
25.	*See* Sexual Behavior
26.	125, 145
27.	9, 13
28.	256
29.	*See* Neuroticism
30.	328, 337, 339
31.	93
32.	22
33.	58, 147
34.	72
35.	97, 140

Item	Strategy Sheets
36.	115
37.	143
38.	157
39.	144
40.	149
41.	48, 83
42.	*See* Authority Conflicts
43.	122, 128, 136
44.	122, *see also* Authority Conflicts
45.	*See* Authority Conflicts; Home Behavior
46.	299
47.	302
48.	270
49.	*See* Attentional Problems
50.	24
51.	349
52.	40
53.	97, 140, 332
54.	305, 306, 307, 308
55.	30, 40, 128, 136
56.	296
57.	218, 219, 220, 222
58.	300
59.	147
60.	238
61.	282, 291, 292, 298
62.	198, 221
63.	239
64.	348
65.	*See* Withdrawn or Overinhibited Behavior
66.	158, 160, 163, 167, 340
67.	330
68.	165
69.	20
70.	264, 293
71.	226
72.	280
73.	301

Item	Strategy Sheets
74.	291, 295, 298
75.	148
76.	280, 283
77.	*See* Withdrawn or Overinhibited Behavior
78.	35, 36, 50, 305, 307
79.	344, 346, 349, 350
80.	282, 294
81.	*See* Impulse Control
82.	16
83.	316
84.	262
85.	255, 259
86.	253
87.	126
88.	134, 137, 138
89.	N/A
90.	255, 260, 261
91.	297
92.	22, 342
93.	336
94.	289, 290, 335, 338
95.	105, 259, 332, 338
96.	*See* Oral Expression; Withdrawn or Overinhibited Behavior; Immaturity; Interaction; Disruption of Classroom Routine
97.	*See* Oral Expression

Hahnemann Elementary School Behavior Rating Scale (Spivak and Swift, 1975)

Item	Strategy Sheets
1.	52, 170
2.	45, 66, 67, 128, 136, 137
3.	55
4.	337
5.	10, 40, 163, 166
6.	55, 337, 339
7.	63, 243

Item	Strategy Sheets	Item	Strategy Sheets
8.	*See* Authority Conflicts	48.	74, 161, 163
9.	211, 212, 215	49.	170, 172, 180
10.	9, 13, 157	50.	*See* Withdrawn or Overinhibited Behavior
11.	60, 64	51.	4, 52
12.	40, 103, 106, 130, 166	52.	39, 45, 63, 66, 67, 79
13.	N/A	53.	170, 172, 173
14.	*See* Authority Conflicts	54.	*See* Interaction; Immaturity
15.	305, 307, 308	55.	150
16.	N/A	56.	76
17.	44	57.	20, 23
18.	*See* Disruption of Classroom Routine	58.	*See* Interaction; Immaturity
19.	161, 305	59.	136, 323
20.	99, 101, 103, 104	60.	65, 69, 239
21.	123, 125, 145		
22.	N/A		
23.	39, 66, 67, 305, 307, 308		
24.	99		
25.	172, 190, 191		
26.	150, 153		
27.	239		
28.	20		
29.	62, 63		
30.	60, 337, 339		
31.	20, 24		
32.	122, 128, 136		
33.	20, 22, 24		
34.	123, 126, 138		
35.	77		
36.	23		
37.	225, 250, 251		
38.	22, 286		
39.	74, 163		
40.	*See* Authority Conflicts		
41.	99, *see also* Authority Conflicts		
42.	6, 219, 220, 222		
43.	122, 127, 143		
44.	102, 103, 104, 106, 152		
45.	36		
46.	68		
47.	23		

Hahnemann High School Behavior Rating Scale (Spivak and Swift, 1971)

Item	Strategy Sheets
1.	39, 57, 58, 63, 67, 137
2.	25, 60, 73, 74
3.	73
4.	39, 66, 67
5.	64, 73, 106
6.	5
7.	25, 163
8.	52
9.	84
10.	51
11.	66, 67
12.	101, 102, 103, 104
13.	25, 28, 32, 99
14.	28, 64, 74
15.	4, 169
16.	99
17.	52, 169
18.	240, 251
19.	61, 62
20.	38, 128, 136

Item	Strategy Sheets
21.	55, 60, 337
22.	165, *see also* Disruption; Authority Conflict
23.	165, *see also* Disruption; Authority Conflict
24.	3, 225, 250, 251
25.	*See* Learning Difficulties: Confusion/Disorganization; Learning Difficulties: Memory
26.	39, 57, 58, 62, 66, 67
27.	240, 256
28.	77, *see also* Authority Conflicts
29.	103, 106
30.	*See* Learning Difficulties: Confusion/Disorganization; Learning Difficulties: Memory
31.	45, 66, 67, 128, 136, 137
32.	49, 51, 74
33.	254, *see also* Withdrawn or Overinhibited Behavior
34.	170–175
35.	22
36.	347, 350
37.	243
38.	74, 163
39.	251
40.	231, 233
41.	74, 163
42.	189, 191, 207
43.	233
44.	*See* Withdrawn or Overinhibited Behavior
45.	55, 69

Louisville Behavior Checklist (Miller, 1981)

Item	Strategy Sheets
1.	133, 135
2.	131, 137
3.	346 *133,862*

Item	Strategy Sheets
4.	128
5.	166
6.	114
7.	14, 107
8.	*See* Learning Difficulties: Reading
9.	348
10.	270, 302
11.	307
12.	266, *see also* Neuroticism
13.	5, *see also* Impulse Control
14.	94, **247**
15.	271, 281, 286
16.	285
17.	241
18.	58, 142
19.	21
20.	N/A
21.	309, 314
22.	244
23.	9, 13
24.	236
25.	51, 225, 240, 251
26.	158, 165, 343, 350
27.	26, 27, 33, 43, 58, 70, 75, 122, 142, 330
28.	272, 274, 277, 288
29.	310, 314
30.	94
31.	154, 349
32.	244
33.	39, 54
34.	218, 219, 220, 222
35.	231, *see also* Impulse Control
36.	311, 315, 316, 318, 320
37.	335
38.	237
39.	146, 175
40.	23, 224
41.	226, 239, 245, 252
42.	132, *see also* Immaturity
43.	122, 123, 126, 130, 131, 134, 137, 145

Item	Strategy Sheets	Item	Strategy Sheets
44.	53, 56, 61, 62, 66, 67, 68	84.	344, 350
45.	N/A	85.	N/A
46.	8, 9, 13	86.	5
47.	234, *see also* Neuroticism	87.	128, 136
48.	5	88.	326, 327, 331
49.	284, 311	89.	*See* Delinquency/Rule Breaking
50.	117	90.	*See* Delinquency/Rule Breaking
51.	132	91.	N/A
52.	115, 116, 128, 136	92.	113, 116
53.	126, 145, 242	93.	216
54.	312, 318, 319, 322	94.	57, 58, 66, 67
55.	171–175	95.	132, *see also* Immaturity
56.	275	96.	133
57.	99, 101, 102, 103, 104, 106	97.	246, 252
58.	N/A	98.	167, 324, 325, 340
59.	226, 344	99.	161
60.	69	100.	227, 244
61.	303	101.	157, 164, *see also* Disruption of Classroom Routine
62.	121, 332	102.	334
63.	170, 171, 172, 173, 174, 175	103.	157, 165
64.	242, 249, 328, 337, 338, 339	104.	246, 252
65.	93	105.	*See* Sexual Behavior
66.	264, 293	106.	33, 36, 58
67.	176, 177, 178, 179	107.	48, 83
68.	82	108.	291, 292, 295, 296, 298
69.	110, 305	109.	111
70.	271, 286	110.	93
71.	118, 126	111.	89
72.	95	112.	277
73.	14, 50, 109, 348	113.	303, 305, 307, 308
74.	296, 300, 301	114.	N/A
75.	65, 68, 69	115.	98
76.	263	116.	108
77.	309, 316, 321	117.	76
78.	239, 245	118.	86, 87, 96
79.	6	119.	317, 320
80.	268, 272, 277	120.	253, 255, 259
81.	5, 19, 20, 24	121.	155
82.	N/A	122.	163
83.	289, 290		

Item	Strategy Sheets
123.	228
124.	90, 315, 316
125.	92
126.	249
127.	229
128.	113, 114, 116, 117, 118
129.	350, *see also* Withdrawn or Overinhibited Behavior
130.	95
131.	115
132.	N/A
133.	95
134.	35, 77
135.	N/A
136.	212, 214, 215
137.	282, 294
138.	97, *see also* Depression
139.	11, 113, *see also* Aggression
140.	235
141.	165, 343, 350
142.	95
143.	5, 71
144.	86
145.	N/A
146.	128, 136, 229, 230, 235, 244
147.	281
148.	231
149.	72
150.	*See* Sexual Behavior
151.	46, 135
152.	265
153.	88, 91, 158
154.	233, 244, 250
155.	N/A
156.	126, 159, 163
157.	264, 293
158.	N/A
159.	N/A
160.	N/A
161.	36, *see also* Immaturity

Item	Strategy Sheets
162.	*See* Authority Conflicts
163.	71, 146, 148, 151
164.	N/A

Ottawa School Behavior Checklist (Pimm and McClure, 1978)

Item	Strategy Sheets
1.	17, *see also* Authority Conflicts
2.	14, 17
3.	93
4.	5, 78
5.	7
6.	7
7.	86, 87, 96
8.	49
9.	26
10.	11
11.	100, 105
12.	89
13.	93
14.	9, 26, 28, 33
15.	8, 9, 11–14
16.	89
17.	22, 23, 24, 39
18.	44, 58, 60, 71, 87
19.	7, 11, 26, 28, 33
20.	7, 9, 11, 12, 14, 17
21.	16
22.	16
23.	44, 58, 60, 71, 87
24.	101, 102, 105
25.	46, 47, 63
26.	7, 9, 11, 27, 28, 43
27.	7, 8, 9, 11, 13, 157
28.	17
29.	17
30.	43, 156
31.	7, 9, 157

Item	Strategy Sheets	Item	Strategy Sheets
32.	101, 102, 105	72.	104
33.	46, 47	73.	268, 272, 277
34.	70	74.	327, 338
35.	7, 11, 16	75.	272, 277
36.	7, 11, 16, 157	76.	270, 302
37.	7, 11, 16	77.	268, 272, 277
38.	9, 13, 164	78.	236
39.	53, 54, 59	79.	236
40.	87	80.	224, 287
41.	237	81.	94
42.	285	82.	299
43.	86, 96	83.	6, 113, 116
44.	17	84.	N/A
45.	86, 87	85.	297
46.	75, 168	86.	327, 338
47.	5	87.	236, 297
48.	17, 43, 101, 219, 221	88.	326, 327, 338
49.	15, 87, 341	89.	6
50.	5, 27, 31, 71, 80	90.	101, 226, 344
51.	5, 70	91.	89
52.	94, 247	92.	344, 349, 350
53.	261	93.	301
54.	331, 332, 338	94.	338
55.	144	95.	344, 349, 350
56.	255, 259, 330, 332, 338	96.	271, 286, 338
57.	103, 106	97.	338
58.	100, 101, 102, 105, 106	98.	136
59.	135, 337	99.	136, 323
60.	101, 103, 104, 106, 148	100.	336
61.	10		
62.	342		
63.	48, 83		
64.	255, 283, 350		
65.	254		
66.	13, 14, 15, 18, 32, 83		
67.	25		
68.	332, 338		
69.	39, 62, 66, 67		
70.	101, 102, 105		
71.	135, 337		

Walker Problem Behavior Identification Checklist (Walker, 1983)

Item	Strategy Sheets
1.	125, 126
2.	8
3.	31
4.	123, 125, 131
5.	160

Item	Strategy Sheets	Item	Strategy Sheets
6.	243	28.	66, 305, 307
7.	255, 261	29.	344
8.	12	30.	12, 58
9.	19, 20	31.	97, 238
10.	5	32.	31, 32, 40
11.	110	33.	115
12.	135	34.	97, 98, 140
13.	65, 69, 208	35.	12, 58
14.	11, 101, 102, 104	36.	244, 252
15.	347	37.	158, 165, 343, 344, 350
16.	242, 249	38.	36, 138
17.	266	39.	7, 9, 11–14, 16, 17, 58
18.	25, 32, 38	40.	304, 305, 307
19.	57, 66	41.	53, 54, 57, 58, 59
20.	224, 236	42.	345
21.	213, 214, 216	43.	158, 321, 344
22.	270	44.	248
23.	332	45.	343, 344, 346, 350
24.	45, 136, 138	46.	25, 26, 29, 32, 39, 40, 42
25.	303	47.	144
26.	23	48.	261
27.	142	49.	20
		50.	22

SECTION FOUR

Strategy Sheets

4

Academic Products

1

Messy Pictures and Drawings

1. Reinforce the student when he produces an assignment that is acceptable or better than usual.

2. Give the student an incomplete grade on the messy picture. Explain that the picture or drawing is not acceptable in its present condition and have him redo the assignment (Williams, 1983).

3. If after revision the picture is still not acceptable, warn the student that he will receive a failing grade for any future unacceptable assignments (K. Schmitt, personal communication, 1985).

4. Encourage the student to do the assignment to the best of his ability by displaying the daily activities in a weekly art show. Have students choose the best one and award the winner something such as a star, a sticker, or money (Konstantareas, 1984).

5. Identify the part of the assignment that is

messy and the part that is acceptable (K. Schmitt, personal communication, 1985).

6. Explain any expectations or necessary rules such as staying inside the lines or on the paper, or not tearing or ripping paper unless told to do so (K. Schmitt, personal communication, 1985).

7. If the student does not finish the assignment in class, include the parents by letting them know what has to be accomplished and when it is due (K. Schmitt, personal communication, 1985).

8. While the student is working on the assignment, watch to see if he is having difficulty holding the drawing instrument or staying on the paper (Kistner, 1985).

9. Work on improving the student's fine motor skills if he is having difficulty staying on the paper or holding objects (K. Schmitt, personal communication, 1985).

10. Have the student complete the assignment in parts. Check each part before allowing the student to continue further.

11. Give the student a paper on which part of

the drawing or picture is already present. Have the student complete the product.

12. Provide two assignments—one that allows messiness (e.g., finger painting) and one that demands neatness (e.g., pencil drawing).

13. Have the student do a rough sketch before attempting the final product.

14. Do not rush the student by placing time limits on the assignment.

2

Poor Penmanship

1. Mold modeling clay around a pencil so that it fills the student's hand and holds the fingers extended (Getman, 1985).

2. Place a wooden bead, such as those used in macrame crafts, on a pencil so that it fills the student's hand and holds the fingers in an extended position (Getman, 1985).

3. Vary the writing implement. Try using implements with larger grips and writing points such as crayons, magic markers, primary pencils, large three-sided pens or pencils, and regular pencils with three-sided rubber grips, which might provide more control over the writing implement (Cieslicki, 1980).

4. To help the student correctly position his paper, tape a corner made from masking tape onto the desk into which he can place the corner of the paper each time he begins to work (C. Bayles, personal communication, 1985).

5. Tape the paper into the proper position on the desk (Cieslicki, 1980).

6. Insist on good writing posture. The student should sit upright at the desk with his lower back against the back of the seat. The upper back and shoulders should lean forward. The elbows should be just off the edge of the desk, and the large muscle of the forearm should serve as the pivot for the writing movement (Harrison, 1981).

7. Use correctly lined paper. Lines should be printed clearly, and it should be possible to identify the baseline, midline, and headline easily (Milone and Wasylk, 1982).

8. Use lined clear contact paper on a desk to provide an interesting alternative for practice (Cieslicki, 1980).

9. Make a writing board using lined, clear contact paper for writing practice (Cieslicki, 1980).

10. Implement activities that foster the hand-eye coordination necessary for writing (e.g., lacing pictures, finger painting, pouring water, tracing on acetate or onionskin paper, stringing beads, clipping clothespins, connecting dots, making clay figures, catching balls, and playing finger games) (Graham and Maden, 1981).

11. Have the student write the numerals, letters, or words in the air (Burton, 1982).

12. Have one student draw the numeral, letter, or word on another's back and have the receiver guess which one was produced (Burton, 1982).

13. Have the student bend pipecleaners into the shape of numerals or letters and trace them with the fingers to get the "feel" of the letter (Burton, 1982).

14. Have the student draw the numerals, letters, or words in sand, cornmeal, or salt that has been poured into a boxtop (Burton, 1982).

15. Have the student write large letters on the chalkboard. These overemphasized movements give the child the feel of the "up and down" of letter formation (Getman, 1985).

16. Group letters to be practiced by a similarity in the direction of movement (e.g., Group 1: o, c, a, g, q; Group 2: e, l, t, i, j, p; Group 3: d, b, h, k, f; Group 4: m, n, x; Group 5: u, v, w, r, s). After practicing each individually, group them together as if making words.

17. Identify the basic strokes in each letter that are incorrectly made and reteach the correct form of these basic strokes (Milone and Wasylk, 1981).

18. Give instructions based on certain copying rules. Three rules govern starting points: (a) start at the top, (b) start at the left, and (c) start with a vertical stroke. Three rules govern progression within shapes: (a) draw verticals from top to bottom, (b) draw horizontals from left to right, and (c) draw with a continuous line (Kirk, 1981).

19. Guide the direction and order of strokes through the use of arrows or colored dots. If necessary, physically direct the student's hand as the letter is formed (Graham and Maden, 1981).

20. Provide guides for the student. The letter or word can be formed by tracing raised letters, an outline, dot-to-dot patterns, dashed letters, or a faded model. To fade the model gradually, lighten the ink on the ditto (Graham and Maden, 1981).

21. Make a flipbook. The letter appears in a manner similar to the animation of a cartoon. Design the flipbook so that when pages are quickly flipped, letters appear to be forming as one would normally write them. Put a stiff backing on the flipbook so that the student cannot form the letter backward by flipping the book in reverse order (Wright and Wright, 1980).

22. Surround the student with models of good writing. Alphabet charts should be displayed prominently, exemplary samples of students' writing should be posted around the classroom, and each time you write something on the chalkboard or on a student's paper, be sure that it is correctly written on ruled lines (Milone and Wasylk, 1981).

23. Group left-handers together with a teacher who is also left-handed in order to provide a model (Harrison, 1981).

24. Provide a model cursive alphabet with a rightward slant for left-handers (Harrison, 1981).

25. Have left-handers practice at the chalkboard to prevent development of the "hook" hand position (Harrison, 1981).

26. Teach left-handers to slant backward or to write vertically (Harrison, 1891).

27. Use calligraphy as a means of improving penmanship. Calligraphy provides motivation to produce lovely writing. The student who starts at the bottom and writes upward must do the reverse or the ink will splatter, and the student whose straight up and down cursive writing causes problems in connecting letters benefits from learning and practicing slanted italic writing style. The student who bears down excessively often finds it helpful to use a calligraphic pen, which will not function properly under excessive pressure, and the student who has difficulty remembering the sequence or direction of letter strokes benefits from consistent practice and repetition of these strokes (O'Donnell and Duncan, 1980).

28. Develop a simple and direct vocabulary of handwriting terms. Teach the terms to the student to insure understanding (Milone and Wasylk, 1981).

29. Determine the criteria of acceptability that are within the ability of this student. If the writing does not meet the acceptability level, do not accept the paper. Have the student rewrite the assignment after you have given specific directions as to what must be changed (Milone and Wasylk, 1981).

3

Poorly Organized Work

1. Reward the student for producing work that is orderly and neat (M. Pierre, personal communication, 1985).

2. Break the work into steps for the student to follow (Winston, 1979).

3. Have the student make a master list of things to do in order to accomplish the assignment (Winston, 1979).

4. Guide the student in achieving stated goals by setting dates for each subtask (Kops and Belmont, 1985).

5. Have the student outline written work before attempting the task.

6. Have the student write math homework on graph paper in order to properly align the problems (M. Pierre, personal communication, 1985).

7. Give the student outlines for written assignments to show sentence order (i.e., where topic sentence should go, supporting details, etc.) (M. Pierre, personal communication, 1985).

8. Give the student a checklist to complete before submitting assignments (e.g., name and date are on paper, all problems are complete, etc.) (M. Pierre, personal communication, 1985).

9. Have examples on the worksheets or board for the student to follow (C. Weyeneth, personal communication, 1985).

10. Have the student write sentences on note paper or ruled worksheets (M. Pierre, personal communication, 1985).

11. Have the student ask a peer to check over his assignments for completeness and neatness before submission (M. Pierre, personal communication, 1985).

12. Accept only that work that meets expectations.

13. Have the student check with you at various points so that any problems are detected early.

14. When the assignment is submitted, review it with the student. Be sure that all stated expectations were met. If they were not, make a list of corrections that must be accomplished before resubmission.

15. Provide the student with a model to which to refer if necessary.

4

Poor Test Performance

1. Devise a program that develops efficient test-taking skills.

2. Have the student attend programs, such as reading labs, to learn independent study skills (Markel, 1981).

3. Have the student set easy daily performance goals. This allows the student to decide on which weaknesses or strengths he wishes to work and it provides him with some responsibility for his own behavior.

4. Provide practice tests similar to the upcoming exam (Markel, 1981).

5. Review the practice test with the student.

6. Provide study guides before testing (Mabee, Neimann, and Lipton, 1979).

7. Give the student practice by providing take-home tests that parents can score and interpret (B. Kreuger, personal communication, 1983).

8. Provide short and success-insured tasks that are similar to the test (Markel, 1981).

9. Have study teams of students so that they can ask each other questions and review as a group.

10. Implement a "study-buddy" system in which two students review and study together. Pair the student of concern with one who is successful in testing (Blanco, 1972).

11. Decide on a goal with the student and plan a program that starts at the level on which he is achieving. To motivate the student to perform better on tests, a reward system can be used for gradual improvement. For example, the student should be reinforced for increasing the number correct by one until he achieves above a set level of percentage correct. At this point, reinforcement should be administered only for the maintenance of this level.

12. Set realistic test-taking goals that can be accomplished (McCall, 1983).

13. Purposely arrange for tests that the student can pass. Carefully prepare the student. After a successful experience, be sure that the student receives praise.

14. Explain how tests are used and how the scores are only a relative measure of strengths and weaknesses.

15. Offer remedial help in areas of subject deficiency.

16. Give more frequent tests so that less material is tested.

17. Promote the importance of having a good night's sleep and eating a meal before testing (Gifford and Fluitt, 1980).

18. Check to be sure that the student is feeling well.

19. Establish good test-taking conditions (e.g., a quiet room, good lighting, removal of distracting stimuli, arrangement of desks).

20. Place the student outside of class in a quiet area away from any source of distraction, or have him take the test when classmates are gone.

21. Before a test, identify the requirements of the test. Discuss format, directions, criteria, test topic, number and type of questions, and time limits (Gifford and Fluitt, 1980; Markel, 1981).

22. Present verbal instructions in a calm, non-authoritative tone, using a short, single-sentence format (Markel, 1981).

23. Instructions that are repeated should be simply stated and consistent with prior statements (Markel, 1981).

24. Have the student repeat the directions.

25. Establish an organized and predictable set of test-taking conditions, including the arrangement of desks and availability of materials (Markel, 1981).

26. Have the student bring a watch to class. When he finishes half the questions, have him look at the watch to see if half of the time allotted for the test has elapsed (Gifford and Fluitt, 1980).

27. Allow the student to mark and make notes on the test question booklets (Gifford and Fluitt, 1980).

28. Be sure that the student can read and understand all of the words on the test.

29. Divide the class into small groups. Make test completion contingent on group cooperation to complete questions, with each student contributing vital input (Madsen and Madsen, 1981).

30. Have the student read the directions aloud.

31. Have the student take a test orally if he prefers to do so (Blanco, 1972).

32. Give the student points for each correct answer rather than demerits for each incorrect answer (Blanco, 1972).

33. Start all tests with "easy" questions to facilitate success.

34. Extend or eliminate time limits during testing (Forness and Dvorak, 1982).

35. Have open-book tests on occasion, or allow certain questions on the test to be answered with assistance from one's notes or book (B. Kreuger, personal communications, 1983).

36. During testing, provide a clock and give the approximate time to be spent on each test section or question (Markel, 1981).

37. Provide periodic breaks every 10 to 20 minutes during testing (Markel, 1981).

38. Have the student recheck his or her answers when finished.

39. After testing, discuss the student's errors in following directions, adhering to time limits, and problem-solving sequencing (Markel, 1981).

40. Try to give immediate feedback on the results of the test.

41. Abandon formal standardized testing and employ short periods of intensive individualized instruction (Forness and Dvorak, 1982).

42. Use computer-generated tests to promote self-pacing by the student (Dunkleberger and Knight, 1979).

43. If the student exhibits symptoms of test anxiety, refer him for evaluation (Markel, 1981).

44. Agree with the student that he might do poorly on tests. This allows an opportunity to avoid being defensive or feeling guilty about not living up to expectations. Telling the student, "You have a right to fail" often relieves anxiety.

45. When a student reports that he "froze up" on a test, listen to him sympathetically and, if at all possible, make provisions for retesting under less stressful conditions.

46. Eliminate grades or marks since they create unnecessary anxiety. If grades must be used in a traditional system, then grade the student leniently.

47. To decrease test anxiety, eliminate use of letter grades, red checks, pouting faces, and other negatively perceived evaluations. Discuss with the student how he would like to be evaluated (B. Kreuger, personal communication, 1983).

48. Recommend counseling in the school setting, as it can be very effective with poor test performance if motivation or personality problems interfere with learning.

49. Reduce punishment for poor performance and increase encouragement for improving performance.

50. Assess self-confidence, motivation, and independence. Ask questions such as: "Do you think you can do the work?" "Are you trying as best as you can?" and "Do you think others are always pestering you and telling you want to do?" (McCall, 1983).

51. Conduct relaxation exercises before starting the test (e.g., close the eyes and take a deep breath, shake limbs, make a tight fist and release).

52. Don't negate achievements (e.g., "You got a C. Now get an A."); reinforce them (McCall, 1983).

53. Give immediate reinforcement for correct test answers and assistance for problems on which help is required (B. Kreuger, personal communication, 1983).

54. Don't say, "You're capable." Let the student's successes prove this (McCall, 1983).

55. Show that you sympathize and understand. Share some of your failures with the student (McCall, 1983).

56. Display a cooperative attitude with parents and the student. Ask: "What can we do together about this?" (McCall, 1983).

57. Discuss the student's poor performance with parents and note their level of tolerance. Note if there is too much urging by the parents for the student to be like a sibling (Blanco, 1972).

58. Have the student take home review materials, and if the parents are willing, let them assist the student.

59. Some students may have problems at home that keep them from studying properly (e.g., having no place to study, distractions, chores, lack of interest by parents). Since teachers usually remain after pupils leave, the school could assign one special room for those who wish to stay after school to study for tests.

60. Make enjoyable activities dependent on good test performance. This should be used only with the student who has the potential to do better.

5

Activity Level

Hyperactive

1. Give the student social attention and praise when desired behaviors occur (Barkley, 1981).

2. Use a variety of tangible and activity-oriented backup reinforcers as a way to increase desired behaviors such as in-seat behavior (Robinson, Newby, and Ganzell, 1981).

3. Give immediate nonverbal recognition as well as verbal or written rewards or tokens (Renshaw, 1976).

4. Maintain a great deal of structure in the classroom (Stone and Sugarman, 1974).

5. Place the student near the teacher's desk (Stone and Sugarman, 1974).

6. Capture interest and improve motivation by controlled and creative use of novelty and surprise (Renshaw, 1976).

7. Use audio-visual aids whenever possible as they draw attention and improve comprehension (Renshaw, 1976).

8. Use a token economy system to control performance (Robinson, Newby, and Ganzell, 1981).

9. When the student displays bad behavior, let him know that you are displeased. Speak frankly to him in a firm adult manner, and express your concern and dislike for his socially unacceptable behavior. Be reasonable and consistent. Don't compare his bad behavior with the good behavior of another student (Stone and Sugarman, 1974).

10. Specifically identify the student's problem. Turn the problem into a goal. Select an appropriate reinforcer and then establish a plan by which the student is able to earn the reinforcement by successively closer approximations to the desired behavior.

11. In order to lessen motor activity, reduce the ordinary restrictions on movement about the classroom and look for substitute outlets for motor activity, including the assigning of physically exhausting tasks.

12. Have the student monitor his behavior during individual work time. On a wall facing

the student, post the rules for individual work time. By the use of a tape recorder, randomly program a bell to sound on the tape at scattered intervals. Instruct the student that at this signal, he is to ask himself if he has been on task, as determined by the rules of the poster. If so, then he is to place a check mark on his recording card. If not, no check is to be given. You should also note if the student was on task. At the end of individual work time, count the number of checks recorded. If the student's tally agrees with yours, he receives the correct number of points (tokens) plus bonus points for honesty in recording. Lesser degrees of accuracy receive fewer points (Barkley, Copeland, and Sivage, 1980).

13. Teach the hyperactive student to use cognitive self-instruction procedures for reducing hyperactive behaviors. These procedures attempt to help the student learn how to focus on tasks and as a result, gain some internal control over interfering hyperactive behaviors. Instruct the student to "stop, look, and think before doing" (Lahey, 1979).

14. Place the student in a time-out room for five minutes when this behavior occurs (Lahey, 1979).

15. Modify the pace of the classroom. The curriculum for the hyperactive student should be presented in short blocks of time. Tasks should progress rapidly from one to another. Gradually increase the length of the lessons in order to aid the student in increasing his attention span.

16. Give short assignments with definite finishing times. Provide the student with periodic breaks when he can move around the room, go on errands to the school office, or do calisthenics.

17. Set clear limits on behavior. Be sure the limits are fair and are consistently enforced. Make certain that the student understands what is expected of him, the consequences of failure to abide by the rules, and that the work is within his capabilities.

18. Be flexible in expectations for the student.

Realize that each student has different needs and must be treated differently.

19. Use role play. Have the student play a part that is different from his usual role in the classroom. By doing this, the student is able to break through the barriers of egocentrism to learn how his behavior is viewed by others and how it influences them.

20. Videotape the student in the classroom. Play the tape and have the student see himself. By doing so, he may become aware of the rapidity of his movements and notice how annoying some of them can be to other people.

21. Play soft background music in the classroom. This will tend to increase the productivity of the work done by the student. The student will also tend to become significantly less active (Windwer, 1980).

22. If the student is on medication to control his behavior, monitor him and keep communication lines open with the physician (Gadow, 1982).

23. Demonstrate to the student a feeling of understanding and acceptance. This can be done through contact with the student verbally, with facial expression and gestures, and personal touch (Connor, 1974).

24. Begin work assignments at the level where the student can surely succeed. Gradually progress as skills are acquired (Connor, 1974).

25. Use methods and materials that are minimally abstract and maximally concrete and tangible (Connor, 1974).

26. Use demonstration instead of verbal explanation whenever possible. Be sure directions are concise and meaningful, consisting of one to two steps at a time, and acknowledged as being understood by the student (Connor, 1974).

27. Be careful not to punish the student for that which he cannot control such as overactivity, short attention span, clumsiness, or learning problems (Heeting, 1978).

28. When correcting the student, keep your

voice firm, quiet, and calm. Keep emotions under control (Heeting, 1978).

29. Focus on the behavior, not the student. When you express disapproval of the student's misbehavior, be careful that you do not "put him down" as a person. Remember that it is his behavior that you do not like, not him (Heeting, 1978).

30. Rules should always have the same consequences from day to day. A predictable environment will lessen the student's anxiety, excitability, and impulsiveness (Heeting, 1978).

31. Discipline is most effective if administered as soon as possible after misbehavior. This is especially important with hyperactive students since they often have a short memory (Heeting, 1978).

32. Redirect the student from a frustrating situation or activity to something less stressful (Heeting, 1978).

33. Do not punish the student by making him sit still for a specified length of time during recess or activity periods. These times are needed to release energy (Yamamoto, 1972).

34. Simplify the environment for the student. Set a model for calmness and consistency (Yamamoto, 1972).

35. Refer the student for a medical evaluation if this has not already been done.

36. Have the student face the wall while working. Place screens around him or have him sit in a cubicle (Cruickshank, Bentzen, Ratzburg, and Tannhauser, 1961).

37. A student's materials should consist of the barest essentials, even to the extent of cutting away the borders of pictures and using covers over reading materials to expose only a small area at a time.

38. Keep the classroom group small and use a large classroom so that each student can be seated at a distance from the others.

39. Use "hands-on" concrete materials that allow the student to move and manipulate objects.

40. When learning new words, have the student trace over the word. He can now attend to the task at hand because he is no longer overly sensitive to the tactile influences of the surroundings (Fernald, 1963).

41. Reduce unessential visual and auditory environmental stimuli (Cruickshank et al., 1961).

42. Establish a highly structured daily program. Write the daily plan on the board each morning. This way the student will know exactly what is expected and when it is to be done (Cruickshank et al., 1961).

43. Increase the stimulus value of the instructional materials by making them more colorful and interesting than the surroundings. This will draw the student's attention to the materials (Cruickshank et al., 1961).

44. Provide a hierarchy of educational tasks. In this way the student will be given tasks to perform at different levels of learning (Hewett, 1964).

45. Reinforce peers for not attending to disruptive behavior (Patterson, 1965).

46. Select high-status peers who are willing to cooperate with adults. Train these students in extinction and reinforcement techniques. Have them apply the behavioral procedures to reduce deviant behavior in the hyperactive student (Solomon and Wahler, 1973).

47. Allow the student to have some free time in one part of the room to read, play, or be alone if he feels restless (S. Kania, personal communication, 1985).

48. During movie or filmstrip time, allow the student to run the video equipment (S. Kania, personal communication, 1985).

49. Food additives and artificial flavors, colors, and preservatives may induce hyperactivity. Suggest to the parents that their child stay away from foods that contain these ingredients (Feingold, 1975).

50. Suggest that the parents consult with their doctor as to whether massive doses of vitamins might help to counteract this behavior (Feingold, 1975).

51. Recommend that the parents consult a physician regarding the use of stimulant medications prescribed for attention-deficit disorders (e.g., ritalin, dexedrine, and cylert) (Levine, Brooks, and Shonkoff, 1980).

52. If the whole class is active, have everyone exercise at their seat to release excess energy (Miller, Galanter, and Pribram, 1960).

53. When class squirming increases, organize a specific playground activity (e.g., a hike or a game where everyone must exert an excessive amount of physical energy) (Miller, Galanter, and Pribram, 1960).

54. Provide outlets for the student's excessive movement needs by assigning extra tasks that involve coordinated movements. This would include activities such as drawing, scissor cutting, pasting, straightening shelves, and taking down or setting up display boards (Miller, Galanter, and Pribram, 1960).

55. Confine a student's learning periods and class participation to those times of the day when he is emotionally prepared and in more control of himself (Miller, Galanter, and Pribram, 1960).

56. Tie one string of sewing thread around the student's lap as a reminder to stay in the seat.

57. Allow time each day for the student to go outside or run around the gym for five minutes to release excess energy. This activity might be made contingent on a period of appropriate work behavior (M. C. Grothaus, personal communication, 1985).

58. Plan classroom activities that will utilize the student's energy (T. J. Grothaus, personal communication, 1985).

59. Use touch when working with the student. For example, if the student is moving his leg back and forth, set your hand on the leg in an attempt to stop the movement (E. M. Connelly, personal communication, 1985).

60. Assign the student a job such as watering the plants or erasing the chalkboard as a means of instilling in him a sense of responsibility, as well as a means of utilizing his energy (M. C. Grothaus, personal communication, 1985).

61. When working one-to-one with the student, imitate the movements made by him. After imitation, slow the movement until it is stopped. Be sure to continue working and talking during the process as well as after the movement has stopped (E. M. Connelly, personal communication, 1985).

62. Have the student record his restless behavior. Every time he is unable to sit still or feels restless, have him place a tally mark on a sheet of paper. At the end of the day, have him plot the number of occurrences on a chart. The student attempts to beat the daily tally during the next day in order to receive a reward (Rowe and Sugai, 1984).

6

Inactive, Lethargic, Lacks Energy, Fatigues Easily

1. Determine if the student is on medication; this behavior may be a side effect. Inform the parents, school nurse, or prescribing physician.

2. Be sure that the student has eaten recently; hunger might cause fatigue.

3. Investigate the student's eating habits. Arrange for a better breakfast and lunch if nutrition might be a factor in the lethargic behavior (C. Young, personal communication, 1983).

4. Suggest a physical examination to determine the cause of the inactivity.

5. Find out if the student works at night or has unusual sleeping habits (D. Otto, personal communications, 1983).

6. Involve the student in enjoyable activities (Royce, 1981).

7. Provide the student with a variety of work to stimulate interest (Royce, 1981).

8. Limit physical activity if this drains the student's energy (Royce, 1981).

9. Shorten the amount of time that the student spends on one subject to keep interest high (Royce, 1981).

10. Make sure that the room is well ventilated and well lighted (Royce, 1981).

11. Allow the student to nap during free time, recess, or lunch period.

12. Allow the student to move about if he feels tired while working.

13. Evaluate the physical environment of the room. Provide bright colors, plenty of light, and fresh air. The room should be tidy and uncluttered (C. Young, personal communication, 1983).

14. Arrange outside activities whenever possible (Bain, 1979).

15. Plan periodic exercise and stretching breaks.

16. Prepare lessons involving the student's interests. For example, if the student likes trucks, devise math problems that involve gas usage, mileage, distance, and cargo weight.

17. Plan hands-on activities to more actively involve the student.

18. Question parents to determine if the student is experiencing a high amount of stress, anxiety, or depression.

19. Seat the student closer to you. Use a one-on-one situation to eliminate any opportunities for the student to doze off (Royce, 1981).

20. Present lessons in an enthusiastic manner (J. Monge, personal communication, 1984).

21. Gain the student's interest by discovering his hobbies, likes, and dislikes.

22. Keep the student active with things to do like cutting and drawing.

23. Whenever possible, give breaks from the more mundane tasks.

24. Vary the presentational mode during the instructional period. Follow a short lecture with a movie, discussion, writing assignment, or other stimulating activity.

25. Allow the student to earn nap time rather than free time or recess.

26. If the pupil is an adolescent, obtain parental permission to allow the student to consume coffee, iced tea, or other caffeine-containing substances.

27. Call on or touch the student to startle him and "get the adrenalin flowing."

6

Aggressive Behavior

7

Bites Others

1. Expose the student to nonaggressive models (Schwartz and Johnson, 1981).

2. Have the student observe models whose aggressive behaviors are disapproved or punished (Schwartz and Johnson, 1981).

3. Show a strong and firm presence to control the student (Weissbourd, 1984).

4. Move around the room during class and be aware of the student's activities and behavior (Gervais and Dittburner, 1981).

5. Stress that biting is unacceptable behavior (Weissbourd, 1984).

6. Teach the student to count to 10, breathe, and relax when he feels the urge to bite (Hawaii, 1983).

7. When the student is about to bite you, leave the situation (Hawaii, 1983).

8. Have the student talk to himself and think about what he is about to do (Hawaii, 1983).

9. Use visual imagery exercises to help the offender reduce the aggression (Hawaii, 1983).

10. Provide an outlet such as pounding, cutting, or sawing (Blanco, 1972).

11. Separate the student from others when he becomes aggressive (Blanco, 1972).

12. Reward those who display appropriate behavior (Schwartz and Johnson, 1981).

13. Suggest to the victim of the offending behavior that he play or work with someone else (Weissbourd, 1984).

14. Encourage other students not to bite back (Katz, 1983).

15. Place the student in time-out as soon as the behavior occurs (Blanco, 1972; Schwartz and Johnson, 1981).

16. When time permits, demonstrate how to handle a situation in which there is conflict between two individuals (Provence, 1985).

17. Use role playing to help the offender understand his actions (Helge, 1983).

18. Show the offending student pictures of a victim who has been bitten by a dog. Stress

the horrible nature of biting (S. Winkler, personal communication, 1984).

19. For persistent biting, refer the student to a school counselor or district psychologist (Weissbourd, 1984).

20. Discuss the behavior with the student's parents to determine if they have observed this behavior at home (Katz, 1983).

21. Console the individual who has been bitten, but do not dwell on the matter (Weissbourd, 1984).

22. Coat exposed areas with the bad-tasting liquid available in stores to stop nailbiting.

23. Use a mild aversive consequence (e.g., squirt the student's face with a water stream, place tabasco sauce in his mouth, splash soapy water in his eyes, etc.).

24. Learn to release a prolonged bite by placing one of your hands on the offending student's forehead to stabilize it, and using your other hand to pull down on his jawbone.

25. If caught in the student's bite, use one hand to push on the student's forehead while pushing the bitten part of your body downward and rolling it out of his mouth.

8

Bossy

1. Ignore the acting-out behavior and reinforce the appropriate behavior (Daniels, 1974).

2. Remind the student to say "please" (Becker, 1971).

3. Respond only to polite requests from the student (Becker, 1971).

4. Model polite respectful behavior (Becker, 1971).

5. Start a cooperative program with the parents to correct the student's behavior.

6. Have the student chart the number of times he uses the word *please*. Require the student to increase the total by at least one time each day.

7. Make the student rephrase the statement before you respond to the request.

8. Say many different requests to the student. Have the student identify which ones are polite and which ones are impolite.

9. Strengthen youth ties to positive value groups. Encourage positive norms and a sense of personal responsibility (Cannon, 1981).

10. Teach and promote positive values in the school. Increase the use of curricular materials and emphases that provide both the incentives and the resources for confronting problems of moral commitment and choice.

11. Refer the student for counseling (Lee and Klopfer, 1978; Lewis, 1978).

12. Use sociodrama or role playing to rehearse proper interaction (Creekmore and Madan, 1981; Ramsey, 1981; Warrenfeltz, 1981).

13. Implement a token reinforcement system (Gable and Strain, 1981).

14. Suggest participation in interscholastic athletics. Athletics positively influence the overall socialization of the individual (Landers and Landers, 1978).

15. Place the student in time-out (Stoops and King-Stoops, 1972; Polsgrove, 1982).

16. Assist the student in channeling energies into acceptable outlets (Millman, Schaefer, and Cohen, 1980).

17. Speak plainly about the degree of common courtesy that is expected from the students. Elicit from the class ways in which they should handle themselves when another decides to boss or manipulate them (Ramsey, 1981).

18. Discuss with students the various things they could do when being pushed around (e.g., "We've decided today that when someone starts bossing us around we'll stare at them."). This way the tables are turned and the all-class agreement gives support to the victim.

19. Discuss the student's behavior during a class meeting. Peer group pressure may assist in behavioral change.

20. Counsel the domineering student. Suggest that he may be dominating situations because he wants to be the big shot, that he wants to put some people in their place and even a score, or simply that he craves attention and doesn't know how else to get it. Help the student identify the cause and set goals for future behavior.

21. Establish time limits for talking or using material. This clarifies the situation and prevents conflict.

22. Tell the student to play in another spot by himself until he is ready to rejoin the group.

23. Videotape small-group activities in which the domineering student is inclined to show bossy behavior. Discuss the film objectively, asking each student to evaluate his own behavior, not that of others (Millman, Schaefer, and Cohen, 1981).

24. Provide opportunities for the student to attract attention in acceptable ways and reward him for desirable behavior (Kiyoth, 1970).

25. Use sustained silent reading as a mood modifier (Millman, Schaefer, and Cohen, 1981).

9

Bullies or Teases Others

1. Punish the student every time he bullies others. Use educational punishments such as asking him to write a paragraph or compose a short story during his leisure time (M. Yusuf, personal communication, 1975).

2. Give the student certain obligations as a leader of the class and remind him that he must assume the responsibility of maintaining the comfort or safety of the class (M. Yusuf, personal communication, 1985).

3. Tell the student that his behavior is not ac-

ceptable and discuss how it might cause him to lose friends (M. Yusuf, personal communication, 1985).

4. Role play a situation in which the student is bullied (M. Yusuf, personal communication, 1985).

5. Suggest that the student avoid playing with other aggressive students because he tends to identify with the successful aggressors (Kirk and Gallagher, 1983).

6. Suggest that the student avoid watching aggressive movies (Lahey and Ciminero, 1980).

7. Suggest to the student's parents that they not let their child watch violent TV programs, as youth are inclined to imitate actions viewed on them (Kirk and Gallagher, 1983).

8. Avoid situations in which the student is likely to become frustrated. Frustrated students tend to be aggressors (Schloss, 1983).

9. Provide the student with a variety of appropriate peer and adult models, hoping that he will be able to observe and then imitate the proper behavior (Kirkland and Gallagher, 1983; Schloss, 1983).

10. Inform the student that aggressive behavior will not produce a reduction in aversive events, nor elicit compliance from others (Schloss, 1983).

11. Engage the student in emotionally enhancing experiences by asking him to read a story about the effect of someone who often bullies friends. The teacher could also compose such a story and narrate it (Schloss, 1983).

12. Actively teach the student skills that are incompatible with aggression, yet equally powerful in producing satisfaction (e.g., self-control skills, social skills, and relaxation skills) (Schloss, 1983).

13. After an incident of bullying, have the offending student identify other ways in which the situation could have been handled.

14. After having bullied another, give the offending student a choice of providing resti-

tution and apologizing nicely, or being given a punishment.

10

Criticizes the Work or Ideas of Others

1. Reinforce the student for complimenting others or avoiding criticism.
2. Place the student in time-out (Walker and Shea, 1980).
3. Send the student to the principal's office (Givner and Graubard, 1974).
4. Use punishment or threats of punishments.
5. Move the student to another part of the room in order to avoid the problem (K. Alvis, personal communication, 1983).
6. Institute a class rule, stating that any disagreements or concerns should be voiced privately to the teacher.
7. Isolate the student in one corner of the room with a cubicle surrounding him (C. Walters, personal communication, 1984).
8. Have the student rephrase negative comments (e.g., "That's stupid") into more objective language (e.g., "I disagree with that view"). Have the student tell why he disagrees.
9. Have the student mention one good thing about the work that he has just criticized.
10. Refocus the student back to his own work and have him evaluate that.
11. Engage the student in group brainstorming in which participants rapidly mention ideas for solving a problem and build on those ideas. No criticism is allowed. The number of ideas, however novel, is important.

11

Fighting

1. Reinforce good behavior by using verbal praise. This should be done frequently when the student displays good conduct toward others (Hammill and Bartel, 1982).
2. Make it clear to the individual that his "fighting behavior" will not be accepted. A rule chart should be made and posted, containing what is and is not acceptable in the classroom (Orlich, 1980).
3. Use response-cost punishment. A warning is given and if the behavior continues, the student loses a privilege. If it occurs again, the student loses another (Orlich, 1980).
4. Place the student in time-out (Kerr and Nelson, 1983).
5. Hold class discussions where everyone discusses behaviors they dislike about others. Names are not mentioned. Discussion centers on how the behaviors can be eliminated, handled, or changed.
6. Explain the democratic form of government. Point out that in a democracy, everyone is free to express his own beliefs and one should respect or debate these beliefs rather than use violence to change them.
7. Have a police officer come to speak to the class about good conduct and the consequences of bad conduct (Payne, Palloway, Smith, and Payne, 1981).
8. Seat the student close to you. Make certain that he can be seen, especially during free time when arguments may arise (Haas, Kasper, and Kryst, 1979).
9. Talk with the student involved in the fight. Gather all sides of the story from every person involved. Have the students think of another and better way that they could have settled their differences. Be certain that they understand that violence was the worst solution that could have been used.
10. Keep the student occupied by giving him interesting and motivating assignments (Myers and Hammill, 1976).

11. When a disagreement begins, intervene and stop it immediately. If the students are fighting about materials or leadership positions, explain to them that if they do not resolve their differences peacefully, you as the teacher will assign materials and positions and these assignments will be final.

12. Put the student near the front of the line so that he can be seen by the teacher (Haas, Kasper, and Kryst, 1979).

13. Give the student a special project when be behaves well (Haas, Kasper, and Kryst, 1979).

14. When the student is out of the room, tell the other pupils that his antics are not appropriate and that you need their assistance to help him control his behavior (Haas, Kasper, and Kryst, 1979).

15. Find reinforcing consequences for the student's positive behavior to develop the desire in him to be good (Haas, Kasper, and Kryst, 1979).

16. For a particularly disruptive student, sit next to him and use some sort of physical contact to calm him (Haas, Kasper, and Kryst, 1979).

17. Use peer reporting of appropriate behavior so that other students reinforce positive behavior (Millman, Schaefer, and Cohen, 1980).

18. Help the student channel energies into acceptable outlets (Millman, Schaefer, and Cohen, 1980).

19. When hitting or threats occur, have the student do 10 exercise sets (Kerr and Nelson, 1983).

20. Enroll in a course on physical restraint of aggressive behavior.

21. Prevent situations in which the student is likely to become frustrated (Schloss, 1983).

22. Implement the "think aloud" program which uses four problem-solving questions: What is my problem? What is my plan? Am I using my plan? How did I do? (Millman, Schaefer, and Cohen, 1980).

23. Restrict opportunities for the student to observe any aggressive models (Schloss, 1983).

24. Seat the student among classmates who display appropriate behavior (Knoblock, 1983).

25. Isolate the student's desk from that of others.

26. Recommend counseling by the school psychologist or guidance counselor (B. Slifer, personal communication, 1984).

27. Set up a values program to teach pro-social skills. To develop a sense of empathy, discuss how the student would feel if someone picked a fight with him (Haas, Kasper, and Kryst, 1979; Kerr and Nelson, 1983).

28. Allow the student to use materials to vent anger in a constructive way. Suitable materials include clay, paint, and punching bags (Bruner and Hall, 1982).

29. Utilize self-mediated strategies:
    a. Obtain the student's cooperation for the program.
    b. Identify the feelings, thoughts, and reactions that he experienced prior to the outburst.
    c. Review a videotape of the student role-playing his reaction to the frustrating situation.
    d. Have the student role play reactions that are incompatible to the earlier behavior.
    e. Train the student to use responses incompatible to the behavior.
    f. Sign a contract with the student that outlines implementation of these steps (Kerr and Nelson, 1983).

30. Assign more responsibilities to the student. In effect, get the student so involved in activities that he has little time to engage in violent acts or make threats (Goldstein and Rusenbaum, 1983).

31. Ignore the undesirable behavior and reinforce appropriate behavior. Use only if the negative behavior is not injuring others or causing damage (Daniels, 1974).

32. Plan punishments for the student but use them infrequently (Schloss, 1983).

12

Flares Up at Classmates if Teased or Pushed

1. Reinforce appropriate behavior to increase its frequency.
2. Increase the student's social skills by increasing the frequency of his contacts with others (Verville, 1967).
3. Encourage the student to become involved in Boy Scouts, Girl Scouts, Cub Scouts, or Campfire Girls. These organizations are open to all students and provide regular opportunities to share in work and play (Verville, 1967).
4. Have the student observe how you and other teachers handle anger. He may model this behavior and learn to handle anger appropriately (Clarizio, 1980).
5. Encourage class discussion of current classroom events and issues. Have a time set up each day so the students may bring any of their problems or concerns out in the open. This will allow for open communication, which may help prevent build up of tension (Verville, 1967).
6. Give praise and responsibility to increase the student's self-esteem. In turn, this may affect his social relationships (Verville, 1967).
7. Allow time each day for the student to partake in vigorous physical activity. This may help to relieve tension (Altrocchi, 1980).
8. Provide the student with extra practice in basic school subjects. This will help keep his mind off other problems. The extra practice will lead to more success in academics and will also improve his self-concept (Verville, 1967).
9. Structure situations to avoid conflict. Review rules and guidelines before each activity. Enforce these restrictions.
10. Intervene in conflicts immediately. Discuss other methods of resolution with the students.
11. Place the student in a nonthreatening environment (Lawrence, Steed, and Young, 1983).
12. Send the student out of the room and have a private talk with him. Explain to him that these kinds of outbursts are not allowed in the classroom (Lawrence, Steed, and Young, 1983).
13. Inspect the student's previous class records. This might help in understanding the causes of the behavior (Lawrence, Steed, and Young, 1983).
14. Praise and identify others who are behaving well. This may motivate the disruptive student to model classroom peers (Lawrence, Steed, and Young, 1983).
15. Do not allow the other students to tease this student.
16. Place the student in time-out if he flares up at others.
17. Utilize self-mediated strategies:
    a. Obtain the student's cooperation for the program.
    b. Identify the feelings, thoughts, and reactions that he experienced prior to the outburst.
    c. Review a videotape of the student roleplaying his reaction to the frustrating situation.
    d. Have the student role play reactions that are incompatible to the earlier behavior.
    e. Train the student to use responses incompatible to the behavior.
    f. Sign a contract with the student that outlines implementation of these steps (Kerr and Nelson, 1983).
18. Implement the "think aloud" program which uses four problem-solving questions: What is my problem? What is my plan? Am I using my plan? How did I do? (Millman, Schaefer and Cohen, 1980).

13

Picks on Others

1. Give attention and respond to the student's cooperative speech and behavior. Ignore the student's aggressive behaviors (Slaby and Crowley, 1977).

2. Plan a seating arrangement in which the student is surrounded by classmates who display good social skills and working habits (LaMancusa, 1966).

3. If the behavior seems to be due to frustration, identify the student's current level of functioning and plan educational activities at a criteria level that is attainable yet challenging (Schloss, 1983).

4. Plan for aversive control, but use it infrequently (Schloss, 1983).

5. Before beginning an activity, provide the student with pretask instruction that includes directions such as: "Do not harm others," "Do not disrupt the class," "Follow the rules"(Zahavi and Asher, 1978).

6. Provide the student with a variety of peer and adult models to imitate (Schloss, 1983).

7. Provide opportunities for the student to participate in emotionally enhancing experiences that are incompatible with aggression (Schloss, 1983).

8. Provide the student with opportunities to engage in physically exerting activities that will safely release muscle tension (Rivers, 1977).

9. Have the student self-record his misbehavior. Interview the student regarding his record at the end of each school day (Lovitt, 1973).

10. Salvage the student's self-respect by providing him with opportunities to erase his former image (e.g., if the student has previously spent much time in the principal's office, allow him to deliver messages to the principal) (LaMancusa, 1966).

11. Teach the student the "turtle technique." Have the student enfold his body into an imaginary turtle shell when the teacher, class, or student expects an aggressive act to occur. While the student is in the "turtle" position, have him apply muscle relaxation techniques while considering alternative strategies for coping with the situation that caused this response (Robin, Schneider, and Dolnick, 1976).

12. Place two chairs facing each other in front of the classroom. When the student begins to pick on another student, have him sit in one of the chairs and imagine that the other student is across from him. Encourage the student to tell the imaginary student anything he wishes. Then have the student change seats and assume the role of the other student by telling how he thinks that student would feel. Finally, allow the other student to sit in each chair and assume each role. Conclude with a rational discussion (Goodman and Timko, 1976).

13. Conduct a "sharing time" at the end of each school day, giving your students the opportunity to report the cooperative and friendly behaviors of their peers (Grieger, Kauffman, and Grieger, 1976).

14. Have a discussion with the student. Listen to him while making attempts to decode or reflect the communications. Provide the student with acceptable labels for feelings of distress to help him better understand his actions (Rivers, 1977).

15. Clarify the situation and define the reaction by making direct statements such as: "Paul insulted you, so you hit him," or "You are too hot and can't do your work" (Harris, 1980).

16. Conduct a three-way conversation with the parent, student, and teacher. Make him face what he has done. Allow him to state his position (Rogers, 1972).

17. Use punishment or threats of punishments, pressuring behaviors, or imperative use of language (Guthrie, 1981).

18. Hold a discussion on the rights of others.

19. Role play the situation followed by different appropriate ways of reacting (T. Marlier, personal communication, 1984).

14

Rejects Classmates in a Hostile Manner

1. Reinforce all appropriate behavior (M. Anderson, personal communication, 1985).
2. Make brief notations about the student's abrasive behavior. Does a pattern appear? (Pearson, 1974)
3. Talk with the student about his hostility after school everyday for a week. Keep a record of your talks, and each day review the previous day's conversation. This may help him to detect the common denominator of the talks.
4. Provide the student with opportunities to discover for himself the reasons for his hostility by videotaping the class and sharing the film during a class meeting.
5. Place the student around others who can help his behavior instead of provoke it (Millman, Schafer, and Cohen, 1981).
6. Anticipate and check the undesirable behavior with a diverting comment (e.g., "Jim, were you about to _____?").
7. Analyze the reasons for the student's hostility. This involves getting to know something about his abilities, experiences, background, physiological and psychological drives, and consulting those best qualified to help.
8. Allow the student to feel that he has some control over the situation, perhaps by drawing up an agreement that focuses on diminishing the hostility (Clarizio and McCoy, 1976).
9. Study the student's art work for clues to his inner-self.
10. Show films that portray students interacting positively with each other.
11. When misbehavior occurs, withhold a privilege, demonstrating that the student must accept consequences for his actions (Millman, Schafer, and Cohen, 1981).
12. Have the student play the role of the student who was rejected. Avoid preaching. Let the activity speak for itself. He may, for the first time, appreciate how his behavior causes another to feel.
13. Discuss the student in a team meeting with or without his presence. Try to pinpoint his hostility and suggest methods of changing the behavior (Clarizio, 1975).
14. Refer the student to a school counselor (M. Anderson, personal communication, 1985).
15. Isolate the student after hostile incidents and allow him an opportunity to "cool-off" in a time-out room (Stoops and King-Stoops, 1972).
16. Place the student in a spot in the classroom where he can be observed by the teacher at all times (Stoops and King-Stoops, 1972).
17. Consult the student's parents about the problem. Indicate your observations of rejection and the consequences it is having on his personality, school work, and the attitudes of others toward him (Stoops and King-Stoops, 1972).
18. Have the student identify and implement alternatives to the rejection behavior.
19. Seat the offending student next to the other students in your class who are least likely to be affected by his behavior.

15

Sarcastic

1. Praise the student for nonsarcastic commentary.
2. Allow the student to talk out his feelings. Do not stop him to scold (Baruch, 1949).
3. The student may be sarcastic because of feelings of hostility and pent-up anxiety. Relaxation exercises or athletic events may be helpful (Reinhart, 1980).
4. Take away privileges if the behavior persists (D. Randall, personal communication, 1985).
5. Require the student to restate the sarcastic

response in proper wording and tone of voice.

6. Use a nonverbal signal that warns the student that he is being sarcastic and must stop.

7. Ask the student to write his feelings of contempt.

8. Give the student a choice between apologizing for his behavior or receiving an appropriate punishment.

9. Chart the number of sarcastic remarks given during a certain period of time. Reinforce the student for reducing the number of remarks each day.

10. Use sarcasm against this student. Later, use it as subject matter for a discussion of feelings of others and the use of caustic humor.

11. If certain students are repeatedly the target of the sarcasm, teach them sarcastic comebacks to use when targeted in the future.

12. Allow the student to record his remarks on audiotape. Replay it to the class during free time. Have them rate the jokes for degree of humor.

13. Help the student to distinguish between friendly sarcasm and hurtful sarcasm.

16

Spits at Others

1. Give reinforcement to the student when he displays positive behaviors or restrains from displaying negative ones (Clarizio and McCoy, 1976).

2. Ask the student what he did. Perhaps hearing himself state the action will help him realize more clearly what was done.

3. Ask the student to write his feelings of contempt.

4. Solicit the help of the class in coping with the spitter (e.g., "Class, right now I am faced with a problem of dealing with someone who just spit on another. Could you help me list on the board some possible reasons for why he might have done that?").

5. Interpret the meaning of the student's act for him (e.g., "Eric, by spitting on me you have just told me that you do not like me very much.").

6. Order the spitter to wait in an isolated place until someone else has time to come to talk to him. Leave the student alone to think for a while.

7. Have another student or the teacher role play the offending student.

8. Use peer pressure (e.g., "Brent spit at someone on the playground today. Tomorrow, if he does not spit at anyone, we will have a puppet show.").

9. Use self-reinforcement of self-control procedures. The student records and evaluates his own behavior and then rewards himself accordingly (Bolstad et al., 1972; Clarizio and McCoy, 1976).

10. Agree with the student on certain times and places in which spitting may be acceptable.

11. Talk to the student about the fragility of people's feelings and how shattering a gesture like spitting can be to others.

12. Note and remember for future reference the things that seem to trigger the spitting behavior. If there is a particular behavior preceding spitting, modify the environment to control this.

13. Have the student wipe the spit off of the other person.

14. Make the student spit into a can or flowerbed until he is thirsty and tired of doing this. Use this punishment each time that the behavior occurs.

16. Embarrass the student into stopping by saying, "John, are you drooling again?" When he insists that he was not drooling, tell him, in public, that it looked that way to you. If you can get others to cooperate with you, ask them, "Didn't it look like drooling to you folks?"

17
Throws Objects

1. Reinforce the student for not throwing objects during a set period of time.
2. Provide highly structured programs to prevent the behavior (Blanco, 1972).
3. Provide adult supervision at all times (Blanco, 1972).
4. Anticipate and prevent situations that are likely to make the student throw objects (Blanco, 1972).
5. Do not force the student to do a task at which he is very poor. This may help eliminate frustration (Blanco, 1972).
6. Seat the student next to someone who will discourage the throwing behavior (Blanco, 1972).
7. Materials not in use should be stored properly or locked in cabinets (Gervais and Dittburner, 1981).
8. Teach the student to think to himself about what he is about to do (Hawaii, 1982).
9. Leave the situation when the student is about to throw an object (Hawaii, 1982).
10. If the behavior is not harming others, ignore it, thereby avoiding reinforcing it through attention (Schwartz and Johnson, 1981).
11. Teach the student to count to ten, breathe, and relax when he feels like throwing something (Hawaii, 1982).
12. Use visual imagery exercises to decrease the aggression (Hawaii, 1982).
13. Use role playing to make the offender feel different about his actions (Helge, 1983).
14. Move around the room during class and be aware of student activity (Gervais and Dittburner, 1981).
15. Take pencils, school materials, crayons, and so forth away from the student if he continually throws them (Blanco, 1972).
16. Utilize regular, private conferences to discuss the student's need for self-control (Blanco, 1972).

17. Allow a free-play period to release tensions and pent-up energy (Blanco, 1972).
18. Allow the student to displace his hostility into neutral objects such as punching bags, tether balls, clay, and fingerpaints (Blanco, 1972).
19. Allow the student to throw nerf balls, sponges, and balloons in the classroom. These objects, when thrown, will not hurt anyone. Phase these out later (S. Winkler, personal communication, 1984).
20. Play throwing games with bean bags, horse shoes, and darts to help the student realize when throwing is acceptable (Reinhart, 1980).
21. Allow the use of soft foam rubber bats to hit another person if aggression must be released (Reinhart, 1980).
22. Involve the student in games of competition, sports, or other physical activities (Senn and Solnit, 1968).
23. Require that the student stay within certain boundaries marked by masking tape on the floor. Remove favorite objects that are thrown from the area.

18
Verbally Abusive

1. Reinforce appropriate behavior (Konczak and Johnson, 1983).
2. Reinforce appropriate behavior, but use time-out for inappropriate behavior (Bostow and Bailey, 1969).
3. Publicly post rules and impose group consequences to bring peer pressure upon the student (Holland and McLaughlin, 1982).
4. Have the student jog at a vigorous rate over long distances at the beginning of each day to relieve pent-up hostility (Backman and Fuqua, 1983).
5. Encourage proper behavior by having the student use self-evaluation techniques (Rhode, Morgan, and Young, 1983).

6. Have peers challenge the targeted student to help that student become aware of his behavior and its effects on others (Bellafiore and Salend, 1983).

7. Sit the student near you (Haas, Kasper, and Kryst, 1979).

8. Ignore the behavior (Haas, Kasper, and Kryst, 1979).

9. Isolate the student from the rest of the class (Haas, Kasper, and Kryst, 1979).

10. When the student is out of the room, tell his classmates that the student's behavior is not appropriate and that you need their assistance in helping the student control his behavior.

11. Tell the student that you care for him as a person, but that you will not tolerate the exhibited behavior (Haas, Kasper, and Kryst, 1979).

12. Don't react emotionally to the student's behavior. State the inappropriate behavior. Tell the student other choices he has in the area of behavior. Tell the student the behavior you expect from him. Implement consequences in a consistent manner (Haas, Kasper, and Kryst, 1979).

13. Have the student write his feelings on paper.

14. Chart the number of verbally abusive statements. Reinforce the student if he lowers that total each day.

15. Discuss with the student how he feels when he is the recipient of verbal abuse.

16. Place the student in time-out (D. Olson, personal communication, 1980).

17. Videotape or audiotape the student's behavior and play it back so that the student can actually see or hear his abusive behavior (D. Olson, personal communication, 1980).

18. Use dance or art to alleviate aggression (D. Olson, personal communication, 1980).

19. Use a consequence totally unrelated to the behavior, such as standing up and sitting down 10 consecutive times after being verbally abusive (Luce, 1980).

20. Require the student to rephrase his comments into socially acceptable form.

7

Attentional Problems

19

Attention Span
Not Increased by Punishment
or Reward

1. Select the student to be Student of the Week. This will make him feel special and important. Seat him in a special chair and give him a badge to wear. Each day ask the other classmates to write something special about the student being honored. They may write positive statements about abilities or personal attributes. Also the students can decide on other special activities that they can do for the student. Some examples would be writing a story about him or playing a favorite game at recess. By doing this, the student will feel important and special and perhaps increase his attention span to better earn praise (Mercer and Mercer, 1981).

2. Have the student self-record his own on-task behavior and academic performance.

Provide him with his own checklist and have him record within a predetermined time period set by you (McLaughlin, 1983).

3. Use touch, movement, variation in voice level and tone, and the student's name to draw his attention.

4. Make a wall chart with the pupil's name across the bottom and numbers in the left-hand column. Record the cumulative number of volunteered responses for the pupil. Do this for a week. At the end of the week, determine if the wall chart should be continued. If so, set weekly goals (Hartman, Lucas, and Stephens, 1982).

5. Write short, personal notes to the student to provide encouragement and to let him know you have an interest in him (Mercer and Mercer, 1981).

6. Tape a temperature sensor to the third finger of the student's dominant hand to detect fluctuations in temperature. By watching a finely tuned meter attached to the sensor, the teacher and the student can monitor the slightest temperature changes. Guided by this instant feedback, the stu-

dent can determine the sensory setting that occurs when he concentrates on his work and can attempt to maintain that setting (Hershey, 1983).

7. Wait until noises and distractions in the room are at a minimum before beginning a lesson (Gold, 1981).

8. Suggest that the student receive "attention training." This training provides the student with strategies for maintaining attention (Kaplan, 1981).

9. Make some academic tasks look more difficult than they really are. The student will gain self-confidence when he successfully completes a task thought to be difficult (Mercer and Mercer, 1981).

10. Set a purpose for listening by providing advanced organizers. Students will have a task in mind before they begin to listen to the message. For example, "Listen carefully and tell me the color of the cat in the poem. Then tell me everything that is the same color as the cat. I will ask you to name these items when I have finished reading the poem" (Gold, 1981).

11. Provide the student or students with a journal. Designate a quiet time of 20 minutes each day for writing in these journals. Assist if necessary. Following the writing, the students will listen to another student read her or his composition (Belensee and Smyth, 1983).

12. Use self-monitoring. This focuses on having the student record his own attending behavior. The typical procedure involves an audiotape with tones or a voice saying "Now" on it that sounds on an average of every 45 seconds, but at irregular intervals. The student is trained by the classroom teacher to ask himself "Was I paying attention?" at the sound of each tone. The student then records by checking a box for Yes or No in response to the question. After recording his response, the student returns to work until the next tone sounds (Hallahan, Lloyd, and Rooney, 1984).

13. Increase the size and color of the instruc-

tional materials. Use vivid colors to highlight instructional materials, thus making them highly stimulating.

14. In a structured learning environment, provide simple tasks at which the student can be successful (Swap, 1974).

15. Implement a task analysis approach whereby the student is taught appropriate cognitive strategies to solve problems (Alford and Brown, 1984)

16. Introduce the forced choice letter recognition task. This is a response to tachistoscopic exposures of displays of letters containing one of two signal letters. The student knows what these signal letters are (e.g., the letter T and the letter F) and that each will be seen in 50 percent of the exposures. Each signal letter is presented within a display that contains irrelevant letters. The student must scan through the letters in the display until the signal letter is found. The number of letters scanned defines the span of attention (Blackwell, Cronin, and McIntyre, 1978).

17. Teach the student to pay attention. Train him to have shoulders squared toward the thing or person to which he is to attend, and lean slightly forward and keep eyes on the thing or person to which he is paying attention (Argulewicz, 1982; George, 1982).

18. Design a curricular activity with a specific starting point and a series of steps leading into a conclusion. Check with the student at each step (Swap, 1974).

19. Use the student as a tutor in peer tutoring situations. This may boost his self-esteem. It also shows that the teacher has confidence in the student's ability to handle the task (Mercer and Mercer, 1981).

20. Make learning fun and interesting for the student. Do this by using materials that are of interest to the student such as a tape recorder, computer, or language master (A. Courtney, personal communication, 1985).

21. Seat students in a circle. This enables students to engage in significantly more on-task behavior than when seated in rows or clusters (Rosenfield, 1985).

22. Allow a stopwatch to run while the student is attending or on task. Stop the watch when the student is off task. Allow the student to earn rewards based on the amount of time accumulated.

20

Distractible

1. While the distractible student is attending to the task at hand, verbally praise him and simultaneously stand near or touch or pat him (Clements and Tracy, 1977; Haas, Kasper, and Kryst, 1979).

2. When the student is distracted by others let him work in a different area of the classroom (Mercer, 1983).

3. Guide the students by giving reasons for becoming better listeners in the classroom.

4. Set an example by being a good listener (Lorayne, 1973).

5. Teach the student how to attend. Teach the proper body posture of squaring the shoulders toward the task, leaning the body forward, and placing the eyes on the work (George, 1982).

6. Have the student make a list of recommendations for reducing or eliminating distractibility. Check the list for feasibility. Implement the suggestions (Lane, 1984).

7. Set up Attending-to-Task training sessions. When the student is on task, actively participating, introduce distractions purposely (M. Quale, personal communication, 1985).

8. Help the student develop a resistance plan to implement when presented with a distraction. Rehearse the plan to improve chances of success (Patterson, 1965).

9. Provide the student with the opportunity to earn rewards by working on lengthy tasks in the face of tempting distractions. Instruct the student to remind himself to say, "No, I'm not going to look. I will re-

main on task" (Mischel and Patterson, 1976).

10. Teach the student to analyze the demands of a specific task and talk to himself about keeping on task (George, 1982).

11. Teach self-monitoring. Set a timer for various intervals. At the sound of the bell, have the student check either the Paying Attention column, or the Off Task column (Hallahan, Lloyd, Kosiewicz, Kauffman, and Graves, 1979; Reinhart, 1980).

12. Seat the student in an isolation booth or carrel when he is doing seat work (Strauss and Lehtinen, 1947; Blanco, 1972).

13. Seat the student near the teacher with his back to the rest of the class (Blanco, 1972).

14. Seat the distractible student next to a student who has appropriate work habits (Broden, Bruce, Mitchell, Carter, and Hall, 1970).

15. Seat the student away from windows, doors, and activity areas.

16. Have the student sit in the front of the room near the teacher (Haas, Kasper, and Kryst, 1979).

17. Create learning centers with a wide variety of materials and activities that can be worked on either individually or in pairs (Gallagher, 1979).

18. Clearly designate special areas of the classroom for certain activities. Do not let others complete projects near the distractible student's desk (Lane, 1984).

19. Designate a time-out area in the room. Place the student there for small periods of time for off-task behavior (Lane, 1984).

20. Reduce distracting stimuli. Arrange the school environment so that exhibits or pictures are kept to a minimum. Have the room painted in a plain, soft color with neutrally colored desks and tables (Berryman and Perry, 1974).

21. Use cupboards or curtained shelves for toys and classroom materials (Berryman and Perry, 1974).

22. Keep extraneous classroom noise to a min-

imum. Select a room away from a street or playground (Berryman and Perry, 1974).

23. Select phonograph records of stories that do not have background music or any sounds other than the story itself (Berryman and Perry, 1974).

24. Use a semicircular arrangement of chairs and separate each chair with a screen. This blocks the student's view of others yet allows you to work with the group of individuals (Berryman and Perry, 1974).

25. Be sure that the material presented is adjusted to the general interest and intellectual level of the students (Dukar, 1971; George, 1982).

26. Simplify tasks and the terms of instruction (Berryman and Perry, 1974).

27. Give school work in small units to accommodate the student's attention span (Blanco, 1972).

28. Use color cues to direct student attention to important information, key words, and directions (Allington, 1975; Special Learning Corp., 1979).

29. Place written or pictorial cues at selected places on a worksheet to help the student focus attention during the individual work (Algozzine, 1982).

30. As soon as a student displays inattention or boredom, change the assignment. Rewards are earned by the student regardless of the type of task, as long as he is functioning appropriately (Hewett, 1967).

31. To increase speed, have the student work against a timer and chart his own progress. For example, record on a graph the number of addition problems completed correctly during a specific period (Bolstad, Johnson, Broden, Bruce, Mitchell, Carter, and Hall, 1972).

32. Use a narrow opening or window cut out of cardboard to direct and focus attention on one line of material (Blanco, 1972).

33. Have the student use ear plugs, head phones, or cotton to reduce auditory distraction (Blanco, 1972; Barklin et al., 1981).

34. Use a colored placemat as the background for assigned tasks. Use the student's favorite color to restrict his tendency to be distracted by other stimuli (L. Levinson, personal communication, 1983).

35. Have the student use a placekeeper for reading work (Haas, Kasper, and Kryst, 1979).

36. Add design and color to the worksheets to make them more interesting and attention getting.

37. Lecture away from windows and open doors.

38. Adjust the length of listening time to the class level of listening span (Lynch, 1967).

39. Alternate listening activities with nonlistening activities. Watch for signs of frustration and reduce auditory activities when these signs are apparent (Berryman and Perry, 1974).

40. Use a less frequently chosen instructional format that may bring higher attention levels than the more frequently used format (Kirley, 1981).

41. Use activities that involve the total body as they serve to focus the attention of the distractible child (Lerner, 1985).

42. Allow choices from a variety of activities within a skill area (R. Smith, personal communication, 1985).

43. Require each student to present a lesson relating to the unit. This may be an individual or group presentation. This method might increase student attention and participation (A. Roger, personal communication, 1985).

44. Give the student opportunities to select projects that have special interest to him (Special Learning Corp., 1979).

45. Provide the student with the opportunity to use a different writing tool (e.g., crayons, pens, markers) (Special Learning Corp., 1979).

46. Provide an area in the room to which the student can go when his problem of maintaining attention becomes overwhelming (Berryman and Perry, 1974).

47. Substitute a desirable behavior for an undesirable one. Ask the student to look at the blackboard or in his book, not out the window. Ask that the student place pencils on the desk instead of tapping them (Hayden, Smith, Saaz, and von Hipple, 1982).
48. Play memory games. The student will have to give full attention to these types of activities to do well (Bush and Giles, 1977).
49. Play games with the student that require attention and concentration (Blanco, 1972).
50. Practice activities such as classification, rhyming, matching, and association. These types of activities may assist the student in learning to stay on task (Bush and Giles, 1977).
51. Teach the student to follow block patterns on the floor while walking down the hall. This may help him to proceed from one classroom to another without being distracted (Barklin et al., 1981).
52. Set up two activities or games by dividing the class into groups. Put the distractible student in the group with which he functions best (Schloss, Schloss, and Segraves, 1985).
53. Require that all work be completed before going home.
54. After each scene of a movie, stop the projector and ask the student to identify what the character was doing.
55. Allow the student to work on computers to learn a new skill or remediate a weak one (Lane, 1984).
56. Videotape the student during regular class hours. Seeing himself on tape may help him to become more aware of the need to change his behavior.
57. Use role playing. Role reversal encourages a student to learn how his behavior is perceived by and influences others.
58. As a means of encouragement, ask everyone in the student's group to help the target student remain on task (Simmons and Wasik, 1976).
59. Hold group discussions centered around the feelings and behaviors of the students. Assign one student to be the listener and one student to be the observer in each group. Each group will also contain a talker. The talker will state something of importance to him. The listener will listen and then ask questions. The observer will watch and later make statements concerning the experience. This method may increase the distractible student's interest level and attention span (Myrick and Kelly, 1971).
60. Make sure the student has a "guardian angel" (another student) to help him through the day when the routine is changed (Haas, Kasper, and Kryst, 1979).
61. Interest the student by using filmstrips, games, and puzzles in lesson instruction (Swap, 1974; Mercer, 1983).
62. Structure the task tightly with clear rules, beginning and end points, and few transitions (George, 1982).
63. Present only one assignment at a time. When the student finishes a task, it is removed and the next activity is introduced (Berryman and Perry, 1974).
64. Present puzzles one piece at a time (Berryman and Perry, 1974).
65. Modify the pace of the classroom. Gradually increase short blocks of time designated for activities and offer periodic breaks.
66. Be sure the student is actively listening. Ask him questions. Ask for opinions or reactions (Edelman, 1984).
67. Be sure all directions and assignments are clearly stated and understandable (George, 1982; Edelman, 1984).
68. Organize the setting to maximize time in a one-to-one teacher/student ratio (George, 1982).
69. Avoid using extraneous materials or jargon when teaching. Too much background can detract from the topic and

often confuse the student with facts that are not necessary to the comprehension of the material (Gallagher, 1979).

70. Provide multisensory instruction to increase the probability of the student attending to the learning task (Thorpe and Borden, 1985).

71. Use direct eye contact whenever talking to the student (Haas, Kasper, and Kryst, 1979).

72. Provide cues to promote attention such as pointing to salient features of the material, giving leading sounds, snapping fingers to demand a response, and hinting at and modeling correct responses (George, 1982).

73. When presenting materials, direct the student's attention to the relevant aspects by saying, "Look at this" and "Look here" while pointing to the picture, word, or figure to which you want the student to attend (Stephens, Hartman, and Lucas, (1978).

74. Use visual aids when lecturing (Commonwealth and Gootnick, 1974).

75. Unravel the lesson in front of the students while they assist in the development of the concepts by either working out given problems or responding to your questions about the lesson (Commonwealth and Gootnick, 1974).

76. Use a sense of humor to keep the student interested and involved (Wegman and Talent, 1982).

77. Keep teacher talk at a minimum (Gold, 1981).

78. Minimize visual and auditory distractions (Underwood, 1976).

79. Establish a good rapport with the listener to promote attention (Lorayne, 1973).

80. Vary volume and tonal quality while speaking (Nicholas, 1957; Wegman and Talent, 1982).

81. Arrange for comfort in terms of temperature, lighting conditions, and seating arrangements to allow for full concentration (Trabasso and Bower, 1968).

82. See that that student's desk is free from clutter and as well organized as possible (Barklin et al., 1981).

83. Avoid being distracted yourself. When you stop to talk to another teacher during a lesson, it could convey to the students that the lesson takes second priority. Show the students that the lesson is of paramount importance. Ask the messenger to come back at another time or leave a note on your desk (National Education Association of the U.S., 1984).

84. Observe the student to distinguish between unintentional and intentional actions. Discuss them with the student. Make up a signal between the two of you to make the student aware of his unintentional actions (Rivers, 1977; Kirwan, 1985).

85. Stand by the student's desk as often as possible when talking to the class (Haas, Kasper, and Kryst, 1979).

86. Combine listening improvement with everyday learning (Lynch, 1967).

87. Point out that failure to listen well to directions in school often can mean the difference between good and poor grades (Dukar, 1971).

88. Ask the student for a first-hand experience of embarrassment caused by careless listening (Nicholas, 1957).

89. Send complimentary notes home when the student displays on-task behavior (Haas, Kasper, and Kryst, 1979).

90. Show a videotape that contains scenes of the school day. After each scene, stop the projector and ask the student to identify what the character is doing. If it is a task-oriented scene, the student is reinforced for correctly identifying the situation. Make further comments about the good things that could happen to the character for studying so hard. Give no praise or reinforcement for nontask-oriented scenes (Nixon, 1969; Daniels, 1974).

91. Chart the student's attending behavior so that he can see his progress (Daniels, 1974).

92. To increase a student's attention span, allow the distractible student to earn rewards for paying attention to taped instructions. Each tape may include 10 directions as part of the lesson, such as: "Raise your hand," "Close your eyes," and so on. The student will receive one point for responding appropriately within two seconds. Points can later be turned in for tangible rewards of the student's choice (Woolfolk and Woolfolk, 1974).

93. Shortly after assigning a task, provide a reward for those students who have started the work and completed several problems (R. Smith, personal communication, 1985).

94. Reward students who have completed tasks so that others are encouraged to work steadily to finish an assignment (Mercer, 1983).

95. Reward "free time" to the entire class for attentive behavior for a designated time period. Use a stopwatch to time each interval (Devine and Tomlinson, 1976).

96. Make time-out a consequence of inattentive behavior (Devine and Tomlinson, 1976).

97. Make teacher social praise and approval contingent with on-task behavior (Lynch, 1967; Broden, Bruce, Mitchell, Carter, and Hall, 1970; Rogers and Baer, 1976; Lewis and Strain, 1978).

98. Agree with the student that if he finishes a specific part of an academic task within a certain amount of time, he may have an additional amount of time added to his break during the day. The contract should specify an accuracy criterion. This will discourage rushing (Daniels, 1974; Mercer, 1983).

99. Set up a token system of reinforcement to motivate the student and reduce distracting behaviors. For example, whenever the student attends appropriately, place a chip or token in a container. When the student does not display attention, remove a chip (Daniels, 1974; Ayllon, Lyman, and Kandel, 1974; Kornswiet and Yarnell, 1981).

100. Discuss with parents the possibility of modifying the student's diet to exclude sugars, additives, colorings, or to include vitamins. This should be done with the approval and supervision of a doctor (Lane, 1984).

101. Recommend that the parents consult with a physician regarding the use of stimulant drugs to improve attending behavior (Underwood, 1976; O'Leary and O'Leary, 1977).

102. Refer the student for counseling to determine whether distractibility is a result of emotional turmoil. Deal with the student in accordance to the results. Make modifications and allowances based on the counselor's recommendations (Lane, 1984).

21

Jumpy; Easily Startled

1. Determine if hearing and sight testing has been conducted recently.

2. Seat the student in a part of the classroom where he can see others approach.

3. Seat the student away from high-traffic areas in the classroom.

4. Approach the student from the front.

5. Walk more heavily and noisily as you approach the student so that he will notice your approach.

6. At a distance, warn the student of your approach.

7. Use a soft, gentle voice when addressing the student.

8. Speak softly at first and raise your voice as you continue to speak.

9. Have consistent, established classroom routines so the student knows what to expect.

10. Use bonding and friendship-building activ-

ities to make the student feel more comfortable in the classroom.

11. After an incident, ask the student how he could have predicted the situation or how it could have been handled differently.

12. If the reaction appears to be insincere or contrived, discuss appropriate reactions with the student.

13. Investigate the possibility of physical abuse.

14. Investigate the possibility of drug use.

15. If the reaction seems to be due to suspiciousness or emotional disturbance, recommend counseling for the student.

22

Oblivious to What Is Happening in Class

1. Reinforce the student when he is paying attention (Hewett, 1968).

2. Look at the student directly. Speak slowly and briefly (Mosse, 1982).

3. Read aloud. This demands attention and counteracts distractibility (Mosse, 1982).

4. Vary the presentation of the task. Introduce novelty. If the student is usually asked to write sentences for spelling words, perhaps he can dictate a story to a peer or into a tape recorder (Mandell, 1984).

5. Use effective questioning techniques to determine if the student understands the assignment. Ask him to explain the assignment in his own words (Mandell, 1984).

6. Consider the personal relevance of the information to the student. Can the student see a relationship between his experience and the task? Can you help to make this connection? (Mandell, 1984).

7. Help the student to attend by giving him the time and opportunity to prepare a response. Rather than saying, "Name the planets in our solar system, John," prepare the student to respond by saying, "John,

(pause) you're next. Name the planets in our solar system" (Mandell, 1984).

8. Reinforce the student when he is attending (Mandell, 1984).

9. Consider whether or not the student has the necessary concepts to understand the information. Using vocabulary that is not understood or building on skills that are not well developed may result in loss of attention (Mandell, 1984).

10. Set the purpose for listening. Create a mindset before reading a passage so the student knows what to listen for (Gold, 1981).

11. Keep teacher talk to a minimum so that what is said draws attention (Gold, 1981).

12. Train the student in physical attending or posturing behavior. Aspects of this are sitting squarely, leaning forward, and focusing eyes on an object or person (Argulewicz, 1982).

13. Create a stimulus-free classroom. This calls for bare walls painted a bland color, covered windows, and student cubicles enclosed on three sides devoid of books and papers. Along with reduced extraneous stimulation, emphasize relevant stimuli on worksheets through novel uses of color, shape, and type size (Harris, 1976).

14. Teachers should not distract the attention of the class away from lesson content unnecessarily. For example, if the student is daydreaming, do not interrupt the lesson to bring him to attention. Rather, incorporate his name into the next set of directions (e.g., "Look at page 26. All of you, including Nancy and Sue, can look at the graph that shows . . .") (Rinne, 1982).

15. Help the student pay attention to lesson content. Before instruction, prepare conditions for learning that promote a high degree of continuous attention to content. Act during instruction to establish, maintain, and reestablish attention to lesson content (Rinne, 1982).

16. When it is time for instruction to begin, the student should sit quietly, hold feet and

hands still, and look at you or the appropriate materials. He should also stop any verbal or motor behavior that may interfere with the learning process (Stowitschek, 1984).

17. Use humor to maintain attention (Mandell, 1984).

18. Investigate the recent history of the student to determine if personal problems are the cause of this oblivious behavior. If so, recommend counseling.

19. Recommend a medical or psychological evaluation if the student seems "lost."

20. Work with the student on an individual basis (J. Bonwell, personal communication, 1984).

21. Try different modalities of presenting material to find one that best keeps the student on task.

22. Have the student work with a partner (J. Bonwell, personal communication, 1984).

23. Have the student keep a chart of accomplishments to stimulate interest in staying on task.

24. Present tasks in a game format.

25. Talk about a subject in which the student is interested (J. Bonwell, personal communication, 1984).

26. Seat the student near the teacher where physical touch and nonverbal signals can bring the student back to task.

27. Stand near the student who is not paying attention. This will focus the attention of the other students in the area where he is seated, placing pressure on him to pay attention (T. J. Grothaus, personal communication, 1985).

28. Use more activities that encourage classroom participation, especially from the student who appears to be in his own world (M. C. Grothaus, personal communication, 1985).

29. Begin the class with an "attention getter" such as a joke, rhyme, story, and so on (T. J. Grothaus, personal communication, 1985).

30. Sit or bend down so that you are on the same level as the student and make eye contact with him (Park, 1972).

31. Vary your routine. Use attention-demanding stimuli (e.g., yelling, bright lights, ice cubes on the neck).

32. Use an intense stimulus to demand attention.

33. Use a large, as opposed to a small, visual stimulus.

34. Present the stimuli more than once.

35. Administer the *Attention Level Inventory* to determine the frequency of inattention and assess his receptivity to primary rewards (Hewett, 1968).

36. Use concrete multisensory experiences (Hewett, 1968).

37. Use a colored stick as an attention wand. This wand is to be used whenever full attention is required (Hewett, 1968).

38. Wear an "attention mask" to indicate that attention is required and to get the student to look at the teacher. If the student looks at the teacher for a designated period of time, give him a reward (Hewett, 1968).

39. As an attention-building exercise, have the student tap the number of beats on his desk that correspond to the number of taps by the teacher on a drum (Hewett, 1968).

23

Perseveration; Attention Becomes Fixated

1. Reinforce the student when he shows the proper behavior and doesn't perseverate (Stephens, Hartman, and Lucas, 1978; Lerner, 1976; Reinhart, 1980).

2. When a child perseverates, simply say, "Stop" and do not get involved in further discussion. This verbal signal may be accompanied by either a tactile or visual cue (Barklin et al., 1981).

3. Keep a supply of self-directed activities or

games to be used during transition times (Barklin et al., 1981).

4. Give a few minutes' warning before a change in activity (Barklin et al., 1981).

5. Always give simple, clear, and concise directions (Reinhart, 1980).

6. Develop activities that teach the following of directions (Bush and Giles, 1977).

7. Use bold lines and thick margins to prevent perseveration in writing.

8. Monitor the student closely or have a peer monitor-assist the student.

9. Develop a magic word with the student's help (e.g., *snarzelpharf*) that will signal the student to stop the perseveration.

10. Have a timer sound periodically. The student determines whether he was perseverating when the sound occurred. This is charted by the student.

11. Place a hand on the student's shoulder as a reminder to cease perseveration.

12. Prepare the student for a change in activities by "counting down" the time left in the present activity.

13. One minute before the end of an activity, ask the student what he should be doing to prepare for the end of the task.

14. Praise another student who has followed directions and ended a task when told to do so (Brinbauer, Hopkins, and Kauffman, 1981).

15. Make an audiotape of someone else's voice giving directions to the student, telling him when to begin and end a task. The recorder would be placed on the student's desk. The recorded directions would end with the voice telling the student to stop, followed by a count to ten and a shrill sound. The sound should continue until the student pushes the Off button, at which time you should intervene to assure that the student does not go back to the task (Warner, 1973).

16. Develop a videotape that demonstrates teacher's instructions and a student following these instructions. Review the tape with the student.

17. Use action songs and a tambourine to interrupt the student's train of thought and behavior patterns (Mahlberg, 1973).

18. Use a back projection of a kaleidescope on the wall or ceiling to distract the student's attention. At that precise moment, obtain his attention and redirect him to the next task at hand (Jellis and Grainger, 1974).

19. Place the student's desk as close to yours as possible. When the student is to end a certain task, sound a buzzer that is located on your desk. The student must get out of his seat and turn it off (Finch and Weinberg, 1976).

20. Time the student to see how long it takes him to stop working on one task and move on to another. Have the student attempt to decrease this time each day.

21. Place a mirror in front of the student when it is time to move on to another task. Take notice of the precise moment the student's eyes catch his image in the mirror and ask a question. Ask for attention or offer praise (Egeland, 1974).

22. Darken the room or flash the classroom lights to signal the end of a task or activity (J. Roth, personal communication, 1986).

24

Quickly Loses Attention When Teacher Is Explaining Something

1. When the student is paying attention, respond with specific verbal praise (Hall, 1968; Bernhardt and Forehand, 1975).

2. When reinforcing attentive behavior, make sure that the student knows how to pay attention; otherwise, you may be reinforcing "looking" behavior (Kauffman, 1985).

3. In instances where the student is extremely distractible, the use of stronger reinforcers than teacher attention may be needed. Candy, trinkets, and other extrinsic rewards should be used. Before the initiation

of such a program, the rules should be reviewed with the student (Hallahan and Kauffman, 1975).

4. Train the student with activities to increase his attention span.

5. Use group responses. This requires all students to respond together and be attentive. Examples include the use of individual chalkboards, group answer cards, or group verbal response (Myers and Hammill, 1976).

6. Reinforce students who attend to directions. When the nonattentive student notices this, he may also attend better (Azaroff and Mayer, 1977).

7. Ignore nonattentive behaviors (Azaroff and Mayer, 1977).

8. Indicate to the student when he is attending appropriately and mention that because he can attend now, he can also attend in other situations (Azaroff and Mayer, 1977).

9. Set a timer initially for short intervals and gradually increase the timed intervals. When the timer rings, everyone who was positively attending is allowed a chance on the "slot machine" (e.g., five paper cups turned over, under which lie slips of paper with a reinforcing activity, prize, or nothing). As attending behavior increases, the timed intervals also increase (Azaroff and Mayer, 1977).

10. Direct the student to listen for a certain word to be said (e.g., a color or name). The student keeps a count and an accurate total is rewarded. Although the student's attention would be directed toward the catch word, he would also have to attend to the directions (C. Frankiewicz, personal communication, 1985).

11. Materials and methods should be geared to the student's ability to succeed. A short attention span or lack of concentration may be the result of material that the student cannot learn or understand.

12. Use repetition of specific guidelines (Lerner, 1985).

13. Give **direct** and specific instructions (Lerner, 1985).

14. Formulate a set of standard questions to act as reminders: "Are you looking carefully at the directions?" "Did you check your answers?" "Did you answer each question completely?" (Lerner, 1985).

15. Materials for the student should be widely spaced and not very detailed. Small portions of printed material should be presented at a given time. Dark underlining or color clues should accompany directions to attract attention to the desired area (McCarthy and McCarthy, 1969).

16. It may be necessary to isolate the student or eliminate extraneous sights and sounds while giving direction (McCarthy and McCarthy, 1969).

17. Move while speaking and make quick, exaggerated movements.

18. Vary your voice tone and volume to be more vivid.

19. Touch the student if he becomes nonattentive.

20. Use humor while speaking.

21. Have the student repeat the directions in his own words to assure understanding.

22. Keep directions short and simple. Avoid elaboration and extraneous information.

23. Give the assignment in steps or segments.

24. Put the directions on audiotape so that the student can review the tape if necessary.

25. Make privileges dependent on the correct completion of the task.

26. If the student completes the assignment incorrectly, have him redo the task after restating the directions.

27. Have the student explain something to you. Look away and yawn during the explanation. Use this as substance for a discussion on listening to others.

28. Give a boring lesson or set of directions. Tell the student that you are doing this purposely and, as a game, you want him to listen attentively so he can later tell what was said.

29. Have the student list reasons why accurate listening is important.

30. Place written directions on the task to avoid having to repeat yourself.

31. When explaining something, establish eye contact with the student (Edelman, 1984).

32. Before explaining something or giving directions, state to the class that one student will be required to do an example on the chalkboard of what is being explained (D. Jasek, personal communication, 1986).

33. Set up a role-playing situation in which the student has the role of a teacher explaining something to the class. Assign another student the role of an inattentive student. Observe how the "teacher" responds to the "student," and the next time he is not paying attention respond to him in the exact same way (D. Jasek, personal communication, 1986).

35. Set up classroom activities that strengthen listening skills. For example, play a game entitled Telephone Book, which requires the student to listen to a tape of instructions that leads him throughout the book with a series of clues until he reaches the designated number (Burnham, 1981).

8

Authority Conflicts

25

Argumentative

1. Positively reinforce cooperative behavior (Carberry, 1978).
2. Avoid confrontations with the student that may result in an argument (Carberry, 1976).
3. Take the student aside to discuss the argumentative behavior privately. Never reprimand him in front of the group (Brennan, 1974).
4. Develop a contingency contract with the student. Initially use a short period of time when the student is expected to avoid arguing. Expand the time period as the behavior improves (Dolly and Page, 1981).
5. Listen carefully to the student's argument without responding. Once he has finished, move on to an unrelated activity (Whong, Fletcher, and Fawcett, 1982).
6. Hold a conference with the student to determine if there are reasons for wanting the argumentative behavior not to occur. Determine appropriate ways that the student

can appropriately and effectively deal with the behavior (Adelman and Taylor, 1983).

7. Allow the student to determine mutually agreeable specific choices to use in order to decrease the behavior (Adelman and Taylor, 1983).
8. Develop a nonverbal cue (e.g., wink, nod) to indicate that you have recognized the student for using one of his alternate choices (Adelman and Taylor, 1983).
9. Have a nonbiased party decide which person is "correct." Abide by this decision.
10. Withdraw from the argument and suggest a meeting later in the day. After the "cooling off" period, discuss the problem in private (Tauber, 1981).
11. Provide structure in the classroom with understandable and attainable goals, rules, and boundaries. Define specifically what is expected of the student so that he has less reason to argue (Murray and Whittenberger, 1983).
12. Identify situations when argumentative situations are likely to occur. Use this knowledge to anticipate and defuse potentially

explosive situations (Murray and Whittenberger, 1983).

13. When developing the IEP, include all mainstreamed teachers and work out a plan to deal with the argumentative behavior that can be carried out consistently in all situations. In the plan, cooperatively motivate the student to work toward a realistic and attainable goal. Reward the appropriate behavior (Munson, Miller, and Berman, 1981).

14. Have the student assess his argumentative behavior through discussions with a small group of peers. Have the peer group suggest alternate responses to use when an argumentative situation arises (Campbell, Dobson, and Bost, 1985).

15. Encourage a reaction by fellow students when the individual argues, indicating that the peers find the argument to be inappropriate (Campbell, Dobson, and Bost, 1985).

16. Give the student opportunities to make positive contributions to the class. Praise his contributions (Campbell, Dobson, and Bost, 1985).

17. Encourage the student to voice his argument in writing. Respond to the argument in writing in a positive and supportive manner (L. Burr, personal communication, 1985).

18. Whenever the student argues about an assignment, require an additional assignment to be completed (Campbell, Dobson, and Bost, 1985).

19. Teachers can be wrong. Be willing to listen to the student's argument. Be willing to admit your own areas of weakness and lack of knowledge (Kerry, 1981).

20. Have the student suggest better ways of dealing with his needs (Floyd and Hughes, 1980).

21. Send the student to time-out when the argument begins. While in time-out, have the student role-play appropriate behavior with you. Reinforce positive verbalizations while role-playing (Floyd and Hughes, 1980).

22. Develop a token economy system. Whenever the student initiates an argument, take away a token (Floyd and Hughes, 1980).

23. Investigate the role of the parents in the argumentative behavior. Involve the parents in a master plan, educating them to the results of their child's behavior. Encourage the parents to deal with it appropriately (Brennen, 1974; Caldwell, 1977).

24. Privately rehearse appropriate responses to arguments with the student (Berler, Gross, and Drabner, 1982).

25. Have the student make a list describing possible appropriate responses to substitute for an argument (Berler, Gross, and Draber, 1982).

26. Lower the student's grade on the particular assignment that caused the argument (Campbell, Dobson, and Bost, 1985).

27. Once a decrease in argumentative behavior is evident, gradually introduce situations in which the student's behavior is usually agreeable. Tell the student you appreciate the fact that he is changing his behavior. Discuss goals and rewards with him (Carberry, 1976).

28. Allow the student to argue for one minute in a nonyelling voice. At the one-minute mark, stop the student and give your final, unwavering decision on the matter. Implement negative consequences if the student continues to argue.

29. Explain exactly what is considered arguing by giving the student different situations to help determine appropriate responses. The student's own responses should be used as examples (Sprick, 1981).

30. Be aware of your facial expressions and tone of voice. How you sound and look can affect a student's willingness to do as expected. Make sure your expression shows caring and concern (Marlin, 1977).

31. Ease the tension through humor. This offers the student an opportunity to ''save face'' (Fried, 1978).

32. Encourage the student to improve his logic

and judgment rather than always trying to win the argument.

33. Upon your direction, have the student stand up and sit down 10 times on the floor. This teaches the student to obey rather than argue. Physical prompting may be necessary (Luce, Delquadri, and Hall, 1980).

34. Set up certain times for argumentation. This way the student can anticipate that time and other tasks will not be jeopardized.

35. Periodically have the student write his arguments instead of speaking them. Have a student that he respects react to the arguments.

36. Require the student to preface at least some of his statements with, "I agree with you on. . . ."

37. Have the student record positive interactions and negative interactions with others. If he has more positive marks than negative ones on the first day, he earns free time. On the following days, free time is earned by decreasing the number of negative interactions (Sprick, 1981).

38. When a student responds without arguing, give verbal praise. After an entire day without arguing, allow the student to spend 10 minutes with the teacher doing something special (Sprick, 1981).

26

Becomes Angry if Asked to Do Something

1. Praise the student when he does something without becoming angry (J. Mitsdarfer, personal communication, 1984).

2. Assure that you are not needlessly arbitrary and restrictive (Tyrrell, 1977).

3. Withdraw from the conflict. Acknowledge the student's power and ask the class to help in getting the student to behave (Dinkmeyer, McKay, and Dinkmeyer, 1980).

4. Allow the student to help establish rules. This gives him a better understanding of the rules and why they are needed (Tyrrell, 1977).

5. Give the student a choice of either doing the work or going to the office (J. Mitsdarfer, personal communication, 1984).

6. Allow the student to have some choice in learning activities (Tyrrell, 1977).

7. Use reflective listening and negotiate with the student (Dinkmeyer, McKay, and Dinkmeyer, 1980).

8. Use rules and reminders to develop appropriate behavior (Becker, 1971).

9. Control the environment to produce fewer frustrations for the student (Walters, 1981).

10. Say, "I'll be glad to talk with you when you're ready to discuss it calmly." Then walk away or busy yourself with other tasks (Dinkmeyer, McKay, and Dinkmeyer, 1980).

11. Reassure the student that he is valued, respected, and loved (Walters, 1981).

12. If the anger is disruptive, remove the student from the classroom (Dinkmeyer, McKay, and Dinkmeyer, 1980).

13. Help the student identify his strengths. Promote these whenever possible (Walters, 1981).

14. Encourage the student to talk about feelings with people who care about him, rather than acting out his emotions (Dinkmeyer, McKay, and Dinkmeyer, 1980).

15. Keep requests short and simple so as not to upset the student (Dinkmeyer, McKay, and Dinkmeyer, 1980).

16. Reword negative instructions to make them positive. Tell the student what *to* do (e.g., instead of saying, "No running," say, "Walk") (Sloane, 1976).

17. Provide the student with opportunities to work off anger through sports and games (Sheviakov, 1969).

18. Eliminate any critical remarks from your instructions (e.g., instead of "Don't be lazy—use your knife and fork," say, "Please use

your knife and fork and show us how well you can eat'') (Sloane, 1976).

19. Discuss with the student which expressions of anger are acceptable and which are not (Sheviakov, 1969).

20. Withhold social reinforcement by ignoring the behavior (Newcomer, 1980).

21. Stress the effect upon you rather than upon the student (e.g., instead of saying, ''You will be nicer if you stop swearing,'' say, ''I will feel happier if you will stop swearing'') (Sloane, 1976).

22. Use humor and encourage the class to laugh together (Sheviakov, 1969).

23. Tell the student that when he finishes with the work he may help other students with their work.

24. Praise the student for good work and effort (Sheviakov, 1969; Blanco, 1972; Wade, 1984).

25. Calmly tell the student that this task must be completed before any privileges are granted or before he may go home that night.

26. Give the student a more appropriate method for expressing angry feelings or releasing tension (e.g., art, sports, bibliotherapy) (Stopps, 1961; Oaklander, 1978).

27. Prepare the student for a request so that it does not surprise him when presented (Becker, 1971).

28. Have one of your class rules state that students must follow teacher directions the first time that they are given.

29. Help the student build a positive self-image via self-concept activities.

30. Model appropriate behavior.

31. Warn the student of what will happen if anger persists (Becker, 1971).

32. Help the student identify with whom or what he is angry and why (S. Williams, personal communication, 1983).

33. If the student sometimes becomes violent, attend a workshop on how to handle aggressive behavior.

34. Do not back the student into a corner.

Allow the student to avoid embarrassment in front of peers.

35. Use punishment by withdrawal of reinforcers rather than also becoming angry and providing an aggressive model (Becker, 1971).

36. Give the student a chance to settle down in the morning. Overlook mild misdemeanors as the class settles down to work. A day that starts without confrontation has more of a chance of continuing that way (Wade, 1984).

37. Discuss reactions to this behavior with the members of the staff and administration who interact with the disruptive student. This helps to achieve a consistency within the school, thus providing a united front and greater sense of security for the student with this kind of need (Wade, 1984).

38. Keep rules reasonable, rather than petty or meaningless (Wade, 1984).

39. Have a routine and timetable so that the student knows exactly what is expected of him and when (Wade, 1984).

40. Try to anticipate the student's feelings and work out coping strategies in advance (Wade, 1984).

41. Use quiet and calm talk with physical contact, such as a hand on the shoulder, to keep the situation low key (Roberson, Lewandowski, Potts, and Michell, 1982).

42. Be sure all worksheets are clear and uncluttered. Be specific in all directions (Department of Instruction and Support Services, 1984).

43. Set objectives that are tangible and reachable (Department of Instruction and Support Services, 1984).

44. Explain to the student why he needs to master certain skills (Department of Instruction and Support Services, 1984).

45. Relate all learning to everyday life to show the need for studying (Department of Instruction and Support Services, 1984).

46. Always be positive and encourage the student to do his best (Department of Instruction and Support Services, 1984).

47. Teach one concept at a time to avoid confusion (Department of Instruction and Support Services, 1984).

48. Encourage questioning to keep the student's frustration from building (Department of Instruction and Support Services, 1984).

49. Give fun assignments occasionally (Department of Instruction and Support Services, 1984).

50. Use a "job form" in which each task that has to be accomplished is listed and must be done within a certain amount of time (Department of Instruction and Support Services, 1984).

51. Recognize that this student may have internalized this behavior as a way of life, in which case a referral to the school psychologist is in order (Berres, 1979).

52. Hold general discussions in which the teacher gets the group to talk about how they handle feelings of anger. It is important to emphasize how normal it is to have feelings of anger and how satisfying it is to talk about them instead of acting them out (Berres, 1979).

53. Have personal meetings with the student and express concern about his behavior. If the student denies the behavior, arrange for a personal signal to give when you feel that the behavior is beginning (Berres, 1979).

54. Allow him to choose between two succinctly stated alternatives. Explanations should be brief as well as nonnegotiable (e.g., the student may choose not to do something, but in choosing this, he misses out on a favorite activity or privilege later) (Blanco, 1972).

55. Try to keep the student separate from those who laugh at or are nonsupportive of him (Blanco, 1972).

56. Set up a program so that there are rewards for being obedient and consequences for being disobedient (Blanco, 1972).

57. Encourage self-direction. Give the student an opportunity to make rules and regulations for his own conduct (Blanco, 1972).

58. If the student appears as though he is trying to invoke physical punishment, make a verbal reflection of the student's feelings by saying something such as, "It seems as though you are trying to get me to punish or hit you" (Blanco, 1972).

59. Send a note home with the student when he has a good day (Blanco, 1972).

60. The behavior may be a sign that the work is too difficult for the student, and he is afraid to admit it. Consider lowering the task level (Blanco, 1972).

61. Place the student in a subordinate position in a group that has a strong positive leader (Blanco, 1972).

62. Try to offer choices. If the student thinks he is choosing to do writing over math, within time he may try to do the things with which he feels less comfortable (Pearson, 1974).

63. Do some role-playing activities. Often the student can devise some reasonable and effective solutions when he "sees" his own behavior (Blanco, 1972).

64. Make a contract with the student in which the student is rewarded for withholding anger (Anderson, 1974).

65. Make "punishment cards" to hand to the student when he is misbehaving. In this way you can spend little time on the behavior. The cards are pre-explained to the student (Anderson, 1974).

66. Hold a conference with the student's parents to discuss the behaviors and gain their support (Stoops, 1961).

67. Give the student special jobs and responsibilities so that he feels you genuinely like him and have trust and faith in his ability (Stoops, 1961).

68. Encourage the student to talk about the underlying things that may be bothering him (Stoops, 1961).

69. Have the student write an autobiography. This may give some insight into his problems (Stoops, 1961).

70. Investigate health conditions, both mental and physical. The student may need a psychiatric referral, family counseling, or medical treatment (Stoops, 1961).

71. Visit the student's home so that he perceives a genuine interest from you (Stoops, 1961).

72. If the student is having trouble participating with the whole group, assign quiet work at his desk. The feeling of isolation may make him want to join the rest of the class and act appropriately (Stoops, 1961).

73. Remember that tenseness in the student may be caused by tenseness in the teacher; therefore, embarrassing the student will not help. If you feel that you are tense, it might be best to avoid contact with the student for a while (Stoops, 1961).

74. Avoid being placed on the defensive. Don't argue with the student. Deal with the student in a calm, controlled manner (Stoops, 1961).

75. Discuss actions, not personalities. Let the student know it is the behaviors you dislike, not him (Stoops, 1961).

76. Make sure all the directions are clearly stated. The student may become angry because he does not know what is expected of him (Walker, 1979).

77. Be consistent and impartial. Certainty of punishment is more of a deterrent than severity (Cultice, 1969).

78. Teach behaviors that you are trying to instill. Most behaviors are learned.

79. Become aware of the student's personal values in order to appeal to them (Mercer and Mercer, 1981).

80. Allow the student to choose between a variety of tasks within one skill area. For instance, allow him either to write sentences, correct punctuation on a ditto paper, or some related task, in order to see if he can use punctuation properly (Mercer and Mercer, 1981).

81. Give rewards to students who start work immediately after being told to do so (Mercer and Mercer, 1981).

82. Start the day by putting 15 slash marks on the board. Explain that the marks are for 15 minutes of free time or can be used toward something larger (e.g., a field trip). Every time the student misbehaves, erase a mark so that he will see that he has lost time (Mercer and Mercer, 1981).

83. Have the student chart his own behavior (Mercer and Mercer, 1981).

84. Play referee for the student. Hold up a yellow card as a warning to cool down. Hold up a red card to indicate that a certain consequence is being administered.

85. Provide a cubicle or corner into which a student can withdraw when angry. The student is allowed five minutes to "cool off" before returning to work.

86. Institute a program whereby the student must stay two minutes after school for each minute of displayed anger.

27

Deliberately Tries to Get into Trouble

1. Immediately reinforce the good behavior that the student exhibits (K. Schmitt, personal communication, 1985).

2. Warn the student when his behavior is disrupting the learning environment (Konstantareas, 1984).

3. Upon the display of undesirable behavior, take away a privilege that the student likes or an activity such as free time (Konstantareas, 1984).

4. Have the student stay after school for a set time period and increase the time as negative behavior increases. Have the student clean chalkboards or perform other duties that will not let the student enjoy his stay (K. Schmitt, personal communication, 1985).

5. Enforce a structured curriculum that will allow the student to receive points or to-

kens for good behavior (Konstantareas, 1984).

6. Have the student do independent work away from other students (K. Schmitt, personal communication, 1985).

7. Eliminate distractors that draw his attention and give him devious ideas (e.g., seat him away from doors, windows, supplies, and other students) (K. Schmitt, personal communication, 1985).

8. When the student is off task, direct his attention back on task by either verbally intervening or nonverbally signaling him immediately before undesired behaviors occur (K. Schmitt, personal communication, 1985).

9. Hold a conference with the parents of the student to implement school discipline consequences at home (e.g., television or phone usage) (Williams, 1983).

10. Ignore the behavior; it might be directed at drawing your attention (K. Schmitt, personal communication, 1985).

11. Forewarn the student that any misbehavior will result in negative consequences for him.

12. Gain other students' cooperation in ignoring or denouncing the undesired behavior.

13. Place the student in time-out.

14. Embarrass the student after misbehavior by sarcastically saying to other students, "Someone wants our attention. Let's all watch him for a while." Then address the student, saying, "Go ahead, you've got our attention."

15. When a confrontation occurs, withdraw and suggest a meeting later. After a "cooling off" period, discuss the problem in private (Tauber, 1981).

28
Disrespectful of Authority

1. When respect is shown, socially reinforce the student with a pat on the back, a smile, verbal praise, a handshake, or a hug (Herbert, 1978).

2. If the behavior is isolated, use planned ignoring (Herbert, 1978).

3. Keep conflicts to areas where others cannot observe the behavior.

4. Discuss with the student how breaking the rules makes it difficult for others in the classroom to work and enjoy themselves.

5. Be consistent with all students in all situations so the student knows that you are being fair (Kerr and Nelson, 1983).

6. Establish rules that state desired behavior in observable terms. Enforce these rules consistently, reteaching when necessary.

7. Use an agreed upon signal to warn the student when his behavior is becoming unacceptable.

8. Arrange to meet quietly with the student for a few minutes after school, just to talk (Karlin and Berger, 1972).

9. If lack of respect for rules is severe, refer the student to a therapist or counselor (Herbert, 1978).

10. Institute time-out (Herbert, 1978).

11. Use punishment by presenting an aversive consequence or by removing a positive event following a display or lack of respect.

12. Teach the student the relationship between his disrespectful behavior and its consequences (Millman, Schaefer, and Cohen, 1981).

13. Ignore disrespect until after class and discuss the problem with the student individually. If improvement is not evident, schedule a parent conference.

14. If the display of disrespect causes a disruption of classroom activities, send the student to the office.

15. Use role play and videotape playback to make the student aware of his actions and attitudes (Millman, Schaefer, and Cohen, 1981).

16. Train the student in self-control so that he is able to stop the chain of events that lead

to conflicts with school authorities (Millman, Schaefer, and Cohen, 1981).

17. Divide students into teams and intermittently give checkmarks for courteous behavior. Take away points when anyone on a team acts in a disrespectful manner. The team with the most checkmarks at the end of a set time is allowed to engage in a chosen activity (K. Christensen, personal communication, 1984).

18. Withdraw all communication from the student until he is ready to behave in a respectful manner (Schaefer and Millman, 1977).

19. Ask the student why he feels the need to be disrespectful. Devise a plan for change (R. Christensen, personal communication, 1984).

20. Use a Rodney Dangerfield comedy record album that includes routines about "I don't get no respect" as an introduction to a discussion about respect for others.

21. React to every incidence of disrespect. Do not let disrespectful behavior occur without a consequence.

22. Allow the student to rephrase his comment in order to avoid punishment.

29
Does the Opposite of What Is Asked

1. Reinforce the student when compliant behavior is demonstrated (Blanco, 1972).

2. Review the directions of the task before allowing him to proceed.

3. Have the student repeat the directions in his own words to assure understanding.

4. Observe the student's work during the initial part of the assignment to assure that it is being done correctly.

5. Have the student check with you at various points during the task to assure that the directions are being followed.

6. Have the student redo assignments or repeat actions until correctly done (Lovass and Bucher, 1974).

7. Explain to the student why following directions is important.

8. Give the student a list of palindromes (e.g., deed, kayak, pep, noon). Tell him to copy these words from "front to back." Even if he writes them backwards, they will still appear to be correct (Lovass and Bucher, 1974).

9. Implement negative consequences for noncompliance (Lovass and Bucher, 1974).

10. Give directions that are the opposite of what you wish to be done. When the student does the opposite of what is directed, he will produce the desired product.

11. If the student has a receptive problem with oral language, give short, simple directions or write them.

12. Model the appropriate behavior for the student (Jones, 1980).

13. Have the student participate in forming rules and procedures to follow (M. Pierre, personal communication, 1985).

14. Have the student check off steps on a list as they are completed.

15. Review with the student what should have been done after he has completed the assignment in an incorrect manner. Have him redo the assignment according to these guidelines.

16. Encourage self-direction. Give the student an opportunity to make his own program, making him accountable for his own actions (Blanco, 1972).

17. When the student does not do what is expected, offer an explanation of the nature of the misbehavior, as he may not understand what was wrong. Offer alternative behaviors that are more acceptable (Blanco, 1972).

30

Does Things in His Own Way

1. Give praise to students who are following directions (Canter, 1974; Lovass and Bucher, 1974).

2. Allow the student a choice of assignments or ways of completing an assignment. This gives him a personal choice within guidelines (Blanco, 1972).

3. Review the student's work while in progress to assure that it is being done correctly.

4. Give the student a verbal cue when he does not follow directions (Lovaas and Bucher, 1974).

5. Have the student experience negative consequences for not following directions (e.g., staying after school) (Lovaas and Bucher, 1974).

6. Set up a token economy for the student (Lovaas and Bucher, 1974).

7. Have the student redo the work or repeat the action until it is correctly done (Lovaas and Bucher, 1974).

8. Have the student keep a record of his behavior (Lovaas and Bucher, 1974).

9. Have the student self-evaluate his behavior (O'Brien, Riner, and Budd, 1983).

10. Contract with the student for setting goals and rewards (Center and Wascom, 1974).

11. Explain to the student why it is important to follow directions (C. Weyeneth, personal communications, 1985).

12. Model the appropriate behavior for the student (Jones, 1980).

13. Have the student participate in forming rules and procedures to follow (M. Pierre, personal communication, 1985).

14. Have the student repeat the directions in his own words. Be sure that the student's interpretation agrees with yours.

15. Have the student complete the assignment in specific segments. Check each part.

16. Have the student check off steps on a list as they are completed.

17. Review with the student what should have been done after he has completed the assignment in an incorrect manner. Have him redo the assignment according to these guidelines.

18. Encourage self-direction. Give the student an opportunity to make his own program, making him accountable for his own actions (Blanco, 1972).

19. When the student does not do what is expected, offer an explanation as to why the misbehavior was wrong. Offer alternative behaviors that are more acceptable (Blanco, 1972).

31

Does Not Conform to Limits

1. Reinforce the student when limits are obeyed (Canter and Canter, 1976).

2. Ignore the student's inappropriate behavior.

3. Give a warning that appropriate behavior is expected.

4. Place the student in time-out.

5. Set specific limits for the student. If the student does not stay within the limits set, then the student loses his privileges. Enforce limits consistently.

6. Start with limits that are not as strict and reinforce the student when limits are obeyed. Then move to stricter limits and reinforce those when met. Use this process until limits correlate with the other students' limits and are obeyed. Gradually fade reinforcements.

7. Use peer pressure to help the student stay within limits by encouraging others to remind the student when limits are breached (J. Bonwell, personal communication, 1985).

8. Use rational-cognitive therapy, a therapeutic approach that promotes the changing of

a student's thoughts, beliefs, perceptions, and attitudes (Newcomer, 1980).

9. Arrange an individual conference with the student to discuss the problem of not conforming to limits. Discuss why limits are important.

10. Use videotaping to show the student the frequency and severity of the inappropriate behavior.

11. Have the student tally the number of limit violations. The student must decrease this total each day to receive reinforcement until an appropriate level is attained.

12. Have the student list events that might happen if society had no laws or limits.

13. Let the student be the "teacher" to see how difficult it is to conduct a learning experience when others refuse to obey the rules.

14. If questioned or confronted by the student, withdraw from the challenge and suggest a meeting at another time during the day. This allows a "cooling off" period before the problem is aired in private (Tauber, 1981).

15. Divert the student's attention to another activity and go back to the problem at another time (Hipple, 1978).

16. Acknowledge the student's excuse, but do not be swayed from administering a consequence (Womack, 1983).

17. When a student complains about the rules, explain that someday he will be able to make some of his own rules. For now, however, you make the rules and he is to follow them (Womack, 1983).

18. Invite the student to come back for a private interview after the class to discuss his behavior (Wilcox, 1983).

19. At the beginning of the year, state that conflicts between the students and yourself are natural and that it is important for them to be resolved. Point out that it is important for: (a) "face saving" on the part of both parties, (b) tempers to cool down, and (c) power struggles not to interfere with the scheduled learning activities (Tauber, 1981).

20. Acknowledge the student's power and solicit his cooperation (e.g., "Yes, I know you could, but I would appreciate it if . . .") (Tauber, 1981).

21. Individualize the command by using eye contact and the student's name. This directs the command at the student and is difficult to ignore (Lasley, 1981).

22. Share the problem with the class and define it. Generate possible solutions. Evaluate the solutions and select the best one. Implement it and assess its effectiveness (McDaniel, 1977).

23. Give a "breather" or time-out activity. This removes the student from a situation. Send the student out of the room on an errand or have him do a job (Hipple, 1978).

24. Set limits on behaviors, but not on feelings. All feelings should be accepted no matter how destructive or outrageous. Reflect the feeling of the "misbehavior" to demonstrate understanding. Set limits on behavior and provide symbolic outlets for the feelings (e.g., art therapy). Acknowledge that the symbolic outlet is not as good as the real thing (*Encyclopedia of Educational Research*, 1982).

25. If you must punish, let the punishment fit the crime. For example, if something is broken, punish the student by having him clean it up or apologize rather than writing 100 times "I will not break . . ." (Wasicko and Ross, 1982).

26. If there are no natural consequences that could serve as a punishment, then try withdrawing a privilege (Wasicko and Ross, 1982).

27. If the student comments, "Everybody's doing it," there may be several offenders and you may have caught only one. Reply, "I'm not talking to everyone, I'm talking to you. Now about your part in this. . . ." You could tell him that next time you'll try to catch everybody, but for now you are talking to him (Womack, 1983).

28. Role play the situation and several solutions. Point out the student's unwarranted behavior and discuss the situation. Then discuss the solutions with the student and pick out the best one.

29. Place the student in time-out. After the student has calmed down, discuss the problem and try to reach an acceptable compromise (Harris, 1980).

30. If the student creates scenes to secure attention, react to the situation in the least noticeable way. When possible, ignore it (Henson, 1977).

31. Help the student maintain control by structuring consequences for the action (i.e. "If you continue to do that, you will have to . . ."). Follow through on the consequences in a firm, but nonvindictive manner (Harris, 1983).

32. Warn the student of logical consequences in private. In this way, there is no one else to be impressed by a show of power (Wilcox, 1983).

32

Impertinence or Sauciness

1. Provide positive reinforcement when polite, respectful behaviors are emitted (Fine, 1977).

2. Remove the student from the environment for a specified period of time when the inappropriate behavior is shown (Fine, 1977; Norton, Austen, Allen, and Hilton, 1983).

3. Use time-out when inappropriate behaviors are exhibited. While in time-out, allow the student to see other students being reinforced for good behavior (Norton, Austen, Allen, and Hilton, 1983).

4. Ignore the behavior (Norton, Austen, Allen, and Hilton, 1983).

5. Use team management of behavior by dividing the class in half. Each time an inappropriate behavior is exhibited by a team

member, that team is penalized one point (Fine, 1977).

6. Award coupons that are exchangeable for participation in certain events. These are given for appropriate behavior. Group rewards for appropriate behavior can also be given (Fine, 1977).

7. Require the student to rephrase the unacceptable statement in acceptable words and tone of voice.

8. Use an agreed upon signal to warn the student when his behavior is becoming out of bounds.

9. Meet quietly with the student and discuss ways to arrive at more appropriate behavior.

10. Tally the number of impertinent remarks during a period of time and require the student to lower that amount each day to receive an agreed upon reward.

11. Inform the student's parents of the behavior and ask for their support.

12. Display this behavior toward the student. Use this as an introduction to a discussion regarding mutual respect.

33

Rebellious if Disciplined

1. Reinforce the student for complying with your intervention.

2. Forewarn the student of the possible implementation of a more severe consequence (e.g., "If you don't do as I say, I will have to . . .").

3. If the student becomes rebellious, implement a stronger consequence. Continue this procedure if the student still does not comply.

4. Videotape or audiorecord the situation. Review the tape later with the student. Discuss how the situation could have been avoided by accepting the first punishment.

5. Figure the percentage of times the student accepts the first punishment without rebel-

lion. Have the student work on increasing this percentage. Reinforce him for progressively higher percentages.

6. Place the burden on the student to use self-control. Say, "Show me that you're in control by following my directions." Reinforce self-control.

7. Review class rules before starting each lesson to avoid noncompliance.

8. Review your sequence of consequences before each class so that the student knows what punishment will be implemented each time he fails to obey.

9. Start a stopwatch when the student becomes rebellious. Stop it when the student is calm. The amount of time accumulated during the day is the amount of time that the student will have to stay after school or stay in from recess.

10. Set a time limit on the length of the rebellion after being disciplined. Count it down for the student. No extra punishment is administered if the student calms himself before the end of the time limit.

34
Lack of Respect for Rules

1. Reinforce the student for following rules and directions (Reinhart, 1980; Dunworth, 1982).

2. Use planned ignoring (Reinhart, 1980).

3. Have the student view his behavior on a videotape recorder. Both you and the student count his inappropriate behaviors. After counting, meet to discuss the behavior (Reinhart, 1980).

4. Allow the student to earn academic credit or free time to work at a paying job if appropriate behavior is shown (Reinhart, 1980).

5. Arrange a parent conference to devise a cooperative plan for changing behavior (Dunworth, 1982).

6. Be sure the student has knowledge of the class rules (Dunworth, 1982).

7. State the rules before each lesson.

8. Present assignments on the student's achievement level; many students are disobedient because of feelings of failure (Dunworth, 1982).

9. Place the student in time-out for displaying maladaptive behavior (Herbert, 1978; Antonelli, 1982).

10. When a persistently disobedient student is unable to tolerate a time-out period, exclude him from school and send him home. No lecture is given; the student merely is told that he cannot remain in school because it appears that he can't be a responsible student. The student is told to return the next day with no penalty being carried over (Johnson, 1977).

11. Modify the assignment to make it easier, different, or more difficult. This may motivate the student to concentrate on the task (Johnson, 1977).

12. Develop a learning center where the student follows directions, thus redirecting him (Johnson, 1977).

13. Role play situations of cooperative behavior (Brophy, 1982).

14. Initiate in-school suspension for the student if the behavior continues (R. Osterman, personal communication, 1983).

15. Ask parents to cooperate by engaging the student in a nonpreferred activity and requiring successful completion while telling the student that he will be allowed to participate in a preferred activity when this task is completed (Hutton, 1983).

16. Teach the student a sense of responsibility so that he can develop self-discipline and begin to move toward desired goals (Millman, Schaefer, and Cohen, 1980).

17. Record occurrences of misbehavior, time of day, and possible reasons for these occurrences. Look for patterns of misbehavior. Restructuring of daily activities may be necessary.

18. Teach the student to accept responsibility for his behavior (Diem, 1984).

19. Direct the student to evaluate the negative effects of his actions and make suggestions for more responsible behavior (Millman, Schaefer, and Cohen, 1980).

20. Encourage peer reinforcement of proper behavior and ignoring of inappropriate behavior (Reinert, 1980).

21. Use compliance training to modify oppositional behavior and to train students to respond quickly to adult directions (Kerr, 1983).

22. Arrange to meet quietly with the student for a few minutes after school just to talk (Karlin and Berger, 1972).

23. Make sure the classroom is very structured and has routines. Students who have a lack of respect for rules often have little structure or discipline in their lives and will abuse the freedom of a loose environment (J. Rogger, personal communication, 1986).

24. If the lack of respect for rules is severe, recommend that the student see a therapist or counselor (Herbert, 1978).

25. Administer sequentially more restrictive or punishing consequences if the behavior does not stop after a teacher request.

26. Explain to the student how breaking the rules makes it difficult for others in the classroom to work and enjoy themselves (C. Young, personal communication, 1983).

27. Use the following guidelines for establishing rules: (a) have the fewest number of rules possible, (b) have different rules for different situations, (c) rules should be stated in observable terms, and (d) rules should be reasonable and achievable, and (e) provide consistent consequences (Kerr and Nelson, 1983).

28. Be consistent with all students in all situations so the student knows that you are being fair (Kerr and Nelson, 1983).

29. Explain the need for rules in the classroom.

30. Use role playing of situations to demonstrate the usefulness of rules.

35
Overly Obedient

1. Be careful in your phrasing of directions.

2. Explain to the student why his behavior is inappropriate.

3. Give vague directions that require interpretations and decisions by the student.

4. Have the student do the opposite of what is requested.

5. Ask the student what he thinks ought to be done. If his idea meets with your approval, allow him to proceed.

6. Determine if the behavior is passive-aggressive in nature. If it is done as a form of disrespect or defiance, implement a negative consequence.

7. Teach the behaviors you wish to see. Have the student practice less "teacher's pet" behaviors.

8. If done defiantly, continually repeat the direction and have him comply until done to your satisfaction.

9. Reduce the number of verbal requests. Give nonverbal signals and gestures as often as possible.

10. Suggest that the student receive assertiveness training.

36
Overly Sensitive to Criticism

1. Reinforce the student when he handles criticism appropriately (Stephens, Hartman, and Lucas, 1978).

2. Give criticism in the best possible atmosphere. Be sure to explain to him the positive aspects of what was done before giving constructive criticism. End on a positive note (Graham, 1984).

3. When the student becomes overly sensitive to your criticism, it may be due to a pattern of failures. Help the student achieve a suc-

cess pattern by giving easier assignments. Work closely with him and use lots of praise. Gradually increase the difficulty of the student's assignments. Interject some criticism, but remain very positive. In time, the student will know success and understand that criticism helps him achieve those successes (Rohrkemper, 1984).

4. When criticizing, speak clearly and simply so that he can understand (Whitehurst, 1984).

5. Do not criticize a student for something not understood. Students sometimes do not understand concepts without training (Whitehurst, 1984).

6. Do not criticize for something over which the student has no control (Brown, 1984).

7. If the student is overly sensitive to criticism, it could be a direct link to feelings of guilt and shame about not doing his best. Work on the student's feelings by helping him reach his potential (Richard, 1984).

8. Teach the class a lesson on criticism and how it helps us to improve ourselves or our work (R. Witkin, personal communication, 1985).

9. Play a game in which each student makes a criticism about a public figure, a movie star, a cartoon character, or the teacher. By doing this, the overly sensitive student may see that there is no harm in being criticized (R. Witkin, personal communication, 1985).

10. After criticism has been given, help the student devise a plan to avoid this criticism in the future.

11. After criticism has been given, have the student restate it in his own words, being sure to include some of the positive comments presented by you.

12. Give your criticism in a good-natured, humorous comment.

13. Demonstrate appropriate behavior in situations that involve teasing (Stephens, Hartman, and Lucas, 1978).

14. Recommend counseling with a social worker or school counselor (C. Scism, personal communication, 1983).

15. Use role playing. Each student plays his real life role and describes what is happening and how he is feeling (Stephens, Hartman, and Lucas, 1978).

16. Discuss appropriate ways of responding to teasing or criticism. Prompt such responses as: one could ignore the teasing; one could walk away from that person; one could change the subject; or one could tease also. You may decide to teach the student to respond in a specific way rather than giving alternatives (Stephens, Hartman, and Lucas, 1978).

17. Reward the student with verbal praise from the other students when a situation is handled appropriately (Stephens, Hartman, and Lucas, 1978).

18. Work on building the student's self-concept and emphasizing his strong points (Stephens, Hartman, and Lucas, 1978).

19. Have the student enroll in assertiveness training (Beall, 1983).

20. Set up an office or study carrel. It sets the student aside in a special place not in the direct fire of criticism (Reinhart, 1980; Barklin et al., 1981).

21. Use the "magic circle." This is a human development approach in which students learn to communicate with other members of their group and learn to understand themselves and others. They verbally explore themselves and each other through teacher guidance. A sample of circle topics are: It made me feel good when I . . . ; and I made someone feel bad when I . . . (Lerner, 1976).

22. Modify your curriculum to reduce frustration (Barklin et al., 1981).

23. Put the student in a position of leadership if his strengths will shine (Barklin et al., 1981).

24. Ask the other students to forward complaints about this student to you.

25. Ignore this behavior if the situation does

not warrant hurt feelings (Newcomer, 1980).

26. Have a counselor come in to talk about criticism (D. Swartsbaugh, personal communication, 1984).

27. Criticize the behavior while complimenting the student as a person (e.g., ''Henry, you're such a good student, but I cannot let you scream in my room.'').

28. Ask the student how the task or behavior could be improved.

9. Provide outlets for anger (e.g., punching bags, art supplies, etc.).

10. Teach the student proper complaint procedures if he feels that he has been mistreated.

11. Ignore the behavior.

12. Reinforce and praise others for cooperative behavior (D. Gerdes, personal communication, 1984).

13. Encourage the student to verbally express his disagreement or concern.

14. Have the student write his complaint.

37

Passive-Aggressive

1. Use positive reinforcement of other appropriate behaviors (S. Stidham, personal communication, 1984).

2. When you see this nondefiant noncompliance, hold a meeting with the student and discuss his concerns.

3. Teach the student to properly voice his negative feelings (e.g., ''I feel as if you've been biased in your decision. Could you please reconsider?''). Listen to the student's request and respond in a polite way.

4. Use peer pressure. Arrange rewards for the class contingent on the student's behavior (S. Stidham, personal communication, 1984).

5. Plan the lesson to be more interesting. Use props, films, audiovisual aids, and the like (S. Stidham, personal communication, 1984).

6. Be assertive. Offer the student a choice between compliance or a negative consequence (S. Stidham, personal communication, 1984).

7. If the behavior continues, use positive practice and overcorrection (S. Stidham, personal communication, 1984).

8. Get the student to vent his anger immediately.

38

Pesters, Nags, or Persists When Told He Cannot Have Something

1. Reinforce the student when he does not pester or nag.

2. Ask the student, ''What did I say last time?'' Have him restate your words. Then say, ''Nothing has changed.''

3. Give the student a warning that he is not to pester again. Be prepared with a consequence.

4. Implement negative consequences that are progressively more restrictive or punitive. Tell the student what will occur if he pesters or nags again.

5. Allow a certain number of questions or interruptions by the student. More than the designated allowance results in punishment.

6. Have a predetermined nonverbal signal to let the student know when his behavior is becoming irritating. This saves time and effort because you don't need to explain verbally.

7. When the student starts to nag, start a stopwatch. When he ceases nagging, stop the watch. The amount of time accumulated over the course of the day is the time that is lost from recess or spent after school.

8. When you say that the student cannot have something, ask him if he understands why. Assure that he does. Then ask the student, "Will we need to discuss this any further?"

9. Create a situation in which you can nag the student. Use this as an opportunity to discuss how irritating this behavior can be.

10. Give the student a chance to use his self-control by asking, "What should you be doing right now?"

11. Ignore the behavior.

39

Refuses to Do Assigned Work

1. Reinforce the student when he is working on an assigned task.

2. Allow no preferred activities until the work is completed.

3. Require that all work be completed before going home.

4. Use a peer tutor to assist the student.

5. Develop learning centers that will provide variety as the student travels from one to another.

6. Seek parental support (J. Pratt, personal communication, 1984).

7. Give an informal interest inventory to determine motivational items and activities.

8. Include the student's interests in the work to motivate him.

9. Be sure that the work is on the student's ability level.

10. Orally do the task with the student (L. Kinman, personal communication, 1984).

11. Present the work in small amounts so as not to overwhelm the student.

12. Have the student chart his work performance. Reinforce him for improvement.

13. Allow the student to complete the required tasks in any order he prefers (P. Bidle, personal communication, 1984).

14. Use agreed upon nonverbal signals as a friendly reminder to the student that he needs to return to the task.

15. Remove all work from the student. Make him sit (in isolation if possible) for the whole period or day. The object here is to bore the student so that he wishes to do work.

16. Reduce any sense of group competitiveness by helping the student see that he only needs to compete with his own record (Carberry, 1980).

17. Offer the student a variety of short tasks, rather than single, longer ones (Carberry, 1978).

18. Give the student assignments that draw on information he has readily available and that capitalize on his major interests (Carberry, 1978).

19. Emphasize the "you-can-do-it" approach, rather than reinforcing the dependency relationship (Carberry, 1978).

20. Emphasize that it is not a catastrophe to make an error (Carberry, 1978).

21. Provide simple tasks in which the student can be successful (Swap, 1974).

22. Require only that a certain percentage of the assignment be completed. The student may choose which parts of the assignment he or she will complete. Raise the percentage periodically.

23. Assist the student with the first part of the assignment to assure that he or she is familiar with the process or procedures.

40

Resists Adult Assistance

1. Give reinforcement for every commendable action or academic achievement in order to soften antagonism and halt rebellion. Let the student know you are there to help (Verville, 1967).

2. Give the student choices in activities to re-

move any motivation for noncompliance (Haswell, Hock, and Werner, 1982).

3. Allow the student to exercise autonomy at some time during the day. This may serve to reduce the need to express it at other times in rebellion against authority (Haswell, Hock, and Werner, 1982).

4. Instead of forcing the student to receive teacher help, have a fellow student help with problems (Hood, 1979).

5. Involve the student in goal setting. Have the student participate in identifying a specific problem, setting a behavioral goal for action, and developing an attainment scale for that goal (Maher, 1981).

6. Do not engage in direct attempts to change the student's behavior through verbal or physical force. Diffuse the tension by reducing your own force. Tone down opposition in order to work toward a resolution. Backing a student into a corner and asserting authority is not helpful. If such a situation should occur, provide the student with a "way out" to keep his self-esteem intact (Perry, 1980).

7. Use the time-out ribbon technique. The students are given ribbons to wear, signaling to themselves and others that behavior is appropriate. For inappropriate behavior, remove the ribbon for three minutes, constituting an in-class time-out, and signaling that no reinforcement from peers or teacher should be given (Foss and Shapiro, 1978).

8. Give detention every night until the student allows you to help with the work. After a short period of detention, the student may finally realize that you really care about his academic progress (Hood, 1979).

9. Have the student remain after school until all work is completed. Offer assistance periodically.

10. Meet with the student to discuss and resolve the problem.

11. Institute progressively more severe consequences as the student continues to resist.

12. Make a deal with the student. If the first segment of a task is completed correctly, you will not intervene. If that segment is done incorrectly, then he must accept assistance.

13. Agree with the student that when he does not want help, you will respect his wishes if his work is 80% (or some other acceptable criterion level) correct. If he has not met the criterion, he is to allow you to assist.

14. Start a stopwatch when the student resists help. Stop it when he accepts assistance. The accumulated time is subtracted from free time or recess. This time might also be used as detention time.

15. Speak with the student's parents to gain their support in convincing the student to accept assistance.

16. Make the assistance sessions very positive and enjoyable to promote future acceptance of help.

41

Satisfied with Negative Attention

1. Be sure that the student is receiving much positive attention.

2. Find positive consequences that are motivating and reinforcing to the student. Use these to develop a contract for better behavior.

3. Base your behavior management program on positive rather than negative consequences. This results in less negative attention as misbehavior is usually ignored (K. Monty, personal communication, 1984).

4. Place the student in an isolated time-out booth after calmly explaining why. He is not to leave the booth until he agrees to display appropriate behavior.

5. Ignore the misbehavior (K. Christensen, personal communication, 1984).

6. When the student misbehaves, ignore it by sending him on an errand or having him assist you in the classroom.

7. Keep the student active and interested in order to avoid misbehavior.

8. Provide more punitive consequences than are presently in use.

9. Be sure that your "punishment" is not actually rewarding to the student (e.g., sending the student to the office where he socializes before seeing the lenient vice-principal) (N. Hammerschmidt, personal communication, 1984).

10. Use boring rather than negative consequences.

11. Make the punishment academic in nature so that the consequence is productive (J. Camp, personal communication, 1985).

12. Ask the parent to implement a home-based punishment (e.g., no television viewing, loss of telephone privileges, having to remain indoors).

13. Have the student tell you what he is doing, not why. Ask him to write a letter to his parents telling them what he did.

14. Send a positive note home to the parents, praising the student's appropriate behavior in the classroom when he is cooperative throughout the day (Martin and Lauridsen, 1974).

15. Don't allow yourself to react emotionally to the student's inappropriate behavior (Haas, Kasper, and Kryst, 1979).

16. Use "face working." Treat the behavior as being appropriate rather than inappropriate. Respond as though noncompliance with the request is acceptable, given the circumstances. For example, suppose you request that students clear their desks, signaling a switch of subjects or tasks. Joe ignores the request and continues to finish what he is doing. After giving him plenty of time to comply, say, "I'm sorry, Joe, I didn't know that you were not finished. I'll give you time to finish it after. . . ." This allows you to deal assertively with the misbehavior without threatening or challenging the self-esteem of the student (Lasley, 1981).

17. Provide the student with opportunities within the classroom and school that capitalize on his strengths and interests. These opportunities should be generally associated with status and prestige (Turnbull and Schulz, 1979).

18. Stress to the student the value of positive relations, and show the negative aspects of the undesirable behavior (Ysseldyke and Algozzine, 1984).

42

Uncooperative and Stubborn

1. Reinforce cooperative behavior (Turnbull and Schulz, 1979).

2. Open your marking book and make a notation when the student becomes uncooperative. Make sure that the student and class see that you are recording his misbehavior (Chernow and Chernow, 1981).

3. Whisper in the student's ear that you would like him to do the work assigned quietly and nicely (M. Sciandra, personal communication, 1985).

4. Give the student a star on a chart every time he is cooperative during an entire lesson (Chernow and Chernow, 1981).

5. Stop talking and stare at the student when he is being uncooperative (Chernow and Chernow, 1981).

6. Speak to the student in the hall or at your desk. Ask the student what is bothering him. Ask why he is being uncooperative (Chernow and Chernow, 1981).

7. Send the student to the principal or counselor to talk over what has just happened in the classroom (Kraft, 1970).

8. Send the student home for the rest of the day when he becomes uncooperative and stubborn. Tell the student that he will be welcomed back as soon as he can get himself under control (Canter and Canter, 1976).

9. Instead of reprimanding the student for being uncooperative, praise an adjacent stu-

dent who is behaving appropriately (M. Sciandra, personal communication, 1985).

10. Sit down with the student and openly confront his inappropriate behavior in the classroom. Tell the student that his behavior is unsatisfactory and you care too much about him to allow this behavior to happen in the classroom (Canter and Canter, 1976).

11. Place a tape recorder next to the student. When he begins to get uncooperative and disrupts the class, turn it on. Discuss the tape later if necessary (Canter and Canter, 1976).

12. Have the student tell you what he is doing, not why. Ask him to write a letter to his parents telling them what he did.

13. Send a positive note home to the parents, praising the student's appropriate behavior in the classroom when he is cooperative throughout the day (Martin and Lauridsen, 1974).

14. Send a note home to the student's parents, telling how uncooperative he was in the classroom (Chernow and Chernow, 1981).

15. Explain to the student, as briefly as possible, what the misbehavior was and indicate what rule was broken (Rivers, 1977).

16. Encourage the student to strive for greater self-control while in the classroom (Rivers, 1977).

17. Have the student lose privileges for the rest of the day when he is uncooperative and stubborn (Chernow and Chernow, 1981).

18. Don't allow yourself to react emotionally to the student's inappropriate behavior (Haas, Kasper, and Kryst, 1979).

19. Use "face working." Treat the behavior as being appropriate rather than inappropriate. Respond as though noncompliance with the request is acceptable, given the circumstances. For example, suppose you request that students clear their desks, signaling a switch of subjects or tasks. Joe ignores the request and continues to finish what he is doing. After giving him plenty of time to comply, say, "I'm sorry, Joe, I didn't know that you were not finished. I'll give you time to finish it after. . . ." This allows you to deal assertively with the misbehavior without threatening or challenging the self-esteem of the student (Lasley, 1981).

20. Give the student time to comply with requests. Rapid-fire repetition of requests may serve to increase oppositional behavior rather than decrease it. Patience and timing are key elements. Allow at least ten seconds for compliance (Haswell, Hock, and Wenar, 1982).

21. Provide the student with opportunities within the classroom and school that capitalize on his strengths and interests. These opportunities should be generally associated with status and prestige (Turnbull and Schulz, 1979).

22. Structure the lesson to accommodate the learning style of the student, and increase the interest level of instructional materials to focus his attention (Ysseldyke and Algozzine, 1984).

23. Stress to the student the value of positive relations, and show the negative aspects of the undesirable behavior (Ysseldyke and Algozzine, 1984).

24. Be careful to reinforce only those behaviors that are cooperative. Although the student may have been reinforced in the past for any behavior, he will only be reinforced for cooperative behavior now.

25. Direct instruction should be used when teaching a complex skill in order to assure that the student will understand what is going on and be more cooperative about participating and doing the work (Cotterell, 1982).

26. Develop a signal to indicate to the student that he is being uncooperative (Lobitz and Burns, 1977).

27. Have the student set up his own goals toward more cooperative functioning in the classroom. Make up a rating scale that shows the degree of goal attainment that has been achieved at the end of the quarter (Maher, 1981).

28. Tell the student in private that you will rate him on a scale of 1–10 every fifteen minutes for "cooperativeness." A rating of 1 would be "uncooperative" and a rating of 10 would be "cooperative." The student is then aware of his progress and what is expected of him (Lobitz and Burns, 1977).

29. Announce to the class that you will be rating the student on a scale from 1–10 every fifteen minutes. At the end of 15 minutes, tell the class how well the student did. The student is reinforced by public feedback and attention if he receives a high rating (Lobitz and Burns, 1977).

30. Break the class into groups and give each group 10 points per day for good behavior. A point is taken away for each inappropriate behavior. The student responsible is informed of the point loss and the reason why it was removed. Positively reinforce those who are being cooperative. At the end of the week, the winning group can earn a prize (Holland and McLaughlin, 1982).

31. Communicate clearly what is expected of the student. He may be uncooperative because he does not know what is expected of him (Lehman, 1982).

32. Be sure that the student is working on material that is at his skill level (Lehman, 1982).

33. Use interesting ways of presenting material, such as varying the methods, involving students, and relating subject matter to relevant experiences, to prevent boredom (Lehman, 1982).

34. Set a timer for every 15 minutes. If the student is cooperating when the timer sounds, then he receives tokens, points, or stars that can be traded in for something reinforcing (Lehman, 1982).

35. Set up a contract with the student. In specific terms write the behavior expected from the student and the consequences for both the appropriate and inappropriate behaviors. You and the student should develop the contract together to decide on

what is expected of each party (Lehman, 1982).

36. Always maintain your options. Avoid "playing your last card." Never threaten a student with something you won't implement (Cangelosia, 1984).

37. Ignore uncooperative behavior (Deibert and Harmon, 1973).

38. Have the student keep self-reports on himself. He should write daily reports of how cooperative he has been. He may even wish to write why he behaved a certain way, which could be discussed with you later. The student then compares his progress to previous weeks to see if positive change has occurred (Schwitzgebel and Kolb, 1974).

39. Involve the students in the formulation of class rules. This assures more cooperation with these guidelines.

40. Appeal to the student's classmates to help deal with the behavior. (e.g., "Class, Jessie is refusing to _____. I'm going to be in the library for the next 10 minutes. I'll ask the class chairperson to engage you in a discussion of Jessie's dilemma.") Peer-group discussion and your withdrawal from the scene may lead to a resolution of the student's stubborn conduct.

41. Ask the student to put into writing the reasons he feels that he must stubbornly resist (Gervais and Dittburner, 1981).

42. Deny the student certain privileges, but then be aware of opportunities to reinforce his cooperative behavior (Wolfgang and Glickman, 1980; Axelrod, 1977).

43. Brainstorm with others who are dealing with the same problem in order to devise a solution.

44. Use nonverbal signals to warn the student that the behavior must cease (Caldwell, 1977).

45. Show films dealing with uncooperativeness and follow them with discussion (Clarizo, 1980).

46. Transfer the uncooperative student to another class. Sometimes such a move

brings about a change in attitude and conduct.

47. With the student, make a list of things or ideas that stimulate strong feelings. (e.g., "List 10 things that make you feel very stubborn. List 10 things about which you wouldn't change your mind. List 10 people from whom you resist taking suggestions. List 10 things about which you couldn't care less.").

48. When the student becomes stubborn or uncooperative, place him in time-out (Wolfgang and Glickman, 1980).

49. Avoid interrupting the student once assignments have been made (Dunworth, 1982).

50. Speak with the parents to obtain their cooperation (Dunworth, 1982).

51. Make sure that the student has knowledge of the class rules (Dunworth, 1982).

52. Politely, but firmly, ask the student to stop being uncooperative and get to work (Rivers, 1977).

53. Have the student make choices of what he would like to do. Give the student a wide range of options related to both content and procedures. Included are the options about materials and when, where, and with whom learning activities are to be pursued (Adelman and Taylor, 1983).

54. Give the student a surprised look or frown when the student is being stubborn (Caldwell, 1979).

55. Snap your fingers at the student or stand from a seated position when he is being uncooperative (Caldwell, 1979).

56. Put your hand gently on the student's shoulder or arm when he is being stubborn (Caldwell, 1979).

57. Establish a rating system for the student that consists of plusses or minuses based on how cooperative he is in the classroom. Every hour put a plus or minus on the chart depending on the student's behavior (Chernow and Chernow, 1981).

58. Send the student to another classroom when he is uncooperative. Send him to a widely different grade level (Canter and Canter, 1976).

59. When the student becomes uncooperative, go over to the student and help him begin the task (Canter and Canter, 1976).

60. Role play an incident of stubbornness, such as a student refusing to do a particular assignment. Follow this activity with a class discussion.

61. Tell the student that it is not fair to the rest of the students when he is being uncooperative (Canter and Canter, 1976).

62. Say the student's name firmly when he is being uncooperative and stubborn in the classroom (Canter and Canter, 1976).

63. When the student is cooperative for an entire lesson, drop a marble in a jar. Each marble can be worth 30 seconds to one minute of free time at the end of the day for the student (Canter and Canter, 1976).

64. Give the student detention after school for being stubborn and uncooperative during class (L. Juron, personal communication, 1985).

65. Tell the student that he must be cooperative in class or you will call his parents (Chernow and Chernow, 1981).

66. With parental permission, devise a plan in which the student is not allowed to go home until the teacher's directions have been followed.

67. For each time the student refuses to obey a direction, add two minutes to the time he must remain after school.

68. Determine if a rescheduling of the activity would minimize the behavior. (e.g., A hot, sweaty pupil who has just finished playing an active game can hardly be expected to settle down immediately to a sheet of long-division problems.) The bulk of the basic academic work should be scheduled for the early morning, and the "winding-down" activities should be scheduled after recess or lunch (Hammill and Bartel, 1978).

69. Set a timer for a specific amount of time. Tell the student that he has to accomplish

the task within this period. Reward him if he finishes the task before the timer goes off. If the student does not complete the task within this time frame, do not give reinforcement (Neisworth and Smith, 1973).

70. Provide sufficient physical guidance, demonstrations, and other prompts for the desired behavior. Gradually remove these prompts as the student begins to respond correctly without them. Begin by physically assisting the student or guiding the appropriate body part. Then proceed to model or demonstrate the desired response. After that, use a "gestural" prompt by pointing, touching, or indicating the correct behavior or responses. Next, use the "verbal" prompt by giving the student hints or directions that will help him to complete the task. Finally, give the student no more help. The student is to start and complete the task by himself (Haring, 1982).

71. Use a peer or an older student as a reinforcing agent. Train the "agent" to ignore inappropriate behaviors and deliver reinforcers for on-task behavior. The agent observes by either sitting next to or to the side of the student. The agent judges whether the student should receive reinforcements (e.g., edibles, praise, touching, smiling, etc.) (Long and Madsen, 1973).

72. Play the game "Simon Says." Group cooperation, individual cooperation, and listening skills are stressed. Additionally, this is a physical activity that can be very motivating to students.

73. Have the class hold trials, which are as authentic as possible, and judge violators by a jury of their peers. Trials deal with classroom issues, uncooperative behavior, rule violations, and so on.

43

Welcomes Punishment

1. Reinforce the student for compliant and on-task behavior.

2. Base your behavior management program on positive rather than negative consequences. In this way, there is less punishment.

3. When the student misbehaves, provide alternative behaviors (e.g., when the student begins to disrupt, send him on an errand).

4. Provide more punitive consequences than are presently in use.

5. Be sure that your "punishment" is not actually rewarding to the student (e.g., sending the student to the office where he socializes before seeing the lenient vice-principal) (N. Hammerschmidt, personal communication, 1984).

6. Avoid trouble situations by keeping the student active and interested.

7. Have the student self-monitor his behavior and attempt to improve each day to receive a desired reward.

8. Videotape the student's behavior for future review and discussions with him (Booth and Fairbanks, 1983).

9. Ignore the misbehavior (K. Christensen, personal communication, 1984).

10. Find a consequence that is boring for the student.

11. Make the punishment academic in nature so that the consequence is productive (J. Camp, personal communication, 1985).

12. Ask the parents to implement a home-based punishment (e.g., no television viewing, loss of phone privileges, having to remain indoors).

13. Have the student tell you what he is doing, not why. Ask him to write a letter to his parents telling them what he did (Collins and Collins, 1975).

14. Send a positive note home to the parents, praising the student's appropriate behavior in the classroom when he is cooperative throughout the day (Martin and Lauridsen, 1974).

15. Don't allow yourself to react emotionally to the student's inappropriate behavior (Haas, Kasper, and Kryst, 1979).

16. Use "face working." Treat the behavior as being appropriate rather than inappropriate. Respond as though noncompliance with the request is acceptable, given the circumstances. For example, suppose you request that students clear their desks, signaling a switch of subjects or tasks. Joe ignores the request and continues to finish what he is doing. After giving him plenty of time to comply, say, "I'm sorry, Joe, I didn't know that you were not finished. I'll give you time to finish it after. . . ." This allows you to deal assertively with the misbehavior without threatening or challenging the self-esteem of the student (Lasley, 1981).

17. Provide the student with opportunities within the classroom and school that capitalize on his strengths and interests. These opportunities should be generally associated with status and prestige (Turnbull and Schulz, 1979).

18. Stress to the student the value of positive relations, and show the negative aspects of the undesirable behavior (Ysseldyke and Algozzine, 1984).

9

Classroom/School Behavior (Academic)

44

Acts as if Work Is Done Correctly When It Is Not

1. Reinforce the student when tasks are completed correctly.
2. Praise the student for the parts completed correctly.
3. Point out the flaws in the student's work.
4. Restate the task criteria. Ask the student to review his paper based upon these criteria.
5. Have the student redo the work until completed correctly.
6. Allow the student to have the choice between a low grade on this paper or redoing it correctly with a five-point penalty attached.
7. Have students work in teams to complete assignments. This provides peer feedback on correctness of the product.
8. Have the student stay after school or stay in from recess until all work is done correctly.

9. Have the student assist you in correcting the work of others to instill in him the need to finish a task correctly.
10. Have an impartial third person evaluate the product to determine if it meets the stated criteria.
11. If asked by the student to do something, give him a partially done or incorrectly completed product (e.g., notes, comments on the top of papers, etc.). Use this as an introduction to a discussion of the need to produce accurate work.

45

Always Asking for Help

1. Reinforce the student if he has attempted or completed the work without assistance (L. Stickelmaier, personal communication, 1983).
2. Ignore requests for help unless the student has earnestly tried to complete his work (Knoblock, 1983).

3. Appoint the student as a teacher's helper to assist other students.

4. Pay attention to the student only when he is working independently.

5. Divide the task into parts. Be available for each part at the beginning, but over a period of time offer help only for every other part. Continue to fade out assistance over time.

6. Appoint another student to be a peer helper for the student in need of assistance.

7. Demand that a certain amount of work be attempted before receiving assistance.

8. Do not assist the student until his hand has been raised for two minutes. This waiting period may deter unnecessary requests for assistance.

9. Initially give the student easier work to let him see that he can complete tasks on his own (L. Stickelmaier and D. Mattingly, personal communication, 1983).

10. Accept anything at first with no criticism. Gradually point out his errors (D. Mattingly, personal communication, 1983).

11. Require the student to stay after school or miss a nonacademic period until the work is finished independently (L. Stickelmaier, personal communication, 1983).

12. Give the student a small amount of work to do at first. When his confidence level is built, increase the amount of work (D. Mattingly, personal communication, 1983).

13. Provide the student with activities that you know he can handle independently.

14. Give simple, sequential, concise directions.

15. Have the student participate in cooperative group work that allows peers to assist.

16. Break down an assignment into smaller parts so that it is less intimidating.

17. Divide the assignment into parts with colored pencils. Tell the student that he must work down to a specific line before you will assist.

18. Have the student monitor the amount of work attempted on his own to demonstrate progress.

46

Cheats on Tests and Assignments

1. Praise the student when he refrains from cheating.

2. Seat the student near the teacher and surround him with peers who will not allow him to cheat from them.

3. Pay close attention to the student during tests or assignments (M. Yusuf, personal communication, 1985).

4. Remind the student that his friends will observe him cheating and that they will lose respect for him (M. Yusuf, personal communication, 1985).

5. Before giving tests or assignments, state that you will punish whoever cheats by taking his paper and giving a failing grade (M. Yusuf, personal communication, 1985).

6. Let the student know that you appreciate his own effort, whatever amount (M. Yusuf, personal communication, 1985).

7. Before giving tests or assignments, ask the student to put his books in a place where he cannot reach them (M. Yusuf, personal communication, 1985).

8. Write a comment on the student's paper to the effect that you believe he was cheating while doing tests or assignments. Indicate that you will give him a failing grade if he is caught cheating on the next test or assignment (M. Yusuf, personal communication, 1985).

9. Compose a story about a student who was expelled and disliked by friends because of his cheating. Read it to the class (M. Yusuf, personal communication, 1985).

10. Allow the student to use his book or notes for a certain percentage of the items.

11. Have the students in the class place their desks in a large circle, facing out.

12. Place the student in a cubicle during testing.

13. Have the student take the test before the rest of the pupils.

14. Give a test in which the student's questions are in a different order than on other pupils' tests.

15. Stand by the student during testing situations.

16. Stand behind the student so that he is unable to tell if you are watching him.

17. Be sure that the student's reading level allows him to read and understand what is on the printed page.

18. Make sure that the guidelines are understandable and relatively easy to remember.

19. Casually mention to the class that no cheating is allowed and that they should keep their eyes on their own papers.

20. Give a stern look to the student suspected of cheating.

21. Stress to the student the importance of doing his best.

22. Have an individual conference with the student and discuss the problem of cheating (Anderson, 1974).

23. Make the student ineligible to participate in an activity if he is caught cheating.

24. Verbally praise the noncheaters (Anderson, 1974).

25. Place folding bulletin boards around the student during test time.

26. Have the student role play different situations dealing with cheating and then hold a discussion (Anderson, 1974).

27. Hold pretest review sessions so that the need to cheat in order to gain a high mark is lessened.

28. Take the test away from the student. Give a failing grade or allow him to retake it later with a penalty attached.

29. Have the student complete the assignments under supervision.

30. Create chaos by encouraging all the players in a game to cheat without penalty. Be sure that the game does not become dangerous, however. Before the game, let the student know that the teacher will be watching him or her.

31. Check typical hiding places for "crib sheets" (e.g., in pockets, inside pens, inside belts, under watchbands, inside shoes, etc.).

47

Copies Other's Work

1. Reinforce the student for completing his own work.

2. When the student is thought to have been copying another student's answers from a homework assignment, respond by giving a lesson to the entire class about being honest with themselves. Explain how they are cheating themselves because they may never really know how much knowledge they have or how smart they really are (Fogg, 1976).

3. Give a failing grade due to plagiarism.

4. If the student resorts to copying, allow him to redo the work. Next time, however, he will receive a failing grade (Fogg, 1976).

5. Penalize the pupils who allowed another to copy from them.

6. If the student has been caught copying, sit down with him and convey your faith in his ability to do assignments alone (Schuman, 1980).

7. Talk to the student alone when you feel that he has copied the work of another. State that he is infringing on the right of the other student by stealing their hard work (D. Jasek, personal communication, 1986).

8. Make the student understand that the submitted work will not be accepted as his own.

9. Inform the student that the value of doing his own work is that it helps you ascertain what he does not know. Prepare lesson plans to help him with the material that is difficult (C. McConneghy, personal communication, 1986).

10. Arrange a conference with the parents to

discuss the copying behavior (Schuman, 1980).

11. Ask the parents to monitor the student's homework to assure that the work is his own.

12. Ask the student to remain after class. When the others are gone, ask him to come to your desk. Give him a stern look until he knows that you are upset about his copying. Let him worry for a minute or so. Tell him that this work is not as hard as he may think and reassure him that if he needs help, all he has to do is ask (Siegel, 1980).

13. Rip up his paper and tell him that copying another's work is wrong (S. Robins, personal communication, 1986).

14. Take the paper from the student. Move him to another area of the room which is isolated and give him another worksheet or sheet of paper.

15. Be sure that the student has the necessary prerequisite skills to be able to complete the task.

16. Assure that the student understands the directions for the task, including that it be his original work.

48

Curses While Working

1. Reinforce the student when he does not curse for a predetermined amount of time.

2. When the student uses obscenities or curses, point out openly and without apology that the obscenities are offensive to you and the others.

3. Ignore the cursing (Pomerantz and Schultz, 1983).

4. Inform the student that you will use drastic action, such as using soap to wash his mouth, if the cursing behavior persists (Pomerantz and Schultz, 1983).

5. Ask the student if he knows the meaning of the curse words that were used. If the student says yes, ask for a definition. If the student's definition is correct, explain that it is a poor word to use. Tell him why the word was a poor choice, and is not to be used again in school. If the student does not know the meaning of the word, you can explain it and say that the word is not to be repeated in school (Pomerantz and Schultz, 1983).

6. Tell the student that it is not a good idea to use words of which one does not know the meaning, if that is the case (Pomerantz and Schultz, 1983).

7. If cursing occurs while the student is working, ask him if he is in need of help. Instruct the student to ask for help rather than use words that are unacceptable (N. Ortiz-Marshall, personal communication, 1985).

8. Privately discuss the cursing with the student (Pomerantz and Schultz, 1983).

9. Allow the student to use certain words such as *hell* and *damn* in an attempt to reduce his repertoire to more acceptable levels.

10. Contact the parents about their child's swearing, telling them which words are and are not appropriate for school.

11. Suggest to the parents that films, television, and books be monitored or censored (Middleton, 1978).

12. Suggest to the student that he is in need of the services of Curseaholics and supply him with the number of the 24-hour hotline.

13. Allow the student to curse when alone (Aman, 1980).

14. Ask the student not to curse around you (Gourney, 1981).

15. Inform the student that people who swear when under pressure are full of fear, uncertainty, or hot air. Then ask him which of the three groups he considers himself to be a member (Gourney, 1981).

16. Explain the difference between language that is profane, and language that is vulgar

or obscene. Discuss the views that people hearing the profanities will form of him.

17. If the student uses curse words, address the situation with humor and acknowledge the common failings in youth and adults who use profanity unnecessarily (Costello, 1984).

18. Set up a system whereby the student is required to pay a monetary fine for each time that he curses. Return the money to his parents (N. Ortiz-Marshall, personal communication, 1985).

19. Have the student say a nonsense word, such as *rosenshankle* or *snarzelpharf* instead of a curse word (W. Jones, personal communication, 1985).

20. Have the student use real words as substitutes for the curse words, such as *heck*, *darn*, or *sugar*.

21. Award the student a predetermined prize for every five consecutive substitute words used in place of curse words (W. Jones and O. Montes, personal communication, 1985).

22. Set aside one day as a class "cuss day." Only on this day is cursing allowed in the classroom. All other days are considered to be non-cuss days and no swearing is allowed (Aman, 1985).

23. Take the student aside and have him tell you all of the curse words that he knows. Discuss why these are not appropriate for classroom use (J. Stern, personal communication, 1985).

24. Have the student chart the number of curses each day. Reward him for lowering the previous day's total.

25. Take the student's work away for five minutes if he curses. Require all work to be completed by the end of the day.

26. Teach the student the derivation of various curse words to lower their "shock value" for the student.

49
Destroys Something He Has Made Rather Than Take It Apart

1. Praise the student's creation frequently during the time he is making it (Wade and Moore, 1984).

2. Ignore the student's behavior. He may be doing it for attention (Lawrence, Steed, and Young, 1983).

3. Discuss the causes of the destruction with the student (Lawrence, Steed, and Young, 1983).

4. Point out other pupil's appropriate behavior to the student (Lawrence, Steed, and Young, 1983).

5. Use a contract agreement with the student. For every creation the student shows you and gently takes apart, he receives 10 extra minutes of free time (S. Blaha, personal communication, 1985).

6. Give support and encouragement to the student as he makes the product (J. Maroon, personal communication, 1985).

7. Place the student in time-out (S. Blaha, personal communication, 1985).

8. Take away privileges from the student each time he destroys something (J. Gallagher, personal communication, 1984).

9. Stand near the student as the activity ends so to prevent destruction.

10. Have the student rebuild the destroyed product.

11. Require the student to say something positive about the project every five minutes.

12. Do not require the student to display his product publicly.

13. Tell the student that he may destroy the product after leaving the room.

14. Communicate with the parents to assure that the product reaches home.

15. Laminate assignments to make them more resistant to destruction (L. Kinman, personal communication, 1984).

16. Do as much oral work as possible (L. Kinman, personal communication, 1984).

17. Make so many copies of the assignment that the student will realize that the work must be done before leaving (L. Kinman, personal communication, 1984).

18. Do not let the student go home until he has given you a completed, undamaged product.

19. Take a photograph of the project before it is destroyed. Display the photo.

20. Do not give a grade for the assignment unless it is presented to you and left in your possession for one day's "evaluation."

50

Disinterested in the Classwork of Others

1. Reinforce the student for *any* comments made about the classwork of others.

2. Tell the student that you would like him to make positive comments to others about their work.

3. Reinforce the student for any positive comments made about the work of others (N. Worstell, personal communication, 1984).

4. Reinforce other students for their interest in the work of others.

5. Have the student tutor other students. If his work is at a low-skill level, have him tutor younger children (N. Worstell, personal communication, 1984).

6. Ignore the behavior and accept it as this student's personal decision.

7. Have the student chart the number of his positive statements given about the work of others. Have him attempt to increase the daily total.

8. Ask the student to render an opinion on a certain student's work. Show work that is of high quality.

9. Have the student compare his work with that of others.

10. Have the student work on a group project with others.

11. Have the student assist you in the correcting of assignments.

12. Have the student list one good and one poor aspect of someone else's project.

13. Have students read each other's opinion papers and react to them.

51

Does More Work than Assigned

1. Reinforce the student when he completes only the assigned class work (C. Ritz, personal communication, 1985).

2. Set up a contract with the student to do only a certain amount of work (C. Ritz, personal communication, 1985).

3. Allow the student to do extra work, but tell him that you will grade only a prescribed amount of what is submitted to you (C. Ritz, personal communication, 1985).

4. When the student is finished with class work, have him read a book instead of going ahead to other material (C. Ritz, personal communication, 1985).

5. Have the student do extra work in weak areas (B. Yakus, personal communication, 1985).

6. Talk to the student and explain that your concern is if he goes ahead he may run into something that he does not understand and practice it incorrectly (B. Yakus, personal communication, 1985).

7. Mark any extra work as being incorrect. This will lower the grade of the task.

8. Refer the student for entrance into a program for gifted students if the work is of high quality.

9. Have the student assist others when done with assigned work.

10. Assign a lengthy project on which this student can work when assignments are complete.

11. Use worksheets. The student will be unable to do extra work in that he has only one sheet in front of him at the moment.

12. After an assigned amount of work is done, have him review it with you.

52
Does Not Bring Correct Materials to Class

1. Reward the student for coming to class prepared (e.g., free time, raisins, gum, etc.) (C. Robinson, personal communication, 1985).

2. Make the student feel the importance of bringing the correct materials by praising him for remembering even one necessary item, or just remembering to come to class (G. Maul, personal communication, 1985).

3. Give the student an index card with necessary materials listed or pictures of the materials on it (Ackerman and Rathburn, 1984).

4. Have a recording chart or checklist in both the classroom and special classes. The student will then be reminded of the proper materials when entering and leaving each room (Ackerman and Rathburn, 1984).

5. Teach the student to self-check by using verbal dialogue (e.g., "It is time to go to math class. I need my math book, paper, and pencil.") (Ackerman and Rathburn, 1984).

6. Show the student pictures of different career specialists such as a firefighter, a painter, a carpenter, and a dentist. State the importance of having the necessary tools or materials in order to work at one's job. Parallel the necessity of the carpenter having wood, a hammer, and nails, to the student bringing his tools (such as pencil, paper, and book) in order to do his work correctly (D. Gluc and G. Maul, personal communication, 1985).

7. Have a guest visitor come to class but needing materials. (e.g., A TV weather personality arrives, but cannot give the weather report because he does not have the necessary materials to help in giving that report.) As the materials are gathered, the student will observe how helpful the materials are in assisting the meteorologist (D. Gluc and G. Maul, personal communication, 1985).

8. Keep a log or notebook with pictures depicting materials needed (D. Gluc, personal communication, 1985).

9. Select and complete a project that requires follow-through (e.g., planting seeds). This type of project requires the gathering of many materials in order to accomplish the task (D. Gluc, personal communication, 1985).

10. Develop a current events or TV news bulletin program announcing readiness for work. Here, the student will relay readiness to go to different classes as he is prepared with the necessary materials for each class. The student would then name the materials needed for each of the classes, and indicate that he is prepared with those materials (D. Gluc and G. Maul, personal communication, 1985).

11. Play a game whereby the student recognizes materials needed by stating what the material is used for and describing the material. The game could use the form of "I Spy" or "Twenty Questions" (D. Gluc and G. Maul, personal communication, 1985).

12. Help the student develop his own symbols to represent the needed materials. The student could then check the symbols as he gathers the materials for class (Ross, 1980).

13. Use maze, dot-to-dot, or design sheets to identify and draw in any missing items before leaving the classroom (D. Gluc, personal communication, 1985).

14. Prepare a formal contract that lists time references for completing a certain amount of activities or assignments using specified

materials. (e.g., For Monday, list as many animals as you can that have a tail. Use a red magic marker.) (D. Gluc and G. Maul, personal communication, 1985).

15. Make a list of supplies needed for a planned trip. The list could be on large newsprint or the chalkboard. Some of the supplies needed would be food, clothing, and money. Each of these categories would be further elaborated to show the need for bringing the materials (Bobowski, 1978).

16. List sequential rules for a well-known game, such as checkers or dominoes, to develop foresight and readiness for a task (Bobowski, 1978).

17. Use reverse role playing with the student. You play the part of the student and the student pretends to be the teacher, asking you to remember to bring the correct materials to class (G. Maul, personal communication, 1985).

18. Develop student identification with work, workers, and work values. As the teacher, you can model the value of preparedness (Bentley, 1980).

19. Showing pictures of different occupations, ask the following questions:
    a. Would you describe this person as happy?
    b. How long does it take for this person to get ready?
    c. How successful would you say this person is?
    d. What values are involved in being prepared? (Bentley, 1980).

20. Develop a verbal code between you and the student who is leaving your classroom to go to another class. The student will tell you that he is leaving, and you will acknowledge the student by saying, "Pizza." The code word *pizza* reminds the student that he should take certain material to where he is going (G. Maul, personal communication, 1985).

21. Have the student learn the meaning and importance of the words *responsible, duty, conscientious,* and *mature* (Bentley, 1980).

22. Write the student a letter reminding him of what materials to bring to class. In response, he would write a letter stating what materials he will bring to class (Bobowski, 1978).

23. Have the student verbalize how he feels when he forgets to bring the correct materials to class. Compare these feelings to those he has when he does bring the correct materials. Stress that you would like him to always be able to have good feelings (Bobowski, 1978).

24. Show the student a list of the correct materials. Next to each material have the student write other words that help to describe it. One of the student's descriptors may help him to remember the correct material (Bobowski, 1978).

25. Allow students who bring supplies to work in groups (D'Amico, 1980).

26. In class, discuss the importance of individual development, responsibility, and consideration (D'Amico, 1980).

27. Ask the school guidance counselor to become involved (D'Amico, 1980).

28. Verbally tell the student what is expected of him (Bailey, 1979).

29. Use new and interesting materials that the student will enjoy bringing (Bailey, 1979).

30. If the student forgets materials in order to gain your attention, plan a conference time for the two of you to meet (Fogelman, 1978).

31. The student may forget classroom books because he has a fear of being seen as an illiterate. Direct instruction to improve reading ability may increase the number of times he comes prepared for class (Fogelman, 1978).

32. Keep the student involved and interested in classroom lessons (Anderson and Scott, 1978).

33. Post a class schedule in the student's locker and write what books and supplies are needed next to each class listed (C. Robinson, personal communication, 1985).

34. Ask parents to have the student keep all books and supplies in one place only at home (C. Robinson, personal communication, 1985).

35. Require the student to complete any work missed or unfinished because he was unprepared for class (C. Robinson, personal communication, 1985).

36. Have alternate materials available (Bailey, 1979).

37. Have oral tasks ready in case the student is unprepared for class (Anderson and Scott, 1978).

38. Show interest and enthusiasm for the materials (Bailey, 1979).

53

Does Not Complete Homework

1. At the beginning of the school year, set a precedent for homework every night. When students know what is expected of them, the expectations are more likely to be met (R. Witkin, personal communication, 1985).

2. Schedule homework for a week at a time so that daily assignments are not surprising.

3. Write all homework assignments on a 3 × 5 card and have the student present the card to his parents each evening. The card must be initialed by them and returned to school the next day.

4. Require the student to keep a daily assignment sheet (Haas, Kasper, and Kryst, 1979).

5. Never let late work extend further than one day if possible. Have the student do it during recess or free time if necessary (Haas, Kasper, and Kryst, 1979).

6. Keep the student after school to do incomplete or late work (Haas, Kasper, and Kryst, 1979).

7. Have the student start or complete the assignment in class or in study hall.

8. Establish guidelines for the student. If these guidelines are not met, he must pay the consequences (e.g., working in the office, staying after school until work is completed) (N. Bashe, personal communication, 1982).

9. Let homework be the completion of unfinished classwork. This is beneficial for the less academic student who can then work at a slower pace and do a competent job. Be sure that the student understands the material (Ashmore et al., 1984).

10. Introduce a daily report card system. On the first intervention day, the cards are taped to each desk and the students are told that their homework will be scored on a scale of 1 to 4, which is circled on the card. The highest score of 4 is given when all homework is completed and totally correct. A score of 3 indicates all complete and largely correct. A 2 indicates all complete but largely incorrect, and the lowest score of 1 is given for an incomplete assignment. The teacher marks the cards individually and makes comments to the students during marking (Dougherty and Dougherty, 1977; Fairchild, 1983).

11. Get the student to set the amount and the nature of the homework. This may lead to a better completion (Jongsma, 1985).

12. Develop a telephone hot line that students can call if they are having a problem or need clarification on a concept when doing homework (Jongsma, 1985).

13. Arrange a very pleasant atmosphere in your school for an after-school homework session. Students could bring in a small contribution for a snack. A radio could be played softly if the students prefer. By combining this type of atmosphere with the social connotations of being able to attend this special session, many students may want to join (R. Witkin, personal communication, 1985).

14. Use a newspaper to make homework interesting. Newspapers can be used to develop creative writing. Use the format of classi-

fied ads to have the students advertise one of their own personal possessions to sell (Crisuola, 1981).

15. Establish a homework contract. Each time a homework assignment is completed on time, a happy face is stamped in the appropriate box. If criteria are met by the end of the day (week or month), reward the student accordingly. Each student has his own contract (A. Courtney, personal communication, 1985).

16. Tear the name off of completed homework assignments and drop names into a container. Hold a drawing for a prize.

17. Have the student write himself a note to do the homework and bring it in the next day (R. Witkin, personal communication, 1985).

18. Teach the student a lesson on the organization of doing homework. This should include the importance of homework, how to do it, when to do it, and evaluation of it (R. Witkin, personal communication, 1985).

19. Make assignments clear, being certain that the student understands the homework assignment (Harris, 1983).

20. Require the student to write down the assignment from the board every day (Harris, 1983).

21. Give the student time in class to do the homework assignment (Strothers, 1984).

22. Give cooperative assignments to the student and a friend.

23. Have another student, whom the target student admires, respects, or likes, serve as a model for reinforcement (Rorschler, 1981).

24. Give a choice of homework assignments.

25. Allow various ways of completing an assignment.

26. Have supplemental activities available if the student is done with the work (Rorschler, 1981).

27. Make the homework interesting. This may include such activities as creative writing, art, music, studying current events, and interviewing community leaders in addition to using textbooks (Strothers, 1984).

28. Give homework assignments that are fun (e.g., riddles, wordsearches, and crossword puzzles) (D. Sadlon, personal communication, 1985).

29. Have the student earn the privilege of being allowed to do homework at home. If the student fails to complete a homework assignment, he must stay after school for five consecutive days and report to the "homework room" to do his homework. Follow-up consists of doing homework at home and school on alternate days for five consecutive days, then full-time homework at home. Repeat the procedure if homework is not done. There is no longer a choice of doing the homework or not. The only choice is to do it in school or at home (Lieberman, 1983).

30. Have the student receive a special privilege for completing his homework assignment (Strothers, 1984).

31. Give some type of feedback regarding the student's performance to the parents on a regular basis (Harris, 1983).

32. Have the class publish a newsletter, written by the students and copied by the teacher, to go home every week. The newsletter could include a short paragraph that states the class performance during the past week and a short preview of the coming week's work. This will allow the parents to review with their child his individual goals for the past week in relation to the class performance. It also helps him schedule next week's work (Harris, 1983).

33. Have the parents become involved. If the parents know that their child has homework to do every night, they will be more likely to arrange an environment conducive to studying. Siblings of your student would also be pulled into the routine devised for doing homework (R. Witkin, personal communication, 1985).

34. Ask the parents to provide feedback for work well done (Spadafore, 1979).

35. Give the parents pointers on setting up a study area.

36. A specific time to do homework needs to be established by the parents. The student should be allowed to finish homework and still have time to relax before retiring for the evening. Many families find 6:30–8:30 P.M. to be the most convenient time. This time slot also allows the student time to relax and unwind after getting home from school (Harris, 1983).

37. Ask the parents to have the student do the homework in segments to promote interest and concentration. (e.g., "Do three problems now. Watch television until the timer sounds. Then we will finish the last four problems.") (Gillet, 1977).

38. Instruct parents to avoid scheduling the homework session when it conflicts with a favorite television show, playtime with a friend, other household requirements, or any time that will require a large sacrifice. Late evening work when both student and parents are tired should also be avoided (Spadafore, 1979).

39. Ask parents to state homework instructions at home without using negatives. This focuses a student's attention on desired behavior. For example, "Don't make mistakes" can be rephrased as "Do your best work" (Baenninger and Ulmer, 1976).

40. Teach parents to state instructions in a manner that indicates that success, not just a show of effort, is expected (Baenninger and Ulmer, 1976).

41. Send home instructions to the parents for each assignment given. Indicate how you hope they will be able to assist their child. On the day that an assignment is sent home, discuss it in class with the student. Allow three or four days for work to be completed and returned to school. This gives busy parents time to spend with their child without feeling burdened (O'Neill, 1978).

42. Ask the parents to work with their child on a specific educational project at home, and to evaluate that project and assign a grade. This grade is then recorded in your gradebook as a major grade for a grading period.

If a parent grade is not returned or not returned on time, an "F" is recorded for that particular activity (Stephens, 1982).

43. Have all the students make large signs to be placed over their desk or study area at home as a reminder to do their homework (R. Witkin, personal communication, 1985).

54

Does Not Complete Tasks

1. Arrange a learning setting to accommodate a small group, yet still provide the target student with as much one-to-one instruction as possible (George, 1982).

2. Be sure that the task is on the student's ability level (George, 1982).

3. Divide a task into several segments of short duration and give easy-to-understand directions at the beginning of each segment (Negley, 1981; George, 1982).

4. Make sure the task is one with a structure that will promote attending as well as task completion (George, 1982).

5. Give the student cues, both verbal and nonverbal, to provide incentive (George, 1982).

6. Teach the student to cue or talk to himself and monitor his own complete or incomplete work (George, 1982).

7. Provide feedback that is immediate and specific to the task (Negley, 1981).

8. Express genuine interest in seeing the student succeed (Negley, 1981).

9. Use activities that the student naturally enjoys as reinforcements and incentives so he will first complete the task that is given (Enright and Roit, 1979).

10. Devise a contract in which the student earns interesting activities for completed work (Stivers, 1977).

11. Work with the student on responsibility until he believes failure to complete a task is the result of his lack of motivation. The

student may then escalate his efforts in an attempt to obtain the goal (Tollefson, 1981).

12. Through your instructions and discussions, show the student that the knowledge he gains when completing a task is of interest and exciting (P. Gray, personal communication, 1984).

13. Use puppets during your instructional period to promote good listening and excitement pertaining to the particular task at hand (M. Montgomery, personal communication, 1984).

14. Allow students to play a quick game that they enjoy at the end of a particularly productive day for all members of the class. This will encourage those that don't complete tasks to do so and will also encourage the rest of the class to support the target student's efforts (Davis, 1982).

15. Take note of the student's expectancy when given a task. Discuss it and work on it through positive, immediate feedback (Keon and Willoughby, 1981).

16. Give the student optional ways to complete the same content material (M. L. Schaefer, 1986).

17. Do not allow the student to engage in desired activities until all work is completed.

18. Require the completion of all work before the student goes home.

19. Call the parents of the student to enlist their help in motivating their child.

20. Allow the students to work in groups.

55
Does Not Show Imagination

1. Have the student play a game called "Imagine if. . . ." For example, have the student tell what might happen if children were 15 feet high, if dinosaurs were found in caves under the city, if the sun shined 23 hours a day, and if there was a law saying that the color red could never be used again.

2. Have the student brainstorm with others to develop a list of 100 uses for an object (e.g., things you could do with a brick: paperweight; tie it into a fisherman's line to make him think that he has a fish on the end; break it in half and tie each half to the bottom of ones' shoes to make one taller; etc.).

3. Have the student write or tell what it would be like to be a certain object (e.g., purse, gym sneakers, etc.). Have him describe a typical day and what the object would say if it could speak (J. Rogger, personal communication, 1986).

4. Show the student pictures of Rube Goldberg contraptions which are elaborate, convaluted machines for doing ordinary tasks. Have the student design one of these useless and unnecessary devices.

5. Have a group of students pass a highly decorated empty box to each other. Each student is to make a wild guess as to the contents of the box. Each student should try to make his guess sillier or more unusual than that of the previous student.

6. Give the student a large piece of paper and a writing instrument. Have him move the instrument to the beat of music. After the music has ended, have him find recognizable objects in the maze of lines and squiggles.

7. Have the student tell what he sees in inkblot pictures. These can be made by pouring ink or paint into a certain crease in a piece of paper and folding the paper in half. Promote creative stories by asking the student to elaborate on his answers.

8. Create an object with no obvious usefulness. Have the student brainstorm with others as to possible uses for this thing.

9. Supply lots of materials and clean trash. Have the student make "modern art."

10. Read part of a mystery, horror, or science fiction story. Have the student complete the story.

11. Promote creative writing on such topics as

"When I met a creature from Mars" or "My last trip to Africa."

56

Does Not Study

1. In a private conference with the student, tell him that by studying, he is practicing or reviewing what has already been learned and that this will enhance his abilities (Youssef, 1984).

2. Ask the student if he feels that good grades are achieved by putting forth a reasonable amount of study time outside of class, or solely by luck (Youssef, 1984).

3. When alone with the student, ask him if he feels that the work is too easy and that studying outside of class isn't needed. If so, revise the level of expectations in your assignments (Youssef, 1984).

4. Distribute a "study time" scale to the student. Have the student indicate how many hours he spends studying each week and the typical days that he might study. After the student has completed the scale, discuss the results (Youssef, 1984).

5. Inform the student that he must assume responsibility for learning, and that providing time for study outside of class is part of this responsibility (Newton and Matthews, 1985).

6. Conduct classroom discussions on the importance of studying (both inside and outside of class) and different studying techniques that can be used (Kristine, 1985).

7. Inform parents by letter that studying is a required part of your class. Also emphasize that studying should be completed before television and/or radio. Request that the parents ask their child each evening if there is any studying to be done. Have the parent sign the letter and return it to school with their child. If the letter isn't returned within a reasonable time, call the parents. If you suspect that a parent's signature has been forged, call him or her (Ashmore et al., 1984).

8. Make sure that the student understands what is expected of him (e.g., specific notes, texts, and text page numbers) (Ashmore et al., 1984).

9. Have the parents write a note saying that their child has studied on the specific nights specified by you. If in doubt about the legality of the note, call the parents (Ashmore et al., 1984).

10. Assume that the student doesn't know how to study. Teach different studying tips and techniques (Gibbs et al., 1979).

11. In class, use current magazines that are interesting to the student and will motivate the student to study (e.g., *Rolling Stone*, *Sports Illustrated*, and *Seventeen*) (Frager and Thompson, 1985).

12. Give an "interest survey" to the student on topics about which he would like to learn and study. Plan some instruction time around the student's ideas (D. Sadlon, personal communication, 1985).

13. Ask the student which occupation he wishes to enter after graduation. Stress the importance of studying to gain entrance into this occupation (D. Sadlon, personal communication, 1985).

14. Verbally state the specific rules of study for the given task (Simpson, 1984).

15. Supply the student with a checklist that contains teacher-posed questions on the specific subject material to be studied (e.g., "Did you read through the vocabulary words twice?") (Simpson, 1984).

16. Check with the student and his parents to find out if he has a quiet place at home in which to study. Ask if the room is properly lighted and ventilated, has an appropriate temperature, and has a desk and the necessary study supplies at home (Castagna and Codd, 1984).

17. Emphasize to the parents that music and television can be used as rewarding activities after the student studies. Ask them to

eliminate these during the study period (D. Sadlon, personal communication, 1985).

18. Ask the parents to withhold a desirable activity until the student studies (e.g., going to the movies or a party) (Salend, Esquivel, and Pine, 1984).

19. Be sure that the student takes all necessary study materials to his studying environment.

20. Allow the student to call you if he is having difficulty while studying.

21. Teach the student to pay special attention to vocabulary words or bold type in his textbooks and notes (Middleton, 1985).

22. Encourage the student to recopy his notes as a means of reviewing the material (Kristine, 1985).

23. Teach mnemonic devices to the student to help him memorize material. For example, Roy G. Biv is a mnemonic for the colors of the visible lights spectrum (red, orange, yellow, green, blue, indigo, and violet). A mnemonic can also be a sentence of words with the same first letters as the words in the list. For example, "King Philio came over for good spaghetti" is a mnemonic for the classification levels of living things (kingdom, phylum, class, order, family, genus, species) (Middleton, 1985).

24. Tell the student to remember to ask questions and admit when something isn't understood (D. Sadlon, personal communication, 1985).

25. Arrange for class time to be used for studying.

26. Guide the student's studying by telling which material and which sections in the text are particularly important.

27. Ask all the students in the class to tell you how long they studied. Correlate this information with the grades achieved by the respective students. Chart this information to show that increased study time results in higher grades.

28. Hold private study sessions after school or during nonacademic times.

57

Easily Frustrated; Gives Up Passively

1. Identify and eliminate the source of frustration by conducting diagnostic pretesting (Gnagey, 1968).

2. Sit the student next to someone who asserts himself and asks questions in order to give the target student a model to observe and imitate (Clarizio and McCoy, 1976).

3. Let him know that it is alright to ask for help when needed (Clarizio and McCoy, 1976).

4. Have the student check with you after every five (or another agreed upon number) questions in order to clear up any problems or questions that the student may have (C. Schwehr, personal communication, 1984).

5. Act out a situation in which the passive student asserts himself and another gives in (Clarizio and McCoy, 1976).

6. Provide an overabundance of opportunities for success and resultant praise. Reinforce the student when he "stands fast" in any situation (Verville, 1967; Clarizio and McCoy, 1976).

7. Break the assignment into smaller parts to prevent overwhelming the student (House and Lapan, 1978).

8. If too difficult for the student, change the lesson, assignment, or teaching method immediately (House and Lapan, 1978).

9. Use the student's strengths to develop interests, confidence, and self-esteem. Plan activities and assignments that involve the student's interests (Karlin and Berger, 1972).

10. Before presenting the assignment, ask the student to tell you the correct way to react if he has difficulty.

11. Hold a discussion with the student to discover his perception of the problem. Test its depth, explore the anxiety level, high-

light reality, explore the student's motivation to change, and establish a plan to change the behavior or the pressures associated with the behavior (Heuchert, 1983).

12. Systematically increase the amount of work required from the student. Begin below the student's frustration level. As the student is successful, increase the requirement (C. Lesinski, personal communication, 1985).

13. Whenever the student accomplishes a small task, reinforce him with praise and attention (C. Lesinski, personal communication, 1985).

14. Use a token economy. Reward a completed task with tokens which can be exchanged for money, goods, or privileges (Mosse, 1982).

15. Have the student help identify the problems and possible solutions. Use his ideas (Mandell, 1984).

16. Be sure that the student understands the purpose for the assignment.

17. Assign a peer tutor to assist the target student when he is experiencing difficulty.

18. Ignore the student when he gives up, but give the student positive attention when he is persevering at a task (C. Lesinski, personal communication, 1985).

19. With the permission of the parent, do not let the student go home until all work is completed. One or two late sessions is usually all that is needed.

58

Quickly Frustrated; Loses Emotional Control

1. Remind the student with a simple gerund. In order to prevent an argument, say in one or two words what a whole sentence says (e.g., say, "Waiting" instead of, "Please sit down and wait your turn") (Cherry, 1983).

2. Distract the frustrated student to a positive model in near proximity (e.g., A student who is having trouble using a paint brush correctly, and is getting frustrated in attempting to do so, can be distracted (and instructed) by drawing his attention to a child next to him. Say such things to the other student as "You're holding your brush so nicely" and "You are pressing so gently and moving your brush so slowly across the paper.") (Cherry, 1983).

3. Inject humor into frustrating situations. "Ooops! We goofed!" is better than saying, "That's not how we do it" (Marshall, 1972; Cherry, 1983).

4. Offer choices to the student who is in a frustrating situation (e.g., "You may pick up the blocks right now or you can come here, have me give you a hug to show you how much I like you, and then pick up the blocks.") (Cherry, 1983).

5. Ask yourself what you are doing that might be causing this behavior in the student. Make a list of such things as yelling, ignoring, threatening, and so on. For the next week, try to refrain from doing these things and see if the behavior improves (Fuller and Fuller, 1982).

6. Allow the student to go for a drink of water if he starts to feel frustrated.

7. Promise yourself that each time the student acts out because of frustration you'll act as though it's the first time he has done so. Do not use phrases such as, "You're doing it again" or "I've told you a thousand times." Avoid doing anything that reminds him that this is repetitive behavior (Fuller and Fuller, 1982).

8. Help the student get started in the desired behavior when he is losing control by walking over to him, touching his shoulder, and saying, "Can you do your work now?" In this way, you are giving the student responsibility for his behavior and demonstrating a willingness to help him get started in the behavior (Fuller and Fuller, 1982).

9. Ask the student, "What are you doing that is against the rules?" Get an answer. Then say, "Are you willing to do your work now?" (Fuller and Fuller, 1982).

10. Make a plan with the student to help him move toward responsible behavior. Make it short, specific, and concrete. The plan should follow all classroom rules (Fuller and Fuller, 1982).

11. When the student who has been emotional regains control, place him someplace close to the class activities where he can see, but not be an active participant. Allow him to listen but not contribute. Bring the student back to general activities when he can answer "yes" to the question, "Are you ready to follow class rules?" (Fuller and Fuller, 1982).

12. To avoid frustration from occurring, teach the student to engage in the following verbal mediations: (a) make questions regarding the nature of the task, (b) answer the questions he makes, (c) give self-guided instructions while performing the task, and (d) give self-evaluation and reinforcement (Glenwick, 1979).

13. Predict when frustration is likely to occur and build in controlling contingencies (Graziano, 1974).

14. If a student becomes frustrated in math, orally model each step of the mathematical procedure to be used in solving the assigned problems. Listen to the student and have him repeat the procedure back to you (Kendall and Braswell, 1985).

15. Play a card game. The playing cards are labeled with situations that are frustrating to the student. Have the student role play an acceptable response to a frustrating situation (Kendall and Braswell, 1985).

16. To prevent frustration when attempting a new task, give the student feedback on his performance as soon as possible (Kerr, 1985).

17. Recognize the underlying feelings a student is experiencing as frustration is occurring (e.g., say, "I know you are angry that your paper got torn, but I cannot let you hurt others") (Marshall, 1972).

18. Remove frustrating objects from the student who has not developed the ability to handle them (Miller, 1984).

19. State the reasons for all rules (Miller, 1984).

20. Positively direct the student to the logical consequences of his own actions without being punitive (e.g., the frustrated student who spills milk would be guided to clean it up) (Miller, 1984).

21. Hold and restrain the badly frustrated student and soothe him with words and strokes until he gains control (Miller, 1984).

22. Ignore inappropriate behavior. Reinforce only appropriate behavior (Sarason, Glasser, and Rargo, 1972).

23. Teach the student to set goals for behavior.

24. Teach the student to observe behaviors that are inappropriate and to discuss these behaviors (Nielsen, 1983).

25. Have the student copy a paragraph, written by you, that describes the poor conduct and the desirable alternative. The paragraph should give the reasons why one type behavior is not acceptable and the other is. After copying the paragraph, have the student rephrase it in his own words (Nielsen, 1983).

26. Teach students to set up their own system of reinforcement and to assign penalties if the goals are not met (Nielsen, 1983).

27. Have the student serve as a rule-following model for others (Toner, 1978).

28. Role play the frustrating situation and demonstrate the manner in which the student should have behaved (J. O'Malley, personal communication, 1985).

29. For the student who is consistently frustrated by a classroom rule, have him present an argument, as a lawyer, to a classroom judge and jury. You could be the witness for the defense. Do this only with a rule that you are willing to change if you lose (J. O'Malley, personal communication, 1985).

59

Fails to Finish Things He Starts

1. Reinforce the student for things that he completes (Salend, Esquivel, and Pine, 1984).

2. Require sequentially larger sections of a task to be completed in order to receive reinforcement.

3. Require that all work on tasks be completed before the student goes home.

4. Set up a work schedule with the student to insure that he works on the project.

5. Give the student a grade of "incomplete" until the project is completed.

6. Give a failing grade if the project is not completed.

7. Do not allow the student to pursue new projects until previous ones are completed.

8. Remove privileges and preferred activities until all work is completed.

9. On a sheet of paper, list the steps that need to be followed in order to complete the task. Have the student check off each step as it is completed.

10. Make a contract with the student that provides reinforcement for the completion of various sections of the task. The reinforcement should become progressively more lucrative to motivate the student to attempt completion of the next section.

11. Assign a task that requires the students to work together in pairs. Match the student who doesn't finish things with a student who does (McDaniel, 1985).

12. Make your assignments interesting and be enthusiastic when presenting them, so the student will want to finish what he starts (McDaniel, 1985).

13. Privately talk to the student about a "good note" that he will take home to his parents at the end of the day. Let the student know what is expected of him in terms of the assignment, and if it is completed, send a "good note" home. Steadily increase your expectations (Gappa and Glynn, 1981).

14. Set up a point system with the student. The amount of points the student earns during the day or week for completing assignments or tasks results in his being able to choose an activity of his liking (Gearheart, 1981).

15. Send home daily or weekly progress reports regarding the student's completion of assignments or tasks (Y. Pingitore, personal communication, 1986).

16. In a private conference, express to the student your concern over the behavior and ask if there is something that you, as a teacher, can do to help correct this behavior (Y. Pingitore, personal communication, 1986).

17. Provide opportunities for the student to choose activities that are of interest to him (Y. Pingitore, personal communication, 1986).

18. Provide the student with many hands-on experiences that will attract his interest (Y. Pingitore, personal communication, 1986).

19. Role play with the student the behavior you are trying to correct (Covington, 1984).

20. Hold a conference with the parents to let them know about the student's behavior. Find out if there is something the parents can do to encourage the student to finish assignments and tasks (Y. Pingitore, personal communication, 1986).

21. Encourage the student, both verbally and nonverbally, while he is working on a task or assignment (Y. Pingitore, personal communication, 1986).

60

Gives Inappropriate Responses or Answers

1. At a predetermined variable time interval, reward all students who are speaking appropriately. Explain to the entire group that

you are rewarding those students who are talking appropriately (L. Burr, personal communication, 1985).

2. Hold a team meeting with parents and other adults who deal with the student's inappropriate responses. Develop a strategy for dealing with the behavior that all the adults can carry out consistently in all of the student's environmental situations (Ysseldyke, 1983).

3. Praise students who respond appropriately and ignore inappropriate responses (Campbell, Dobson, and Bost, 1985).

4. Give the student a nonverbal cue (e.g., nasty look, nod of the head) to indicate that the response is inappropriate (Campbell, Dobson, and Bost, 1985).

5. Record the frequency of responses and share the data with the students. Arrange a contingency contract agreement with the student in which he attempts to lower the amount of inappropriate responses. Involve the student in self-recording his inappropriate responses. Set up a review time with the student each day. Compare your recordings with the student's (Dampf, 1977).

6. Record the student's inappropriate responses. Share and discuss these with the student when he is calm. Have the student make up a list of acceptable responses that can be used in place of the inappropriate remarks (Floyd and Hughes, 1980).

7. When the student makes an inappropriate response, insist that the student apologize and rephrase the remark (Campbell, Dobson, and Bost, 1985).

8. When a student makes inappropriate remarks, give the student detention after school and have him practice appropriate responses (Campbell, Dobson, and Bost, 1985).

9. Have the student leave the room temporarily until he can make appropriate remarks (Campbell, Dobson, and Bost, 1985).

10. Instruct peers to model the appropriate be-

havior by prompting and reinforcing appropriate responses (Gresham, 1984).

11. When a student responds inappropriately, say, "Excuse me." If the student continues to speak inappropriately, continue to say, "Excuse me" until the student changes his response to the appropriate language (L. Burr, personal communication, 1985).

12. Remove a classroom privilege such as participation in a fun activity (Campbell, Dobson, and Bost, 1985).

13. Isolate the student in a section of the classroom away from the class activity for a predetermined time period (Campbell, Dobson, and Bost, 1985).

14. Divide the entire class into two teams, equally distributing behavior offenders. Appoint a team captain who emits appropriate responses. Draw a chart on the board and each time a student makes an inappropriate response, put a slash under his team's side. After a given time period, count the number of slashes and reward the team with the least number of slashes with a predetermined reinforcer (Johnson, Turner, and Konarski, 1978).

15. Take the time to determine what prompts the student to give the appropriate response. Control the environment by insuring that needs are met and by stating positive prompts for the desired behavior (Munson, Miller, and Berman, 1981; Murray and Whittenberger, 1983).

16. Teach the student how to graph. Have him graph the number of inappropriate responses each day. Encourage him to be artistic and creative on the graph, allowing him to draw happy faces or other pictures to indicate his feelings about the day's response level. Reward any daily decrease in the number of responses (Paquin, 1978).

17. When the student gives an inappropriate response, stand close to him and maintain eye contact while giving a verbal reprimand (Van Hauten, Nau, MacKenzie-Keating, Sameoto, and Cdaneichia, 1982).

18. When reprimanding the student verbally

for an inappropriate response, praise an appropriate response that the student has given previously (Van Hauten, Nau, MacKenzie-Keating, Sameoto, and Cdaneichia, 1982).

19. When the student gives an inappropriate response, touch the student lightly on the arm. Maintain eye contact (Van Hauten, Nau, MacKenzie-Keating, Sameota, and Cdaneichia, 1982).

20. Have small groups of students demonstrate appropriate responses in similar circumstances. Discuss the responses with the student (Wietig and Elston, 1980).

21. Videotape role-playing demonstrations of the target student giving appropriate response. Play it back for the student and discuss the differences in the reactions of others when he responds appropriately (Wietig and Elston, 1980).

22. Inform the student that he has five seconds to rephrase the inappropriate comment. If this direction is disobeyed, implement a consequence.

23. Draw a certain number of boxes on the chalkboard. Place a checkmark in a box for each inappropriate response. If all boxes are filled, implement a negative consequence. If less than the total amount of boxes are checked, provide a reward (B. Kreuger, personal communication, 1984).

24. Ask the student to explain his answer and how it relates to the question (Ferreday, 1980).

25. Give hints as to what you are expecting in order to cue the student as to what is appropriate (C. Calvano, personal communication, 1984).

26. Give the student a question early in the lecture. Tell him to think about this and prepare a good response. Call on him later for an answer (Ferreday, 1980).

61

Hands in Assignments Late

1. Send home daily progress reports to the student's parents (Y. Pingitore, personal communication, 1986).

2. Provide special privileges for those students who hand in assignments on time (Y. Pingitore, personal communication, 1986).

3. When the student hands in an assignment on time, praise him and use nonverbal gestures to communicate your acceptance of his behavior (Salend, Esquivel, and Pine, 1984).

4. Role play with the student the behavior you are trying to correct (Covington, 1984).

5. Set up a contract with the student that will result in rewards for performing the behavior (Gappa and Glynn, 1981).

6. Keep the student after school for every two assignments that are handed in late (Y. Pingitore, personal communication, 1986).

7. Have a supervised study period in which the student cannot leave until he finishes his assignment (Strothers, 1984).

8. Do not accept the assignment if it is late. Give the student an incomplete or failing grade for the assignment (Y. Pingitore, personal communication, 1986).

9. Take away a special privilege for each assignment that is not handed in on time (Y. Pingitore, personal communication, 1986).

10. Tell the student that when he hands in his assignment late, he owes you something (e.g., cleaning up the classroom, staying in from recess to straighten up the reading corner, etc.) (Y. Pingitore, personal communication, 1986).

11. Make your assignments interesting and be enthusiastic when presenting them, so the student will want to finish what he starts (McDaniel, 1985).

12. Set up a point system with the student. The amount of points the student earns during the day or week for handing in assign-

ments results in his being able to choose an activity of his liking (Gearheart, 1981).

13. Have the parents of the student sign a contract agreeing to review the assignment sheets, look at completed work, help provide a quiet place for their child to study, and listen to the summary of what he has studied (Quasius, Koppman, Goldman, McQueen, and Little, 1984).

14. Give parents a monthly calendar that lists scheduled assignments and suggested activities that they can do with their child (Quasius, Koppman, Goldman, McQueen, and Little, 1984).

15. Have the parents and student set an agreed upon goal for how much time at home the student will spend on the assignment. Parents will chart this daily to determine the progress of the student on the assignment (Quasius, Koppman, Goldman, McQueen, and Little, 1984).

16. When the student hands in a late assignment, place him on a five-day probation and have him stay after school to do the assignments for that week. After the five days, a follow-up program begins, in which the student alternately does his assignments at school and home for the next five days. This is followed by full-time assignment completion at home. If at any time the student fails to comply with on-time assignments, he will be required to do the assignment in school and the cycle repeats (Lieberman, 1983).

17. When assignments are repeatedly handed in late, a daily report card may be used. This involves writing the assignment on the card along with the date it is to be completed by. The parents are required to sign the card and return it to the teacher. Failure to return the card will be followed by a phone call to the parent at work or home, and a conference with the parent and student (Fairchild, 1983).

18. Schedule homework one week at a time, Sunday through Thursday, with weekends off. Inform the parents of this schedule (Harris, 1983).

19. Ask parents to chart the homework behaviors that are completed daily at the agreed upon level, and have them reward their child frequently for the completed assignments (Harris, 1983).

20. Make the assignments clear and be certain the student understands them (Harris, 1983).

21. Require the student to write down the assignments from the board into a notebook (Harris, 1983).

22. Clearly communicate the expectations as to how the assignment is to be done. This includes a proper heading, due date, order of questions, and writing style (Harris, 1983).

23. When assignments are late, deduct points or penalize the student for each day. This system may also be used in reverse. For everyday the assignment is handed in early, the student receives bonus points.

24. Be specific in terms of assignments. Tell the student when assignments must be done and the quality that will be expected (Haas, Kasper, and Kryst, 1979).

25. Do not let an assignment deadline extend further than one day. Have the student complete it during recess or free time if necessary.

26. Have the student complete all corrections during recess or free time.

27. If the student finds a project to be overwhelming, break the task into smaller steps (Kerr and Nelson, 1983).

28. Make a chart for the student to record how many assignments he has turned in on time for one week. Decide with the student beforehand how many must be turned in to receive special privileges. Slowly increase the criterion each week (D. Parker, personal communication, 1983).

29. Send home a certificate with the student for completing a week's worth of assignments on time. This also builds relationships with parents. Gradually fade out certificates as the student takes responsibility and pride in doing work (Cooper, 1981).

30. For long-term projects, establish time

guidelines or checkpoints to assist the student in getting started and continually working to meet the daily portion.

31. Allow the student to collect the assignments from the class when his is done on time (C. Schawel, personal communication, 1983).

32. Have the student play a game with you in which he is the secret agent and must get the top-secret information (homework assignment) to you on time or else the mission has failed (C. Schawel, personal communication, 1983).

33. Have the student stay after school to finish the task (C. Schawel, personal communication, 1983).

62

Has Trouble Starting a Task

1. Read the directions together in class and start the class as a whole (K. Alvis, personal communication, 1983).

2. Have the student read the directions to the teacher, and in his own words, state what is expected for each assignment (K. Alvis, personal communication, 1983).

3. Put the assignment directions on a tape recorder so that the student can refresh his memory if directions are forgotten (K. Alvis, personal communication, 1983).

4. After getting the rest of the class on task, individually assist the student in starting (K. Alvis, personal communication, 1983).

5. Ask a friend of the student to assist in starting (Reinhart, 1980).

6. If the student is not starting the task because it is too difficult, simplify the task (Reinhart, 1980).

7. Rewrite or restate the task with simpler directions (Reinhart, 1980).

8. After giving instructions, review them with the student (Roberts, 1975).

9. Teach the student a new skill in a tutorial situation. Then give the student a work-sheet to be completed within a stated time period. When the student completes the task, reward him. The reward should only be given if the student completes the task within the time limit (Glazzard, 1981).

10. Verbally praise a student who sits close to the slow starter for his speed when starting an assigned task. Hopefully, the slow starter will begin the task upon hearing this. Reinforce the slow starter when he does start.

11. Reinforce the student for any steps that resemble procedures that indicated he is starting the task (e.g., picking up a pencil, writing name on paper).

12. Give the student a brief look at the reinforcer he will receive if the task is started on time.

13. Pair the student with a peer who quickly starts on tasks.

14. Assist the student initially before having the student continue on his own.

15. Make a game out of the task (D. Olson, personal communication, 1983).

16. Assure success through short, easy tasks.

17. Break the task into shorter sections so that the student does not feel overwhelmed by the amount of work (House and Lapan, 1978).

18. Use peer tutoring.

19. Use a timer set at one-minute intervals. If the student starts the task before the first interval has ended, he gets more reinforcement than if he starts during the second interval.

20. Give a "countdown" to the start of the task.

21. Time the student to see how fast he can complete the task.

63

Looks to See What Others Are Doing Before Starting

1. Provide choices for various activities (Reinhart, 1980).
2. Provide examples of how to do the task (K. Alvis, personal communication, 1983).
3. Ask the student to rephrase the directions to gauge his level of comprehension.
4. When appropriate, have the student include his own opinion in the work to show that there is not always one correct answer (D. Brown, personal communication, 1984).
5. Check to determine if the cause for looking at other's work is due to the situation (e.g., work is too difficult, irrelevant work, long papers, etc.) or whether it is the immorality of the student as he cheats (Fogg, 1976).
6. Use peer tutoring for the student (D. Brown, personal communication, 1984).
7. Make sure the student is physically, academically, and emotionally able to do the work given to him (D. Brown, personal communication, 1984).
8. Provide activities to build the student's self-concept (D. Brown, personal communication, 1984).
9. Provide the student with as many open-ended, creative activities as possible (D. Brown, personal communication, 1984).
10. Place the student in a study carrel or other segregated area to do his work (D. Grey, personal communication, 1984).
11. Inform the student of the meaning of plagiarism and outline specific guidelines regarding the consequences (Fogg, 1976).
12. Seat the student near your desk.
13. Seat the student near model students who will not allow him to look at their papers.
14. Tell the student that he may look at other's papers after doing part of the assignment.
15. Give a different assignment or a variation of the assignment to the students near the target student.

64

Raises Hand But Doesn't Know the Answer

1. Praise the student when he does raise his hand and answer correctly.
2. Praise the student when he doesn't raise his hand during a lesson because he doesn't know the answer.
3. Only call on the student when you are sure that he knows the answer.
4. Before accepting a response from the student, ask him if he knows the answer.
5. Before the start of the lesson, remind the student that he is to raise his hand only when he knows the answer.
6. Prepare the student for an upcoming question by requesting that he listen closely to the information that will be presented next.
7. Talk with the student in an effort to determine why the behavior is being demonstrated.
8. Provide a negative consequence whenever the student displays the behavior.
9. Have all students write the answers to your questions. After this is done, review the questions orally while the students correct their answers. Ask the target student to answer a question that he correctly answered on paper.
10. Appreciate the effort of the student in an attempt to be like others. Give him hints to assist in answering.

65

Satisfied with Inferior Performance

1. Praise the student when acceptable performance is displayed.
2. Have the student redo the assignment until it meets acceptable criteria.

3. Post well-known slogans in the room to motivate the student (e.g., "Quality is job 1," "We're talking proud," etc.).

4. Hold class discussions regarding doing one's best and taking pride in one's work.

5. Ask the student which future occupation he wishes to enter. Point out the need to do well in school in order to enter and progress in his field of endeavor.

6. Make participation in desired activities dependent on meeting a stated criterion on assignments.

7. Do not let the student go home until all assignments meet an acceptable criterion.

8. Have students work in groups. Assign the underachieving student to a group of high-level achievers.

9. Have the student review his paper and determine how it could have been done in a better manner. Offer reinforcement if the student makes these changes.

10. Ask the student to correct the assignments of others. Have him give praise for quality work and offer constructive criticism as to how the other assignments could have been improved. Hopefully, this will draw his attention to high-quality performance.

66

Says He Is Not Capable of Doing Something

1. Praise the student for completing tasks.

2. Ask the student to "give it a try." Offer encouragement throughout the assignment. If done correctly, review the student's earlier comment and point to the finished product.

3. Check to determine if the task is on the student's ability level.

4. Read and discuss the book *The Little Engine that Could*.

5. Institute a point system. With the student, decide what the odds are of the student be-

ing able to complete the assignment. Bet on the student being able to complete the task. The possibility of winning points, based on the odds, may motivate the student.

6. Ask the student what aspects of the assignment would cause him difficulty. Address these points to reassure the student of his ability.

7. Divide the task into sections. Have the student complete one section at a time and review it with him upon completion. Direct him to attempt the next section.

8. Ask the student what must be done to complete the task. Ask if he has ever done these things before. If he has, then encourage an attempt. If he has not done some things before, assist him during these parts.

9. If the student is capable of completing the task, do not allow him to engage in desired activities until the work is completed.

10. Do not allow the student to go home until work is completed.

11. Have the student work with a peer.

67

Says School Work Is Too Difficult

1. Use "face working." Treat the behavior as if it were appropriate rather than inappropriate. For example, say, "You know, this work is too difficult." This shows your ability to deal with misbehavior without threatening the self-esteem of the student (Lasley, 1981).

2. Praise the student for attempting the task in addition to praising work done. Call attention to completed work by displaying it when appropriate and inform the student of his achievement. Let the student know that he has done well (National School Boards Association, 1979).

3. With the student, list various ways of correcting the situation and agree on one of

these possible solutions (National School Boards Association, 1979).

4. Permit the student to complete the assignment at any chosen time, but he must complete it (Verville, 1967).

5. Require the student to remain at school until all work is completed.

6. Reward work completion. Give the student free time or allow him to listen to records or engage in recreational activities (Groten and Cautela, 1981).

7. Do not assign easier work unless the work really is too difficult. Conduct an assessment and assign appropriate work (Sloane, 1976).

8. Break the assignment or directions into smaller parts to insure understanding and prevent overwhelming the student (House and Lapan, 1978).

9. Change the lesson assignment or teaching methods in the middle of the assignment if warranted.

10. Make a deal with the parents to require that unfinished work accrued during the week be done on Saturday starting at 9:00 A.M. All unfinished work is sent home with the student on Friday, along with a listing of what needs to be accomplished. If all work is completed in school, a note is sent home verifying this (Millar, 1980).

11. Review the necessary skills with the student before giving the assignment.

12. Before giving the assignment, point out its similarity to previous work that was completed successfully.

13. Tell the student that he must attempt a designated part of the assignment before you will come over to check it and possibly assist him.

68

Will Not Review Work

1. Verbally encourage the student to review the finished work (J. Grant, personal communication, 1983).

2. Praise the student for any attempt at reviewing.

3. Make work materials more attractive (J. Grant, personal communication, 1983).

4. Have the assignments revolve around the student's interests to make it more interesting for him.

5. Have a class discussion after everyone has finished the assignment by reviewing each question (P. Brewer, personal communication, 1985).

6. Divide the class into small groups to review the assignment together (J. Grant, personal communication, 1983).

7. Give the student a checklist of steps needed to complete the assignment. The last step should be "Recheck your work for possible errors."

8. Do not let the student engage in preferred activities until the work is reviewed.

9. Keep the student after school until the work is reviewed.

10. Review the material with the student.

11. Make a deal with the student in which he will review his work for one week. Record his grades on these assignments. Have him compare his grades with and without rechecking. This may help him to see the efficacy of review.

12. Allow the student to use a calculator or key sheet for the rechecking.

13. Invoke a penalty for refusing to recheck the work.

69

Works Below Potential

1. Demonstrate to the student that your standards are not too high (Baksh and Martin, 1984).

2. Positive expectations should be present in all the students' tasks (Baksh and Martin, 1984).

3. Give positive feedback on any amount of progress (Baksh and Martin, 1984).

4. Motivate the student through classroom incentives (e.g., grading systems; provision of stars, tokens, or rewards for doing academic work; and praise or recognition for correct responses for academic efforts) (Slavin, 1984).

5. Set up a small group of students to work toward a common goal. Individuals who are working together toward a common goal are likely to encourage one another to do whatever helps the group to be rewarded. This should encourage the underachiever to work up toward his potential (Slavin, 1984).

6. Use the underachiever as a peer tutor (Slavin, 1984).

7. Give the student a list of materials needed for each class. A student not working to potential needs to be organized (Kops and Belmont, 1985).

8. Put upcoming academic events on the board to allow the student advanced knowledge of what is expected of him (Kops and Belmont, 1985).

9. The student should be aided in starting a task and have many check points at which the teacher can guide him in staying on task (Blair, 1984).

10. Privately talk to the student about any problems that could be hindering his progress (Wellington and Wellington, 1979).

11. Recommend that the student be tested to eliminate any medical reason for not working up to potential (Rocks, 1985).

12. Set up a study time for exams, giving the underachiever time to study without cramming for the test (Lake, 1984).

13. Have an informal question-and-answer period where there is less pressure to give correct answers.

14. Start with a task the student knows and show a common bond to the new task (Bricklin and Bricklin, 1976).

15. Have the student participate in activities geared toward improving his self-image. A poor self-concept may hinder a student reaching his potential (Rocks, 1985).

16. Have a reason for the student to achieve his potential. Some students are not motivated by grades. Determine what is motivating to him (Bricklin and Bricklin, 1976).

17. Set up a performance contract with the student. Make it progressive, so that it guides the student toward his potential (Braun, 1976).

18. Conduct a course in study habits for the student (Lake, 1984).

19. Allow more time or give more help to the student (Wellington and Wellington, 1979).

20. Plan high-interest activities to stimulate the desire to learn (Wellington and Wellington, 1979).

21. Help the student plan what he is going to study, where he should study, and the best time to study (Lake, 1984).

22. Build assignments around the student's interests.

23. Break a long assignment into shorter segments so as not to overwhelm the student. Check the work after the completion of each section (Messerer, 1984).

10

Classroom/School Behavior (Nonacademic)

70

Attempts to Run Away from Classroom or School Grounds

1. Reward the student with a reinforcer for each period or day that he does not try to run away. Gradually increase the amount of times required before the reinforcer is given (J. Mette, personal communication, 1984).

2. After an infraction, do not allow the student on the school grounds. Have the student stay inside during recess, P.E., or other outside activity for one week.

3. Allow the student to choose which activity he wants to engage in and make him a central figure in the game. He will be too interested and involved to run away.

4. If the student is leaving between classes, place him in a self-contained room with supervised breaks.

5. Escort the student to lunch, the bathroom, and other activities (K. Monty, personal communication, 1984).

6. Give the student the responsibility of being assistant supervisor for an area of the playground (C. Gingerich, personal communication, 1984).

7. Place the student in a walking harness when traveling about the school (D. Gerdes, personal communication, 1984).

8. Give the student important responsibilities that need to be completed throughout the day (e.g., hanging the school flag in the morning, reading the school announcements at noon, helping correct papers at the end of the day) (T. Marlier, personal communication, 1984).

9. If the student leaves during recess, give him the responsibility of being playground manager. Have him be in charge of taking equipment out to the playground, monitoring use of equipment, making sure all equipment is brought back inside and properly stored after use, and checking equipment periodically to make sure it is in

good condition (D. Brown, personal communication, 1984).

10. Reinforce the student for staying within boundaries which are, over a period of time, steadily decreased in range.

11. Take away the student's recess time. Have him complete homework during this time (C. Walters, personal communication, 1984).

12. Arrange for a truant officer to meet with the student and discuss the consequences of leaving the school (N. Hammerschmidt, personal communication, 1984).

13. Assign staff to watch the student (J. Camp, personal communication, 1984).

14. Design a program whereby the student works at home with a teacher and is gradually integrated into the school setting (J. Camp, personal communication, 1984).

15. When the student feels the urge to run away, let him verbalize this urge, sign out, and go home. This privilege is slowly removed over a period of time (D. Bloom, personal communication, 1984).

16. Seat the student far from doors.

17. Place your desk near the door.

71

Behaves in Ways Dangerous or Frightening to Self or Others

1. Reinforce the student for behavior that does not endanger his safety.

2. Reinforce the student for behavior that does not endanger the safety of others.

3. Punish the student for behavior that is dangerous to his safety.

4. Punish the student for behavior that is dangerous to others.

5. Set rules and restrictions before activities are undertaken.

6. Review the behavior with the student after it has occurred. Analyze its danger factor

and discuss alternative actions that could have been demonstrated in the previous situation.

7. Provide more supervision for the student.

8. Restrict privileges based on the student's recent behavior.

9. With the student, agree on a signal that, when given by you, will result in a stoppage of the present behavior with no argument.

10. Warn the other students to avoid the student when he behaves dangerously.

72

Daydreaming

1. Praise the student when he is paying attention.

2. Praise nearby attentive students when the target student is daydreaming.

3. Verbally check with the student at regular intervals (J. Lowry, personal communication, 1984).

4. Touch the student when he is daydreaming.

5. Use a signal to regain his attention (e.g., clearing throat, snapping fingers, slapping your hand on his desk).

6. Drop a marble in a glass jar near the student when daydreaming is noticed. The student attempts to lower the number of marbles in the jar each day (D. Lathrop, personal communication, 1986).

7. Make the materials more colorful and vivid.

8. Include the student's interests in the assignments.

9. Use more hands-on activities (K. Cowell, personal communication, 1986).

10. Do more assignments in the outside environment (K. Cowell, personal communication, 1986).

11. Make lessons shorter and more interest-

ing (K. Cowell, personal communication, 1986).

12. Seat the student near your desk or the usual area from which you instruct (K. Olsen, personal communication, 1980).
13. Make an audiotape with periodic beeps or the word *now*. The student is reinforced if he is attending when the beep or word sounds.
14. Give pop quizzes periodically.
15. Forewarn the student that there may be a pop quiz and that he should be attentive.
16. Make your presentations more vivid and interesting.

73

Does Not Ask Questions

1. Pay the student in cash to ask appropriate questions (Menkin, 1976).
2. Use token reinforcement when the student does ask appropriate questions (Menkin, 1976).
3. Offer the student increased play time for asking the appropriate questions (Menkin, 1976).
4. Use contingency contracting (Mithaug, 1976).
5. Have students work with partners who help cue questions to be asked (Mithaug, 1976).
6. Check your presentation rate to maximize the questioning rate (Carnine, 1976).
7. Give the student a choice of sample questions to ask and have him ask the discussion question that he deems most appropriate to the presentation given (B. Takagi, personal communication, 1985).
8. Make the student a spokesman for a small group of students. He asks the questions formulated by the group (B. Takagi, personal communication, 1985).
9. Make the student lead a small group of other students in asking questions about a subject. He will be the only one to have access to cue

cards that aid in formulating questions (B. Takagi, personal communication, 1985).

10. Have the student play the "Answer Game" with you or a peer. The second person supplies the answer and the target student is responsible for formulating the question (B. Takagi, personal communication, 1985).
11. Have the student ask questions of the class and give classmates proper credit for answering those questions (B. Takagi, personal communication, 1985).
12. Have the student play quizmaster in a question-answering game between two teams (B. Takagi, personal communication, 1985).
13. Have the selected student ask trivia questions of the class in his greatest area of knowledge (B. Takagi, personal communication, 1985).
14. Have the student interview relatives or friends on a given topic (B. Takagi, personal communication, 1985).
15. Have the student develop and ask questions of people in a polling procedure to gather data for a class (B. Takagi, personal communication, 1985).
16. Have the student go to a news conference and see how reporters ask questions (B. Takagi, personal communication, 1985).
17. Have the student interview a local celebrity after preparing questions with teacher guidance (B. Takagi, personal communication, 1985).
18. Have the student read a newspaper article before preparing and asking questions about information not fully covered in the article (B. Takagi, personal communication, 1985).

74

Dogmatic and Opinionated

1. Praise the student when he is open-minded.
2. Ignore the dogmatism displayed by the stu-

dent. The student may tire of not getting attention.

3. Give the student a warning about inappropriate behavior.

4. Ask the student to explain or support his opinion (Ferreday, 1980).

5. Recommend rational-cognitive therapy, an approach that promotes the changing of a student's internal cognitive operations (Newcomer, 1980).

6. Praise nondogmatic students.

7. Have the student read a book about opinionated people who talk out of turn and what may happen to them (J. Bonwell, personal communication, 1985).

8. Have the student list the pros and cons of each side of an issue.

9. Mediate a debate on a topic in which the target student defends his viewpoint.

10. Mediate a debate on a topic in which the target student must defend a viewpoint with which he does not agree.

11. Inform the student that the classroom is not the proper place to express these opinions unless it is done during designated times.

12. Have the student identify one positive point about opinions on the other side of the issue.

13. Encourage the student to join groups that represent his opinions (e.g., Young Republicans, National Rifle Association, National Organization of Women, Nader's Raiders, Guardian Angels, etc.).

75

Fails to Return Promptly from Bathroom or Errands

1. Praise the student when he returns within a reasonable time.

2. Ignore the behavior and praise the student for being good at other things (Reinert, 1976).

3. Have the student take a timer or watch with him. Require him to make it back to class before a designated time is expired (K. Fisher, personal communication, 1984).

4. Choose a responsible friend to go with the student to remind him when to return (K. Fisher, personal communication, 1984).

5. Place a red sign on the door when the student has taken too long before returning to class. Upon returning to the room, the student sees the sign and knows to report to the office for discipline.

6. Channel misbehavior by placing the student in charge of bathroom and hall monitoring (Dinkmeyer, Mckay, and Dinkmeyer, 1980).

7. Tell the student that each minute spent outside the classroom beyond the set time limit will result in a loss of two or three minutes from recess, free time, or class dismissal.

8. Escort the student.

9. Have the student obtain a note stating the time of arrival at and departure from a certain place. An adult's signature must also be obtained.

10. Have an aide or other adult secretly follow the student to determine if his route and behavior were expedient.

11. Have the student attempt to beat his previous travel times for reinforcement.

76

Indecisive; Difficulty Choosing

1. Reinforce the student when he makes a quick, firm decision (D. Grove, personal communication, 1984).

2. Use "values clarification" as an exercise in deciding between alternatives (Hansen, 1981).

3. Use a model designed for decision making in citizenship education. The first phase includes awareness and problem confrontation; the next phase considers options; the third phase analyzes and interprets; and

the fourth phase plans a strategy (Hansen, 1981).

4. Ask the student to imagine the consequences following several different choices (Richardson, 1981).

5. Have class members use values rating. The students must make individual decisions on questions involving values. They affirm their decision by voting for their position (Simon, Howe, and Kirschenbaum, 1972).

6. Use an "either-or" forced choice exercise. The student must make a decision between two things (Simon, Howe, and Kirschenbaum, 1972).

7. Assign one of two choices to the student. Have this student defend that viewpoint.

8. Set time limits for decisions. For example, tell a student that he has one minute to decide which of two free-time activities he would like (D. Grove, personal communication, 1984).

9. Use the "decision story strategy." It provides an open-ended situation requiring a person to make a decision (Smith, Hamrick, and Anspaugh, 1981).

10. Teach the student the "decision-making model." This model has four parts: defining the problem, identifying the possible solutions, gathering and processing information, and making the decision (Smith, Hamrick, and Anspaugh, 1981).

11. Teach the student the following steps in decision making: (a) identify the decision, (b) decide what is most important, (c) seek information, (d) study the consequences, (e) rank the choices, (f) make the decision, and (g) decide on a plan of action (Richardson, 1981).

12. Use constructive daydreaming to have the student project himself into the future a few weeks later, then a year later, and finally to age 50, after having made a certain decision (Richardson, 1981).

13. Assign a peer tutor to assist the student.

14. Materials and procedures should be programmed so as to minimize the student's experience of failure. When the student makes the wrong choice from two or more possibilities, he should be told to try another way instead of just being told that he is wrong. This method emphasizes where he can look to succeed instead of where he has failed (Scott, 1970).

15. Have the student tell you what is wrong with the problem or task after you have pointed out the incorrectness. Verbalizing the problem may help the student look at all the alternatives (Scott, 1970).

16. Give the student a few possible answers to a problem. Insist that he choose one within 30 seconds.

17. Have the student list the pros and cons of each choice and make a decision based upon this analysis.

18. Have the student flip a coin to decide on a choice.

19. Teach the student general rules for approaching tasks, including: defining task demands accurately, assessing one's own relevant knowledge and/or the available cues in a situation or problem, considering all possible solutions, evaluating the relative effectiveness of the solutions considered, and checking work carefully (Douglas, 1980).

20. Discourage passivity and indecisiveness by addressing the student by a title like "Mr. (or Ms.) Problem Solver." Encourage the student to produce his own strategies and to restate instructions in his own words, helping him learn to differentiate between careless errors and errors that reflect genuine problems with understanding (Douglas, 1980).

21. Role play techniques for improving decisiveness by acting out self-monitoring techniques or scanning strategies (Hammill and Bartel, 1975).

22. Use art and music to encourage the student to express himself freely and without fear. Students often can derive a feeling of success from art and music when no judgment of quality is involved (Hammill and Bartel, 1975).

23. Use nondirective play therapy in which students are given permission to express themselves in any way they choose (Guerney, 1983).

24. Guide the student through a task by teaching him problem-solving routines or how to talk himself through the task. Also have him monitor his skills. When students attribute their success or failure in a particular task to the amount of personal effort put into the task, they are more likely to try harder in similar situations in the future. Many students can be taught to attribute success or failure in a task to effort instead of luck or difficulty of the task (Anderson and Prawat, 1983).

25. Introduce a program such as "Think Aloud" or "Copycat" to teach the student cognitive strategies to eliminate indecisive behaviors. These two approaches place heavy emphasis on modeling cognitive strategies and developing answers to: "What is my problem?" "How can I do it?" "Am I following my plan?" and "What are my alternatives?" Gradually fade the prompting and have the student verbalize his own strategy (Camp, 1980).

26. Focus the student's attention on the relevant properties of the task. If the student gives an incorrect response, then shift the student's attention from the irrelevant to relevant properties. Point out the alternatives and provide correct practice trials following incorrect responses (Sulzer-Azaroff and Mayer, 1977).

27. Present clear and concise instructions.

28. Train the student in self-management techniques. These include self-observation, self-recording, self-instruction, and self-reinforcement (Haring, 1982).

29. Promote participation in tasks that have high intrinsic motivational properties and require reflective behaviors. Puzzles, finding mistakes in other students' work, and games of concentration might be tried (Levine, Brooks, and Shonkoff, 1980).

30. Separate the class into teams. Intersperse the indecisive students throughout the teams. The team that completes the task correctly in the quickest time wins. Team members help each other find alternatives (Neisworth and Smith, 1973).

77

Offers to Help the Teacher Too Often

1. Thank the student for his offer, but decline.

2. Ask the student, "What did I say last time you asked?"

3. Have a set procedure for choosing classroom helpers.

4. Have the student earn the privilege of assisting you.

5. Assign one daily helper from those who have completed their homework or done well during the previous day.

6. Assign a weekly duty for each student in the class.

7. Tell the student to stop offering assistance. Implement negative consequences if he continues.

8. Only choose helpers from those who are quiet and in their seat (J. Rogger, personal communication, 1986).

9. Make it clear that only you decides who the helpers will be and that volunteers automatically eliminate themselves from competition.

10. Have chores ready for the student when he completes his work.

11. Ignore the offer.

78

Out of Seat

1. Have the student earn out-of-seat time (or another appropriate social reinforcer) by staying in his seat. The initial length of time

required for the student to stay in his seat would be slightly longer than he is usually able to accomplish. Increase the time as he becomes better able to sit in his seat.

2. Extinguish the out-of-seat behavior by ignoring it.

3. Give attention and praise to the student when he is sitting in the seat (Sulzer-Azaroff and Mayer, 1977; Salend, Esquival, and Pine, 1984).

4. Be sure that the student is not receiving attention for out-of-seat behavior through peers.

5. Give specific praise and attention for sitting to the students who are in their seats at the same time as the student in question is out of his seat (Y. Pingatore and C. Lesinski, personal communication, 1985).

6. Give the student a "bogus buck" for in-seat behavior. This money could be used later to buy things provided by the teacher, such as snacks, free time, music time, and the like (Reyes, 1981).

7. When the students in the class have free time, play music (assuming that music is a reinforcer). If the student gets out of his seat, shut off the music until he returns (Ford and Veltri-Ford, 1980).

8. If you are using a token economy, fine the student for out-of-seat behavior and reward him for in-seat behavior (Salzer-Azaroff and Mayer, 1977).

9. Have the student try to reduce the number of times he is out of his seat each day. For each day that the student meets or beats the previous total, reward him (M. Steiniger, personal communication, 1985).

10. Have a friend of the student record the number of minutes the student is seated. Both students will be rewarded according to an agreement made with the teacher (M. Steiniger, personal communication, 1985).

11. Have the student tie an apron on backwards. This apron and the seat have a small piece of velcro attached. If the student attempts to leave the seat, the tug on the apron and the sound of the velcro separat-

ing will remind the student to sit down. The velcro strip should be small and the apron should be tied in a bow so as not to be a safety hazard. A variation on this procedure would be to use a safety pin to attach a strip of velcro to the student's clothing.

12. Tie a thread over the student's lap as a reminder. This thread would easily break in case of emergency.

13. Place the student in time-out (Sulzer-Azaroff and Mayer, 1977).

14. For every two minutes that the student is seated, drop a candy into a "sharing jar." Allow him to distribute the candies to classmates at the end of the day (Kubany, Weiss, and Sloggett, 1971).

15. Talk to the student and tell him that the out-of-seat behavior is not complying to the classroom rules that he had agreed to follow (G. Mecca, personal communication, 1985).

16. Separate the student's desk from the other students or place him in a carrel. This will eliminate the problem of distractions which may be causing him to be out of his seat (D. Shumsky, personal communication, 1985).

17. Talk to the student and write a contract that will result in rewards for performing the behavior in the contract (Gappa and Glynn, 1981).

18. When the student gets out of his seat, have a project or paper ready that requires him to be sitting in his seat. Say nothing about out-of-seat behavior—just interest him in the task at his desk (Evans and Meyer, 1985).

19. Set up a star chart that will be taken home every other day. After each class, the teacher evaluates the behavior. If the student has been in his seat, place a star on his chart (Gappa and Glynn, 1981).

20. Give the student five strips of paper. Tell him that for a period of one hour, each time he gets out of his seat, he has to give up a strip of paper. Having more strips of paper left results in a better reward (Lovitt, 1978).

21. Instruct the aide in your room to physically walk the student back to his seat each time he leaves it without permission (Evans and Meyer, 1985).

22. Role play with the student. Let him be the teacher while you exhibit the behavior that he normally displays (Y. Pingitore, personal communication, 1986).

23. Allow the student mobility. Have learning centers where the student can get up from his desk and go to another area of the room to work (Y. Pingitore, personal communication, 1986).

24. Have frequent stretching breaks so students who cannot sit for long periods of time can move (Y. Pingitore, personal communication, 1986).

25. Shorten the work periods so the student is not working on one task too long (Sinclair, Guthrie, and Forness, 1984).

26. Give the student a tape recorder with a tape that has tones that sound periodically. If he is in his seat when the tone is heard, he records this on the tally sheet. If he is not in the seat when the tone sounds, he records this. The in-seat marks may be turned in at the end of the day for an activity (Rhode, Morgan, and Young, 1983; Rooney, Hallahan, and Lloyd, 1984).

27. At the beginning of the day, ask the student if he is going to remain in his seat. At the end of the day state how the student did.

28. Have peers challenge the targeted student to make him more aware of the out-of-seat behavior and its effect on others (Haas, Kasper, and Kryst, 1979; Bellafiore and Salend, 1983).

29. Have the student sit in the front of the room near your desk (Haas, Kasper, and Kryst, 1979).

30. Give the student specific times when he may be out of his seat (Haas, Kasper, and Kryst, 1979).

31. Send complimentary notes home when the student's behavior is appropriate or improving (Haas, Kasper, and Kryst, 1979).

32. Have the student set daily goals to increase academic performance and in-seat behavior.

33. In order to keep the student on task, present the information at a faster rate (Millman, Schaefer, and Cohen, 1981).

34. List the student's name on the blackboard with a check mark for each out-of-seat occurrence. Each check mark represents five minutes to be spent in detention after school (J. Posteher, personal communication, 1984).

35. Assign the student who is out of his seat the task of walking around the classroom for the entire period (J. Posteher, personal communication, 1984).

36. Form two teams to compete on in-seat behavior (J. Posteher, personal communication, 1984).

37. Provide a chance for the student to engage in appropriate out-of-seat behavior by making him class messenger (J. Posteher, personal communication, 1984).

79

Says Too Much Work Has Been Assigned

1. Praise the student when he works without complaining (McLaughlin and Malaby, 1972).

2. Give the student a worksheet with the first few problems already completed (Mercer, 1983).

3. Break the task into smaller parts so as not to overwhelm the student.

4. Place the complaining student next to a student with appropriate work habits (Bandura and Kupers, 1984).

5. Give the student a choice of format. For example, instead of writing the answers to questions, have the students answer orally in complete sentences.

6. Use humor or reassurance to reduce tension and anticipation of failure.

7. Alter the planned schedule to accommodate student fatigue or lowered tolerance for stress (Gnagey, 1968).

8. Alter the length or difficulty of tasks to accommodate student fatigue or lowered tolerance for stress (Gnagney, 1968).

9. Make the assignments more interesting by including the student's interests or "hands-on" activities.

10. Place the complaining student in time-out.

11. When the student is being lazy, state that he is wasting time complaining. Tell him that the work will not disappear unless he does it (R. Smith, personal communication, 1985).

12. Inform the student that he will not be allowed to participate in extracurricular activities (e.g., gym, art, music, school talent show, etc.) unless he gets to work (R. Smith, personal communication, 1985).

13. Develop an agreement with the parents whereby the student is not allowed to go home until all work is done.

80
Show-Off Behavior

1. Praise the student when he displays acceptable behavior.

2. Praise other students for their appropriate behavior.

3. Ignore the behavior and have the rest of the class ignore it too.

4. When the student is disruptive, respond by stating that he is stealing the time of the entire class and that this is not fair to other class members (Karlin and Berger, 1972).

5. When other students are not present, quickly inform the student that he will not be allowed to participate in the class as long as this behavior persists (Brown, 1971).

6. Talk to the student and help him understand that his show-off behavior will turn people away from him (Karlin and Berger, 1972).

7. Have the student devise a self-recording check plan that will help him realize the extent of the problem.

8. Conduct a group conference with the student and with the significant others who have a negative influence on his behavior. Speak with the student's peers about their input into his behavior. Explain to the student how he is being influenced by others. Conclude with an emphasis on the need for both the student and his peers to modify their behavior (Rivers, 1977).

9. Have the entire class engage in the student's attention-seeking behavior and then call a halt to the activity.

10. Turn the misbehavior into a learning experience. For example, if the student is making and shooting paper planes, have him teach the whole class how to fold paper planes.

11. When the student is showing off, praise him for something that has nothing whatever to do with his misbehavior.

12. Videotape the student during class to provide an opportunity for him to give feedback, offering an opportunity for the student to receive a clear perception of his actual behavior (Esveldt, Patrick, and Forness, 1974).

13. Provide an outlet for this student by allowing him to be the monitor of a class discussion (Karlin and Berger, 1972).

14. Provide the student with new and more constructive ways of gaining attention by giving him extra responsibilities in the classroom (Galloway, 1976).

15. Have the student write you a letter explaining why he is behaving in this manner and whether he feels this is appropriate (Karlin and Berger, 1972).

16. Involve the student in active rather than passive learning (Usova, 1980).

17. Keep students on task by being prepared and organized for instruction, and presenting lessons in a lively and interesting manner (Usova, 1980).

18. Place the student in a part of the room

where others will be less likely to view his show-off behavior. Place the student so that he is unable to view the reactions of others.

19. Teach the student in a one-to-one or small group setting. This will decrease the number of people available for which to show off.

20. Say to the class, "Someone wants our attention. Let's all look at him and give him that attention." The target student will most likely feel awkward after a few seconds, at which time you can say, "Is that all?" Upon receiving affirmation, continue the usual routine.

81

Skips Classes; Refuses to Attend Certain Classes

1. Reinforce the student for the other classes that he does attend.

2. Reinforce the student when he does attend the class often missed.

3. Develop a contract with the student to motivate him to attend.

4. If the student has a past history of this behavior, get to know him personally at the beginning of the year to develop a bonding and emotional obligation to attend your classes.

5. Report the student's behavior to the administration of the school.

6. Give the student detention.

7. Call the student's parents to see if they can motivate the student to attend classes.

8. Transfer the student to another teacher's class.

9. Upon finding the student, require him to stay after school until your presentation is given and all work is done.

10. Give daily grades to students. The student who skips would receive a failing grade.

11. Make part of the final grade dependent on class participation or attendance.

12. Point out the necessity of attending this class to meet graduation requirements or to obtain a job.

13. Assure the student that if he attends and attempts all work, he will receive a passing grade.

82

Sneaky

1. Reward open and honest behavior exhibited by the student (T. J. Grothaus, personal communication, 1985).

2. Seat the student near your desk.

3. When the student appears to be doing something sneaky, walk toward him and stand near him (M. W. Connelly, personal communication, 1985).

4. Administer punishment for sneaky behavior (M. W. Connelly, personal communication, 1985).

5. When the student is sneaky in terms of cheating in a game, take the student out of the game either for a portion of the game or the remaining time (M. W. Connelly, personal communication, 1985).

6. Send the student to the principal's office to discuss the consequences of his actions (M. W. Connelly, personal communication, 1985).

7. Ignore sneaky behavior (T. Folsom, personal communication, 1985).

8. Refer the student to the school psychologist (M. C. Grothaus, personal communication, 1985).

9. Teach the student to be assertive and to indicate wants and complaints rather than being devious.

10. Make surprise observations of the student so that he can never feel that the behavior will go undetected.

11. After catching the student being sneaky,

warn him that being caught again will result in specific undesirable consequences.

12. Determine the type of sneaky behavior most often seen. Devise a plan to prevent the behavior from occurring by changing the classroom environment in some way.

13. If you are unable to catch the student being sneaky, reward your class for no occurrences of sneaky behavior during the day. This will provide peer pressure for the student to behave appropriately.

83

Swears

1. Make clear to the student which swear words, if any, are allowed in your classroom.

2. Praise the student for using nonvulgar language.

3. Have the student rephrase his words into more acceptable language.

4. Ignore the swearing.

5. Place the student in time-out.

6. Speak with the parents to enlist their assistance.

7. Conduct a class meeting to discuss the origin of the words, why they are used, and why people are often offended by them.

8. Discuss the use of alternate words that are less offensive (e.g., *hell, damn*).

9. Suggest nonoffensive replacement words (e.g., *shoot, sugar, heck*).

10. With the student, devise a nonsense word that will carry the same meaning as the offensive word (e.g., *snarzelpharf, blickick*).

11. Have the student apologize to those present for using vulgar language and have him tell of his feelings in more acceptable language.

12. Wash the student's mouth with soap.

84

Tardy for School or Class

1. Have the student write a composition about why he was late for class (E. McGriff, personal communication, 1985).

2. Have the student write 100 times "I must not be late for class" (P. Olszewski, personal communication, 1985).

3. Have the student write a composition about why it is important to be on time for class (J. Cummins, personal communication, 1985).

4. Have the student stay after school and complete a writing assignment (W. Finnegan, personal communication, 1985).

5. Have the student placed in the in-school detention class (J. Cox, personal communication, 1985).

6. Have the student receive a reward of some kind when he arrives on time for class (M. Hannon, personal communication, 1985).

7. After the student has arrived on time for class for a one-week period, allow him to have one free period to do something of his choice (J. Cox, personal communication, 1985).

8. For each time the student is late to class, subtract one point from his class average for that grading period (V. Rosenthal, personal communication, 1985).

9. Do not let the student participate in any classroom special activity or free time on the day that he is late to class (M. Hannon, personal communication, 1985).

10. Have the student keep track of the days that he is on time for class. When he has accumulated a full week of being on time, give one point to be added on to his average (J. Walsh, personal communication, 1985).

11. Determine the shortest route between classes. Have teachers in rooms along the way remind the student to keep moving.

12. Assign a peer to escort the tardy student.

13. Set up a system whereby quicker arrival at your room results in more reinforcement.

14. Start class on time. Students learn to be late when they know that they will not miss anything of importance (W. Wayson, personal communication, 1984).

15. Do something important during the first part of class to motivate students to be on time (W. Wayson, personal communication, 1984).

16. Do not repeat material missed by the tardy student. This bores the other students and penalizes them for being on time.

17. Present an oral graded quiz at the beginning of the class. Do not repeat questions presented before the student arrived (K. Monte, personal communication, 1984).

18. Have the student make up the missed time after school or during free time or recess (T. Marlier, D. Brown, S. J. Matte, personal communication, 1984).

19. Have the student make up two or three times the amount of class time that was missed.

20. For homework, give an extra question or problem for every minute that the student is late (S. Stidham, personal communication, 1984).

21. Do not allow the student to enter the classroom without a late pass from the office. This forces him to deal with the administration.

11

Delinquency/ Rule Breaking

85

Belongs to a Gang

1. Suggest the start of a program similar to *Positive Action through Holistic Education* (PATHE) which recognizes that forces outside the school environment play a major role in shaping classroom performance. PATHE brings the total community into the process of positive change. It provides for special tutoring and upgrading of math and language, training in effective communication, problem solving, and decision making (Buckholtz, 1981).

2. Move the student away from values of toughness, autonomy, and easy money to values such as honesty and hard work, necessary for success in adult life (Weisfield and Feldman, 1982).

3. Make the student aware of the advantages of legitimate work and effort (Weisfield and Feldman, 1982).

4. Make the student aware of employment opportunities as employment promotes nongang values (Weisfield and Feldman, 1982).

5. Recommend affirmation counseling which helps the student face the reality of the nature of his life, affirm and embrace the nature of himself, and see that he has chosen to lead the life he is leading (Larrabee, 1982).

6. Provide instruction in social skills (Kerr and Nelson, 1983).

7. Use role playing of appropriate social situations to teach new skills (Kerr and Nelson, 1983).

8. Suggest the use of rational-cognitive therapy in which an individual's thoughts, beliefs, perceptions, and attitudes are changed in a positive direction (Newcomer, 1980).

9. Provide opportunities for the student to interact in appropriate group situations in class (K. Christensen, personal communication, 1984).

10. Ask the gang to get involved in a public service or school service activity. This may

promote a desire to engage in positive activities more often. Attempt to gain publicity for these events.

11. Have the student list the pros and cons of belonging to a gang. Attempt to show how gang membership hurts school-related items. Suggest that the gang behavior should be left outside of the school setting.

12. Get the student involved in nongang-oriented groups (e.g., clubs, sports teams) (Trojanowicz, 1978).

13. Recommend that the student be sent to school in another district or state.

14. Contact the local prison to find out if they have a "Scared Straight" program in which convicts tell of the terrible conditions in jails.

86
Destroys Property

1. Set up programs and activities to teach students to respect other's property (D. Brown, personal communication, 1984).

2. Show a videotape of the consequences of vandalism (e.g., property damage, monetary loss, etc.) and have the students lead a class discussion afterwards (Faily and Roundtree, 1979).

3. Involve the student in youth centers and after-school activities in order to occupy spare time (Trojanowicz, 1978).

4. Find an acceptable outlet for the student's emotions (D. Brown, personal communication, 1984).

5. Offer a reward to witnesses who supply information regarding an act of vandalism (D. Brown, personal communication, 1984).

6. Publicize the names of those persons caught vandalizing (D. Brown, personal communication, 1984).

7. Have the student repair the damage (Trojanowicz, 1978).

8. Have the student pay to have property repaired or replaced (Bayh, 1979).

9. Suggest guidance and counseling programs for those students caught vandalizing (Bayh, 1979).

10. Hold seminars to educate teachers, parents, and persons in the community about the effects of vandalism. Ask for their help in preventing vandalism in the community (D. Brown, personal communication, 1984).

11. Suggest the use of tough vandal-proof materials in building and repair (Bayh, 1979).

12. Install adequate indoor and outdoor lighting for night use (D. Brown, personal communication, 1984).

13. Install alarms and intrusion-detection systems (e.g., closed-circuit television cameras, etc.) (Faily and Roundtree, 1979).

14. Install unbreakable glass or plastic windows (Connecticut State Board of Education, 1979).

15. Install deadbolt locks on all outside doors (Connecticut State Board of Education, 1979).

16. Engrave the school name on all property and equipment (Vestermark and Blauvelt, 1978).

17. Hire uniformed police or security officers to patrol the school grounds before, during, and after school hours (Faily and Roundtree, 1979).

18. Set up a direct telephone line to the local police department for quick reporting of vandalism attempts (Faily and Roundtree, 1979).

19. Encourage community groups to hold meetings and activities to occupy parts of the school building after school hours (Bayh, 1979).

20. Identify isolated areas of the school where problems are most likely to occur and close them off or provide for increased supervision (Connecticut State Board of Education, 1979).

21. Institute 24-hour custodial services in the

school building (Connecticut State Board of Education, 1979).

22. Involve students in a school vandalism patrol system. Have students take shifts and routinely patrol hallways, bathrooms, cafeteria, and auditorium during school hours (Faily and Roundtree, 1979).

23. Have patrols made up of students, teachers, and aides work in locker rooms during the times they must be open (D. Brown, personal communication, 1984).

24. Keep an up-to-date inventory of all school property (Vestermark and Blauvelt, 1978).

25. Empty all vending machines of coins each day (Vestermark and Blauvelt, 1978).

26. Do not leave money in the school building overnight (Vestermark and Blauvelt, 1978).

27. Insist on adult supervision at all extracurricular events (Vestermark and Blauvelt, 1978).

28. Require all teachers to be in the hallways during class change times (Vestermark and Blauvelt, 1978).

29. Ask school neighbors and community residents to keep an eye on the school building (Bayh, 1979).

30. Have written school codes that specifically spell out the consequences for violating the rules (Bayh, 1979).

31. Have a faculty member monitor halls and bathrooms between classes (Sexton and Hamilton, 1979).

32. Recommend expulsion from school for extreme cases (Sexton and Killian, 1979).

33. Assign the student to detention (Sexton and Killian, 1979).

34. Institute a vandalism repair program. Set aside an amount of money at the beginning of the year for the repair of any vandalism. Whatever is left at the end of the year is spent on various class or school improvements that are chosen by the students (Kratcoski, Kratcoski, and Washburn, 1979).

35. Give the student a verbal reprimand (Patsey, 1981).

36. Recommend counseling by a principal, dean, teacher, or specialist (Patsey, 1981).

37. Involve outside agencies such as police, the juvenile probation department, or juvenile court in very severe cases (Patsey, 1981).

38. Have the student clean the wall, desk, or stall he has defaced, or have him clean every one in the class or school (American School and University, 1980).

39. If defacement is done during class, place the student in time-out (S. Thomas, personal communication, 1983).

40. Have a large tablet in the time-out corner to give students a chance to write all the graffiti they wish. Each of these sheets goes with the student as he leaves the corner. It is then thrown out.

41. Have a large bulletin board covered with blank paper. Students are allowed to write nonvulgar, nondemeaning comments upon it.

42. Repair vandalism immediately to avoid the image that it is condoned by the school.

43. Enlist trouble-making students for a repair crew. This might stimulate pride in one's school or at least protectiveness of one's repair work.

44. Use role playing. The student acts out a situation in which a possession he values has been destroyed.

45. Repair all property after school. If you are not sure which student destroyed the property, involve the whole group of students in the repair crew.

46. Invite a guest speaker. This should be someone who has suffered greatly due to an act of vandalism, or someone who got caught vandalizing when young and tells how it affected his or her life later.

47. Invite a police officer to speak to the class or school.

48. Encourage students to help clean and improve their school and community.

49. Help students develop a sense of pride in their school and community. Allow them to decorate bulletin boards. Get them in-

volved in a competition with another school in improving the appearance of their school.

50. Have a class discussion on why vandalism is wrong.

51. Provide other, more appropriate ways for the student to get attention. For example, publicly show the students class work or find something else at which he is proficient and show that.

52. Get the student involved in recreational activities.

87

Graffiti; Writes on Walls and Stalls

1. Form clean-up squads to remove graffiti.

2. Have a faculty member monitor halls and bathrooms between classes (Sexton and Hamilton, 1979).

3. For extreme cases, expel the student (Sexton and Killian, 1979).

4. Give the student attention (Sexton and Killian, 1979).

5. Develop student pride in the school and classrooms through awareness lectures (Sexton and Killian, 1979).

6. Institute a vandalism repair program. Set aside an amount of money at the beginning of the year for the repair of any vandalism and graffiti. Whatever is left at the end of the year is spent on various school improvements that are chosen by the students (Kratcoski, Kratcoski, and Washburn, 1979).

7. Give the student a verbal reprimand (Patsey, 1981).

8. Recommend counseling by the principal, dean, teacher, or specialist (Patsey, 1981).

9. Involve outside agencies such as police, juvenile probation department, or juvenile court in very severe cases (Patsey, 1981).

10. Have the student clean the wall, desk, or stall he has defaced, or have him clean every one in the class or school (American School and University, 1980).

11. Place the student in time-out.

12. Have a large tablet in the time-out area to give students a chance to write all the graffiti desired. Each of these sheets must go with the student as he leaves and is then thrown out.

13. Set up a bulletin board where nonvulgar and nondemeaning graffiti is allowed.

14. Set aside one section of the building where graffiti is allowed.

15. Do not allow the student to take writing instruments to the bathroom or while passing in the hallways.

16. Escort the student to the bathroom.

17. Have someone check the bathroom for new graffiti after the student goes to the bathroom.

18. Have the student causing the damage pay to have the object cleaned, fixed, or replaced (American School and University, 1980).

19. Attempt to eliminate potential causes, factors, or motivations before the actual behavior takes place (Trojanowicz, 1978).

88

Has Bad Companions

1. Reinforce appropriate behavior in the classroom (N. Mulchrone, personal communication, 1985).

2. Encourage individual activities in the classroom (Serrano, 1981–82).

3. Encourage the student to be independent both in school and out.

4. Have units or discussions on values and morality (Youniss, 1982).

5. Hold units and discussions on friendship and expectations of friends for each other.

6. Take the class on a field trip to a prison. Discuss how bad companions pressure

friends to break the law. Ask if this is the future desired by the student.

7. Assign the student to work with a "nice" peer on a required assignment (N. Mulchrone, personal communication, 1985).

8. Discuss the importance of peer relationships and friendship qualities and have the class talk about these (Youniss, 1982).

9. Have the student keep a daily log of activities with his friends (Serrano, 1981–82).

10. Teach the student that it is alright to say no to companions (Booraem, Flowers, and Schwartz, 1978).

11. Help the student get involved in clubs, sports teams, or other socially acceptable groups.

12. Ask the student and his companions to assist you in socially acceptable tasks.

13. Help the student and his companions in earning money by doing odd jobs such as lawn mowing and house cleaning.

14. Ask a group of well-behaved students to adopt the student of concern into their group.

89

Has Forbidden Objects in Possession

1. Post rules regarding objects and assure that students are aware of these rules.

2. Praise students who obey the rules.

3. Make a contract with the student that rewards him if he, his locker, and his desk are devoid of forbidden objects. Allow for surprise searches. Failure to agree to these searches results in punishment or in no reinforcement.

4. Have a check-in point where students may submit forbidden objects for safe-keeping until the end of the school day.

5. Have surprise school-wide locker searches.

6. Report the student to the school administration.

7. Give the student a choice of giving you the forbidden object or receiving a negative consequence.

8. Hold class discussions regarding why certain objects are forbidden in school.

9. Talk with the student about his need to have the object. Attempt to find another way to meet the need.

10. Have students pass through a metal detector when entering the school.

11. Contact the parents of the student to obtain their assistance.

12. Inform your class that you will conduct a search after the next hallway passing between classes. This gives the student the opportunity to take the object to his locker.

90

Has Sexually Assaulted Another Person

1. Attend to the needs of the victim if the incident just occurred.

2. Report the student to the authorities or school administration if the incident has just occurred.

3. Follow any established school policy procedures designed to deal with this type of behavior (e.g., call the parents, inform the authorities, contact a rape crisis center, etc.) (E. Smith, personal communication, 1984).

4. Document and date anything you witnessed or any information told to you by the student (E. Smith, personal communication, 1984).

5. Recommend counseling by the school counselor or psychologist (E. Smith, personal communication, 1984).

6. After authorities have investigated and the student is back in class, treat him as you would any other pupil (E. Smith, personal communication, 1984).

7. Find out from the principal or counselor if any special procedure is to be used with

this student (E. Smith, personal communication, 1984).

8. Be cooperative with any family therapists, legal representatives, or counselors involved with this incident (E. Smith, personal communication, 1984).

9. Help other students treat the student fairly (S. Smith, personal communication, 1984).

10. Assure that the student's behavior is monitored while on the school grounds.

91
Loyal to Delinquent Friends

1. Reinforce the student and his friends for appropriate classroom behavior (D. Randall, personal communication, 1985).

2. Suggest that parents, teachers, and siblings provide support, encouragement, attention, and positive reinforcement for the student so that he does not need to look to others for reinforcement of these needs (Krumboltz and Krumboltz, 1972).

3. Interest the student's friends in acceptable activities such as starting a gardening service or a car-washing business (B. Tankersley, personal communication, 1985).

4. For various tasks, assign the student to a buddy who displays appropriate behavior (Reinhart, 1980).

5. Talk with the student on a one-to-one basis about his values and morals without sounding judgmental (Reinhart, 1980).

6. Raise the student's self-esteem through success-oriented activities (L. DiMarzio, personal communication, 1985).

7. Engage students in value exercises and discussions (B. Tankersley, personal communication, 1985).

8. Have a successful person who has previously been in trouble with the law come in and talk to the class or have a one-to-one discussion with the student (B. Tankersley, personal communication, 1985).

9. Have the student talk with a counselor (D. Randall, personal communication, 1985).

10. Help the student become involved in socially accepted groups (e.g., sports teams, clubs, church groups).

11. Discuss the pros and cons of socializing with delinquents.

12. Discuss the possible implications that delinquent acts can have on one's future.

13. Ask socially acceptable groups and groups of friends who display morally/legally acceptable behavior to "adopt" a delinquent.

14. Attempt to get the student and his friends to volunteer their time to neighborhood service activities such as playground clean-up and repair. In return they might receive some award or be allowed to write their names beside the project.

92
Poor Sense of Right and Wrong

1. Praise the student for socially correct behavior (Goldstein, Sprafkin, Gershaw, and Klein, 1983).

2. Provide negative consequences for socially inappropriate behavior.

3. After providing a positive or negative consequence for behavior, tell the student why you felt that his behavior was right or wrong.

4. Discuss moral issues and values, and what is right and wrong in daily group meetings.

5. Have peers comment on the student's behavior each day.

6. After an incident, talk with the student about whether his behavior was morally correct and whether the rights of others were violated (Beck, Roblee, and Johnes, 1982).

7. With the student's agreement, have yourself and the rest of the class (and perhaps the parents) "pick on" the student for a

whole day to allow him to have a "taste of his own medicine."

8. Have the student keep track of his interactions with others and rate them on a five-point scale as being "right" or "wrong" or some degree of each. You should also rate the behavior and compare your ratings with those of the student.

9. Videotape the student's behavior and have it rated by you, the student, and the student's peers. Use it as a basis for discussion.

10. Present the student with hypothetical situations. Have him identify acceptable and unacceptable responses or actions.

11. Refer the student to the school counselor or psychologist.

12. Have the student role play appropriate behavior in typical situations. This role playing might also involve real-life protagonists or antagonists (Goldstein, Sprafkin, Gershaw, and Klein, 1983).

13. Have peers who have viewed the role playing comment on the student's performance and make suggestions for further improvement (Goldstein, Sprafkin, Gershaw, and Klein, 1983).

14. Institute a lottery system in which students who display appropriate behavior in various situations receive tickets. Have a drawing at the end of the week for a prize. As behavior improves, the student will have a greater chance of winning the lottery (Witt and Elliot, 1982).

15. In order to increase awareness of different opinions about what is right and wrong, tell the following story to the students: "A group of students are in a discount store and Mary notices that her friend Sue has slipped away from the group and is putting a pair of earrings in her purse. Mary notices a man watching Sue and sees him point to the group. What would you do if you were Mary?" Have the students write a short answer on a 3 × 5 card. Collect them and read anonymously. Then generate an open discussion. Encourage disagreement in what

would be the right thing to do. As the discussion progresses, bring up the issue of right and wrong behavior (Chase, 1975).

16. In order to help students discover that they have the ability to do the right thing, have several group members recall a time when they did the right thing. Accept and reflect their contributions. Help them to see that all of them have the ability to act the right way (Chase, 1975).

93

Steals

1. Praise the student for not stealing.

2. Provide negative consequences for stealing.

3. Require that the student return the stolen object and give an apology to the person whose possession was taken.

4. Monitor the student closely.

5. Make a contract with the student in which he is rewarded if no stolen objects are found on his possession, desk, or locker. Search these before the student leaves school. Allow for surprise searches. Withhold reinforcement or punish the student if stolen objects are found.

6. Keep valuables locked in the your closet or in another secure area.

7. Encourage students to keep their personal belongings and valuables locked in their lockers or in another secure area.

8. Plan a field trip to a jail. Ask the student if this is the future life he desires.

9. Recommend counseling.

10. Call the student's parents to enlist their support.

11. Discuss the feelings of theft victims who worked hard for their possessions or received special gifts from loved ones.

12. Secretly take one of the student's valued belongings. Later, use this incident as an opportunity to discuss the feelings of theft victims.

94

Truant; Skips School

1. Reinforce the student for attending school.
2. Punish the student for missing school.
3. Exempt students from exams if they have limited absences.
4. Give daily quizzes or participation points.
5. Have attendance check days. If the student attends, he receives prizes, bonus points, and so on.
6. Make sure a relationship exists between attendance and grades. If the student displays regular attendance, he should score higher than those with irregular attendance patterns.
7. Give students without truancy over a period of time privileges such as early dismissal.
8. Display attendance charts that show the attendance of all students.
9. Display charts that show the best monthly attendance for each grade, and the top classes in the school.
10. Have contests between classes, grades, or schools. Award the winners with special prizes and privileges.
11. Recognize perfect attendance in newspapers and other media.
12. Fail students who exceed a certain number of absences per semester.
13. If any student is not on the list of excused absences from the previous day, do not accept him into the class until he has met with the school office staff or administrator.
14. Have the student attend an equivalent number of hours after school or during Saturday morning sessions.
15. Give a certain amount of attendance points for a semester. The student loses points for tardiness or truancy. If the student falls below a designated number of points he must receive a failing grade or other negative consequence.
16. Recommend that the school purchase a computer that is used to make phone calls to parents in the evening to let them know their child was absent or tardy from school that day.
17. Have representatives from industry, business, or public service come in to discuss the importance of attendance in the work world.
18. Make immediate phone calls to the student's home if he is tardy or cuts class.
19. Send home a weekly report card that addresses improvements in attendance and achievement.
20. Recommend that office staff be assigned to make telephone calls for students who missed classes during the previous day.
21. Send a letter home indicating dates of absences.
22. Recommend that office staff phone frequently absent or late students with a wake-up call.
23. Suggest that the PTO collect alarm clocks to be given out to tardy students from needy families.
24. Suggest forming an attendance committee made up of school personnel, students, and parents to develop school-wide programs to promote attendance.
25. Have older students counsel younger ones about the importance of attendance.
26. Recommend that the school place students who had more than a designated number of absences the previous year in the same homeroom. Give them all the same schedule to develop a feeling of comradery and security.
27. Provide a shorter day for the nonattending student.
28. Arrange for special events to be presented on Mondays and Fridays.
29. Start a program of activities before school starts each day. Encourage the student to participate.
30. Arrange the school schedule to meet the individual needs of the student.

31. Inform the truancy officer or police of the student's unexcused absences.

32. Require attendance only for necessary academic subjects.

33. If the student attends school for the first four days of the week, allow him to miss school on Friday.

34. Help the student find full-time or part-time work and enroll him in a GED program to complete his diploma.

35. With the parent's permission, go to the family's home and bring the student to school.

36. Pay the student to attend school.

37. Insist that the primary function of teachers is to teach, not to entertain (Teachman, 1979).

38. Encourage the adoption of attendance policies that lead to acceptance of personal responsibility on the part of the student for his attendance (e.g., the student must be punished if he skips) (Duke and Meckel, 1980).

39. Recommend counseling for those who are truant for the first time in order to correct problems that are remediable. If truancy continues, punish the student. If punishment fails to stop truancy, then he should be removed from the normal classroom. If an alternate classroom is available, it must be more demanding than the regular classroom (Teachman, 1979).

40. Suggest incorporating a program that combines counseling with the real threat of significant negative consequences. If the student and his family do not accept counseling and the student remains truant, the district takes legal action (Hanson and Hoeft, 1983).

41. Suggest the start of a program that teaches students the skills necessary to succeed in school. When the student is identified as a chronic truant, the skill deficiencies that cause his problems should be diagnosed and corrective lessons begun (Unger, Douds, and Pierce, 1978).

42. Counsel the student and parents first. Then

report it to the administrator who should seek a solution by any available method. Lastly, transfer the student to another school (Teachman, 1979).

95
Uses Illegal Drugs

1. Closely supervise the student during class breaks and lunch time to prevent the taking of drugs.

2. If the student is using a nonaddicting drug, require that all work be completed before he goes home. This will require that the student wait out the effects of the drug before starting on the work. When the student stays after normal school hours once or twice, he may see the stupidity of coming to school in a drugged state of mind.

3. Encourage the student to join a self-help group. This type of group stresses the rights and obligations of the private person, either alone or in voluntary association with others. Individuals are expected to accept responsibility for their problems and understand that help must come from themselves and from others who have suffered from the same problem (Nurco, 1981).

4. Make use of a reality therapy stratification system. This involves levels in an ascending order of responsibility and privileges. It is concerned with establishing immediate consequences for behavior, minimizing manipulation and externalization, developing good judgment and responsibility, and promoting adequate social relationships (Schuster, 1978).

5. Develop a program with the parents in which all allowance or earned money must be accounted for and proof of purchase given. If this is not done, next week's allowance or paycheck is withheld.

6. Implement drug education in the school. Presentation of information regarding the dangers and risks of drug use may quiet

curiosity about drugs and the desire to use them (Reasons and Seem, 1978).

7. Encourage the parents to join a support group. The aim is to restore supportive family life by promoting positive communication, equitable societal standards, and rewarding value systems for family members as a means of combating the pressure of peers and the enticement of teenage drug use (Garfield and Gibbs, 1982).

8. Encourage the school to institute locker and personal searches if there is reasonable suspicion that drugs are being hidden.

9. Escort the student to the bathroom to prevent drug use there.

10. Suggest that school personnel patrol bathrooms and isolated areas of the school.

11. Suggest that workshops be held to educate school personnel as to the symptoms and signs of drug use.

12. Post anti-drug posters.

13. Plan drug awareness and anti-drug use units and activities.

14. Reward students to inform school officials of the names of drug pushers and drug users.

96

Vandalism

1. Praise the student for appropriate behavior.

2. Work with others to devise activities to develop school pride in students.

3. Hold formal class discussions on attitudes and feelings concerning public property (Greenstein, 1970).

4. Take a few minutes each day to discuss the importance of school and classroom orderliness and cleanliness (How Schools Combat Vandalism, 1980).

5. Involve the students in the care and decoration of the school or classroom (Greenstein, 1970; Richardson, 1976).

6. Allow student groups to meet in your classroom after school (Irwin, 1976).

7. Conduct hourly inspections of vandalized areas or classrooms (Blauvelt, 1981).

8. Evaluate and change the environment to prevent vandalism (Allen and Greenberger, 1978).

9. Make areas bright and colorful so students will not feel that vandalism will improve the looks of those areas (Allen and Greenberger).

10. Repair damaged areas immediately so that students will not feel that vandalism is acceptable (Allen and Greenberger, 1978; Irwin, 1976).

11. Keep valuable equipment in a locked or secure place (Irwin, 1976).

12. Have school personnel patrol bathrooms, isolated parts of the school, and other vandalized areas.

13. Ask school neighbors to keep an eye on school property.

14. Develop activities to help students develop a feeling of "ownership" in the school or class (Vestermark and Blauvelt, 1978).

15. Develop a volunteer student-monitoring force (Vestermark and Blauvelt, 1978).

16. Obtain the following useful books to develop a vandalism prevention program:
   a. Vestermark, S. D., and Blauvelt, P. D. (1978). *Controlling crime in the school.* West Nyack, N.Y.: Parker Publishing Co.
   b. Zeisel, J. *Stopping school property damage.* Available from ASSA, 1801 North Moore Street, Arlington, VA 22209.
   c. *Working together for safe schools.* Available from the Connecticut State Board of Education, Hartford, CT.

17. Involve the student in a repair crew.

12

Depression

Depressed

1. Help build self-esteem by insuring some successes in academics (Rehm, 1981).

2. Develop a meaningful relationship with the student so he feels comfortable in talking to you (Brussel, 1975).

3. Have students make a pleasant events schedule. Make a list of events ranked according to enjoyment and reinforce "happiness" by giving students a chance to do an activity from this list (Rehm, 1981).

4. Get the student involved in an activity that he does well (D. Gerdes, personal communication, 1984).

5. Alleviate stress by having a relaxation period (Hansen, 1976).

6. Promote cooperative play with someone who is a "happy" person (Beck, 1967).

7. Provide as much positive feedback as possible to the student (Gillette and Hornbeck, 1973).

8. Involve the student in physical activities to release tension (Brussel, 1975).

9. Involve students in reading comedies or performing comedy plays (Beck, Ruch, Shaw, and Emery, 1979).

10. Focus the student's energy on someone other than himself (Brussel, 1975).

11. Vary the daily class routine (Brussel, 1975).

12. Help the student set realistic goals in order to avoid depression when unrealistic goals aren't met (Hansen, 1976).

13. Initiate as much group play as possible. This shows the depressed student how to be "happy" (Cammer, 1969).

14. Talk to other students and have them ask the student to join in different groups or activities in which they are involved (Papalia and Olds, 1979).

15. Encourage students to spend time on their appearance. This is based on the view that if one looks good, one will feel good (Forrest, 1983).

16. Have the student justify his existence. Thus, the student is prompted to empha-

size the positive aspects of his life. It may help the student to see that he has qualities others like (Crosby, 1982).

17. Try to provide a gay, bright environment to promote "happiness" (Funkabiki, 1981).

18. Teach the student to praise himself for good work (D. Gerdes, personal communication, 1984).

19. Recommend counseling for the student.

20. Have the student list the negative and positive points of himself or a situation. Accentuate the positive points.

21. Recommend that the student be evaluated by a physician who can determine the feasibility of administering antidepressant medication.

98

Suicidal

1. Closely monitor the student's behavior in school (J. Gustafson, personal communication, 1984).

2. Have the student contact a prevention center or intervention agency.

3. Inform the administration of your concern and document this interaction.

4. Contact the school guidance counselor or psychologist. Document this contact.

5. Start a continuous (preferably daily) monitoring of the student's feelings (Shneidman, 1981).

6. Be willing to deal with some of the reality problems of the student where advisable. Give directions and take a side of living life (Ross, 1980).

7. Contact and utilize community resources including employment firms, social agencies, and psychiatric social worker assistance (Ross, 1980).

8. Talk to the parents and investigate the existence of any home-life problems such as remarriage, adoption, jealousy of another, or death in the family that might be causing the suicidal thoughts (Ross, 1980).

9. Show concern, interest, and understanding in a nonjudgmental manner (Schneidman, 1981).

10. If the student attends church, contact the priest, minister, or rabbi for assistance.

11. Have the student list the pros and cons of suicide. Accentuate the advantages of living.

12. With the student, read and discuss articles and books by and about persons who were despondent, but overcame their suicidal feelings.

13. Talk with the student daily. At the end of each session, get the student's affirmation that he will talk with you tomorrow.

14. Help the student develop outside interests (e.g., part-time employment, sports, clubs).

13

Disruption of Classroom Routine

99

Belittles Subjects Being Taught

1. Reinforce the student for appropriate behavior.
2. Ignore the belittlement attempt.
3. Have the student privately explain to you why he feels that the subject is unimportant.
4. Have the student give his view, followed by your explanation as to why the subject is important. Have a jury of classmates decide in favor of one view. Choose the time and jury carefully.
5. Explain to the student why this lesson, unit, or course is important to his future.
6. Have the student rephrase his comment into more acceptable language.
7. Implement sequentially more punitive consequences for continued attempts at belittlement.
8. Analyze the content or presentation to determine if the student is correct. Make necessary changes.
9. Determine if the student's behavior is due to a low-skill level. If so, tutoring or remedial assistance may be necessary.
10. Belittle the student. Wait. Apologize for your behavior and use this incident to start a discussion regarding the student's behavior and your feelings.
11. Seat the student near you.
12. Seat the student away from peers who may be promoting or reinforcing this behavior.
13. Call the student's parents and enlist their assistance.
14. Monitor the frequency of these remarks. Reward the student if he lowers the total each day.

100

Class Clown

1. Reinforce the student immediately when he behaves well (Dickerman, 1971).

2. When the student interrupts the classroom, move him to an isolated seat (Book, 1983).

3. Give the student token reinforcements for proper behaviors at 30-minute intervals (Book, 1983).

4. Allow the student a certain number of inappropriate acts during a specific length of time. If the student's disruptive behavior is below or equal to the agreed number, reward him (Usova, 1980).

5. Give tickets for desirable classroom behavior. The tickets can later be exchanged for free time with records, games, and the like (Usova, 1980).

6. Speak with the student in private to ascertain the reason for the disruptive behavior (Rivers, 1977).

7. Politely, but firmly, ask the student to stop the disruptive behavior (Rivers, 1977).

8. Explain to the student, as briefly as possible, about the classroom rules that are broken when he is "clowning around" (Rivers, 1977).

9. Encourage the student to strive for greater self-control in the classroom (Rivers, 1977).

10. Identify significant "actors" in the classroom who have a negative influence on the student's behavior. Develop a plan to control their behavior (Rivers, 1977).

11. Ignore the student when he is disruptive, and try to "catch him being good" (Sarason, Glasser, and Rargo, 1972; Swift and Spivak, 1975).

12. Give the student the extra attention that is needed by giving him different classroom jobs and responsibilities (Galloway, 1976).

13. Meet with the student and find out what really interests him. If possible, plan class discussions in this area (Kohut and Range, 1979).

14. Refer the student to a school counselor (Kohut and Range, 1979).

15. Ex-students who had an attitude similar to this student's, but who "saw the light," could be brought in to talk about their experiences (Kohut and Range, 1979).

16. Send the student to the principal, counselor, or study hall to complete his lessons, thus denying him the desired attention and interaction with peers (Kohut and Range, 1979).

17. Give the student attention before he feels the need to act up in a clowning, disruptive way. For example, talk to him each morning or call on him periodically (Wolfgang and Glickman, 1980).

18. Give the student a responsibility that demands concentration. Find an isolated place for him to work. The task should make the student feel important as well as convince him that he is taken seriously (Collins, 1981).

19. Explain that there are times and places for everything and that class time is for academic goals to be met (Collins, 1981).

20. Praise the student about something that carries the inference that he is sensitive, not just a clown (Collins, 1981).

21. Reverse roles with the student (Collins, 1981).

22. Show and discuss a film focusing on the class clown (Collins, 1981).

23. Use a questionnaire to learn more about the student, his background, and interests. Use these to motivate the student (Collins, 1981).

24. Use puppetry as a mode of expression. The class clown may realize that he doesn't have to be "out front" in order to entertain (Collins, 1981).

25. Talk to the student privately about his ways of asking for attention. It may not have occurred to the student that he was doing such. Between the two of you, devise a check plan that will help him realize the extent of the attention-getting behavior (Collins, 1981).

26. Develop ways in which other adults can distract you from the student who is being disruptive, so that you don't find yourself giving the student attention (Kerr and Nelson, 1983).
27. Make a contract with the student to reward more appropriate behavior (Goodwin and Coates, 1976).
28. A review of the student's past academic performance should be undertaken to see if there is any correlation between that and the clowning behavior (Rivers, 1977).
29. Praise other students for appropriate behavior (Long and Frye, 1977).
30. Reinforce peers for ignoring the student's inappropriate behavior (Silverman, 1980).
31. Praise improvements in behavior. Never expect 100% improvement immediately. When the student's clowning disrupts less than usual, praise that improvement (Silverman, 1980).
32. Provide "entertainment time" on a weekly basis so that time is intentionally set aside with this student in mind. Hopefully, this will teach the student that there is a time and place for joking (L. Schaefer, personal communication, 1985).
33. Place the student in time-out.
34. Call the student's parents to enlist their help.
35. Use signal interference in which you catch the student's attention with a signal before the disruptive behavior gets out of hand (Swift and Spivack, 1975).
36. Have the student monitor his own behavior and attempt to improve it daily (Swift and Spivack, 1975).
37. Allow the student to tell jokes to the class if he has refrained from silly behavior for a specific period of time (Swift and Spivack, 1975).
38. Make the student entertain the class for 5 or 10 minutes (J. Noirfalise, 1983).
39. Give the student a typed copy of a paragraph describing the misbehavior, desired behavior, and the consequences for both.

Have the student copy, paraphrase, and orally recite the paragraph (Swift and Spivack, 1975).
40. Build time into your schedule when the student may be the class clown without censure.
41. When the student misbehaves, say, "Class, someone wants our attention. Let's all look at him. Go ahead, class clown." When the misbehavior ceases, ask, "Is that all?" Upon receiving an affirmative response, restart the lesson or activity.

101
Disruptive Behavior

1. Praise the student for nondisruptive behavior.
2. Ignore the behavior.
3. Implement sequentially more punitive consequences as the behavior continues.
4. Seat the student near you.
5. Ask the student if help is needed.
6. Put a hand on the student's shoulders and ask him, in a quiet tone, to settle down.
7. Be sure that the work is on the student's level of ability to assure that this is not avoidance behavior.
8. Intervene by talking to the student and getting him involved in an activity.
9. Send the student on an errand to allow time for him to cool off (Algozzine, Schmid, and Mercer, 1981).
10. Place the student in time-out (Reinhart, 1980).
11. Videotape the student's behavior to show him or others the extent of the problem.
12. Send the student to another classroom as previously arranged with another teacher. That other teacher should act angry and direct the student to sit down and start working.
13. Send the student to the counselor's or principal's office to sit quietly. Incomplete work

should be completed after school in his home room (Givner and Graubard, 1974).

14. Contact the student's parents to enlist their aid.

15. Allow the student to remove himself from the classroom to a time-out area when he sees his own behavior becoming disruptive (Givner and Graubard, 1974).

16. Present the problem to the class. Enlist class cooperation in nonreaction to the student's disturbing behavior. Record all incidents, both successful and unsuccessful. Use a group prize as a motivator. All or none receive the reward (Blackman and Silberman, 1980).

17. Have the student record points for each time his positive behavior evokes praise or a smile from you (V. Croll, personal communication, 1983).

18. Structure time in the day when students can engage in antics that otherwise would be disturbing behavior (V. Croll, personal communication, 1983).

102

Disturbs Others While They Work

1. Reinforce appropriate behavior (Murphy and Ross, 1983; Osborn, 1985).

2. Implement sequentially more punitive punishment as the disruptive behavior continues.

3. Before the lesson, remind the student that he is not to disrupt others.

4. Prevent the misbehavior by establishing classroom routines, clearly stated and enforced rules, and rewards for proper behavior (Eyde and Fink, 1983).

5. Be sure that the student understands the rules and regulations.

6. Monitor the student's behavior closely, circulating around the room as needed to observe his performance (Sanford, 1983).

7. Consistently enforce work standard expectations, one of which is "working quietly" (Sanford, 1983).

8. Use responses to the student's disruptiveness such as physical presence, touching, distracting the student, waiting, and giving facial expressions of disappointment (Maurer, 1977).

9. Make the student's school work interesting to prevent misbehavior due to boredom (Murphy and Ross, 1983).

10. Ash the student to share his important information with the entire class (P. Sztaba, personal communication).

11. Have the student record the frequency of disruptive behavior. Each day, reinforce him if he betters his total from the previous day (Murphy and Ross, 1983).

12. Adapt instructional methods to the student's individual learning needs (e.g., if the student is an auditory learner, adapt visual assignments so that they involve an auditory component).

13. Develop an individual contract with the student concerning his disturbance of other students. The contract should contain a description of clearly specified outcomes that are needed to satisfy requirements (Murphy and Ross, 1983).

14. Running and jogging are said to improve visual and auditory attention span. A running or jogging program might help the student control impulses, therefore allowing him to stay on task longer without bothering other students (Bass, 1985).

15. Give the problem over to the class and let them decide what to do about the disturbing student. Mediate this discussion (P. Sztaba, personal communication, 1986).

16. Seat the student to the edge of the seating cluster or move him nearer to you.

17. Redirect a student who is bothering another. Have him help you start another task.

18. Talk about the problem with the student. Make him aware that his bothering of other people is distracting to the whole class.

19. Provide a time-out. It should last as long as the student feels is needed to settle down and finish what he is doing. It can also be time for you and the student to talk about feelings (Kendal, 1984).

20. As soon as the student misbehaves and starts to threaten the general atmosphere in the class, give him the choice of remaining in his seat without disturbing others or leaving the classroom (P. Sztaba, personal communication).

21. Provide structured free time or a special privilege to those who complete work early. This may motivate all students to work diligently on their tasks.

22. Teach self-coaching to the student. This method teaches him to talk himself into constructive study (i.e., "I want my classmates to like me, so I am not going to bother them while they are working on an assignment") (Collins, 1981).

23. Teach self-instruction verbalizations. The student does the following: Asks a question (e.g., "What does the teacher want me to do?"), answers the question (e.g., "Stop bothering Eric and finish my work"), provides direction on how to do the task (e.g., "I will sit down and finish my assignment"), and reinforces himself for completing the task (e.g., "Great! I have finished my assignment, I did a good job") (Collins, 1981).

24. Provide a cue directing the student not to bother other students. This could be done by some prearranged signal between you and the student such as touching your nose or putting your hand on your elbow. This signals the student to stop bothering others (Burgio and Whitman, 1980).

25. Stop class and tell the misbehaving student that you will wait for him before continuing. Students are aware that all work must be done before privileges and free time are available (P. Sztaba, personal communication).

26. Instruct the other students that if someone is bothering them, they should nicely tell him that they want to get their work done and ask him to please leave them alone for now (R. Witkin, personal communication, 1985).

103
Excessive Talking

1. Praise the student when he talks at the appropriate time (J. DeMonge, personal communication, 1983).

2. Use videotaping or audiotaping to make the degree of behavior evident to the student (Reinhart, 1980).

3. Have the student monitor the frequency of his behavior and attempt to lower the total from the previous day (Algozzine, 1982).

4. Ignore the behavior if it does not disrupt class routine.

5. Seat the student near your desk (B. Merrick, personal communication, 1984).

6. Have a friend seated near the student to assist in reminding him not to speak at certain times (J. DeMonge, personal communication, 1983).

7. Seat the student away from friends.

8. Seat the student in a carrel or office to prevent interaction.

9. Use a nonverbal signal to remind the student to be quiet. The student signals back to indicate that he will comply.

10. Allow whispering in your class.

11. Have a stop watch running on your desk while students are quietly working. Shut it off while someone is talking. Minutes recorded add up to a special event or privilege.

12. Interpret for the excessive talker what he has done (e.g., "Do you realize that by talking too much just now you deprived Monica of a chance to tell us what she thinks?").

13. Introduce team competition and reward. Peer-group pressure may prove an effective

deterrent (e.g., "The team that talks the least during the next thirty minutes may be excused one minute early for lunch").

14. Keep a tally on the board of the talker's hourly behavior in order to determine when the most talkative times are exhibited.

15. Provide the student with opportunities for talking within an acceptable framework.

16. Set aside 10 minutes each day for *absolutely no talking*.

17. Speak frankly to the entire class about your concern and enlist their cooperation. Solicit ideas from the class and formulate a plan of action, paying reasonable attention to the student's offense and the consequences thereof.

18. Try an approach that does not flatly deny the privilege of talking, but limits it (e.g., "Try to limit your talking to supportive and unsarcastic comments for the next half-hour").

19. Have the student attempt to teach a lesson or talk to the class while you talk excessively. Use this as a springboard to discussion of the need to control one's talking.

20. Use class discussions to uncover why there is so much talking.

21. Talk to the student privately and ask him if he is aware of his excessive talking. Listen to him. Try to work out a reasonable plan to help him control the behavior. Better still, encourage the student to suggest his own plan of control.

104

Interrupts Others

1. Reinforce the student for waiting quietly while others talk.

2. Reinforce the student for talking in turn (J. Grant, personal communication, 1983).

3. Instruct the student that he is not to enter the conversation of others without being asked to do so.

4. Tell the student that if he has something relevant to add to the discussion, he should raise his hand and wait to be called on.

5. Ignore the student until he raises his hand.

6. Reinforce other students when they raise their hands.

7. Ignore the student's interruptions and continue to talk.

8. Place the student in time-out for excessive interruptions (Walker, 1979).

9. Make a contract with the student to reduce the frequency of interruptions (Walker, 1979).

10. Use videotaping to show the student the frequency of the behavior (J. Grant, personal communication, 1983).

11. Have the student stay after school five minutes for each time he interrupts (C. Schwer, personal communication, 1984).

12. When the student interrupts, place all attention on him and have him talk for five minutes to "get it out of his system."

13. Have the student attempt to lower his total frequency of interruptions from the previous day. If he is successful, reinforce him.

14. Interrupt the student when he speaks. Use this as a springboard for discussion of the behavior.

105

Makes Noises in Class

1. Reinforce proper class behavior (Poteet, 1973).

2. Develop a signal system to nonverbally let the student know that the noises are not acceptable (House and Lapan, 1978).

3. Change the seating arrangement by moving the student closer to you or away from other reinforcing students (Atlanta Teacher Corps Consortium, 1978).

4. Reinforce other students for ignoring or not

reinforcing the student's noise making (Clarizio, 1980; Poteet, 1973).

5. Introduce new activities while students are still interested. Keep specific activity periods short (Sloane, 1976).

6. Give students ribbons to wear, which signals to themselves and others that their behavior is appropriate. For disruptive or inappropriate behavior, remove the ribbon for three minutes, constituting an in-class time-out and signaling that no reinforcement from peers or teacher should be given (Foxx and Shapiro, 1978).

7. Place the student in time-out. Before the student can return to class, he must devise a plan that is acceptable to the teacher. The plan states specifically what the student will do differently the next time he is in a similar situation (Fischer, 1981).

8. Require the student to record each time he makes a sound during the work period (Reese, 1978).

9. Have the student attempt to lower his previous day's total of sound making.

10. Tell the students that unless the noise maker refrains this behavior, the class will not have recess or free time (C. Schwer, personal communication, 1984).

11. Have the student teach a lesson or talk to the class while you make noises. Use this as material for a discussion on noise making.

12. Implement sequentially more punitive punishment as the noise making continues.

13. Call the student's parents to enlist their help.

106
Talks Out; Speaks Without Raising Hand

1. Reinforce the student for raising his hand and being recognized before speaking (Donaldson, 1980).

2. Ignore the student's comments (Vargas, 1977).

3. Ask the student to talk to the class for a certain length of time (Hardy and Cull, 1974).

4. Do not respond to the student until he raises his hand and waits to be called on before talking (D. Brown, personal communication, 1984).

5. Have the student do extra work each time he talks without raising a hand or talks out of turn (Vargas, 1977).

6. Place a check mark on a card each time the student raises his hand appropriately. Reward the student for a designated number of checks (Miller, 1973).

7. Place a large, colorful, teacher-made hand on the student's desk and ask him to raise it when wishing to speak (T. Marlier, personal communication, 1984).

8. Have the student role play proper behavior (J. Camp, personal communication, 1984).

9. Remind the students of the rules and the consequences if one is broken (C. Walters, personal communication, 1984).

10. Implement sequentially more punitive punishment for each talk out (N. Hammerschmidt, personal communication, 1984).

11. Reinforce other students for raising their hands (C. Rodriquez, personal communication, 1984).

12. Show the student his behavior through the use of videotaping (D. Gerdes, personal communication, 1984).

13. Make a "baseball" rule for classroom. If a student talks out without raising his hand, it is a strike against him. Three strikes and he misses part of recess (D. Anthony, personal communication, 1984).

14. Give nonverbal signals to remind the student to raise his hand (L. Bevins, personal communication, 1984).

15. Explain to the student that it is inconsiderate behavior to speak without recognition (K. Knight, personal communication, 1984).

16. Place a check on the blackboard every time

the student talks out without raising his hand. Take one minute or more from recess for each checkmark (L. Massie, personal communication, 1984).

17. Have the student write the response before speaking (Newcomer, 1980).

18. Allow the student to earn participation in desired activities by demonstrating self-control (Newcomer, 1980).

19. Remove pressures that the student may interpret as a signal that an immediate response is required (Newcomer, 1980).

20. If the behavior is disruptive to the class, have the student put his head down for one minute (Newcomer, 1980).

21. Devise a four-step procedure for the student: stop, think of what you want to say, raise your hand, and talk when called on (B. Yakos, personal communication, 1985).

22. Use humor as a way of reminding the student to raise his hand (e.g., ''That hand was raised so quickly, I didn't even see it'') (Donaldson, 1980).

23. Chart or have the student chart the number of talk outs during a class period or whole day. He must talk out one time less than this total on the next day in order to earn a reward. Continue to lower the allowed total until an acceptable level is met.

14

Empathy/Concern for Others

107

Cruel to Animals

1. Reward kind treatment of animals (Stephens, Hartman, and Lucas, 1982).
2. Show movies and read stories about animals with great courage, compassion, or other personal traits (D. Grove, personal communication, 1984).
3. Show movies and read stories about comraderie between humans and animals.
4. Model the desired behavior (Stephens, Hartman, and Lucas, 1982).
5. Set up structured situations where the student interacts with a favorite animal while being supervised.
6. Praise other students for their kind treatment of animals.
7. Give the student a chance to write compositions using aggressive words of his choice to serve as a release for emotion (Bettelheim, 1979).
8. If the student is angry, help him distinguish between appropriate and aggressive behavior (Coleman, 1979).
9. Refer the student to the school psychologist (D. Grove, personal communication, 1984).
10. Let the student prove his progress by allowing him to take care of the ant farm or goldfish before being allowed to care for hamsters or gerbils.
11. Teach a unit on animals that benefit humankind.

108

Exploits Others for Own Advantage

1. Hold an open-ended discussion to help the student discover how you and the other students view his behavior (Novack and Bennett, 1983).
2. Hold a classroom discussion about respect (B. Yokus, personal communication, 1985).
3. Have the student write a paper about respect before presenting it to the class (C. Ritz, personal communication, 1985).

4. Have a guest speaker that the student admires talk to the class about respect for others (B. Yokus, personal communication, 1985).

5. Give each student a copy of "Our Civil Rights," which are class guidelines (Fuller, 1984).

6. Arrange for more supervision of the student.

7. Reward others for avoiding exploitation by the student.

8. If the behavior is illegal, inform the school administration.

9. Have the exploiter apologize to those who were exploited and repay them in some way.

10. Punish the student when he is caught exploiting others.

11. Talk with those who were exploited and attempt to devise a way to keep this from occurring again.

12. Role play situations in which the student exploited others. Hold a group discussion following the skit.

13. Have the student identify how he could have had his needs met in another way.

109

Laughs When Others Are in Trouble

1. Praise the student for not laughing when others are in trouble (Stephens, Hartman, and Lucas, 1978).

2. Praise other students for their concerned behavior (Stephens, Hartman, and Lucas, 1978).

3. Describe the behaviors that the student is expected to demonstrate (Stephens, Hartman, and Lucas, 1978).

4. Teach the student to give a nonverbal cue to you when he feels like laughing at someone hurt or in trouble. This will indicate to you that immediate help is needed (C. Scism, personal communication, 1983).

5. Demonstrate appropriate behavior for the student (Stephens, Hartman, and Lucas, 1978).

6. Use role-playing situations. Discuss what is happening and how each student feels (Reinert, 1980; Stephens, Hartman, and Lucas, 1978).

7. Place the student in time-out.

8. Promote social reinforcement from peers in the classroom when the student displays concerned behavior (C. Scism, personal communication, 1983).

9. Refer the student for psychological testing or treatment (Lerner, 1976).

10. Teach the student good-natured "ribbing" in which friends support each other by joking about the situation.

11. Recommend individual counseling with a school counselor or social worker (C. Scism, personal correspondence, 1983).

12. Teach the student to analyze behavior through the "stop-look-and-think" technique. When involved with a potentially conflicting interpersonal situation, the student should speak to himself and say; *"Stop*, before I do anything. *Look around* and determine what is happening. *Let me think* about what will happen if I do this" (Webster, 1981).

13. Tell the student that it is inconsiderate to laugh at another's plight and punish him if this happens again.

14. Institute a "Magic Circle." This is an approach in which students learn to communicate with other members of their group and learn to understand themselves and others. They verbally explore themselves and each other through teacher guidance. Samples of circle topics are: "It made me feel good when I . . ." and "I made someone feel bad when I . . ." (Lerner, 1976).

110

Overremorse for Wrong Doing

1. Praise the student when he "shakes it off" quickly without being overremorseful.

2. Insure that the student realizes that everyone makes mistakes (J. Steele, personal communication, 1985).

3. Relate to the student some of the things other students have done and what those students did to make up for their wrongful acts (J. Steele, personal communication, 1985).

4. Be sure that the student understands that all is forgiven and forgotten now (J. Steele, personal communication, 1985).

5. Take a matter-of-fact approach when the student does something wrong so that he realizes the wrongful act is not something upon which to dwell (J. Steele, personal communication, 1985).

6. Insure that the student's environment is as free of stress as possible. Some stressors to be identified and reduced include: fear of punishment, fear of rejection or abandonment, and self-doubt. By labeling and dealing with these specific stressors, it may be possible to control a major portion contributing to the student's overremorse (Curtis, 1982).

7. Suggest play therapy for the student (Keith, 1981).

8. Suggest counseling (Hinsie and Campbell, 1970).

9. Have the student evaluate the damage done and tell what he has learned from the experience. Help him see that if he won't do wrong again, remorse serves no purpose.

10. Have the parties that were wronged assure the student that all is forgiven if the incident won't recur.

11. Have the student make a public apology or restitution so he can feel that he has "paid back" his debt.

12. Have the student list the pros and cons of dwelling on the incident. Help him to see that it serves no purpose.

13. Have the student identify different ways of making restitution. Ask him to choose one and implement it.

111

Shows No Shame or Guilt in Being Caught

1. Provide positive incentives when the student does show concern about his behavior (McKown, 1935).

2. Have the student role play a past experience in which he did not show concern about his behavior. Then have him demonstrate the appropriate behavior (Hall, 1979; McKown, 1935).

3. Have the student keep a diary and record when he did and did not accept responsibility. Have him analyze these experiences (McKown, 1935).

4. The school staff should be good models who take responsibility for their own actions (Forish and Forish, 1976).

5. Emphasize the good rather than the bad. Let the student know that he does show positive traits in character (McKown, 1935).

6. Reason with the pupil and explain why his behavior is inappropriate (McKown, 1935).

7. Introduce the concept of responsibility in taking the blame for one's own actions.

8. Have the student identify the pros and cons of taking the blame for one's own actions (Hall, 1979).

9. Meet with the student to discuss what will happen to him if the behavior continues (e.g., people will not like him, he will have a hard time finding a job, etc.) (McKown, 1935).

10. Have the student write a puppet show about assuming responsibility. Then have him perform the script (McKown, 1935).

11. Use selected literature to help the student make more responsible judgments about his behavior (Perine, 1978).

12. Design a "dilemma" situation in which there is an individual who never shows shame or guilt. In a small discussion group, the students discuss the situation and try to resolve the problem (McKown, 1935; Scharf, McDoy, and Ross, 1979).

13. Collect data on the frequency of the individual's behavior and present this data to the student (McKown, 1935).

14. Have the student attempt to lower his total weekly frequency to receive a reward.

15. Use situation cards. (e.g., A person has just stolen a candybar from a store and been caught, how should he feel?) Divide the class into small groups. Present the groups with the situation cards and ask each student to tell their group how they would respond to a particular situation. Promote discussion.

16. Have a continuing discussion group on "accepting the responsibility of growing up" (Hall, 1979; Hartford, 1958).

17. Have victims tell of their feelings regarding the incident.

18. After the student has victimized another, ask him how he would have felt in that situation if he were the other student.

19. Require restitution in order to make the victimization of others undesirable.

20. Encourage the student to show feelings (Yamamoto, 1972).

21. Help the student develop social interests and a feeling of adequacy in helping others and working with others (Yamamoto, 1972).

15

Home Behavior

112

Approaches Strangers Who Come to Visit the Unit or Home

1. Tell the youth that an adult must answer the door and escort strangers.

2. Tell the youth that he is not to approach strangers unless a familiar adult is present and invites him to join them.

3. Move social areas away from main entrances.

4. Review procedures with the youth before the arrival of the visitor. Reward the youth for following procedures.

5. Reinforce others who follow procedures regarding the approaching of strangers.

6. Punish the youth for approaching strangers without following procedures.

7. Ask the visitor to ignore the youth.

8. Tell the youth that you wish to talk to the visitor alone.

9. Distract the youth to an activity in another area before the visitor arrives.

10. Teach the youth to greet strangers appropriately.

11. Devise a nonverbal signal system in which the youth can ask if he can approach the stranger. Signal back to him to indicate if this is allowed.

113

Comes Home Late at Night

1. Set a curfew and enforce it. Punish the youth if he is late by keeping him inside for one week (K. Christensen, personal communication, 1984).

2. For every minute the youth is late, make him do household chores for double the time (N. Hammerschmidt, personal communication, 1984).

3. Shorten the curfew for each time the youth

151

is late (C. Mattox, personal communication, 1984).

4. Inform the youth that every minute he is late becomes a debt. He will have to "pay up" next time by coming home that much earlier (T. Marlier, personal communication, 1984).

5. Do not allow the youth to go out at all until he learns to come in at the set curfew (C. Walters, personal communication, 1984).

6. For every minute late, make the youth wait that much longer before he can leave when going out next time (Schinke, 1981).

7. Make a contract with the youth to set limits and rewards (Schinke, 1981).

8. Pick up the youth at his hangout when it is time to come home.

9. Every time the youth comes home late, take away a privilege that he enjoys (P. Moore, personal communication, 1984).

10. Find out why he is coming home late. Express your personal concern for his well being (T. Miller, personal communication, 1984).

11. Limit the number of nights the youth may go out (S. LeSage, personal communication, 1984).

12. Allow the youth extra time outside during the day each time he comes home early (C. Poteet, personal communication, 1984).

13. Create an incentive for him to come home earlier (e.g., extra money, use of the car, parties at home, etc.) (L. Honey, personal communication, 1984).

14. Assign the youth early-morning chores so he has to get up earlier (J. Honey, personal communication, 1984).

15. Devise a cooperative program between home and school (Stumphauzer, 1973).

16. Reinforce the youth when he comes home on time (Stumphauzer, 1973).

17. Plan an activity at home that the youth enjoys so he will want to come home (Stumphauzer, 1973).

18. Withhold allowance and other funds to discourage late-night escapades (Stumphauzer, 1973).

19. Have the youth stay after school and do extra academic work every time he comes home late (B. Yakos, personal communication, 1985).

20. Provide a workshop about applied behavior analysis for the parents (B. Yakos, personal communication, 1985).

21. Talk with community officials about starting a program for youths that will give them something to do after school (Trojanowicz, 1978).

114
Demands Parents Do What He Wants

1. Praise or reward the student when he asks for something rather than demands it.

2. Make it clear to the youth that only requests are considered, not demands.

3. Ask the youth to rephrase his demand into a request.

4. Do what the youth desires if he has asked nicely and assists you in doing the task.

5. Ignore the demands.

6. Tell the youth that he must behave or he will be punished (Canter, 1982).

7. Punish the youth if demands continue (Canter, 1982).

8. Use the "broken record" technique in which the parents or supervisors repeat their viewpoint or response without being distracted by the antics of the youth (Canter, 1982).

9. Require that the youth earn privileges by completing housework first.

10. Inform the youth that disrespectful or demanding behavior automatically results in a refusal by the parents or supervisors.

11. If appropriate to the situation, have the youth perform the task demanded of you.

12. Help to promote improvements of commu-

nication between the youth and his family (Trojanowicz, 1978).

13. Promote the exchange of information and improvement of communication between the school and all other groups within the community in order to devise a cooperative program (Trojanowicz, 1978).

14. Assist the youth in looking for part-time work so he will have to rest before or after work (B. Yakos, personal communication, 1985).

115

Has Bad Dreams and Nightmares

1. Ask the youth to share the dreams with you or another trusted adult (Hendricks and Roberts, 1977).

2. Bring the dreams to a positive completion through story telling (Hendricks and Roberts, 1977).

3. When the youth expresses fear, comfort him (Hendricks and Roberts, 1977).

4. Complete a check of closets, drawers, and under-bed spaces with the youth (Ketterman, 1983).

5. Create a quiet atmosphere at bedtime through the use of soft music or reading (Ketterman, 1983).

6. Investigate possible manipulation. Is the youth saying this to have the parents sleep with him? (Ketterman, 1983).

7. Do not let the youth sleep with adults (Levine and Seligmann, 1973).

8. Install a night-light in the room.

9. Settle any disagreements with the youth before he goes to sleep (Mack, 1970).

10. Eliminate foods that are rich in protein, such as eggs, meat, and cheese (Shulman, 1979).

11. Examine eating habits, how much is eaten, and how late (Shulman, 1979).

12. Upon advice of a physician, gradually withdraw medication before sleep (Shulman, 1979).

13. Change the usual sleeping position (Shulman, 1979).

14. Have the youth take a nap during the day (Mack, 1979).

15. Have the student fall asleep while a familiar person is in the room (Mack, 1970).

16. Read a nonthreatening, comforting story to the student before sleep.

17. Allow the youth to take a favorite stuffed animal to bed.

18. Have the youth stay awake (Mack, 1970).

19. Consult a physician, psychologist, or psychiatrist (Mack, 1970).

116

Resists Going to Bed; Stays Up as Late as Possible

1. Ignore the youth when he calls for a drink, story, and so on (Graubard, 1977).

2. Keep stimulating activities to a minimum before bedtime (Graubard, 1977).

3. Allow the youth to stay up late, but make sure that he is up early the next morning. A set wake-up time will demand an earlier bedtime.

4. Establish a set routine to be followed for bedtime (Graubard, 1977).

5. For every 15 minutes the youth is up past his bedtime, require that he goes to bed 15 minutes earlier the next night.

6. Use the ''One Minute Scolding'' technique. Devote 30 seconds to your statement of feelings about the behavior, using and expressing anger and annoyance. This is followed by a pause that is used to compose feelings. Then 30 seconds is devoted to telling and showing the youth that he is loved. During this 30 seconds the youth is also asked what he did wrong. This is fol-

lowed by a hug (Nelson, 1984, citation unavailable).

7. Provide a relaxing activity before bed such as a game, reading, or soft music.

8. Have the youth drink a glass of milk. An enzyme in milk makes one drowsy.

9. Remove stimulating objects from the bedroom.

10. Turn the clocks ahead without notifying the youth.

11. Allow the youth to earn the privilege of staying awake longer and let him sleep in longer the next morning.

12. If the hesitation to go to bed is due to fear, allow the youth to have a nightlight turned on, take a favorite stuffed animal to bed, or fall asleep while a familiar person is present.

13. Allow the youth to earn an "all-nighter" on the weekend by going to bed on time for a designated number of nights. (The youth will probably fall asleep in front of the television during the "all-nighter") (M. Reich, personal communication, 1985).

6. Contact a "tough-love" support group (V. Croll, personal communication, 1983).

7. Make a contract in which the parent and youth negotiate and compromise to make the home situation more livable for both parties.

8. Organize a support group composed of past and potential runaways.

9. Have a past runaway tell of the terrors and drawbacks of running away.

10. Recommend family counseling for the parents and youth.

11. Arrange for a "cooling off" period in which the youth lives with a friend or relative for a few weeks.

12. Allow the youth to earn desired curfews or privileges by doing housework or meeting designated obligations.

13. Allow the youth to "run away" on weekends if he displays proper home and school behavior on weekdays. The youth must keep parents informed of his whereabouts on weekends.

117
Runs Away from Home

1. Inform the police (Blackman and Silberman, 1980).

2. Call the houses of the youth's friends to determine if he is staying with them (Blackman and Silberman, 1980).

3. Hold a parent-teacher conference to discuss the situation and possible solutions or alternatives for the runaway (Madison, 1979).

4. Schedule conferences with the potential runaway at the beginning or end of each day in order to defuse the situation (V. Croll and K. Roza, personal communication, 1983).

5. Recommend counseling for the runaway (W. Roza, personal communication, 1983).

118
Sibling Rivalry; Complains That Siblings Are Favored

1. Evaluate the student's complaints to determine if he is correct.

2. Explain to the student that, due to age and sex differences, parents must treat their children differently.

3. Allow the student to earn desired objects and privileges.

4. Have the student say one positive comment about his sibling(s) each day.

5. In the classroom, set up an environment of overall fairness. Do not show favoritism to one student when a problem arises. In a fair classroom, the youth will be helped to understand conflicts at home (Bank and Kahn, 1982).

6. Provide the youth with opportunities to in-

teract with the others in class. This may be done through group projects or discussions. Working with others may help improve social relationships and self-concept. This in turn may help at home in sibling relationships (Bank and Kahn, 1982).

7. Allow the youth to fantasize about aggression toward a sibling. This may be done through a creative writing assignment or telling a story. Allowing the youth to express his anxieties in a creative, nonviolent form such as writing or speaking may help resolve the conflict (Bank and Kahn, 1982).

8. Make a set of rules, enforce them, and administer consequences for undesirable behavior. Let students work problems out themselves if possible. With rules and consequences at school, the youth can then understand rules at home (Bank and Kahn, 1982).

9. Teach the concept and advantages of cooperation. This will help the youth understand the importance of getting along with others. This may in turn help the youth better understand his siblings and their relationships with the parents (Martin and De-Gruchy, 1938).

10. To be an effective referee of jealousy and aggression, apply consistent moral principles and communicate them clearly to quarreling. If these moral principles are developed in the school setting, they may carry over to the home environment. When sibling quarrels occur, the youth may be better able to resolve them (Bank and Kahn, 1982).

11. If the student continues to complain of problems at home, contact the parents and get their input on the situation. Discuss suggestions for intervention. A cooperative plan may be possible (Smith, personal communication, 1984).

12. Have the student identify strengths in the family and the behavior of family members (Downing, 1983).

13. Assist the student in adopting a positive focus on himself, other family members, and

what goes on in the family (Downing, 1983).

14. Set up a written contract agreement with the youth. Reward him when he does not complain about brothers and sisters for a specified amount of time. If the contract is broken, there is a consequence (Fatis and Konewko, 1983).

119
Video Game Fanatic

1. Reinforce the student for avoiding video games.
2. Encourage the undertaking of another hobby (J. Rose, personal communication, 1983).
3. Set a time or game limit for the student (J. Rose, personal communication, 1983).
4. Suggest that the parents prohibit the student from entering a video arcade.
5. Carefully monitor the amount of money available to the student.
6. Have the student set an upper limit on the amount of money he will spend. All other money should be held by a friend or adult who will not give it back to him until at home later.
7. Require that the student earn his money or allowance.
8. Discuss whether video games are worth the money spent.
9. Give the student credit for his allowance rather than real money. This can be saved to buy a desired object or activity (J. Rose, personal communication, 1983).
10. Require that the student immediately return home from school.
11. Pack a lunch for the student rather than give him lunch money.
12. Have an adult at school require that the youth buy a lunch whether he is hungry or not.
13. Support and pursue zoning laws that pre-

vent the establishment of video arcade machines near schools.

14. Recommend counseling for the youth.

120

Watches Too Much Television

1. Reinforce the student for engaging in other activities.

2. Encourage the parents to make it clear that in time of stress, the youth can turn to them rather than television (Hickey, 1975).

3. View shows with the youth to open discussions and clarify misconceptions (Schramm, 1961; Miller, 1978).

4. Write the Federal Communications Commission, National Association of Broadcasting, or the networks if you are unhappy with programming (Hickey, 1975).

5. Provide creative toys and family-centered activities to keep the youth from becoming overly involved in television (Kaye, 1974).

6. Sit down with a television guide on Sunday and discuss shows that the youth may watch during the week. Select only those programs on which both the adults and youth agree (Winn, 1977).

7. Select programs for the youth (Kiester, 1978).

8. Offer more interesting pastimes (Kiester, 1978).

9. Encourage hobbies, participation in sports, and reading (Waters, 1978).

10. Limit the number of hours that the youth may watch television (Muson, 1978).

11. Do not allow the youth to watch television until homework is done (Muson, 1978).

12. Lock the television in a closet.

13. Install a pay box on the television set. The youth must earn money to watch. He most likely will become more selective in his viewing habits.

14. Set a price on various television shows and collect money from the youth before each program.

15. Establish curricula in the schools that include consumer education regarding the nature and purpose of television advertising (Reid, 1978).

16. Allow the student to watch television beyond a certain set time limit if he watches educational public broadcasting channels.

16

Immaturity

121

Acts Silly

1. Reinforce the student for displaying appropriate behavior (Clarizio, 1980).

2. Ignore the silly behavior.

3. Punish the student for displaying silly behavior.

4. Use the student's name kindly and often. This gives the student a modicum of attention so he may not seek much more (Catterall and Gazda, 1978).

5. Ask the entire class to engage in the attention seeker's gimmick and then call a halt to the activity. For example, if a student groans when a pop quiz is announced, say, "Let's all complain together before we start the quiz." Then ask the student to perform an appropriate behavior (e.g., hand out quizzes, take a note to the office). Praise the student for this behavior.

6. Talk to the student privately about his behavior. It may not have occurred to him

that the behavior was demonstrated or irritating to others (Clarizio, 1980).

7. Devise a check-mark plan with the student that will help him realize the extent of the attention-seeking behavior (Clarizio, 1980).

8. Build times into the schedule when it's acceptable to act silly (Gervais and Dittburner, 1981).

9. Show a film that focuses on the class clown. Discuss it objectively.

10. Praise the student about something that carries the inference that he is sensitive, not just silly (e.g., "We enjoy your clowning around in small doses. I'm glad to see you can set your own limits.").

11. Allow the student sufficient opportunities to release tension (Walker, 1979).

12. Give the student responsibility that demands concentration. Find an isolated place for the student to work. The task should make him feel important as well as convince him that you take him seriously (e.g., "These flash cards are mixed up and need to be sorted before reading groups. A few are missing too, so please write the

numbers of the missing ones on a sheet of paper.'') (Collins, 1981).

13. Present yourself as a role model who displays proper behavior (L. Saxton, personal communication, 1986).

14. Inform the student that the other students in class do not appreciate his silliness and that this is not a good way to make friends (L. Saxton, personal communication, 1986).

15. Praise the student nearest to the student who is acting silly. This shows that appropriate behavior earns praise and reinforcement.

16. Take the student aside and ask him how he would feel if someone else was trying to distract others and disrupt their work.

17. Explain to the student that he is wasting your time and you cannot spare the time to speak with him (L. Saxton, personal communication, 1986).

18. Videotape the behavior. Show this to the student privately. Ask the student how he feels about this and ask if he feels that it is appropriate.

19. Videotape the behavior and show it to the parents with the student present. Discuss appropriate behavior.

20. If other student's attention is reinforcing the behavior, remove the student from the situation (L. Saxton, personal communication, 1986).

21. Involve the student in the reinforcement of proper behavior in the classroom. If he is in charge of presenting awards, he may become aware of what a student must do to earn them.

22. Role play one on one, or have another person play the part of the student. Talk about this behavior as a group (L. Saxton, personal communication, (1986).

23. If the student is ''performing'' for someone in particular, have the student ''pay'' the other with a token (Center and Wascom, 1984).

24. Set up a timed schedule with the student. If he can act appropriately for a designated amount of time, reward him.

25. Place signs and posters around the room. Have students develop slogans for appropriate behavior (Long, 1984).

26. Send the student to the office (L. Saxton, personal communication, 1986).

27. Have the student show the principal how he has been acting.

28. Remove the student from view and have him perform the act repeatedly for a prescribed period of time. Have someone observe periodically to assure that the student is still demonstrating the behavior.

29. Tell the student that every time he acts out, he will owe you a minute's worth of work. Keep track in full view of the class. The longer the behavior lasts, the more is owed by the student. Take the time out of a special class, lunch, or recess period to make it more effective.

30. Work out a set of nonverbal cues with the student that you can use to encourage the student to stay on task or return to task (L. Saxton, personal communication, 1986).

31. Seat the student near an appropriate peer model (Bixenstine and Abascal, 1985).

32. Seat the student near you.

33. Work with the family to get them involved. If the student can go a full day without acting silly, have a parent take him fishing or out for ice cream.

122

Attention-Seeking Behavior

1. Praise the student for displaying appropriate behavior.

2. Ignore the attention-seeking behavior.

3. Give the student a direction or command (e.g., ''Sit down and work on your project''). Punish the student for noncompliance. Reward the student for compliance.

4. Discuss the behavior with the student. Devise a plan for the student to display more appropriate behavior.

5. Videotape the behavior. Show this to the student to make him aware of the intensity and frequency of the behavior.

6. Show the videotape to the parents to make them aware of the behavior and to enlist their assistance.

7. Say to the class, "Someone wants our attention. Let's all look at him." Watch the behavior until it ceases. Then say, "Are you finished?" Upon receiving an affirmative answer, say, "May we get back to work now?"

8. Ask the entire class to engage in the attention seeker's behavior, then call a halt to the activity. After, ask the student to perform an appropriate behavior (e.g., hand back papers, deliver a note). Praise the student for this behavior (Collins, 1981).

9. If the student is receiving reinforcement from other students, isolate him.

10. Praise other students for ignoring the attention-seeking behavior.

11. Move the student closer to you if he is reinforced by other students.

12. Have the student reward others for appropriate behavior. This may make him aware of desired behavior.

13. Remove the student from the view of his peers and have him perform the behavior repeatedly for a prescribed period of time (Luiselli, 1985).

14. Count each behavior as one minute of extra work owed to you.

15. Devise nonverbal cues to indicate to the student that his behavior is inappropriate. Have him signal back to you to indicate compliance.

123

Becomes Hysterical, Upset, or Angry When Things Do Not Go His Way

1. Avoid placing the student in frustrating situations.

2. Praise the student for appropriately handling frustration.

3. Ignore the demonstrative behavior.

4. Punish the student for the demonstrative reaction.

5. Place the student in time-out.

6. Explain to the student how you expect him to act as you announce to him that something will not occur as he had hoped.

7. Discuss with the student alternative ways of responding to frustration.

8. Model appropriate behavior in frustrating situations.

9. Praise other students for mature reactions.

10. Forewarn the student of possible outcomes of a situation. Speak with him about appropriate reactions to the various outcomes.

11. Review the situation with the student to determine if there was anything that could have been done to make things go his way, but also discuss the importance of being a good loser.

12. Role play hypothetical, past, or future situations with the student to practice appropriate responding.

124

Blushes Easily

1. Accept the blushing as a positive trait of a sensitive individual.

2. If the student blushes when praised, praise the student in private.

3. Have the student say one nice thing about himself each day.

4. Devise activities that boost the student's self-confidence (K. Luebke, personal communication, 1985).
5. Teach the student to say "Thank you" to praise if this is not already being done.
6. Teach the student to be more assertive if the blushing is due to embarrassment caused by others.
7. Do not allow others to embarrass the student.
8. Prepare the student for activities that may make him blush.
9. If extensive or prolonged blushing occurs after physical exertion, recommend a physical examination by a physician.
10. Teach "quick comebacks" so that the student can respond assertively to the embarrassing comments of others.
11. Establish a permissive atmosphere that encourages the shy student to participate and gives him the freedom to express himself openly (Yamamoto, 1972).
12. Develop a feeling of adequacy in the student through encouragement, love, and guidance (Yamamoto, 1972).
13. Reduce social anxiety. Do not react to the student overanxiously. Be natural so he feels just like anyone else (Eliott, 1982).

125

Complains About Other's Unfairness or Discrimination Toward Him

1. Determine if the student's claims have any validity.
2. If the claims have validity, speak with the others involved.
3. Discuss ways of overcoming perceived barriers.
4. Praise the student for not complaining.
5. Ignore the student's complaints.
6. If the student is a victim of discrimination by others due to his inadequate social skills, make the student aware of this, and teach him appropriate social interaction skills.
7. Hold class meetings with prepared questions and discuss topics regarding discrimination against others.
8. Devise ways for the student to show positive skills and capabilities in front of others who perceive him negatively.
9. Each day, choose a "student of the day" who is to receive one positive comment from all others who are present.
10. If the complaints are unjustified, review the situation with the student and help him discover his misperception.
11. Supervise potential trouble situations to insure that rules and fairness are enforced.
12. Place the student in situations that require cooperative efforts with others to attain success.

126

Complains That He Never Has Fair Share of Things

1. Determine if the student's claims have any validity.
2. Praise the student when he does not complain (C. Ritz, personal communication, 1985).
3. Ignore the student's complaints (B. Yakus, personal communication, 1985).
4. Create situations where you can demonstrate that he did receive his fair share.
5. Inform the student that sometimes life is not fair.
6. Wager with the student regarding whether he has his fair share. He must prove his point to collect.
7. Allow the student to earn various desired items.
8. Role play proper responses to perceived unfairness.

9. Have the student write his complaint which will be reviewed by you later.

10. Allow a group of peers to decide whether the student was treated fairly.

11. Organize your classroom so that there are consistently enforced rules, more routines, and fewer judgment calls by you.

127

Denies Responsibility for Own Actions

1. Praise the student when he accepts responsibility for his actions.

2. Ignore the blaming behavior (Highland, 1984).

3. If you observed the incident, ask the student what happened. If he lies to you, administer a negative consequence.

4. Do not punish. Without punishment the student will not need to resort to coping techniques such as denial or excusing the behavior (Gentile, 1984).

5. Do not accept excuses for the failure of the student to adhere to the rules. Instead, have the student commit himself to a new and better behavior, and try again (K. Smolarek, personal communication, 1985).

6. Ask, "What did you do?" If the student begins to mention another student's name, ask, "But what did *you* do?" (K. Smolarek, personal communication, 1985).

7. Hold court. Each side has an equal amount of time to state its case, but hearsay evidence is not allowed (e.g., "He said that she said . . ."). Lead the students to a solution. If no solution is obvious, the case goes to a higher court, held during lunch, with a jury of peers. If a solution is not reached, an arbitration hearing is held involving the teacher and the administration's representative. The decisions of the arbitrators are final (K. J. Smolarek, personal communication, 1985).

8. Discuss and review with the student the facts of the incident (Allan, 1981).

9. Point out to the student why he is wrong, and provide alternate solutions to the denial behavior (Highland, 1984).

10. Do not assume a rescuer role. If the problem is between two students, have the students handle it by writing out their complaints along with some suggestions for improving the situation (Gentile, 1984).

11. Invite the involved individuals to a conference. In this small group, the offender might lose concern about his image in front of peers and admit guilt (National Education Association, 1969).

12. Role play the situations with the student who denies responsibility by playing the role of the student who was scapegoated (Highland, 1984).

13. Teach these problem-solving steps: fact finding, identification of feelings, understandings, solution finding, blocks to the solutions, and commitment to the solutions. When this has been accomplished, take the scapegoated student through the same problem-solving steps before he is returned to the class (Allan and Thompson, 1983).

14. Make a contract with the student insuring a reward for appropriate behavior (Allan, 1981).

15. Provide activities whose completion guarantees built-in success, and praise for appropriate behavior (W. Jones, personal communication, 1985).

16. Help the student discriminate between the sources of anger that he can do something about and those that he cannot. Discriminate also between taking responsibility for his own actions and failures, and distributing blame elsewhere or not at all for events that are beyond his control (Tarvis, 1983).

17. Refer the student to the guidance counselor (M. Guidice, personal communication, 1985).

128

Dependent on Others

1. Praise the student's efforts to become more independent (K. Cearlock, personal communication, 1983).

2. Provide the student with meaningful activities or jobs to build independence and self-confidence (D. Brown and G. Heleine, personal communication, 1984).

3. Allow the student to tutor peers in order to build self-confidence (D. Brown, personal communication, 1984).

4. Provide opportunities for the student to succeed early in the project or task to build his belief that he is capable of finishing it independently (D. Brown, personal communication, 1984).

5. Show the student how to use what has been learned (e.g., "Bill, you have learned your multiplication facts. Now use them to solve these problems.") (K. Cearlock, personal communication, 1983).

6. Assess the student's learning style and favored mode of production. Gear as much instruction and performance requirements as possible to fit the student's style (D. Brown, personal communication, 1984).

7. Seat the student by an independent classmate who will not provide assistance, but will provide a good model (K. Cearlock, personal communication, 1983).

8. Confer with the parents to agree on strategies that will develop the student's independence (Karlin and Berger, 1972).

9. Encourage the student to name something that troubles him about which he would like to find an answer. Help him cope with this problem. Begin by naming the problem, determining its cause, choosing a solution that might succeed, and trying out the favored hypotheses.

10. Brainstorm with the student regarding ways to attack a problem. Help him to choose one. The student then attempts the task independently (Walker, 1979).

11. Give attention to students who are performing independently.

12. Explain to the student why his behavior is not appropriate.

13. Give vague directions that require decisions on the part of the student.

14. Insist that the student attempt part of the task or assignment before you check it.

15. Task analyze the assignment or task. Have the student progressively complete more parts each day.

129

Does Not Have Age-Appropriate Interests

1. Reinforce the student for any level of interest shown in age-appropriate activities.

2. Group the students with peers for activities.

3. Expose the student to various age-appropriate activities.

4. Teach the student about an activity that interests others of his age so that he can converse about the topic and perhaps develop an interest in it.

5. Ask a club, team, or group of peers to "adopt" this student and teach him "the ropes."

6. Contact the parents in order to devise a cooperative plan.

7. Refer the student for counseling.

8. Require the student to engage in various age-appropriate activities.

9. Give the student a choice of participating in one of a few age-appropriate activities.

10. Figure out a way to revise or modify activities that are not age-appropriate into ones more appropriate for his age.

130
Gets Upset When Not the Center of Attention

1. Praise the student when he accepts not being the center of attention.
2. Ignore the student's behavior.
3. Tell the student that he must raise his hand and ask for your attention.
4. Count the number of times that you interact with this student. Compare this amount with the number of interactions with other representative students. Show the student that he is receiving his fair share of attention.
5. Using a stopwatch, figure the duration of time spent interacting with the student. Compare this with the time spent with other representative students. Show the student that he is receiving his fair share of attention.
6. Send the student to an isolated spot to regain control.
7. Forewarn the student that he will have to "share the stage" with others during a certain activity.
8. Give a firm direction to the student to sit quietly and await your assistance or attention.
9. Implement sequentially more punitive consequences if the student continues his demonstrative behavior.
10. Role play the student's behavior in a skit. Have the class respond to the behavior.
11. Videotape the student's behavior to serve as a point of discussion.

131
Gives Picture of "Poor Me"

1. Reinforce the student when he does not complain.
2. Ignore the complaints.

3. Each day have the student mention one good thing that happened to him that day or the night before.
4. Have the student devise possible solutions for all of his complaints about what is wrong.
5. Use sarcastic humor in a good-natured way. (e.g., "Oh! You poor, poor boy! It sounds like a Russian conspiracy to me. Have you been to Moscow lately? Have you seen anyone in a raincoat and hat following you around?")
6. Inform the student that people don't like complainers and suggest that he withhold the "poor me" comments.
7. Play a Rodney Dangerfield or Jackie Vernon comedy album in which they talk about how everything goes wrong for them. Discuss with the student how one can laugh at one's problems.
8. Recommend counseling for the feelings of persecution.
9. Assist the student in analyzing various situations to determine how he contributed to the outcome.
10. Assist the student in analyzing various situations to determine what he could have done to alter the outcome.

132
Immature

1. Praise the student when he displays mature behavior (L. Evans, personal communication, 1985).
2. Ignore the behavior if it is nondisruptive.
3. Use a nonverbal signal to indicate your displeasure.
4. Use a nonverbal signal system to remind the student that his behavior is inappropriate. To let you know that he will behave, have him signal back to you.
5. Use proximity control. Stand next to the student who is demonstrating immature

behavior and continue teaching (A. Stein, personal communication, 1985).

6. Remove whatever object is distracting the student (A. Stein, personal communication, 1985).

7. Hold a group discussion on appropriate behavior (A. Stein, personal communication, 1985).

8. Sometimes immaturity is due to a cultural or social deficit in the student's environment. Expose him to as many cultural experiences as possible (Lindgren, 1982).

9. The immature behavior may be due to a lack in physical maturity. Try to be sympathetic with the student and realize that he is going through some emotional adjustments also (Lindgren, 1982).

10. If the immature behavior is exhibited at a very high rate, consider placing the student on a schedule of differential reinforcement of low rates (DRL). Reinforce the student when he can reduce the immature behavior exhibited to a lower rate (Sulzer-Azaroff and Mayer, 1977).

11. Teach the six areas of maturity: intelligence, articulation, responsibility, empathy, sexuality, and philosophy (Jelinek, 1979).

12. Give the student certain jobs or tasks for which to be responsible each day (Jelinek, 1979).

13. The behavior might be due to the classwork being too difficult. Break the assignments into component parts and systematically teach the components via task analysis (Algozzine, 1982).

14. Recommend that the student be seen by the school psychologist (Algozzine, 1982).

15. Provide the student with social skills training (Algozzine, 1982).

16. Recommend that the student be retained for the next school year (Algozzine, 1982).

17. Since limited expressive ability and shyness are behaviors categorized as immature, a language experience program might be helpful (e.g., assign an older student to

become this student's buddy or friend and converse with him on a regular basis) (Algozzine, 1982).

18. To combat immature behaviors such as insecurity, anxiety, and inadequate self-concept, purposely find as many positive things as possible for which to sincerely praise the student (Algozzine, 1982).

19. Expose the student to the presence of older or more mature students.

20. Model appropriate behavior (K. Roza, personal communication, 1983).

21. Place the student in charge of a group or an activity within the classroom in order to build responsibility (Reinert, 1980).

22. Encourage the student to join organizations such as Boy Scouts or Girl Scouts which deal with peer relationships, responsibility, and working together in a group to obtain a desired goal (Drucker and Hexter, 1923).

23. Have the student seek friendship within the Big Brother or Big Sister programs in the community (Drucker and Hexter, 1923).

24. Arrange for participation in work and community programs.

25. Role play appropriate behavior in mock situations.

26. Give a multiple-choice quiz on proper behavior in various situations. Discuss the answers with the whole class.

27. Require the student to rephrase immature statements and requests with proper wording and tone of voice.

133

Irresponsible

1. Praise the student when he behaves in a responsible manner (Clarizio, 1980).

2. Punish the student for irresponsible behavior.

3. Be friendly but firm about the fact that

he must face up to the consequences of his irresponsibility (Gervais and Dittburner, 1981).

4. Confront the irresponsible student directly, without rancor. Tell him that word is getting around that he is irresponsible.

5. Let him know that his credibility is being questioned.

6. Offer assistance. (e.g., "I think I know how we can gain the trust of your classmates again and perhaps raise your self-esteem. Drop by and see me some day this week. We'll talk about it.")

7. Convey to the student the message that a responsible person is independent and that an irresponsible one remains dependent, which is a sign of immaturity. Hopefully, being immature is the last thing the student wants to be (Clarizio, 1980).

8. Reward other students who display responsible behavior (Collins, 1981).

9. Help the student construct a daily list of things that must be accomplished or remembered (Collins, 1981).

10. Inform the student, ahead of time, what the consequences of responsible and irresponsible behavior will be.

11. Teach time-management skills to the student to insure that all responsibilities are met.

12. Have the student make a promise or say that he will do something. Have him do it immediately. Gradually make these promises more long-term, yet attainable.

13. Do not allow the student to make promises that cannot be fulfilled.

14. When a promise is made, talk to the student about it. Ask questions to see how serious he is about fulfilling it.

15. Have the student list steps necessary to fulfill the promise. The student must then sequentially complete each substep.

16. Have the student make restitution for his irresponsible behavior.

17. Use role playing to practice responsible behavior in mock situations.

134

Jealous of Adult Attention Given to Others

1. Reinforce appropriate behavior (Reese, Murphy, and Filipczak, 1981).

2. Let the student know that you will be with him in a moment (Felker, 1974).

3. Do not put too much emphasis on the student's jealous behavior as you may make the student feel that he is a bad person (Yamamoto, 1972).

4. Be attentive to the needs of the student who requests attention (Felker, 1974).

5. Upgrade the quality and quantity of your response to the student. Be less critical, distant, indifferent, and busy (Yamamoto, 1972).

6. If the jealousy is due to the student's lack of self-confidence about his ability to do the work, change assignments to allow the student some measure of success in completing the task (Gervais and Dittburner, 1981).

7. Give the jealous student some responsibility. Since your attention is positively reinforcing for the student, use the student as your aide (Gervais and Dittburner, 1981).

8. Be certain that the student understands your directions. In this way, the student will not need your help and attention as much (Ashmore et al., 1984).

9. Increase the student's positive interactions with other classmates to aid in building confidence and decreasing jealousy toward others. Praise the jealous student when he interacts with others (Ashmore et al., 1984).

10. Conduct class discussions on topics such as individuality, accepting others, and making friends. Point out that it is better to be accepting of others than jealous of them (Ashmore et al., 1984).

11. To alleviate jealous feelings between classmates, set up an activity in which a different student is honored each week. Put the student in a special chair and give him a

badge to wear. Classmates can write positive statements about the honored student (Ashmore et al., 1984).

12. Make assignments on which small groups of students can work together. This will encourage the formation of new friendships and allow you to give attention to a group rather than each individual student (Ashmore et al., 1984).

13. Conduct a lesson in which students role play situations where the character relates effectively and ineffectively with others. Then discuss appropriate methods of dealing with jealousy in given situations (Ashmore et al., 1984).

14. Provide a time-out area for students whose jealousy causes difficulty in self-control (Ashmore et al., 1984).

15. To decrease dependence on teacher attention, set up an independent learning center with self-correcting materials and activities that students can use independently (D. Cambrini, personal communication, 1985).

16. Read a story about a student who was envious or jealous of others. Ask the students to describe how the main character felt and what he thought and did. This technique can be used to minimize the expression of jealousy and get the students to realize how their jealousy affects others (Bers and Rodin, 1984).

17. Do not compare one student to another. Jealousy may arise from the pain of unfavorable comparisons to other students (Salovey and Rodin, 1984).

18. Do not emphasize competition among students (Ruble, Feldman, and Boggiano, 1976).

19. Training in coping-skill strategies may be helpful if it has been determined that the student has a deficit in these skills. Together, the student and you can generate some coping skills for him to use (Jaremko and Lindsey, 1979).

20. If the jealousy is caused by the lack of coping skills, then specific adaptive behaviors must be taught. Use role playing, modeling, and behavior rehearsals around specific situations to promote social learning (Schloss and Sedlak, 1982).

21. Model and practice appropriate positive social behaviors immediately following an outburst of jealousy (Schloss and Sedlak, 1982).

135
Lies

1. Describe the expected behavior to the student (Anderson and Scott, 1978; Stephens, Hartman, and Lucas, 1978).

2. Reinforce the student when he tells the truth (Blackman and Silberman, 1980).

3. Use planned ignoring (Blackman and Silberman, 1980).

4. Punish the student (Krout, 1932).

5. Role play the telling of exaggerated stories and encourage the student to indicate when he hears "silly talk."

6. Record the conversation or story. Have the student listen to the tape and hold up one finger when he recognizes fantasy and two fingers when he recognizes a fact (V. Croll, personal communication, 1983).

7. Give the class printed and oral exercises for fact-opinion and fact-fantasy discrimination (V. Croll, personal communication, 1983).

8. Have the student keep a log of his statements. Direct him as to which ones to record. At the end of the day, review the log with the student and discuss which statements are fantasy and which are fact (V. Croll, personal communication, 1983).

9. During creative writing sessions, encourage the student to write stories using fantasy. When the story is read aloud, have a class discussion about fiction, nonfiction, fantasy, and fact (V. Croll, personal communication, 1983).

10. Enact a classroom TV news program with a daily feature story entitled "Truth is

stranger than fiction" to demonstrate that truth can be interesting (V. Croll, personal communication, 1983).

11. During language arts, introduce and discuss examples of fiction that use fantasy as opposed to fact (e.g., *Alice in Wonderland* versus *Huckleberry Finn*) (V. Croll, personal communication, 1983).

12. Analyze "tall tales" as to what constitutes deviation from truth (V. Croll, personal communication, 1983).

13. Recommend counseling for the student.

14. Prove the student's story to be wrong.

15. Ask the student to prove his story. If he lies or exaggerates, take away a privilege (L. Frank, personal communication, 1983).

16. Explain that lying is wrong.

17. If the student tells a lie, tell him that now is not the time for stories. Ignore the story.

18. Train the student to think before answering. Instruct him to wait 10–15 seconds before answering questions or telling a story (M. Burns, personal communication, 1983).

19. In a group situation, use story telling as a vehicle for questioning fact versus fantasy. (e.g., "Do you think what Huckleberry Finn said was true or just made up?" "Why do you think so?") (Spivak and Swift, 1975).

20. Establish a "buddy system" or group activities so that the student can have more peer interaction and less chance to lie or exaggerate without contrary responses from others (Reinert, 1980).

21. If you know that the student is lying, say so and focus on a solution to the problem (Lerman, 1980).

22. Ask the student to write or tell a story "that could happen, but didn't." Finally ask him to write a story that is clearly impossible. Engage the student in a discussion about how the stories are different (Spivak and Swift, 1975).

23. Draw the student into the classroom activities rather than causing him to pull away by "pinning him down" about an exagger-

ation. Quickly point out that the statement is difficult to believe, or raise the possibility of a slight exaggeration in a way not embarrassing to the student (Spivak and Swift, 1975).

24. If the student says, "It's true, don't you believe me?" say, "Most of the time. All a teacher can do is listen carefully to what is said and ask more about everyone's interesting ideas." (M. Burns, personal communication, 1983).

25. Read statements and ask the class to identify which parts of them are true, possibly true, probably not true, or never true. Students involved in a discussion of such stories may argue about evidence, but the goal is to make it clear that some things are true and some things are not (Spivak and Swift, 1975).

26. Ask the student to put his ideas into a story. Tell him that he has a very good imagination and could probably be a good writer of stories, books, or plays. If the student is too young to write, he can tell the story while you write it down (M. Burns, personal communication, 1983).

27. Remind the student how books are separated in libraries by fact, fiction, and fantasy. Also explain the difference between the three and the difference between a true story on television and a fantasy movie or cartoon (M. Burns, personal communication, 1983).

28. When you judge that a student is exaggerating and has perhaps slipped into it without realizing, try talking with him after class about the statements. (e.g., "Is what you said today really true or is it part of a story?" "Are interesting stories good sometimes?" "Is it important to say whether something really did happen or whether it didn't?") Tell the student that you value both fact and fantasy, but there is an important difference (Spivak and Swift, 1975).

29. If the student has a good sense of humor or you know that he is aware of what he is doing, say, "Yes, I always take what you

say seriously, but sometimes you tell a good story!" (Spivak and Swift, 1975).

30. Read and discuss the story of *Pinnochio* (M. Burns, personal communication, 1983).

31. Read and discuss the story of *The Boy Who Cried Wolf* (M. Brunagin, personal communication, 1985).

32. Use role playing to show that lying is undesirable (Stephens, Hartman, and Lucas, 1978).

33. Hold a group discussion regarding the difference between telling the truth and lying, how it affects individuals involved, and the consequence of each in various situations (K. Roza, personal communication, 1983).

34. Recommend that the student talk to a school counselor or psychologist (Reinert, 1980).

35. Work on developing the student's self-image. Lying may be a defense associated with failure, low self-esteem, or anxiety (Anderson and Scott, 1978).

36. Establish trust through nonthreatening conversation. This shows interest and fairness. If you are honest and up-front with the student, there is a good chance that student is being honest with you (Webster, 1981).

37. Teach the student to analyze behavior through the "stop-look-and-think" technique. The student should speak to himself and say, "*Stop*, before I do anything; *look around*. What is happening? *Let me think*. If I do this what could possibly happen?" (Webster, 1981).

38. Teach the student to give a nonverbal signal to the teacher when he is exaggerating or lying. This will indicate that immediate help is needed to assist him in getting "out of the spotlight" (C. Scism, personal communication, 1983).

39. Use humor to indicate your detection of a lie. (e.g., "You know, that reminds me of the time I slew a dragon and was awarded a small Kingdom by the grateful people. I still vacation there during school vacations.")

40. Place the student in time-out (Reinert, 1980).

41. Tell the student if he tells you the truth he won't get punished (L. Frank, personal communication, 1983).

42. Arrange a parent conference to gain home support (B. Carey, personal communication, 1983).

43. Stress the benefits of telling the truth instead of dwelling on the falsehood (Lerman, 1980).

44. Offer a sympathetic ear to the student's failures. When a student fails, don't show your disappointment. This will only cause the student to lie about successes (Warren, 1977).

45. Encourage honesty of expression (Warren, 1977).

46. Help the student retrace the steps of his lie in order to get to the truth (Warren, 1977).

47. Recognize what the student is trying to say and help him to say it honestly (Isenstein and Krasners, 1978).

48. When the student tells a falsehood, let him know how he could have told the truth in the same situation (Isenstein and Krasners, 1978).

49. Share your honest feelings of anger, embarrassment, and shame when a student makes a mistake, and help him to find alternatives to his behavior (Isenstein and Krasners, 1978).

50. Demonstrate your own honesty, thus setting an example and providing a model (Isenstein and Krasners, 1978).

51. Listen carefully to a student's feelings. Is the student angry, sad, empty, or needy? Help him find more constructive ways of handling these feelings than lying (Isenstein and Krasners, 1978).

52. Minimize placing a student in a situation where he will react dishonestly (Isenstein and Krasners, 1978).

53. Recommend a peer-support group for the student. This involves group meetings of students who have the same problem of

dealing with the truth. The student must be sure that others in the group trust him and is certain he won't need to lie to impress the group. Here, the student will have the strength to face up to his mistakes and failures without trying to cover up (Virden, 1984).

54. Don't nag, back the student into a corner, or expect too much from him. These things promote lying (Hill, 1983).

55. Explain the social, personal, and academic consequences of a lie. Don't ask a lot of "why" questions. Demanding answers places the student in the position of either lying again to accommodate the teacher or saying nothing (Hill, 1983).

56. Praise good examples of honesty in front of your students (Hill, 1983).

57. Be prompt in dealing with lies. Don't allow them to build (Krout, 1932).

58. Show students the filmstrip *The Trouble with Truth*. It deals with two different dilemmas. In one case, Patrick faces a problem where he must either lie to cover up for his friends or tattle and get them in trouble. In the second case, Debbie must decide if she wants to lie about her age to get into an amusement park (distributed by Guidance Associates, 1972).

59. Catch the student lying and check on his story. Keep track of the number of lies a student has committed by placing chips in a jar. Take away a privilege that the student really enjoys if he gets a certain number of chips in the jar (Millar, 1985).

60. Emphasize to a student privately that by lying he will only be placing friendships on the line. Mention that his friends will not be impressed with lies, only with the truth (M. Brumagin, personal communication, 1986).

136

Reliant; Likes to Be Close to Teacher

1. Reinforce the student's independent behavior (Blackman and Silberman, 1971).

2. Ignore incidences of dependent behavior (Blackman and Silberman, 1971).

3. Encourage the student's independent behavior in small steps (Blackman and Silberman, 1971).

4. Seat the student at increasingly farther distances from you.

5. Require that students raise their hands to receive your attention. Do not respond if the student approaches you.

6. Require the student to earn private and personal time with you.

7. Set a limit on the number of minutes that the student may be close to you. Have the student keep track of this time with a stopwatch.

8. Have the student write all requests. This may deter the behavior.

9. Require that the student pay for staff time with tokens that have been earned by being self-reliant.

10. Tell the student when his behavior is inappropriate (Walker and Shea, 1980).

11. Explain the correct steps needed to solve the problem. Require that the student then attempt the task (Walker and Shea, 1980).

12. Help the student develop his own self-discipline by the consistent use of specific limits and consequences, predetermined procedures and schedules, definite chores and tasks, and appropriate support and guidance (McWhirter, McWhirter, and McWhirter, 1985).

13. Put the student in charge of his own schedule and choice of task (McWhirter, McWhirter, and McWhirter, 1985).

14. Negotiate tasks. Assign a time for completion and consequences if not accomplished

(McWhirter, McWhirter, and McWhirter, 1985).

15. Teach the student to analyze the task and determine whether increased effort alone, or increased effort plus an alternative strategy such as self-questioning, is necessary to produce success (Sheltan, Anastopoulos, and Linden, 1985).

16. Implement a carefully supervised individual reading program that encourages independence and self-motivation while monitoring and improving reading skills (Lindon, 1985).

17. Measure persistence by time on task or by the number of attempts at completing the task. Alter the task until the student can successfully complete it in one or two tries (Luchow, Crawl, and Kahn, 1985).

18. Have the student refer to directions on the board to minimize teacher guidance (Gettinger, 1985).

19. Teach the student to attribute his successes to his ability and effort (Luchow, Crawl, and Kahn, 1985).

20. Encourage the student to try harder and let him know that you believe he can accomplish the task.

21. Design tasks within the student's range of success and encourage with praise.

22. Create play situations where the less confident student is either the leader or the teacher of a game (C. Poliseno, personal communication, 1985).

23. Each time the student is able to go for a longer period of time without the need to be close to you, let him know that he is becoming more mature (Sprick, 1981).

24. Devise a buddy system to make each student feel a part of a group (C. Gingerich, personal communication, 1984).

25. Contact parents of the student to determine if the behavior is typical (G. Leitz, personal communication, 1985).

26. Develop a cooperative plan with the parents to help the student become more self-reliant.

27. Introduce the student to a small group-play activity (G. Lietz, personal communication, 1985).

28. Use "Show and Tell Time" to encourage the student to bring items of interest from home to share with the class. This will increase sociability and make the student feel special and comfortable with peers (G. Lietz, personal communication, 1985).

29. Let the student be a special helper for an errand so he can feel important (G. Lietz, personal communication, 1985).

30. Assign small tasks and responsibilities that can be done alone by the student, such as emptying the waste basket or collecting the erasers, and build to bigger tasks (B. Ballichino, personal communication, 1985).

31. Encourage group activities to promote acceptance by one's peers and cooperation with others (Anderson, 1985).

32. Structure learning experiences so the student can demonstrate that he has more ability and skill than he thought he had (Rogers and Scklofske, 1985).

33. Encourage the self-esteem of the reliant student by emphasizing strengths and praising his strong points (e.g., good penmanship, getting along well with others, etc.), and minimizing criticism of weak points (McWhirter, McWhirter, and McWhirter, 1985).

34. Let the student tell you what he sees as his strengths and weaknesses and then encourage the strengths (McWhirter, McWhirter, and McWhirter, 1985).

35. Teach the student cognitive strategies to encourage self-direction, and monitor progress. This involves talking through a task or problem, or giving oneself advice such as "take time to think," "stick with it," or "consider the alternatives" (Lindon, 1985).

36. Teach the student to take responsibility for his own learning through story telling in which the story presented requires him to determine who was responsible in a given situation and why (Lindon, 1985).

37. Assign seating so that the student is strategically placed away from you (C. Gingerich, personal communication, 1984).

38. Get the student started on an independent activity, and praise him frequently from a distance to keep him on task alone (Sprick, 1981).

137
Says Teacher Doesn't Help Him Enough

1. Praise the student when he is on task and does not make a verbalization (Chance, 1982).

2. Establish peer assistance for the student (Chance, 1982).

3. Make a rule that all students must try their best before raising their hand for help (Blumenfeld, Pintrich, Meece, and Wessels, 1982).

4. Praise other students for doing their work by themselves (Blumenfeld, Pintrich, Meece, and Wessels, 1982; Bernstein, 1982).

5. Check to be sure that the classwork is at the student's level of ability.

6. Develop a plan to help the student accept personal responsibility for his own success or failure (Tollesfson, 1982).

7. Assist the student in setting goals for behavior (Tollesfson, 1982).

8. Give the student a choice of tasks. The most interesting task should have the requirement that the student must work without assistance.

9. Require the student to complete a section of the assignment before your attention is given.

10. Chart and graph the number of times each student asks for help. Discuss the results with the student.

11. Chart the amount of time given to this student and a few other representative students in the class. Show these results to the student and discuss the results.

12. Check with the student periodically to monitor progress.

13. Allow the student a certain number of questions for each task or time period.

14. Reinforce the student for lowering his number of questions per period.

138
Seeks Constant Praise

1. Reinforce occurrences of independent behaviors (Becker, Engelmann, and Thomas, 1975; Allington, 1975).

2. Make a chart and record the number of times the student seeks praise. Break the chart into recognizable time periods. Perhaps the frequency of the requests is not the problem. The problem might be the student's timing of the requests, or how the student seeks praise (K. J. Smolarek, personal communication, 1985).

3. Record what occurs in the class before each request is made by the student. Something might be occurring to cause this student to feel insecure (K. J. Smolarek, personal communication, 1985).

4. Ignore the dependent behavior by appearing to be busy with other things (Becker, Engelmann, and Thomas, 1975).

5. Use the physical arrangements of the classroom to encourage independence (Altman and Grose, 1982).

6. Discuss the problem with the student. Give him your point of view about the number of times he makes requests. In this discussion, decide on an acceptable number of student-teacher interactions for each time period and give him that number of passes or tickets to meet with you. When tickets are gone, no more requests for praise or interaction are honored (K. J. Smolarek, personal communication, 1985).

7. Have the student record the number of

times he seeks praise. Reward substantial decreases by a lunch date or other agreed upon reinforcer (K. J. Smolarek, personal communication, 1985).

8. Insure that each student receives a fair amount of praise in your classroom for working independently, following procedures, finishing work, and so on by marking on a chart or in a roll book each time you praise a student. Make sure you are not praising only a few students or only one section of the classroom (K. J. Smolarek, personal communication, 1985).

9. Use a wooden flag or symbol on your desk to indicate that you are available to review student work (Gallagher, 1971).

10. Sit at a special desk, seat, or table as an indicator to the students that you are ready to review individual progress (K. J. Smolarek, personal communication, 1985).

11. Use a sign-up sheet for student-teacher meetings during independent work times. Do not discuss work with the students except in the order of the names on the sheet (K. J. Smolarek, personal communication, 1985).

12. For each 15-minute time period that the student has worked independently, give him a token. At the end of the two-hour (or some other appropriate) time period, each token can be exchanged for minutes of direct, uninterrupted teacher attention (Gallagher, 1971).

13. Have the student begin the day or period with a set number of tokens. Each time he seeks praise he must pay you with a token. At the end of the day, each token in the student's possession is worth a set amount of time doing a preferred activity (Gallagher, 1971).

14. Constantly roam about your classroom, praising desired behavior of all students and ignoring inappropriate behavior.

15. Praise only genuine accomplishments. False praise is soon identified and becomes ineffective, causing students to seek genuine praise from you (Allington, 1975).

16. Never give praise unless it is deserved, even if the student is asking for it (Allington, 1975).

17. State the positive in praising. Avoid such words as *right*, *good*, and *better*. Specifically tell what was done correctly. In doing so, the student who is in need of praise is getting it instead of being judged or compared (Berne, 1985).

18. Written comments last longer and thus can reinforce more than a verbal comment. The student can read, share, and enjoy a written statement about his work long after school is out. Use certificates as well as statements written on papers (Cheek, 1981).

19. Too much praise increases the student's desire for praise. Students should be taught to think independently about their own work and make value judgments (Elkins, 1981).

20. Use "I" messages that reflect thoughts and feelings without passing judgments (e.g., "I enjoyed reading your composition"). Wean students gradually from the "I" messages (Curwin, 1980).

21. Praise genuine accomplishments and things done that are worthwhile in their own right, not done simply to please you (Brophy, 1981).

22. A student who is overly dependent on praise should be encouraged to evaluate accomplishments for himself (Curwin, 1980; Brophy, 1981).

23. Students from classrooms where praise is abundant often interpret lack of praise as criticism and therefore beg for it. Watch the amount of praise you use (Wolfgang, 1982).

24. Instead of responding with praise to the student who asks for it constantly, respond with comments such as, "I see you are holding your picture. Tell me about it." This lets the student know that his feelings and ideas are respected (Wolfgang, 1982).

25. Praise can be interpreted by the student as showing that he is a valuable person. Because insecure students need to see value

in themselves and interpret lack of praise as lack of self-value, switch to encouraging statements that place emphasis on the student's action (e.g., Praise: ''I like what you have done.'' Encouragement: ''You're trying harder.'') (Wolfgang, 1982).

26. Use praise statements for desired behavior only. Withdraw them as behavior improves (Wolfgang, 1982).

27. Carefully word your statements to give the student needed praise in a variety of ways, making it more meaningful (Academic Therapy, 1981; Brophy, 1981).

28. Teach the student to evaluate his work and praise himself for good effort and quality of product.

29. Arrange a private signal between you and the student that will take the place of a compliment. A wink may mean that the student is working nicely (J. O'Malley, personal communication, 1985).

30. Make a bulletin board called ''Hats Off to _____!'' On hats, have students write good behaviors of the featured student (J. O'Malley, personal communication, 1985).

31. Have the student write behaviors that he feels should be praised in a notebook. Look at the book at the end of the school day and praise the student as appropriate (J. O'Malley, personal communication, 1985).

32. Tell the student that praise means more if others are given the opportunity to initiate it. Point out that it may well work in reverse if he is constantly asking others for it (J. O'Malley, personal communication, 1985).

33. Tell the student that you would like him to share some of the praise he gets from you with others. For example, if a student comes to you and asks, ''Do you like my picture?'', answer that you do and that he has done a good job of coloring it. Direct him to tell the same thing to another student who has done a good job (J. O'Malley, personal communication, 1985).

139

Self-Conscious; Easily Embarrassed

1. Give positive feedback when the student speaks in a group setting (C. Ritz, personal communication, 1985).

2. Have the student interact with others in small groups, then progress to larger groups (S. Nowak, personal communication, 1985).

3. Help the student avoid situations in which he becomes embarrassed.

4. Give messages that help the student see himself as valuable, able, and responsible (Novak and Bennett, 1983).

5. Prepare the student for upcoming situations in which he might be embarrassed.

6. Set aside a few minutes each day when the student boasts or brags about himself and his accomplishments.

7. When the student becomes embarrassed in a group situation, quickly change the focus of the group away from the student.

8. When the student becomes embarrassed privately with you, distract him to a different subject.

9. When the student becomes embarrassed privately with you, continue to talk about the topic until embarrassment regarding it wanes.

10. Do not allow others to embarrass the student intentionally.

11. Create an atmosphere of acceptance, supportiveness, and friendliness in your classroom. Be sure that students understand that putting forth their best effort is the only requirement.

140

Sulks

1. Praise the student when he accepts consequences without withdrawing and being mad.
2. Reinforce a voluntary return to group participation (Krumboltz and Krumboltz, 1972).
3. Ignore the sulking behavior and continue on with your duties (Krumboltz and Krumboltz, 1972).
4. Send the student on an errand to allow him to cool off.
5. Use humor to draw a smile and reinitiate positive contact.
6. Show the student that you hold no grudge by speaking to him in a gentle, upbeat voice and touching him gently on the shoulder. Have him work on a favored activity or task.
7. Speak with the student privately, telling him to vent his feelings without fear of punishment.
8. Review the situation with the student, explaining why you needed to react in the manner that you did.
9. Allow the student to vent his anger through physical exertion such as running, hitting a punching bag, or pounding clay.
10. Reinforce the student for the sulking behavior if it represents withholding aggressive behavior and respect for your power and authority.
11. Require that the student show you a smile and shake your hand before leaving for recess, lunch, or some other preferred activity.
12. Have another person (e.g., aide, friend) speak with the student about the situation that preceded the sulking.
13. If the student sulks because he feels that he has a better way of doing something, let him attempt the task his way with your guidance (Dreikurs and Grey, 1970).

14. Use role playing so that the student can observe how his behavior appears to others (B. Tankersley, personal communication, 1985).
15. Allow the student to do the task his way this time with the understanding that it must be done differently next time (D. Randall, personal communication, 1985).
16. Give the student two minutes to "straighten up and fly right" (L. DiMarzio, personal communication, 1985).

141

Tattles

1. Tell the student that you do not wish to hear tattling (J. Mette, personal communication, 1984).
2. Praise the student for not tattling (Swift and Spivack, 1975).
3. Ignore the student when he attempts to tattle (J. Noirfalise, personal communication, 1983).
4. Provide a negative consequence for tattling on another person.
5. Have the student monitor the frequency of his tattling. Discuss the results.
6. Have the student attempt to lower his daily total of tattling to receive reinforcement.
7. Require that the student have proof for his claims before he reports the behavior of another.
8. Accept reports of others' behavior only in written form. Tell the student that you will review his note later.
9. After the student tattles, have him say something nice about the other's behavior (J. Noirfalise, personal communication, 1983).
10. Thank the student for the information and ask him to return to his task. Use this information to keep you informed.
11. Hold class discussions on the proper times

to report the behaviors of others and what types of behaviors should be reported.

12. Be alert in group situations in order to spot misbehavior so that students do not need to report it to you.

13. Focus the student's behavior back on task by asking, "What should you be doing?" Repeat this until he returns to task.

14. Tell both of the involved students that you want them to return to their work immediately.

142
Temper Tantrums

1. Praise the student for appropriate reactions to frustration.

2. Ignore the behavior (Stumphauzer, 1977).

3. Make a list of specific tantrum behaviors (Sprick, 1981).

4. Use modeling to show expected behavior (Morse, 1975).

5. Use role playing to demonstrate desired behaviors (Morse, 1975).

6. Place the student in time-out to allow him to escape temporarily from group pressure and cool off (Morse, 1975).

7. Discuss with the student alternate methods of dealing with anger (Harris and Mayhew, 1979).

8. Videotape the undesired behavior so that the student can view it (Alberto and Troutman, 1982).

9. Use verbal warnings or distractions before the temper tantrums occur (Haswell, 1981).

10. Isolate the student. Ignore him and give attention later when he shows productive behavior (Stumphauzer, 1977).

11. Use affection as a management strategy (Mullen, 1983).

12. Help the student verbalize his discomfort prior to the tantrum (Mullen, 1983).

13. Empty the classroom by sending the students to the playground. One adult should accompany these students, while another watches the tantrum from outside the classroom door. This removes attention to this behavior.

14. Tell the student that you are providing the control while restraining him (Mullen, 1983).

15. Have the other students imitate this behavior during a tantrum

16. Imitate the behavior yourself when the situation arises.

17. Afterward review the sequence of events in the tantrum with the student. Communicate understanding, not approval (Mullen, 1983).

18. When you see the student becoming angry, suggest that the two of you talk privately.

143
Uses Others as Scapegoats; Blames Others

1. Stress the importance of honesty to the whole class.

2. Talk to the student and explain that scapegoating is an unacceptable behavior in your classroom (K. Irwin, personal communication, 1983).

3. Give positive reinforcement for telling the truth and accepting responsibility for one's own actions (K. Irwin, personal communication, 1983).

4. Ignore the blaming behavior (Highland, 1984).

5. If it is known that the student is responsible for a certain action, do not ask if he performed the action, thus providing an opportunity for lying. Administer a negative consequence (J. Mette, personal communication, 1984).

6. Discuss the situation with both of the students who were involved in order to sort out the facts (J. Mette, personal communication, 1984).

7. Remove the possibility of punishment. This may reduce the scapegoating of others to avoid negative consequences. Then ask the student how he can best resolve the situation (Gentile, 1984).

8. Role play scenes that act out the telling of the truth and the accepting of responsibility for one's actions (K. Irwin, personal communication, 1983).

9. Role play the incident with the roles of the students reversed (Highland, 1984).

10. Have students provide witnesses or other documentation to prove that they were not responsible for an action (J. Mette, personal communication, 1984).

11. Require the student to apologize to the person who was blamed for the action (J. Mette, personal communication, 1984).

12. Ask the student what he did. If he starts to mention the name of another, say, "Yes, but what did *you* do?" (K. Smolarek, personal communication, 1985).

13. Insist that the students involved resolve the problem (Gentile, 1984).

144

Weeps or Cries with Little Provocation

1. Reinforce the student for not crying.

2. Determine the frequency of the weeping or crying. Reinforce the student for exceeding the average time without an emotional outburst (K. Cowell, personal communication, 1986).

3. Ignore the behavior (J. Grant, personal communication, 1983).

4. Reassure the student that everything is alright (J. Grant, personal communication, 1983).

5. Comfort the student by gently rocking him (J. Grant, personal communication, 1983).

6. Initiate a favorite activity to distract and in-terest the student (Beck, Roblee, and Johns, 1982).

7. Model the proper handling of emotions.

8. Use response cost by taking a marker away from the student each time he cries. Markers that are left over may be traded for rewards.

9. Ignore the student until crying stops. Then approach the student and initiate an interesting activity (Brown and Avery, 1974).

10. Use a metaphor or story that parallels the situation and can be used to indicate a more desired result (Bandler, 1978).

11. Search for ways to show that no one is good at everything (Cook, 1983).

12. The student should be encouraged to express how he feels about his performance. Have him chart a record of his progress (Cook, 1983).

13. For each half hour of time that the student has worked appropriately without crying, suggest that he deserves a break. Allow him to get a drink or play a game (Cook, 1983).

14. Use peer reinforcement and peer prompting to increase positive social behavior. Train students to ignore inappropriate behavior and reinforce appropriate behavior (Bellafoire and Salend, 1983).

15. Frequently use verbal approval. Frequent praise directed at the student, coupled with his name preceding each statement, helps him feel capable of achievement (Kazdin, 1977).

16. Use classroom discussion so the student can recognize that others in the classroom share his fears. It could be very supportive for him to see that others have similar fears (Moracco and Camilleri, 1983).

17. Use simple hand-made puppets as a vehicle for telling stories with themes centered on fear or anxiety. The stories can then become the springboard for classroom discussion (Moracco and Camilleri, 1983).

18. Listen for feeling and content when a student speaks. Reflect the feeling to the student (Tindel, 1983).

19. Provide success. Start at a level already mastered to prevent frustration and build confidence (Tindel, 1983).

20. Praise the student before offering constructive criticism (Tindel, 1983).

21. Praise in public; correct in private. Correct acts, not the person (Tindel, 1983).

22. Compare the student's progress with his beginnings, not with others. Help the student set clear, short-term goals (Tindel, 1983).

23. Teach assertiveness training and give the student opportunities to practice being assertive rather than passive (Tindel, 1983).

24. Help the student identify scripts he may be playing out. Show him how to choose to act differently (Tindel, 1983).

25. Allow the student to use art media to express emotions. The release or redirection of energies experienced through art may lessen the tendency to be overly sensitive (Noah-Cooper and Richards, 1983).

26. Prepare a cube with four faces: glad, sad, mad, and scared. When the student is upset, ask him to turn the cube so it shows the face that describes the way he is feeling. The student should then close his eyes and tell what made him feel that way (Grabow, 1981).

27. Listen carefully and thoughtfully to what the student has to say. With eyes closed, the student visualizes the events that led to the current situation. Encourage discussion with frequent questions (Grabow, 1981).

28. Demonstrate different ways to respond to a problem. Show the student his options and have the class practice together. Tally sheets can be kept to record how many times the student responds in the new response and old response patterns (Self, 1982).

29. Recommend counseling for the student (M. Grey, personal communication, 1983).

145
Whines or Complains

1. Praise the student when he makes his needs known in an appropriate manner (S. Blaha, personal communication, 1985).

2. Ignore the whining or complaining (S. Blaha, personal communication, 1985).

3. Punish the behavior by removing one minute of recess or preferred activity for each complaint.

4. Talk to the student after class. Try to get the student to bring out the reason behind his complaining (S. Blaha, personal communication, 1985).

5. If the student whines or complains, have an agreed upon number of times that he will have to perform an undesired activity (J. Maroon, personal communication, 1985).

6. Set a goal for the number of times that whining will be allowed. Reward the student for meeting that goal. Lower the number each day.

7. Have the student list complaints on paper. Decide whether the complaints are justified. If the student disagrees, he may request a hearing. No complaining is allowed until the hearing.

8. If work related, require that the student attempt a portion of the task before verbalization is allowed.

9. Speak with the student about alternative ways to make one's needs known.

10. Provide a helpful peer to assist the student. All complaints or requests for help must come from the peer tutor (D. Lathrop, personal communication, 1986).

11. Require the student to restate his complaint in more appropriate wording and tone of voice.

17

Impulse Control

146

Acts Before Thinking

1. Praise the student for behavior that appears to be planned and thoughtful (Williams, 1983).

2. Reinforce other students for showing thoughtful behavior.

3. Warn the student when his behavior is disrupting the learning environment (Konstantareas, 1984).

4. Ignore temporary behaviors. The student may notice that what he did was wrong and correct it before a decision is made by you (Williams, 1983).

5. Talk with the student about his behavior. He may not be aware of the impulsive nature of it (K. Schmitt, personal communication, 1985).

6. Have a conference with the parents to see if these impulsive behaviors occur at home. Plan a cooperative program (Kistner, 1985).

7. If behavior occurs both in the home and

school, recommend that the student be tested for hyperactivity (Witt, 1985).

8. Talk to parents about the student's diet. Perhaps it can be controlled (Witt, 1985).

9. Seat the student near your desk for better observation and control (K. Schmitt, personal communication, 1985).

10. Forewarn the student of possible consequences for misbehavior.

11. Have the student develop a plan for behaving correctly in an upcoming situation and have him consider the consequences for appropriate and inappropriate behavior.

12. Stop the student during the inappropriate behavior and ask him to state what he *should* be doing.

13. Review the situation after it has occurred. Discuss proper behavior if this situation were to present itself again.

14. Teach the student to analyze behavior through the "stop-look-and-think" technique. The student should speak to himself and say, "*Stop*, before I do anything; *look around*. What is happening? *Let me think*. If

I do this, what could possibly happen?" (Webster, 1981).

147
Easily Overexcited

1. When the student becomes excited, take him aside to talk, giving him guidance in how to control his behavior (Pomerantz and Shultz, 1983).
2. Train the student to recognize the inappropriate behavior.
3. Instruct the student to think before acting or speaking so that he will have time to preview the planned response (Webster, 1981).
4. Train the student to use the technique of stopping, listening, and looking (Brown, 1980).
5. Teach the student the technique of talking his way through various activities with self-directed verbal commands and reinforcement (Douglas, 1972).
6. Interrupt the sequence of behavior and thought prior to the production of overexcitement (Brown, 1980; Campbell, 1983).
7. Manipulate the environment so the behavior is less apt to happen. Stop the activity and substitute, temporarily, a more desirable behavior (Fried, 1978; Walden and Thompson, 1981).
8. Explain the situation that caused the reaction in order to assist the student in understanding and reacting properly (Fried, 1978).
9. Confer with parents, former teachers, the school nurse, physicians, and counselors. Study the available school records to find an effective strategy.
10. Tape-record the student's oral responses so they can be reviewed and discussed later.
11. Use self-observation and self-recording to allow the student to record the number of times he engages in inappropriate behavior.
12. Have the student use self-reinforcement

anytime he is acting appropriately and self-punishment when acting inappropriately.
13. Provide structure by establishing routines that are understandable and acceptable, enabling the student to work within limits that are consistently enforced (Collins and Collins, 1981; Walden and Thompson, 1981).
14. Remove the student from distracting stimuli or situations that cause the overexcited behavior (Walden and Thompson, 1981).
15. Avoid activities that provide too much stimulation (Walden and Thompson, 1981).
16. Provide greater amounts of movement more often (W. Jones, personal communication, 1985).
17. If the excited behavior occurs during academic periods, adjust the amount of work, the rate at which the student is expected to complete assignments, and/or the sequence of the material presented (Walden and Thompson, 1981).
18. If the student becomes overexcited due to frustration with the level of the material on which he is working, reduce the difficulty of the work (L. Evans, personal communication, 1985).
19. If a game has many pieces to the gameboard that cause excitement, bring out one item at a time for the student to see. Do not bring everything out at once if that would be too stimulating (J. Wells, personal communication, 1984).
20. Develop a signal system in which you give a nonverbal sign to remind the student to calm down. The student then returns a signal to indicate that he will comply.
21. Prepare the student for an upcoming activity by describing it. Also talk about appropriate and inappropriate behavior during the activity.
22. Determine which particular situations, activities, or remarks cause the student to become overexcited. Use relaxation exercises before these events (Loffredo, 1984).
23. Give the student an alternative experience

that might prove to be less exciting (L. Evans, personal communication, 1985).

24. Go through an assignment or a test with the student, step by step, immediately after he has become overexcited about a task (Collins, 1981).

25. Evaluate the amount of work that is expected from the student and make any necessary adjustments (Sprick, 1981).

26. Walk over to the student and place a firm, calming hand on his shoulder.

27. Seat a self-controlled student near the one who becomes easily excited (L. Evans, personal communication, 1985).

28. Model desired behavior for the overexcited student (Copeland and Weissbrod, 1983).

29. Define explicitly to the student what behavior is expected of him and what behavior will not be tolerated (Pihl, 1980).

30. Tell the student to calm down. Then discuss the cause of the overexcitement.

31. When he becomes overexcited, remind the student that his response is not the one you wish to see (Copeland and Weissbrod, 1983).

32. Provide structure and consistency in the learning environment (Martin and Martin, 1984).

33. Reduce extraneous visual stimuli by masking reading material and having the student do his work in a carrel (Martin and Martin, 1984).

34. Overcrowded conditions might cause the student to become overexcited. Assure that he has been given sufficient personal space (Martin and Martin, 1984).

35. If the student is displaying tactile defensiveness, don't touch him needlessly, and seat him away from heavy traffic areas in the classroom.

36. If the behavior occurs during transition periods, forewarn the student of the end of an instructional period or activity and use a special sound to indicate transitional times (Martin and Martin, 1984).

37. Make sure that the classroom temperature

and lighting conditions are adequate (Martin and Martin 1984).

38. Institute a classroom token economy, with rewards dispensed at home (Truhlicka, 1982).

39. When the student responds appropriately, give verbal praise and reward him for appropriate academic and social behaviors (Collins and Collins, 1975; Truhlicka, 1982).

40. When the student demonstrates inappropriate behavior, ignore it (Lamberg, 1984).

41. Provide the opportunity to work at activity-oriented learning centers as a balance for quiet, independent seat-work tasks (Walden and Thompson, 1981).

42. Have the student observe a filmed model before discussion of the behavior (Rieberg, Parke, and Hetherington, 1971).

43. When the student becomes overexcited, place him in time-out (Lamberg, 1984; Sulzer-Azaroff and Mayer, 1977; Wolfgang and Glickman, 1980).

44. Allow the student sufficient opportunities to release tension.

45. Set aside a 10-minute period each day to work on relaxation techniques (Sprick, 1981).

46. Train the student to relax forehead muscles by giving him auditory and visual feedback that corresponds to the level of muscle tension. This teaches him to relax and inhibits overactivity in the classroom (Christie, 1984).

47. Have the student participate in a relaxation exercise each time he becomes overexcited. Have him breathe deeply and then slowly exhale, make a fist and release, and shake limbs (Loffredo, 1984).

48. If the student becomes overexcited, have him participate in a muscle-relaxing exercise such as "the clock" or "curled stretch" (Loffredo, 1984).

49. Suggest to the parents that the student be enrolled in a relaxation training program (Williamson, 1980).

50. Suggest to the student's parents that they

take their child to a hypnotist (Williamson, 1980).

51. Chart behavior and activity levels. Identify possible causes of the high-activity levels by observing what happens before the undesired behavior and what happens after it. Choose appropriate intervention strategies (Sulzer-Azaroff and Mayer, 1977).

52. Give the student compensatory writing to complete when he exhibits overexcited behavior (Book, 1983).

53. When the student gets overexcited, he should have a specific place to which he can retreat until he regains self-control (Book, 1983).

54. Give the student only one assignment at a time (Book, 1983).

55. When given an assignment, have the student verbally explain what is to be done and have him demonstrate the proper behavior on the initial items.

56. Play calm music in the beginning of class to help the student relax (L. Evans, personal communication, 1985).

57. Perhaps the student has an abundance of energy that needs to be released. Get the student involved in a sport or activity that might serve as an outlet for this extra energy (C. Johnson, personal communication, 1985).

58. Provide an opportunity for physical exercise and movement both at home and at school (Fried, 1978).

59. Review the medical history of the student. The overexcited behavior of the student could be due to some sort of brain damage that might require medical treatment (Martin and Martin, 1984).

60. The overexcited behavior could be due to an allergic reaction to food and/or the environment. Suggest that the student get a medical exam to determine whether allergies are a problem (Martin and Martin, 1984).

61. If you suspect that the student's overexcitement is due to emotional problems, recommend that he be seen by the school

psychologist (L. Evans, personal communication, 1985).

62. Suggest that the parents consult a physician regarding the use of drug therapy in conjunction with behavior therapy (Brown, 1980; Truhlicka, 1982).

148

Impatient; Impulsive; Unable to Wait

1. Reinforce the student for showing patience.

2. Have a structured schedule and inform the student of it so that patience is mandatory.

3. Show the student the correct behavior by modeling it or having other students do so (Carberry, 1979).

4. Reinforce other students for displaying patient behavior.

5. Give directions and ask questions about them to be sure that the student understands the task.

6. Have the student repeat all directions before starting a task in order to insure that he has been listening (Swift and Spivak, 1975).

7. Place the student in situations where he must wait for a turn (Reinert, 1980).

8. Have the entire class complete a worksheet to promote following of directions. Question #1 would state, "Read through all the questions before filling in any of the blanks." Questions #2 through #19 ask about age, address, and any other general questions. Question #20 says, "Do not fill in any of the blanks for questions #2–#19. Sign your name to show you've read this entire sheet." The student who impulsively rushes through this worksheet will probably complete the whole questionnaire before realizing his mistake (Kaplan and White, 1980).

9. Present activities that involve following directions. These demand concentration on

each step and not just the finished product (e.g., treasure hunts in which notes and directions, placed at various points, lead to the final treasure) (Kaplan and White, 1980).

10. The use of precision teaching may relieve impulsiveness by allowing a short span for the student to work at top speed. It emphasizes that there is an appropriate time for speed whereas other times require neatness and quality (J. Ivarie, personal communication, 1983).

11. Short assignments should be given so that the duration of a task will not lead to building tension over time. Present lengthy tasks in segments (C. Zell, personal communication, 1980).

12. Deemphasize the value of speed at the expense of quality by reinforcing correct answers, no matter how long it takes to derive the answer (Swift, 1975).

13. Do not allow the student to respond to an answer until a specified amount of time has passed. This will allow the student time to think before responding. Gradually decrease the allotted time (Bornstein, 1980).

14. Supply the student with alternate choices to a problem. Encourage him to carefully find the best choice or solution (Millman, Schaefer, and Cohen, 1981).

15. Encourage the student to use self-verbalization when working individually. Encourage him to talk to himself before answering a question in order to gain control and decrease impulsiveness (Millman, Schaefer, and Cohen, 1981).

16. Teach the student to search for differences in solutions or choices. Looking for differences leads to better problem-solving techniques and less impulsivity. Show the student pictures of similar objects and have him state the dissimilar details (Millman, Schaefer, and Cohen, 1981).

17. Seat the impulsive student next to reflective students (Millman, Schaefer, and Cohen, 1981).

18. Teach the impulsive student to "stop, look, and listen" before answering a question or responding to a task. "Stop" is the injunction addressed at impulsivity and "look and listen" instruct him to attend selectively (Brown and Conrad, 1982).

19. Hang flash cards of the "stop-look-listen-think" approach around the classroom to remind the student to think before responding (Millman, Schaefer, and Cohen, 1981).

20. Assign a specific amount of time to an assignment. Do not accept the assignment until the time has passed.

21. Encourage the student to check his answers. This may be done through individual self-checking, checking the work with another student, or skimming the work before submitting it (A. Rogers, personal communication, 1985).

22. Instruct the student to practice self-verbalization in conjunction with strategy training. This involves asking oneself questions and giving directions. (e.g., "What is the task?" "What is required of me?" "Let's restate the directions in my own words.") (Bender, 1976).

23. Sit with the student and review his present behavior and work habits. Develop options or alternatives for present behavior. Also develop positive consequences for each option. When all is agreed upon, suggest a written commitment. This may motivate the student to improve (Bourgeois, 1979).

24. Provide the impulsive student with a very structured environment. Enforce rules with consistency (Shrigley, 1979).

25. Vary the activities. Give the student an activity for 5–10 minutes, then another activity of related subject matter. Gradually increase the length of the assignment (M. Sheahan, personal communication, 1985).

26. Assign the student four tasks, allowing 10 minutes for each. Give him a 5-minute break between each task. Observe him daily, and give feedback on his previous day's work based on the percentage of problems completed correctly (Friedling and O'Leary, 1979).

27. Include the student's interest in assignments to decrease impatience (A. Rogers, personal communication, 1985).

28. To decrease the student's "blurting out" behavior, require that he raise his hand when wishing to speak (Gervais and Dittburner, 1981).

29. Explain to the student why interruptions such as blurting out and impulsiveness are disruptive and poor manners and infringe on the rights of other students (Gervais and Dittburner, 1981).

30. Require the student to record his "blurts" and submit it at the end of the period. Set criteria together and if he meets the criteria, give a reward (Gervais and Dittburner, 1981).

31. Remove the student from the classroom or place him in time-out (Gervais and Dittburner, 1981).

32. Structure the class day so that there are periodic times for the class to stretch or move (Martin and Martin, 1984).

33. When the student acts out impulsively, remove an earned reinforcer (Thompson, Teare, and Elliott, 1983).

34. Impose a time delay to force the student to wait before responding. This will force him to slow down when solving problems. Reinforce him after successful waiting (Thompson, Teare, and Elliot, 1983).

35. If the student is unable to wait for instructions before writing, promote waiting by saying, "Take your time" and by taking the pencil away from the student until directions are given (Lin, Blackman, Clark, and Gordon, 1983).

36. Do not promote quick task completion in your classroom (Becker, 1976).

37. To teach reflective thinking, show the student a videotape in which a model is looking closely at various response alternatives, thereby providing behavioral clues of the reflective tempo. In the videotape, the model should verbalize his strategy during the interval after responding. The model's verbalizations stress responding slowly, avoiding selecting the first figure that appears correct without checking the remaining stimuli, and providing a description of the whole strategy used (Brown, 1980).

38. Discuss with the parents, school nurse, and physician the possibility of implementing a low-phosphate diet to decrease the student's hyperkinesis (Walker, 1982).

39. Teach the impulsive student attention strategies that encourage him to scan and identify similarities and differences in a task before answering impulsively (Maggiore, 1983).

40. If the student is acting impulsively during a lesson, stop talking and wait until you have everyone's attention. (D. Cambrini, personal communication, 1985).

41. Recommend that the student be evaluated by a physician for possible medication treatment.

42. Begin each lesson with an attention-getting device, involving each student as much as possible. As the student begins to establish internal controls and proper habits of attention, these "attention getters" can be reduced (Johnson and Myklebust, 1967).

43. Make work interesting and use short periods of instruction (Silberman, 1985).

44. Provide modified free time that allows the student to play, explore, laugh, and generally be unstructured (Silberman, 1985).

45. Teach relaxation techniques to your entire class. Later, discuss with the student how these techniques could be utilized in other situations (Amerikaner and Summerlin, 1982).

46. Have the student think of three or four ways of handling a specific situation in a better way. Write them down and then decide, with the student, which would be best (VanNagel and Deering-Levin, 1984).

47. Give the student an ultimatum. He is to act appropriately, or a privilege is lost (VanNagel and Deering-Levin, 1984).

48. Practice situations that could cause this student difficulty. Use modeling, coaching,

and behavioral rehearsal with feedback (La-Greca and Mesibov, 1979).

49. A student may need to be told that something else is occurring, and that it is not appropriate to interrupt (J. Richter, personal communication, 1985).

149

Jumps to New Activity Before Finishing Previous One

1. Praise the student when he fully completes a task.

2. Create a schedule that allows the students 10 minutes of jogging or running in place. Students who jog everyday evidence less disputive behavior and exhibit more on-task behavior (Henderson, 1976, citation unavailable).

3. Set a timer for varying intervals during individual or small group instructions. If everyone is on task when the timer rings, the group earns a reward (Milburn and Lemke, 1977).

4. Tell the student that he is to work on the assigned task until a timer rings. After the timer has sounded, the student may then leave that particular task (Milburn and Lemke, 1977).

5. Use a token economy to reward on-task behavor. Continue to increase on-task time demands and gradually decrease the reward (Christensen, 1975).

6. Focus attention and concentration on the major content of the task, not on trivia (Brown, 1980).

7. Help the student learn how to recover from disruptions and distractions (Brown, 1980).

8. Teach internal speech, which takes the form of a dialogue. Teach the student to change what he says internally, using reflection, explanation, interpretation, information giving, and cognitive modeling (e.g., "I can and I will be able to finish

my math page before I begin my social studies") (Meichenbaum, 1978).

9. Stress to the student that taking time to complete a task will actually save time, as he probably will not have to do the task over again.

10. Assign tasks in which the student must focus on one thing (e.g., if listening to a cassette, attend only to a certain voice) (Harvey, Weintraub, and Neale, 1984).

11. Present one task or trial at a time (e.g., when listening to a series of digits on a cassette, write nothing until the series is complete) (Harvey, Weintraub, and Neale, 1984).

12. Have the student observe how a peer completes one task before beginning another (Brown, 1980).

13. Give directions clearly, concisely, slowly, and in the order in which they are to be followed. Write them down if necessary (Interrelated Teacher Education Project).

14. Be sure that one of your directions is "Complete all of this before starting anything else."

15. Limit the size and complexity of the task (Interrelated Teacher Education Project).

16. Be sure that the student sees an end product as a result of his work (Resource, 1969).

17. Withhold other assignments and materials until the first task is completed (Rimm and Masters, 1974).

18. Make the assignment bright and colorful. Use manipulatives if possible (Resource, 1969).

19. Include the student's interests in the assignment.

20. Break large tasks into smaller units so that they do not appear to be so overwhelming (Reinhart, 1980).

21. Allow the student one minute of free time at the end of the day for each worksheet or activity completed that day (Hammill and Meyers, 1969).

22. Have the student keep a list of tasks to be completed so that he can see what has yet

to be accomplished (S. Thomas, personal communication, 1983).

23. Use various jobs within the classroom as rewards for completing assignments (Wallace and Kauffman, 1973).

24. Allow the student to work on an assignment or activity of his choice upon completion of all work (Rimm and Masters, 1974).

25. Let the student decide on which order he would like to complete assignments.

26. Have the student stay after school to complete the whole assignment again from the beginning.

27. Allow the student to check his own answers as soon as he finishes.

28. Make up a daily report card on which to record the number of tasks assigned and number of tasks completed. At the end of each day, have the student bring the report card to the principal if there is the same level or a higher performance from the previous day.

29. Do not allow participation in preferred activities until the assignment is completed.

30. Assign a peer tutor to assist the student.

150

Rushes Through Work and Makes Many Mistakes

1. Praise the student when he works on his assignments in a reflective manner.

2. Give assignments in small parts so that the student is not overwhelmed by the amount of work and resorts to rushing (Reinhart, 1980).

3. Use the student's interests so that he will want to spend time on the work (e.g., if the student likes trucks, devise math problems involving gas usage, mileage, and cargo weight).

4. If the completed assignments are too brief, encourage the student to write more by saying, ''I really like reading what you write. Whenever I reach the end of one of your papers I wish I had more to read.'' (D. Pfeister, personal communication, 1983).

5. Place the student near another who works neatly and carefully. Reinforce the other student.

6. Have the student stay in during recess or after school until the work is done correctly.

7. Have the student recopy the messy or incorrect part of the assignment in addition to completing an additional assignment.

8. Have the student verbalize his thought processes while working (Danforth, 1978).

9. Put problems, questions, or activities on separate sheets of paper. Hand these to the student one at a time. Do not give the next one until the first is done correctly.

10. Tell the student that he does not need to be the first person to hand in his assignments (Reinhart, 1980).

11. Use a buddy system in which students check each other's work after completing small sections. The buddies pass inspection as a pair (Reinhart, 1980).

12. Have the student complete a checklist before handing in work. Some items on the list might be: Did you read the paper over? Did you fill in every blank? Did you check for errors? Did you correct mistakes? (Reinhart, 1980).

13. Divide the page into sections with colored pencil. Check each section before allowing the student to go on to the next (Reinhart, 1980).

14. Graph assignment productivity. Have the student attempt to beat his daily markings (J. Lowry, personal communication, 1983).

15. Do not allow the student to engage in postassignment fun activities unless he meets an 80–90% criterion level.

16. During class, emphasize accuracy rather than speed. Also stress the advantages of checking work for errors before turning it in to be graded (K. Woodrich, personal communication, 1983).

17. Grade the work as soon as possible after completion and return it if changes need to be made.

18. Inform the student that each incorrect answer will require him to do two more problems in its place.

19. Work with the student on a one-to-one basis.

20. Do not allow the student to hand the paper to you until a designated time period has passed.

21. Require the student to proofread his product before the work is accepted.

22. Devise games that require paying close attention to details. Make the directions progressively more complex (Swift and Spivack, 1975).

23. Periodically check the student's work for accuracy.

24. Present words or math examples using flashcards or a tachistoscope to slow the student's response speed.

25. Cut a rectangular slot in a card to allow the student to see only a few words on a page.

26. Have the student underline word meanings and outline stories to encourage attention to details (Smith, 1983).

27. Ask comprehension questions after the student reads a few paragraphs rather than after a whole story to draw attention to detail (Swift and Spivak, 1975).

28. Develop ways to slow the student's response rate in math (e.g., handing the student one peg at a time and requiring the student to complete only one step at a time before teacher monitoring).

29. To slow the student's counting, use a board with holes drilled in it, and have him use a screw-driver and screws. He must turn a screw in for each counted (Strauss and Lehtinen, 1947).

151
Unable to Predict Consequences of Personal Behavior

1. Review the demonstrated behavior and its consequences after each incident.

2. Ask the student how he will react in an upcoming situation. Have him predict the consequences of this behavior. Review the results after the situation.

3. Role play hypothetical situations in which a student makes wise and unwise decisions. Discuss the results.

4. Tell the student the type of behavior you expect and the consequences if he does or does not comply.

5. Teach appropriate social skills.

6. Team the student with a peer who can provide direction and guidance.

7. In a group discussion, have students talk of various situations familiar to all, their past behavior, and the result.

8. Create a classroom environment in which rules are consistently enforced by providing positive consequences for good behavior and negative consequences for misbehavior.

9. Call the student's home to devise a cooperative plan to provide consistent consequences for behavior.

10. Require the student to "relive" certain classroom situations and practice appropriate behavior.

11. Partially show television programs or partly read a story. Have the student predict the outcome of a character's behavior.

152
Unable to Refrain from Talking

1. Praise the student for being quiet (Bowman, 1983).

2. Give positive reinforcement to the student when talking contributes to the lesson (C. Meyer, personal communication, 1986).

3. If the student is not contributing to the topic of the conversation, stop him before he begins talking about other things. Explain to him that he must listen and contribute information only about the topic that the class is discussing (D. Johnson, personal communication, 1986).

4. Make a game of being quiet. Tell the student that he will be rewarded for each five-minute interval during which he can remain silent (D. Johnson, personal communication, 1986).

5. Require all students to raise hands (Gervais and Dittburner, 1981).

6. Record the number of talk outs. Reinforce the student for talking out less than the previous day.

7. Sometimes individuals are unaware that they are exhibiting inappropriate behavior and do not understand why the behavior is undesirable. Explain why this behavior is inappropriate and discuss how this might be remedied (Martin and Quilling, 1981).

8. Set up a contract with the student that focuses on talking only when it is appropriate (Spaulding, 1983).

9. Change the student's seating. It could be the person next to him that is facilitating talking behavior (L. Evans, personal communication, 1985).

10. Move the student to the back of the room, away from others (L. Evans, personal communication, 1985).

11. Keep the violator after school for a private conference. Explain to him how his behavior is disrupting the class. Solicit cooperation (Gervais and Dittburner, 1981).

12. Never try to speak over and above talking. Require silence before teaching (Gervais and Dittburner, 1981).

13. Never give instructions until everyone is quiet and looking at you (Gervais and Dittburner, 1981).

14. Allow students to discuss critical issues and "let off a little steam" prior to indulging in quiet work (Gervais and Dittburner, 1981).

15. Explain to the student that interruptions are considered poor manners in adult society (Gervais and Dittburner, 1981).

16. Ask the student to apologize for interruptions (Gervais and Dittburner, 1981).

17. Remove the student from the classroom (Gervais and Dittburner, 1981).

18. Require the student to keep a record of times he is quiet and set up a reward system with which to reinforce him (Gervais and Dittburner, 1981).

19. Set up a system where the teacher always calls on students and no one raises their hands or yells out answers (Gervais and Dittburner, 1981).

20. If the student has made five or fewer talkouts in 50 minutes, give him a reward (Sulzer-Azaroff and Mayer, 1977).

21. Run a stopwatch while the class is quiet. Stop the watch when someone talks inappropriately. The recorded time can be used toward earning a class privilege.

22. Have a sharing time at the beginning or end of the day when students can talk about things (e.g., where they are going for vacation, what they got for their birthday, etc.) (P. Bazulka, personal communication, 1985).

23. Provide the student with five minutes at the end of class in which he can talk freely with a classmate if he is able to refrain from talking at inappropriate times during the class (L. Evans, personal communication, 1985).

24. Ignore the student completely when he is talking and attend to him when he is quiet (Martin and Quilling, 1981).

25. Have the student conduct research and give an oral report to the class to promote appropriate talking (L. Evans, personal communication, 1985).

26. Set up a specific time for the student to talk freely with you. Tell him that there are appropriate times for talking and this is one of them. Give him some examples of other appropriate times to talk (L. Evans, personal communication, 1985).

27. If the student is able to refrain from talking inappropriately for a set period of time, allow him to tape himself speaking on a tape recorder (L. Evans, personal communication, 1985).

28. Set a limit on calling-out behavior or talking. The student should know what his limits are and what the consequences will be if he stays within these limits or breaks them (Bowman, 1983).

29. Allow the student to read orally during part of reading class (L. Evans, personal communication, 1985).

30. Give the student a short article to read aloud to the class each day (L. Evans, personal communication, 1985).

153

Writes Down Answers Without Thinking

1. Praise the student for reflective writing.

2. Hold the student's writing instrument until he tells you what he will be writing.

3. Have the student recite his ideas onto audiotape before writing. Allow him to use the tape to assist in writing.

4. Review the student's paper with him to discuss the good and poor points of the product.

5. Do not accept papers that are below a designated criterion level.

6. Have the student revise his work until it meets criteria.

7. Promote the production of rough drafts that are later developed into more thoughtful products.

8. Assign the student a peer who is a reflective writer to produce a product with dual authorship.

9. Encourage the student to use self-verbalization when working individually. The student talks to himself before answering a question in order to gain control and decrease impulsivity (Millman, Schaefer, and Cohen, 1981).

10. Discuss all possible alternatives and answers with the student before allowing him to start writing.

11. Work with the student on a one-to-one basis.

12. Review each answer with the student as it is written.

13. Give questions one at a time and only after the previous answers have been reviewed by you.

18

Interaction

154

Acts Like a Little Adult, Doesn't Know How to Have Fun

1. Reinforce the student when he engages in age-appropriate activities.
2. Reinforce other students when they are participating in fun activities.
3. Encourage enrollment in after-school groups and programs that promote involvement in age-appropriate activities.
4. Arrange for increased interaction with age-group peers.
5. Plan games and fun activities that involve the student's interests.
6. Recommend a home visit by school officials to determine if the parents are going to the extreme in giving their child responsibilities or power (Rimm, 1984).
7. Teach the student to play popular games so he will be more likely to join in and enjoy activities.

8. Ask a group of students to "adopt" this student and involve him in their activities.
9. Require that the student participate in activities that you think that he might enjoy. Reinforce the student for participating.
10. If the behavior is due to a fear of getting dirty or messy, bring in old clothing that the student can wear, and provide facilities for washing or cleaning oneself.
11. Recommend that the student speak with the school counselor or school psychologist.

155

Afraid to Be Different

1. Reinforce the student for showing independent behavior.
2. Have the student defend one side of an issue while his friends defend the other side in a debate.
3. Organize a school-wide special day entitled "Start a new trend." Students are encour-

aged to wear unusual clothing and items, or to act or speak in a different manner.

4. Hold discussions that start by having students privately write their opinions on a sheet of paper. Students then read their opinion to the class as you stand by them.

5. Have people with unusual ideas or lifestyles come to your class to speak to the students.

6. Choose an issue on which you expect students to agree. Separate them so that they cannot view each other's work. Give the students one of two versions of a question (e.g., Should music albums be rated like movies? Should we avoid assigning ratings to records?). Ask the students to give you their yes or no answers only while you tally the results on the board according to yes and no answers. If the student changes his answer to be like that of his friends, you can review the question formats and why he changed his answer. If he reports his true choice, which appears to be different from that of his friends, lead a discussion on the initial feelings of each party. Develop this into a discussion on the right to disagree with friends.

7. Disagree in public with a person known to be a friend or friendly colleague. Ask the class if it appeared to hurt your relationship with the other. Let it be known that personal opinions vary among friends.

8. Have a friend of the student state an opinion and support it. Have the student mention a point of agreement and one flaw in his friend's viewpoint.

9. Assign a creative writing task in which students imagine what it would be like if everyone in the world dressed the same, talked the same, preferred the same foods, and so on. Ask the student exactly which clothes, foods, and languages should be eliminated. Have others discuss the choices.

10. Have students taste unusual foods or view unusual customs, clothing, and the like before writing their opinions on taste, beauty,

and so forth. Have the students share their opinions.

156

Aloof; Socially Reserved

1. Reinforce the student when he socially interacts.

2. Encourage parallel activities, giving the student a chance to be near group activities, but not forcing him to interact with other students (Reinert, 1980).

3. Devise activities that guarantee success in order to encourage social participation (Reinert, 1980).

4. Empathize with the student. Share your own problems about getting involved in school activities (Reinert, 1980).

5. Provide specific areas in the room for individual as well as group activities (Reinert, 1980).

6. Have the student practice social skills (Byrnes, 1984).

7. Give the student an opportunity to practice social skills with only one other student. Then gradually increase the number of students involved (Hazen, Black, and Johnson, 1984).

8. Match the student with popular peers for special projects (Byrnes, 1984).

9. Model specific social skills (Byrnes, 1984).

10. Use role playing to assist the student in seeing how his behavior affects others (Byrnes, 1984).

11. Require the student to drop his "stuck-up" attitude and participate like the other students (J. Kitchner, personal communication, 1985).

12. Arrange activities in which a person's skills and talents matter, not social status.

157

Annoys or Provokes Others into Hitting or Attacking Him

1. Closely monitor the student's behavior.
2. Reinforce the student for cooperative play.
3. Punish the student when he annoys or provokes others.
4. Tell other pupils that they are not to hit the student.
5. Reinforce other pupils when they refrain from hitting the provoking student.
6. Have other pupils bring their complaints about the provoking student to you.
7. Teach the student proper social skills via practice in hypothetical or past situations.
8. If the student actually wishes to entertain or be friendly with others, teach him to notice cues that indicate that others are becoming irritated and annoyed.
9. Review behavior expectations with the student before potential trouble situations.
10. Discuss situations with the student after they have occurred. Identify appropriate actions that should have occurred.
11. Have the student set goals for his behavior. Reinforce goal accomplishment.
12. Have the student apologize to those he provoked.
13. Recommend that the student be seen by the school counselor or psychologist.

158

Associates with Loners

1. Reinforce the student for expanding friendships and associating with new peers.
2. Accept the student's choice of friends.
3. Develop activities in which the student and perhaps his loner friends can interact with others.
4. Talk to other pupils and ask them to allow the student to join in groups or activities with which they are involved.
5. Start subgroups or clubs within the classroom, making sure that the student will be interested in at least one club (J. Bonwell, personal communication, 1985).
6. Appoint the student to assist other pupils in an academic area in which he does well.
7. Role play situations where more friends are needed (J. Bonwell, personal communication, 1985).
8. Seat the student by others who are popular and friendly.
9. Give the student jobs in the classroom that bring him into contact with many other students (J. Bonwell, personal communication, 1985).
10. In a group, have every student say or write something positive about every other student. This promotes positive interaction between students.
11. Teach the student social skills that will assist him in meeting and interacting with others.
12. Instruct the student in games and interests of other groups of students so that he can converse and play with them.

159

Attempts to Monopolize

1. Praise the student when he allows others to participate.
2. Ignore the student when he attempts to take control of a situation.
3. Ask the student to give at least two other students a chance to respond before he contributes again (N. Mulchrone, personal communication, 1985).
4. Chart monopolizing attempts and reward the student for each day that the number is decreased (N. Mulchrone, personal communication, 1985).
5. Remove the student from the situation

(N. Mulchrone, personal communication, 1985).

6. Praise other students for waiting their turn so that their behavior will serve as a model.

7. Have a "Personal Current Events" part of each day so that each child can have a chance to be the center of attention (N. Mulchrone, personal communication, 1985).

8. Allow students to speak only after having raised their hands and being recognized by you.

9. Assign duties to various students to prevent one person from assuming control.

10. Channel the student's desire by allowing him to supervise others. However, he is not to do a task assigned to another; he is only there to guide and support others.

11. Have the student mediate a debate or discussion. He is only to ask questions and clarify, not comment.

160
Comments That No One Understands Him

1. Ask the student where you can get more information to better understand him. Obtain the information from these sources.

2. Schedule a time for you and the student to talk in a personal and private manner.

3. Schedule a time each week when a different student tells the others about himself. Help the students to prepare and practice.

4. Allow the student to express his feelings or opinions in a group situation.

5. Assist the student in developing and expressing his viewpoint by teaching him the vocabulary he lacks.

6. Assist the student in supporting his views by directing him to sources of information. These research efforts will provide background information with which he can support his views and opinions.

7. Allow the student to play his favorite music and display his favorite items for others to appreciate.

8. Recommend that the student be seen by the school counselor or psychologist.

9. Have the student and his counselor/psychologist/representative tell others about his feelings or views. The student's representative may be able to translate the student's words so that others better understand.

10. Have the student make a collage from magazine pictures that shows his interests, beliefs, and feelings. Have him tell about his product.

11. Assign a bright, responsible pupil to do a report on the student of concern. The reporter spends time with the student, both in and out of school, and presents a report to the class.

12. Plan an activity in which the student plays the role of a visiting dignitary. The class plays the role of reporters who interview him by asking questions from the gallery.

161
Gullible; Easily Led by Others

1. Reinforce the student for speaking an opinion that differs from others (Reinhart, 1980).

2. Praise other students for responsible independent behavior.

3. Reinforce independent behavior.

4. Place the student in a role of authority or leadership such as team captain or line leader (Reinhart, 1980).

5. Use activities to build the student's self-confidence in order to remove the need to please others.

6. Work with the student on being assertive.

7. Provide the opportunity for the student to participate in group activities. Emphasize

the importance of each member of that group (Diamond, 1974).

8. After an incident in which the student was swayed by others, review that situation with him. Help him list alternative behaviors that could be used if this happens again. Have him choose one to use in the future.

9. Use role play and practice to teach independent behavior.

10. Team the student with a responsible, independent peer (K. Roza, personal communication, 1983).

11. Teach the student to engage in reflective thinking as he enters into spontaneous group activities. Have him ask himself: Why do I want to do this? What are the possible consequences of my actions? Are the others being friendly to me or are they trying to "use" me for their own pleasure?

12. In a debate, have the student defend one side of an issue while his friends defend the other side.

13. Present a hypothetical situation in which a group is trying to influence someone to do something. List various reactions by this individual. Have the student list the pros and cons of each choice.

162

Holds a Grudge

1. Pinpoint the specific reason for the dislike of a particular person.

2. Reinforce the communication between the involved students. Arrange for the students to be around each other more often in order to ease the tension (Harris, 1980).

3. Provide alternatives to this behavior (e.g., instead of having a grudge toward another, positive feelings with one another might be a better alternative) (Harris, 1980).

4. Increase the student's tolerance level for behavior (Walker, 1979).

5. Have the involved students work together

in interesting cooperative activities (J. Mette, personal communication, 1984).

6. Tell the students that what has happened is in the past and should stay there. Now it is time to move on. Have them shake hands (J. Mette, personal communication, 1984).

7. Require apologies for wrongdoings (J. Mette, personal communication, 1984).

8. Have the student list five nice things about the other student.

9. Ask the student to forgive, even if he can't forget.

10. Accept the grudge holding as long as the student does not attempt to gain revenge.

11. Have the student list the pros and cons of holding a grudge against a person.

163

Not Receptive to Opinions of Others

1. Reinforce the student when he listens receptively to the views of others.

2. Provide for brainstorming and other creative exercises that allow the student to broaden his opinions (K. Webster, personal communication, 1985).

3. Role play situations in which the student must react in a way contrary to his own opinion (K. Webster, personal communication, 1985).

4. Inform the student that his opinions are not the only ones and that respect for others is important (K. Webster, personal communication, 1985).

5. Provide for an accepting and unintimidating classroom atmosphere to increase the degree of receptiveness to the opinions of others (J. Webster, personal communication, 1985).

6. Ignore the nonreceptive behavior and leave the student to himself (Dreikurs, 1972).

7. Have the student identify one positive aspect of the other side of the argument.

8. Have the student mediate an opinionated discussion between two persons without stating his opinion. Have the student model television news interviewers.

9. Teach debating skills and hold a debate.

10. Have the student restate another's opinion in his own words before stating the flaw in that statement.

11. Have the student defend a viewpoint contrary to his own during a debate.

12. Do not allow the student to use demeaning remarks (e.g., "That's stupid" or "What's wrong with you?"). Require him to use more polite language (e.g., "I disagree with your statement" or "Your statement is not backed by facts").

13. Videotape a news program in which persons with opposing viewpoints discuss an issue. Choose one in which the participants are respectful of each other.

14. Have the student and another with an opposing viewpoint negotiate and present to you a written compromise. Explain how this is often done when countries disagree on an issue. Devise a treaty.

7. Require that the student apologize to those who were tricked.

8. Have the misbehaving student do something nice for those who were tricked (J. Noirfalise, personal communication, 1983).

9. Reinforce other students for proper behavior (Spivak and Swift, 1975; Kerr and Nelson, 1983).

10. Catch the student's attention with a nonverbal signal before disruptive behavior gets out of control. Reinforce the student if inappropriate behavior ceases (Spivak and Swift, 1975).

11. Use role playing and behavioral rehearsal to teach new social skills (Kerr and Nelson, 1983).

12. Recommend rational-cognitive therapy which changes an individual's thoughts, beliefs, perceptions, and attitudes (Newcomer, 1980).

13. Play a prank or trick on the student. Use this as an opportunity to discuss his behavior and the feelings of others.

14. Contact the student's parents to enlist their assistance.

164

Plays Tricks or Pranks on Others

1. Reinforce the student when he forewarns another of a planned trick or does not follow through on a prank.

2. Implement negative consequences for these behaviors (Sprick, 1981).

3. Discuss the problem and have the student set goals for proper behavior (Sprick, 1981).

4. Ignore the behavior as long as it is tolerable (Spivak and Swift, 1975).

5. Place the student in time-out (Kerr and Nelson, 1983).

6. Provide instruction for appropriate social skills (Kerr and Nelson, 1983).

165

Rejected by Peers

1. Complete a sociogram and set up activities in which the rejected student is paired with accepting, considerate students (K. Hitchler, personal communication, 1983).

2. Reinforce the other students when they are accepting, working, or playing with the students who are often rejected (K. Hitchler, personal communication, 1983).

3. If rejection is caused by an acting-out behavior on the part of the student, set aside a secluded area where he can act out. However, set a time limit on how long he can stay in this area, and reinforce him when he is not in the area (K. Hitchler, personal communication, 1983).

4. Set up a group activity and assign duties so

that the student won't be left out (K. Hitchler, personal communication, 1983).

5. Incorporate a buddy system. Arrange a one-to-one relationship in which the student works with another more accepted student on a project that is fun for both (K. Hitchler, personal communication, 1983).

6. Encourage peer reinforcement of appropriate behavior and ignoring of inappropriate behaviors (K. Hitchler, personal correspondence, 1983).

7. Plan activities that demonstrate the strengths and skills of the student.

8. Create as many successful experiences for the child as possible (C. Walters, personal communication, 1984).

9. Have the student present a successful project to others (K. Szumlas, personal communication, 1983).

10. Influence the other students to praise the student occasionally (C. Walters, personal communication, 1984).

11. Teach social skills to the student.

12. Teach the student about topics and activities that are of interest to others so that he can converse and play with them.

13. Ask a group of students to "adopt" this student and teach him "the ropes."

166
Rude; Unmannered

1. Reinforce the student when he is polite and respectful to others.

2. Reinforce others for respectful behavior.

3. Punish the student for rude behavior.

4. Have the student restate his rude words into more appropriate language.

5. Require the student to apologize to the offended person.

6. Have the student do something nice for the offended person to make restitution.

7. Role play situations and have the student practice being polite and respectful.

8. Give the student a listing of unmannered reactions and rude comments. Have him revise these into polite words and actions.

9. Be rude to the student. Use this as an opportunity to open a discussion on this behavior and the feelings of others.

10. Contact the student's parents to request their assistance.

11. After each rude or unmannered interaction, ask the student how he could have handled the situation differently. Have him list alternatives and choose one that he will use in the future.

12. If you see the student about to engage in rude behavior, ask him, "How are you going to handle this politely?"

13. Teach the student to speak silently to himself when he feels hostile. Some possible thoughts might be: "Stop. How can I let this person know how I feel in a polite manner?" and "What is the best way to react in this situation?"

167
Style of Behavior Is Deliberately Different from Others

1. Set limitations on classroom behavior. Enforce your rules.

2. Reinforce the student when he behaves as others do (K. Luebke, personal communication, 1985).

3. Work with the student on an individual basis to develop social skills (M. Lantero, personal communication, 1985).

4. Do not laugh, show anger, or otherwise reward his behavior (Yamamoto, 1972).

5. Firmly take the student aside and let him know immediately that such behaviors or speech are not acceptable (Yamamoto, 1972).

6. Isolate him from others until he is able to control himself (Yamamoto, 1972).

7. Explain that behaving cooperatively with others can be a positive experience (K. Luebke, personal communication, 1985).

8. Explain to the student that rewards in life are usually earned by behaving in a way that is valued by other people and satisfies their needs or conforms to their expectations (Cohen, 1966).

9. Provide the student with a better position in the school group and give much more recognition for positive accomplishments (Yamamoto, 1972).

10. Have the student set a personal behavioral goal each week. Reward the student if goals are met.

11. Work with others to develop a respect for individuality.

12. Use role playing to provide practice in displaying more accepted behavior.

13. Give presentations and conduct discussions on how societies and groups develop flags, customs, and values to form a cohesive, functioning group. Explain that there are bounds to nontraditional behavior beyond which one's rebellion causes rejection by others.

14. Refer the student to the school counselor or psychologist.

19

Learning Difficulties

Confusion/Disorganization

168

Confused About Directions and How to Get Around the School Building or Grounds

1. Send an escort with the student who will assist him only if necessary.

2. Give the student written directions to carry.

3. Teach the student how to read a map and give him a map of the school to carry.

4. Review the route to be taken before the student leaves the classroom.

5. Take the student on a tour of the school. Point out important landmarks.

6. Ask the school administration to paint or create landmarks to assist students in finding their way.

7. Teach the student the proper way to ask for directions.

8. If the student does not yet know his left and right, draw a red mark on the right hand and a blue mark on the left hand. Tell the student to "turn red" or "turn blue" at various points.

9. Ask the school administration to paint different colored footprints on the floor or lines on the walls that extend from various important places in the school (e.g., office, gym). This would serve to help students follow the correct route.

10. Conduct a practice walk with the student and return to the classroom with him. Have him then retrace the route alone.

11. Go with the student to his destination. Have him return alone.

12. Follow the student at a distance and assist if needed.

13. Build an open model of the school. Have the student move a doll or toy figure through the correct corridors.

169
Disorganized

1. Reinforce organized behavior or attempts at organization.

2. Have students fill out a time use chart indicating how many hours a week are used for recreation, studying, TV, and so on. Make no judgment on the initial list. For the second week, schedule additional study time of 30 minutes for each class. Discuss modifications of this time after the second week. Continue to work on this throughout the semester (McCabe, 1982).

3. Have parents assist at home by providing "homeplay." This will most likely be a daily task that requires sequencing and organization, such as setting the table (Silberman, 1985).

4. Practice sentence writing by making word cards, each containing a word or phrase. The student needs to put them in a logical order to form sentences (Johnson and Myklebust, 1967).

5. Use jigsaw puzzles as a free-time activity. This helps the disorganized student see and work toward whole relationships and not just see meaningless parts (Johnson and Myklebust, 1967).

6. Work in small time slots of 15 to 20 minutes with everything that needs to be completed written down. The student will see that things have a beginning that lead to an end (Silberman, 1985).

7. Begin the school day with a five-minute writing exercise for both the students and the teacher. Everyone is required to write about anything he wishes for exactly five minutes. When the time is up, everyone must stop. If the student insists that he has no ideas, a standard list of "old favorites" can be used, such as "What I did on my summer vacation," "What I would do with three wishes," and so on. Getting down to business immediately upon entering school helps the student to organize himself better (Douglass, 1984).

8. Have the student color-code essential materials, such as using a different color notebook and book cover for each subject (Cohen, 1984).

9. Assist the student with a time table of due dates by using a large calendar to note when each assignment must be completed. Refer to this often (Weiss and Weiss, 1982).

10. Ask the parents to assign a spot where all school materials can be placed that need to be brought to school the next day.

11. Ask the parents to post a list to be checked by the student before leaving for school each day.

12. Give written sequential directions for task completion to the student.

13. Point out that each assignment is a different kind of task and requires a different amount of time spent on it. Discuss and organize with the student how to go about attacking homework assignments each day (Simms, 1983).

14. Develop a study skills questionnaire that includes such points as location of studying, environment, attitude, methods, and planning the length of time needed. Discuss the weak areas and how to improve them (McCabe, 1982).

15. Explain to the student that his brain is like a computer program without a manual. In order to understand the material, it must be broken down into small chunks and the brain must be trained to understand a specific task (Dansereau, 1985).

16. A disorganized student needs to be taught to use multiple passes in his reading assignments. That is, read through the assignment at least twice—the first time to gain a broad picture of material, and the second to gain a more intensified understanding (Dansereau, 1985).

17. Explain and review with the student the concept that each textbook chapter has three parts. The beginning introduces the idea, the middle gives the detail, and the end gives examples and summaries. He can use this information in attempting to find

specific information for test review or for completion of a worksheet (Dansereau, 1985).

18. Have the student work along with a prerecorded audiotape message to complete assignments.

19. Insist that the student date every paper he receives in classes along with the notes taken. This will help organize and sequence the order of the instruction (J. Richter, personal communication, 1985).

20. After each incident of disorganization, review with the student what should have been done.

21. At the beginning of each class, tell the student what will be covered, what materials are needed, and what behaviors are expected.

22. For young students, chart (with words or pictures) all necessary activities, such as hanging up coat, changing into sneakers, sitting at desk, and the like, including everything that needs to be completed in both the morning and the afternoon routines. He can then check off each activity as it is completed (J. Richter, personal communication, 1985).

23. Help the student organize his desk by having a specific place for everything: crayons in boxes, pencils and erasers in pouches, and so on. He will be able to prepare for work in a much shorter period of time (J. Richter, personal communication, 1985).

24. Complete daily sequencing activities to help the student learn that there is a pattern to everything. These might include following a pattern of beads or paper chains, lining up the class alternately according to sex or eye color, and so on (Johnson, 1967).

25. Teach the student to use keywords and pegwords to memorize items in a sequence. One especially good technique is a mnemonic device of rhyming words *one* through *ten* (one–bun, two–shoe, etc.). Once he learns this list, he can learn to memorize information dealing with all academic areas (Mastropieri, 1984).

26. Use the other students in the room to help the student organize his opinion, such as, "The drinking age should be changed to 21." Students then move to a corner of the room, with each corner being marked with one of the following: approve, strongly approve, disapprove, and strongly disapprove. Each group then discusses its feelings, writes down ideas, and reports to the others (Caldwell, 1976).

27. Help the disorganized student make a crossword puzzle, starting with an easy word search or fit-type puzzle. Begin by listing words common to an area of study. Take the two longest words and make one vertical and one horizontal. Insert as many others as possible. Have another student in the class do the puzzle first to check for flaws. The "creator" can then share this puzzle with others. As he begins to develop confidence with these, start to use puzzles with clue words and sentences, assisting him as much as necessary (Caldwell, 1976).

28. Use a timer to encourage the student to complete work and use free time more effectively (Martin and Martin, 1984).

29. In printed material, make sure that all letters are complete on the student's copy. A blurred sentence may cause the student to misunderstand what is to be done, or to lose some important point of the assignment (Johnson, 1967).

30. Begin each day with an itinerary of what is to be completed during the course of the day. As each is completed, check it. This can also be done on an individual level where the student reads the plan with the teacher at the beginning and then checks each item as it is completed (J. Richter, personal communication, 1985).

31. Have a "buddy" in the room make sure that the student has all assignments written down and all books and notebooks ready to take home before he leaves school for the day (J. Richter, personal communication, 1985).

32. Preview material to be read by checking

topics and subtopics found in the chapter. Form some questions that he should be able to answer after completing the reading assignment (J. Richter, personal communication, 1985).

170

Does Not Seem to Understand Materials or Directions Given

1. Make the directions clear and simple (Davis, 1981).
2. Present the student with the information and then ask others to present the same information in other words (Clubok, 1983).
3. Repeat the directions a number of times through a variety of approaches before having the student attempt the task (Clubok, 1983).
4. Carefully explain the assignment to the student and give him many drills, examples, illustrations, and reviews (Davis, 1981).
5. Ask the student to repeat the directions in his own words (Davis, 1981).
6. After carefully giving the student the directions, ask him to write them down for future reference (Swift and Spivak, 1975).
7. Have a logical sequence of learning assignments so that the student can see the transition from one step to the next (Davis, 1981).
8. Task analyze the task that the student is to do and present the directions through step-by-step modeling (T. Marlier, personal communication, 1984).
9. Work with the student and make a list of the steps to follow when doing the assignment (Landers, 1984).
10. Structure the information by presenting it in graphic form. For example, outline the directions through a diagram, map, or chart (T. Marlier, personal communication, 1984).

11. Make a card containing the steps of the directions and tape it to the right-hand corner of the student's desk (Swift and Spivak, 1975).
12. Present the steps needed to complete a task in picture form on the blackboard (Swift and Spivak, 1975).
13. Ask the student to analyze information. Ask him, "What needs to be done first?" (Davis, 1981).
14. Encourage and teach the student to ask questions for clarification by being a "good" questioning model and by reinforcing the student's questioning behavior (Kidder, 1984).
15. Overcome your frustration and the student's resentment with understanding, patience, and encouragement (Crowley, 1969).
16. Send work home with the student and insure his success by working with the parents. Establish a session routine and set session goals for team work between parent and student (Landers, 1984).
17. Allow the student to practice following directions on a microcomputer (Lovett, 1973).
18. Find materials that are of interest and hold relevance to the student.
19. Start at a lower level of instruction so that the student can be successful (J. Bonwell, personal communication, 1984).
20. Work individually with the student (J. Bonwell, personal communication, 1984).
21. Assign a peer assistant to help the student with assignments and projects.
22. Present material through different learning modalities (auditorily, visually, kinesthetically).
23. Teach the necessary prerequisites to complete a task.
24. Place directions on an audiotape so that the student can review as necessary.
25. Have the student complete one step before you give the next direction.
26. Play "Simon Says."

27. Play a game that involves following sequentially longer directions each time.

171

Easily Confused; Problem-Solving Difficulties

1. Reinforce the student when he thinks or acts in a nonconfused manner.

2. Teach mnemonic strategies to assist the student in memorization (Gelzheiser, Solar, Shepherd, and Wozniak, 1983).

3. Provide the student with extended practice to enable the skills to become automatic and for generalization to occur (LaBerge and Samuels, 1974).

4. Provide the student with a plan or strategy to approach a learning situation (Miller, Galanter, and Pribram, 1960).

5. Provide a clear understanding of the goal and encourage the student to value that goal in order to motivate him (Miller, Galanter, and Pribram, 1960).

6. When speaking to the student, speak clearly. Understanding of the sentence, instructions, and so on is affected by the context of the sentences heard before. A student often selects some parts of the context and ignores others (Broadbent, 1977).

7. Provide a demonstration or model the procedure to reduce student confusion (Davey and Porter, 1982).

8. Some television shows present interesting, life-related problems and also demonstrate creative and systematic ways of solving them. Encourage the viewing of these programs (Brown, 1983).

9. Play problem-solving games with the student.

10. Give the student practice in real-life problem solving (Brown, 1983).

11. Allow the student to work with a skilled peer.

12. The process of solving problems requires a blend of knowledge and skills related to the content areas. Teach the student the skills and knowledge together. Too often such skills and knowledge are taught in isolation (Brown, 1983).

13. Practice, although necessary, is not sufficient. Direct instruction is also required, along with gentle encouragement, for the student to think a little more about what he does and how he does it (Brown, 1983).

14. Have the student keep a daily "learning log." The student will then be able to identify points of confusion, formulate questions for further study or clarification, and recognize important insights (Bondy, 1984).

15. Provide opportunities for feedback on the student's understanding. For instance, allow the student to adopt the role of teacher and present information to another student. Additionally, the student can attempt to carry out activities about which he has studied, such as science experiments (Bondy, 1984).

16. Provide instruction in self-questioning techniques so the student does not rush through an assignment simply to "get it done." Discussion and practice of "fix-up" strategies (e.g., rereading, looking back for examples of similar assignments, studying examples provided, and surveying the body of the assignment for clues) may reduce the number of times a teacher needs to repeat the information or the number of times a student needs to redo the assignment (Bondy, 1984).

17. Ask the student to repeat the directions to be sure that he understands (M. B. Dean, personal communication, 1985).

18. Orally read or tell a story to the student about someone who gets easily confused, and discuss the story after you are finished. Talk about different ways the person could have handled the situation (L. Abernethy, personal communication, 1985).

19. Have the student ask for help when needing assistance.

20. Break the assignment into smaller sections.

Have the student check with you after the completion of each part.

21. Allow the student to ask a friend for clarification.

22. Be sure that the student has the prerequisite capability to engage in actions appropriate to goal attainment (Miller, Galanter, and Pribram, 1960).

23. Eliminate extraneous visual and auditory stimuli (Mosse, 1982).

24. Allow the student to work at his own pace (Mosse, 1982).

25. Instruct the student in concentration exercises that combine body movements with relaxation, breathing, and rest periods. All movements are connected with a logical thought or idea so that the student has to keep a "set" of attention in mind while he is exercising. This strengthens his concentration span (Mosse, 1982).

26. Instruct the student to use external retrieval cues that can prompt remembering of an event to help reduce confusion (e.g., a timer, an alarm) (Meacham and Colombo, 1980).

8. Provide a model or demonstration to assist understanding (Davey and Porter, 1982).

9. Allow the student to work with a peer.

10. Encourage the student to browse, skim, or survey written material before reading it more closely (Anderson, 1980).

11. Encourage the student to question himself during the task (e.g., "Does this make sense?" "Did I do that correctly?") (Anderson, 1980).

12. Encourage the student to ask questions when he doesn't understand.

13. Give one direction at a time. Require the first one to be completed before giving another.

14. Task analyze the task and have the student do one part at a time.

15. Present directions in many ways (e.g., visually, auditorally, tactually).

16. Be sure that the student has the prerequisite skills and knowledge to understand the presentation or task. If not, teach them.

17. Allow the student to ask a friend for clarification.

172
Never Seems to Understand

1. Praise the student when he listens well and understands.

2. Give directions and statements in short, simple language.

3. Have another student explain the material in different words.

4. Have the student repeat your directions in his own words.

5. Be sure that the student is maintaining eye contact and is attentive when you speak.

6. Preface your remarks by saying, "Now listen carefully."

7. Remove distracting auditory and visual stimuli (Mosse, 1982).

173
Poor Deductive Reasoning

1. Reinforce the student when good deductive reasoning is demonstrated.

2. Teach the student how to perform deductive reasoning.

3. Give hints and cues to assist the student.

4. Give the student a list of randomly ordered items that must be placed in order to reach a conclusion.

5. Give a list of randomly ordered items that may or may not help derive a conclusion. Have the student eliminate extraneous information and place pertinent items in order.

6. Have the student use inductive reasoning. Then have him reverse the order to reach a conclusion.

7. Pair the student with a peer who is a good deductive reasoner. Have the peer assist and explain.

8. Give examples of poor deductive reasoning (e.g., All men are mortal. Socrates was a man. Therefore, all men are Socrates). Have the student point out flaws in the reasoning.

9. Use classroom exercises to make the logic clearer to the student.

10. Give a conclusion. Have the student research why that conclusion is valid.

11. Engage the class in philosophical dialogue (Alvino, 1984).

174

Poor Inductive Reasoning

1. Reinforce the student when good inductive reasoning is demonstrated.

2. Teach the student how to perform inductive reasoning.

3. Provide hints and cues to assist the student.

4. Give an answer to a problem. List steps to arrive at the answer in random order. Have the student order the steps correctly.

5. Give an answer to a problem. List items that may or may not lead to that conclusion. Have the student eliminate extraneous information and order pertinent steps.

6. Give the student a conclusion and have him research information that would lead to this conclusion.

7. State a classroom rule. Have students give reasons why it is important.

8. Give a hypothetical event (e.g., a snowstorm that lasts for one year). Have students list possible implications.

9. Give examples of poor inductive reasoning. Have the student point out flaws in the reasoning.

10. Have the student use deductive reasoning

to reach a conclusion. Then have him reverse the process.

11. Pair the student with a peer who is a good inductive reasoner. Have the peer assist and explain.

12. Engage the class in philosophical dialogue (Alvino, 1984).

13. Suggest to the student that to understand something is to "reinvent" it. Advise the student to put himself into the inventor's shoes and then describe the events.

175

Poor Thinking and Reasoning Skills

1. Reinforce the student's behavior when he puts together simple thoughts (S. Kennedy, personal communication, 1984).

2. Cut out frames of comic strips and have the student sequence the frames together in a logical order (B. Smith, personal communication, 1984).

3. Have the students write correctly formed sentences (Axelrod, 1977).

4. Teach the student how to make an outline (Axelrod, 1977).

5. Verbally lead the student through a thought process (S. Kennedy, personal communication, 1984).

6. Have the students practice group brainstorming on a problem (Axelrod, 1977).

7. Teach logic, inductive reasoning, and deductive reasoning.

8. Ask the student about consequences of behavior, next steps in a project, and so on.

9. Help enhance a student's critical thinking skills by pointing him toward independent, logical, and even ethical thinking through encouragement of philosophical dialogue (Alvino, 1984).

10. Provide direct, systematic classroom instruction in how to use thinking skills in all

appropriate content areas and across all appropriate grade levels (Beyer, 1984).

11. Fuel the mind of a student with perceptions—the basic activity of thinking. To sharpen his thinking is to stimulate creativity (Crow, 1984).

12. Improve memory skills by promoting closer attention, rehearsing the information to remember, linking new information to something already known, and forming mental pictures (Farrell, 1984).

13. Challenge a student by using a computer. Select software that asks the student to solve problems, not merely indicate predetermined answers (Naiman, 1985).

14. Teach the student what processes to use, when and how to use them, and how to combine them into workable strategies for task solution (Sternberg, 1985).

15. Suggest to the student that to understand something is to "reinvent" it. Advise the student to put himself into the inventor's shoes and describe the events.

16. Screen out seatwork activities that require low-level cognitive (factual) response. Convert them from rote, "single-correct answer" activities into thinking activities (Wassermann, 1984).

17. Promote the association of events that surround an experience, as this has a great bearing on how a student will remember. Much of his memory depends on the context in which an event occurs (Weingartner, 1985).

18. Generate repeated opportunities to apply the skill (Beyer, 1984).

19. Recognize, respect, and give reinforcement for questions, mental manipulations, or unusual thinking (Alvino, 1984).

20. Help the student focus on the problem task by first analyzing it step by step, testing hypotheses, and gradually building up an accurate mental model (Naiman, 1985).

21. Select instructional materials that require a student to process data cognitively instead of merely regurgitating facts (Wassermann, 1984).

22. Devise measures of competence in the use of thinking skills that are congruent with the skills chosen to teach. They should be valid and reliable (Beyer, 1984).

23. Suggest that the student use whatever tricks his imagination can devise to aid in memory (Berkowitz, 1983).

24. Collect a series of reading materials to engage the classroom in discussions and exercises that help in identifying, simulating, and learning ways that better thinking can be distinguished from poorer thinking (Steinberg, 1985).

25. Encourage a student to apply logical thinking to all kinds of assertions and situations. Provide opportunities to practice behaviors that reinforce analysis and open-minded reflection (Alvino, 1984).

26. Allow a student to select a partner to work together as a pair to solve problems. One student thinks through a problem aloud while the other student checks for accuracy and keeps the problem solver verbalizing his thoughts and actions (Beyer, 1984).

27. Assess teacher-student interactions by tape-recording them. This will help you decide if you are eliciting a single correct answer as opposed to promoting an independent student functioning level. The student should ask questions, accept fewer things at face value, and become more critical in his appraisals (Wassermann, 1984).

28. Help the student recall hard-to-remember information by using memory aids such as mnemonics. For example, *Sam's Horse Must Eat Oats* is a way to remember the Great Lakes: Superior, Huron, Michigan, Erie, and Ontario, from west to east (Farrell, 1984).

29. Shift the emphasis in education from the routine, repetitive activities that have been identified as basic skills to a higher order of critical thinking or reasoning skills.

30. Introduce, explain, and demonstrate a thinking skill in considerable detail, after which the student immediately applies the skill, reflects on it, and discusses the procedures he used to do it (Beyer, 1984).

31. Deal with problems thoughtfully. Promote an attitude of "Look and think before you leap." The main aim is to help the student simplify his pattern of thinking into a habit of "reasonableness" instead of "impulsiveness" (Blanshard, 1984).

32. Devise a game-like activity that uses cards to distinguish between fact and opinion (Hanford, 1984).

33. Remembering numbers can be recalled by dividing them into chunks and associating the chunks with other known numbers. For example, 747-1225 could be remembered in two chunks: 747 as a type of airplane, and 1225 as the date of Christmas (Farrell, 1984).

34. To solve a fixed problem from a different perspective or to come up with new ideas, new experiences help sharpen the student's thinking ability (Crow, 1984).

35. Include all kinds of mental operations (e.g., broad, general processes, discrete micro-operations, and the combination of operations involving analysis and evaluation that is commonly designated as critical thinking) for an effective program designed to teach thinking skills (Beyer, 1985).

36. Use repetition. Focus on the overlearning of materials (Berkowitz, 1983).

37. Teach the student to think intensely about what is being read or heard. Have the student relate those facts to information he already knows (Weingartner, 1985).

38. Develop a sequential approach in teaching thinking skills, beginning from grades K through 12. This approach assigns responsibility for instruction, reinforcing and expanding specific skills in specific subject areas at specific grade levels or when the skills are appropriate for the student's cognitive development (Beyer, 1984).

39. Capitalizing on concentration is the first step in memory improvement. To get the student back on the track of thought after he has been distracted, recommend that he take three seconds to visualize himself doing the original task before returning to work (Berkowitz, 1983).

40. Engage the student in the use of problem-solving software; for example, a maze game where he attempts a simple maze until he understands the process. Then he moves into more complex patterns, forming a mental map of each maze (Naiman, 1985).

41. Reserve time in the classroom for conversation, analysis, and reflection. Provide 20 minutes each day for discussion of such things as the value of work, the nature of cooperation and competition, and the role of developing relations between governments (Kohl, 1985).

42. Teach the student that all problem solving must begin with the internalization of the problem. Learning proceeds best when based on a student's need to solve a problem (Shermis and Barth, 1984).

43. Think about the things you want the student to encode and make them meaningful by relating them to something already known (Weingartner, 1985).

44. Identify and clearly define a core of thinking skills and the components of these skills. For example, comprehension involves translation interpretation and extrapolation. Then devise and implement a developmental curriculum that integrates the teaching of selected thinking skills and their combined use within various content areas (Beyer, 1984).

45. Require the student to be responsible for defining a problem. The adequacy of the definition will depend largely on the intelligence, information background, and ability of the teacher to guide him to information sources (Shermis and Barth, 1984).

46. Model the desired behavior. Draw reasonable conclusions from information found in various sources, whether written, spoken, tabular, or graphic, and defend conclusions rationally (Hanford, 1984).

47. Encourage a discussion and sharing of peer procedures used to solve a problem successfully (Beyer, 1984).

48. Stress the importance of patience and persistence in order to tolerate repeated failure

and learn from it. This also includes learning from success by eliminating notions that prove not to fit and by testing and retesting hunches that seem to work (Naiman, 1985).

49. Provide exercises in recognizing inductive and deductive reasoning. Supply the student with opportunities so that he can identify and formulate problems as well as propose and evaluate ways to solve them (Hanford, 1984).

50. Utilize activities in which the student lists pros and cons of an argument. This is a high-order thinking skill.

51. Become familiar with Bloom's taxonomy. Be sure to give questions and assignments that include the higher levels of thought.

Math

176
Lacks Basic Arithmetic Processes

1. Begin with blank index cards. Write 10 problems on each card with the answer next to each. Clip a slip of paper over the answers and have the student complete the problems as fast as he can. Record the student's time and errors. Reward the best time and least errors with the title of "Arithemetic Champ of the Day" (Purcell, 1985).

2. Have the student put together math puzzles. On one side of the puzzle piece, write a math sentence. The middle pieces will contain the answer and the end piece will contain the inverse operation problem. Have him match the problem to the answer and to the inverse operation problem (Hiebert, 1984).

3. Make a game with two math wheels with numbers from 0–9 along the outside. In the center between the wheels make a slide rule with the different operations. Have the student choose the operation and spin each wheel and complete the operation using the two numbers that come up on the wheel. Students may compete or work independently (M. Hannon, personal communication, 1985).

4. Have the student figure out the value of different words when the consonants in the word are assigned a numerical value (e.g., $B = 2$, $C = 3$, etc.) and vowels are assigned a negative value (e.g., $A = -5$, etc.). The words that are "worthless" are those whose letters add up to zero. Have him make a list of "worthless" words (Putnam, 1984).

5. Give the student a math sentence with a sign missing. Have him decide which operation is needed to make the sentence true. This may be expanded to include a sentence with several operations. Have the student try to make up his own sentences to stump his classmates (Houghton Mifflin, 1984).

6. Have the student make number line sections the length of each number (e.g., 5 would be 5 inches long). Give him problems and have him solve them by using the sectional pieces placed end to end along the number line (M. Hannon, personal communication, 1985).

7. Have the student complete the math problem using concrete objects in the classroom (e.g., students, desks, etc.) (L. Davis, personal communication, 1985).

8. Drill the student's counting abilities by having him count backward and forward on a given number line. As he improves, increase the interval of counting (e.g., counting by 2s, 3s, etc.) (Baroody, 1984).

9. Have a student move a game piece around

a game board while completing math problems. The board may include optional spaces such as free space, go back one, lose a turn, and so on. The student advances one space for each problem that he solves correctly (L. Davis, personal communication, 1985).

10. Have the student figure out the solutions to real-life problems with concrete materials. For example, John and Mary went to the store and bought 2 quarts of milk and 3 loaves of bread. How many items did they bring home? The student could use pictures of the items or the actual items to supply the answer (M. Hannon, personal communication, 1985).

11. Have the student participate in the "Take Away Game." (This can be modified for use with the other operations.) He counts out a number of marbles and places them under his hand. Another student takes away a certain number of marbles and gives the mathematical sentence to indicate the process just illustrated. The answer is checked by counting the remaining objects under the hand (Thompson and Van deWalle, 1984, citation unavailable).

12. Have the student play the "Comparative Game" in which he lines up blocks or pulls apart beads into two different columns. The opposing player compares the two columns and gives the mathematical sentence to indicate the comparison. This may be modified for multiplication and division operations (Thompson and Van deWalle, 1984, citation unavailable).

13. Have the student practice addition problems by adding up the objects found in a set of little drawers. Fill match boxes with small objects and have the student count all the objects in the boxes he chooses. The student may then do the inverse operation of the problem (Learning, 1984).

14. Give the student cut-outs or articles of clothing with different word problems on them. The student must solve the problems and hang the article and the answer on the clothesline with a clasp clothespin (Learning, 1984).

15. Have students wear signs with numbers on them. Give them directions to find the person who is wearing the number needed to solve their math problem (e.g., Who is twice your number? Find the person who is the sum of your multi-digit number.). Have the students make up their own problems.

16. Have the students make a deck of "Math Cards." Deal the cards face down. Have each student turn one card up and tell the solution to the designated problem. If the student fails to answer correctly, his opponent gets a turn. If both parties fail, the card is put in a kitty. The student with the most cards at the end of the game is the winner.

17. Have the student compute a page of math problems in 60 seconds. These should be basic facts. The student receives credit only for the problems answered correctly up to the first error. He does not receive any credit for problems after the first error. Graph results to show improvement.

18. Have the student make graphs to indicate the multiplication tables. On the left side of the graph the student would indicate the answer, and on the bottom side he would indicate the multiplier. The bars up the graph would be the product of the multiplier times the number that the graph represented. A separate graph would be used for each multiple (e.g., for the 2s tables, the student would look on the 2s graph and find the 4 along the bottom, follow it up the bar, and get the answer of 8) (Friebel, 1974).

19. Have students race around a game board by moving the number of spaces indicated by the answer to a problem. The first person to reach the end is the winner. The problems can be written on flash cards or given by the teacher.

20. Have the students lay out a series of cards that are the answers to the problems you want to reinforce. The number of cards is optional, but a good figure is about 10.

Have him roll dice and complete the operation desired. He then removes the card with the answer on it. The winner is the person who ends up without any cards on the table (Friebel, 1974).

21. Using two sets of cards numbered from 1 to 18, the player chooses to roll one, two, or three dice in any given turn. The object of the game is to pick up one card equal to the sum of the dice. The game is over when all the cards are picked up. The player with the most cards is the winner (Friebel, 1974).

22. The student rolls five dice. By using any and all operations, he tries to come up with the mathematical sentence of the highest value for the series of numbers. The student calls out the largest answer he can find and the other students compare their answers to the one called out (Friebel, 1974).

23. Have the student make himself a set of domino cards. Each card has dots spaced equally apart and in columns and rows so that there are the same number of dots across as there are down. The student will then use the cards to complete the different math questions. Addition will be completed by adding the number of dots on the two cards, and subtraction will be used by turning over the smaller card and covering up the number of dots it represents (Friebel, 1974).

24. Draw an outline of a football field on the board. Divide the class into two teams of players. The offensive team takes turns answering questions. For each correct answer, the team advances 10 yards. If the first student cannot answer, the next two players get to try. If all three cannot answer, the teacher will provide it. They will then roll a die with the following rules: 1—the team kicks a 50-yard punt; 2—a 40-yard punt; 3—a 30-yard punt; 4—a 20-yard punt; 5—a block and the defensive team recovers the ball; and 6—the defensive team recovers and runs with the fumbled ball. The die is then rolled to tell how far the defensive team advances (each number on the die stands for 10 yards). When one team reaches its goal line, it scores six points and has the option of attempting a one- or two-point conversion. Any player on the team may answer either conversion question. The ball then goes back to the opponent on the 50-yard line (Best, 1985).

25. Prepare 45 pairs of cards, each pair containing an addition fact whose sum is 10 or less. Shuffle all 90 cards and deal 5 to each player. The object of the game is for the players to take turns and get books of cards that add up to the same number (e.g., $4 = 1 + 3$ and $4 = 2 + 2$). The players who cannot make a pair choose either the face-up card or the top card in the draw pile. If the player chooses a card that goes along with one of the books on the table, he places it with the book. If not, one card must be discarded. If a player picks up from the discard pile he may take the card he desires and any card after it. The winner is the player with the most books on the table at the end of the game (Learning, 1985).

177
Poor Arithmetic Reasoning

1. When teaching mathematics to the student, try to keep in mind two language and one math considerations: (a) What am I saying? (b) What is the student saying? and (c) What are the mathematics saying? (Fisher, White, and Fisher, 1985).

2. To make language meaningful in mathematics, teach words for situations. Point out that when words come together in a particular arrangement, the meaning comes from that situation. If the problem states "There were 18 players who were going to be broken up into three teams," the student may think that the players were going to be hurt and may not understand "divide" in this situation. Drawing pictures demonstrating the division of 18 players into three teams may help clarify the use of the division process (Fisher, White, and Fisher, 1985).

3. Help the student look at the context as a way of distinguishing two homonyms (e.g., *some* means a part of, a few, as in some of the cake or some of the money; *sum* means the result of adding two or more numbers as in the sum of 2 and 3, or the sum of *x* and *y* (Fisher, White, and Fisher, 1985).

4. Show the student that relationships change as situations change. Do this so he understands that the rules are not being changed arbitrarily. For example, if the student thinks that the multiplication of two numbers always results in a larger number, and that the division of two numbers always results in a smaller number, then he may feel tricked when instructors multiply 5 × 2/5 and get 2. The student must see that the relationship changes as the situation changes, and that if you multiply a given number by a number less than one, then the answer is less than the given number (Fisher, White, and Fisher, 1985).

5. Clarify the words *reduce* and *cancel* when using them in the classroom. *Cancel* is really dividing in mathematics. One doesn't cancel anything. Something is still there. The student might think of *reduce* as "make smaller." *Reduce*, as it is used sometimes in math, means write in a different form. It does not mean "make smaller" (Fisher, White, and Fisher, 1985).

6. The division process refers to a combination of steps. Refer to division as "the division process" so the student sees there is a progression with several pieces that must be put together (Fisher, White, and Fisher, 1985).

7. Help the student learn the concept of naming things differently. Show him that using a number and a word is possible in a compound name. Use a dash between the number and the word. When the problem says "eight 8 cent flowers," the student may think, "I know what a red flower is. What does an 8 cent flower mean? Is this two 8s and a cent?" Place the dash so that the "eight 8 cent flowers" would look like "eight 8-cent flowers" (Fisher, White, and Fisher, 1985).

8. Construct a money line. Use the money line to develop skill in counting various combination of coins (Frank, 1978).

9. Use two money lines to demonstrate equivalent forms of money (e.g., 25 cents = two dimes and one nickel or four nickels and five pennies).

10. Use concrete materials to aid in problem solving. Concrete symbols such as fingers, lengths of wood, or pebbles are symbols that behave in accord with the rules of mathematics. The student is better able to generalize a reasoning principle when he works with a concrete medium (Williams, 1952).

11. Correct the student's learning while it is in progress. This is extremely important in a subject like mathematics in which various parts of the subject matter are so interdependent. If a student acquires a mistaken idea about one part, he is unlikely to be able to make sense of other parts. The student becomes habituated to inefficient methods of problem solving unless he is continually given information about his progress (Williams, 1952).

12. Create a positive atmosphere when teaching or talking about mathematics.

13. Organize your math program around a topic in which your student is highly interested.

14. Use motivational methods, such as earning a piece of candy for a homework fact sheet, as opposed to a more traditional method, such as "Do pages 19–21 for homework."

15. Train the student to determine the "wanted-given" structure in problems. All one-step problems are in one of four major categories:
    a. If what is *wanted* is the "size of the total (sum)" and what is *given* is the "size of each part (addends)," then add.
    b. If what is *wanted* is the "size of a part" and what is *given* is the "size of the total and the size of one part," then subtract.

c. If what is *wanted* is the "size of the total (product)" and what is *given* is the "size of equal parts (factor) and the number of equal parts (factor)," then multiply.

d. If what is *wanted* is the "size of the equal parts" or "how many parts of equal size" and what is *given* is the "size of the total," then divide (Glennon, 1952, citation unavailable).

16. Define words and concepts when assisting the student in order to help him understand the process of reasoning.

17. Encourage the student to discover patterns in mathematics such as the commutative property, based on specific observations in the physical world (e.g., 3 cuisinaire rods + 3 more cuisinaire rods = 6 cuisinaire rods).

18. Urge the student to explore and discover using concrete objects, which will help develop his thoughts about mathematics (e.g., discovering the next color in a pattern using attribute blocks: "Red, white, red. What should the next block be?").

19. Have the student substitute smaller and easier numbers for problems with larger or more complex numbers so that he can understand the problem and verify the solution more easily.

20. Have the student restate the problem in his own words. The verbalization may help the student structure the problem and show whether he understands it.

21. Supplement textbook problems with your own. These might deal with classroom experiences. Include students' names to make the problem more realistic.

22. Allow the student enough time to complete the problem. Ask for alternative methods for solving the problem. Try to determine how the student thought about the problem and went about solving it.

23. Create a key to which the student can refer in order to choose the correct operation in a problem story. The key could be similar to the following:

Total, all together, *in all*—ADD

How much more? How many more?—SUBTRACT

One weighed 10 pounds. How much did *seven* weigh?—MULTIPLY

Joey shared *equally*—DIVIDE

(G. Maul, personal communication, 1985).

24. On a large chart, show a step-by-step sequence of operations.

178
Poor Math Concepts

1. Use concrete objects (e.g., formboards, pegboards) to teach size relationships such as big/small, long/short, and the like. The student must be able to differentiate and grade sizes, quantities, and measurements before he can use abstract number concepts (Frierson and Barbe, 1967).

2. Use colors (e.g., crayons, chalk) to teach the differentiation of rows and such concepts as "beginning of the row," "end of the row," "next row," "first," "middle," and "last" (Frierson and Barbe, 1967).

3. Have the student perform activities to help him understand concepts (e.g., form a row versus walk in single file) (Frierson and Barbe, 1967).

4. Teach the student to use the "Finger Scheme." Many students have difficulty making appropriate use of their fingers. This is our native structure of the number system and one on which the student can always rely (Frierson and Barbe, 1967).

5. Employ vividness or imagery to develop number word-object associations. Tell the student to picture one close friend or two close friends in his mind (Reisman and Kauffman, 1980).

6. Emphasize patterns that generate the sequence to be matched. For example, match a set of dominoes to a set of playing cards (Reisman and Kauffman, 1980).

7. Use familiar songs (e.g., "The Twelve Days of Christmas") that contain words involving numbers. Introduce Pascal's triangle—a

pyramid of numbers in six rows with many variations to teaching addition and subtraction, to reinforce the song by using special colors and making certain designs in the figure to create and expand understanding of the number concepts used (Dugle, Brown, and Cook, 1982).

8. Provide the student with multimodel input. Encourage him to handle, see, and talk about an object's properties (Reisman and Kauffman, 1980).

9. Teach about number concepts, especially the concept of one-to-one correspondence, through role playing. Have the student classify characters (e.g., doctors, fire fighters) with their specific jobs. To take the role playing one step further, re-create a particular work environment in the classroom. During the building, mathematical questions should arise: How high? How long? How wide? and many more (SanAndres, 1979).

10. Use a token reinforcement system to increase correct student responses to math worksheet exercises (Ayllon, Layman, and Kandel, 1975).

11. Model correct procedures for the student while describing each step involved. The procedure is then left on the student's desk as a permanent model to which he can refer when necessary (Smith and Lovitt, 1974).

12. Supply the student with immediate feedback. Scoring the correct and incorrect responses on his paper may be enough to induce permanent changes (Blankenship and Lovitt, 1976).

13. Use peer tutors to help underachievers. Train high-achieving students to speak clearly, praise appropriate behavior, ignore inappropriate behavior, correct errors, and provide appropriate instructions (Johnson and Bailey, 1974).

14. Have the student verbalize the requirements of a math exercise and give the answer aloud (Lovitt and Curtiss, 1969).

15. Train the student by using a sorting presentation of pictures to improve memory and conceptual development. Show the student pictures and ask him to classify by conceptual aspects (Worden, 1976).

16. Present unrelated words. The student classifies the words with pictures using free or constrained sorting (Worden, 1975).

17. Teach the student to use a *start state* and an *end state*. The *start state* helps the student identify the referential and contextual sources of the relevant information from which a solution may be extracted. An *end state* specifies the goal that must be reached for the problem to be solved (Wilkinson, 1976).

18. Use concrete objects or pictures when teaching concept analysis (Markman and Siebert, 1976).

19. Use concrete objects paired with number concepts to teach one-to-one correspondence (Reisman and Kauffman, 1980).

20. Use paired-associate learning (i.e., the student pairs a relationship between particular stimuli and responses). At every opportunity, match number words with objects (e.g., "I have one cookie." "I have two cookies.") (Reisman and Kauffman, 1980).

21. Use redundancy and point out relevant dimensions (Reisman and Kauffman, 1980).

22. Employ familiarity to develop number-word-object associations. Label various sets of familiar objects with different number qualities (e.g., one color, two legs, five fingers) (Reisman and Kauffman, 1980).

23. Use familiar categories to insure meaning for the student. Have the student sort familiar pictures or objects into two groups (Reisman and Kauffman, 1980).

24. Control irrelevant stimuli that may be included in a learning activity. If the student is to attend to the shape of the geometric figure, omit unnecessary attributes such as colors and textures (Reisman and Kauffman, 1980).

25. Combine paper-pencil practice with moderate amounts of calculator practice. The hand-held calculator is an effective alternative device for reinforcing the student's un-

derstanding of basic math concepts such as place value and counting (Bitter, 1979).

26. Use numbers that are interesting to the student (e.g., the number of hockey games the New York Islanders have won) (Arnsdorf, 1979).

27. Ask the student to show answers to problems on his fingers (Arnsdorf, 1979).

28. Give special directions such as, ''I want you to pay very close attention to this'' (Arnsdorf, 1979).

29. Pause after saying something of importance.

30. Use questions to encourage guessing (Arnsdorf, 1979).

31. Give appropriate verbal praise to encourage repeated student participation (Arnsdorf, 1979).

32. Allow the student to use the chalkboard and overhead projector (Arnsdorf, 1979).

33. Include choral reading. Have the entire class read important facts aloud (Arnsdorf, 1979).

34. The interactivity, graphics, and motion capabilities of the microcomputer, as well as its ability to store information, make it a useful tool in the formation of mathematical concepts. Program a computer to varying instructional formats that can serve as drill and practice, tutorial, simulation, dialogue, game, or diagnosis and remediation modes for the teacher and student (Billings, 1983).

35. Have the student do sorting tasks. Give him objects that differ in only one attribute. Continue to increase the complexity of the classification to two and three attributes (Lerner, 1985).

36. Provide activities to help the student focus on and recognize a single object or shape (e.g., matching and sorting). Such activities can include looking in a box of beads for a yellow one, choosing the forks from a box of silverware, and so on. (Lerner, 1985).

37. Help the student develop the concept of

groups by using domino games, playing cards, felt boards, magnetic boards, and mathematic worksheets (Lerner, 1985).

179

Poor Math Skills

1. Provide written practice with soft verbal praise (Kelly and McLaughlin, 1983).

2. Use materials that relate to the student's experience, interest, and creativity (e.g., if the student likes trucks, devise math problems that involve gas usage, mileage, and cargo weight) (Jones, 1983).

3. Use concrete materials and real-world situations (Danforth, 1978).

4. Use daily short drills as review (Osborn, 1980).

5. Present directions in several different ways to insure understanding (Danforth, 1978).

6. Provide the student with a list of steps that, when followed, will help him complete the math problems.

7. Institute peer tutoring (Sharpley, 1983).

8. Use bulletin boards for pictorial graphs, tally charts, and other activities (Alton, 1982).

9. Use music and songs to teach math rules and procedures.

10. Set up learning centers (Manning, 1980).

11. Use computers to stimulate interest (McDermott and Watkins, 1983).

12. Use precision teaching techniques (Montana State Board of Education).

13. Use visual cues and notes written on the assignment paper to remind the student of proper procedures.

Memory

180

Forgets Learned Material

1. Praise the student when he remembers learned materials.
2. Provide hands-on experience when it is possible to do so.
3. Teach the same material in different ways.
4. Review material daily.
5. Use game-like activities for difficult subjects.
6. Establish a regular study routine (Robinson, 1975).
7. Motivate the student in particular areas of study by using materials and topics of interest to him.
8. Develop the student's interest in the material (Robinson, 1975).
9. Teach patterns, rules, or general principles (Highbee, 1977).
10. Teach the student to associate the new materials with something already known (Highbee, 1977; Elliot and Carrol, 1980; Torgesen, 1985).
11. Be sure that the student is paying attention and concentrating (Underwood, 1976).
12. Reduce interferences and distractions in the room (Highbee, 1977).
13. Help the student organize information and material so it will be easier to retrieve when wanted (Lorayne, 1973).
14. Teach acronyms as a memory enhancer (Lorayne, 1973).
15. Have the student recite to himself what has been learned (Robinson, 1975).
16. Develop memory games.
17. Be sure that prerequisite material is learned before moving on to more advanced material (Underwood, 1976).
18. Use the SQ3R technique: Survey, Question, Read, Recite, and Review (Highbee, 1977).
19. Give hints to the student to remind him of the answer.
20. Let the student know what you consider to be a "good answer" (K. Keefer, personal communication, 1983).
21. Provide a cue item to the student along with each new item learned (Goodson, 1984).
22. Review cues frequently and practice the association with learned material (Goodson, 1984).
23. Activate recall in different settings and at different times of day (Thompson and Shapiro, 1984).
24. Use a picture reinforcement of material to be memorized (Baumeister, 1984).
25. Use the iconic memory by videotaping material to be learned and utilize pictorial essays to reinforce new material (Baumeister, 1984).
26. Create a happy and cheerful atmosphere of learning so as to maximize retention (Clark and Teasdale, 1982).
27. Have the student attempt to recall learned materials at different intervals with varying moods, times, and methods (Frame and Oltmann, 1982).
28. Use rehearsal to aid recall of learned material. Practice recalling in short term so as to maximize long-term memory (Swanson, 1983).
29. Use pig Latin to rehearse the student's memory (Mann and Liberman, 1984).
30. Have the student use rhymes to increase word retention (Mann and Liberman, 1984).
31. Use games such as counting in multiples and number patterns to increase memory span (Mann and Liberman, 1984).
32. Have the student repeat poetry and spoken sentences (Mann and Liberman, 1984).

33. Have the student recite learned passages (Mann and Liberman, 1984).

34. Use simple and immediate repetition in presenting new materials (Worden, Malmgren, and Gabourie, 1982).

35. Have the student label simple objects and then attempt to recall the names as they are shown (Lewis and Kass, 1982).

36. Have the student make posterboards of objects to be learned and recalled (Lewis and Kass, 1982).

37. Present immediate recall tasks like concentration games when parts are shown, concealed, and then recalled (Lewis and Kass, 1982).

38. Promote verbal rehearsal over visual imagery to insure auditory memory for future recall (Rose and Cundick, 1983).

39. Have the student use melody patterns to strengthen auditory memory (Valett, 1983).

40. Have the student utilize songs and jingles to retain new material (Valett, 1983).

41. Have the student utilize chants and singing to strengthen auditory memory (Valett, 1983).

42. Use pegboard word pictures and flash cards to aid in learning new material (Mastropieri, 1985).

43. Have the student label items and make cue cards to be used for learning new material (Bayliss and Livesey, 1985).

44. Have the student perform some simple retrieving tasks that involve memory. For example, present a display board that shows pictures of items located around the room. Request that the student locate the items and bring them back to you in the same order as they appear on the board (Kops and Belmont, 1985).

45. Use a display board of letters and have the student retrieve letter cards that are exactly the same as those on the board. Color code the cards to assist memory.

46. Using a display board, introduce some words. Instruct the student to find the word cards that are exactly the same as

the ones on the board, and return them to the board in the order that they appear (Kops and Belmont, 1985).

47. Use a display board to present a math problem (e.g., exhibit 4 pencils and 5 books). Encourage the student to count the items and to give his answer. Then encourage him to retrieve the number of pencils and number of books from the room that is equal to the number presented on the board. Have him count them to see if the answer is correct (Kops and Belmont, 1985).

48. Use a mnemonic association strategy to help the student retain learned material (Mastropieri, 1985).

49. Use multisensory instruction to increase time on task, which subsequently increases student learning (Thorpe and Borden, 1985).

50. Reinforce memory of words from a list by requiring the reader to decide whether a word fits into a given sentence (Torgsen, 1985).

51. Encourage control strategies to enhance memory performance on a specific task. Examples of some control strategies are: rehearsal (repeating items over and over); elaboration (thinking of verbal or visual associates); clustering items by meaningful relationships; or proper apportionment of study time by using the study-test-study method (Torgsen, 1985).

52. Recall of subject matter can be facilitated when students are allowed to listen (e.g., audiotaped lessons) and when the information is presented in conversational form (Deshler, Schumaker, and Lenz, 1984).

53. Cue students when lecturing or reading to them to activate the monitoring strategies of when, who, how, why, and where (e.g., "Following this passage, I will be asking you questions regarding the content of what we have just read") (Bos and Filip, 1984).

54. Reduce the size of the unit of response in order to create a high probability of suc-

cess, and provide consistent positive reinforcement for correct performance. Present only one or two sentences followed by a commanded response. Build toward a paragraph and so forth after the former is mastered (Treiber and Lahey, 1983).

55. Have the student say items aloud (Swanson, 1983).

56. Work on improving memory with short-term, free-recall tasks. Present the student with stimuli (e.g., words or pictures) for several seconds and then ask him to remember as many of them as possible (Hallahan and Sapona, 1983).

57. Offer the information from a variety of media (e.g., textbooks, films, lectures, discussions, overhead transparencies) (Hallahan and Sapona, 1983).

58. Encourage the student to paraphrase, question, or summarize the material presented (Hallahan and Sapona, 1983).

59. Use associative clues. Instruct the student to visualize previous associations and to verbalize his idea of the word, sentence, or paragraph (Grant, 1985).

60. Use the "keyword" method. Think of a good word that sounds as much as possible like the word to be learned and picture it in some interactive way with the information to be learned. For instance, to teach the Shakespearean word *bodkin*, which means dagger, the learner is taught to think of a picture of a dead *body* stabbed by a dagger (Scruggs and Mastropieri, 1984).

61. Use the "pegword" method, which involves retrieval of ordered information. This is a rhyming scheme in which a pictured word, which rhymes for each number, is given (e.g., one = bun, two = shoe, etc.). For instance, to remember that Jackson was the seventh president, the learner first thinks of a keyword for Jackson, which could be *jacks*, and associates it with its pegword for 7, which is *heaven*. An image of angels playing jacks in heaven might be pictured (Scruggs and Mastropieri, 1984).

62. Use attribute learning whereby one phe-

nomenon is associated with several others. For example, to remember that bauxite is number 1 on the hardness scale, white in color, and used in making aluminum, one could picture the keyword for bauxite as *box*. The box may be colored white. Aluminum foil in the box with buns can represent the use and the buns represent the hardness level (Scruggs and Mastropieri, 1984).

63. Enhance **visual** imagery by encouraging dream **recall**, listening to descriptive stories, playing memory games such as concentration, watching cloud formations, retaining after-images, and doing all forms of drawings including free, programmed, doodling, sketching, and upside-down (Forrest, 1981).

64. Promote visual imagery to build vocabulary. For example, for the word *annual*, write: "once a year." Ask the student to see himself in his mind, blowing out candles on his once-a-year birthday cake. Ask him to use the word *annual* in a sentence. Ask him once again to close his eyes and think of another situation that he could do "annually" (Grabow, 1981).

65. Use visual imagery to teach writing. Place dots with numbers along the outline of a large capital letter and have the student say each number as he traces from dot-to-dot with his finger. Then he closes his eyes and traces the letter on his imaginary chalkboard with the numbers and later without (Grabow, 1981).

66. To facilitate recall, have the student categorize related material into groups (Bousfield, 1953).

67. Provide the student with organized input or encourage him to organize it (Becker and Morrison, 1980).

68. Avoid lessons utilizing "semantic" questions (i.e., those restricted to the recall and processing of factual information) rather than "episodic" questions (i.e., those that encourage the student to relate personal experiences to lesson content) which enable him to recall new information better (Dalton and Lynch, 1976).

69. Create a mindset for listening. Say, "I will ask you to name the items in this poem that are the same color as the cat" (Gold, 1981).

70. Move throughout the class. Gesture and pause. This activity has a positive correlation with student recall of presented material (Henson, 1980).

71. Incorporate music into lessons. Familiar tunes may trigger the recall of words or phrases (B. Furmanek, personal communication, 1985).

72. Have the learner continue to repeat the names of items that are no longer available or visible in order to keep them alive in memory (Brown, 1972).

73. Provide the student with as many visual cues as possible. Associate these with the auditory channel. For example, have the student follow a book while hearing it read, or have him read aloud (Berryman and Perry, 1974).

74. Turn your back, clap your hands twice, slap your knees three times, and so on. Then have the student imitate the sequence of sounds (Berryman and Perry, 1974).

75. Give the student a list of nonsense syllables or proper words. Repeat the list, leaving out one syllable or word. Have him identify the one left out (Berryman and Perry, 1974).

76. Have the student listen to a record or the radio each day to obtain specific information, such as a weather forecast (Berryman and Perry, 1974).

77. Play the restaurant game. One student plays the waiter and must remember the orders to give to the chef (Berryman and Perry, 1974).

78. Use concrete, manipulable objects during reading to tie the abstract words to meaningful situations. For instance, as the student finishes a sentence such as "The cow jumped over the fence and crossed the river," he manipulates the arrangement of objects on a flannel board (Elliot and Carrol, 1980).

79. Play "Do This." Place five or six objects in front of the student and give a series of di-

rections to be followed (e.g., "Put the green block in Jean's lap and the yellow flower under John's chair"). Increase the number of directions as the student improves (Lerner, 1985).

80. Ask the student to answer questions about a series of numbers (e.g., "Write the fourth one: 3, 8, 1, 9, 4") (Lerner, 1985).

81. Play "Going to the Moon." Say, "I took a trip to the moon and took my space suit." The next student repeats the statement but adds one item to the list (e.g., helmet). Continue through the group (Lerner, 1985).

82. Dictate and have the student repeat. Start with short, simple sentences. Later, use compound and complex sentences (Lerner, 1985).

181

Forgets Names of Classmates, Teachers, and School Personnel

1. Reinforce the student when he remembers the names of others.

2. Play "add a word" games involving names. For example, "When my grandmother went to China she met Bill." The next student would add another name after "Bill" (L. Schiffman, personal communication, 1986).

3. Speak to the school staff and explain to them that this student has difficulty remembering the names of individuals. Tell the staff you will be sending this student with "written messages" and when he arrives, to engage him in a casual conversation. Familiarization with these individuals might help his memory (L. Schiffman, personal communication, 1986).

4. Ask the forgetful student to ask other students about their families, pets, and favorite pastime. Associating his classmates with "mind" pictures might help him to remem-

ber names (L. Schiffman, personal communication, 1986).

5. Ask the student who he does remember. Try to figure why and how he does remember certain people, and then apply that information to others (L. Schiffman, personal communication, 1986).

6. Tell the student how much more well liked he will be if he calls others by their names. The student will be more accepted by everyone when he can refer to them personally (Carnegie, 1936).

7. Have the student draw a picture of the principal with the principal's name underneath. For fun, you can say the principal is sponsoring a contest for a portrait and will be giving a reward for the best selection (J. Feder, personal communication, 1986).

8. Give the student hints when he is having difficulty remembering someone's name.

9. Teach the student to associate a person's name with a prominent personal characteristic (e.g., Nice Nancy, Tall Ted, Laughing Larry).

10. Make a schedule that lists the people the student is most likely to meet at certain times. Before these times, review the names of these people.

11. Have a board containing the pictures of persons whose names are often forgotten by the student. Review these with the student.

12. Have the student refer to certain persons by initials, nicknames, or shorter names (e.g., Mr. B., P.J., Red).

182
Forgets What to Do

1. Reinforce the student when he remembers what is to be done (B. Foote, personal communication, 1985).

2. Attempt to help the student mediate his moods. Recall of material is much better if a student is in the same mood during recall as when the material was first learned (Fallone, 1985).

3. Study the student's mood; severely depressed students often have recall problems. If necessary, suggest the student be examined by the school psychologist (Fallone, 1985).

4. Utilize external retrieval cues to remind the student (e.g., pinning a note to the student, writing the task to be done on paper, and placing the object in plain sight of the student) (Ceci and Bronfenbrenner, 1985).

5. Work on organizational skills with the student (Weingartner, 1985).

6. Provide frequent breaks or varied activities to allow for mental rest and absorption of material (Weingartner, 1985).

7. Describe events that are associated with an experience and give proper cues. Events surrounding an experience have a great bearing on how students remember it (Weingartner, 1985).

8. Think about the things the student is encoding and make them meaningful by relating them to something that he already knows (Weingartner, 1985).

9. Suggest to the parents that they consider having their child eat foods with the substance lecithin, which is a building block for the chemical that is known to piece learning and memory together (Weingartner, 1985).

10. Insure that the student is paying attention. Anything that diminishes the student's attention detracts from the encoding process that fixes memory (Berkowtzi, 1983).

11. Have the student study "What you have to do" line by line, not all at once. Remembering information is influenced by whether the information was memorized by linear, beginning-to-end fashion, or all at once. Linear is better for more successful recall (Parks, 1985).

12. Remembering is a skill that gets better with practice. You can help the student improve a faulty memory just by having him pay closer attention, rehearse the information

to be remembered, link new information to something already known, and form mental pictures (*Good Housekeeping*, 1984a).

13. The time of day is very important in immediate recall. The best time for recall ability is late in the morning, especially around 10:00 A.M. For learning information you want students to remember for a long period of time, studies indicate that studying should be done at home between 6:00–8:00 P.M. (*Good Housekeeping*, 1984b).

14. Promote eustress (positive anxiety). Up to a point, moderate stress stimulates memory. Extreme stress, the kind produced in a life-threatening situation, impairs memory (*Good Housekeeping*, 1984b).

15. Promote nonalcoholic studying. Alcohol interferes with the ability to remember (*Good Housekeeping*, 1984b).

16. Use leading questions to influence how a student remembers something (e.g., "What are you going to study tonight Michael?") (*Good Housekeeping*, 1984b).

17. Suggest to the parents that they consider having their child eat more fish. Some scientists say fish contains large amounts of choline, a chemical that is a precursor of acetycholine, a neurotransmitter utilized in memory.

18. Sing your assignments to a popular song melody.

19. When your students forget what to do, don't become annoyed. Forgetting occasionally can be a valuable tool. It is said that the human brain remembers only 1 out of every 100 pieces of information it receives. Scientists claim that if we remembered everything, then all humans would be paralyzed by information overload (Finn, 1985).

20. Teach the student to classify information systematically. If a student classifies well, his chances of remembering are greater (Elwell, 1985).

21. Recommend that the student and parents paste, hang, or tape large notes in a visible place (e.g., on a mirror, refrigerator, bath-room sink, or in a shoe or wallet) (B. Lynch-Herod, personal communication, 1985).

22. Have the student make a list of all things he must accomplish in a specific time frame (e.g., in an hour, a day, week, or month). Tape the list to his desk. When he remembers to accomplish a task and actually finishes it, he should scratch it out (B. Lynch-Herod, personal communication, 1985).

23. Have the student utilize mnemonic devices to create mental pictures of what has to be done (Berkowitz, 1983).

24. Purchase a paper pad with the title, "Things I Gotta Do!" List the things that must be accomplished underneath (M. Herod, personal communication, 1985).

25. Train your student to concentrate and relive previous events that took place. He could remember what his mother wanted from the store by closing his eyes and replaying in his mind what happened and what was said (L. Smielinski, personal communication, 1985).

26. During the school day, occasionally stop teaching, put on a popular record, and conduct exercises. This may awaken students, and motivate them.

183

Has Difficulty Drawing Designs and Symbols from Memory

1. Praise the student when he draws accurately from memory (A. Arnbold, personal communication, 1986).

2. Point out the distinguishing properties of each shape (Gibson, 1969).

3. Have the student analyze the distinctive properties of the shapes (Woodworth, 1938).

4. Differentiate as many attributes of the shape as possible (Maccoby and Bee, 1965).

5. Provide many opportunities for practice and review (Hodges, 1982).

6. Develop a story mnemonic. Draw the shape as you tell a story about it (Hodges, 1982).

7. Have the student trace inside and outside cardboard stencils while noting the distinctive features of each shape verbally (Beloit Public Schools, 1980).

8. Cut shapes from construction paper. Draw a pencil border approximately one inch from the edge. Have the student staple around the perimeter of the shape on this line (Sorrell, 1978).

9. Have the students identify strengths and weaknesses in their shapes drawn from memory (Columbia Department of Education, 1981).

10. Have the student observe someone else making the shape (Columbia Department of Education, 1981).

11. Have the student tear paper into given shapes (Columbia Department of Education, 1981).

12. Encourage the student to verbalize what he is doing as he is drawing a shape from a model or from memory (Barkin, 1981).

13. Have the student trace over the teacher's shape using a marker of another color. Provide auditory directions (Barkin, 1981).

14. Guide the student's hand or place the student's hand on yours as the shape is formed (Barkin, 1981).

15. Have the student close his eyes while drawing the shape. This helps to "fix" the image (Burton, 1982).

16. Ask the student to analyze the parts of the shape aloud. Many students profit from a "first we do this and then we do this" approach (Burton, 1982).

17. Use the fading process. Fading involves the presentation of a stimulus first in a strong, clear fashion, then gradually reducing the clues until the learner can function without them (Burton, 1982).

18. Reinforce concepts particular to the writing act to help the student focus on the writing process. These concepts include: up and down, top and bottom, and vertical and horizontal (Kaminsky and Powers, 1981).

19. Enhance motor memory by activating the large muscle system. Encourage the student to write in the air and to work on large surfaces such as the chalkboard or newsprint (Kaminsky and Powers, 1981).

20. Have the student copy a shape or a drawing in a step-by-step fashion (Van Witsen, 1979).

21. Use color cues to highlight the lines composing the shape (Barkin, 1981).

22. Prepare a series of large cards, each containing a shape. Use white cardboard and a black marking pen or black construction paper letters or shapes. While in a dark room, have the student trace over the outline of the shape using a small flashlight. Demonstrate the strokes and have the student verbalize directions (Wedemeyer, 1975).

23. Fill a shallow tray or cookie sheet with damp sand. Following your directions and demonstration, have the student draw shapes with his finger or a stick. Prepared cards containing shapes can be given to the student to copy in the sand prior to having the student form shapes from memory (Wedemeyer, 1975).

24. Make shapes with a stylus on "magic" toy slates (Burton, 1982).

25. Have the student form shapes in the air with a nose or an elbow (Burton, 1982).

26. Have one student draw a shape on another's back and have the receiver guess what was drawn (Burton, 1982).

27. Practice forming shapes in the air on an imaginary blackboard with and without a model (Burton, 1982).

28. Provide a set of sandpaper shapes for tracing. Several sets, using sandpaper ranging from very coarse to very fine, is even better (Burton, 1982).

29. Encourage the student to remember what he sees. Show the student a shape. Wait a

while and then ask the student to point at or talk about the shape (Ford, 1983).

30. Draw two figures. Make one a dot-to-dot outline and the other a complete shape with connecting lines. Have the student study the complete shape and then connect the dots on the outline figure to make it like the complete shape (Molnar and Reighard, 1984).

31. Draw several shapes on white paper using heavy black ink. Place paper, thin enough to see through, over the shapes. Have the student trace the shapes first with his finger and then with a pencil or crayon (Molnar and Reighard, 1984).

32. Have the student close his eyes and describe a shape (Molnar and Reighard, 1984).

33. Make a shape in a clay pan. Have the student trace it. Next, have the student write it. A clay pan is made by using a foil pan or box lid and spreading modeling clay in the bottom (Molnar and Reighard, 1984).

34. Have the student form shapes using geo-blocks or sets of geometric figures made from cardboard. Begin by having the student imitate the procedure. Then, move to designing of cards. Finally, have the student form the shape from memory (Wolf, 1982).

35. Draw a shape leaving out one part. Have the student draw the missing part (Warner, 1973).

36. Arrange craft sticks to form shapes. Rearrange them while the student's eyes are closed. Then ask him to place them in the original order (Warner, 1973).

37. Play a memory game. Describe several shapes as you show them to the student. Remove the shapes from sight, give the student clues, and have him guess the one of which you are thinking (Warner, 1973).

38. Using a slide projector or overhead, flash a shape on a screen momentarily. Have the student tell what he saw (Warner, 1973).

39. Have the student practice forming shapes in sand, cornmeal, salt, and fingerpaint (Burton, 1982).

40. Have the student stretch elastic bands to form shapes on geoboards (Burton, 1982).

41. Play "Humpty-Dumpty Dominoes." Decide what shape is to be constructed. Place dominoes on their edges so they are standing upright and so that upon toppling one, it topples the next, and so on, until the newly constructed design has the same design as when the dominoes were standing. The game may be played with or without a shape pattern card on which to arrange the dominoes (Sorrell, 1978).

42. To assist the student in drawing a shape from memory, mark a starting point for each shape and verbalize the direction and shape of the stroke (Frostig and Maslow, 1973).

43. Use rhymes and songs to aid recall. For example, the fingerplay below helps the student focus on the distinguishing features of three basic shapes (Hodges, 1982).

Draw a Circle

Draw a circle, draw a circle
Round as can be;
  (Draw a circle in the air with pointer finger)
Draw a circle, draw a circle
Just for me.
  (Point to self)

Draw a square, draw a square
Shaped like a door;
  (Draw a square in the air with pointer finger)
Draw a square, draw a square
With corners four.

Draw a triangle, draw a triangle
With corners three;
  (Draw a triangle in the air with pointer finger)
Draw a triangle, draw a triangle
Just for me.
  (Point to self)

44. Teach prerequisite skills, such a directional-

ity and topography: *in-out, right-left, up-down, top-bottom, under-over, beginning-end, tall-short, on-off, big-little, oblique, diagonal, slanting, one, two, three, around, across, middle, center, curve, trace, vertical, horizontal, circle,* and *straight line.* With the acquisition of these key vocabulary words the student and teacher can describe the images to be mastered (Ebersole, Kephart, and Ebersole, 1968).

45. Task analyze the components of the design or symbol and teach a simple shape component first. When the student can reproduce the shape, add another component, until the whole design has been mastered (R. Hayes, personal communication, 1985).

46. Have the student feel the shape by tracing a sandpaper letter. Next, have him trace the letter in a shallow plate of salt or sand. Repeat the procedure until the student can trace the letter in the salt without feeling the sandpaper letter first (J. Curlington, personal communication, 1985).

47. Have the student first trace an image or symbol. Gradually fade the image by decreasing the intensity of the image that the student is tracing, until it is barely visible. Next fade out parts of the image and have the student trace the shape, thus connecting the parts together. Continue to fade the image (R. Hayes, personal communication, 1985).

48. Using chocolate pudding on a plate, draw a letter or shape while the student is watching. Wipe the plate clean, and have the student draw the same shape with the pudding and his finger. If the student draws the shape correctly, he can eat a fingerful of pudding (L. Stern, personal communication, 1985).

49. Guide the student in imaging by having him listen to verbal cues, which become more and more specific (e.g., "Close your eyes and imagine an apple. Can you see it? Do you have a small picture of it in front of you that you can see? If so can you count the blemishes on it?"). After he has had

some success envisioning, have him draw what he saw (Hendricks and Wills, 1975).

50. Have the student frequently reproduce the same design or symbol. The item will quickly become stereotyped and thereafter suffer little change (Frostig and Maslow, 1973; Bartlett, 1964).

51. Present the student with a shape or figure drawn on a card and then remove it from his sight. Ask him to copy it from memory (Mott, 1974).

52. Use guided imagery to have the student rehearse an act of drawing from memory. For instance, "See yourself, in your mind, getting up from your chair and walking to the chalkboard. There is a piece of colored chalk, whatever color you see is fine. Pick it up and write or print your name as large as you can across the board. (Pause) Now, starting from the last letter, erase your name, one letter at a time, backwards." After the student imagines this, provide colored chalk and have the student enact the image (Shorr, Sobel, Robin, and Conella, 1980).

53. Have the student add a novel detail to a symbol or design as a cue to trigger the memory (Bartlett, 1964).

54. Have the student use a verbal description, name, secondary association, or analogy to aid recall (Bartlett, 1964).

55. Using an etch-a-sketch, create a simple shape while the student is watching. Erase it and have the student repeat the process with the same design (L. Stern, personal communication, 1985).

56. Using a "magic slate," draw a simple image or letter on the screen while the student is watching. Lift up the screen to erase the image. Have the student draw the same design on the "magic slate" (L. Stern, personal communication, 1985).

57. Use cues to trigger the memory for the desired response. In a group of symbols, choose a target symbol that will be the trigger cue (Ackerman and Rathburn, 1984).

58. Give the student several simple symbols on

a piece of paper. Allow the student to look at them for as long as he wants and then remove the paper. Give him a piece of paper in which several of the symbols are present and one or two are missing. Have the student draw the missing symbols (Cruickshank, 1977).

59. Expose a simple pattern for a few seconds. Remove it and have the student draw it from memory (Faas, 1972).

60. Have the student look at something that will deeply impress the student (e.g., a burning candle). Next, have the student close his eyes and imagine the sight in his mind, after which the student will discuss or draw the image from memory (Hendricks and Wills, 1975).

61. Take the student on a nature walk and point out items of interest on the way. Have the student draw some items from the walk when he returns to the classroom (Hendricks and Wills, 1975).

62. Using symbols drawn on cards, show the picture to the student and then cover it with a plain card the same size. Gradually remove the cover, exposing a little bit of the picture at first and increasing the visible amount as it moves down the card. As soon as the student recognizes the shape, have him stop and draw the shape on a piece of paper (Cruickshank, 1977).

63. Begin with a simple word like *was*. Have the student slowly underline the word with his finger as he says the word. Then have him trace the word with his fingers as he says the sound for each letter. After that, have him copy the word using a pencil and paper. Finally, have him cover the written word and write it from memory (Hall, 1969).

184

Has Difficulty Remembering the Sequence of the Alphabet

1. List the letters A–H on a ditto. Then make a recording containing the following script: "Look at number one. The letter next to it is an *A*. Point to it and say, 'A.' Look at it very carefully and say 'A' again." Continue through the list of letters in a similar fashion. The student may also be requested to trace or write the letters. Once these letters have been mastered by the student, this process can be repeated with the remaining letters (Ekwall, 1985).

2. Ask the student to arrange upper- and/or lower-case letters sequentially on a flannel board, using a model if necessary (Herr, 1961).

3. Paste pictures representing the letters of the alphabet on 4 × 6 cards. Also paste a half-inch strip of cardboard at the bottom of each to form a pocket. Ask the student to place small upper- and/or lower-case letter cards in the pocket of the card whose picture begins with that sound. Then have the student arrange the cards in proper sequential order (Herr, 1961).

4. Make a ditto with the letters of the alphabet listed sequentially, leaving some letters out. Ask the student to fill in the blanks. As the pupil becomes more proficient, more and more blanks may be used (D. Pernick, personal communication, 1986).

5. Make tagboard cards with the letters of the alphabet written in dotted lines for the student to trace. Cover the cards with clear contact paper so that they may be reused (D. Pernick, personal communication, 1986).

6. Give the student dot-to-dot activities that require him to join letters sequentially to form a picture (D. Pernick, personal communication, 1986).

7. Draw a long snake or caterpillar on heavy colored posterboard. Write the letters of the

alphabet sequentially on the body and use a razor knife to cut each letter into a puzzle piece. Present the student with these pieces and ask him to assemble the puzzle, using the letters on the pieces as cues (D. Pernick, personal communication, 1986).

8. An alphabet chart may be used to teach the letters in proper sequence. Make a large chart with the letters Aa, Bb, Cc, and Dd printed in large block letters. Teach these letters, and have the student say each letter as you point to it. Repeat this process each day as a new letter is added (Platts, 1972).

9. Tell the student that he will be playing a game to see if he can tell what letter you are thinking of. Give the student various hints (e.g., "I'm thinking of a letter that comes before H," "This letter is the tenth letter of the alphabet," etc.) (Platts, 1972).

10. Make 9″ × 12″ letter cards and ask the student to draw or paste pictures to represent the letters of the alphabet. Then have him either arrange these letter cards on the chalktray in proper order, or sequence them on a bulletin board (Herr, 1961).

11. Give the student a selection from a newspaper or magazine and ask him to circle the very first A, then the next B, then the following C, and so on (Herr, 1961).

12. Glue 26 library envelopes onto a piece of sturdy cardboard and write the letters of the alphabet in proper order. Present the student with letter flashcards and instruct him to match the letters to their respective envelope sequentially (D. Pernick, personal communication, 1986).

13. Create several sets of tactile alphabets from sandpaper, pipe cleaners, wood, felt, styrofoam, cardboard, wallpaper, material, and so on. Have the student arrange these letters in alphabetical order, using a model. Give verbal cues when necessary (D. Pernick, personal communication, 1986).

14. Have the student make an accordion alphabet book. Give him a very long strip of tagboard that has been folded back and forth to make 26 "pages" and a cover. Have the

pupil print letters, one each page, in proper sequence, and draw or paste pictures to represent each of the letters (Herr, 1961).

15. Use puppets to motivate memory drills. Use a finger or hand puppet to present the student with a series of letters, digits, or words that you want him to remember in order. Ask the student to repeat the sequence of items to the puppet (Fitzmaurice et al., 1974).

16. Say two or three letters to the student and ask him to repeat them. Continue adding another letter each time until the child cannot repeat all of them to you (D. Pernick, personal communication, 1986).

17. Using a model, allow the student to practice typing the letters of the alphabet, in sequence, on a typewriter or computer (D. Pernick, personal communication, 1986).

18. Display a set of large alphabet flash cards on the chalktray. Point to a letter at random and ask the student to find the letter that comes before or after the letter you have chosen (D. Pernick, personal communication, 1986).

19. Present the student with an envelope containing alphabet cards and ask him to arrange them on a tabletop in alphabetical order (Platts, 1972).

20. Have the student make a picture dictionary, allowing one page for each letter. Help him select pictures from magazines, old texts, and so on (Herr, 1961).

21. Provide the student with a set of all 26 letter cards. Say a letter sequence (e.g., q,r,s,t,u,v) and have the student repeat the series orally. Ask him to find the letter cards and arrange them sequentially on the table (Labrie, 1973).

22. Say a group of letters to the student out of order (e.g., r,u,s,q,t,v) and have the pupil put them in proper order (Labrie, 1973).

23. Cut out a large tagboard lollipop tree and print the alphabet in sequential order. Cut out acorns and print the lower-case letters on them. Direct the student to match the

letters on the tree to the acorns (Mallet, 1975).

24. Turn over 3 empty egg cartons and print the lower-case alphabet on the bumps. Cut apart 26 egg cups and print the upper-case letters on them. Ask the student to match the letter by placing the cups over the bumps (Palewicz and Madaras, 1979).

25. Teach the alphabet in thirds, rather than in its entirety. Place the first third on a chart and clearly display it. Work with the student until he is able to instantly tell you which letter comes before or after a given letter (Ekwall, 1985).

26. Have the student make an alphabet book, putting one letter on each page. Instruct the student to cut out matching letters from old workbooks, magazines, coloring books, and so on (Sparkman and Saul, 1977).

27. Create an alphabet center. Place alphabet cards, blocks, books, records, songs, lotto games, magazines, scissors, paste, paper, and pencils in an attractive arrangement in an independent work area. Allow the student to match letters, pair upper- and lower-case letters, sequence alphabet cards, write letters, and make a dictionary (Aulls, 1982).

28. Have the student sing "The Alphabet Song" while a manuscript chart is displayed. Point to each letter as it is sung (Ekwall, 1985).

29. Make a ditto with two letters on each row. Instruct the student to circle the letter that comes first in each group. If necessary, he may refer to a chart (D. Pernick, personal communication, 1986).

30. Place four or five tactile letters in proper sequence in front of the student. Ask him to trace each letter in proper order. Then jumble the cards and ask him to re-create the pattern (Berryman and Perry, 1974).

31. Allow the student to recite the alphabet from A to Z. Then isolate three letters and give them to the student, omitting the middle letter (e.g., $m, \_\_, o$). Require the pupil to supply the missing letter (Berryman and Perry, 1974).

32. Print the letters of the alphabet on a sheet of posterboard and cut it apart into a jigsaw puzzle. Instruct the student to assemble the puzzle so that the letters are arranged alphabetically (Herr, 1961).

33. Play the "Alphabet Rhythm Game" with a group of students. Seat the pupils in a circle and teach them to clap twice, hit their knees twice, and snap the left then the right fingers in a rhythmic patter. The first pupil will hit his knees twice, clap twice, snap his left fingers, say, "A," snap his right fingers, and say the sound of a. The rhythm is repeated and the second student says, "B" and the sound of b. The game is continued until the entire alphabet is recited in proper order. If a student misses, he must sit in the center of the circle. When another pupil misses, the first student may return to his place in the circle (Platts, Shumaker, and Marguerite, 1960).

34. Line up students in groups of five or six and instruct them to remain 10 feet from the chalkboard. When the teacher signals, the first student goes to the blackboard, writes the letter A, and walks back to the next student on his team. The next student writes the letter B. This will continue in relay race fashion until one team has successfully written the alphabet (Platts, Shumaker, and Marguerite, 1960).

35. Divide the class in groups of five to seven children and present each student with a word or picture card. Instruct the students to arrange themselves in proper alphabetical sequence. The first completed "train" wins (Bloomer, 1961).

36. Play "Alphabet Tap" with your students. Begin reciting the alphabet slowly while walking around the room. At random intervals, stop and tap a student. That student must then identify the letter that follows. Continue this process until the alphabet has been recited three or four times (Platts, 1972).

37. Write the letters of the alphabet across the blackboard. List the students' last names in the appropriate columns (Herr, 1961).

38. Make two complete sets of alphabet flash cards, shuffle them, and distribute them evenly between two students. Have the students play "War." Each pupil simultaneously turns a card over from the top of his or her deck. The pupil with the card that comes last in the alphabet gets to take the pile. In the event that both students have the same letter, another card is placed on top of each. The first student to get all of the cards is the winner (D. Pernick, personal communication, 1986).

39. The game "Head Down" may also be played to aid the student in remembering the alphabet. Select one pupil to put his or her head down. Select another student to stand up and recite the alphabet in his or her own voice or a disguised voice. Then say, "Head up," and allow the student to have three chances to guess who was reciting (Platts, 1972).

40. Instruct a student to begin reciting the alphabet as quickly as possible. When you say "Stop," the next student must begin reciting where the other student left off. If a student reaches z, he should begin again with a (Platts, 1972).

41. Draw several balloons on the blackboard and write a different letter in each. Point to a balloon. Tell the student if he can name the letter that follows the letter you have chosen, he may buy the balloon. The student may play against another student, and points may be given for each balloon (Platts, 1972).

42. Have the student hop through a hopscotch figure taped or drawn on the floor in sequential order, saying the names of the letters as he proceeds (Herr, 1961).

43. Have the student trace his shoes on paper or cardboard 26 times. Print one letter in each footprint and arrange them in alphabetical order on the floor. The student must step from one to another, in proper order, and say the names of the letter as he proceeds (Herr, 1961).

44. Play "Alphabet Rummy." Make three sets of 3" × 2" letter cards. Shuffle the cards and deal six to each player. Place the remaining cards face down on the table. The students should take turns drawing. When four letters are in sequence, the pupil may lay the cards down. If he cannot play, a card must be discarded. The student may build on another player's sequence, but he must keep the card in front of himself. At the end of the game, the student with the most cards down is the winner (Herr, 1961).

45. Arrange 26 chairs in a row and tape the alphabet cards in sequential order to the backs of the seats. Then distribute "train tickets" (cards containing the letters of the alphabet) to the students. Instruct them to find their reserved seat. Then the "conductor" checks the seats (Bloomer, 1961).

46. Play the "Echo Game." Have the student stand in a corner of the room opposite you. Then say a series of letters in a clear voice. The "echo" must repeat what you said (Fitzmaurice et al., 1974).

47. Prepare an "Alphaland" game board with several colored spaces. Place a set of alphabet flash cards in the center of the game. Direct the students to take a card, in turn, and name the letter and the letter that would immediately precede it in the alphabet. If the student answers correctly, he may roll two dice and move his game piece the proper number of squares. The student who reaches the finish line first is the winner (D. Pernick, personal communication, 1986).

48. Play games that improve auditory memory. These help to develop the skills necessary in sequencing the alphabet (Fitzmaurice et al., 1974).

49. Give the student a pencil and paper. Tell him that you are going to say a series of letters and that he is to write the second to last one on the paper. Directions may increase in difficulty (e.g., write the letters that are closest to M in the alphabet, or write the letters that would come last if the list were in alphabetical order) (Fitzmaurice et al., 1974).

50. Engage the student in activities that improve visual memory and sequencing skills. These help the child who has difficulty sequencing the alphabet (Labrie, 1973).

51. Play concentration games with the student to develop visual memory (Bornstein, 1980).

185

Has Difficulty Remembering the Sequence of Numbers

1. Give the student a hopscotch board that is numbered. Tell him to start on the first block and correctly name the number that comes before and after the number he is on. If the student answers correctly, he can move on. If not, the student puts a tile or stone on that block and waits until it is his turn again. The first one to home base wins (Lucas and Barbe, 1974).

2. Ask the student to bounce a ball any number of times between 2 and 10. The student who bounces the ball asks another student how many times the ball was bounced. If the student answers correctly, it is his turn to bounce the ball. If he does not answer correctly, ask the original ball bouncer to bounce the ball again (Dumas, 1960).

3. Give a sequence of numbers and display them to the student. Ask the student to close his eyes while another student removes one of the numbers. Ask the student who had his eyes closed to guess which number is missing (Dumas, 1960).

4. Draw a house on the board and draw smoke coming from it to make it look like there is a fire. Draw a ladder next to it with a number on each step. Choose a student to read the numbers up the ladder, then down. Each student who rescues a person from the burning house receives a fire fighter's cap or badge (Dumas, 1960).

5. Follow the same steps as in the previous item, but erase the numbers and have the student recall the sequence in order to rescue the person (Dumas, 1960).

6. Construct a large chart having only the numbers 1, 2, 3, and 4 in the first squares. Ask the student to finish the sequence of numbers (Dumas, Howard, and Dumas, 1960).

7. Give the student a clock face with certain numbers deleted. Ask him to fill in the clock face in numerical order (Dumas, Howard, and Dumas, 1960).

8. Construct a bulletin board that has a calendar with only the days of the week and the first day of the month on it. Have small cards with numbers 2 through 31 available. Ask the student to place the number cards in proper order on the calendar (Dumas, Howard, and Dumas, 1960).

9. Give a student a few markers and a number line. Ask him to place a marker on top of the number that is read aloud. Remove some of the markers and ask the student to name the numbers that are still covered (Sharp, 1971).

10. Using a deck of playing cards, ask a student to shuffle and deal out all the cards. Ask to see which student has the lowest card in his hand, and have him put the card on the table face up. The student next to him has to put a card down that follows the sequence. The suit does not matter. If the student cannot follow, he must pass. The first one to get rid of all his cards wins (Kazarinoff, 1981).

11. Give students three four-inch squares with dots on one side. Make one square for number 1, two squares for number 2, three squares for number 3, and so on. Ask a student to count out the appropriate number of given objects for each numbered square. Have the student look at each side of the square (Basic Skills Curriculum Guide/ Teaching Resources, 1977).

12. Ask the student to stack the squares (see the previous item) in sequence from 1 to 10

(Basic Skills Curriculum Guide, Teaching Resources, 1977).

13. Print numbers 1 through 8 on large felt circles. Make one circle with a face. Make four or five of each of the lower numerals. Turn all numerals face down on flannel board. Give each student a face circle. Have each student take a turn at turning over one numeral circle at a time and trying to build the number sequence from one to eight. Each student must find 1 first, then 2, and so on. The first to complete the sequence is the winner (Basic Skills Curriculum Guide, Teaching Resources, 1977).

14. Draw a 10″ × 10″ grid on a sheet of tagboard. Print numbers 1 through 10 across the bottom row of spaces, 11 through 20 across the second row from the bottom, and so forth up to 100. Leave one die as is, with the dots for 1 to 6. Print *left, right, up,* and *down* on pressure-sensitive stickers (make two *rights* and two *ups*). Put them on the second die. Ask each player to roll both dice and to move his or her marker according to what is on the dice. The labeled die tells the direction in which the player is to move. If there is an impossible move, the player must pass. The first player to reach 100 wins (Basic Skills Curriculum Guide, Teaching Resources, 1977).

15. Using a connect-the-dots exercise, the student must connect dots in numerical order. When finished, the student should have a picture (Pope, Edel, and Haklay, 1979).

16. Say a sequence of numbers to a student. Repeat the sequence as the student listens. Have the student repeat the pattern (Pope, Edel, and Haklay, 1979).

17. Seat the students in a large circle. Whisper a sequence of four numbers into the student's ear. The student then turns to the next student and repeats the same sequence. The last student repeats the numbers out loud (Pope, Edel, and Haklay, 1979).

18. Tell the student to repeat after you. Say a sequence of numbers, using a tap to hold the place of a number that is left out. (e.g.,

"1, 2, 3 (tap on the table), 5, 6″). Sequences can be changed and numbers can be added (Jocquot, Shelquist, and Breeze, 1973).

19. Ask the student to insert an appropriate number of golf tees into a number line on numbered cardboard with holes punched out (Jocquot, Shelquist, and Breeze, 1973).

20. Ask the student to place numbered race cars in order from 1 to 10 (Sunny, Courington, and Stephens, 1978).

21. Make a list of sequences on the board, with the last five numbers missing (e.g., 1,2,3,—,—,—,—,—). Ask the student, "What comes next?" (Sunny, Courington, and Stephens, 1978).

22. Make a number line with the numbers 0 through 10 on the floor, using masking tape. Make a set of 25 number cards (4″ × 4″). Lay these along the line to identify points. Label cards in domino style, having dots on cards one through ten. Have the student pick a domino card and then count off the number of dots on his domino card on the number line (Kennedy and Michon, 1973).

186

Has Difficulty Remembering the Sequence of Sounds

1. Reinforce the student when he remembers a sequence of sounds correctly.

2. Make three very different sounds. Replay one sound and ask the student which position it occupied in the sequence (K. Cowell, personal communication, 1986).

3. Have the student make a short sequence of sounds. Have him attempt to repeat that sequence.

4. Give a short sequence of sounds. Play another sequence and have the student tell you if the two sequences were the same or different.

5. While the student's eyes are closed, make

a short series of sounds. Have the student reproduce the sequence (Moyer, 1976).

6. Give progressively longer sequences of sounds as the student reproduces them.

7. Have the student hum familiar tunes played for him in order to build his confidence in his ability to remember a sequence of sounds.

8. Use repetition to assist the student's memory.

9. Practice with meaningful sounds to assist the student in remembering (e.g., environmental sounds, names, animals sounds).

10. Have the student watch you making the sounds. This may assist recall.

11. Involve movement in the student's reproduction of sounds (e.g., clapping, slapping, snapping fingers).

12. Practice by playing auditory sequencing games with your class. Seat the group in a circle and say, "I went to the store and bought a _____." The next student must repeat your sentence and add an additional item to the list. Continue this process until each student has had a turn. Other starters that may be used are: "I'm going on a trip and I'm packing a _____," "I went to the zoo and saw a _____," and "I'm making vegetable soup with _____ in it" (Bornstein, 1980).

187

Has Difficulty Remembering Verbal Directions

1. Reinforce the student when he correctly follows verbal directions (K. Cowell, personal communication, 1986).

2. Give one-step directions (Kaplan and White, 1980).

3. Have the student repeat directions to determine if he heard them correctly (Haas, Kasper, and Kryst, 1979).

4. Have the student rephrase the directions in

his own words (Haas, Kasper, and Kryst, 1979).

5. Give the directions in short, concise sentences with simple terminology.

6. Define word meanings that may be confusing to the student (Haas, Kasper, and Kryst, 1979).

7. Pause between each idea presented (Haas, Kasper, and Kryst, 1979; Buttery and Anderson, 1980).

8. Place verbal directions on an audiotape so that the student may review them as necessary.

9. If using longer words when repeating the directions, use simpler synonyms with which the student might be familiar. The repetition of the concept in more than one way is less redundant than repeating the same direction over again (Haas, Kasper, and Kryst, 1979).

10. Break the direction into a sequence of steps. Number the steps. Have the student complete the steps one at a time (Haas, Kasper, and Kryst, 1979).

11. Prepare the student by saying, "Now listen carefully."

12. Use direct eye contact when giving directions (Haas, Kasper, and Kryst, 1979).

13. Give the student several simple tasks to perform using earphones in a listening center (e.g., "Draw a big red square on your paper. Put a small green circle underneath the square. Draw a black line from the middle of the circle to the upper right-hand corner of the square.") (Lerner, 1985).

14. Use masking tape to make various line patterns on the floor. Number each pattern. Place a book, eraser, glass of water, spoon with a marble, or ball at the start of each line pattern. Give oral instructions, indicating the number of the pattern to follow, which object to hold, and whether to walk, run, or hop (Wedemeyer and Cejka, 1975).

15. Play games that involve following directions.

16. Have the student read the directions dur-

ing verbal presentation to assist with memory (D. Lathrop, personal communication, 1986).

17. One minute after presentation of directions, ask the student what he is supposed to do.

18. Limit the repetition of questions and directions. When students realize that questions and directions will be repeated as often as they ask, they may soon become unaware of their personal listening responsibilities, depending on the repetition of statements rather than attending to the initial communication (Buttery and Anderson, 1980).

19. Place three or four simple picture cards on a table. Seat yourself and the student about four feet away. Ask the student to bring you a certain picture. When he can do this correctly, use new pictures. Gradually add more pictures to the group, then increase the distance to eight feet. Increase the number of pictures you request. Next, remove the visual clues and have the student remember the command auditorily. Seat the student about eight feet from the cards and face him away from them. Repeat the previous step. Gradually increase the complexity by giving a sequence command (e.g., get the car and put it under the table) (Chaney and Kephart, 1968).

20. Give oral tests. This requires the student to listen attentively and prepare a response (Buttery and Anderson, 1980).

188

Unable to Retell a Simple Story in Sequential Order

1. Place pictures in sequential order and ask the student to tell a story about them (Bornstein, 1980).

2. Sequence pictures in accordance with poems and stories (Bornstein, 1980).

3. Establish an environment in which the student feels secure and relatively free from tension (James, 1976).

4. Arrange objects in a sequence. Ask the student to reproduce the sequence of objects previously seen (Novakovich and Zoslow, 1973).

5. Read a story to the class. Ask the students to mark appropriate characters presented visually (Bornstein, 1980).

6. Ask the student simple questions after reading a story (Bornstein, 1980).

7. Have the student retell the day's events in sequence (Bornstein, 1980).

8. Help the student tell the sequence of steps in making something (Bornstein, 1980).

9. Cut a story on the group's reading level into different parts and paste them on cardboard. Mix the pieces and pass them to group members. The student who thinks he has the first part of the story reads it. The other students follow until all parts of the story have been read. Don't be surprised if the story is quite different from the original one (Fitzmaurice et al., 1974).

10. Give hints to assist the student.

11. Give two events from a story. Ask which happened first.

12. With the student, take turns telling parts of a story.

13. Retell a story. Stop when the student says that he knows what comes next. Allow him to continue as long as he is accurate. Continue the story as necessary.

14. Tell a story and use flannel board characters that go with it. Ask the student to repeat the story and place the characters in order as the story is retold (Fitzmaurice et al., 1974).

15. Tell a simple story and have the student repeat the events in order of their occurrence. Help the student by asking, ''What happened after that?'' (Fitzmaurice et al., 1974).

16. Review longer stories that have been read to the student several times. Ask the student to tell the events in order of their occurrence (Fitzmaurice et al., 1974).

17. Read a story to the student. Ask him to tell the story back to you. Write what he says on the chalkboard at his vocabulary level (Fitzmaurice et al., 1974).

18. Ask the student to write a story in chronological order, based on his own past experiences (Barasch, 1974).

19. Use simple repetition to improve story recall (Worden, Malmgren, and Gabourie, 1982).

20. Put stories on tape. Have the student listen to the tape and then recall the stories (Chvany, 1972).

21. Have the student listen to stories that are told on tape. Ask him to write a story (Chvany, 1972).

22. Using a felt-tipped marker, divide a circular piece of cardboard into eight sections. Ask the student to think about events of his daily routine, such as dressing, eating meals, and going to bed. Write these ideas, in sequence, around the circle. The student may get a sense of sequence by examining the completed ring and seeing the repeated events of his daily life (Baker, 1982).

23. Help the student construct a timeline of his life, beginning with birth and including events up to the present. Allow room for expansion as new events occur (Baker, 1982).

24. Listen to a recording of a biography. Discuss the important events with the student. List these events on a timeline (Baker, 1982).

25. View a videotaped TV show or a film that contains a logical sequence. Discuss the events with the student and list them, in order of their occurrence, on the chalkboard (Baker, 1982).

26. Help the student select a current topic in a daily newspaper and have him follow it for two weeks. Paste the articles on posterboard in sequence and date them. At the conclusion of the two weeks, discuss the changes that occurred in the items over time. The student may wish to continue this procedure if the topic remains in the news (Baker, 1982).

27. Have the student follow written directions on how to master a clever card trick, construct a paper boat or a slippery snake, whip up a milkshake, or use salt and lemon juice to remove corrosion from an old penny. Sentence strips copied from the original instruction page serve as tests of sequence understanding. When the student has completed the project, he can test himself by arranging these strips in the proper order (Baker, 1982).

28. Using magazines or discarded books, have the student search for "time" words or phrases. Ask him to locate and underline words such as *later, soon, tomorrow, in the future*, and so on. Discuss the meaning of these words and their relevance to sequence. For instance, a sentence beginning with *later* would not describe the first event of a series (Baker, 1982).

29. After the student has had the experience of putting comic strips in correct sequence, ask him to make his own strip. He can then ask a friend to reconstruct the story (Baker, 1982).

30. After reading a story, ask the student and friends to dramatize the story in sequence (A. Russ, personal communication, 1986).

31. Give the student picture cards and ask him to place the events in sequential order. For example, the first picture shows a tall candle with a fresh wick. The second picture shows a hand lighting the candle. The third picture shows the candle starting to burn. The fourth picture shows the candle burned down (A. Russ, personal communication, 1986).

32. Use a computer program that is designed to enhance sequencing skills (A. Russ, personal communication, 1986).

189

Has Difficulty Finding Smaller Words in Larger Words

1. Reinforce the student when he is able to find smaller words in larger words.

2. Strengthen the student's understanding of the concept by assigning "word search" sheets.

3. Strengthen the concept of finding items in a larger mass by using figure ground exercises (e.g., "Find the _____ in the picture").

4. As a first step, tell the student which word he is to find. Upon mastering this, have him search for unknown smaller words.

5. Give a hint by circling one end of the smaller word to provide a reference point cue.

6. Give hints as to the number of letters, which vowel is contained in the word, and so on.

7. Teach grammar rules regarding prefixes, suffixes, double consonants, and so on.

8. Decrease the length and complexity of the words until the student becomes proficient at this task.

9. As a hint, provide the definition of the word to be found.

10. Teach a sequential elimination strategy (e.g., "Look at the first and second letters of the large word. If you see no smaller word, then look at the first three or four letters. If you see no smaller word, then eliminate the first letter and look at the second and third letters.").

11. Use smaller words that are nouns familiar to the student.

190

Misinterprets Written Directions

1. Reinforce correct responses (Treiber and Lahey, 1983).

2. Be sure that the student is capable of reading the directions correctly (Haas, Kasper, and Kryst, 1979).

3. Have the student repeat the instructions to you (Hallahan and Sapona, 1983).

4. Have the student relate the instructions back to you in his own words or by a partial demonstration of the directed task.

5. Progress toward self-monitoring by having the student repeat instructions to himself and question himself as to what is being asked (Hallahan and Sapona, 1983).

6. Obtain microcomputer software that mechanically reads the print on the screen for the student to prevent misreading (Rosengrant, 1985).

7. Teach the student to monitor and "look over" his work (Hagin, 1983).

8. Read the directions aloud while the student silently reads the directions.

9. Place your directions on audiotape and allow the student to review them as necessary (B. Ballichino, personal communication, 1985).

10. Frequently monitor the student's work (Haas, Kasper, and Kryst, 1979).

11. Monitor the student's work. Have him show you the work and explain it when it is half completed (Haas, Kasper, and Kryst, 1979).

12. Break the directions into a sequence of steps. Have the student complete one step at a time (Haas, Kasper, and Kryst, 1979).

13. Use short complete sentences in the directions (Haas, Kasper, and Kryst, 1979).

14. Assign a peer assistant to monitor and help the student (Haas, Kasper, and Kryst, 1979).

191

Poor Comprehension of Reading Passages

1. Reinforce the student for displaying good comprehension.

2. Tell the student which question you will ask of him after a passage is read (e.g., "I'm going to ask you how many men were on the team") ((R. Schwab, personal communication, 1986).

3. Tell the student that you will call on him after the reading of a passage (V. Condino, personal communication, 1986).

4. Tell the student which line or paragraph contains the answers (N. Cedrone, personal communication, 1986).

5. Ask questions in order around the group so that the student knows when he must attend (P. Gailey, personal communication, 1986).

6. Ask questions in random order around the group as that the student feels that he must always attend (G. Boudreau, personal communication, 1986).

7. Provide the student with a list of questions before reading. This will help the student attend to important points (B. DiLoretto, personal communication, 1986).

8. Use materials other than the text, such as magazines and newspapers, to help build motivation (S. Thomas, personal communication, 1983).

9. Stop the student frequently and have him explain, in his own words, what has been read thus far (L. DiLoretto, personal communication, 1986).

10. When the student has difficulty answering questions, give him hints to assist in recollection (B. Borsari, personal communication, 1986).

11. Have the student read the passage silently before reading it aloud (J. Cannon, personal communication, 1986).

12. Underline or mark important information in a reading passage (M. McIntyre, personal communication, 1986).

13. When you read aloud, use special voice emphasis on important points (B. Covert, personal communication, 1986).

14. Choose passages of interest to the student to provide motivation to attend (K. Cowell, personal communication, 1986).

15. Paste or draw pictures in the margin of a reading passage to assist with comprehension (P. Barnett, personal communication, 1987).

16. Be sure that the material is within the student's reading ability level (S. Pilgrim, personal communication, 1987).

17. Omit every fifth word of a paragraph. Have the student insert a word that keeps the basic sense of the passage (Fischer, 1985).

18. Using a paragraph, omit every fifth word. Have the student select an answer from a group of four possibilities (Fischer, 1985).

19. Give the student sentences with a word underlined. This word should have multiple meanings listed below the sentence. Using context clues, he must select the meaning best suited for that sentence (Nagy, Herman, and Anderson, 1985).

20. Give the student simple sentences in which an obvious contextual mistake has been made. He must underline the mistake and substitute the correct word (Carnine, Carnine, and Gersten, 1984).

21. Have the pupil read a story and answer the who, what, where, when, and why about it (Bielawski and Pomerleau, 1973).

22. Facilitate reading comprehension by requiring the student to read a passage and create visual images representative of the passage. The steps are: (a) read the passage, (b) image a picture in one's mind, (c) describe the image, (d) evaluate the image for its completeness, and (e) repeat this with the next sentence or passage (Clark, 1984).

23. Teach the student to form questions while reading to maintain interest and enhance recall. The steps are: (a) read the passage, (b) ask who, what, where, why, how, and

when questions, (c) answer the questions after one reads, and (d) mark the answers with the appropriate symbol (e.g., a clock face for "when") (Clark et al., 1984).

24. Look for overt signs of frustration in the student's behavior while reading (e.g., hesitation, pauses, looking around rather than at the passage, puzzled facial expression, etc.) (Klesius and Homon, 1985).

25. Substitute other questions for those that are not passage dependent. Perhaps a new wording will aid in the student's ability to properly interpret a passage (Klesius and Homon, 1985).

26. Make a list of additional responses to questions that are equally acceptable or more appropriate than the ones provided by the author. In some instances the acceptable responses provided in the teacher copy are never given by the students (Klesius and Homon, 1985).

27. Carefully observe the student's reading and comprehension once he is placed in reading materials to insure that the placement is not at a frustration level (Klesius and Homon, 1985).

28. Use microcomputers to lessen the degree of difficulty and frustration that the student experiences in trying to gain reading and working skills. There are computer programs that say the letter and/or word as the student types at the keyboard. Then, to assist their reading, the software could be used to say aloud any and/or every word of text on the monitor screen as often as needed (Rosengrant, 1985).

29. Have the students open their books to a selection they have not yet read. A number of puzzlers to be defined are listed on the board with the page and line where each is to be found. Students may make full use of all clues present, but they are not to turn to the dictionary (Thomas and Robinson, 1972).

30. When presented with an unfamiliar word, students should be encouraged to examine the word for familiar parts. They may rec-

ognize a part as familiar, but if they do not know its meaning, help the student think of other words in which the part appears. Then help them reason out the meaning of the part (Thomas and Robinson, 1972).

31. Facilitate reading comprehension by requiring students to read a passage and create visual images representative of that passage (Clark et al., 1984).

32. Encourage verbal rehearsal to improve recall and comprehension. Have the student pause after reading a few sentences and talk to himself about what has been read (Rose and Cundick, 1983).

33. Encourage the student to pause after reading a few sentences, close the eyes, and make a picture or a movie in the mind about what has been read (Rose and Cundick, 1983).

34. Facilitate reading comprehension by teaching students to form questions while reading to maintain interest and to enhance recall. Steps include: (a) reading the passage, asking who, what, where, why, how questions while reading; (b) answering the questions while reading; and (c) marking answers with an appropriate symbol (e.g., a clock face for "when") (Clark et al., 1984).

192
Poor Word Attack Skills

1. Reinforce the student when he correctly pronounces a difficult word.

2. Teach the student to use story pictures to assist in identifying a word (N. Cedrone, personal communication, 1986).

3. Teach the student to use sentence or passage context to identify the difficult word (Cushenbery, 1972).

4. Present new words before reading (N. Cedrone, personal communication, 1986).

5. Use flash card drills to assist in word recognition.

6. Teach phonics skills to students as a tool to use in word attack (Della-Piana, 1968).

7. If the student has been trained by the phonics approach, encourage him to attempt to sound out the word.

8. Give contextual hints to the student.

9. Provide the student with the initial sound of the word.

10. Read the passage aloud to the student while he follows along before asking him to read aloud.

11. Flash word cards to individual students and ask them to pronounce the words as quickly as possible. Whenever a pupil misses a word, he is given that word and makes a copy of it to keep. He can then give the original word back to you. Each student develops his own "pack of trouble," which he can use for study with another individual (Ekwall, 1985).

12. Have the student write troublesome words on cards (8 1/2″ × 3″). Have him trace the word, using the index and middle fingers, and say the parts of words traced. After the pupil knows the word, use cards to form sentences. Also give sentences with the sight words omitted. Have the pupil fill in blanks with the appropriate word from his pile of cards (Ekwall, 1985).

13. Use pictures to illustrate words such as: *play, wash, work, small*, and *sing*. Use a picture with a sentence describing it and the sight word underlined (Ekwall, 1985).

14. Have the pupil write troublesome words on a card (8 1/2″ × 3″) and then pantomime the action described by the word (e.g., *pull, sleep, right, jump*, etc.) (Ekwall, 1985).

15. Place one word in a line that is different from the rest. Ask the pupil to circle that one (Ekwall, 1985).

16. Use words commonly confused in multiple-choice situations. Have the pupil underline the correct word (e.g., "He wanted to (walk, wash) his clothes") (Ekwall, 1985).

17. Cut letters from sandpaper or velvet to form troublesome words. Let the student feel the word as he pronounces it. Make a master pile of "sandpaper words" and go over them daily (Ekwall, 1985).

18. Put a thin layer of salt or fine sand in a shoe box lid and let the student practice writing the word in the granules (Ekwall, 1985).

19. Place a piece of paper over a piece of screen wire such as that used on the screen doors of a house. (Before doing this, it is a good idea to cover the edges of the screen wire with book-binding tape so that the rough edges do not cut anyone.) Writing on the paper on the screen wire with a crayon will leave a series of raised dots. Have the student trace basic sight words in this manner and then have him trace over the words, saying them as they are traced (Ekwall, 1985).

20. Each day, pass out a few basic sight words on cards to students. Each student goes to the board, in turn, and writes his word. The class should try to say it aloud. After it is pronounced correctly, have the class write it in a notebook. On some days have students select words from their notebooks and write them on the chalkboard. Then ask various members of the class to say these words (Ekwall, 1985).

21. Make "domino" flash cards divided in half by a line, in which a different word is on each side of the card. Make sure that the words are repeated several times on different cards. After mixing the cards, the game proceeds the same as dominoes. The student pronounces the word as he matches it (Ekwall, 1985).

22. Make group-size (6″ × 3″) and individual-size cards with words on them. One set is given to the group of students and one is kept by the captain. Each student is given one or several words (passports). In order to get aboard the boat, they must show their passports to the captain. When the captain calls their port (their word or words) from his deck of cards, the student who has a card matching the captain's must show it to him to get off the boat. The same game can be played with the sound

of the consonants and vowels. In this case, the student who has a letter that matches the sound of the first letter in the word called by the captain shows his passport (letter) and is allowed to leave the boat (Ekwall, 1985).

23. Have available a large box and cards with troublesome words printed on them. The students sit in a circle around the box. Read or play a tape recording of a story. Before hearing the story, each student is given a card on which there is a word from the story. When that word is read in the story, the student says, ''_____ goes in the box'' and puts the word in the box. The student is then given another word so that he may continue in the game (Ekwall, 1985).

24. Make the student aware of specific types of clues and the mental processes involved as he uses all the hints at hand to identify unknown words. The following are types of clues: direct explanation clue, experience clue, mood or tone clue, explanation through example, summary clue, synonym or restatement clue, comparison or contrast clue, familiar expression or language experience clue, words in a series clue, and inference clue (Thomas and Robinson, 1972).

25. Draw a football field on a large piece of paper. The game begins at the 50-yard line where the football is placed. (The football can be a small replica of a football made out of thick paper or cardboard.) Place word cards face up on the table and two students or two teams take turns reading them. When a student reads the word correctly, he moves the ball 10 yards toward the opponent's goal. If the student reads the word incorrectly, it is considered a fumble and the ball goes 10 yards toward his own goal. Each time the ball crosses into the end zone, six points are scored. The scoring side then gets to read one more word to try for the extra point (Ekwall, 1985).

26. Encourage parental involvement. Some suggestions that you can give to a parent are: (a) read to your child every day, (b) have books available, (c) provide the opportunity to visit the library, (d) converse and listen to him, and (e) provide trips to places of interest (Biggins and Sayre, 1980).

27. For visual presentation, select only lowercase letters that are the same size. Avoid any distractible stimuli when presenting a new word. If possible, avoid capital letters (Greenwood, 1981).

28. Develop those skills and abilities that are most necessary for immediate successful word attack. No remedial method has universal application. Methods of instruction should be selected that are in harmony with the best mode of learning for a given student (Dechant, 1969).

29. Teach new vocabulary words by linking the new word or label to a previously learned concept. Set up a situation where a conceptual network common to most students will be activated. For example, for the word *peculiar*, talk about strange happenings and other appropriate labels for *peculiar*. Then have students write down something they have heard of or experienced that they found to be very peculiar. Later, have them write a nonexample (something not peculiar). Finally, in their own words, have them write what the new word means (Eeds and Cockrum, 1985).

30. Provide practice in structual analysis clues. The following are some structual analysis clues that can foster adequate word attack skills: syllabication (division and accent), prefixes, suffixes, contractions, words ending in *ing*, doubling the consonant before adding *ing*, compound words, the apostrophe *s*, the past tense with *ed*, and the plural of *es* (Steere, Peck, and Kahn, 1966; Dechant, 1969).

31. Lead the student to work out, syllable by syllable, the pronunciation of words that seem forbidding. Once he reduces these polysyllabic words to a series of short, easy-to-manage syllables, he may be able to pronounce the word (Thomas and Robinson, 1972).

32. Help the student develop a ''shift-the-

accent'' strategy. The student should be aware that if the first try at pronouncing the word doesn't yield a word that fits the context, he can sometimes get a breakthrough by shifting the accent to another syllable (Thomas and Robinson, 1972).

33. Using a tape of several letter sound pronunciations, have the student select felt letters when he hears the appropriate phonetic cue (Ehri and Wilce, 1985).

34. After reading an article or a story, give the student a crossword puzzle with the new words learned from the story or article (Gentile, 1983).

35. Use a tachistoscope to provide drill practice. A teacher-made tachistoscope can be made using a piece of cardboard or index card and putting a small slit in it so that only one word or a small group of words can be seen at one time.

36. Make a word wheel by fastening two circles together, with the smaller one fastened so that it rotates in such a way that initial consonants and consonant blends can be matched to family words or prefixes, or suffixes can be matched to root words.

37. Teach an initial vocabulary of sight words learned (memorized) as visual configurations.

38. Using the cloze method, have the student select his answer from a group of words in which one is spelled correctly and the others are nonsense words (Fischer, 1985).

39. Set up a single board game by having the student move from a starting point to a finishing point by matching letters to taped phonetic sounds (Ehri and Wilce, 1985).

40. Have the student match boundary letters (first and last letters) to pictures of the word. For example: *b, k* for a picture of a book, or *l, t* for a picture of a light (Ehri and Wilce, 1985).

41. Provide practice with the pronunciation guide of a dictionary so that students can ''take a stab'' at the pronunciation of an unknown word (Robinson, 1975).

Visual Perception/Visual Motor

193
Cannot Discriminate Between Shapes

1. Point out the distinguishing properties of shapes (Gibson, 1969).

2. Have the student analyze the distinctive properties of figures (Woodworth, 1938).

3. Present several large shapes that are identical and one that is different. Have the student point out the one that is different and tell why it differs (Sperling, 1985).

4. Have the student trace inside and outside cardboard stencils while noting the distinctive features of each shape verbally (Beloit Public Schools, 1980).

5. Play ''Shape Bingo.'' Make a set of Bingo cards, each containing four circles, four squares, four triangles, and four rectangles. Make a set of flash cards with one shape on each card. Make enough flash cards so that you have one color for each shape (Ali, 1980).

6. Provide shape dominoes and have the student match them according to shape. Matching according to color will also reinforce discrimination skills (Armfield, 1977).

7. Provide parquetry blocks and ask the student to sort them into separate piles according to shape (Armfield, 1977).

8. Place round and square shapes in a box and ask the student to remove the round shapes (Armfield, 1977).

9. Make up a variety of shape patterns by

placing washers and nuts on a piece of cord or a long bolt. Ask the student to duplicate the pattern (Wedemeyer, 1975).

10. Turn a sectional packing box on its side and tape a shape tab to each section. Prepare a set of shape cards that match the tabs used to label each section of the box. Ask the student to sort the shape cards (Wedemeyer, 1975).

11. Paint shapes at the easel using a big brush and verbally describing your strokes. Then have the student engage in this activity (Burton, 1982).

12. Have one student draw a shape on another's back and have the receiver guess what was drawn (Burton, 1982).

13. Provide a set of sandpaper shapes ranging from very coarse to very fine in texture (Burton, 1982).

14. Bend pipe cleaners to form simple shapes. Verbally identify and compare these shapes (Burton, 1982).

15. Present a selection of containers with different shaped lids. Encourage the student to put the appropriate lid on each container by matching shapes (Ford, 1983).

16. Draw a picture of a circle, triangle, square, or some other shape. Have the student copy the drawing. Ask him to draw a picture using that shape. For example, a square can be made into a house or a truck (Molnar and Reighard, 1984).

17. Show a picture of a shape. Ask the student to name the shape. Ask him to find other things in the room that are the same shape (Molnar and Reighard, 1984).

18. Have the student draw or trace shapes in sand or fingerpaint (Molner and Reighard, 1984).

19. Develop awareness of shapes through fingerplays. For example, the following fingerplay helps the student focus on the distinguishing features of three basic shapes (Molnar and Reighard, 1984).

Draw a Circle

Draw a circle, draw a circle

Round as can be;
  (Draw a circle in the air with pointer finger)
Draw a circle, draw a circle
Just for me.
  (Point to self)

Draw a square, draw a square
Shaped like a door;
  (Draw a square in the air)
Draw a square, draw a square,
With corners four.

Draw a triangle, draw a triangle
With corners three;
  (Draw a triangle in the air with pointer finger)
Draw a triangle, draw a triangle
Just for me.
  (Point to self)

20. Draw two figures. Make one a dot-to-dot outline and the other a complete figure with connecting lines. Have the student study the complete figure and then connect the dots on the outline figure to make it like the complete figure (Molnar and Reighard, 1984).

21. Draw several shapes on white paper using heavy black ink. Place paper, thin enough to see through, over the shapes. Have the student trace the shapes first with his finger and then with a pencil or crayon. Have the student verbally identify the shape and describe it as he traces (Molnar and Reighard, 1984).

22. Prepare geometric forms from posterboard, cardboard, or wood. Blindfold the student and have him compare the forms and identify those that are the same or different (Molnar and Reighard, 1984).

23. Show the student a shape for approximately five seconds. Remove the shape and present a second. Ask, "Is this shape the same as the first one?" As the student progresses, decrease the time of presentation of the first shape and wait longer before presenting the second (Molnar and Reighard, 1984).

24. Arrange three or four shapes in a specific

order. Have the student close his eyes while you rearrange them. Have him put them back in order or name them in order from memory (Molnar and Reighard, 1984).

25. Arrange five or six shapes on the table. Cover the shapes. Show one duplicate shape to the pupil for five seconds. Remove the duplicate. Then uncover the original shapes and have the student identify the matching form (Molnar and Reighard, 1984).

26. Have the student match playing cards by suit (Molnar and Reighard, 1984).

27. Have the student cross out one of a series of pictures that is different from the rest (Molnar and Reighard, 1984).

28. Have the student pair design cards that are almost alike. Have him tell what part, size, or color makes them different (Molnar and Reighard, 1984).

29. Make outlines of shapes with rope on the floor. Ask the student to walk along the edge of the rope. Have him move inside of the shape, find the corners, and describe the shape (Molnar and Reighard, 1984).

30. Present a series of shapes in which one is rotated. Have the student identify the one that is rotated (Molnar and Reighard, 1984).

31. Ask the student to identify the geometric shapes of square, circle, rectangle, and triangle in such common objects as baking pans, checkerboards, floor tiles, and traffic signs (Wolf, 1982).

32. Have the student experiment with geoblocks or sets of geometric figures made from cardboard to form new shapes. Discuss the characteristics of the shapes (Wolf, 1982).

33. Have the student make shapes using geoboards and rubber bands (Wolf, 1982).

34. Make shape mosaics using bathroom tile pieces (Sorrell, 1978).

35. Describe several shapes as you show them to the student, then remove the shapes from sight. Give the student clues and have him guess the one that you are thinking of (Warner, 1973).

36. Have the student complete form-board activities with the shapes (Warner, 1973).

37. Cut shapes out of felt for use on a flannelboard. Have the student arrange the shapes. Ask him to identify the ones that are alike and discriminate between the ones that are different (Warner, 1973).

38. Using materials or objects large enough to manipulate, have students turn shapes in different directions to demonstrate differences in appearances (Warner, 1973).

39. Have the student use materials such as straws, pipe cleaners, wire, and tinker toys to explore shapes. Through discussion and questioning, elicit such ideas as the rectangle has four corners and four line segments, the triangle has three corners and three line segments, and the square has four line segments that are the same length (Wolf, 1982).

40. Shine a flashlight at a surface. Have the student trace the beam of light to the illuminated part of the shape and tactilely follow the shape it makes (Bernstein, 1979).

41. Spatial awareness can be reinforced by using a blindfold and asking the student to verbally respond to the tactile sensations of varying shapes (McCulloch, 1971).

42. Promote good posture. Tilting the head too far to one side causes distortion (Liepmann, 1973).

43. Using copper plates, have the student burnish shapes that have been predrawn. The student begins with a two-dimensional representation of a shape and produces a three-dimensional representation (L. Carelli-Lang, personal communication, 1986).

44. Using different colored blocks, both you and the student place a block in your hands without seeing which block the other has chosen. When both of you open your hands, the student must state whether the blocks are the same or different in shape and color (Bernstein, 1979).

45. Reinforce the concept of shapes by relating them to animal and human body parts

(e.g., circle for head, rectangle for torso) (L. Carelli-Lang, personal communication, 1986).

46. Relate shapes to familiar objects within the home and classroom. Discuss the similarities of shape among these objects (Liepmann, 1973).

47. Improvement in a visually impaired student's functioning can be accomplished by enlarging the object through reproduction, magnification, a telescopic device, moving the student closer to the object, regulating the illumination of the object, and manipulating foreground-background contrasts (Gardner, 1985).

48. Use capsule paper to assist the student with tactile stimulation as an aid to visual identification. Capsule paper is specially treated to raise when heat is applied to blackened surfaces (Andrews, 1985).

49. Have the student place pegs into a pegboard with a predrawn shape on it. Have the child string the pegs together using a shoelace (L. Carelli-Lang, personal communication, 1986).

50. Recommend a complete medical eye exam to detect any eye pathologies (Casey, 1984).

51. To improve the student's ability to discern flat shapes to solid form, have him draw and cut out a flat rectangle and a flat half circle. After he cuts them out, fold them to form a solid cylinder and a pyramid (Liepmann, 1973).

52. Give the student a predrawn shape and have him make a person, animal, or object using this shape as the foundation for the picture (L. Carelli-Lang, personal communication, 1986).

53. Have the student use clay to form shapes that provide a three-dimensional and tactile approach (Liepmann, 1973).

54. Provide a page full of predrawn shapes. Using a color key (e.g., square = blue, circle = red), have the student color the shapes (L. Carelli-Lang, personal communication, 1986).

194

Cannot Match Pictures or Symbols

1. Reinforce the student for correct matching.

2. Provide lotto games for picture or symbol matching. Use the letters or symbols with which the student is having difficulty to make the lotto cards. Use other cards to cover the pictures or symbols and proceed as in a regular lotto game (Ebersole, Kephart, and Ebersole, 1968).

3. Prepare large bingo cards for image matching. Use flash cards to "call" the image. Have the student cover the image if it is found on his card (Ebersole, Kephart, and Ebersole, 1968).

4. Use printed exercises in which the student is required to circle identical images. A printed exercise is more difficult when he is required to pick out the image unlike the others (Ebersole, Kephart, and Ebersole, 1968).

5. Purchase a set of rubber stamps that illustrate a variety of objects and symbols. Have the student stamp the object on paper, choose the name of the stamped object from a list, and write the object's name on the paper (Ebersole, Kephart, and Ebersole, 1968).

6. Have the student reproduce bead patterns on a string (Frostig and Maslow, 1973).

7. Ask the student to point out various categories of objects in a room or play yard, such as round things, red things, wooden things, and so on (Frostig and Maslow, 1973).

8. Play a game of "Police Officer, Find My Child!" Play the part of a parent and have the student play the part of the police officer. Tell the officer that your child is lost and ask him to help. Describe the child, the kind and color of clothes he is wearing, and other details. The student then finds the student who fits the description (Frostig and Maslow, 1973).

9. Have the student sort shapes. Provide cubes, spheres, and three- and four-sided pyramids. Next, add more irregular shapes (Frostig and Maslow, 1973).

10. Set aside spaces on shelves for blocks of specific shapes. Directly above each space, tape or tack a small drawing of that shape. When the student puts away the blocks, ask him to be sure to put each block in the correct space, thus matching the block with the picture (Frostig and Maslow, 1973).

11. Make or purchase puzzles. Puzzles require the student to match the positive space with the negative space (R. Hayes, personal communication, 1985).

12. Make puzzles with two copies of a simple picture, like large apples. Leave one whole and cut the other in half, quarters, thirds, or fourths. Give the student the whole picture and the parts of the second. Instruct him to put the pieces together such that they match the whole picture (Cruickshank, 1977).

13. Paint and construct a box to look like Noah's ark. Place pairs of small plastic toy animals inside the ark. Have the student match the pairs (R. Hayes, personal communication, 1985).

14. Have the student match pairs of cards with pictures or symbols on them. Ask him questions (e.g., "Why should these two cards go together? What is this? What is it called?") (Cruickshank, 1977).

15. Begin with a few pairs for the student to match and gradually increase the number as the student successfully works with more stimuli. At first, present identical pictures or forms on color-cued cards. Eventually pictures or forms may be similar rather than identical (Cruickshank, 1977).

16. Provide matching through various aspects: color, shape, configuration, picture, picture-word, picture-sentence, pattern, symbol, configuration-symbol, symbol-word, object-word, word-word, rhyming pictures, antonyms, synonyms, sums (e.g., 6 + 3 and 4 + 5), shapes in different sizes, identical items with missing parts, gross likeness, gross difference, size, internal detail, actions, parts of a whole, lower-case letters, upper-case letters, and lower-case and upper-case letters (Cruickshank, 1977).

17. Use the overhead projector to project shapes, colors, or symbols. Have the student discuss the properties of the shape. Place another shape on the projector alongside the first one and have him discuss the properties of that shape. Have him determine whether or not the two shapes are the same (R. Hayes, personal communication, 1985).

18. Have the student do dictionary work by giving words from his reader and having him match the letters and words with the ones in the dictionary. To make a simpler task, tell the student which page of the dictionary contains the word (R. Hayes, personal communication, 1985).

19. Have the student match mirror images by pointing out relevant similarities and differences using overlays and directional markings (Casey, 1984).

20. Using a 100-hole pegboard with three colors of pegs, have the student copy a simple design that has been made on paper (Faas, 1972).

21. Draw a series of four symbols, in which two of the symbols match. On another piece of paper cut out windows that correspond to the drawn symbols. Fasten the two pages together. Have the student open the doors until he finds two symbols that match (R. Hayes, personal communication, 1985).

22. Have the student fish for pairs. Attach a magnet to the end of a fishing pole made from a stick and a string. Fasten paper clips to pairs of different objects or symbols on paper cutouts of fish. Scatter the fish on the floor and have the student fish for matches (R. Hayes, personal communication, 1985).

23. Take a student to a small parking lot. Copy two or three license plate numbers from the cars. Have the student find the cars that

match the written license plate numbers (Hall, 1969).

24. Using a polaroid camera, take two or three photographs of several students. Shuffle the photographs and have the student sort them into piles of each person (R. Hayes, personal communication, 1985).

25. Make a matching game by drawing and cutting several simple figures with large feet. Paste these onto a cookie sheet. With bits of magnetic tape on the back, prepare several pairs of shoes for the student to match and place on the feet of the figures (R. Hayes, personal communication,1985).

26. Using commercially prepared hidden item pictures, trace the hidden items (to be used as a cue sheet). Have the student match the items on the cue sheet with the ones hidden in the picture. To increase the difficulty, have him match the cue words to the hidden pictures (R. Hayes, personal communication, 1985).

27. Prepare two copies of the same symbol. In each drawing, remove part of the outline. Instruct the student to complete each drawing so that they match each other (R. Hayes, personal communication, 1985).

28. With small wooden tiles in various angular shapes, such as triangles and squares, have the student match exact size and shape patterns of the design sheets provided. Initially, he can match the materials by placing them directly on the design sheets. As he becomes more skilled, the design can be assembled on a space next to the picture (J. Curlington, personal communication, 1985).

29. Halve several pieces of fruit and ask the student to match the two halves together by smell and sight (K. Bondi, personal communication, 1985).

30. Draw a number of different geometric figures on a portable blackboard and take it outside. Have the student race to the corresponding figures on the playground (e.g., baseball diamond, rectangular benches, etc.) (Cratty and Martin, 1969).

31. Have the student cut out shapes and match them with objects in the lunch room and on the playground (Cratty and Martin, 1969).

32. Draw figures on a piece of paper and have the student walk in a similar pattern in a sandbox (Cratty and Martin, 1969).

33. Have the student match the letters and objects shown with the letters on a large grid. Have the student throw a bean bag on the square of the correct letter or object (Cratty and Martin, 1969).

34. Draw the outline of an object on the blackboard and then place the same object on it (e.g., a key, scissors). Give the objects to the student and let him place the objects on their proper outline. Change the position of the drawings so he can't memorize the original order (Barrett, 1965).

35. Using paper of various colors, paste very distinct shapes on the floor. Give the student the same shapes with the same colors and let him match them. Later, give him the same objects to match, but with different colors (Bornstein and Stiles-Davis, 1984).

36. Have the student look at parts of pictures from left to right and pick out similarities to find their matches.

37. Use map reading. Have the student match the objects in the key with objects on the maps (Ekwall, 1985).

38. Have the student play "Candyland" (Milton Bradley). Match colors and various types of candies (M. Olscamp, personal communication, 1985).

39. Give the student puzzle pieces. Put a finished picture of the puzzle by his side. Have him look at the designs and colors in both, and match them (Wagner, 1971).

40. Ask the student to look around the room or outdoors and name different kinds of objects that have a certain similarity (e.g., show all things which are round, square, triangular, blue, pink, long, thin, vertical, hortizontal, etc.) (Wagner, 1971).

41. Give the student a variety of objects to hold, such as a disc, ball, or colored stick.

Place other objects of the same shapes on his desk. Some objects should be the same size as the one the student is holding. Have the student identify the same shapes of the same size (Ghent and Bernstein, 1963).

42. Play "I Spy" with the student (e.g., "I spy something shaped like this" (show a picture) "What is it?") (Buktenica, 1968).

43. Give the student a row of pumpkin pictures with various faces, or Christmas trees with various ornaments, and ask him to circle the ones that match the original (Jolles, 1958).

44. Give the student a letter of the alphabet on a card and some modeling clay. Ask him to look at the letter *L* and make it with the clay. Then show him the letter *M* and ask him to make it. Last, ask him to look at the letter *T* and ask him to make it. Now take the cards and arrange them in various orders. Ask the student to match the picture with the clay models (Keogh and Keogh, 1967).

45. Buy or make some cutout Christmas cookies. Have the students match the cookies with the correct cookie cutters (M. Olscamp, personal communication, 1985).

46. Cut two sets of identical pictures from two magazines. Have the student match the pictures (M. Olscamp, personal communication, 1985).

47. Have two or more students play "Find a Pair." Make four sets of 12 pairs of cards, each card differing only slightly from the other in its pairs. The sets promote fine visual discrimination (Piazza, 1979).

48. Play "House Lotto." The houses in this lotto game differ only in small details. Have the student match the similar ones and tell the differences between the others (Gervais, Harvey, and Roberts, 1984).

49. Have the student play "Store." Give the student a shopping list with pictures on it instead of words. Have him match the things on the list to what is on the shelf. Have him put what he buys in a cart (Frostig and Horne, 1964).

50. While playing music, show the student pictures of instruments and have the student match the sound of the instrument with its picture (Bornstein and Stiles-Davis, 1984).

51. Show the student various types of flowers that are near the school. Take him outside and have him match the picture with the flower (Cratty, 1969).

52. Use flannel board objects. Have the student put all the apples in one group, circles in another, and pears in another. Try this with objects that are the same and different color to see if he is grouping them by color (Gibson, Gibson, Pick, and Osler, 1962).

53. Have the student take a sheet of paper with the classroom desks shown on it and draw the objects from the room that are missing (Ekwall, 1985).

54. Give the student two words that are similar and let him tell you what letters differ (e.g., *ate, at*) (Orton, 1966).

55. Have the student draw a house in vertical and horizontal positions. After his drawings are completed, match them with other vertical-horizontal drawings (Perner, Kohlmann, and Wimmer, 1984).

195
Depth Perception Difficulties

1. Recommend a medical eye exam to detect any pathologies (Casey, 1984).

2. If no evidence of eye pathology is found, recommend referral to a psychologist (J. Twist, personal communication, 1986).

3. Determine if this difficulty occurs only in darker environments or at night, or if it becomes worse at these times. Accurate depth perception is more difficult in low light.

4. Promote good posture. Distortion occurs when the head is tilted too far to one side (Liepmann, 1973).

5. A person playing a musical instrument in the foreground, another in the middle-

ground, and another in the background would allow the student to hear the closeness of the sound and correlate that with the closeness of the player (L. Carelli-Lang, personal communication, 1986).

6. Use optical illusions to increase the student's ability to understand spatial surroundings (Liepmann, 1973).

7. Teach the student that increased distance makes objects look smaller (Liepmann, 1973).

8. Teach the student to use contextual and environmental cues to determine size and depth of field.

9. Stand with your students in front of a window or outdoors where you can see both stationary and moving objects. Ask your student which ones are closest and how he can tell (Liepmann, 1973).

10. Have the student watch a person approach. Tell him to notice how more of the visual field is occupied as objects get closer.

11. Have the student walk away from one person, past another, and turn around. Direct him to notice how the first person appears to be smaller due to the longer separation distance, whereas the second person appears to be larger due to closeness.

12. Obtain a photograph or painting that shows perspective. Show the student that even in two dimensions, we interpret smaller objects as being farther away (Liepmann, 1973).

13. Teach the student about Renaissance art which first used perspective and depth in painting. Compare such paintings with paintings from the Medieval era.

14. While driving in a vehicle, point out to the student that the cars closest to him are clearer than those in the distance. Quiz the student by asking him to identify cars by certain characteristics. He will find that it is easier to identify these qualities on cars closest to him. Cars in the distance will appear as flashes of color (Liepmann, 1973).

15. Use optical illusions to discuss and teach

depth perception and manipulation of perspective.

196

Has Difficulty Finding Hidden Pictures in the Background (Figure-Ground Problems)

1. Help the student improve figure-ground perception by using everyday opportunities for practice. For example, while out walking, ask, "Do you see the white house?" "Do you see the little bird sitting in the grass?" "Do you see the colored stone?" (Frostig and Maslow, 1973).

2. While reading a story aloud, hold up pictures that have considerable detail in them and ask the students to identify separate objects in each picture (Frostig and Maslow, 1973).

3. Provide various collections of objects. Ask the student to find a specific object in a collection. For example, ask the student to find a green marble among blue ones (Frostig and Maslow, 1973).

4. Mix objects of two or more types together and ask the student to sort them (Frostig and Maslow, 1973).

5. Ask the student to sort a collection of shapes (Frostig and Maslow, 1973).

6. Draw a picture of a circle, triangle, square, or some other shape. Have the student copy your drawing. Ask him to draw a picture using that shape (e.g., a square can be made into a house or a truck). Have the student find the original shape (Molnar and Reighard, 1984).

7. Show a picture of a shape. Ask the student to find other things in the room that are the same shape (Molnar and Reighard, 1984).

8. Draw outlines of three or four objects superimposed on each other. Have the student outline each in a different color (Warner, 1973).

9. Draw designs and figures on printed wallpaper. Have the student identify the forms (Warner, 1973).

10. Have the student draw pictures on printed wallpaper for classmates to identify (Warner, 1973).

11. Using overlays, show the process of drawing an object. Add plastic sheets with other designs. Ask the student to identify the original object. Reverse the process as necessary (Warner, 1973).

12. Draw or print with a felt marker on newspaper. Ask the student to identify the figure (Kephart, 1960; Warner, 1973).

13. Ask the student to fill in missing parts of a figure, first on plain ground, then on more complex ground (Warner, 1973).

14. Ask the student to outline pictures in one color, color the picture in another color, and then color background in another color (Warner, 1973).

15. Create picture pages in which the main figure is blended into the background. Have the student color only the main figure (Warner, 1973).

16. Use markers or stencils to help students frame hidden words or shapes (Warner, 1973).

17. Ask the student to pick out certain details in a picture (Warner, 1973).

18. Work with students to find hidden figures in pictures. Describe the object to be found or show a picture of it (Warner, 1973).

19. Print random letters on a paper. Ask the student to locate a certain letter (Warner, 1973).

20. Have the student complete word search puzzles (Warner, 1973).

21. Show the student a letter or a word on a card. Ask him to find examples of it in books, magazines, or catalogs and circle the letters or words (Ali, 1980).

22. Cut out approximately six each of various shapes in different sizes and colors. Place the shapes in various places in the room. Ask the student to hunt for the shapes. After the shapes have been found, have him name other objects in the room that have the same shape (Wedemeyer, 1975).

23. Using a stencil, draw a large letter, number, or shape onto a piece of paper. Draw lines dissecting the form and the remainder of the paper. In each section of the form, indicate that it should be darkened with a certain color. Have the student color in the designated sections. The hidden form becomes apparent when the coloring is complete (Wedemeyer, 1975).

24. Prepare a ditto grid with 1/2" × 1/2" squares, six spaces horizontally and seven spaces vertically. Write the letters *A* through *F* across the top and the numbers 1 through 6 down the left column. Prepare a design by placing dots in the appropriate squares. Write directions for the design. For example, "Draw a straight line connecting the dot in *A* to the dot in *1F, 1F,* to *5D,* and *5D* to *1A.*" When the student completes the design, he colors the shape in a solid color (Wedemeyer, 1975).

25. Use parquetry blocks to provide finer discrimination in recognition and reproduction of forms and training in visual memory (Wold, 1969).

26. Add or reduce large cue differences on the relevant shape dimension as necessary (Matson and McCartney, 1981).

27. Add or fade redundant color dimensions as necessary (Matson and McCartney, 1981).

28. Use a variety of textures for the background or main figure. Have the student touch the main design to help discriminate (M. B. Dean, personal communication, 1985).

29. Construct boards using marbles of different colors. Design a specific picture against a marble background. Give the student opportunities to reconstruct the picture, against the strong influence of the background, on his own board (Werner and Strauss, 1941).

30. Have the student trace the main picture with his finger and then draw the picture on another sheet of paper (Werner and Strauss, 1941).

31. Make a board with flat enameled thumb tacks as the background and semi-spherical rubber tacks of the same diameter rising 5 mm above the background to form a hidden picture, shape, or design. Cover the board so the student cannot see it. Allow him to use his touch only. Once he thinks he knows what the shape is, have him draw it on a piece of paper (Werner and Strauss, 1941).

32. Rely heavily on color. Outline the hidden shapes and pictures with bright colors and gradually change to duller and duller colors (Cruickshank, 1961).

33. Make puzzles in such a way that the student sees the entire picture immediately with a plain background. Gradually add backgrounds to the puzzles (Cruickshank, 1961).

34. Expose a magazine picture that contains a number of familiar objects. Cover it and have the student tell as many things as he remembers seeing (Cruickshank, 1961).

35. Using a shoebox and predrawn objects (e.g., people and cars) with tabs, make a diarama. The student first makes the environment in which the objects should be placed, then glues the objects in the foreground (L. Carelli-Lang, personal communication, 1986).

36. Have students put on a puppet show. Scene design reinforces background while the props are placed in the foreground along with the puppets (L. Carelli-Lang, personal communication, 1986).

37. Use overlays and markers as visual cues to assist the student in discerning foreground and background (Casey, 1984).

197

Has Difficulty Imitating Body Movements, Positions, or Patterns

1. Reinforce the student for imitating observed movements (W. Grimm, personal communication, 1985).

2. Stand in front of a pair of students. Move a certain part of your body. The students attempt to imitate you. If needed, one student helps his partner into the correct position (K. Diehl, personal communication, 1986).

3. Stand in front of a large mirror with the student at your side. Move a specific body part. Have the student imitate the action (Valett, 1974).

4. Have your pupils stand one behind the other while they imitate your movements. Have the student who will have more difficulty stand toward the back. This allows him to copy the others without feeling intimidated (Rosner, 1973).

5. Have the students stand behind each other facing forward. The students take turns being the leader. The leader makes body movements. The rest of the students imitate him (K. Diehl, personal communication, 1986).

6. Have the students stand in a circle holding hands. As they walk around, they sing:

"Here we go loop-te-loo
Here we go loop-te-lie
Here we go loop-te-loo
All on a Saturday night."

Players then drop hands and continue singing:

"I put my right foot in
I take my right foot out
I give my foot a shake, shake, shake
And turn myself about."

Students continue singing and changing body parts (Rosner, 1973).

7. Tie a balloon around the student's wrist and your own wrist. Tell him what part of his body should hit or touch the balloon. Demonstrate the actions if necessary. He then calls out the next body part to touch the balloon (Leary and von Schneden, 1982).

8. Write positional concepts on index cards that are cut into the shape of fish. Put a paper clip on each. Tie a string with a magnet attached to the end of a yardstick. One student, who is the "fisherman," goes fishing while the other students watch. He then demonstrates the directions on the index card (e.g., raise right leg, etc.). The other students imitate this action. Then choose a new fisherman (Leary and von Schneden, 1982).

9. Provide hula hoops for yourself and the student. Twirl the hoop on a body part. Move the specified body part to keep the hula hoop moving. Have the student imitate this action (Leary and von Schneden, 1982).

10. Make an old-fashioned wooden or cardboard movie box. Using rolled paper, draw stick figures that show different movements. The student stands facing the box and imitates the movement shown by the stick figure (Leary and von Schneden, 1982).

11. Give a specific direction involving body movements (e.g., touch your nose, shake your right hand, etc.). Have the students follow the directions. When the students perform correctly, give them a small piece of tape to be placed on the specified body part used. The student with the most tape wins (Leary and von Schneden, 1982).

12. Move like a robot and have the student imitate. Costumes may be added (Leary and von Schneden, 1982).

13. Have students sit in a circle. Give directions to a chosen student (e.g., touch Bill's shoes, rub John's arm, etc.) (Leary and von Schneden, 1982).

14. Have students listen to the record "Basic Motor and Ball Skills" by David G. Rem-

baugh. Follow directions and imitate each other. The record can be obtained from Bowmar Records, Inc., 622 Rodier Drive, Glendale, CA 91201 (213/247-8995) (Farrald and Schamber, 1973).

15. Have the students line up one behind the other. The first student makes body movements while walking on a board. The other students follow and imitate. Change leaders periodically (Cejka and Needham, 1977).

16. Assign the student a partner. One student creates the movement patterns and is designated as the person looking into "a mirror." The other student attempts to imitate the movements and is designated as "the mirror" (Simpson, 1977).

17. Set up a simple obstacle course. Go through the obstacle course using many body movements and patterns. Have the student imitate the movements (Cejka and Needham, 1977).

18. Place tape or rope on the floor in straight and curved lines. Have the student walk on the line (Cejka and Needham, 1977).

19. Have the students stand in a circle. Going in order, have each student call out the name of an animal or object. All the students pretend to be that animal or object (Valett, 1974).

20. Play "Simon Says." Call out a body movement including the phrase "Simon Says . . . ." The student should only imitate the movement if the phrase *Simon says* is included. Otherwise, he is eliminated from this round or moved to the back of the group (Shelquist, Breeze, and Jacquot, 1973).

21. Put marching music on the record player. Stand in front of the students who are in a line, one behind the other. As you are marching, call out a variety of commands that the students follow (e.g., put your hands on your head) (Shelquist, Breeze, and Jacquot, 1973).

22. Choose an animal and imitate how the animal would walk around the room. The stu-

dent imitates and suggests different animals. Costumes may be added (Cratty, 1973; Shelquist, Breeze, and Jacquot, 1973).

23. Make a life-sized human body with movable parts. Stand behind the dummy while the students stand in front of it. Move a part of the dummy while the students imitate the specified movement (S. Kennedy, personal communication, 1986).

24. Sing a simple song containing or referring to a body part, such as, "I'm being swallowed by a hippopotamus, hippopotamus, hippopotamus. I'm being swallowed by a hippopotamus." After the beginning, continue with different verses. For example:

"Oh no, he's got my toe.
Oh gee, he's got my knee.
Oh fiddle, he's got my middle.
Oh darn, he's got my arm.
Oh heck, he's got my neck.
Gulp."

The student touches the specified body part when mentioned (Melear, 1973).

25. Have the students sit in a circle. The leader touches a part of his body and says that it is a different body part. For example, the leader touches his eye and says, "This is my arm." A second student does the opposite and touches the body part named and calls it the name of the part to which the leader pointed. For example, the second student touches his own arm and says, "This is my eye." (Melear, 1973).

26. Pretend you are rowing a boat, peddling a bicycle, flying like a plane, and so on. Have the student imitate you (Cratty, 1973; Lerch, Becker, Ward, and Nelson, 1974).

27. Take photos of students. Cut the picture into puzzle pieces. Have the student piece the puzzle together and imitate the pose in the picture (Stock, 1970).

28. Present an aerobic dance class for your student.

29. Obtain pictures of popular movie or sports personalities. Have the student imitate the poses in the pictures.

30. Have the student watch a movie or television show and imitate the body position of a character when you say, "Now."

31. Encourage the student to plan his movement pattern before he responds (Kephart, 1971).

32. Remove distractions so that the student can develop control for mastering a difficult task (Freischlag, 1973).

33. Have the student watch himself performing movements in the mirror as directed. Once a certain movement has been mastered, have him attempt the movement without a mirror (Adler, 1964).

34. Conduct dancing lessons and improvisations in front of a mirror (W. Gramm, personal communication, 1985).

35. Have one student assume and maintain a certain pose. The problem student tries to imitate this pose. Since the leader holds the pose over time, the student has an opportunity to check his response (Kephart, 1971).

36. Seat the students in a circle. Give the first pupil an object and ask him to pass it to a second student. The second student must pass it on with the same movement that the first student used in delivering it (Kephart, 1971).

198
Has Difficulty Tracing, Drawing, and Forming Letters

1. At the chalkboard, have the student draw large circles with both hands, first counterclockwise and then clockwise (Cohen, 1974).

2. Have the student make a large star by drawing lines in and out of a chalked X on the chalkboard (Cohen, 1974).

3. Have the student use paper or plastic stencils to trace outlines of objects or letters (Cohen, 1974).

4. Have one student at the chalkboard while another student gives explicit directions for drawing a simple shape (B. Rex, personal communication, 1985).

5. Have the student trace over a motif that is placed directly in front of him. Tracing should be done with both hands and in both directions. Vary the size of the motif and the speed of the tracing (Chaney and Kephart, 1968).

6. Instruct the student to draw lines between goals, both vertically and horizontally. Have him draw in one direction several times, then the other (Chaney and Kephart, 1968).

7. Place 10 dots on a piece of paper and have the student join the dots to make figures. Color the enclosed area with different textures and colors (Haskell, 1979).

8. Provide continuous opportunities for the student to draw and paint (Haskell, 1979).

9. Allow the student to explore lines and shapes by drawing at an easel on a large sheet of newsprint (Haskell, 1979).

10. Let the student follow over his pencil lines with a squeezable bottle of glue. He then sprinkles chalk flakes, glitter, or sawdust over the glue to complete a picture (Haskell, 1979).

11. To gain control of a crayon, the student should lift the crayon and repeat lines and curves (Lindberg and Swedlow, 1976).

12. Provide the opportunity for the student to scribble to develop coordination (Lindberg and Swedlow, 1976).

13. Provide repeated experiences with the drawing of symbols of familiar shapes and objects. This will enable the student to perceive relationships and develop a concept of distance (Lindberg and Swedlow, 1976).

14. Help the student hold his writing implement correctly. It should be held in a relaxed yet firm manner between the thumb and first two fingers (Cratty, 1971).

15. Help the student determine which hand works best for him. Give the student a reasonably difficult task, such as cutting with scissors or combing hair three times a week for several weeks. Keep a record of the hand preference the student indicates for each task (Cratty, 1971).

16. Stabilize the hand with which the student writes while he moves it to draw or trace (Cratty, 1971).

17. While guiding the student's hand for drawing or tracing, encourage him to watch the movements. Eventually allow him to write without guidance (Cratty, 1971).

18. Place bright lining tape on a table outlining various figures and letters to help the student draw vertical and horizontal lines (Cratty, 1971).

19. Provide various grooved surfaces through which the student can trace geometric figures and block-printed letters (Cratty, 1971).

20. Have the student connect dots as an exercise to encourage him to move accurately through his space fields. Especially useful are dots around the perimeter of the paper which connect with one dot in the center (Cratty, 1971).

21. Arrange dots so that connecting them will result in various block-print letters (Cratty, 1971).

22. When specific letters prove difficult for the student to draw, have him walk a large replica of the letter made with chalk on the schoolyard pavement. Have him walk the letter several times, then go to the chalkboard, trace the letter there, write in on the chalkboard, and then transfer this skill to lined paper (Choate and Young, 1982).

23. Direct the student in drawing letters on sandpaper with a crayon or piece of chalk (Choate and Young, 1982).

24. Have the student draw letters or shapes in a box filled with sand or salt. A magic slate is also useful (Choate and Young, 1982).

25. Give the student sandpaper letters and a pencil and paper. Blindfold him and have him trace a letter. Remove the blindfold and have him say the letter and write it (Choate and Young, 1982).

26. Use transparencies to project the image of a shape or letter on the chalkboard or a large sheet of paper. Have the student trace over the image (Choate and Young, 1982).

27. Write a complete word and have the student trace it. Then write the first part of the word and have him trace it before completing the word (Choate and Young, 1982).

28. Draw a complete figure, then an outline of the same figure using dots. Have the student make the figure by connecting the dots (Choate and Young, 1982).

29. Using an overhead projector, project large letters with arrows to indicate starting points and changes of direction so the student can trace over the image (Choate and Young, 1982).

30. Have the student make letters in the air before making them on the chalkboard. Prior to putting letters on paper, have him make the letters about two inches above the paper, gradually move closer to the paper, and finally make the letter on the paper (B. Rex, personal communication, 1985).

31. Have the student say the motions being made while drawing the letters (Choate and Young, 1982).

32. Purchase a 2″ plastic guide (available at most department stores). The triangular piece slips onto the pencil, allowing the student to grip the pencil on two of the three sides correctly as the third side rests on the middle finger (Choate and Young, 1982).

33. Provide the student with a ball of clay. Instruct him to roll the clay into a thin slab. Lightly scratch letters or words onto the clay. Tell him to trace over the words with a stick, pencil, or nail (Karstadt, 1976).

34. Have the student roll a ball of clay into strips and use them to form words or shapes. The shapes or words can then be traced with the finger and later drawn on lined paper (Karstadt, 1976).

35. Print a word lightly in pencil on a sheet of cardboard. Have the student trace over the lines with an eraser, thus erasing the word (Karstadt, 1976).

36. Clap an eraser filled with chalk dust. Instruct the student to trace in the chalk dust (Karstadt, 1976).

37. Instruct the student to dip his finger or a paintbrush in water and trace out letters, words, or shapes on a slate or chalkboard (Karstadt, 1976).

38. Draw shapes or letters on a sheet of typing paper. Clip it over a sheet of carbon paper with another sheet of paper underneath. Have the student trace the letters to make a carbon copy (Karstadt, 1976).

39. Print letters or words in short, broken lines for the student to trace (Karstadt, 1976).

40. Give directions for the student to follow as you demonstrate how to create a drawing in steps on the blackboard.

41. Provide numbered reference points on the chalkboard and the student's paper to assist him in drawing a design.

42. Provide cardboard cutouts that the student can use to draw a shape.

43. Have the student frequently reproduce the same design or symbol. The item will quickly become stereotyped and thereafter suffer little change (Frostig and Maslow, 1973; Bartlett, 1964).

44. Have the student complete connect-the-dots sheets which result in a completed drawing of an object.

45. Have the student complete partially completed drawings.

46. Teach prerequisite skills, such as directionality and topography: *in-out, right-left, up-down, top-bottom, under-over, beginning-end, tall-short, of-off, big-little, oblique, diagonal, slanting, one, two, three, around, across, middle, center, curve, trace, vertical, horizontal, circle,* and *straight line.* With the acquisition of these key vocabulary words, the student and you can describe the images to be mastered (Ebersole, Kephart, and Ebersole, 1968).

47. Task analyze the components of a design or

symbol and teach a simple shape component first. When the student can reproduce the shape, add another component until the whole design has been mastered (R. Hayes, personal communication, 1986).

48. Have the student feel, by tracing, a sandpaper letter. Next, have him trace the letter in a shallow plate of salt or sand. Repeat the procedure until he can trace the letter in the salt without feeling the sandpaper letter (J. Carlington, personal communication, 1985).

49. Have the student first trace an image or symbol. Gradually fade the image by decreasing its intensity until it is barely visible. Next, fade out parts of the image and have him trace the shape, thus connecting the parts together. Continue to fade the im-

age (R. Hayes, personal communication, 1985).

50. Using chocolate pudding on a plate, draw a letter or shape while the student is watching. Erase the letter and have him draw the same shape in the pudding with his finger. If the student draws the shape correctly, allow him to eat the pudding (L. Stern, personal communication, 1985).

51. Guide the student in imaging by having him listen to verbal cues that become more and more specific (e.g., "Close your eyes and imagine an apple. Can you see it? Do you have a small picture of it in front of you that you can see? Can you count the blemishes on it?") After the student has had some success envisioning, have him draw what he saw (Hendricks and Wills, 1975).

Written Expression

199

Can't Take Notes Properly

1. Reinforce the student for well-organized, accurate note taking.

2. Review the student's notebook and give written feedback to the student (Simms, 1983).

3. Indicate when it is important to put certain information into one's notes. Tell the students or use nonverbal signals (e.g., tie thrown over your shoulder).

4. Help the student to develop an outline or summary style that is comfortable for him (Dansereau, 1985).

5. Have the student take notes with a peer (Dansereau, 1985).

6. Science experiments need to be done slowly and meticulously. Sequencing of steps is vital to make the experiment work. This type of activity can help demonstrate

how important sequencing is, while training the student to jot notes as each step is completed (Bond and Tinker, 1967).

7. Use a co-study method by having both you and the student read required material before outlining it. Compare ideas (Bond and Tinker, 1967).

8. Use oral interviewing of students by each other. This will require the student to jot down notes of interest. Later, a summary paragraph can be written from it (Bond and Tinker, 1967).

9. Prepare a ditto for the student before a lecture. The sheet should give three or four of the major points, but leave space so that he can fill in the examples, details, and evidence given during the lecture (Devine, 1981).

10. Use an encyclopedia with the student. Show him how the authors summarize material. If another set of encyclopedias is available, compare this author's summary to another one (Devine, 1981).

11. Teach basic outline format to the student. At first it should be teacher prepared, but later he can complete his own (Devine, 1981).

12. Use the outline form in all content areas, and encourage other teachers to do the same. Whenever an essay is to be written, the student should use this format (J. Richter, personal communication, 1985).

13. Have the student prepare an oral report, using a required outline. Give assistance in formulating the report (Devine, 1981).

14. Encourage an individualized note-taking system for this student if other methods seem to fail. For example, he might use color coding, arrows pointing from the main topic to the subtopic, or circular arrangements. Remember that note taking should be used and understood by the student. Any system that works for him is appropriate (Devine, 1981).

15. Have the student tape his notes. He can then listen to these notes as a review before a test (Devine, 1981).

16. Discuss positive suggestions for note taking with other members of the class. Have others share ideas that have worked for them (Devine, 1981).

17. Have the student work with others in preparing a study guide of material that is to be covered next week. Prepare questions, a list of new vocabulary, difficult terms, and the like. Make copies of this to be distributed to the rest of the class (Devine, 1981).

18. Have the student prepare to teach a lesson to younger students in the school. In order to do this, he must make notes of what is to be done and in what order. After he teaches the lesson, review the notes with him to see how they helped to keep the lesson moving (J. Richter, personal communication, 1985).

19. Provide the student with an outline format to be filled in during instruction.

20. Provide the student with partially completed notes on a ditto.

21. Have the student write a sentence that the teacher reads aloud. Then have him monitor his own material by reading it aloud very slowly, checking for accuracy (Johnson, 1967).

22. Follow an oral discussion with a review before having the student convert it to written language (Johnson, 1967).

23. List all the major points of the lesson on the chalkboard. During the lecture, stop and indicate the points being discussed (Devine, 1981).

24. Have students explain to the class how to make fudge, how to repair a flat tire, and so on. The other students jot down notes, using transitional devices, such as *first, next, finally,* and the like. When completed, all students compare their lists to see if all points were covered (Devine, 1981).

25. Let the student choose a magazine article of interest. Together, highlight topic sentences and key words and write an outline from the highlighted sentences (J. Richter, personal communication, 1985).

26. Have the student classify word lists according to categories and tell how two things are the same or different. For example, milk and crackers can both be found in a grocery store, and they are both something to eat, but one must be kept in the refrigerator one is a dairy product (J. Richter, personal communication, 1985).

27. Develop a core vocabulary for a specific topic before the presentation of the unit. Review these terms with the student, making sure he understands what they mean and how they are related to one another (Weiss and Weiss, 1982).

28. Use the who, what, where, when, why, and how questions to organize a report. Make up questions for the student that he must answer (Weiss and Weiss, 1982).

29. Create a bulletin board in the classroom with cards indicating topic and subtopics. The student must then place notes in the appropriate envelopes as he finds information for his report (Weiss and Weiss, 1982).

30. Have the student take a survey about a par-

ticular product. He can then write a summary of what was found, and mail this to the company. Another variation of this is to take a survey, asking questions of everyone who has read a specific book. Once again, the research is tabulated and sent to the publisher or author (J. Richter, personal communication, 1985).

31. Tape record an entire lecture. Later, sit down with the student, play the tape, and write notes together from the lecture (J. Richter, personal communication, 1985).

32. Have the student preread the assignment. Then, as the material is read a second time, have him use a pen and notebook to jot down all the important information (J. Richter, personal communication, 1985).

200

Difficulties in Written Expression

1. Reinforce the student for good effort and production (Smith, 1973).

2. Have the student read two or more short, simple sentences and combine them into one longer, more complex sentence (Straw, 1982).

3. Have the student focus on an object, idea, or event and think of words that relate to it. The student can then choose the terms he would like to include in the composition (Humes, 1984).

4. Provide the student with first-hand experiences about which to write (e.g., field trips, movies, sports) (Lerner, 1985).

5. Write a story on the board that the student expressed in oral language. Have the student copy the story from the chalkboard (Lerner, 1985).

6. Give the student an object to describe orally. Have him tell what he saw, felt, and heard. Record all details and phrases offered by him. Have him rewrite these in greater detail (Gleason, 1982).

7. Give the student a story in which words are left out. He must complete the story by writing words in the blank areas (Thoburn, Schlatterbeck, and Terry, 1983).

8. To provide practice in description, devise hypothetical situations and let the student describe them aloud. For example, you might say, "I have my eyes closed and am entering a store where chocolate candy is made and sold. What do I smell? Can you describe it?" (Staudacher, 1972)

9. Have a student recall an incidnet that he would like to tell others. He then writes three sentences recounting the incident. One sentence explains what happened at the beginning, one at the middle, and one at the end (Giordano, 1983).

10. Have a student read a story and summarize it in one sentence (Giordano, 1983).

11. Display idea-generating questions on a bulletin board or chart so that the student can see them as he writes (Humes, 1984).

12. Have the student write in a journal each day. This is not corrected by you. It could be a journal of feelings, a historical journal, or a home economics journal (Humes, 1984).

13. Write to each other in a dialogue notebook. The student could write about something he saw, thought about, was confused about, or wanted to complain about. Respond to this while you model proper writing (Giordano, 1983).

14. Have students share the talk-write process with one another. They work in pairs, one as a talker/writer and the other as questioner/clarifier. They discuss what they want to write and then write it together (Rubin, 1980).

15. Have the student draw a picture for a story before writing about it (M. Sciandra, personal communication, 1985).

16. Create a story with the whole class and write in on chart paper. Each student supplies one sentence to the story (M. Sciandra, personal communication, 1985).

17. Demonstrate how to make something (e.g.,

peanut butter and jelly sandwich) and have the student write down the simple steps involved. Then demonstrate the steps as the student wrote them so that he understands that one must be explicit in writing instructional paragraphs (Thoburn, Schlatterbeck, and Terry, 1983).

18. Require writing in other subjects so the student sees the many purposes of writing (Rubin, 1980).

19. For motivation, have the student use any object that he desires as the stimulus to develop a poem, using an outline of the object for margins (Rubin, 1980).

20. Have the student create newspaper poetry, which involves choosing and cutting out words from newspapers and magazines that express certain feelings and thoughts. Words can be of various sizes, shapes, and colors. He then arranges these in a pattern that best expresses the thought or feeling he would like to portray (Rubin, 1980).

21. Avoid discouraging a student through grading procedures. Grade only the ideas, not the technical form, for some assignments. You might also want to give two grades—one for ideas and one for technical skills (Lerner, 1985).

22. Give the student a set of pictures of an event in sequential order. Have him write his own paragraph for each picture (Thoburn, Schlatterbeck, and Terry, 1983).

23. Create a writing center in a corner of the classroom. Have several unfinished sentences on the table and have the student fill in the blanks from a list of appropriate words. Another activity would be to have him choose from a set of pictures and pretend that he is in that scene. He then writes about the events that are happening in that scene (Staudacher, 1972).

24. Promote reading. A student who reads widely will have a broad range of ideas from which to draw for his writing. Through reading, the student may also come to recognize the skills necessary to be a good writer (Rubin, 1980).

25. Give the student a five-line story in which the sentences are not in sequential order. Have him rearrange the sentences to make a story before copying the story (Hurwitz and Goddard, 1972).

26. Help the student learn the importance of opening paragraphs by cutting one from a magazine and reading it to the student. Discuss the paragraph with the student, asking if it captured his attention and motivated him to continue reading (Rubin, 1980).

27. On the board, show the purposes of revision and proofreading and how to revise a composition (Rubin, 1980).

28. If the student cannot seem to get started on a story, present the first part of a story and let him write the ending. Choose a story that leaves the listener "up in the air" or with a problem to solve (Staudacher, 1972).

29. Play dramatic music to provoke thought and stimulate imagination. Have the student jot down any words or mental pictures that came into his mind. He can then write a story or create a poem from his notes (Staudacher, 1972).

30. Have students work together to make up stories (Smith, 1973).

31. Have the student diagram sentences (Reed, 1977).

32. Write several separate kernel sentences. Have the student connect the sentences and make more complex ones by using connectors and adding clauses (Lerner, 1985).

33. Keep an idea sheet for all students in the front of the room. Anyone in the class may write down an idea and anyone else may use it for writing inspiration (Smith, 1973).

34. Encourage the student to copy a favorite passage from his favorite story to experience what the writer must have felt when writing the story (Hersey, 1977).

35. Conduct workshops to provide experiences about which to write. Use media, filmstrips, films, and story books (Fern and Foster, 1977).

36. When writing, have the student use pencil

so that errors can be erased easily and re-written correctly (Hayes, 1975).

37. Encourage the student to read aloud what he is writing as it is being written (Hayes, 1974).

38. Use the cloze method by writing a sentence and leaving out a word. Have the student insert as many different words as possible (Lerner, 1985).

39. Have the student write every day for varying time intervals (Fern and Foster, 1977).

40. Make up stories so your class sees you experiencing the joy of creating (Smith, 1973).

41. Read or tell a story to the class. Focus on and discuss the plot. Chart the progression of the story on the blackboard by having students identify the introduction, development obstacles, climax, resolution, and solution. Keep practicing the routine until the students need little assistance from you (d'Alelio, 1976).

42. Have the student develop his compositions on a tape recorder. Play it back, allowing mistakes to be corrected. Have the student play "secretary" and write the auditory composition (L. Burr, personal communication, 1985).

43. No matter what opinions are conveyed in the student's writing, provide encouraging comments and responses (Klein, 1977).

201
Poor Spelling

1. Reinforce the student for improvement in spelling.

2. Difficult spelling words should be anticipated and listed on the board. Allow the student to ask for the spelling of difficult words (Lerner, 1985).

3. Correct spelling errors not by marking them wrong, but by writing the word correctly for the student to rewrite (Hayes, 1975).

4. Proofread the rough draft for spelling er-

rors. Circle any misspelled words and have the student revise them independent of instruction (L. Burr, personal communication, 1985).

5. Teach the student to use a dictionary while writing.

6. Have the student write misspelled words correctly 20 times each.

7. In order to strengthen the visual impression that is left with the student, use contrasting colors in handouts to emphasize words that are especially difficult to revisualize (Johnson, 1967).

8. Write sentences that contain errors. Read them as they should be and have the student note if the sentence is the same or different (Johnson, 1967).

9. Present spelling words with letters missing. Have the student fill in the blanks with the correct letters.

10. Present words with letters out of order. Have the student unscramble the letters to spell words (Swisher, 1984).

11. Present three or four spellings of a word. Have the student identify the correct spelling.

12. Teach spelling rules (e.g., i before e, except after c) (Chittenden, 1984).

13. Impress upon the student the value of proofreading papers before submission (J. Kush, personal communication, 1985).

14. Develop a spelling consciousness. The student needs a reason for spelling and a desire to spell correctly (Durkin, 1978).

15. Hold a spelling bee (L. Adeseye, personal communication, 1983).

16. Tell the student to think of the words he knows that use the same pattern as the spelling word in order to remember how to spell it (M. Sciandra, personal communication, 1985).

17. Write a number of words on the chalkboard that portray a regular pattern. Have the student look at the words and discover the pattern (Rubin, 1980).

18. Instruct the student to look and listen for

small familiar words within target words or use his knowledge of root words.

19. Provide speech synthesis for the student who has problems with auditory discrimination, auditory memory, sequential memory, or fine motor skills. This artificial production of speech by electronic means provides assistance in spelling instruction (Fisher, 1983).

20. Use phoneme counting tasks in which the student must indicate the number of phonemes in a syllable (Treiman, 1985).

21. Use the multi-sensory "Accordion" method. Have the student look at the whole word, enunciate it, break it into syllables, and write the syllables while pronouncing each one (Chittenden, 1984).

22. Teach memorization techniques such as association and mnemonic aids (J. Kush, personal communication, 1985).

23. Promote self-correcting of tests (Ganschow, 1983).

24. Design and structure spelling drill into popular activities such as solving word searches and word twists (Swisher, 1984).

25. Have the student look at the word and say it. Then have him cover the word and try to reproduce it exactly as seen.

26. Have the student look at the word carefully, check it in a dictionary for meaning or pronunciation, and say it distinctly (Chittenden, 1984).

27. Have the student delete a specified phoneme from a syllable and pronounce the remaining sounds (Treiman, 1985).

28. If the student's errors consist of deletions and insertions of similar letters, ask him to spell the words orally. If he can do so correctly, the spelling errors are probably caused by the method of writing. Such a student should be cautioned to be on guard for this kind of error and to get into the habit of lifting the hands from the paper more often (Rubin, 1975).

29. Reintroduce phonemic analysis skills by providing experiences in spelling-sound correspondence rules (Treiman, 1985).

30. Structure your spelling program so that the following components are included: copying, proofreading, rewriting, writing from memory consciously, and spelling automatically without conscious thought (Struthers, Struthers, and Williams, 1983).

31. The tactile learner should concentrate on writing words in cursive so as to get the feel of the whole word through the flowing motion. Also, he can strengthen his visual image of words by tracing and feeling three-dimensional letter blocks (Chittenden, 1984).

32. Provide phoneme recognition tasks in which the student must judge whether a syllable contains a specified phoneme (Treiman, 1985).

33. Improve spelling accuracy on weekly tests by the use of social reinforcement, competition, practice, correction, and peer tutoring (Delquadri, Greenwood, Stretton, and Hall, 1983).

34. To increase the students' ability to score correctly on weekly review tests, give a portion of the words each day and test daily (Struthers, Struthers, and Williams, 1983).

35. Compose spelling lists with words the student frequently uses. Teach words in which he has an interest, need, and can use (Rubin, 1975).

36. Draw boxes for each letter shape of the word to be spelled. These configurations will help the student identify letter shapes (Cohen, 1974).

37. Have the student work with another to draw visual configuration boxes for a short list of spelling words. One student says the word, and the other draws the configuration (B. Rex, personal communication, 1985).

38. For visual reinforcement, have the student identify some words by using a color code (e.g., red apple, yellow banana, and green grass) (Cohen, 1974).

39. Have the student use a telephone to dial the letters of a spelling word, repeating

each letter as dialed. The student should then try to write the word on paper (Cohen, 1974).

40. Provide practice in spelling nonphonic pattern words so that the student will overlearn the correct spelling (Durkin, 1978).

41. Use high-interest reading materials. The more a student reads, the more familiar he becomes with the standard spelling of frequent words and consistent spelling principles (Groff, 1984).

42. Have the student make flash cards of all weekly spelling words for home study (Scarrozzo, 1982).

43. Give the student a spelling pretest in the beginning of the week. Have him study only those words missed on the pretest. Give the final test at the end of the week which counts for a grade (Wallace, 1984).

44. Write a word on the chalkboard. Ask the student to close his eyes for 10 seconds. Remove a letter from the word. Ask him to identify the missing letter and fill it in. Then have him close his eyes while you remove the first letter in addition to another letter. The game continues until all the letters of the word have been removed (Hillerich and Gould, 1981).

45. Write the second part of compound words on tagboard cards. Write the first part of each compound word on a clothespin. Have the student match the correct clothespin with the card and snap it on. He then reads the compound words (Bigler, 1979).

46. Give the student sentences that have picture clues in them. Have him write the word that is missing from each sentence (Geedy, 1981).

47. Write a spelling word on the chalkboard. Underline each letter of the word. Tell the student that he is to make a complete sentence from the letters of the word. Tell the student that each letter of the word must be used as the first letter of one word in the sentence (Wallace, 1984).

48. Help the student compile an individualized list of spelling words. Prepare three pockets or envelopes. Write the student's name in red on one pocket, in yellow on another, and in green on the third. The red pocket is for words to be learned, yellow is for words under study, and green is for words known (Johnson, Langford, and Quorn, 1981).

49. Produce a monthly magazine incorporating the students' writings and activities. This will generate a concerted effort to learn to spell (Durkin, 1978).

50. Cover all but the last letter of a word. Have the student say the letter, look away, and say it again. Uncover the next to the last letter so that the last two letters are exposed. Have him look and say the two letters. Proceed until all the letters are exposed and the student spells the whole word, looking first, then looking away (Choate and Young, 1982).

51. Trace letters or short words on the back of the student's hand. He then writes the word on paper (Choate and Young, 1982).

52. Provide an opportunity for the student to study the entire configuration of a word. Gradually omit letters from various positions and ask him to write in the missing letter(s). At the end, only blank spaces remain and the student must write the entire word from memory (Choate and Young, 1982).

53. Instead of counting a misspelled word as being wrong, give credit for each letter that is in the proper sequence (Choate and Young, 1982).

54. Have the student spell the word using cardboard or wooden letters and a stamp pad (Serio, 1984).

55. Have the student use colored pencils for either beginning, medial, or ending letters or sounds (Serio, 1984).

Other Problems

202
Cannot Imitate Sound Patterns or Noises

1. Provide the student with a model that he can imitate (McLean, Yoder, and Schiefelbusch, 1972).

2. Pair a vocalization with a motor act. The motor act is then faded so that the phoneme production is all that remains (McLean, Yoder, and Schiefelbusch, 1972).

3. Reinforce the student for any kind of vocalization that immediately follows your presentation of sound (McLean, Yoder, and Schiefelbusch, 1972).

4. Encourage the student to use the various muscles used in speaking for nonspeech activities (e.g., smiling, chewing, swallowing, whistling, yawning, blowing, laughing, and various tongue movements) (Lerner, 1985).

5. Let the student feel vibrations of sound by touching your face or throat when you make sounds (Lerner, 1985).

6. Let the student observe mouth movements and shaping during the production of sound (Lerner, 1985).

7. Use a mirror for enabling the student to observe himself in producing sounds (Lerner, 1985).

8. Call attention to the sounds in the student's environment (e.g., barking dog, car horn, jets). Begin with loud sounds and, as they become noticed by the student, introduce less noticeable ones (e.g., ticking clock, buzzing bee, sound of wind) (Bangs, 1968).

9. Initiate activities of interest to the student to take advantage of his initiative (e.g., go for a walk outside and pick flowers to make him aware of the environmental sounds) (Bangs, 1968).

10. Emphasize discrimination between sounds of different pitches, different loudnesses, and different qualities. Have the student indicate whether the stimuli are same or different (Adler, 1964).

11. Drill on recognition of and discrimination between vowel and consonant sounds. Have the student indicate whether the sounds are the same or different (Adler, 1964).

12. Devise group play activities such as marching, clapping, singing, and reciting simple rhymes. Teach the student to imitate or reproduce rhythmic patterns (McLean, Yoder, and Schiefelbusch, 1972).

13. Let the student perform a noise that the other students are asked to imitate. Then he should attempt to imitate a noise produced by another student (W. Grimm, personal communication, 1985).

14. Form a rhythm band with drums, triangles, and bells in order to involve body movements for awareness of rhythm and sound (Adler, 1964).

15. Use a rhythm record. The change in tempo of rhythm records is convenient for having the student walk like a turtle, hop like a rabbit, or fly like a bird. Then have him imitate the animals' noises (Bangs, 1968).

16. Let the student creep on all fours in the pretense of being jungle animals trying to make their noises (W. Grimm, personal communication, 1985).

17. Place a toy turkey, duck, and a bird on a table. Demonstrate the sound each makes and have the student imitate the sounds. Have him turn his back and listen while you produce the sounds. He then should point to the appropriate one and imitate the sound (Bangs, 1968).

18. Use a sound-effects record to play a household sound, such as the ringing of a telephone. Have the student identify the object (Bangs, 1968).

19. Look at pictures of animals, trains, cars, and so on with the student. Name and imitate the sounds they make. Then ask him to identify and imitate their sounds (Bangs, 1968).

20. Utilize sound objects until the student can recognize them in isolation. Progress to more abstract sources (Adler, 1964).

21. Show the student pictures that begin with the same sound. Use a sound that the student omits or substitutes in his speech (Bangs, 1968).

22. Produce a sound and repeat it like an echo. Encourage the student to do the same (W. Grimm, personal communication, 1985).

23. Include parents and age peers in your efforts (W. Grimm, personal communication, 1985).

24. Refer the student to a speech and language clinician.

203
Has Difficulty Identifying Objects by Feel or Touch

1. Cut a hole in the middle of the lid of a shoebox. From underneath, staple the top of a sock. Cut off the foot section of the sock. Place objects into the box that will be identified by touch (Wilt and Watson, 1977).

2. Have a student move part of his clothing to have skin showing on the leg, back, or arm. Have another student place a common object on the body part. Have the first student attempt to identify the object (Wilt and Watson, 1977).

3. Have the student take his shoes off. Place objects under a blanket. Have the student identify the objects by feeling with his feet (Wilt and Watson, 1977).

4. Take an oversized pocketbook and place familiar objects in it (e.g., lipstick, earrings, bobby pins, wallet, tissues, gum, mirror, money, etc.). Have the student identify each by touch (Wilt and Watson, 1977).

5. Make a number of containers. Place a small object in each. Have index cards with the picture and name of the objects on each. Have the student feel the object and match it with the appropriate picture on the index cards (Wilt and Watson, 1977).

6. Place different articles of clothing in a large plastic bag. Have the student put on a blindfold. He then reaches into the bag, pulls out one article of clothing, and identifies it by touch. Have him put the clothes on over his own (Wilt and Watson, 1977).

7. Put a large apron on the student. The student closes his eyes while you place an object into the pocket. By feeling the outside of the pocket, he attempts to identify the object (Wilt and Watson, 1977).

8. Supply a number of lunch bags with an object in each. Have the student feel the bag and attempt to identify the object. Have the student match an index card with the name of an object on it with the correct bag (Wilt and Watson, 1977).

9. Blindfold the student. Hand him a thick piece of yarn threaded into a needle without a sharp point. Have the student string an assortment of objects that contain a hole and identify each by touch (Wilt and Watson, 1977).

10. Give the student two similarly textured objects or two differently textured objects. He then attempts to tell you if the objects have the same or different texture (Pennsylvania Materials Center, 1980).

11. Place students in pairs. One student wears a blindfold. The other student gives his partner an object and describes it in detail. The blindfolded student guesses what the object might be.

12. Make a collage of familiar items with velcro strips attached. Place them on the wall within reach of the student who is blindfolded. Have him identify objects by touch. If needed, take a particular object off the collage board so the student can feel it separately (Young, 1967).

13. Write a word in wet sand or a flat clay surface. Have the student feel it and trace it.

Have him identify it by touch (Young, 1967).

14. In a small pool or sink, place a variety of floating toys (e.g., dolls, ducks, blocks, boats, etc.). The student identifies each by touch. If able, he should also provide details about the object (Schattner, 1971).

15. Set up a doll house with dolls and furniture. Blindfold the student. Place his hand in a specific room. After feeling the objects in the area, he should identify that room (Schattner, 1971).

16. Paste coins face-up on a felt strip. Blindfold the student and give him a variety of coins. Using the guide provided, he should place the coins in groups. He identifies which coin he is feeling by the size and texture of the edge (K. Dieh, personal communication, 1986).

17. Put a variety of clothing attachments (e.g., zippers, buttons, snaps, laces, etc.) on a large poster board. Blindfold the student and have him identify the attachment and perform the appropriate action (Ebersole, Kephart, and Ebersole, 1968).

18. Put hard and soft objects in a pillow case. Have the student close his eyes and touch one object at a time. He is to identify the object and whether it is hard or soft. Also use objects that are sharp or blunt, rough or smooth, warm or cool, or sticky or slick (Van Witsen, 1979).

19. Have the student make his own scrapbook containing examples of objects that are hard, soft, rough, sticky, and so on. Have him identify each object. If more than one student makes a scrapbook, they can exchange books and identify the objects in each other's book (Van Witsen, 1979).

20. Paste different shapes on a bulletin board. Have the student feel each and identify the shapes (Van Witsen, 1979).

21. Cut out the letters of the student's name from blocks of wood. Spread glue on the surface of each letter. Before it dries, put a specific material on each letter (e.g., sprinkles, glitter, sandpaper, felt, etc.). The student feels each letter separately and identifies it. He then arranges the letters to spell his name correctly (K. Diehl, personal communication, 1986).

22. Use a stencil of an object or animal. Paste the stencil on a poster board. Shellac the inside and sprinkle it with sand. If desired, paint it also. Have the student feel it and identify it. He might label it using velcro strips and index cards (Cruickshank, Bentzen, Ratzeburg, and Tannhauser, 1961).

23. Mold a pipe cleaner into a letter or an object. Have the student identify it by feel. He can also mold pipe cleaners into different objects (Ellingson, 1967).

24. Mold a piece of clay into an object. The student feels the clay and identifies the object (Ellingson, 1967).

25. Blindfold the student. Hand him a letter of the alphabet to feel. While still blindfolded, he writes the letter on the blackboard (Ellingson, 1967).

26. Make a puppet from a tight-fitting plastic glove. Add eyes, nose, hair, mouth, and so on. Blindfold the student and give him a variety of objects that can be identified by the shape and not just the texture. Using the "puppet glove," he feels the object and identifies it (B. McNeely, personal communication, 1986).

27. Hide objects under the sand in a large sandbox. The student feels through the sand and finds objects. He then identifies them (B. McNeely, personal communication, 1986).

28. Fill an aquarium with water. Use plastic objects shaped like the real objects found in an aquarium. The student feels the objects and identifies them (K. Diehl, personal communication, 1986).

29. Use felt strips to make a picture. Connect the strips with buttons and button holes. Have the student complete the picture by connecting the buttons to the corresponding holes. Have him feel the completed picture and describe it (Ebersole, Kephart, and Ebersole, 1968).

204

Has Difficulty Judging Time and Punctuality

1. Reinforce the student when he is punctual.

2. To help the student become aware of the differences between seconds and minutes, make a chart that is divided into two sections: seconds and minutes. Have the student list things that take seconds or minutes to be completed under the appropriate heading (Markle, 1983).

3. Make a list of everyday activities such as brushing teeth, baking cookies, and walking to school. Have the student estimate how long these activities take to complete. After the student has recorded the estimates, have him actually time these activities to compare how close the guess is to the actual time (C. Bayles, personal communication, 1985).

4. To help aid in the ability to compare time segments, show the student the second hand on the clock and how it works. Give him a pair of activities to estimate which of the pair would take longer to complete. Then have the student do the tasks while another student times him (Markle, 1983).

5. To attune the student's awareness of amount of time spent on daily activities, make charts labeled "My Time" on plain paper with five vertical columns labeled *eating, at school, playing, watching television,* and *sleeping.* Make two horizontal rows labeled *estimate of time* and *time spent.* The student should first estimate the time spent on each item and then total the time to see if it is close to 24 hours. He should then compare these with the guesses of others. He could also set aside a day when he actually logs the amount of time spent on these activities and compares them with the estimates (Markle, 1983).

6. List events in the day such as eating lunch, catching the school bus, and doing math. Have the student draw or collect four or

five pictures representing these events. He can then practice putting them in order and ordering the events of the other students (Horak and Horak, 1983).

7. To learn to estimate time, give the student opportunities to experience one-minute intervals. For example, reading a book for one minute or running in place for one minute. The next step is to have him estimate one-minute intervals by putting his head down until he thinks one minute is up. From this step, have him estimate the time while doing something such as singing a song (Horak and Horak, 1983)

8. Hold discussions about longer time intervals such as lunch time and reading time. Students often underestimate the time spent on fun activities and overestimate the time spent doing tedious ones. This activity can lead to meaningful discussions about factors that affect one's ability to estimate the duration of time (Horak and Horak, 1983).

9. Frequently use time words such as *now, before, later, yesterday, first, soon,* and their opposites. Encourage the student to use these words. Do not use phrases that can cause confusion (e.g., "I'll be ready in a minute") in which a minute may not equal 60 seconds (Burton and Edge, 1985).

10. Sequencing helps develop a sense of time. Some activities to promote the development of the concept of sequence are: ordering objects such as straws, paper strips, or ribbons cut to different lengths; assembling a comic strip that has been cut apart; ordering photographs of the growth of a plant or animal; and drawing pictures of activities of a typical day and ordering them chronologically (Moyer, 1983).

11. Have the student determine the amount of time between two given times. Use questions such as: "It is 9:20 now and recess is at 10:05. How many minutes do you have before recess?" This will help the student become aware of how much time is left before recess (Moyer, 1983).

12. Approximate the amount of time it takes to

perform a task or activity. The student writes down the starting and finishing time of the activities. Then he determines how long the activity lasted. Choose a useful or realistic everyday activity such as. "How long does it take to ride to Jimmy's house on a bicycle?" rather than "How long does it take to walk around the room four times?" (Moyer, 1983).

13. Have the student predict what the actual clock time will be after the passage of a specified amount of time (e.g., "You have six more minutes to finish your spelling assignment. What time will you have to put your spelling book away?") (Moyer, 1983).

14. Have the student determine the actual clock time prior to the passage of a specific amount of time. Once a student has determined the approximate time it takes to accomplish an activity and knows the starting time of the second activity, he can start to plan ahead. For example, if Kelly knows chores take 20 minutes to complete and his favorite television program comes on at 4:00 P.M., then he can determine that 3:40 is the latest that he can start the chores in order to be finished by the start of the program (Moyer, 1983).

15. The student should learn to determine the amount of precision required in various time-telling situations. If a class starts at 10:30, a student can probably arrive at 10:32 without much consequence except making the teacher angry, but if a bus is scheduled to arrive at 7:21 and the student gets to the bus stop at 7:23 he will probably have missed the bus. Determining the amount of precision required in various time-telling situations will help him develop a sense of appropriate urgency (Moyer, 1983).

16. Duration helps develop a sense of time. Some activities to promote the development of the concept of duration are: providing experiences that include estimating and checking how long it will take something to happen (e.g., comparing the melting of an ice cube with the melting down of a birthday candle); having students time

activities with a stopwatch; collecting data for a class graph on how long it takes different students to complete a task such as inflating a balloon; and making a timeline that shows the length of time spent on daily events over a long period (Burton and Edge, 1985).

17. Have the student be a time watcher while other students are assigned a task. He is to tell the others when a predetermined time limit is up (Burton and Edge, 1985).

18. To help curb tardiness, stand at the door. When the bell rings, close the door immediately and begin the class activity. Students will soon realize that this gesture means that class has started and that they need to move faster to get to class on time (Pirvis and Leonard, 1985).

19. Schedule a student-centered activity or game that begins immediately after the tardy bell. Only students who are in class when the tardy bell rings will be allowed to participate. These preclass activities should be related to the topic currently being studied. Those students who participate in the preclass activities should receive academic credit (Purvis and Leonard, 1985).

20. Institute a reward system that enables on-time students to accumulate tokens that can be exchanged for various activities or privileges (Purvis and Leonard, 1985).

21. Identify realistic "time-using" situations from a typical day in the student's life that are recurring and require the use of a watch. These situations, such as class times, dinner times, and the like, can then be used as the basis for formulating instructional "time-using" goals (Moyer, 1983).

205

Has Difficulty Telling Time

1. Encourage the student to associate various times and clock-hand positions with getting up in the morning, eating, school be-

ginning, and so on (R. Gawrecki, personal communication, 1986).

2. Use lots of time-oriented language. Mention times, parts of a day (such as morning, noon, afternoon, evening), and descriptors (such as late, early, on time, later, before, and after).

3. Have the student make a clock out of cardboard, brads, and colored paper to familiarize himself with the various components, numbers, and the like (A. Swartz and R. Gawrecki, personal communication, 1986).

4. Have the student place a different sticker next to each number on a play clock. Then have him number 1 through 12 on a sheet of paper. Ask him to identify hourly times set by you on the play clock. For each correct guess, he gets to place the type of sticker that is next to that number on the clock onto his paper next to that number. Do the same as you teach quarter and half hours (A. Swartz, personal communication, 1986).

5. Draw clock faces with set times on paper cutouts of fish. Attach paper clips and drop them into a container. Have the student use a stick with a string that holds a magnet to "fish" the cut-outs from the container. Have him identify the time on the figure (R. Gawrecki, personal communication, 1986).

6. Make a bulletin board on which the students connect times with the correct clock faces using string.

7. Have the student make a number line from 0 to 12 on a strip of paper. Have him bend it in a circle so that the 12 overlaps the 0 to show that a clock is merely a circular number line.

8. Have the student make a time booklet in which he completes the following statement: I wake up at _____. I leave for school at _____. I go to lunch at _____.

9. Have the student choose cards turned face down with times written on them. Have the student set that time on a play clock (G. Gawrecki, personal communication, 1986).

10. Using a digital clock, ask the student which time will appear next after the minute change. For more advanced students, ask if the time is before or after the half hour, etc.

11. Make bingo cards with clock faces that show various times. If the student has a time on his card that is called, he covers it with a chip (R. Gawrecki, personal communication, 1986).

12. Give a sheet with two or more clock faces with different times. The student crosses out the clock which shows the time called.

13. Place 60 marks in a circle on the floor. Every fifth mark should be a different color from the ones on either side. Have the student count from 1 to 60 while walking around the circle and counting aloud for each step on the marks. Have him begin at the number 12. To review concepts of counting by 5s, grouping of sets of 5s, and the concept of the fraction 1/2, use the same technique on the color-coded circle. Hopping may be used instead of walking to internalize the concept of groupings of 5s (T. Chlosta, J. Neuner, and V. Homewood, personal communication, 1986).

14. Put your daily time schedule on the board using clock faces to show each time (L. Williams, personal communication, 1986).

15. Have the student copy the daily time schedule for your class. As each period starts on time, have the student look at the clock, make the corresponding time on the play clock, and say that time. Later, have the student set the time on his play clock that corresponds with reading time, calendar time, and so on (J. Feinstein, personal communication, 1986).

16. Make domino cards with clock faces on each side of the card set to different times. The game is played as in dominoes (R. Gawrecki, personal communication, 1986).

17. Have a student who knows how to tell time set times on a play clock and quiz another (R. Gawrecki, personal communication, 1986).

18. On a ditto full of clock faces, have the student draw hand positions that correspond

to a time designated by the teacher (R. Gawrecki, personal communication, 1986).

19. Make clock face flash cards for drill.

20. Have the student arrange times on cards from earliest to latest.

21. To teach the concept of a half hour, have the student fold a paper clock face in half. This idea can also be used for teaching the quarter hour concept by folding the paper into quarters.

22. Create problems that involve time (e.g., "You left home at 7:00 A.M. and arrived at school at 7:25 A.M. How long was your walk?"). Allow the student to use a play clock to solve the problem.

23. Make a sun dial by putting a strip of tape on a window that receives direct sunlight. Mark hourly shadows on surfaces.

206

Has Difficulty Locating and Naming Body Parts

1. Have the student lie down on a large piece of mural paper. Trace around him. Have him color and draw in the details on his outline. Ask him to point to a particular part on his paper body. Repeat the procedure until all the body parts have been quizzed (D. Levy, personal communication, 1986).

2. Place various flannel pieces of body parts on a table. Have the student come to the table, choose a flannel piece, name the body part, then place it in its appropriate place on the flannel board (Instructo Corporation, 1973).

3. Construct a body of flannel, point to a part on the body, and ask a student to name the part. If he answers correctly, he may then point another part and call on another student to identify that part (Instructo Corporation, 1973).

4. Remove some flannel pieces from a body

and ask the student to name which parts are missing (Instructo Corporation, 1973).

5. Place one flannel body part on a table. Ask a student to name another part that is needed to make a whole body. Then have him find the piece and place it in its proper place (Instructo Corporation, 1973).

6. Review the major parts of the body with the student. Then present a picture of a more detailed arm, leg, or face and have him point to and name known parts. Present the new parts by pointing to them, one by one, and naming them. Have the student identify the part on his body (P. Martone, personal communication, 1986).

7. Using a template of various individual body parts, have the student name each part of the body on the template by pointing to it. Then have him trace a body part requested on a piece of paper and hold up the paper to show answers (Developmental Learning Materials, 1969).

8. Given a template of various individual body parts, have the student trace one part on a piece of paper. Then have him trace each connecting part on the paper to form a completed body (Developmental Learning Materials, 1969).

9. Give dittos with incomplete outlines of various body parts. Have the student draw in the parts that are missing (Lerner, 1985).

10. Guide the student in a game of "Hokey-Pokey" or "Simon Says" to teach various body parts (Lerner, 1985).

11. Allow the student to play with various people and animal puzzles in order to learn the parts of the body (Lerner, 1985).

12. Give the student modeling clay and allow him to form the body parts he has learned (P. Martone, personal communication, 1986).

13. Have the student look into a mirror and point to various parts of his body while naming each (P. Martone, personal communication, 1986).

14. Have the student close his eyes. Touch a part of his body and have him name the

part that was touched (P. Martone, personal communication, 1986).

207

Has Difficulty Understanding Spatial Concepts

1. Use four sets of six to eight cards with each set being a different color. On the cards are written directions concerning how students are to move. The directions on each set of cards are the same. Divide the students into four teams. Each team is the color of one set of cards. The teams line up in relay formation. Shuffle all the cards together. Take a card from the top of the pile. Call out the color team that is to move and read the directions from the card. Each student begins beside the student who moved before him. The team that first reaches the goal line wins. Vary the game by adding different locomotor movements to the directions (Werner and Burton, 1979).

2. Supply an object of interest to the student (e.g., doll, toy truck, etc.). Have the student place, walk, or drive the object under, over, beside, and around various objects.

3. Have the student walk or run in left and right directions, varying the speeds of the walk and run and the intensity of the steps from light to heavy. As the student moves, he should verbally indicate in which direction he is going or which foot is moving (Harvat, 1971).

4. Have the student walk up and down stairs in a combination of steps (e.g., two steps up, one step down, three steps up). As he is going up and down the stairs, he should verbally indicate which way he is moving (Harvat, 1971).

5. From a standing position, have the student lift his knees up and grasp them with both hands pulling them tightly to his chest. As he performs the action, he should repeat the words *up* or *down*, as indicated by his actions (Harvat, 1971).

6. Give a command, then model it and have the student imitate it. Be sure to repeat the word at the moment the student performs the action so he can relate the word to the activity (Chaney and Kephart, 1968).

7. When an action or direction has an opposite (such as in *up* and *down*), introduce only one until it is reasonably well learned. Then teach the opposite.

8. Have students scatter out around the room and find a space. Guide their exploration of the spatial dimensions by giving them verbal instructions (e.g., "Point to something that is above you." "Point to something below you." "Point to the right with your right hand.") (Werner and Burton, 1979)

9. Instruct the student to move in the direction you point. Gradually increase the speed of the changes (Werner and Burton, 1979).

10. Instruct the student to move in different directions as you call them out (Werner and Burton, 1979).

11. Have the student execute different locomotor movements in each of the directions (e.g., hop forward, jump backward, stretch up, stretch down) (Werner and Burton, 1979).

12. Have the student move through space, changing direction each time you clap or beat the drum (Werner and Burton, 1979).

208

Performance Below Potential

1. Downgrade the difficulty of the task.
2. Give the student exercises in completing progressively more difficult tasks.
3. After giving a class assignment, have the student repeat what is supposed to be done. This assures that that task is understood.
4. Use a multisensory approach to the student's work to allow him to use many senses to evaluate materials (e.g., hearing

with tapes, touching forms and surfaces, seeing colors, etc.).

5. Use the student's interests to make the task more interesting (e.g., sports, cars, cheerleading, etc.) (B. Kreuger, personal communication, 1983).

6. Highlight positive grades and provide positive comments on papers to motivate the student (Millman, Schaefer, and Cohen, 1980).

7. Have another student in the class act as a tutor for the one who does not know the material.

8. Have the student set goals to improve performance. Evaluate these goals periodically (Millman, Schaefer, and Cohen, 1980).

9. Outline for the student exactly what must be done to achieve the desired level of accomplishment.

10. Give attention in the form of smiling, chatting, and physical proximity for adequate academic performance (Brown and Avery, 1974; Donaldson, 1980).

11. Make early dismissal contingent upon the student's academic performance (Harris and Merrill, 1972).

12. Make the reading of a story to the entire class contingent upon the student's academic performance (Harris and Merrill, 1972).

13. If academic performance improves, give the student a note saying that he did well in the targeted academic area. He can then bring it home and receive praise and outside play from the parents (Harris and Merrill, 1972).

14. Have the student receive attention and praise from the principal or other highly regarded school official if performance standards are met (Millman, Schaefer, and Cohen, 1980).

15. Have the student compete against himself by trying to better the previous day's or week's performance.

16. Have the student revise work that is unacceptable (Sprick, 1981).

17. If free-time activities follow the successful completion of work, be sure that they are enjoyable to the student (Sprick, 1981).

18. Have the student reward or fine himself with tokens, depending on the rate and quality of the work (Millman, Schaefer, and Cohen, 1980).

19. Model careful performance of tasks while thinking out loud. Train the student to instruct himself verbally while performing the task.

20. As a motivational activity, pair students and have one describe a picture or scene to his partner. The second student attempts to draw what was described. The first student then gives suggestions for improving the picture after saying something positive (Jackson, Jackson, and Monroe, 1983).

21. Change positive phrases such as "nice job" to current positive slang expressions used by students (Clarizio, 1980).

22. Use contracting with contingent pay procedures (Kelly and Stokes, 1982).

23. Teach through the student's strongest learning modality.

24. Be sure that class assignments for the underachiever are well structured and within range of his ability level.

25. Allow the student in upper grades to tutor in the primary grades with students who also demonstrate below-average achievement in specific areas. Often students with learning problems relate well to others who are experiencing similar problems while reinforcing their own skills.

26. Capitalize on interests in isolated subject areas by seeing that the student completes assignments in these areas. With the introduction of new material, these positive attitudes may generalize to other subject areas.

27. Prevent possible learning fatigue by incorporating rest breaks during the course of the lesson or assignment.

28. Set up a "study-buddy" system with a neighborhood friend for study sessions at their homes.

29. Time should be set aside to give the student special help or attention. Tell the student that the time is available if needed. If the student refuses, remain available in case he decides to take advantage of the offer.

30. Do not sit the student next to superior students, but rather with average students whom he likes and who like him. Ask them, with his knowledge, to "keep him on the track" in a friendly and helpful way in terms of desk work, writing down assignments, and reminding him of due dates on reports and projects.

31. Institute a program that emphasizes arts, crafts, shop, or other courses that will make use of an underachiever's strengths and underplay his weaknesses. Participation in these courses might be made contingent upon good academic performance in underachievement areas.

32. The underachiever may have problems at home that keep him from studying and completing homework assignments. Since teachers often stay after pupils leave, the school might assign one special room for those who wish to remain after school to study and complete assignments.

33. Encourage parents to set aside a quiet place and time for study at home.

34. When achievement drops at a particular grade level, consider the possibility of changing teachers, even in mid-semester.

35. Use a reinforcement chart. When the student has earned a certain number of points, allow him to take the chart home where it is traded for some prearranged activity with parents (e.g., playing checkers, making a cake, going shopping).

36. If the student provides an incorrect answer or appears to be on the verge of giving no answer, provide hints. When the student does respond correctly, praise him.

37. Encourage participation in summer school enrichment programs.

38. Encourage counseling in a school setting if motivation or personality problems interfere with learning.

39. Reinforce any and all efforts on the part of the student as he tries to achieve. Reduce the amount of punishment and increase encouragement. Grade him, if at all, at the level at which he is functioning.

40. Provide shorter assignments so as not to overwhelm the student. Assure that the first part of the assignment is easy or already known to the student. This provides initial success.

41. Set limits within which the work should be done. These should be longer than necessary so that the pupil can "beat the clock."

42. Give marks and report card grades on the basis of effort and production, rather than in relation to the rest of the class. Help parents understand the meaning of these marks.

209
Poor Vocabulary

1. Reinforce the student's use of new vocabulary.

2. Have the student write the words he is studying and use them in sentences.

3. Have the student tell you what he did last night or over the weekend (Haas, Kasper, Kryst, and Young, 1982).

4. Have the student list as many words as possible that describe an object.

5. Give the student a list of words he commonly uses. Have him use a book of synonyms to find 5 to 10 words that mean the same thing.

6. When speaking to the class, use many synonyms. For instance, say, "That gorilla was big. I mean that anthropoid was humongous."

7. Have a group of students find objects on the school grounds and write down as many descriptive words as possible. Have the group write a story using these words.

8. Utilize the Dolch Basic Sight Vocabulary list consisting of 220 sight words. List these

words from the lowest level to the highest. The student starts reading from the beginning until there is an error. A sticker is put by the error. Next time the student reads, he starts from the sticker and tries to advance to the end (Kauffman, 1983).

9. Make 12 lists. Each list contains common sight words frequently found in out-of-school reading material (e.g., books, newspaper, periodicals) pertaining to living areas. When the student has mastered a living area word in print, it is placed in his envelope. It is also checked on your master list. To prove that the student has mastered this word, the assignment can be one of the following: present a picture from a magazine or newspaper to illustrate the word; write a sentence using the word correctly, present a newspaper or magazine article with the word encircled, or identify the word in a multiple-choice setting (Aukerman and Aukerman, 1981).

10. Dictionary etymologies (i.e., word origins) are useful in vocabulary development. Have the student find the words in the dictionary. Then have him draw a simple cartoon depicting the origin of the chosen words (Aukerman and Aukerman, 1981).

11. Throughout the school year, there are opportunities in class observation of scientific phenomena such as hatching chicks, the freezing of water, and the creating of steam. Vocabulary, as it is learned, should be presented on tagboard to the student immediately. This involves the use of the principle of learning contiguity whereby the visual symbol is learned immediately with the pronunciation of the new word and the observation of its meaning (Aukerman and Aukerman, 1981).

12. Do not teach words in isolation. Teach vocabulary words in clusters (e.g., teach all the modes of transportation, which are further divided into categories such as land vehicles and water vehicles) (Holbrook, 1985).

13. Teach vocabulary related to upcoming field trips and excursions via books, discussions, magazines, and newspapers.

14. Every workable machine, process, or complex thing has parts that have names. Vocabulary can be developed by learning the correct names of those parts. Use only appropriate things for the student's age and grade level. Utilize a large diagram of a process or a cutaway diagram of the interior (Aukerman and Aukerman, 1981).

15. Be an enthusiastic teacher of new words rather than a "mentioner" of them. Plan systematic, educationally sound vocabulary instruction. This instruction can be enhanced by a variety of fun-filled, thought-provoking activities with words (Monroe and Hicks, 1985).

16. Read vocabulary words in meaningful context and work on related activities afterward (Eeds and Cockrum, 1985).

17. Teach vocabulary in connection with spelling. The spelling of words often reflects the meaning of the sound (e.g., *sign* would be taught for *signal* and *signature*) (Holbrook, 1985).

18. Have the student start a "Vocabulary Savings Bank." The book consists of 28 sheets of lined paper, one for each letter of the alphabet, plus one for each cover. When he has learned a new word, it is deposited in his account under the proper letter. Later, the words can be withdrawn for use in writing exercises assigned by the teacher (Aukerman and Aukerman, 1981).

19. Play "Word War." Utilize word cards with several sets of identical words. Shuffle the cards and deal them to the players. All players simultaneously turn one card at a time. When two (or more) identical cards are turned up, the first player to name the word correctly takes the turned up stack of cards from the players involved in the "war." The winner is the player who gets all or most of the words within a set time period (Mercer and Mercer, 1981).

20. Play "In Other Words." In this synonym game, a simple sentence is printed on the

chalkboard with one word underlined. For example, ''The children were *loud*.'' The class might respond with, ''In other words, the children were noisy or boisterous.'' The new words should be printed on the board (Searls and Klesius, 1984).

21. Create word search puzzles for any vocabulary words you want to drill with your students (Kauffman, 1983).

22. Give each student a bingo card and several discs. Read a word from the list and check it off. The players look for the word on their bingo card and if a player has it, he covers it with a disc. Continue to call out words one at a time. The first player to cover five spaces in any direction calls out. After the player calls out, he must also pronounce each of the covered words. Another variation would be to have definitions on the bingo card for the words called out (Mercer and Mercer, 1981).

23. Teach vocabulary words through their translation into other words borrowed from foreign languages (Holbrook, 1985).

24. Construct a set of puzzles. On one piece of the puzzle write a word. On the second part write the word's definition. All pieces fit each other, but in order for the student to use self-correction immediately, there are two identical symbols on the back of matching pieces to represent success (T. Gorski, personal communication, 1985).

25. Choose a few words. Then shuffle together a number of word cards, each containing a substitute for one of the main words. Have the students go through the deck of word cards and put each card under the correct main word (Aukerman and Aukerman, 1981).

26. Play ''Ping Pong.'' Make a card with a word printed on each side, each word synonymous with the other. Hold these aloft between two students. One student reads aloud his word. The other student ''returns the serve'' with the synonym on his side of the card. This can also be utilized with antonyms (Aukerman and Aukerman, 1981).

27. Play ''Charades'' to review words in subject matter areas (Monroe and Hicks, 1985).

28. Teach ''Tom Swifties'' (e.g., ''I broke my leg,'' Tom said lamely) (Monroe and Hicks, 1985).

29. Have the student produce his own sentences for words, put definitions in his own words, and create categories for word lists. This forces him to engage in deeper processing than just copying definitions (Stahl, 1985).

30. Play ''Clothespin.'' The student reads a word definition on a chart and looks at the words on clothespins to find the correct one. He clips the clothespin containing the answer to the section of the wheel with the definition and then turns over the circle. If the response is correct, the symbol on the back of the circle and clothespin will match (Aukerman and Aukerman, 1981).

31. To enrich vocabulary, select a specific part of the room to be designated as a News Bulletin Board on which are printed some different news items or notices each day. Strive to introduce new vocabulary (Mercer and Mercer, 1981).

32. Add new vocabulary words to a classroom by creating ''Word Mobiles.'' Have several mobiles, each one holding words of a single category (Aukerman and Aukerman, 1981).

33. Select a noun and instruct the student to suggest adjectives that ''maybe'' modify it (e.g., if the word is *car*, the student responds with ''maybe it's a green car'' or ''maybe it's a sports car'') (Aukerman and Aukerman, 1981)

34. Select a part of your class as the ''Word of the Day'' area. Select a different word daily and post it in the section. Utilize different activities with each word (B. Lynch-Herod, 1985).

35. Design a deck of cards composed of words that are opposites. An equal number of cards are distributed to each player until all cards are dealt. The student finds any opposite combination and lays those cards down in front of him. He then picks a card

in turn from any player. The game continues until one player wins by pairing all cards in his hand (L. Mann, personal communication, 1985).

36. Select several comic strips from the newspaper. Cut out the narrative from each frame, but do not disorientate the comic strip as a whole. Have the student paste the comic strip on a sheet of white paper. Then have him utilize specific vocabulary words and create a narrative to accompany the comic (B. Lynch-Herod, personal communication, 1985).

37. Write a new word on the chalkboard, pronounce it, and tell what it means. Ask the students to imagine a simple pantomime for the word's meaning. Give a signal for the students to do their pantomimes simultaneously. Select the most common pantomime from those that the students presented. Have it shown to all and have them do it while saying the word. Repeat each new word. The class does the pantomime for each and says a brief meaning or synonym. Have the students read a selection containing the new words (Casale, 1985).

38. Teach words with audiovisual aids. Use pictures, photographs, models, graphs, charts, maps, and diagrams to portray the meanings of words. Use slides, films, and recordings for extending listening and speaking vocabularies (Durkin, 1978).

39. Teach words by reading to the student. This should promote interest in words and a curiosity about their meanings (Durkin, 1979).

40. Make lists or charts of special-interest words, such as those related to football, television, and cooking (Hammill and Bartel, 1982).

41. Have the student write his own "Book of Word Lists." Briefly describe *The Book of Lists* and give examples of how he can develop his own word list (e.g., rhyming words, funny words, words that are hard to spell, words that are hard to say, words that describe pretty things, etc.). The possibilities are endless and the best ideas often come from the student himself. Make duplicate copies of the lists and bind them to look like books. Present a copy of the book to the library for the student to share with his friends and classmates (Smith and Elliott, 1979).

42. Make crossword puzzles out of words that you wish to teach. Provide some letters on the crossword puzzle to give added clues (Smith and Elliott, 1979).

43. Make your own picture cards. Just print the word and attach a picture or illustration. The student will then be able to associate a picture or a meaning to a specific word (Smith and Elliott, 1979).

44. Ask the student to select an article from a newspaper or magazine. Circle all unknown or technical terminology. Encourage him to find these words in the dictionary and provide a definition or a synonym. Have the student share his story or article with the rest of the class (Gentile, 1983).

45. Have each student bring to class a useful new word in clue-rich context and read the sentence aloud to the group. The others try to deduce the meaning. The student who answers correctly presents the next sentence (Thomas and Robinson, 1972).

46. Encourage the student to keep a vocabulary notebook of the new words that he encounters in reading. A short definition and sentence with the word included may be helpful for later use. Students should be encouraged to use the new words in future assignments (Cushenbery, 1972).

47. Compile a list of words with interesting stories. Each student selects a word that interests him, researches it, and presents its life story. The classroom can be stocked with books on derivations (Thomas and Robinson, 1972).

210

Reversals

1. Write large letters on the chalkboard or sheets of paper. Ask the student to trace over the letters with his finger many times, saying the letter as he traces. Watch him so that he starts and completes his strokes at the proper point (Heydorn, 1984).

2. Ask two or more students to participate in a game. One student writes a letter that has been causing him difficulty, and another student must name it. If the student reverses the letter, the other students have an opportunity to identify and correct the error (Heydorn, 1984).

3. Use a mnemonic device to teach the student to differentiate between *b* and *d* by imagining the word *bed*. The word is in the shape of an actual bed. The student learns that the *b* and *d* are inside the headboard and footboard (Heydorn, 1984).

4. Have the student make cards with the words that are causing problems. Then have the student finger trace the word while saying it. After practice, remove the card and have the student write the word from memory. Repeat this procedure until the word has been mastered (Heydorn, 1984).

5. Have the student form the "thumbs up" sign with each hand. Inform him how the left hand looks like a *b* and the right hand looks like a *d*. Have him bring the two hands together and notice how they look like a bed. This mnemonic device will help him remember that the letter that looks like his left hand is a *b*.

6. Make up paired flash cards for reversed words. Present the paired words until the student can choose the correct response without errors (Heydorn, 1984).

7. Have the student write letters in a salt box or make letters out of clay. Stress the correct formation. The student might also use tactile letters for tracing (Kaminsky and Powers, 1981).

8. Have the student write letters or words in the air and work on large newsprint (Kaminsky and Powers, 1981).

9. Color code letters that the student frequently reverses. This will help in the visual discrimination of those letters (Doyle, 1982).

10. Have the student trace over a word that has been causing difficulty. The word should be written in fairly large letters. As the student traces each letter, he should vocalize the sound of that letter, making the sound last as long as it takes him to write the letter, thus coming out even at the end of the word with both sound and tracing. Encourage him to blend the sound of one letter into the next (Kampwirth, 1983).

11. Draw an arrow pointing to the right under those words that are frequently reversed (Kampwirth, 1983).

12. Slide a pencil or finger along the text to keep the student's eyes moving toward the right (Kampwirth, 1983).

13. Print frequently reversed words with the first letter in green and the rest in red, or the first letter underlined with green and the last underlined in red. Tell the students to observe the "traffic signal," starting on the green and stopping at the red. The same words printed in pencil should then be placed beside the colored words and read after them (Kampwirth, 1983).

14. Dust fine sand over a word that has been painted with mucilage made with coarse thick paint. Have the student trace the word and spell it (Kampwirth, 1983).

15. Have the student select from among *b, d, p,* and *q* the letter that matches a sample letter *b* while the sample is available for comparison. Emphasize the directional differences between the letters by pointing them out and explaining them to the student (Moyer and Newcomer, 1977).

16. Use the same procedure as in the previous strategy except this time the student must remember the orientation of the letter while looking for a match (Moyer and Newcomer, 1977).

17. Give the student a paper ruled off into as many blocks as there are letters in the word to be studied. Number the blocks from left to right. He then writes the letters in the correct boxes. This provides training in the habit of reading from left to right (Kampwirth, 1983).

18. Let the student use a typewriter to get a clearcut notion of the order in which the letters must be observed (Kampwirth, 1983).

19. Hold up a card that is covered with a marker or sheet of paper. The marker or sheet of paper is moved slowly to the right so that the letters are exposed in proper sequence (Kampwirth, 1983).

20. For an exercise in discrimination, first show the student that *b* has a hump on its right side, *d* has a hump on its left side, and *p* has a tail that goes down. Make an exercise on a ditto sheet that has the *b, d, p,* and *q* interspersed among each other. The student must identify the ones requested (Kampwirth, 1983).

21. Show the student how to trace confusing letters by writing the script form of the letter over the printed form. A cursive *b* will fit nicely over a printed *b* but will not fit over a printed *d*. By superimposing the movements of writing over the printed letters until one ''fits,'' the student learns to identify the printed letters (Kampwirth, 1983).

22. Provide three small cardboard boxes with slits on the tops. Arrange them in front of the student, who is instructed to draw letters from a pile of *b*s, *d*s, and *p*s. Using alphabetical order, each *b* goes in the first box, *d* in the second box, and *p* into the last box. These letters should have a line under each one to avoid inversion. After the student has sorted the pile of letters, the boxes are opened and any error is noted and corrected (Kampwirth, 1983).

23. Print the letter *b* on a card and the letter *d* in identical size on tracing paper. Place the paper on the card and have the student point out the differences. Remove the tracing paper and show the letter *b* again. The same techniques may be used with sets of words beginning with confusing letters (e.g., *big* and *dig*) (Kampwirth, 1983).

24. Make all *b*s and *d*s blue like the sky to indicate that these lines point up; all *p*s and *q*s orange or brown or green to show that these lines point down (Hardin and Bernstein, 1976).

25. Work with cursive writing as soon as interest develops. Some teachers find that this is a great aid in correcting directional habits as it is more difficult for the student to reverse letters (Hardin and Bernstein, 1976).

26. Encourage the student to point with a finger or guide as he reads. This is a means of establishing sequence (Hardin and Bernstein, 1976).

20

Motivation

211

Bored with Schoolwork

1. Vary teaching techniques to maintain student interest (Karmos and Karmos, 1983).

2. Use novelty items (e.g., crossword puzzles, word searches) to interest the student (Karmos and Karmos, 1983).

3. Couple novelty and variety techniques with substance in terms of what is to be learned (Karmos and Karmos, 1983).

4. Use individual instruction (Karmos and Karmos, 1983).

5. Take students on field trips to show a correlation between the outside world and what is being learned (Delattre, 1983).

6. Do not allow the student's boredom to anger you (Karmos and Karmos, 1983).

7. Talk openly with the student about boredom as a natural occurrence (Karmos and Karmos, 1983).

8. Make the student aware that when bored, he has a choice between misbehavior and more constructive activities (Karmos and Karmos, 1983).

9. When the student states that he can not get started on an assignment, ask, "Any reason why?" Good reflective listening on your part often results in renewed interest (Karmos and Karmos, 1983).

10. Try to reduce boredom through wide choices of instructional materials and procedures and through ideas from professional publications (Karmos and Karmos, 1983).

11. Attend workshops, inservice training, and professional meetings to develop new ideas (Karmos and Karmos, 1983).

12. Use the resources available in the community (Karmos and Karmos, 1983).

13. Promote and encourage new learning, causing the student to become committed to learning (Karmos and Karmos, 1983).

14. Use hands-on activities. The student should be a participant in activities (Karmos and Karmos, 1983).

15. Revolve instruction around the student's interests (Hamilton, 1983).

16. Use a change-of-pace technique to prevent boredom. Some seat work, a film, work with manipulatives, and problems to do at the chalkboard can all break classroom routine and energize the student (Karmos and Karmos, 1983).

17. Ask hypothetical questions that require the student to generate ideas and involve his own experiences (Hamilton, 1983).

18. To encourage his best performance, tell the student what the test measures and for what purpose the test is being used (Brown and Carroll, 1984).

19. Use different types of questions so that the student does not become bored with the test (Brown and Carroll, 1984).

20. Ask questions that force the student to answer creatively. These would include opinions (Brown and Carroll, 1984).

21. Provide an atmosphere that promotes optimal academic performance (Frick, 1985).

22. The classroom should be cheerful and clean, and display examples of the student's work (D. Fegatilli, personal communication, 1985).

23. Use audio-visual materials (D. Fegatilli, personal communication, 1985).

24. Provide brief but frequent rest breaks.

25. Motivate the students by allowing personal time as soon as the lesson is completed.

26. Draw the student's attention back to task with a loud handclap, hand on the shoulder, or mentioning of his name.

27. While presenting, tie concepts and information to his present lifestyle (e.g., ''Is your family 'nomadic' or 'seditary'?'').

28. Do not allow the student to go home until all work is completed in a satisfactory manner.

212

Bright But Doesn't Apply Self

1. Reinforce the student when he applies himself to his work (B. Loomes, personal communication, 1984).

2. Keep samples of good work in folders so that the student can evaluate his present work against these desired examples (Dolgins, Myers, Flynn, and Moore, 1984).

3. Encourage self-evaluation of work so the student can judge whether goals have been achieved (Reis and Cellerino, 1983).

4. Encourage traits such as cooperation, collectivity, and interdependence, which are important motivating factors (Castenell, 1983).

5. Expose the student to role models of successful professional people in the home, school, and community (Callahan, 1982).

6. Use guided fantasy as a technique for motivating reluctant students (Hershey and Kearns, 1979).

7. Discourage female students from thought patterns that husbands will take care of them (Lee, 1984).

8. Discourage students' thought patterns that they will live on their inheritance.

9. Plan lessons around the interests of the student (e.g., if the student likes trucks, devise math problems that involves gas mileage, cargo weight, and speed).

10. Have a student set goals for himself, including rate and criteria. If the goal is met, reinforce the student.

11. Find interests or areas in which the student excels and let him do extra credit work in these areas (J. Hoseman, personal communication, 1984).

12. Give a special project that is related to what the rest of the class is doing (J. Camp, personal communication, 1984).

13. Give the student a chance to make up activities for other students (S. LeSage, personal communication, 1984).

14. Have the student help others with their homework (C. Potlet, personal communication, 1984).

15. Send home a certificate of merit when a week's worth of high-quality assignments is turned in on time (D. Gerdes, personal communication, 1984).

16. Hold an individual conference with the student and discuss the problem (D. Haut, personal communication, 1984).

17. Talk to the parents to find out what might work to motivate the student (P. Lammon, personal communication, 1984).

18. Hand out a "Hard Worker of the Day" award at the end of each day (A. Clark, personal communication, 1984).

19. Give extra attention to the student and compliment his work (Brown and Avery, 1974; Donaldson, 1980).

20. Ask the student for advice on what he thinks the class would like to do next and thank him for the input (Donaldson, 1980).

21. Make a chart for the student. Have him set attainable goals and chart accomplishments (Donaldson, 1980).

22. Have someone the student admires talk about the importance of working to one's ability (Hardy and Cull, 1974).

23. Highlight positive grades and provide positive comments on papers (Millman, Schaefer, and Cohen, 1980).

24. Allow personal time as soon as an assignment is completed correctly.

25. Have the student revise unacceptable work (Sprick, 1981).

26. Use contracting (Kelly and Stokes, 1982).

27. Do not allow the student to partake of recess or go home until all work is done.

28. Discuss the student's desired future occupation and the need to study to become the best in that field.

213

Dislike for School

1. Give the student something to look forward to each day (Reinhart, 1980).

2. Give the student choices of academic assignment (Reinhart, 1980).

3. Plan experiences at which the student can succeed (D. Kirby, personal communication, 1984).

4. Involve the student in social activities at school (D. Kirby, personal communication, 1984).

5. Make the classroom visually attractive (Lovitt, 1978).

6. Have the student assist another (D. Kirby, personal communication, 1984).

7. Be enthusiastic and make lessons interesting (D. Kirby, personal communication, 1984).

8. Determine the interests of the student and try to revolve lessons around them (e.g., if the student like trucks, devise math problems that involve gas usage, mileage, and cargo weight (Hammil and Bartel, 1982).

9. Provide the student with activities that are attainable yet challenging (Schloss, 1983).

10. Encourage the student to bring hobbies and crafts to class and speak about them (Swift and Spivak, 1975).

11. Pair friends for simple activities (Mayer, 1982).

12. Make the school curriculum motivating and interesting. Use hands-on activities, filmstrips, speakers, and field trips (K. Kirby, personal communication, 1984).

13. Make school work simple enough so that the student will experience a degree of success.

14. Give the student a leadership role or a role that requires encouragement from his peers.

15. Speak to the parents and ask them to encourage their child in his school work and attitude toward school.

16. Ask the student what he would like to do in school. Perhaps one of his suggestions could be done as a class project. This might improve the student's image of school as a learning place (C. Zimarowski, personal communication, 1985).

17. Try to expand the curriculum so that it covers a variety of areas and topics. This will help keep the student attentive. Do not linger on the same topic for long periods of time, as this may cause boredom and increase the student's dislike for school (A. Brulle, personal communication, 1985).

18. If frequent absences occur, make the student feel welcomed when he attends. Let the student know that the class wishes that he would come to school more often because they enjoy his presence (Duanne, 1980).

19. Display the student's work in the classroom.

20. Involve the student in school-related clubs, groups, and activities.

21. Make instruction relevant to his interests or homelife.

22. Reinforce the student for accomplishments.

23. Discuss with the student the importance of schooling.

24. Allow the student to earn fun activities by completing work successfully.

25. Solicit suggestions from the student regarding how to make school a more positive place.

26. Refer the student for special services or evaluation.

214
Has "I Don't Care" Attitude When Faced with Failure

1. Reinforce the student when he appears motivated or works well (D. Jeckovich, personal communication, 1986).

2. When a student says, "I don't care," respond by stating, "I care. I care how well you are doing in school" (D. Perkins, personal communication, 1986).

3. Stop the regular classroom routine and have a class discussion regarding things people care about. Set initial goals to meet the desired future (D. DelSanto, personal communication, 1986).

4. When the student refuses to participate in the classroom assignment, tell him privately that if he does not do it now, he will do it after school or during extracurricular activity time (D. Jeckovich, personal communication, 1986).

5. Privately talk to the student about his "I don't care" attitude. If the student has a personal problem, tell the student it is difficult, but to try not to let it interfere with his school responsibilities. If the attitude stems from the classroom routine, ask him for input. Devise a contract that fits the needs of both of you (B. Miller, personal communication, 1986).

6. Ask, "If you don't care, then why should I?" Give the student enough time to answer that question. If he does not answer, then ignore the behavior (D. Jeckovich, personal communication, 1986).

7. Provide a grade for effort. Require only that the student give his best effort.

8. Inform the student of short- and long-term consequences of continual failure.

9. Ignore the behavior and exclude the pupil from the lesson. Require that he ask for permission to reenter the activity (A. Conde, personal communication, 1986).

10. Break a large task into small parts so it will seem less overwhelming (Millman, Schaefer, and Cohen, 1981).

11. To promote success, give the pupil easy assignments (J. Posteher, personal communication, 1983).

12. Assign a friend to motivate the student (Simons, 1982).

13. Write positive written comments on the student's correct classwork or homework

(J. Posteher, personal communication, 1983).

14. Provide an opportunity for the student to air feelings about school in an appropriate manner (Swift and Spivak, 1975).

15. When the student responds correctly, immediately give a compliment (Swift and Spivack, 1975).

16. Check the student's work frequently to insure that he is doing the work correctly (C. Gingerich, personal communication, 1984).

17. Discuss the problem with the student at a neutral time (C. Gingerich, personal communication, 1984).

18. Have the student compose a listing of positive things about himself to build self-confidence (Sprick, 1981).

19. If the student is working and following directions, then suddenly responds with "I don't care" to the next assignment, he may need a break in the routine. Give him something else to do for a few minutes (e.g., run an errand, clean off a shelf). Perhaps it is also time to give the whole class a five-minute break (D. DelSanto, personal communication, 1986).

20. If a student is persistent and refuses to do anything in the classroom, tell him that this cannot continue. State that you have a responsibility to teach and he has the responsibility to participate (D. Jeckovich, personal communication, 1986).

21. Use the student as a tutor for another (D. Jeckovich, personal communication, 1986).

22. Inform the student that his uncaring attitude and unwillingness to work could cause him to lose special privileges such as free time or playtime (D. Jeckovich, personal communication, 1986).

23. Give the student a zero mark in the grade book (D. Jeckovich, personal communication, 1986).

24. Refer the student to the school psychologist or counselor.

25. Require that the work be revised until it is done correctly.

215

Lacks Motivation

General Strategies

1. Reinforce the student for displaying motivation and completing work (Meihofer, 1974; Dinkmeyer, McKay, and Dinkmeyer, 1980).

2. Ignore the lazy behavior (Meihofer, 1974).

3. Devise a checkbook learning activity. Make deposits into the student's accounts to compensate for "fines," "rent," and other regularly deducted items so that grades (subsequent "deposits") are based on his academic performances. Give him a checkbook containing 75 checks for a nine-week period at the first of the year. Make extra checks available for "fines" and "taxes." Offer to make deposits into his account for doing extra credit work and special projects. Enable the student to make deposits for doing homework and taking tests. Have him make deposits at the end of each week and at the end of the nine-week period in order to determine a grade (Hendrikson, 1980).

4. Use the "perfect pass roll" system to encourage good quality work on time. Students who pass all their classes during a given 4½-week session get to leave one period early on Fridays during the next 4½-week session (Diers et al., 1983).

5. When the student finishes a test, give him a "three cheers" note to take home and share with his family (Diers et al., 1983).

6. Use coupons from fast-food restaurants as rewards for good work (Diers et al., 1983).

7. Give a "Student of the Week" award to one who has had perfect attendance, completed a sufficient amount of work, and been cooperative. The reward might be computer time, food, or a small gift (Diers et al., 1983).

8. Set up a competition with another class to enhance learning. Students in the winning

class get doughnuts or cookies (Diers et al., 1983).

9. Let the student become "Teacher for a Day." Have him make up worksheets, crossword puzzles, word finds, art projects, and so on (Diers et al., 1983).

10. Use promotional posters of popular music albums as rewards (Diers et al., 1983).

11. Draw up contractual agreements between the student and his employer to encourage appropriate behavior at school. Completion of daily requirements at school allows the student to go to work and earn money. Incompletion means suspension from a day's work (Diers et al., 1983).

12. Permit oral, taped, or written reports (Broening, 1983).

13. Privately talk with the student about setting up a behavioral contract concerning his laziness in class. The goals of the contract as well as the consequences of misbehavior are mutually agreed upon by both of you (Covington, 1984).

14. Set up a token economy system. Initially, the student would earn tokens for attempting to do work (Azaroff and Mayer, 1977; Brophy and Evertson, 1981).

15. Provide special privileges (e.g., free time, games, or puzzles) when the student attempts and completes work (American Education Coalition, 1983).

16. Withhold a desirable activity until the student completes the task (Salend, Esquivel, and Pine, 1984).

17. Role play with the student concerning the behavior. Let the student pretend that he is the teacher. Pretend that you are the student. Do your best to act like the student (Jones, 1980).

18. Pair the student with others who are good workers and can serve as appropriate role models (Slavin, 1984).

19. Have a bulletin board in the classroom set aside for the "Hardest Workers" of the week. Display pictures of two to five students who really worked hard that week. Emphasize to the lazy student that he could

be on that board also (D. Sadlon, personal communication, 1985).

20. Help the pupil establish a close relationship with a person who can supply positive reinforcement for his educational attempts (Watson, 1963).

21. Help the student set short-term and easily achieved goals (Watson, 1963).

22. Use high-interest and well-programmed materials (Watson, 1963).

23. Make the activities relevant to the student's life (Hamachek, 1968).

24. Have the student compete against himself by use of charts to plot progress (Hamachek, 1968).

25. Provide immediate feedback on completed work (Hamachek, 1968).

26. Provide parents with a list of activities they can do at home with their child (Swift and Spivak, 1975).

27. Use popular songs for motivating the student in listening, vocabulary, comprehension, and poetry (Ciani, 1981).

28. Have the student take photographs related to the unit of study or his interests. Have him show them to the class (Ciani, 1981).

29. Give the student choices whenever possible so that he feels more in control of the environment (deCharms, 1977).

30. Stress personal reasoning and values clarification over correct answers to help build students' confidence in their own thinking ability (Broening, 1983).

31. Allow the student to pop a balloon at the end of the day if all work has been completed with 85% accuracy. Rewards are written on paper placed inside the balloons (D. Grey, personal communication, 1983).

32. Tell the student that you have very high standards for him. Let him know that you really believe in him and his abilities. Emphasize that one must believe in one's abilities (Dinkmeyer, McKay, and Dinkmeyer, 1980).

33. Let the student know that you will check

with him every 15 minutes to see what work has been completed (Jones, 1980).

34. Provide opportunities for the student to choose activities that are of interest to him (Adelman and Taylor, 1984; Nicholls, 1984).

35. Verbally recognize those students who are working when the lazy student isn't (e.g., "I like the way Russ is working") (D. Sadlon, personal communication, 1985).

36. Let the student know that his time and effort spent on school work is worthwhile (Adelman and Taylor, 1984).

37. Allow the student to earn the privilege of being hallway monitor or office helper (K. Westray, personal communication, 1983).

38. Allow the student to earn the privilege of assisting you in class (K. Westray, personal communication, 1983).

39. Send home a weekly report card that the parents review, sign, and return to school (K. Westray, personal communication, 1983).

40. Do not allow the student to go home or engage in activities until all work is done.

41. Have the student present a talk or teach the class something that is of interest to him (Blanco, 1977).

42. Have a private conference with the student regarding his laziness in school (Salend, Esquivel, and Pine, 1984).

43. Call the parent to find out if the student is taking any medication that may be producing this behavior (D. Sadlon, personal communication, 1985).

44. Ask the parent about the student's sleeping and eating patterns (D. Sadlon, personal communication, 1985).

45. Talk to teachers who have had the student in their classes regarding successful practices (D. Sadlon, personal communication, 1985).

46. Seat the student in the front of the room in order to observe his behavior and monitor his work patterns (Emmer, 1984).

47. Send notes home on a daily basis regarding the student's behavior (Emmer, 1984).

48. Discuss past school experiences with the student and his attitudes toward school (Ames and Ames, 1984).

49. Talk to the student and let him know that you are concerned about his welfare. Let him know that you will help him in any way that you can (Ames and Ames, 1984).

50. Have the student list his goals in school. Privately talk with him about these goals (Ames and Ames, 1984).

51. Use jackdraws, which are collections of interesting artifacts (e.g., photos, recordings, clothes, movies, news articles, biographical sketches of authors) that provide information about a particular subject, period, or idea to build background and interest in a subject area (Rasinski, 1983).

52. As students become familiar with jackdraws, ask them to add to existing ones or construct their own as an extension activity following the completion of a unit (Rasinski, 1983).

Motivation Strategies for Reading

1. Introduce alternate reading materials such as advertisements, airline schedules, comic strips, drivers' manuals, filmstrips, greeting cards, insignias, jackets from books, jingles, jokebooks, labels, letters, lyrics from familiar songs, movie information, menus, occupational bulletins, pamphlets, plaques, price tags, radio logs, rulebooks, sports material, travel brochures, trick and magic books, wills, wrappers, and zoo signs (McDaniel et al., 1982).

2. Organize the dramatization of stories with puppets, shadow plays, role playing, and pantomime (McDaniel et al., 1982).

3. Have the student create clay models, wire sculptures, or wood carvings of book or historical characters (McDaniel et al., 1982).

4. Follow up television shows or movies with book displays (McDaniel et al., 1982).

5. Encourage students to share books they have read with peers (McDaniel et al., 1982).

6. Use group storytelling. A narrator tells the story and the group provides the action and sounds (McDaniel et al., 1982).

7. Hold individual conferences in which students talk about favorite books with the teacher (DiSibio and Savitz, 1983).

8. Hold a mock trial. Charge a prosecutor with the task of criticizing a story and permit the defendant to justify the story or book of his choosing. The class renders a decision on the relative merits of the case (DiSibio and Savitz, 1983).

9. Have the student write a book review and submit it for publication (DiSibio and Savitz, 1983).

10. Broadcast a book review on your school public address system (DiSibio and Savitz, 1983).

11. Have the student read a story to or work with a lower-grade student (DiSibio and Savitz, 1983).

12. Provide a list of items to locate in the local newspaper. Ask the student to find a dog food, tear out an important current event, or locate an editorial dealing with professional sports (DiSibio and Savitz, 1983).

13. Set up a point system for reading class with 90 points as the total required for course completion. Each completed assignment is worth a certain number of points. When the student has earned 60 points, his picture is taken with an instant camera and displayed on a "Club 60" chart (Diers et al., 1983).

Motivation Strategies for Language Arts

1. Ask the student to find pictures or cartoons and write dialogue for them that reveals something about the character, the relationship between the characters, or the situation (McDaniel et al., 1982).

2. Ask the students to bring their baby picture to school. Have a bulletin board of baby pictures with numbers under each. Encourage students to guess whose pictures they are. Students can then write a story about themselves as they were in the picture (McDaniel et al., 1982).

3. Choose a picture of a door. Have the student write or tell about the life of someone he imagines lives, or once lived, behind it (McDaniel et al., 1982).

4. Play unfamiliar music for the class. Ask the following questions: "What ideas or mental pictures do you get? How does the music make you feel? If this were background music for a motion picture, what would you expect to see on the screen?" Students can write an appropriate response (e.g., anecdote, poem, paragraph) or draw what the music makes them feel (McDaniel et al., 1982).

5. On a file-folder panel, have students paste a display of magazine and catalogue pictures reflecting their own personality and interests. On another part of the folder, the students attach a brief writing sample that explains the creation. When all have completed their "personality" folders, display them (with names hidden) on the bulletin board under the banner "Guess Who?" (McDaniel et al., 1982).

6. Have the student describe life as viewed by a razor blade, skillet, pencil, telephone, pair of shoes, mirror, and so on (McDaniel et al., 1982).

7. Pick an unusual name from the phone book. Have the student characterize the person, using the name alone as the basis (McDaniel et al., 1982).

8. Divide students into teams of two or four. Each team member gets an assignment card to write directions for locating an object that is in the room. When it is the student's turn, he gets a copy of someone else's directions. Scores are awarded by the length of time it takes the member to locate the items (McDaniel et al., 1982).

Motivation Strategies for Social Studies

1. Have the student examine ideas presented in popular songs for the impact that con-

temporary songwriters have had on shaping American culture (Cooper, 1981).

2. Have the student investigate a singer's personal background, history of recording success, and social and political themes in songs (Cooper, 1981).

3. Have the student develop lyrical biographies of socially alienated, politically powerless individuals (Cooper, 1981).

4. Spark interest in historic periods by examining some of the customs related to eating and by tasting particular dishes (e.g., French pastries) (Indiana State Department of Public Instruction, 1981).

5. Cut out different sections of a newspaper and mount them on construction paper. Label them "Editorial," "Ad," and so on. Have students contribute their articles and discuss them (Indiana State Department of Public Instruction, 1981).

6. Play "Mystery Location" in which the student identifies and locates specific places in the United States with the aid of geographic cues (Pelow, 1981).

7. Play "*Geoging* the Mind" in which the student reviews information related to the meaning of geographic terms (Pelow, 1981).

8. Have students write a list of rules that will govern their class (Adams, 1982).

9. Have students participate in U.S. history skits (Adams, 1982).

10. Have students draw or construct maps of their neighborhoods (Adams, 1982).

11. Analyze humor and its relation to historical periods. Analyze the humor of presidents and other famous people (Kelly, 1983).

Motivation Strategies for Science

1. Take trips to participatory science museums to provide visual and kinesthetic learning experiences associated with classroom lessons or printed texts (Flexer and Borun, 1984).

2. Inform students attending a science museum of what they will be seeing in order to enhance cognitive gain (Gennaro, 1981).

3. Issue a challenge to increase experimentation and problem solving. Consider these activities:

    a. Design a hand-powered airplane that will fly 30 feet. The heaviest plane to travel the required distance wins.

    b. Design a sailboat that will travel across a linoleum floor when placed in front of a fan. The boat that travels the farthest wins. No wheels are allowed.

    c. Build a container that will prevent an ice cube from melting. Fill the containers with equal amounts of ice and set a time limit. The container with the least amount of water at the end of the limit wins (Flindt, 1985).

4. Try new categories for science fairs such as: science in history wherein students recreate famous experiments; science today in which students design projects to explain recent discoveries in medicine, space, electronics, and so on; and consumer products testing in which students test common household products for safety, effectiveness, and value (Flindt, 1985).

5. Provide many hands-on experiments.

Motivation Strategies for Mathematics

1. Set up a mathematics laboratory to free students to think for themselves and provide opportunities for them to discover the order, pattern, and relations, which are the very essence of mathematics (Travers et al., 1972).

2. Encourage the use of calculators to help students find patterns or errors in computation (Travers et al., 1972).

3. Introduce manipulative devices such as an abacus, cuisenaire rods, geoboards, scales, thermometers, erector sets, levers, pulleys, stopwatch, compass, and the like (Travers et al., 1972).

4. Give the student an opportunity at the end of the week to use a computer to strengthen math skills or play games if he has done well all week (Diers et al., 1983).

5. Have the student bring candy bars to divide into fractional parts (Diers et al., 1983).

6. Have the students prepare budgets (Adams, 1982).

7. Use holiday themes when presenting material (Smith, 1981).

8. Use the student's interests when developing word problems.

216

Planning to Drop Out of School

1. Reinforce the student when he mentions remaining in school.

2. Explain the importance of a high school diploma (e.g., better jobs, increased job opportunities, increased wages) (Cervantes, 1965; Miles and Killingsworth, 1984).

3. Have employers from different occupations discuss how they view employment of high school dropouts (Miles and Killingsworth, 1984).

4. Provide information and statistics to the student regarding how high school dropouts are perceived in society (e.g., uneducated, poorly motivated, lacking in dedication) (C. Robinson, personal communication, 1985).

5. Teach each subject by showing its relevance to his future (C. Robinson, personal communication, 1985).

6. Ask past high school dropouts to come to the classroom and discuss their experiences and problems since dropping out (C. Robinson, personal communication, 1985).

7. Explain to the student that the unemployment rate for dropouts is higher than for graduates (Howard and Anderson, 1978).

8. Be familiar with community opportunities and make the information available to the student (Hampton, 1977).

9. Inform the student about various higher institutional opportunities available to him if he should decide to drop out of school (Hampton, 1977).

10. With the student, list the pros and cons of dropping out of school and discuss each item (C. Robinson and D. Sadlon, personal communication, 1985).

11. Recognize that school is not a positive environment for this student. Therefore, all learning has to be the result of a desire on his part, brought on by his being able to recognize a real need to improve his skills or seek a high school diploma (Lindsay, 1977).

12. Take advantage of spontaneous learning when it occurs (e.g., in woodshop, assemblies, etc.) (Lindsay, 1977).

13. Teach by "doing" as much as possible. Use hands-on activities (Lindsay, 1977).

14. Individualize the curriculum to meet the student's needs and interests (Howard and Anderson, 1978).

15. If you notice grades lowering or the skipping of classes, talk with the student immediately (Howard and Anderson, 1978).

16. Reduce the pressure placed on the student in the educational environment. Reduce homework or provide alternatives to written tests (C. Robinson, personal communication, 1985).

17. Encourage alternative programs or studies that may interest the student (e.g., typing, computers, auto mechanics, cosmetology) (C. Robinson, personal communication, 1985).

18. Make the subject matter interesting and as fun as possible so that the student enjoys attending class (C. Robinson, personal communication, 1985).

19. Have a social worker or psychologist talk with the student (C. Robinson, personal communication, 1985).

20. If there is an economic problem at home, contact a social worker to help alleviate the problem (Kaplan and Luck, 1977).

21. Enroll the student in a "Dropout Prevention Program" if available (Kaplan and Luck, 1977).

22. Make efforts to improve the rapport among

students, teachers, parents, and administrators (Kaplan and Luck, 1977).

23. Visit the pupil's home and meet with him and his parents to encourage school attendance (Kaplan and Luck, 1977).

24. Develop a more flexible curriculum to allow the student to seek vocational, community, and academic education outside of the schools (Kaplan and Luck, 1977).

25. Devise alternative schedules to ease voluntary reentrance to the educational process (Kaplan and Luck, 1977).

26. Help the student feel comfortable and relaxed in the classroom (C. Robinson, personal communication, 1985).

27. Find out how the school can best meet the student's needs (Laird, 1980).

28. Include the student's culture and experience into everyday lessons when possible (Laird, 1980).

29. Recommend the student for special educational services (e.g., counseling, tutoring, etc.) (Laird, 1980).

30. Suggest counseling (Laird, 1980).

31. Have the student participate in self-concept activities to improve his self-image and attitude toward success (Laird, 1980).

32. Teach through the mastery style so the student does not have to experience as much failure as previously (C. Robinson, personal communication, 1985).

33. Hold value clarification discussions (Laird, 1980).

34. Locate training programs to enable the student to learn skills that will help him obtain a job (Lindsay, 1977).

35. Inform the student of opportunities offered by the armed forces (Kaplan and Luck, 1977).

36. Set up a work-study program (Lindsay, 1977).

37. Place the student in a workshop that simulates an actual place of work (Gorman, 1978).

38. Teach the student about the world of work (e.g., employer-employee relationships, human relations, personal hygiene, and completing job applications) (Gorman, 1978).

39. Reinforce the student for coming to school (C. Robinson, personal communication, 1985).

40. Use diagnostic training techniques to assay the assets of a potential dropout (Hampton, 1977).

41. Go out of your way to get to know the student. Find out about his interests, family history, feelings, and so on (Howard and Anderson, 1978).

42. In a private conference with the student, discuss past school experiences and his attitude toward school. Focus on why he feels that quitting school is the answer (Ames and Ames, 1984).

43. Have the student list his goals in school. Privately talk with him about these goals and whether or not these goals have been met (Williamson and Crewell, 1984).

44. Gain more knowledge of the student. Review past social history and psychological testing that has been done on the student (Cooper, 1984).

45. In the classroom, provide the student with incentive activities such as field trips and extracurricular events that can be utilized in conjunction with school work (Fagan, 1984).

46. Talk with the guidance counselor about the student's desire to drop out of school. Arrange for a meeting between the counselor and the student (Quimby, 1984).

47. Within the classroom, locate a student who is doing well in school and enjoys it. Have this student talk with the one who wants to drop out of school (Gallagher, 1985).

48. Arrange trips to local colleges, universities, and occupational skills centers within the community in order to promote and enhance the benefits of an education (Coca-Cola, 1985).

49. Recommend that the student be vocationally assessed in order to determine his skills potential (Doughtery and Davies, 1984).

50. Contact the guidance counselor for booklets on jobs and careers (Miles and Killingsworth, 1984).

51. Within the classroom, provide a "Job Awareness Center." Have catalogs, brochures, directories, pamphlets, and newspapers available. Materials should represent job opportunities and training programs available in the community (D. Sadlon, personal communication, 1985).

52. Provide the student with literature on the Job Corps Program. Emphasize some of the benefits of the program (e.g., increased independence and self-esteem, vocational training) (Job Corps Amendments, 1984).

53. Have a discussion with the student concerning part-time job openings in the community. Have him tell how he could learn of job openings within the community (e.g., newspaper, store window) (Miles and Killingsworth, 1984).

54. Have the student look for information on part-time job openings in the local community (Miles and Killingsworth, 1984).

55. Provide the student with worksheets that ask him to obtain information on two part-time job openings within the community. Give him two days to complete the sheets and return them to class (Miles and Killingsworth, 1984).

56. Go to the local businesses within the community to obtain job applications. Have the student practice completing these (D. Sadlon, personal communication, 1984).

57. During a class discussion, emphasize the advantages and disadvantages of students working while in school (D. Sadlon, personal communication, 1985).

58. During a private conference with the student, discuss ways of obtaining occupational training within the community. Mention to the student the possibility of enrolling in a vocational-technical center as an alternative to a regular high school program (Miles and Killingsworth, 1984).

59. Have a private conference with the student and discuss alternative high schools. Emphasize that if accepted he would only go to school part-time and then work the remainder of the day. Provide the student with literature on this type of program (D. Sadlon, personal communication, 1985).

60. Discuss the possibility of evening high school with the student. Emphasize that this is another alternative that he should consider. Provide information (e.g., names, contacts, and specific schools) regarding this (D. Sadlon, personal communication, 1985).

61. Role play with the student. Let him pretend that he is the teacher. Pretend that you are a student wanting to drop out of school (Jones, 1980).

62. Send home weekly progress reports on the student's academic work and behavior in school (Quimby, 1984).

63. Call the student's parents on a weekly basis. Discuss the student's attitude, behavior, and academic work (D. Sadlon, personal communication, 1984).

64. Purchase a textbook on preparing for the high school equivalency exam. Provide time for instruction and review (D. Sadlon, personal communication, 1985).

65. Take the student on a trip to the local jail. Point out to the student that dropouts are more likely to get into trouble and end up in jail. If possible, let the student experience what it feels like to be in a jail cell (D. Sadlon, personal communication, 1984).

66. Explain a W-2 form to the student and have him practice completing one (L. Dodd, personal communication, 1985).

67. Encourage participation in school activities so that the potential dropout may gain some positive reinforcement from the school environment (Lower, 1964).

68. Draw up a monthly budget to demonstrate that the money he will be earning will be inadequate to support private housing, a family, and pleasure purchases.

69. Change standard grading procedures. Instead of the usual A, B, C, D, F system, try something new. Perhaps the criteria for dif-

ferent grades will need to be adapted to the student's learning needs. A point system is also a possibility for keeping track of a student's progress (National Education Foundation, 1984).

70. Keep communication lines open to the student. Let him know you are available and can be trusted. Be a friend as well as a teacher (National Education Foundation, 1984; Kaufman and Lewis, 1968).

71. Treat absenteeism as a symptom, not a cause for dismissal. Don't punish the student for not showing up for classes. Instead, reinforce him for attending (Kaufman and Lewis, 1968).

21

Movement

217

Constricted Flexibility

1. Encourage the student to "warm up" with gentle movement before stretching.
2. Encourage physical activity.
3. Involve periodic "stretch breaks" in the day or lesson (Piazza, 1979).
4. Gently move the student's body parts until resistance occurs.
5. With the student's feet back, push the body part past the range that the student is able to accomplish alone.
6. Have the student grasp a stationary object or attach a body part to it. He then uses this to assist himself in moving beyond his usual range of motion.
7. Have the student grab a body part and gently pull it just beyond the usual range of motion.
8. Have the student and a partner do mutual stretching of body parts by pulling against each other.

9. Have the student do athletic warm-up stretches.
10. Allow the student to attach light weights to assist himself in moving beyond the usual range of motion.
11. Suggest enrollment in an aerobic dance class.
12. Suggest enrollment in a gymnastics instruction class.
13. Have the student place the palms of his hands on the seat by his hips and lean forward so the wrists bend backward. Repeat this action several times (Matson, 1982).
14. Have the student stretch out over a table, letting the body weight stretch the shoulders (Matson, 1982).

218

Difficulty with Balance

1. Have the student place his feet within a square. While guiding him, have him shift his weight from one foot to the other. The

285

foot on the ground should remain within the square (Stanley, Waglow, and Alexander, 1973).

2. Holding the student at the hip from behind, guide him in a walking pattern (Kline, 1977).

3. Have the student push a weighted cart, buggy, or chair across the room, which provides a moving point of balance (Kline, 1977).

4. Have the student shift weight from one leg to another with arms extended outwards (Ayres, 1979).

5. Have the student walk between the rungs of a ladder that has been laid on the floor (Ayres, 1979).

6. Have the student climb up the ladder of a slide using one foot at a time while you support him from behind (Newson, 1979).

7. Have the student walk on footprints cut from rubber or paper on a course in which the feet may cross over the midline (Knickerbocker, 1980).

8. Ask the student to touch his shoulder, knees, and ankles while he is balancing on a balance board (Radler and Kephart, 1960).

9. Teach tasks incorporating static and dynamic balancing in which the student's attention is directed toward achieving the optimal amount of tension only in the body parts being utilized (Freischlag, 1973).

10. Using a board or the broad side of a balance beam, have the student cross one foot in front of the other until he walks the length of the beam (Knickerbocker, 1980).

11. Have the student jump rope to help distribute body weight from one side to the other (Knickerbocker, 1980).

12. Use an indoor climber to encourage the student to explore a wide range of movement (Kirchner, Cunningham, and Warrell, 1979).

13. Play make-believe games using an indoor climber to encourage the student to climb. Tell the student that the floor is water and an alligator lives in it. Every time his feet touch the floor, the alligator will tickle them (Smidt, 1984).

14. Place a strip of tape on the floor in a straight line. Have the student follow the tape, placing one foot in front of the other until he reaches the end (Wells and Luttgens, 1976).

15. Place large automobile tires on the floor. Guide the student through the tires using one foot in a tire at a time until he has stepped through all of them (Wells and Luttgens, 1976).

16. Have the student stand up immediately after he falls. Assure the student that falling is part of learning to balance oneself (Rogers and Mann, 1980).

17. Hold both of the student's hands. Stand in front of him, holding his hands forward at his shoulder level. Slowly walk backward, pulling gently so that the student will tend to step toward you (Held and Hein, 1963).

18. Stand the student facing a wall. Have him stretch his arms over his head. Make a point on the wall where his fingers reached. Ask him to try to touch it again (Wessel and Body, 1970).

19. Have the student stand on one foot, then the other. Count to see how long he can stand on one foot at a time (Holland, 1968).

20. Place a beanbag or book on the student's head. Have him walk forward trying not to let the object fall (Van Witsen, 1984).

21. Have the student carry a glass half filled with water (Steindler, 1979).

22. Have the student walk backward, then forward, turning frequently (Knickerbocker, 1968).

23. Position the student prone over a large therapy ball. Rotate his hips while you are standing between his legs. Bring him to a standing position while he is leaning on the ball. Stand the student on one leg at a time (Click and Davis, 1982).

24. Position the student on a prone stander, giving support and restraint to his hips and legs (Click and Davis, 1982).

25. Place the student prone on a large therapy ball. Slide the student down until he is standing, supported by the ball in front of him (Click and Davis, 1982).

26. Place the student on his back on a large therapy ball and rock him back and forth while holding his legs straight and apart. Guide him to a standing position (Click and Davis, 1982).

27. Have the student walk back and forth across a ladder, stepping over the side rail into the space between two rungs, then over the other side rail (Basmajian, 1978).

28. Have the student walk the length of a ladder, stepping over each rung and bringing both feet together in each space (Basmajian, 1978).

29. Have the student walk the length of a ladder, stepping over rungs with alternate feet (Basmajian, 1978).

30. Have the student walk on a ladder, stepping on rungs with one foot and into spaces with the other. Repeat, reversing feet (Basmajian, 1978).

31. Position the student so that he is standing straddling a tilted bolster, leaning with his hands on the bolster. Roll the bolster slightly to simulate weight shift.

32. Have the student kneel with or without support (Chaney and Kephart, 1968).

33. Assist the student to stand when he is sitting in a low chair, astride your leg, or on a bolster. Have the student keep his hands free or lean them on something at wrist level or lower (Chaney and Kephart, 1968).

34. Place the student in a standing position while you support him at the hips or elbow. Gradually withdraw your support until he is standing almost unaided (Elkind, 1969).

35. Stand the student in front of a full-length mirror in order to give him additional feedback (Elkind, 1969).

36. Have the student shift his weight while standing.

37. Hold the student at the hips. Pull his hips in the direction you want him to step. Help him bring one leg toward the other one.

38. Support the student's trunk when he walks (Espenschade and Eckert, 1967).

39. Walk short distances in the beginning to help the student gain confidence (Espenschade and Eckert, 1967).

40. Have the student walk on uneven surfaces such as a playground (Hoberman, 1951).

41. Have the student step over or around obstacles and into and out of boxes (Hoberman, 1951).

42. Have the student stand in the middle of a room. Stand beside him. Place one hand on his stomach and one hand on his lower back. Tap the student front to back alternately (Click and Davis, 1982).

43. Hold the student under the armpits and tip his body backwards. The student's head, shoulders, and arms should move forward and the student's feet should point upward and bend at the ankles (Click and Davis, 1982).

44. Have the student stand on a balance board, facing you and holding your hand. Slowly tilt the board from side to side so that one of the student's knees bends (Basmajian, 1978).

45. Have the student sidestep along a line drawn on the floor. Hold the student at the hips and assist him in shifting his weight (Basmajian, 1978).

46. Have the student practice "ballet" kicks by standing with his side toward the wall, one arm outstretched while leaning into the palm of the hand of his other arm. He then kicks outward with his leg.

47. Have the student play kickball or soccer-type games (without support if possible).

48. Have the student go up and down steps, using one foot on a step at a time (Chaney and Kephart, 1968).

49. Engage the student in a game in which he alternately stands then squats to pick up a number of items from the floor (Chaney and Kephart, 1968).

50. Allow the student to use the wall for support while walking.

51. Allow the student to use a loosely strung rope for balance as needed. Securely tie each end to a stable base.
52. Have the student imitate a number of quick moves used in sports (e.g., backhand stroke, baseball batting, throwing, etc.). Supply equipment for reality and motivation.
53. Allow the student to push a chair while ice skating.
54. Outfit the student with a helmet with face-mask, knees and elbow pads, and pillow tied to the buttocks while he attempts to learn roller skating or skateboarding.

219
Difficulty in Moving

1. Have the student assessed and a recommended therapy program developed.
2. Have the student use magnetic card machines to do lessons in reading, spelling, and math. Students with little or no muscle control can then see and listen to a lesson. A message recorded on tape is heard while the card runs through the machine, presenting auditory and visual information at the same time (Calhoun and Hawisher, 1979).
3. Allow the student to use a typewriter if he has difficulty writing (Calhoun and Hawisher, 1979).
4. Attach a steel grate over the typewriter to help the student find and keep his place on the keys.
5. A student who cannot move his arms might benefit from a head wand. A head wand is a long stick attached to a helmet the student wears on his head. He uses the wand to type (Calhoun and Hawisher, 1979).
6. Allow the student to type rather than write (Calhoun and Hawisher, 1979).
7. Obtain "talking books" if the student has difficulty holding a book comfortably.

These books are distributed by the Library of Congress, New York (Calhoun and Hawisher, 1979).
8. If the student has difficulty turning a page, obtain a page turner. This is a plastic stick with a curve on the end for the student to hold. The other end has a piece of rubber on the tip (Bigge, 1982).
9. Engage the student in a game of ping pong to strengthen arm movement for handwriting. The ping pong table should have walls on the sides so the ball does not fall to the floor (Bigge, 1982).
10. Strap the student into a prone board. The board allows the student to do his work at a table (Bigge, 1982).
11. Build or obtain a wedge. This is a box built off the floor about six inches. The student lays down and puts his arms through the top openings so he can write, read, etc. (Bigge, 1982).
12. The student who cannot write his vocabulary or spelling words can read them off index cards. The index cards are held up with sticks inserted in foam bricks (Bigge, 1982).
13. Allow the student who cannot write to use pictures to describe his project's theme. This can also be done in reading groups to answer questions about a story (Love, 1978).
14. Show slow-motion movies or filmstrips to teach various movements (e.g., nodding the head, raising the hand) (Piazza, 1979).
15. Pair the student with a nonimpaired student for activities (Piazza, 1979).
16. Allow a severely impaired student to raise his finger or make a noise to answer to a question (M. Olscamp, personal communication, 1985).
17. Have the student do motor sequencing strategies. Motor sequencing strategies are movements the student does in a particular order (e.g., wiping the table) (David, 1985).
18. Instruct the student on how to use a motor sequence board. An action such as turn, point, or slide is shown on a picture with an arrow to guide directions (David, 1985).

19. Instruct the student in his weak areas. Work on his impaired activities and intellectual instabilities (Steinberg, 1980).

20. To aid the student in arm movements from left to right, use an electrogoniometer. This is a device with plastic straps that are attached to the student's elbows. A pendular protentiometer is attached to the student's headcap. The student moves his hand to the left and then right. The student's movements are recorded on a graph (Smith, 1984).

21. Keep instructions short and allow time for the accomplishment of activities and movement (M. Olscamp, personal communication, 1985).

220
Poor Eye-Hand Coordination

1. Have the student do training activities (Stamatelos and Mott, 1983; Lerner, 1985).

2. Use various sized balls, beginning with large and working down to smaller sizes while playing bouncing and catching games with the student (Capon, 1977).

3. Use a tether ball or punching bag to teach the student to direct and guide arm movements (Capon, 1977).

4. Have the student tap balloons to keep them in the air or have them on a string to use like a punch ball (Capon, 1977).

5. Instruct the student to walk on masking tape lines, ropes, arrows, or footprints to develop eye-foot coordination. Have him start with the left foot first, then switch to starting with the right foot first. Use music with different beats to add interest to the activity (Capon, 1977).

6. Give the student nails to hammer into a board, first in a random pattern and later in designs, numbers, or letters (Capon, 1977).

7. Use ring toss and bean-bag throw games for improving accuracy in aiming at a target (Capon, 1977).

8. Have the student attempt to thread a needle.

9. Have the student pick up small objects (e.g., paperclips, coins) from a flat or contoured surface.

10. Have the student touch the point or edge of various classroom furnishings.

11. Have the student carry and pour water into larger containers, filling them to a specified level (Lerner, 1985).

12. Have the student use scissors to cut along lines (Lerner, 1985).

13. Have the student draw outlines of stencils or templates (Lerner, 1985).

14. Have the student do lacing activities (Lerner, 1985).

15. Engage the student in a game of jacks (Lerner, 1985).

16. Have the student copy designs onto a separate sheet of paper (Lerner, 1985).

17. Engage the student in paper folding or Japanese origami activities (Lerner, 1985).

18. Have the student complete dot-to-dot connecting activities (Lerner, 1985).

19. Ask the student to assemble jigsaw puzzles, beginning with simple wooden puzzles. Gradually increase the number of pieces and decrease the size of the pieces (Payne, Palloway, Smith, and Payne, 1981).

20. Given a target and ball darts with sticky adhesive on them, have the student throw the balls at the target (Dowell, 1975).

21. Cut various shapes into a plastic milk carton. Have the student place various sized and shaped blocks into these holes (Fallen, 1978).

22. Teach the student to play jacks as a means of further enhancing intricate muscle movements (Payne, Palloway, Smith, and Payne, 1981).

23. Let the student play a game of dropping marbles into a box with holes cut into it (Cratty, 1973).

24. Allow the student to practice pounding large wooden pegs into a play wooden

workbench (Bluma, Sherer, Frohman, and Hilliard, 1976).

25. Have the student draw a picture in crayon or marker onto tagboard or heavy construction paper. Then have him cut them into puzzles and reassemble them (Hamill and Bartel, 1975).

26. Mark two parallel heavy black lines on paper and ask the student to cut between them. As he becomes more proficient, the lines may be placed closer together (D. Pernick, personal communication, 1986).

27. Construct various mazes on dittos. Have the student complete these mazes without backtracking, retracing, or crossing barriers (Payne, Palloway, Smith, and Payne, 1981).

28. Direct the student to "drive" his toy cars or blocks along tape on table tops, arranged in a zigzag fashion (Cratty, 1973).

29. Have the student place small plastic rings around a peg mounted on a wooden block (Bluma, Sherer, Frohman, and Hilliard, 1976).

30. Suspend an object from a string and have the student attempt to catch it while it is moving.

31. Have the pupil further develop eye-hand coordination by stringing beads or threading nuts onto bolts. This activity may be made more challenging by asking him to create and repeat patterns (Payne, Palloway, Smith, and Payne, 1981).

32. Have the student string noodles, cheerios, buttons, and popcorn (D. Pernick, personal communication, 1986).

33. Allow the student to practice dribbling and bouncing small rubber balls (Bluma, Sherer, Frohman, and Hilliard, 1976).

34. Direct the student to throw rubber balls against a wall and retrieve them.

35. Have the student practice hitting balls with bats, sticks, or old racquets (Bluma, Sherer, Frohman, and Hilliard, 1976).

36. Using a "pitch-back net," the student aims for a target for more accurate direction and control in throwing and catching activities (Capon, 1974).

37. Have the student throw bean bags into pie tins, saucers or holds in vertical wood figures.

38. Present the student with two columns of letters or objects and have him draw lines to match them (Payne, Palloway, Smith, and Payne, 1981).

39. Design various closure activities in which two objects are drawn (one with missing parts) and ask the student to complete the second drawing (Payne, Palloway, Smith, and Payne, 1981).

40. Have the student practice writing letters and words using visual cues such as channels, bars, dots, and lines (Cratty, 1973).

41. Straighten out a coathanger and bend it into a path with several curves and loops. Place a washer onto the end of the wire and make handles by bending both ends before taping them. Ask the student to turn and tip the hanger to get the washer from one end to the other (Fallen, 1978).

42. Make a gameboard with several different colored squares pasted on a narrow piece of sturdy cardboard. Present the student with colored wooden clothespins that correspond to the colors on the gameboard and allow him to match the colors by clipping them onto the appropriate square (Fallen, 1978).

43. If the student is not ready to use scissors, have him tear various shapes from paper (Bluma, Sherer, Frohman, and Hilliard, 1976).

44. Present the student with small colored blocks and design cards. Ask him to replicate the designs using blocks. Designs may range from two or three blocks to highly complex and intricate patterns (Payne, Palloway, Smith, and Payne, 1981).

45. Give the pupil a selection of colored triangles, squares, rectangles, and squares cut from heavy poster board. Present him with design cards and instruct him to replicate the designs (D. Pernick, personal communication, 1986).

46. Direct the student to manipulate various

shapes and forms to create shapes, pictures, and letters (French and Jansma, 1982).

47. Instruct the student to practice dropping ping pong balls or coins into a tennis ball can.

48. Instruct the student to pour salt into empty ketchup bottles with different levels marked on them. Allow him to use a funnel (D. Pernick, personal communication, 1986).

221
Poor Fine
Motor Coordination

1. Instruct the pupil to roll modeling clay into small balls, using different finger combinations and other parts of the hand (Cratty, 1973).

2. Present the student with a scrap of felt and a button. Direct him to sew the button on the patch (D. Pernick, personal communication, 1986).

3. Fold a piece of felt approximately 3" × 13" long, and have the student sew the edges together to make an eyeglass case (Mott, 1974).

4. Provide the student with ample opportunity to manipulate flashlights and other devices with intricate on-off switches (Mott, 1974).

5. Provide the student with opportunities to manipulate timers, alarm clocks, wind-up toys, and the like (Mott, 1974).

6. Have the student play store. Let the cashier press the numbers on the machine to increase finger dexterity (Frostig and Horne, 1964).

7. Teach knotting to the student (C. Frankewicz, personal communication, 1985).

8. Engage the student in a game of "pick-up sticks" (Wessel, 1982).

9. Give the student experience in unwrapping various packages and wrappings (Bluma, Sherer, Frohman, and Hilliard, 1976).

10. Involve the student in unscrewing lids from jars and bottles (Bluma, Sherer, Frohman, and Hilliard, 1976).

11. Design activities in which the pupil must manipulate twist ties around objects (e.g., storage of modeling clay in plastic bags, cleanup of art supplies, snack distribution) (D. Pernick, personal communication, 1986).

12. Instruct the student to place the palms of his hands together and touch the corresponding fingertips to each other in order (Cratty, 1973).

13. Have the pupil touch each fingertip, one at a time, to the tip of his thumb (Cratty, 1973).

14. Allow the student to experiment with various ways of interlocking and clasping hands together (Cratty, 1973).

15. Teach the student beginning sign language, allowing him to practice manipulating fingers and hands (D. Pernick, personal communication, 1986).

16. Have the student play "Mailman." If you have notices or papers to send home, the chosen mail person folds the papers once, matching corners. The student then stamps it in the upper right corner with an ink stamp (Jackson and Randell, 1971).

17. Play "Chinese Checkers" with the student (Jackson and Randell, 1971).

18. Given different kinds of fruits and vegetables, have the student use a peeler to remove the skin (Jackson and Randell, 1971).

19. Direct the student in activities that involve assembling Legos, Tinker Toys, Lincoln Logs, and other commercially made stacking and connecting blocks (D. Pernick, personal communication, 1986).

20. Have the student practice dialing various phone numbers on rotary and push button telephones (D. Pernick, personal communication, 1986).

21. Give the student an assortment of small

containers or baby food jars with the numbers 1–20 printed on them. Instruct the pupil to place the corresponding number of plastic bingo chips or beads in each of the jars (D. Pernick, personal communication, 1986).

22. Have the student practice bundling small sticks or straws into groups of 10 and binding them with a rubber band (D. Pernick, personal communication, 1986).

23. Have the student practice turning door knobs (Bluma, Sherer, Frohman, and Hilliard, 1976).

24. Provide the student with experience in turning pages while being read to (Bluma, Sherer, Frohman, and Hilliard, 1976).

25. Ask the student to pick up small pellets and drop them into a bottle (Boyd, 1974).

26. Allow the student to place small objects, such as acorns, buttons, raisins, stones, and blocks, into various containers (Bluma, Sherer, Frohman, and Hilliard, 1976).

27. Give the student experience in counting small objects, such as beads, chips, cereal, and M&Ms (D. Pernick, personal communication, 1986).

28. Play "Simon Says." Call out commands that require fine motor coordination (e.g., "Simon Says, unbutton your top button") (Jackson and Randell, 1971).

29. Have the student play "Bowling" using small table pins and a small ball (Dowell, 1974).

30. Have the student practice cutting by fringing the borders of precut shapes and objects (Mott, 1974).

31. Instruct the student to round or cut the corners off of a sheet of paper (Mott, 1974).

32. Use modeling clay to provide the student with sculpturing and pottery activities (Lerner, 1985).

33. Cut a series of vertical strips into a sheet of paper, leaving approximately one inch at the top and bottom of the page. Have the student weave strips of colored paper through this paper loom (Lerner, 1985).

34. Have the student further develop weaving skills by using commercially prepared miniature looms (Lerner, 1985).

35. Further develop weaving skills by using a teacher-prepared loom. A small loom can be constructed by cutting small slits into the ends of a piece of sturdy cardboard and stringing kite string vertically through it. The student may then weave brightly colored yarn through the loom to make a decorative wall hanging (D. Pernick, personal communication, 1986).

36. Allow the student to gain an awareness of his fingers and their manipulation using thick finger paints and making movements in all directions (Cratty, 1973).

37. Direct the student to make paper chains using pre-cut strips of construction paper and paste (Cratty, 1973).

38. Given a drawing of a candle with a missing flame, have the student paste the flame on the candle (Jackson and Randell, 1971).

39. Have the student decorate cookies (Jackson and Randell, 1971).

40. Have the student trace a quarter on paper (Jackson and Randell, 1971).

41. Create a large gadget board with locks, latches, plugs, zippers, levers, snaps, buttons, and so on and allow the student to practice manipulating these devices.

42. If the student has difficulty holding writing utensils, wrap a sponge around a regular-sized pencil to improve grip (Fallen, 1978).

43. If holding or steadying paper is a problem, tape the student's paper to the table, or make a paper-holding frame from two sheets of cardboard (Fallen, 1978).

44. If grip is a problem for the student, glue small wooden pegs or beads to puzzle pieces (Fallen, 1978).

45. Lay a jar on the floor. Have the student aim water into the jar with a squirtgun (Dowell, 1974).

46. Display paper dolls. Allow the student to punch out clothes and clasp them to the dolls (D. Pernick, personal communication, 1986).

47. Use command drawings to practice handwriting. Instruct the student to make a certain design (e.g., a circle and a line, a triangle inside a square, etc.) (Mott, 1974).

48. Instruct the student to make chains by linking paper clips together (Payne, Palloway, Smith, and Payne, 1981).

49. Have the student independently construct model planes and cars (Lerner, 1985).

50. Have students form a straight line standing behind one another. The first student passes the ball under his legs, the second person over his head, the third person under his legs, fourth person over his head, and so forth (Nagel and Moore, 1968).

51. Have the student practice "air writing." Present him with a letter or word and have him write the letter(s) with his fingers in the air (D. Pernick, personal communication, 1986).

52. Have the student place large ring-shaped blocks around a peg mounted to a block of wood (Bluma, Sherer, Frohman, and Hilliard, 1976).

53. Provide the pupil with a set of cans, boxes, or plastic containers, that he can fit inside one another when arranged according to size (Watrin and Furfey, 1978).

54. Play board games with the student such as dominos, bingo games, and card games involving small muscle movements (D. Pernick, personal communication, 1986).

55. Give the student experience in locking and unlocking padlocks with keys (Mott, 1974).

56. Allow the student to practice fastening and unfastening paper clips (D. Pernick, personal communication, 1986).

57. Have the student practice operating crank toys, such as a jack-in-the-box or an eggbeater (D. Pernick, personal communication, 1986).

58. Have the student paper clip various papers and pictures together (D. Pernick, personal communication, 1986).

59. Have the student participate in simple fingerplay activities (J. Bonwell, personal communication, 1984).

60. Provide the student with the opportunity to operate finger and hand puppets (D. Pernick, personal communication, 1986).

222
Poor Gross Motor Coordination

1. Encourage the student to watch the movements of other people. Have him imitate these (Chaney and Kephart, 1968).

2. Have the student move forward, backward, and sideward without touching objects or people in a given area (Capon, 1977).

3. Have the student skip, gallop, trot, run, and prance, changing the pace periodically (Capon, 1977).

4. Set up an obstacle course with chairs, boxes, tunnels, ropes, and the like. Have the student go over, under, between, through, into and around these objects (Capon, 1977).

5. Have the student use roller skates and skateboards on paved areas of the playground (Capon, 1977).

6. Practice pantomime techniques.

7. Have the student rollerskate or skateboard with your support. Gradually remove the support (Arnheim, 1979).

8. Have the student ride a bike. Use training wheels and support. Gradually remove these (Arnheim, 1979).

9. Play frisbee (Arnheim, 1979)

10. Play basketball after enlarging and lowering the hoop (Cratty, 1975).

11. Arrange some benches in a large square. The student tries to get a soccer ball through the opponent's benches while preventing it from going through his own "goal."

12. Play "Two Squares." In this game, the student bounces the ball in the opponent's square only. If it bounces in his square or

is out of bounds, he loses his turn (S. Williams, personal communication, 1983).

13. Have the student jump or hop into obstacles such as old tires, hula hoops, boxes, and inner tubes (Capon, 1977).

14. Give sequential directions (e.g., "do a forward roll, hop once on your right foot, place your hand on top of your head, and sit down") (Simpson, 1977).

15. Draw two dots on the chalkboard and have the student connect them using chalk (Lerner, 1985).

16. Have the student practice drawing concentric circles on the blackboard (Lerner, 1985).

17. Using stilts and pogo sticks, have the student move forward, backward, or sideways (Capon, 1977).

18. Allow the student to practice writing letters and shapes on the chalkboard (Lerner, 1985).

19. Have students use a small hand-held apparatus when moving through space to music. Use balls, hoops, ribbons, and scarves to encourage the student to move more freely and smoothly (Willoughby and Plumton, 1983).

20. Have the student play "Blackboard Follow." Draw an irregular wandering line on the chalkboard and instruct the student to follow with different colored chalk (Cratty, 1973).

21. Have the student play "Make the Clock." Draw a large circle on the chalkboard with markings where numbers would be on a clock. Place a dot in the center of the circle. Instruct the pupil to draw a line from the center dot to each of the markings on the clock (Cratty, 1973).

22. Have the student squat like a baseball catcher and tuck his chin to his chest. The student should then put his hands on a mat below his knees, push with his feet, and roll forward (Simpson, 1977).

23. Have the student toss beanbags into small hoops or shallow boxes (Fallen, 1978).

24. For body and space awareness, have the student move body parts in a special way (e.g., nod the head, clap the hands, bend the elbows, shrug the shoulders). Do this both slow, fast, and with music (Capon, 1977).

25. Attempt to involve the student intellectually in the movement tasks. Teach him to think and plan before moving (Cratty, 1971).

26. Integrate gross motor training into the curriculum of the student. In math, let him jump and hop on numbers. Practice language by describing gross motor activities. Let him imitate movements of zoo, farm, and circus animals in social studies. In writing, teach him to perform a gross motor movement with a crayon in the air and to transpose it later onto paper. In music, sing rhymes while jumping (Lowenthal, 1983).

27. Conduct swimming activities. Water offers resistance to movement, thus increasing the tactual-kinesthetic information coming from the movement of the limbs (Kephart, 1960).

28. Roll the ball to the student so that he can pick it up before catching a smaller ball coming from a considerable distance (Cratty, 1971).

29. Make the student aware of the problem. He may not be aware that he moves differently, since it has always been this way for him (Kephart, 1975).

30. Use foam rubber "nurf" balls in activities to alleviate the student's fear of on-coming objects.

31. Utilize hula hoops as objects to step into in obstacle courses as well as tossing and catching them. Twirling the hoops around the waist without letting them hit the ground promotes smoother movement (Capon, 1977).

32. Have the student ride a bicycle or scooter on lines and paths through obstacles such as cones (Capon, 1977).

223

Poor Rhythm

1. Have the student run to the beat of the music (Kephart, 1975).
2. Have the student march to music (Kephart, 1975).
3. Using a metronome, have the student tap his foot to the beat (Simpson, 1977).
4. Inform your students that in many eastern European countries, audiences applaud in synchronized fashion. Have your class clap in synchronized fashion for various student accomplishments.
5. Provide instruments such as drums, tambourines, rhythm sticks, and triangles for experimentation (Morrison, 1978).
6. Ask the student to play an instrument in beat to your clapping.
7. Instruct the student to match the beat of the music while clapping or playing an instrument.
8. Suggest enrollment in an aerobic dance class.
9. Have the student imitate your repetitive rhythmic movement as you move to music.
10. Teach the student "classic" dance steps (e.g., foxtrot, waltz, polka).
11. Have the student bend his knees to a beat.
12. Have the student snap his fingers to a beat.

224

Tics

1. Observe the school and family environment for possible emotional conflicts that might be creating the tics. Focus on eliminating the existing emotional conflicts (Dreikurs, 1972; Bakwin and Bakwin, 1972).
2. Search for physical sources of the irritation and work on improving physical aspects of the tic (Bakwin and Bakwin, 1972).
3. Make use of the "competing response practice" technique. This involves teaching the student an appropriate behavior that is incompatible with the tic (Schaefer and Millman, 1977).
4. Utilize the "habit control motivation" technique. In order to increase the student's drive to eliminate the tic, make the student aware of the inconvenience and embarrassment created by the motions (Schaefer and Millman, 1977; Eyde and Fink, 1983).
5. Use the "massed practice" technique. The student repeats the tic as often as possible until he can no longer repeat it even once a minute (Miller, 1970; Sue, Sue, and Sue, 1981).
6. Advise the student to read about his disturbances so as to develop an understanding of it. This understanding may strengthen the process of treatment (Shapiro, Shapiro, Brunn, and Sweet, 1978).
7. Assist the student in performing mirror drills and exercises with the involved muscles (Shapiro, Shapiro, Brunn, and Sweet, 1978).
8. Recommend counseling for the parents so as to involve them in the process of treatment (Schaefer and Millman, 1977; Shapiro, Shapiro, Brunn, and Sweet, 1978).
9. Suggest group therapy (Shapiro, Shapiro, Brunn, and Sweet, 1978).
10. Advise parents to seek information from their physicians on the use of drug therapy (Bakwin and Bakwin, 1972; Schaefer and Millman, 1977; Sue, Sue, and Sue, 1981).
11. Videotape the tics and replay the tape for the student's viewing.

22

Neuroticism

225

Achievement Anxiety

1. Make learning fun in order to relax the atmosphere. Showmanship is important. Make fun of yourself or do something silly to make a point (Smith, 1983).

2. Place the students in groups according to their achievement thus far. When the individual is with other students achieving at his level, the achievement anxiety level may be lower (Schwarzer and Schwarzer, 1982).

3. Allow the student to categorize himself in a reference group according to the anxiety level felt (Schwarzer and Schwarzer, 1982).

4. Use positive suggestions and comments whenever the student is beginning a task that involves feelings of anxiety (Kahn, 1977).

5. Have the student repeat suggestions to himself (e.g., "I am calm," "I am working with great efficiency") (Kahn, 1977).

6. Experiment with a different teaching style

to see if there is a difference in the anxiety level (Wade, 1981).

7. Use an invitational approach to reduce anxiety-related reactions. In this approach, the student decides the strategy to be used and how he will incorporate it (Howarth and Wagner, 1983).

8. Show the student the way to deal with anxiety by modeling. Have the student choose an anxious situation for you. Perform a model reaction through self-talk and a positive attitude (Parker and Johnson, 1981).

9. Encourage the student to set realistic goals. At first, this may require some assistance so that the goals are realistic and attainable (Parker and Johnson, 1981).

10. Give encouragement and support for effort, whether goals are met or not (Parker and Johnson, 1981).

11. Use a special code for grading. Each student has his own code so that comparisons cannot be made.

12. Give constant reminders to the student that working to his best ability is important, and

that making mistakes in the process is all right as long as he learns from them.

13. Request that the student have a thorough examination to make certain that none of the problems he is experiencing has a physical basis (Goldfried, 1976).

14. Give partial credit for problems and exercises attempted even if the answers are not correct (Wegman and Talent, 1982).

15. Give positive feedback on assignments (e.g., "You got six right" rather than "You got five wrong") (Wegman and Talent, 1982).

16. Have the student read about others who are like him. In a discussion or follow-up activity, draw out the similarities (Dreher, 1978).

17. Encourage the student to participate in lessons by calling on him only when you are sure that he knows the answers, or by having him hold materials or demonstrate something (H. Bongiorno, personal communication, 1985).

18. Encourage the student to select projects of special interest (Special Learning Corp., 1979).

19. Give the student alternative assignments (e.g., "You may either read pages 30–35 and answer the questions about the story, or you may write a story about ships"). Be sure the alternatives cover the same concepts you intended the original assignment to include (H. Bongiorno, personal communication, 1985).

20. Make mistakes intentionally with something that is very routine and have the student point out your error. When he does so, thank him for correcting you, showing him that there is a positive way to handle corrections (M. L. Schaefer, personal communication, 1985).

21. Reduce the criterion for success or correctness of completed work (Special Learning Corp., 1979).

22. Give praise for small efforts. Praise can be either verbal or nonverbal (Special Learning Corp., 1979).

23. Guarantee the student success in learning. For example, if he is fearful of reading in class, have him tape his reading at home and play it back for you the next day (Special Learning Corp., 1979).

24. Structure new learning situations so the student fully understands the process and does not worry as much about what might go wrong. Let the student work on subskills before being presented with the whole task (Wegman and Talent, 1982).

25. Present the new skill in a familiar context along with a skill the student has mastered in order to avoid or lessen anxiety and frustration (Hayden, Smith, Saaz, and Hippel, 1982).

26. Reduce the sense of group competitiveness by helping the student see that he is not competing with the others in the class. Place a personal progress chart on the student's desk or in a place where it can be seen. Allow him to graph his successes (H. Bongiorno, personal communication, 1985).

27. Involve counselors when necessary. Family counseling may be in order if the student is driven by anxious parents. Follow the suggestions of counselors in the classroom whenever possible (H. Bongiorno, personal communication, 1985).

28. Isolate specific incidences of achievement anxiety and work on lowering the level of anxiety in just one area at a time (Goldfried, 1976).

29. Stand or sit next to the student and offer assistance when needed as a precaution against him becoming too frustrated (Hayden, Smith, Saaz, and von Hippel, 1982).

30. Present work to the student in small quantities. Tear out the pages of a workbook instead of presenting him with an amount of work that might seem overwhelming (Special Learning Corp., 1979).

31. Camouflage materials. If the student reads on a lower level than is expected of him, tear off the covers and make colorful book

jackets to disguise the materials (H. Bongiorno, personal communication, 1985).

32. Provide the student with opportunities to earn extra credit in areas that he is successful (Special Learning Corp., 1980).

33. Take pictures of the student working hard. As added encouragement, display photos where they can be seen (Meyer, 1979).

34. Allow the student to complete the odd-numbered problems on a page, or the first five, to ensure that he knows the concept without providing frustration (Special Learning Corp., 1979).

35. Invent learning games and situations where performance is not judged with paper, pencils, or books (e.g., field trips, discussions, films, etc.) (Lane, 1984).

36. The use of medication may be warranted if the student is extremely high strung and nervous. This should be left to the discretion of a physician (Lane, 1984).

37. Insist that the student think the situation through before attempting an academic achievement (Goldfried, 1976).

38. Listen for key thoughts when a student is talking about a situation. These thoughts are put into words like, "I *must* do something" or "I *can't* possibly do this." These thoughts should serve as a signal to stop and examine what the student is thinking (Goldfried, 1976).

39. Tell the student that no matter what anyone else does or says, he only needs to be concerned with himself and know inside that he has done his best (Goldfried, 1976).

40. Discuss the out-of-class experiences that the student may have had concerning anxiety about achievement (Tobias, 1980).

41. Encourage the student to work *with* mistakes and learn from them rather than being upset and defeated by them (Tobias, 1980).

42. Avoid timed tests, frequent pop quizzes, and excessive competitiveness in the classroom (Tobias, 1980).

43. Highlight directions on materials. Give clear and concise instructions before handing out the work. Have the student repeat directions back to you in his own words to insure understanding (Special Learning Corp., 1979).

44. Set up two or three instructional groups. Place the student into the group within which he functions the best. If need be, one-to-one remediation can be done later in the day (Hayden, Saaz, Smith, and von Hippel, 1982).

45. Gear the lesson below the student's frustration level. Gradually increase the difficulty and the amount of teaching time as he can cope with it (Hayden, Smith, Saaz, and von Hippel, 1982).

226

Afraid of Being Hurt in Physical Play

1. Reinforce the student when he participates in games.

2. Let the student know that fear is a normal reaction in order to reduce his feelings of shame, if any.

3. Develop the student's awareness of the fear. If he tends to withdraw in physical activities, point this out to him so that he will face the fear and better cope with the anxiety (Kellerman, 1981).

4. Give private instruction in a physical activity that will occur later in the week or month.

5. For activities that involve physical movement, conduct a task analysis in order to insure success and accomplishment. Begin with small exercises and progress (Kellerman, 1981).

6. The student may be afraid of not mastering a task. Insure mastery activities are done in order to gain confidence in physical activities.

7. Set rules for games that will help prevent physical contact.
8. Enforce the rules consistently to avoid dangerous play.
9. Videotape or tape record the student as the behavior occurs so that he can see for himself how he acts (Reinhart, 1980).
10. Show the student how other students act in the same situations (Carberry, 1979).
11. Use soft "nurf" balls to lessen fear of being hit by the ball.
12. Encourage participation in solitary sports (e.g., track, swimming, golf).
13. Encourage participation in noncontact games and sports (e.g., volleyball, baseball).
14. Provide the student with protective equipment.
15. Have the student participate in these activities as a coach or referee.

227
Afraid of Dirt and Germs

1. Reinforce the student when he is not expressing his fear of dirt and germs.
2. Allow the student to quickly clean his desk and materials. Set a time limit on this.
3. Discuss the problem with the student and point out how others react to him, germs, and dirt, and how they are not concerned.
4. Recommend counseling for the student.
5. Obtain an ultra-violet light and have the student watch as you kill bacteria on surfaces.
6. Ask a health-care expert to talk with the student about his overconcern with germs and dirt.
7. Read to the student about the later life of Howard Hughes. With the student, discuss how Mr. Hughes's life was affected by the phobia and how others perceived him.
8. Assist the student in building his resistance to germs by recommending adequate sleep,

good nutrition, and proper cleanliness. Stress how he now needs to be less concerned with germs and dirt (K. Cowell, personal communication, 1986).
9. Allow the student to wear gloves or a mask if it will enable him to engage in activities.
10. Ask others not to sneeze or cough in the student's proximity.
11. Ask others not to touch the student.
12. Encourage other age and sex peers to include the student in their activities. Modeling, support, and peer pressure may influence the student.
13. Suggest that the student's parents have him immunized to give him a greater sense of protection and security (D. Bastible, personal communication, 1986).

228
Afraid of Doctors

1. Reinforce the student when he undergoes medical treatment or evaluation in a calm or brave manner.
2. Recommend counseling for extreme cases (Clarizio and McCoy, 1970; Dupont, 1969; Haring and Phillips, 1962; Segraves, 1978).
3. To help build understanding, teach a unit about doctors and the medical profession (S. Thomas, personal communication, 1983).
4. Have the student meet and talk with a physician or nurse away from a medical facility (S. Thomas, personal communication, 1983).
5. Have a nurse or doctor come and talk to the class about their job (Dupont, 1969).
6. Use role playing to help deal with the student's feelings (Haring and Phillips, 1962).
7. Conduct play therapy with toy medical equipment included (Haring and Phillips, 1962; Hill, 1973).
8. View movies and filmstrips about going to

the doctor or hospital (S. Thomas, personal communication, 1983).

9. Recommend the "flooding technique" in which the student is placed at once in the fear-induced situation (Segraves, 1978).

10. Have the student draw or write about what frightens him (Hill, 1973).

11. Have the student read and discuss the children's book, *Curious George Goes to the Hospital*.

12. Ask medical personnel to remove their outer smocks so that they look less threatening.

13. Speak with the student beforehand to reassure him.

14. Reassure the student that the treatment will "make him better."

15. If the student is afraid due to past unpleasant experiences, ask him if the treatment "made him better." This may help him understand the need.

16. Allow the student to hold a favorite toy or stuffed animal (D. McKnight, personal communication, 1986).

17. Allow the student to have a friend or favorite adult present for support. Allow the student to hug or be hugged or touched by the escort (D. McKnight, personal communication, 1986).

18. Ask that a certain medical person be present at repeat visits so that the student feels more comfortable and has a familiar "expert" nearby.

19. Have the student talk with other pupils who have been through the same procedure.

20. Ask the medical personnel to tell the student what they will be doing in order to familiarize him with what is occurring.

21. Ask medical personnel to allow the student to tell them when he is "ready" for a procedure. Tell the student he has two minutes to prepare himself. This allows the student to summon his courage and have some control over the situation.

229

Afraid of Social Events and Crowds (Agorophobia)

1. Reinforce the student when he reacts to groups of people in a calm manner (Morris and Kratochwill, 1983).

2. Expose the student to progressively larger groups of people (Morris and Kratochwill, 1983).

3. Have the student engage in an activity with a small group, the size of which he is not frightened by. This group should be comprised of familiar individuals. Tell the student the number of people in the group and inform him that he will work with this same sized group later. This second group includes some strangers.

4. Expose the student to controlled group settings (e.g., people seated in bleachers rather than milling about on a street).

5. Allow the student to observe groups from the edge of the setting or as close as the student still feels comfortable.

6. Have friends escort the student to provide support.

7. Include the student in group activities of interest to him (e.g., a movie or magic show) in order to allow him to focus on something other than the crowd.

8. If the student is small, place him on your shoulders or carry him on your back to suppress the fear of being trampled.

9. Have the student enter the crowded event for as long as he can control his fear. After withdrawal, discuss the situation with him (D. McKnight, personal communication, 1986).

10. Drive the student through crowded areas (e.g., a college campus, carnivals, field days). This provides physical protection for the student.

11. For more ideas, see the strategy sheet in this book entitled "Phobic."

230
Afraid of Unfamiliar People

1. Reinforce the student when he reacts in a nonfrightened manner to the presence of strangers.
2. Have the unfamiliar person smile and wave to the student.
3. Have the unfamiliar person enter with an item of interest to the student.
4. Have the stranger engaged in one of the student's favorite activities. Ask the student to join the activity or allow him to watch.
5. Show your pleasure in meeting this unfamiliar person. Smile, shake hands, and joke with this person in the presence of the student.
6. Escort the student and the unfamiliar person to provide support for the student.
7. Allow the student to observe this new person from a distance as he interacts positively with other pupils.
8. Allow the student to have a friend available while interacting with the unfamiliar person.
9. Have the unfamiliar person return frequently to promote familiarity.
10. Have a familiar person arrive in disguise and then remove it.
11. Prepare the student for the arrival of the stranger. Tell him about this person and discuss ways of greeting him or her.
12. Use field trips to introduce students to people in the neighborhood, authority figures, and "every day" people (D. Otto, personal communication, 1983).
13. Arrange for guest speakers in order to familiarize students with people.
14. Make use of the outdoors; social interactions are often easier to undertake there (Bain, 1979).
15. Conduct class activities such as speeches and self-introductions so as to familiarize

the students with presenting themselves to others (Tunnel, 1981).
16. Use role playing in which you or a pupil plays the role of a stranger. Have the student greet the unfamiliar person and carry on a conversation about general topics (e.g., sports, weather, activities in progress) (Barrow, 1979).
17. For more ideas, see the strategy in this book entitled "Phobic."

231
Appears Tense or Nervous

1. Help the student recognize and accept his feelings and behavior. Help him devise more rational ways of thinking and taking behavioral risks.
2. Play music to lessen tenseness and anxiety (Blanchard, 1979).
3. Have a friend who can be helpful under conditions of high stress be available to the student to help calm him. Specific observable behaviors as well as attitudes and values can be learned through exposure to this helper (Gerber, 1983).
4. Encourage the student to externalize anxiety through art (Algozzine, 1982).
5. Conduct stress management techniques such as deep breathing, imagining pleasant things, or biofeedback.
6. Initiate relaxation exercises (Lang, 1980).
7. Massage the student's shoulders while calmly talking to him (C. Thompson, personal communication, 1984).
8. Teach the student to argue with his tense feelings. The student tells himself why these feelings are not necessary in this situation.
9. Inform the student about how nervousness impairs performance. Encourage him to relax and "just try your best."
10. Help alleviate peer pressure by encouraging the student to be a leader and individualistic (Lang, 1980).

11. Reduce competitiveness in the classroom (C. Thompson, personal communication, 1984).

12. Be sure to let the student know exactly what is expected of him (Barger, 1983).

13. Help improve the student's attitude by setting realistic goals. Goals beyond the student's ability to achieve may cause nervousness or anxiety (Ivancevich, 1982).

14. Investigate the student's health and level of exercise. Nervousness and anxiety are often linked to health (Crisp and Stonehill, 1976).

15. Initiate behavioral rehearsals. Practice appropriate behaviors in mock anxiety-producing situations to show the student how to overcome nervousness (Massong, Dickson, Ritzler, and Layne, 1982).

16. Have the student pick out anxiety-producing situations and videotape him in these situations. Replay the tape. This will either show that there was really nothing to worry about, or, in some cases, it will show the cause of the nervousness. Discuss how to change the behavior (Massong, Dickson, Ritzler, and Layne, 1982).

effect on others. The peers can provide suggestions for alternatives to the undesirable behavior (Appollini and Cooke, 1978).

6. Create more noncompetitive games and activities in which everyone wins.

7. Stress that winning or losing is irrelevant if the student has tried his best.

8. Have students attempt to beat their former scores or performance during a task or game. Focus on personal performance rather than group performance or final results.

9. Work with the student to develop the skills necessary to compete without embarrassment.

10. If the student is afraid of being hurt by a ball, use "nurf" balls.

11. Enforce firm, consistent game rules so that the danger of being injured is lessened.

12. Implement rules that burden the winning team and assist the team that is losing in order to even the score.

13. Require supportive team spirit by all players. Degrading remarks should not be allowed.

232

Avoids Competition

1. Reinforce the student when he engages in competitive activities.

2. Teach peer modeling to the students (Apollini and Cooke, 1978).

3. Teach peers to prompt the student into joining competitive activities (Strain, Keer, and Ragland, 1979).

4. Pair students together in any competitive or noncompetitive situation. Explain to the students that as partners they should work together cooperatively (K. Feeley, personal communication, 1985).

5. Implement a peer confrontation system in which the peers challenge the student to become aware of the target behavior and its

233

Becomes Flustered or Ill When Asked to Express Self Verbally

1. Reward the student for answering appropriately (Blanco, 1972).

2. Give the student a task that involves the coordinated efforts of two or more students in order to provide support (Blanco, 1972).

3. Place the student and his desk near friends where he might feel more secure (Blanco, 1972).

4. Give the student more time for response. Let him practice answers at home. Ask

questions from a prepared list (Blanco, 1972).

5. Minimize criticisms. Emotional support should be maximal (Blanco, 1972).

6. Encourage the student to join extracurricular activities such as scouting, booster club, and so on (Blanco, 1972).

7. Ask questions in areas that are strong points for the student (Blanco, 1972).

8. Encourage participation in games and sports to promote verbal interaction with others (Blanco, 1972).

9. Encourage expression through creative writing or art (Blanco, 1972).

10. Make sure the student is doing work at his level so that he is not reporting on material that he doesn't understand (Blanco, 1972).

11. Be consistent in telling the student that he is capable of doing the work (Blanco, 1972).

12. Explore the possibility of suggesting counseling (Blanco, 1972).

13. Use role playing. It sometimes gives the student a chance to be more verbal and outgoing under the "guise" of being another personality (Blanco, 1972).

14. Eliminate the grading system for this student to lower anxiety (Blanco, 1972).

15. Try working with this student in small groups or one on one where he will feel more comfortable in contributing.

16. Assure the student that it is healthy to feel afraid or angry, but unhealthy to retreat or assault (Long, 1979).

17. Encourage the student to develop a vocabulary that expresses feelings like afraid, worried, and so on (Mercer and Mercer, 1981).

18. Inspire the student's confidence in his ability. Conduct a lot of activities to build self-concept (Blanco, 1972).

19. Be supportive. Avoid appearing impatient or angry when asking the student to speak (Stoops, 1961).

20. Call on the student when he volunteers an answer. Do this with a smile and a sense of appreciation and affection (Stoops, 1961).

21. Use modeling techniques to teach appropriate behaviors (Mercer and Mercer, 1981).

22. Provide verbal phrases like "You've almost got it" when the student gives a wrong answer (Mercer and Mercer, 1981).

23. Have the student videotape his verbal presentation in private and present it to you or the class.

24. Have the student practice his presentation in front of you or a few friends before presenting to the whole class.

25. Have all students write a response then read it to the class.

26. Offer to rescue the student or provide cues if he has trouble expressing himself.

27. Have a session labeled "STP" (socially terrific person). The whole class lists things that constitute a STP. Students look at the list to see which they have learned. Hopefully, this will help the student realize that he can learn to express himself (Biemer, 1983).

28. Have the student make two columns for pros and cons of conquering this behavior. He might realize there is a bigger advantage to conquering the behavior (Biemer, 1983).

29. Try role playing using a small group and short scenes (Biemer, 1983).

30. Allow the student to write responses on paper that will be read to the class by a friend (Bruch, 1983).

31. Identify objects of interest to the student. The student then says one thing about each object (Beisler and Tsai, 1983).

32. Have the student start talking to a good friend. Then add another friend after the student feels comfortable. Slowly ease the student into verbalizing in front of a group (M. Montgomery, personal communication, 1984).

33. Conduct relaxation exercises before a verbal activity. These include turning of the head from side to side, trunk bending, dropping the jaw, and the like (Biemer, 1983).

34. Before the student is to speak, use humor whenever possible. Laughter is an excellent way to place students at ease (Biemer, 1983).

35. Along with laughter, allow the student to verbalize first so that he is still loose and does not have time to get tense while others speak (M. Montgomery, personal communication, 1984).

36. Allow the student to speak first, last, with introduction or without, with notes, or whatever way makes him most comfortable.

37. Encourage the student to look at the back wall when giving presentations.

234
Compulsive Behavior

1. Reinforce the student when he avoids compulsive behavior.

2. Recommend counseling for the student (Biehler, 1974).

3. Ignore the compulsive behavior (Stanley, 1980).

4. List situations that elicit compulsive behavior and grade them according to "upset" value. Present the mildest situation first and prevent the student from engaging in the compulsive behavior. Later, focus on the more severe situations (Stanley, 1980).

5. Institute various operant procedures (e.g., desensitization, thought stopping, contingent shock) (Gelder, 1979).

6. Have the student set goals for decreasing the compulsive behavior (e.g., switching a pencil between hands only two times rather than three before writing).

7. Consider that the behavior is useful for relieving anxiety and perhaps normal, especially if the student is around the age of two years, seven to eight years, or in early adolescence (Kessler, 1972).

8. Encourage the student to substitute a less demonstrative or involved compulsive behavior in place of the present one.

9. Allow the behavior to occur only at prescribed times. Direct the student to avoid the behavior at certain times.

10. Discuss with the student the purposeless nature of the behavior. Ask him to refrain from the behavior in a certain situation and determine if anything undesirable happened due to the lack of compulsive behavior. Reconvene your discussion later.

11. Use overcorrection to reduce the compulsive behavior. The student is required to display the compulsive behavior until he tires of it and begins to dislike it (Luiselli and Michaud, 1983).

235
Fearful of New Situations

1. Encourage and reinforce the student when he enters new situations or attempts to overcome his fear (Marks, 1969).

2. Promote and enhance the student's self-confidence in order to help overcome the fear of the new situation. Experiencing anxiety in new situations is frequently indicative of low self-esteem (Canfield and Wells, 1976).

3. Conduct a task analysis if the situation is known. Break the fearful situation into a list of subtasks and its essential components. Present them to the student in teachable units. Give the student the opportunity to unlearn the fear (McLoughlin and Lewis, 1981).

4. Recognize the fear and back up to the step where the student is having a difficult time but is less fearful. Then continue with careful guidance and explanation (M. Hewitt, personal communication, 1986).

5. Hold a group discussion where each student discloses his fears. Have the students hear the fears of others. Reassure them that it is all right to fear, yet fears must be overcome (Goodwin, 1977).

6. Allow the student to have an escort, friend, or good luck charm as he enters the new situation.

7. Relate the experience to past fears that were overcome.

8. Help the student identify the fear. Grade the fear in its various aspects from the least fearful to the most fearful. Tell the student to visualize a situation involving the least threatening aspect of the fear. Next, have him combine the visualization with a pleasant experience to counteract the fearful aspect of the new situation. Finally, move up the hierarchy, step by step, until the student is able to visualize the most fear-arousing aspect in the hierarchy and not experience the fear (Goodwin, 1977).

9. Expose the student to a *real-life* fearful new situation. As a teacher, do not become overinvolved. The student must learn to confront the fear and do well without the teacher (Goodwin, 1977).

10. Couple the student experiencing the fear with another student who does not fear the same particular situation. The "brave" behaviors may transfer and replace the fearful behaviors (S. Rothchild, personal communication, 1986).

11. Teach the student to substitute negative thoughts with positive thoughts (Goodwin, 1977).

12. Use humor to put the fear in perspective (Goodwin, 1977).

13. Simulate a potential new fearful situation. Provide the student with the opportunity to practice appropriate behaviors and strategies to attack the fear (P. Kennedy, personal communication, 1986).

14. Provide feedback and be reflective when the student is discussing a fear of a new situation. Listen actively. Be empathic (S. Clark, personal communication, 1986).

15. Keep the student in the fearful state of maximal panic for as long as necessary for the panic level and fear of the new situation to drop. Continue exposure until the student gets accustomed to it (Goodwin, 1977).

16. Expose the student to the new situation gradually. First, show the student pictures of the new situation then gradually have him spend longer and longer periods of time exposed to the real situation (Marks, 1969).

17. Ask the parents to consult a physician regarding the use of chemotherapy or psychotherapeutic measures as a general treatment for fear of new situations and its connected anxiety reactions and consequences (Kahn, 1977).

18. Return the student immediately to a fearful traumatic experience. Prevent the development or escalation of more intense fear through repeated avoidance and cognitive rehearsal (Marks, 1969).

19. Have the student make a list of treatment targets. Include all the new situations the student fears. Tell the student to list the different items in order of the difficulty of getting him into the situation. Have the student put himself in the least threatening situation and stay there. Practice this daily. Remind the student to be prepared for setbacks even after successful experiences (Fensterheim, 1976).

20. Have the student visualize himself in an anxiety-provoking situation. Instruct him to "handle it" in an assertive manner.

21. For more ideas, see the strategy sheet in this book entitled "Phobic."

236

Fingernail Biting

1. Reinforce the student for avoiding nail biting (J. Kurschner, personal communication, 1984).

2. Pull the student's hand away from his mouth (J. Kurschner, personal communication, 1984).

3. Provide the student with a nail care kit to promote pride in the appearance of one's nails.

4. Arouse interest in better nail care by cutting out magazine advertisements that show the beauty of well-manicured nails.

5. Show the student pictures of a famous figure in which his or her hands show nails that are well-manicured.

6. Purchase bad-tasting nail polish which is marketed to prevent nail biting.

7. Purchase nail polish that hardens the nails, thus inhibiting nail biting (J. Kurschner, personal communication, 1986).

8. Take a surprise photograph of the student while he nail bites to show him how this behavior appears to others (J. Kurschner, personal communication, 1986).

9. Videotape the student while he bites his nails and play this for him.

10. Provide the student with something else to do with his hands (e.g., squeeze a ball, bend a paper clip, etc.).

11. Provide the student with something else to chew on (e.g., gum, a piece of inner tube rubber, etc.).

12. Ask a friend to remind the student not to bite his nails.

13. Reinforce the student for each day that you can see white space at the outer end of the nail.

14. Promise a prize when the white space at the outer end of the nail reaches a certain length.

3. Search the student for matches, lighters, and flammable liquids as he enters the class.

4. Have a burn victim give a guest lecture to the class and tell, in detail, what happened in the fire.

5. Have the student participate in youth club with supervision in structured activities to occupy spare time (Kvaraceus, 1966).

6. Show a film on fire and its hazards. Discuss in depth the results of the fire and the many lives it can affect (e.g., firefighters, burn victims, neighbors, the family of a pyromaniac, doctors, etc.).

7. Have the pyromaniac visit a fire station and spend the day with them going on calls. He will see all the time and specialized training needed to extinguish a fire. This may show him all the troubles that fires can cause (Stratton and Stratton, 1968).

8. Encourage preventive programs for students (Kvaraceus, 1966).

9. Recommend a policy in which the student who caused the damage pays the cost for whatever he has set on fire in the school (Taming campus vandals, 1980).

10. Threaten punishment under the hypothesis that punishment will forestall the criminal act (Trojanowicz, 1978).

11. Attempt to eliminate potential causes or motivations before the actual behavior takes place (Trojanowicz, 1978).

237

Firesetting (Pyromania)

1. Recommend family and individual counseling if the firesetting behavior of the student is severe or if the severity of the behavior is increasing (Kvaraceus, 1966).

2. Fireproof the classroom as much as possible. Use the chalkboard instead of paper. Keep notebooks, workbooks, and other easily flammable items locked away and out of reach of the student.

238

Moody

1. Have the student monitor his moods using a daily chart. Keep additional data to pinpoint frequency and to identify problem behaviors. Use this information as a basis for discussion, attempting to enhance his self-awareness and control of the problem (Safran and Safran, 1984).

2. Use the mood chart to promote the student's awareness and understanding of the

feelings of others, and to improve social skills and sensitivity toward others (Safran and Safran, 1984).

3. Complete mood charts independently and compare results. This will encourage communication about feelings and determine the accuracy of mood perceptions (Safran and Safran, 1984).

4. Express positive emotions toward the student, such as a smile or a friendly greeting (Bower, 1985).

5. Teach prosocial alternatives to moody behavior, such as taking a deep breath and counting to 10 (McGinnis, Sauerbry, and Nichols, 1985).

6. Have the student practice prosocial behaviors in real-life situations (McGinnis, Sauerbry and Nichols, 1985).

7. Provide feedback to the student as to his performance of acceptable behaviors (Schloss, 1983; McGinnis, Sauerbry, and Nichols, 1985).

8. Catch the student successfully performing and using the skills taught. Provide reinforcement (McGinnis, Sauerbry, and Nichols, 1985).

9. Prepare the student for events that may cause a mood change.

10. Start the school day for your students with a fun, positive activity to set the tone for the day.

11. Remind the student what to do, rather than what not to do (McGinnis, Sauerbry, and Nichols, 1985).

12. Role play and model social skills (Schloss, Schloss, and Harris, 1984).

13. Use a coaching system in which you provide the student with oral descriptions of the importance of each skill. Ask him to name example situations in which the skill could be used, and tell him to use the skill in a play session immediately following instruction. Review and evaluate what happened after the play session (Schumaker and Hazel, 1984).

14. Encourage the student to verbally label the

association between his behavior and achievement outcomes (Schloss, 1983).

15. Actively teach and reinforce interpersonal skills, assisting the student in gaining satisfaction through prosocial responses, behavior rehearsals, modeling, and small group activities (Schloss, 1983).

16. Alter consequences by insuring that depressive episodes do not produce positive reinforcement in the forms of sympathy or assurance. The student should be redirected to other topics rather than attending to depressive ones (Schloss, 1983).

17. Follow negative self-statements by the student with a reference to some positive aspect of performance (Schloss, 1983).

18. Implement problem-solving training. Allow the student to play an active role in choosing the problem to be worked on and in generating his own solutions (Fleming, Ritchie, and Fleming, 1983).

19. When the student effectively applies the skill in a real-life setting, report the success with much fanfare to the class, and give him bonus points or stars in his skills performance booklet (Fleming, Ritchie, and Fleming, 1983).

20. Identify the antecedents or causes for the moodiness and attempt to prevent them from occurring.

21. Investigate the health and exercise level of the student. The amount of sleep and the types of food one eats affects one's mood (Crisp and Stonehill, 1976).

22. Have the student write down feelings felt at different times and make him aware of what feelings go with what moods (Golding-Mather and Singer, 1981).

23. Use music either to calm or excite a student (Hansen, 1976).

24. When the student is in a "good" mood, encourage as much peer interaction as possible. When a "bad" mood comes along, interaction with others may induce a "good" mood (Wessman and Ricks, 1966).

25. During a "down" mood, give the student

a hands-on activity to vent the mood (Wollert, 1981).

26. If the student becomes angry, allow him to vent this anger through exercise.

239

Obsessed with Persistent Ideas That Occupy the Mind

1. Reinforce the student for attentive behavior (Carter, 1972).

2. Maintain an accurate check on the inattentive student's behavior for reference (Pearson, 1974).

3. Recommend counseling for the student (M. Anderson, personal communication, 1985).

4. Capitalize on the students' chief interests and use this to help them focus their attention to more appropriate thoughts (Collins, 1981).

5. Talk with the student privately about these persistent ideas and the reasons behind them (M. Anderson, personal communication, 1985).

6. Capitalize on every opportunity to change the undesirable thoughts into a new train of thought.

7. Avoid responding to the student with anger or sarcasm (Pearson, 1974).

8. Keep the student busy with activities that require movement. Ask him to run an errand for you, stack books, sort papers, and so on.

9. Keep the student attentive to classroom activities by touch, verbal reminders, calling his name, and so on.

10. Allow frequent breaks for the student to think of these obsessive thoughts after which he is to attempt to work diligently on a school task.

11. Provide art and writing activities to assist the student in release and expression of feelings.

240

Overly Concerned About Right Directions

1. Verbally reward the student for reading and following directions without question (Schunk, 1982).

2. Train the student to identify specific self-verbalizations that he often says when faced with directions. Model and reinforce alternative constructive self-verbalizations (O'Leary and Wilson, 1975).

3. Train for self-instruction by having the student ask questions of himself about the nature of the problem (e.g., stimuli, accuracy, or quality of performance) (Morris and Kratochwill, 1983).

4. Give verbal or nonverbal prompting for the student to follow directions independently (M. Pierre, personal communication, 1985).

5. Give practice opportunities for following directions (Morris and Kratochwill, 1983).

6. Provide feedback of the student's performance in following directions (Morris and Kratochwill, 1983).

7. Discuss grade-emphasis pressure with the student's parents (M. Pierre, personal communication, 1985).

8. Give examples and illustrations whenever possible (Siedow and Fox, 1983).

9. Give oral directions to support written directions (Siedow and Fox, 1983).

10. Keep directions in short, simple sentences, giving only one direction per sentence (Siedow and Fox, 1983).

11. Keep the direction vocabulary simple, avoiding difficult technical terms where possible (Siedow and Fox, 1983).

12. List steps in sequence, numbering each step (Siedow and Fox, 1983).

13. Have the student repeat directions in his own words.

14. Require that the student attempt a portion of the task before inquiring about further directions.

241

Overly Religious

1. If religious views are being expressed at inappropriate times, reinforce the student when he refrains from expressing his opinions and provide negative consequences for inappropriate religious remarks.
2. Empathize with the student when he is willing to discuss his feelings (J. Steele, personal communication, 1985).
3. Encourage and lead the student to develop a wide variety of interests. Expand his horizons (McGinnis, 1983).
4. Have class discussions about the similarities present in all religions (J. Steele, personal communication, 1985).
5. Insure that the student is taught that God is a benevolent figure. Tell students that "God loves you" and that "God is everywhere—in people, in nature, in church." Avoid statements like "God rewards you if you're good and punishes you if you're bad" (Shaver, Lehauer, and Sadd, 1980).
6. See that role models endorse "healthy-minded" religion. That is, they characterize God as loving, benevolent, and nonpunitive (Shaver, Lehauer, and Sadd, 1980).
7. Suggest the administration of the Eysenck neuroticism scale, which provides an index of emotional stability against which psychological accounts of the function of religion in a normal population can be tested (Frances, Pearson, Carter, and Kay, 1981).
8. Administer the Frances scale of attitude towards religion Form ASC4B to qualify that the student is, indeed, affected with religiosity (Frances, Pearson, Carter, and Kay, 1981).
9. Religiosity and perceived sanctioned threats are often common components. Investigate the student's perceived threats and remove them if possible (Rowe, 1982).
10. Recommend professional counseling for the student (J. Steele, personal communication, 1985).
11. Inform the student that he is not to discuss or purport his religious views in school.
12. Mediate a debate on religion. Allow only those statements that can be backed by proof or logic. Do not allow opinion.
13. Hold a discussion regarding the declaration on the separation of church and state in the U.S. Constitution.
14. Tell the student that he may only purport his views during hallway passing, lunch, or before or after school.

242

Paranoia

1. Reinforce the student when his thoughts and reactions are reality based.
2. Assist the student in trying to relax (Kleinmuntz, 1974).
3. Confront the student with the absurdity of the present situation (Kleinmuntz, 1974).
4. Allow the student to act out his thoughts (Kleinmuntz, 1974).
5. Help the student replace his present thoughts with other thoughts (J. Anderson, personal communication, 1985).
6. Recommend art therapy.
7. Recommend group "theraplay" (Jernberg, 1979).
8. Advise the parents to seek psychiatric treatment for the student (Kleinmuntz, 1974; Slavson, 1952).
9. Advise the parents to seek therapy in order to understand the student's behavior (Slavson, 1952).
10. Advise the parents to consult a physician for information concerning drug therapy (Kleinmuntz, 1974; Layton, 1982).
11. Give the student the necessary direction in understanding the precipitating factors (Layton, 1982).
12. Provide information to the contrary of the paranoid thought.
13. After the incident is over, review it and talk

about how it might be avoided in the future.

243

Perfectionist/Meticulous

1. Compliment the student whenever he shows spontaneity (Adams, 1973).

2. Model spontaneous work techniques (Adams, 1973).

3. Give permission to make mistakes in every area in which the student is working. Tell him that it is all right to make mistakes because they are good learning tools (L. Nicolai, personal communication, 1985).

4. Focus the student's learning on generalizations and concepts rather than rote learning by asking questions pertaining to the larger concept. Reward the student's completed tasks (M. Gunther, personal communication, 1985).

5. Include many spontaneous activities in the student's program so the opportunity to focus on details is less available (e.g., role playing, finger painting) (Adams, 1973).

6. Use more manipulative and concrete materials so the student views the idea in another perspective and is able to view the concept as a whole rather than in its parts (e.g., Montessori materials) (R. Hayes, personal communication, 1985).

7. If the compulsiveness is a reaction to previous impulsivity, this behavior is to be encouraged, as it may be the best adjustment the student can make under the circumstances of his underlying inner chaos (Buxbaum, 1970).

8. Deemphasize right and wrong by providing activities that encourage creative and individual responses rather than correct answers. Let the student know that his thoughts and feelings are important (Buxbaum, 1970).

9. Establish a relationship that permits the student to speak about his problems without fear of ridicule or criticism. Free and easy discussion can help him air his feelings (Bakwin and Bakwin, 1972).

10. Ask this student to role-play the part of a sloppy student (Blanco, 1972).

11. Set a time limit for each part of the task, thus preventing the student from dwelling on details. This will also enable him to perceive the task as a sum of parts even though all of the parts may not be completed (Blanco, 1972).

12. Play a game of "Beat the Clock," gradually shortening the time intervals allotted for task completion. This allows less time for perfectionism (M. Minkoff, personal communication, 1985).

13. Encourage spontaneity through the use of cue words, such as: *At ease, tension free, spontaneous, natural, freedom, letting go,* or *letting loose* (Adams, 1973).

14. While the student is working, encourage, cajole, and reassure him with humor (Adams, 1973).

15. Give the student tasks that have discrete endings, obvious solutions, and that are easy to accomplish (J. Stith, personal communication, 1985).

16. Obtain familial background information in addition to having an interview with the student's parents. Discuss ways that the student's home life may be promoting perfectionism (J. Pitell, personal communication, 1985).

17. Do not allow the student to erase.

18. Give the student pencils without erasers.

19. On a written assignment, have the student circle his mistakes instead of erasing. Grade for content, not for errors (E. Stein, personal communication, 1985).

20. Gradually reduce the number of erasures allowed (J. Martin, personal communication, 1985).

21. Demonstrate the inevitability of human imperfection by modeling errors on the blackboard, allowing the students to catch and correct them (E. Stein, personal communication, 1985).

22. Have all work done in nonerasable ink.

23. Provide assignments that challenge the ability of the student so that some mistakes will occur on a regular basis (Sprick, 1981).

24. Discuss with the student appropriate reactions to making a mistake (Sprick, 1981).

25. Praise the student when he can be corrected without getting upset (Sprick, 1981).

26. Find alternate ways for the student to evaluate his performance other than being "the best" (e.g., evaluate overall performance) (Sprick, 1981).

27. Use precision teaching to encourage the student to work quickly. This technique counts the number of correct responses given during a timed test (J. Ivarie, personal communication, 1985).

28. Provide the student with an opportunity to engage in messy classroom work (e.g., fingerpainting, paper mache, pottery making) (S. Stidham, personal communication, 1984).

29. Provide the student with the least amount of paper needed to finish the assignment (S. Stidham, personal communication, 1984).

30. Videotape the behavior so the student can view his actions later (J. DeMonge, personal communication, 1983).

31. Have the student count his own behavior occurrences and record these on a chart. Have him attempt to lower his total each day (J. DeMonge, personal communication, 1983).

32. Provide relaxation exercises to keep stress, which may cause the compulsive behavior, at a minimum (J. DeMonge, personal communication, 1983).

33. Split the assignment into outline, rough draft, and final draft stages. Perfection is promoted only on the final draft.

34. Have each student do something different. The student who is a perfectionist then has nothing with which to compare his own work (S. Kania, personal communication, 1985).

35. Tell the student that this particular project is not going to be graded. This may relieve pressure to perform to perfection (S. Kania, personal communication, 1985).

36. Construct assignments where there are no right or wrong answers (Myers, 1961).

37. When giving an assignment, give an ending goal. Tell the student to strive only for this particular goal so he does not go beyond the expected behavior (S. Kania, personal communication, 1985).

38. Have the student work on things at which he is not very good. This will demonstrate that he cannot be perfect at everything (S. Kania, personal communication, 1985).

39. Have the student work with a peer who is a perfectionist in something else (S. Kania, personal communication, 1985).

40. Use gentle physical restraint to stop the compulsive behavior (Luiselli and Michaud, 1983).

41. Give the student hand signals or verbal cues to remind him to control his behavior (D. Brown, personal communication, 1984).

42. Teach other appropriate behaviors to replace the compulsive one. The behaviors should be incompatible so that when the new one is developed, it interferes with the occurrence of the undesired behavior (Luiselli and Michaud, 1983).

43. Use overcorrection to reduce the compulsive behavior. The student is required to display the compulsive behavior until he tires of it and begins to dislike it (Luiselli and Michaud, 1983).

44. Have the student set up a self-regulation program consisting of self-goal setting, self-monitoring, self-evaluation, and self-reinforcement (Neilans, Israel, and Pravder, 1981).

244

Phobic

1. Praise the student when he engages in a previously feared activity (Algozzine, 1982; Morris and Kratochwill, 1983).

2. Model the appropriate behavior in situations that are frightening to the student (Rimm and Masters, 1979; Morris and Kratochwill, 1983).

3. Use rational-cognitive therapy in which the student learns to control illogical thought patterns (Newcomer, 1980).

4. Use implosive therapy in which the original traumatic events are re-created in the student's imagination. Sights, sounds, and smells are imagined with intense anxiety, which diminishes as the student realizes that nothing is really happening to him (Millman, Schaefer, and Cohen, 1980; Morris and Kratochwill, 1983).

5. Help the student externalize his fears through art (Algozzine, 1982).

6. Use facts to reduce the fear. Read nonfiction materials to the student about things that are frightening to him (Algozzine, 1982).

7. Use music and dance to help the student express his anxieties (Algozzine, 1982).

8. Have parents discuss stories about the student's fears with him and have him go over these at school (Algozzine, 1982).

9. Role play frightening experiences (Alogozzine, 1982).

10. Recommend "flooding," in which feared stimuli are presented for an extended period of time (Morris and Kratochwill, 1983).

11. Recommend individual systematic desensitization. To desensitize a fear, the student is exposed gradually to the fear (Rimm and Masters, 1979; Morris and Kratochwill, 1983).

12. Recommend group systematic desensitization. The progressive exposure is geared toward the most affected student in the group (Morris and Kratochwill, 1983).

13. Recommend automated systematic desensitization. In this method, a series of tape-recorded scene presentations that are feared by the student are presented. The tapes lead the student through the desensitization process at his own rate (Morris and Kratochwill, 1983; Foa, 1981).

14. Institute emotive imagery. The first phase is to list a gradual hierarchy of feared events from least to most threatening. Then the student is instructed to imagine a story of his everyday life that includes his favorite hero. Next, the therapist introduces from lowest to highest the items on the hierarchy and the student tells how he and the hero overcame them (Morris and Kratochwill, 1983).

15. Institute contact desensitization. Model the behavior in the feared situation. Then use physical and verbal prompts to encourage the student. Finally, gradually withdraw assistance and contact with the student as he deals with the situation (Morris and Kratochwill, 1983).

16. Institute rational-emotive system. Show the student that his emotions arise because of irrational thinking. Show the student how emotional problems are maintained by the irrational thinking (Kerr and Nelson, 1983).

17. Teach the student to use the symptoms of anxiety as an ally or as a cue for coping, rather than a cue for worry (Bell, 1979).

18. Have the student make a list of things that used to cause anxiety, but don't anymore, and recall what happened to those feelings and why they are no longer present (Fensterheim, 1977).

19. Teach skills to help the student cope with the anxiety and fear (Morris and Kratochwill, 1983).

20. Have the student confront a situation of which he has unrealistic views (e.g., fear of dogs because of his mother's fear) that increase anxiety. Have confrontations on a regular basis to reduce anxiety levels (Goldfried, 1976).

21. Have the student put together a "tension ladder," which is a range of situations ranging from least to most upsetting. Discuss one of these situations and talk about the tension and anxiety that the student would feel (Goldfried, 1976).

245

Preoccupied with Thoughts of Death

1. Reinforce the student when he avoids the topic of death.
2. Recommend counseling for the student.
3. Recommend that the student meet with a member of the clergy to discuss death and a possible afterlife.
4. Encourage the student to read *On Death and Dying* by Kubla-Ross.
5. Supply activities in which the student can externalize his thoughts and feelings (e.g., art, writing, play therapy, etc.).
6. Use poems, readings, biblical passages, and movies on death as stimulants for discussion on the topic.
7. Create a unit on the beliefs of various groups regarding what occurs after death.
8. Allow the student to observe a funeral.
9. Ask a mortician to explain the symbolism and significance of the funeral rite.
10. Provide readings regarding people who have been pronounced clinically dead and came back to life.
11. Have the student complete a research paper on a topic related to death and dying.
12. If the student appears to be suicidal, see the strategy sheet in this book entitled "Suicidal."

246

Questions Indicate a Worry About the Future

1. Reinforce the student when he presents a positive outlook on the future.
2. Reinforce the student when he shows an interest in dealing with the present.
3. Recommend counseling.
4. Speak with the student to determine a specific worry, if any.
5. Have the student read literature related to his topic of concern.
6. Have the student list all the possible future outcomes regarding the topic of concern. Have him decide how he will react in each of the possible outcomes should they occur.
7. Encourage the student not to worry and to deal with the future when it happens.
8. Encourage the student to take a benign interest in the future as he has little affect on its path.
9. Teach the student to respond to his concern with statements such as "Que sera sera" (kay sir-rah sir-rah), which loosely translated from Spanish means "whatever will be will be" (D. McKnight and S. McKnight, personal communication, 1986).
10. Use the recording *Que Sera Sera* by Patti Page as a stimulant for discussion (S. McKnight, personal communication, 1986).
11. Encourage the student to write a letter to his governmental representative or a newspaper editor about his concern.
12. Help the student prepare for the upcoming event so that he can perform or react more effectively.

247

School Phobia

1. Reinforce the student for positive statements about school (Blackman and Silberman, 1980).

2. Reinforce the student when he attends school (Blackman and Silberman, 1980).

3. Bring the student to school (against his will if necessary) (A. J. Pappanikou, personal communication, 1980).

4. Advise the parents to ignore physical complaints and send the student to school (Blackman and Silberman, 1980; Levine and Seligmann, 1973).

5. Force the student to attend school and stay in the classroom. The parent may visit, but cannot stay (Blackman and Silberman, 1980; Brulle and McIntyre, 1984).

6. Gradually fade out the presence of the parent in the classroom (e.g., the parent stands inside near the door, then in the hallway, then the office, then at home by the phone if a reassuring word to the student is necessary) (A. J. Pappanikou, personal communication, 1980).

7. Allow the student to bring a special stuffed animal or good luck charm to school for support.

8. Encourage the parents to seek counseling for the student soon after the problem is discovered to avoid it becoming ingrained (Blackman and Silberman, 1980).

9. Systematically expose the student to a graded series of situations involving the actual fear-arousing stimulus. Have the student move progressively closer to the school each day and for longer periods of time. Fade out escorts as appropriate (Doleys and Williams, 1977; Meyer and Osborne, 1982).

10. Recommend hypnosis in resistant cases (Meyer and Osborne, 1982).

11. Have the student think of a fictional character involved in feared school situations. Have the student give verbal reassurance to the fictional character (Blackman and Silberman, 1980).

12. Hold a brief counseling session with the student after he is in school for a few hours (Blackman and Silberman, 1980).

13. Encourage the student to return (e.g., "I hope to see you tomorrow") (Levine and Seligmann, 1973).

14. Tell the student about a fun situation that will occur the next day.

15. Involve the student in his own rehabilitation by using reflective listening techniques (Brulle and McIntyre, 1984).

16. Give the student a job in the school (e.g., janitorial assistant, tutor to younger children, office errand boy, etc.) and stress how important it is that he show for "work" each day.

17. If the cause of a faked illness is rooted in a feeling of wanting to stay home to be with and take care of an ill family member, recommend that the school psychologist or social worker conduct individual sessions with the student to relieve guilt feelings and encourage independence. Group family sessions might also be held to clarify each member's role. This may take the pressure off the student so that he does not feel the need to stay home from school (Bauknight, 1978).

18. Set up a support program in a building other than the school. The program focuses on increasing the student's self-esteem and making the return to school a more positive experience for him (Church and Edwards, 1984).

19. Desensitize the student by using emotive imagery in which very pleasant memories are interspersed with anxiety-provoking images (Trueman, 1984).

20. Have the student imagine his storybook hero being afraid of and not attending school. The student is then asked to help the hero to overcome the fear (Trueman, 1984).

21. Implement a desensitization approach for school phobia. It involves five steps: (a) in-

struct the student in relaxation procedures; (b) remove reinforcement in the home (e.g., the student is not allowed to watch television while absent from school); (c) begin formal systematic desensitization treatment; (d) reinforce for achieving actual progress toward school attendance; and (e) implement the program on a daily basis (Prout and Harvey, 1978).

248

Steals (Kleptomania)

1. When the student shows appropriate behavior, reinforce it (Wilcox, 1983).

2. Administer negative consequence for stealing (D. McHugh, personal communication, 1984).

3. Recommend counseling for the student.

4. Always require the student to return a stolen article, confess, and apologize (Verville, 1967).

5. Teach the student that taking something that doesn't belong to him is never permissible, regardless of need or provocation (Verville, 1967).

6. The student who steals from need should have this need fulfilled in other ways. Give the student something to do (Verville, 1967).

7. Allow the student to earn the desired item (Verville, 1967)

8. At the beginning of the school year, make a set of classroom rules with "no stealing allowed" being one of them. Enforce the rules (Wilcox, 1983).

9. Discuss the concept of property rights (Verville, 1967).

10. Have children check out materials at the teacher's desk. This will allow you to keep track of many items (Gnagney, 1968).

11. Keep tempting objects locked away. This will reduce the opportunity for stealing (Gnagney, 1968).

12. Verbally attack the improper actions, not the student himself (Wilcox, 1983).

13. At the beginning of the day, lock up any valuables the students may have (e.g., lunch and book money, radio, etc.) (Wagner, 1983).

14. Expect common classroom supplies to be returned to their proper places and let your conduct reflect only the highest form of behavior. It would be more effective to use statements such as "Thank you for putting the scissors in the box, Don. You might make a count of them, so we know how many we have" rather than "O.K., I know you kids are swiping the scissors! If I catch you, it won't be funny" (K. Cearlock, personal communication, 1983).

15. Give recognition to students who have had a conspicuous opportunity to steal but have not done so (e.g., "It feels good to live in a community of mutual trust. In some classrooms, I would be very foolish or careless ·to leave my purse unattended") (K. Cearlock, personal communication, 1983).

16. Conduct an inspection for the lost item on a large-group basis (K. Cearlock, personal communication, 1983).

17. Elicit suggestions from the offender regarding restitution, and establish a fair payment for the offense (J. Rose, personal communication, 1983).

18. Encourage students to try to identify the thief and settle the matter themselves (Kozloff, 1974).

19. Give the student an opportunity to return the stolen item with no questions asked (Kozloff, 1974).

20. Retain all students in the room until the missing item is returned (Kozloff, 1974).

21. Require the student to pay for the stolen article.

22. Monitor the student closely.

23. Allow the student to "borrow" items for one day before returning them. Gradually shorten the "borrowing" time.

24. Search the student's locker and desk.

249

Suspicious or Distrustful of Others

1. Reinforce the student when he is trusting of others (Millman, Schaefer, and Cohen, 1981).

2. Show films that portray students interacting positively toward each other. Later, discuss ways of making meaningful contact with others (Collins, 1975).

3. Help the student feel secure and ''at home'' in the classroom. Talk with the student about topics with which he is familiar and directly assure him that he is needed and loved (Millman, Schaefer, and Cohen, 1981).

4. Discuss the student's need to participate and share with others. For example, talk directly with the student, pointing out how much more fun he would have if he joined the others (Millman, Schaefer, and Cohen, 1981).

5. Gently move the student toward group participation (Ramsey, 1981).

6. Ask the student for advice in areas where he is able to be helpful, such as teacher-student planning (Millman, Schaefer, and Cohen, 1981).

7. Find activities in which the student feels secure enough to participate (Ramsey, 1981).

8. Arrange the environment to encourage the student's contact with his peers. This includes placing the student in group activities with friendly peers, encouraging the others to interact with the student, and seating the student near friendly, outgoing peers (Millman, Schaefer, and Cohen, 1981).

9. Require participation in all group activities (Ramsey, 1981).

10. Demonstrate warmth and affection for the student by touching, hand holding, and patting.

11. Read stories to the class concerning trust and caring (M. Anderson, personal communication, 1985).

12. Speak with the student's parents and urge them to talk with their child about school and his interaction with others.

13. Recommend counseling for the student (M. Anderson, personal communication, 1985).

14. Have the student analyze interactions with others and whether they were trying to ''use'' or ''hurt'' him in any way. Assuming that most interactions are positive, the student should realize that he can usually be less suspicious.

15. Follow through on all promises made. Require that students do the same.

250

Test Anxiety

1. Design tests so that the questions progress from easiest to more difficult. Difficult questions at the beginning can cause frustration and panic (Spielberger, 1966; Plake, Ansorge, Parker, and Lowry, 1982).

2. Tell the student the precise material, chapters, and class notes that will be on the test so that studying will focus on those areas (Spielberger, 1966).

3. Tell the student what type of test will be given (e.g., essay, short answer, true and false, multiple choice, etc.) in order to help him to study more efficiently (Spielberger, 1966).

4. Help the student develop skills of memory and recall so that he is more successful in selecting material from recall for objective or short-answer questions (Spielberger, 1966).

5. Word the test items very clearly and specifically (Spielberger, 1966).

6. Make the testing environment as comfortable and anxiety-free as possible (Spielberger, 1966).

7. Be sure that the testing environment is free of distracting noise, sounds, and interrup-

tions that could cause anxiety (Spielberger, 1966).

8. Make sure the room is neither too hot, cold, bright, dark, or crowded (Spielberger, 1966).

9. Encourage the student to share and discuss feelings of stress, fear, and anxiety regarding tests. Knowing that he is not alone can help him deal with the feelings that are upsetting (Spielberger, 1966).

10. Explain what it is you expect from the students (Spielberger, 1966).

11. Teach the student how to budget time to include enough time for studying, distractions, responsibilities, work, social demands, and interruptions (Spielberger, 1966).

12. Make the testing situation less of a "potential" failure situation by giving it less importance (Doll and Fleming, 1966).

13. Avoid including tricky questions on the test (Doll and Fleming, 1966).

14. Tape lectures for the student to use for studying (Barabasz and Barabasz, 1981).

15. Give the student homework similar to the test (Barabasz and Barabasz, 1981).

16. Make sure the student is well prepared with pen, pencil, eraser, calculator, and so on (C. Robinson, personal communication, 1985).

17. Review notes with the student the day before the test (C. Robinson, personal communication, 1985).

18. Have the student study with a peer (C. Robinson, personal communication, 1985).

19. Teach the student to organize his notes and materials (Kirkland and Hollandsworth, 1979).

20. Have the student discuss new material with another person (Kirkland and Hollandsworth, 1979).

21. Teach appropriate preexamination behavior such as note taking, completing assignments, and participating in class (Kirkland and Hollandsworth, 1979).

22. Tell the student that improving academic performance decreases test anxiety (Kirkland and Hollandsworth, 1979).

23. Teach the student to meditate for relaxation purposes (C. Robinson, personal communication, 1985).

24. Give sample tests for practice (C. Robinson, personal communication, 1985).

25. Encourage the student to think positive thoughts throughout the test (Galassi, Frierson, and Sharer, 1981).

26. Have the student participate in a test-anxiety desensitization workshop (Hudesman, Wiesner, and Abramson, 1981).

27. Teach and practice muscle relaxation 10 minutes before the test (Hudesman, Wiesner, and Abramson, 1981).

28. On the exam, write brief, written relaxation instructions for the student to follow (Deffenbacher and Deitz, 1978).

29. Discuss test anxiety with the student, and why he has it (Hudesman, Wiesner, and Abramson, 1981).

30. Inform the student that you really care and are genuinely interested in his progress. He should know that the test is to help so that weak areas can be remediated, and that this is not a punishment or threat (Doll and Fleming, 1966).

31. Give instructions that are clear, concise, and do not use the word *test* (Trentham, 1984; Bergman, 1981).

32. Be positive and establish a positive atmosphere in the classroom so that the testing situation is just a part of the whole learning process, not something with which to "get" the students (J. Rossow, personal communication, 1985).

33. Use humor in the classroom and testing situations so students can relax and "lighten up," which in turn reduces anxiety (Koppel, 1982).

34. Eliminate time limits (Gaudry and Spielberger, 1971; Plake, Ansorge, Parker, and Lowry, 1982).

35. Give the student memory support by allowing the tests to be open book, open

notebook, and so on (Gaudry and Spielberger, 1971; Francis, 1982).

36. For severe cases of test anxiety, recommend the services of a psychologist (Phillips, 1981).

37. Teach the student effective study habits, methods, and skills so that he is prepared to study more effectively for tests and exams (Spielberger, 1966; Phillips, 1981).

38. Use sensitivity training, positive reinforcement, and modeling for the student to decrease the stress regarding testing situations (Phillips, 1981).

39. Alleviate the stress of the testing situation by using many other means of evaluating the student's work and knowledge of the material. Homework, class participation, daily work assignments, projects, oral presentations, and so on should be the main way a student is graded, rather than by testing (Doll and Fleming, 1966).

40. Discuss the test so that the student can correct his wrong information and benefit from the experience (J. Rossow, personal communication, 1985).

41. Use frequent testing over smaller amounts of material (Fulkerson and Martin, 1981).

42. Administer the test in a location that is familiar and comfortable for the student (Plake, Ansorge, Parker, and Lowry, 1982).

43. Encourage the student to put his pencil down for a few moments during the test to take deep breaths and relax (Deffenbacher and Deitz, 1978).

44. Manipulate the test format to suit the student. For example, if the student has writing problems or a visual problem, test him orally (Deffenbacher and Deitz, 1978).

45. Tell the student to concentrate on the task and not on himself. Explain that there is not time to worry because it interrupts performance (Reister, Stockton, and Maulsby, 1977).

46. Teach the student to recognize irrational thoughts and to practice formulating rational beliefs (Reister, Stockton, and Maulsby, 1977).

47. Try to make "waiting time" for a test as short as possible. Anticipation can affect performance (Sarason and Stoops, 1978).

48. Allow the student to do something quietly at his desk while waiting for a test in order to reduce anticipatory anxiety (Sarason and Stoops, 1978).

49. Have the student name three of his personal strengths and decide how he can apply them to test taking (C. Robinson, personal communication, 1985).

50. Use other names to refer to tests (e.g., *evaluation, quiz*, etc.) (C. Robinson, personal communication, 1985).

51. Be sure that tests are free of cultural or language bias (C. Robinson, personal communication, 1985).

251

Worries About Knowing the Correct Answer

1. Reinforce the student for attempting a task without expressing worry (Daly and Friedrich, 1981).

2. Explain to the student that it is all right to be wrong and that the most important thing is to try one's best (Watson and Dodd, 1984).

3. Give the student a choice of different ways to respond to the question (e.g., to the entire group, to one member of the group, or to the teacher only) (Bozigar and Hansen, 1984).

4. Provide the student with experiences that mix failure with success rather than only successful experiences. This may help him understand that it is all right to be wrong (Balk, 1983).

5. Praise the student's efforts even if he gives the wrong answer (Frey and Young, 1979).

6. Establish a relaxing, informal atmosphere in the classroom. The student will feel more comfortable and be more likely to take chances (Watson and Dodd, 1984).

7. Teach the student to recognize and refrain from negative self-talk (e.g., "Everyone will think I am foolish" or "That really sounded stupid") (Glaser, 1981).

8. Point out the logical consequences of the student's behavior (e.g., if he won't speak, he may perform poorly in school, risk possible retention, or be socially stigmatized by his peers) (Bozigar and Hansen, 1984).

9. Present subjects with which the student is familiar and comfortable to promote chance taking and to reduce anxiety (M. D'Arcy, personal communication, 1985).

10. Focus the student's attention on needed effort, not on personal ability (Balk, 1983).

11. Conduct group role-play sessions on asking for clarification and answering direct questions. Then have group discussion of the role play. Stress the positive aspects.

12. Give the student suggestions, cues, and hints for answering the question (Daly and Friedrich, 1981).

13. Teach the student to use positive coping thoughts (e.g., "It is unlikely that people are spending much energy evaluating my every word") (Glaser, 1981).

14. Allow the student to answer in a whisper at first. Then progressively move to a more appropriate level of volume (Bozigar and Hansen, 1984).

15. Build the student's self-confidence through various activities (Watson and Dodd, 1984).

16. Teach the student to perform self-instructions that pertain to the task (e.g., "Slow down," "Think before saying") (Balk, 1983).

17. Establish goals for the student to achieve (e.g., "Answer two questions in history class this week") (Glaser, 1981).

18. Show confidence and high expectancy of the student. Show that you believe he can do the work (Watson and Dodd, 1984).

19. Teach the student to interpret failure as being feedback that more information was needed (Balk, 1983).

20. Assign activities that require opinions and have no "right" or "wrong" answers.

21. Give assignments with more than one correct answer.

252
Worries Excessively

1. Keep the student busy with small chores so he won't have time to worry (K. Renfro, personal communication, 1983).

2. Give activities with no wrong or right answer in order to reduce anxiety (K. Renfro, personal communication, 1983).

3. Request assistance from the guidance counselor or school psychologist (K. Renfro, personal communication, 1983).

4. Use humor and laughter to get the student to "loosen up" and be less apprehensive (Beimer, 1983).

5. Help the student acquire a positive self-esteem (Beimer, 1983).

6. Have students write a paragraph that includes describing situations when they worry (Beimer, 1983).

7. Have the student list ways to reduce anxiety in the identified situations.

8. Have the student sit in the front of the room near the teacher to give him a sense of security (C. Gingerich, personal communication, 1984).

9. Use free time once a week to brush up on any academic or social problems the student may be having (C. Gingerich, personal communication, 1984).

10. Teach stress management techniques.

11. Be flexible in criteria and assignment deadlines.

12. Present anxiety-producing activities in a game format.

13. Have the student evaluate situations that are causing worry in order to devise reaction patterns or coping strategies.

14. Role play threatening situations. Have the student practice appropriate coping behavior.

15. Help the student prepare for the situation that worries him.

16. Teach the student to develop a benign attitude toward situations over which he has little control.

23

Oral Expression

253

Echolalia

1. Recommend a speech/language and psychological evaluation.
2. Reinforce the student each time he makes some nonrepetitive, consistent sound for actions, people, or things (DeMyer, 1979).
3. Use negative consequences when the student engages in echolalia (DeMyer, 1979).
4. Teach the student simple sign language while simultaneously teaching words (DeMyer, 1979).
5. Use formal drilling to teach words and phrases. Consult with a speech clinician (DeMyer, 1979).
6. Provide the student with alternative responses to the echoed phrase to promote the discontinuance of the echoing (Fay, 1981).
7. Put the student's verbal repetition to use, as it can serve to sustain talking with the other students (Fay, 1981).
8. Do not try to extinguish echolalia entirely because repetition and imitation of nonverbal and verbal behaviors seem to play a major role in maintaining a communicative interaction. It demonstrates turn taking and social awareness (Fay, 1981).
9. Be aware that the echolalic behavior may express the desire to communicate. Acknowledge this desire (Fay, 1981).
10. Use the student's ability to repeat in a conversation for joint activity language acquisition with other students (Fay, 1981).
11. Teach the student when echoing is appropriate and inappropriate (Fay, 1981).
12. Have people who are important to the student encourage him to respond in an appropriate manner (Van Riper, 1978).
13. Show examples of your own self-talk as you play a game. Use short and simple utterances only, and no questions or requests that the student say anything (Van Riper, 1978).
14. Make food, drink, toys, or other things the student likes contingent on appropriate speech (Watson, 1973).

15. Place your hand over the student's mouth and firmly say, "No."

16. Talk with the parents to determine if they have found effective techniques to reduce repetition (M. Smith, personal communication, 1984).

17. Ignore the echolalic behavior. Require the student to carry on a conversation or respond appropriately before giving attention to him (Campbell, Scaturro, and Lickson, 1983).

18. Develop and encourage socialization. Reward interpersonal relations. Learning to communicate with others may help eliminate the repetitive speech and other bizarre, disruptive behaviors (Coffey and Widner, 1967).

19. To help in speech training, present some verbal stimulus. Prompt the student to make the appropriate response. Reward successive approximations and then fade the prompts (Kozloff, 1973).

20. Form a peer tutoring group. Peer tutoring helps students to interact socially with peers in a structured environment. It allows students to model appropriate language, academic, and social skills (Campbell, Scaturro, and Lickson, 1983).

21. Promote physical activity. This helps decrease self-stimulating behavior and may increase appropriate academic and language skills (Kern, Koegel, Dyer, Blew, and Fenton, 1982).

22. Place the student in time-out during echolalic speech episodes.

23. Use a designated verbal or nonverbal signal to inhibit echolalia.

254

Elective Mutism

1. Give rewards for speaking (Kupietz and Schwartz, 1982).

2. Have the student tested for immaturities of speech or other speech difficulties (Fundudis and Kolvin, 1981).

3. Refer the student for a psychological evaluation (Blotcky and Looney, 1980; Kupietz and Schwartz, 1982).

4. Establish nonverbal compliance (Andrews, Davis, Nash, and Thorpe, 1979).

5. Improve teacher and peer relationships with this student (Fundudis and Kolvin, 1981).

6. Use physical contact. Hugging, touching, and holding hands with the student helps develop interaction and may help him feel more comfortable (Cowen, 1982).

7. Promote modeling by peers. A student's language is affected by the speech of others (Ianfolla, Sonnschien, and Whitehurst, 1981).

8. Use communication games, such as Bingo, Lotto, guessing games, and action directive games (Budoff and Conant, 1982).

9. Recommend or use play therapy (Andrews, Dais, Nash, and Thorpe, 1979).

10. Use behavior rehearsal and role playing to teach the desired behavior (Kerr and Nelson, 1983).

11. Use instructional strategies such as prompting, chaining, and role playing (Andrews, Davis, Nash, and Thorpe, 1979).

12. Establish verbal compliance training (Andrews, Davis, Nash, and Thorpe, 1979).

13. Use well-sequenced, highly structured programs involving operant techniques (Andrews, Davis, Nash, and Thorpe, 1979).

14. Make snack food, privileges, and the like dependent on the utterance of a verbal response.

15. Speak with the student's parents to find out if certain words or sounds are uttered at home. Attempt to elicit those words in your program.

16. Encourage any appropriate verbal sounds (e.g., making animal noises for stuffed animals, making motor sounds while riding a bike, etc.).

255
Incorrect Articulation

1. Reinforce accurate pronunciation of words (Pearson, 1974).
2. Avoid making mention of the speech problem before a large group.
3. Use commercially programmed materials to handle increasingly complex speech and language patterns.
4. Compliment the student about his improved speech.
5. Communicate with the parents concerning the specific speech problems.
6. Refer the student to a speech clinician (M. Anderson, personal communication, 1985).
7. Tape record or write down the student's pronunciation of various words to give to the speech clinician.
8. Make sure that the student has many opportunities to communicate with people he really likes and in situations where he is comfortable.
9. Enlist the cooperation of the other students in not ridiculing the student.
10. Be a good speech model for the student.
11. Ask the speech clinician which hints or cues to use to remind the student to say sounds correctly. Use these hints in the classroom.
12. Ask the speech clinician for activities that can be used to improve speech in the home and classroom.
13. If the student's pronunciation of certain words and sounds is inconsistent, require the student to use correct pronunciation when asking for privileges.
14. Consult books on articulation. These can usually be found in libraries at universities that have a speech or language therapy program.

256
Jumps from One Topic to Another When Talking

1. Reinforce the student for staying on topic (S. Thomas, personal communication, 1983).
2. Ignore the student when he goes off on a tangent.
3. Have a time set aside each day for the student or class to work on oral communication skills. Complete thoughts and sentences must be used (Adamson, 1978).
4. Use flash cards of familiar objects. Have the student say as much as possible concerning the topic before the next card is shown. If the student has something to add to the previous topic, he must raise his hand and say it before he moves to the new topic (S. Thomas, personal correspondence, 1983).
5. If the student begins a new topic in the midst of the previous one, ask, "Are you through with _____?" (S. Thomas, personal correspondence, 1983).
6. Prepare a dialogue or monologue for the student to memorize and read aloud to a group (Jensen, 1980).
7. Have students hold a debate in which each has an allotted amount of time to talk. They must then listen to the other students (Jensen, 1980).
8. Have the student orally read a paper or report that he has written (Jensen, 1980).
9. Use story starters as oral cues (e.g., "If I were a frog . . .") and have the student tell an organized story (S. Thomas, personal correspondence, 1983).
10. Have a show-and-tell time. Have the student tell about an object and the personal experience he has had with that object (Higginbotham and Davis, 1981).
11. Using the show-and-tell technique, have students exchange objects and information and tell about the new object (Higginbotham and Davis, 1981).

12. Teach a unit on outlining and organization in class. Show how it relates to what is spoken (S. Thomas, personal correspondence, 1983).

13. Have the student give a small "how-to" presentation. The steps should be written down before he begins (Higginbotham and Davis, 1981).

14. Be a model of organization. Point out repeatedly how what you say and do is organized (Jensen, 1981).

15. Have the student practice "thinking through" and writing down what he is going to say (S. Thomas, personal correspondence, 1983).

16. Sound a buzzer or bell when the student strays from a selected topic in order to remind him to return to the subject under discussion.

17. Have a preselected word that is said when the student goes off on a tangent.

18. Ask the student, "What does this have to do with _____?"

19. Record the behavior and play it back for the student. Have him identify where he strayed from the topic under discussion.

257

Non-English Speaking

1. Recommend a language and academic skills evaluation for the student.

2. Reinforce the student when he uses English words.

3. Use name-labels to identify many of the objects the student uses so that he can see the English word for that object (C. Calvano, personal communication, 1983).

4. Use flash cards to drill everyday, common phrases such as *thank you, come here, I need help,* and so on (C. Calvano, personal communication, 1983).

5. Use pictures or visual materials to accompany your lessons. Even though the student may not know what something is called, he can still comprehend the meaning through the pictures (Hyde, 1971).

6. Assign a buddy to work with the student on a one-on-one basis to give aid during academic subjects (Newman, 1981).

7. Make instructions short and to the point, using words the student understands. Have the student restate the directions or do part of the assignment to show understanding (C. Calvano, personal communication, 1983).

8. Tutor the student after school or send instructions home to parents to review several of the concepts covered that day in class. Be sure that the parent will understand the written words (C. Calvano, personal communication, 1983).

9. Simplify and shorten assignments. Do not expect in-depth complex work from the student until he grasps the use of the language (Hyde, 1971).

10. Encourage the student to read. Begin with very basic, well illustrated books (Hyde, 1971).

11. Suggest enrollment in a bilingual program.

12. Place the student in group activities in and out of class. By interacting with others, the student can learn the language and its use (Hyde, 1971).

13. Work on vocabulary building. Each day, ask the student to bring to class at least three names of objects, places, and people that he has seen and can identify (C. Calvano, personal communication, 1983).

14. Work on the days of the week, months, holidays, and seasons by using games or interesting student-made projects (Hyde, 1971).

15. Allow the student to use a two-language dictionary containing the native language and English so that he can compare words and their meanings (C. Calvano, personal communication, 1983).

16. Allow the student to write in his native language. Together use a two-language dictionary to translate the composition.

17. Work on building grammar. Explain the S-V-O structure of our language, which may be very different from the structure of the native language.

18. Quiz vocabulary and spelling words frequently to spot problem areas (Newman, 1981).

19. Learn some interaction phrases (e.g., *hello, thank you*, etc.) in the student's language to make him feel more comfortable and to promote "bonding" between the two of you.

20. Make use of the "language master" machines.

21. Take the student on walks during which the two of you exchange words for environmental objects.

22. Provide cards that have either the English or native language word for objects on them. Have the student match the corresponding words.

258

Poor Oral Grammar

1. Reinforce the student when he uses proper grammar.

2. Refer the student for a language evaluation.

3. Teach proper grammatical rules.

4. Be a good language model for the student (Peppard, 1925; Pearson, 1974).

5. Include the student in group activities where peers can serve as language models (Pearson, 1974).

6. Have the student initiate phrases and sentences (Peppard, 1925).

7. Tape the utterances and play them back for the student. Have him correct his grammar.

8. Have the student listen to various versions of a statement and identify the correct one by saying it.

9. Have the student identify the correct grammatical statement from various ones written on paper by saying them aloud.

10. If the grammar is due to a cultural influence, stress that while it is certainly acceptable to speak that way to friends and family, you would like him to practice a different way in school.

11. Role play situations where students dress up and act the part of rich sophisticates who are conversing at an opera or other social event.

12. Have the student translate his utterances, either written or on audiotape, into proper grammatical terms.

13. Provide practice in using correct grammar by having the student read a short story repeatedly until he can retell it to others using the language of the author (D. Becker, personal communication, 1986).

14. Have the student listen repeatedly to an audiotape of a short story and practice retelling it with as many of the author's words as possible. This provides experience in attending to and using proper language structure, as well as appropriate voice inflection (D.Becker, personal communication, 1986).

15. Write the proper form of grammar for frequently used sentences (e.g., "I have to go to the bathroom." "May I get a drink?"). Post them and require their usage (L. Williams, personal communication, 1986).

16. Have the student rate each sentence of dialogue from television, movies, or books as being appropriate or inappropriate (T. Chlosta, M. Diggins, and V. Homewood, personal communication, 1986).

17. Tell the student that you would like to tape record an interview with him about his interests, a hobby, or any topic that he wishes. Listen to the tape and assess the oral grammar used. On a worksheet, make a list of incorrect usages. Examples of correct usage should be listed opposite these. Review relevant English grammar rules with the student. Have him practice using proper oral grammar (T. Chlosta, M. Dig-

gins, and V. Homewood, personal communication, 1986).

259

Speaks in Incoherent or Meaningless Way

1. Refer the student for a language evaluation.

2. Refer the student for a psychological evaluation.

3. Reinforce the student for meaningful coherent speech (Pearson, 1974).

4. Ignore the student when he engages in incoherent speech.

5. Provide a good language model for the student (Peppard, 1925; Pearson, 1974).

6. Have the student imitate phrases and sentences (Peppard, 1925).

7. Include the student in situations where peers will model appropriate language (Pearson, 1974).

8. To keep from frustrating the student by inquiring as to what was said, choose one important word that you did understand and repeat it either in statement or question form. For example, if the student says, "Erha stru merhn car" say, "Car?" or "Car." This will show that you are listening and will encourage the student to continue talking.

9. Enlist the cooperation of other students in avoiding ridiculing the incoherent speaker.

10. Record some of the student's utterances over a period of time to get a varied sample and listen to the recording carefully to analyze any patterns. Play the recording at various speeds to determine if any sense can be made of the utterances (K. Christensen, personal communication, 1984).

11. Have the student speak into a tape recorder. Play it back so that the student can hear how he speaks in relation to others (J. Mette and D. Brown, personal communication, 1984).

12. Have the student read preselected sentences aloud slowly (C. Gingerich, personal communication, 1984).

13. When the student purposely speaks inappropriately, reply in a foreign language or jibberish as a "shock" technique (T. Marlier and D. Gerdes, personal communication, 1984).

14. By role and drill, teach simple sentences such as, "My name is _____" and "I live at _____" in response to personal information questions (C. Walters, personal communication, 1984).

260

Speaks Rapidly

1. Give a cue to the student to slow his speech rate (M. Pierre, personal communication, 1985).

2. Praise the student when he speaks at an appropriate pace (M. Pierre, personal communication, 1985).

3. Have the student repeat himself, slowing the speech rate (N. Mohrman, personal communication, 1985).

4. Request that the student stop talking when he speaks rapidly (Marshall, 1983).

5. Carefully phrase questions so he can respond with only one word (Marshall, 1983).

6. Talk to the student about how people may not listen to him when he talks fast (Marshall, 1983).

7. Have the student self-monitor his speech rate by timing readings (N. Mohrman, personal communication, 1985).

8. Have the student read passages aloud and try to get the speech rate between approximately 145 to 175 words per minute (Glenn, Glenn, and Forman, 1984).

9. Have the student practice reading a selection purposely prolonging vowel sounds within the syllables of words (Elson, Peck, Willey, Hirsch, Moore, and Wynn, 1966).

10. Have the student participate in choral reading exercises (Elson, Peck, Willey, Hirsch, Moore, and Wynn, 1966).

11. Have the student read groups of words separated by varying punctuation marks (e.g., the student would pause less for commas than semi-colons and periods) (Glenn, Glenn, and Forman, 1984).

12. Ask the student to speak one word for each beat of a metronome or each hand clap by the teacher.

13. Use a speech compressor-type tape recorder that can slow or quicken speech without changing in tone or comprehension level. These are often housed in programs for individuals with sight impairment. Demonstrate how his speech ought to sound.

261
Stutters or Speaks Words or Phrases in a Repetitive Manner

1. Recommend a speech evaluation (De Hirsch, 1984).

2. Give the student opportunities to express himself freely, taking the time to listen. Let the student feel that he is an important individual. Give encouragement (Schasre, 1978).

3. Suggest to the student that he speak slowly in a sing-song or monotone, to slur the consonants and prolong the vowels, to shorten the vowels and stress the consonants, to hold the tongue this way or that way, or to pay attention in one manner or another to his rate, phrasing, or breathing (Blodstein, 1969).

4. Train the student to avoid exaggerated movements that often accompany blocks. Teach him to speak without making faces, stamping feet, or exaggerating mouth movements. A mirror may help in this work and a tape recorder can be used to

show the student that the worst part of his speech could be looking at it, not listening to it (Pennington and James, 1967).

5. Do not draw the student's attention to his repetitiveness if you begin to notice a hesitation in his speech. Hesitation is perfectly natural during the transition from first language "baby talk" to English. This should not be mistaken for stuttering (Bolles, 1982).

6. Exclude the student from an oral reading group if this creates problems. He should read to the teacher alone until ready to read for a small group (Van Riper, 1971).

7. Have the student breathe slowly and concentrate on what he is going to say before it is said (Shaw and Lucas, 1970).

8. A classroom list of speaking situations should be given to the speech clinician and may consist of the following: a listing of the student's mannerisms, statements the student may make about his speech, and any reactions of listeners (Liebergott, Favors, Saaz, vonHippel, and Needleman, 1980).

9. When holding group activities, have the student participate. He can participate in many activities in ways other than speaking (Dunn, 1963).

10. Try to relax the student in a stressful situation by having him do exercises such as breathing deeply and exhaling slowly before speaking (Van Riper, 1973).

11. Tell the student to count to 10, breathe, and relax (Hawaii, 1982).

12. Have the student stop talking, think about what he wants to say, and then slowly speak (S. Winkler, personal communication, 1984).

13. Encourage the student not to attempt to speak while in an excited state. Have the student calm himself and then continue speaking (S. Winkler, personal communication, 1984).

14. Have the student construct a mask on a stick. Through mask making, the student can express himself nonverbally and ver-

bally in a nonfrustrating atmosphere (Murphy and Fitzsimons, 1960).

15. Use creative dramatics during the language arts program to help the student gain self-confidence and speech adequacy (Murphy and Fitzsimons, 1960).

16. If an object is part of the repetitive syndrome, hide that object and try to divert the student's attention (DeMeyer, 1979).

17. During repetitive situations, try to read to the student or point out objects in nature (DeMeyer, 1979).

18. Sit face-to-face with the student and use a firm tone and simple phrases or sentences. This helps gain attention and understanding from the student (DeMeyer, 1979).

19. Have the student relate his repetitions to aspects of the environment and communicative interactions (Fay, 1981).

20. When the student starts to perseverate, give him a new stimulus, question, or topic.

21. Recommend structural therapy. In this approach, emphasis is placed on increasing stimulation to the body of the student. This may be done verbally or physically (e.g., talk to the student about himself; hug or tickle the student). In doing this, the student is encouraged to focus on his body boundaries rather than internal fantasies.

22. Tape record the speech to develop awareness of the problem.

23. Have the student record the number of repetitions and attempt to lower the tally over a period of time.

24. Have a designated cue word that is used to tell the student to stop repeating.

25. Reinforce the student when he does not repeat words and phrases.

26. Refer the student for a psychological evaluation.

262
Uses Name Instead of ''I'' When Referring to Self

1. Positively reinforce the student for using ''I'' correctly (K. Webster, personal communication, 1985).

2. Model the use of ''I'' when referring to yourself (K. Webster, personal communication, 1985).

3. Overemphasize the use of ''I'' in the content of conversation (J. Webster, personal communication, 1985).

4. Correct the student when he uses his name and encourage ''I'' usage (K. Webster, personal communication, 1985).

5. Investigate the possibility of autism as a cause for this behavior (K. Webster, personal communication, 1985).

6. If autism is suspected, refer the student for a psychological/medical evaluation.

7. Encourage the parents to use modeling and repetition at home (J. Webster, personal communication, 1985).

8. Refer the student for speech and language evaluation.

9. Ask the student to rephrase the improper statement using ''I.''

10. Tell the student that his requested need will not be met until he uses ''I'' in the sentence (e.g., ''*I* want a drink of milk'').

24

Physical Health Concerns

263

Alcoholic

1. Attend an alcohol education workshop or educational program on alcoholism to become better informed.
2. Check with local and state social service agencies for information.
3. Suggest Al-Anon as a support group for the family of the alcoholic.
4. Talk with an alcoholic who is an active member of Alcoholics Anonymous. Perhaps this person can give advice based on experience.
5. Educate or inform the parents and help them learn the nature of alcohol and what they can do to help their child.
6. Go to the school board, administrators, other teachers, and counselors to establish policies related to alcohol (Foster, 1982).
7. Help students who are having problems with alcohol usage get an insight into their own behavior through discussion of the reasons for drinking (e.g., appear more

adult, "get high") (Hoch and Olszowy, 1981).
8. Present an alcohol awareness unit of study.
9. Refer the student to qualified counselors or adolescent treatment centers (Foster, 1982).
10. Have the school nurse check the student for signs of alcohol consumption before and during the school day.
11. Check the student's possessions for alcoholic beverages.
12. Closely monitor the student's movement about the school to prevent consumption of alcoholic beverages.

264

Anorexic

1. Recommend a medical evaluation.
2. Reinforce the student for eating.
3. Ignore noneating behavior.
4. Have the student chart the amount of food

or calories ingested each day to monitor progress and motivate her.

5. Monitor and chart the student's weight. Reinforce weight gain.

6. Make enjoyed activities and privileges dependent on food consumption.

7. Obtain information on the condition for the student to read.

8. Educate the student regarding the drawbacks and dangers of this behavior.

9. Show pictures of a youth before and during anorexia. Ask the student and peers in which picture the youth looks best.

10. Help the student find interest in something other than an obsession of being fat (B. Barbieri, personal communication, 1983).

11. Have the student keep a daily diary of food intake.

12. Refer the student to the guidance counselor to help her correct faulty body image, to alleviate feelings of depression, guilt, and anxiety, and to develop self-esteem and confidence.

13. Teach the student the principles of healthy eating habits and nutrition (P. Barnett, personal communication, 1988).

14. Encourage the parents of the student to give their child independence and speak to her as an individual, not just part of the family as one organism (Bankmand and Knickerbocker, 1983).

15. Give the student an opportunity to talk about her obsession. This helps defuse the explosive, "itchy" feeling that anorexics often report shortly before going on a "reduction binge" (Bankman and Knickerbocker, 1983).

16. Encourage family therapy (Bankman and Knickerbocker, 1983).

265

Asthma

1. Recommend that the parents consult a physician (Smith, 1978).

2. Remind the student to use prescribed medications at the various administration times (Foster, 1980).

3. Check to see if the student is on a special diet. Be sure that the student adheres to it while in school (Foster, 1980).

4. Be sure the student drinks enough liquids. A proper fluid balance is necessary to help break up the mucus within the lungs and maintain hydration (Foster, 1980).

5. Good posture should be encouraged. This promotes drainage of mucus (Smith, 1978).

6. Remind the student that if he exercises in cold weather, he should breathe through the nose rather than the mouth and cover his face with a scarf (Boyd and Strunk, 1980).

7. Remind the student to avoid overexertion and to get a sufficient amount of sleep (Effects of Relaxation Training, 1979).

8. Keep the classroom as free from allergens as possible (Foster, 1980; Kaercher, 1980).

9. Avoid having pillows stuffed with feathers, down, or kapok; instead, use synthetic, machine-washable pillows (Kaercher, 1980).

10. Because they gather dust easily, venetian blinds should be dusted with a wet cloth at least once a week (Kaercher, 1980).

11. Suggest that cleaning products with strong, pungent odors be avoided as often as possible. These include products such as insecticides, camphor, mothballs, pine oils, floor waxes, or furniture polishes (Kaercher, 1980).

12. If possible, keep doors and windows closed during the pollen season in the spring and early fall (Kaercher, 1980).

13. If possible, keep the room dry and warm. Damp and excessively cold air should be avoided (Kaercher, 1980).

14. Allow the asthmatic student to rest when asthma symptoms develop (Kaercher, 1980).

15. If an air conditioner is being used during pollen season, set it on "recirculate" rather than "fresh air" (Kaercher, 1980).

266
Becomes Physically Ill from Stress

1. Provide a means of success at a meaningful task (Pine, 1985).
2. Utilize a combination of relaxation and fantasy journeys. The student learns to relax while you take him through an imaginary journey that relates to the topic being studied (Wood, 1984).
3. Do something silly everyday. Talking back to TV commercials is a possible activity (Cox, 1985).
4. Create positive experiences for the student while he is in the school building. This is not necessarily academic success, but success in sports, achievement in music, having a good relationship with a teacher, and so on. All exert an important protective effect on a student (Pine, 1985).
5. Have the student participate in physical exercises and music activities as aids in coping with stress (J. Kush, personal communication, 1985).
6. Identify the stress-producing situation in order to reduce it. Once the stressor is identified, it should be managed. Systematic decision-making guidelines and problem-solving steps should be followed (Hamilton, 1984).
7. Provide an "oasis." This is an activity in which the student can feel successful (e.g., the act of creation in writing, painting, composing, and developing new ideas) (Pine, 1985).
8. Reduce rather than increase pressure to perform when the student seems "out of sorts" (J. Kush, personal communication, 1985).
9. Use acupressure as a relaxation technique. Learn acupoints to release pain, tension, and stress (St. John, 1984).
10. Train the student to use the following problem-solving format for stress management: (a) get the facts, (b) verbally express

the exact nature of the stress, (c) devise a goal, (d) develop a plan, (e) suggest alternative approaches, (f) try the plan, and (g) discuss progress at regular intervals and evaluate the original plan making changes as necessary (Kuczen, 1984).
11. Encourage innoculation against stress. This includes getting enough sleep, eating healthy foods, and venting the inevitable stress-generated energy that builds up each day (Tingey-Michaelis, 1985).
12. Teach the student to concentrate on reestablishing equilibrium as quickly as possible when physical signs of stress appear. Physical reactions can be cut short by using a deep-breathing technique or by practicing progressive relaxation, in which a student learns to tense and relax muscle groups on command (Kuczen, 1984).
13. Suggest to the student that he outwardly play-act the opposite emotions of his feelings of fear or helplessness. Often the positive feelings take over (Kuczen, 1984).
14. Allow the student to take a walk or get a drink of water when feeling stressed.
15. To reduce anxiety, provide activities with no right or wrong answer (K. Renfro, personal communication, 1983).
16. Give specific instructions so that the student doesn't worry if he is doing it correctly (K. Renfro, personal communication, 1983).
17. Involve the student in physical activity to release stress (K. Renfro, personal communication, 1983).
18. Present stressful activities in a game format (K. Renfro, personal communication, 1983).
19. Allow the student to leave the room whenever stress becomes too overpowering (K. Renfro, personal communication, 1983).
20. Have the student compose a list of things in the classroom that cause stress and devise a way to reduce this stress (C. Gingerich, personal communication, 1984).
21. Emphasize the productive and good qualities of the student to help promote a posi-

tive self-image (C. Gingerich, personal communication, 1984).

22. If stress is caused by testing, make modifications such as oral testing, private testing, and so on (C. Gingerich, personal communication, 1984).

267

Bulimic

1. Recommend a medical evaluation.

2. Recommend psychological counseling.

3. Monitor the student's movements about the school to prevent vomiting.

4. Escort the student from lunch to class. Do not allow her to stop at bathrooms or drinking fountains.

5. Escort the student to the bathroom and drinking fountain.

6. Monitor the student's weight. Reinforce weight maintenance.

7. Encourage the student to engage in physical activity if she wishes to lose weight.

8. Plan a daily diet with the student to provide proper nutrition and control caloric intake that is of concern to the student.

9. Obtain information on bulimia for the student to read.

10. Educate the student regarding the drawbacks and dangers of this behavior.

11. Since bulimia victims usually eat secretly, have the student keep a record of times and places of eating, amount of food consumed, and what happened before and during the binge. After she does this, go over the chart with her to pinpoint the problem areas (Mule, 1981).

12. With the help of a dietician or doctor, place the student on a disciplined diet. Educate her in proper eating habits and proper weight for different heights (Bakwin and Bakwin, 1967).

13. Help the student become involved in positive school activities in order to provide so-

cialization and to build esteem (J. Mills, personal communication, 1984).

14. If possible, remove situations that are stressful for the student. Revise her class schedule, change the seating arrangement, have a conference with the parents about any home problems, or meet with other people in her life who can offer you insight to the causes of stress for her (Mule, 1981).

15. If possible, have a buddy or parent help monitor the student and offer encouragement during and after school hours (J. Mills, personal communication, 1984).

16. Encourage the student to join an encouraging, supportive program such as Weight Watchers.

17. In extreme cases, recommend hospitalization if the student's weight and health is past the point where outpatient care is sufficient (Kerr and Nelson, 1983).

268

Complains of Illness to Avoid Work

1. Reinforce the student when he does not complain of illness (Kirschner and Levin, 1975).

2. Discuss the behavior and its consequences with the student so that he knows what to expect if he performs the behavior again (Payne, Palloway, Smith, and Payne, 1981).

3. Conduct simulations and role-playing activities (Payne, Palloway, Smith, and Payne, 1981).

4. Have a doctor or nurse come into the classroom and discuss various symptoms of sickness and what constitutes being sick (Payne, Palloway, Smith, and Payne, 1981).

5. Tell the student a story that involves a situation when a student complains about being sick and the consequences he has to face (M. Cruz, personal communication, 1985).

6. Help the student differentiate between be-

ing really sick and faking sickness to avoid doing work (Lerner, 1981).

7. Ask the entire class to discuss various circumstances in which they have faked sickness (A. Correa, personal communication, 1985).

8. Inform the student that if he continues to pretend to be sick, no one will believe him when he really is ill and claims to be (Buhler, 1952).

9. Read and discuss the story entitled *The Boy Who Cried Wolf*.

10. Encourage the student to "work for a few more minutes."

11. Require all work to be completed before the student is allowed to go home or participate in nonacademic activities.

12. Discuss the matter privately with the student. Open confrontations and accusations between you and him may encourage lying so that he can "save face" (Gervais and Dittburner, 1981).

13. If illness and pain are viewed by the student as a way to avoid difficult situations, reduce threats to his self-esteem by developing skills and competencies that he can reach in a successful manner (Smith, Snyder, and Perkins, 1983).

14. When sickness is used as an excuse to stay home, involve the parents in the remediation program. They can take the student's temperature and decide whether he is telling the truth. When the student attends school voluntarily, a star is given and placed on a home chart. Five stars equal a special treat or trip with the family (Allyon, Smith, and Rogers, 1970).

15. Have the parents give rewards to the student contingent on a report of noncomplaining behavior in school (D. Cambrini, personal communication, 1985).

16. If the student is being reinforced by staying home with the mother, restructure the mother's behavior. Instruct her to ignore the complaining behavior and only reinforce reports of fun activities in school.

Also, you should ignore all crying or complaints of illness (Cooper, 1973).

17. Implement a procedure that contains checks and double checks to help prevent lies, fibs, and excuses (Gervais and Dittburner, 1981).

18. As a general rule, require written excuses from parents. A consistent policy will avoid the feeling of personal stigma (Gervais and Dittburner, 1981).

19. Call the student's parents to find out if there is a true illness (B. Battaglia, personal communication, 1985).

20. Recommend that the school's physician do a complete physical check-up on the student (B. Battaglia, personal communication, 1985).

21. Review the student's diet to see if the illness is being caused by something he eats during the day (B. Battaglia, personal communication, 1985).

22. Keep a record to see if a pattern is developing (B. Battaglia, personal communication, 1985).

23. Do a unit in class that shows how being healthy can be a positive experience (B. Battaglia, personal communication, 1985).

269

Encopresis (Fecal Incontinence)

1. Recommend an examination by a physician.

2. Reinforce the student when the behavior is not exhibited.

3. Ignore the inappropriate behavior (Keystone Area Education, 1983).

4. Investigate the toilet facilities. Notice out-of-the-way toilets and those located in cold, dark places that the student may be avoiding (Kleinmuntz, 1974).

5. Retrain the student (Kleinmuntz, 1974; Finch and Kendall, 1979).

6. Recommend that parents ask a physician about the use of suppositories so that the student will defecate at fixed times until the colon regains normal shape and muscle tone (Wright, 1975; Finch and Kendall, 1979).

7. Suggest the use of mechanical devices that detect appropriate elimination (Finch and Kendall, 1979).

8. Develop a positive self-concept within the student through the use of positive remarks and the avoidance of negative comments.

9. Advise the parents to contact a psychologist in order to provide therapy for the student (Wooden, 1985).

10. Recommend art therapy.

11. Advise parents to see a physician for further treatment such as drug therapy (Bakwin and Bakwin, 1972).

270

Enuresis (Bedwetting)

1. Recommend an examination by a physician.

2. Positively reinforce the student for dryness (Morgan, 1972).

3. Recommend hypnotism (Baller, 1975).

4. Recommend psychological consultation (Kolvin, Mackeith, and Meadow, 1973).

5. Suggest that the parents ask a physician about the use of stimulant drugs that are often effective in the treatment of enuresis (Baller, 1975).

6. Recommend mild punishment following an accidental wetting (Turner, 1973).

7. Restrict fluid intake at night (Silberstein and Blackman, 1965).

8. Awaken the student periodically during the night to go to the bathroom.

9. Use a bell and buzzer alarm pad in the bed at night (Kolvin, Mackeith, and Meadow, 1973).

10. Have the student wear a "diaper" and plastic pants when sleeping to prevent leakage into the bedding.

11. If the student is afraid to get out of bed in the dark, install a night light.

271

Epilepsy

1. Recommend that the student get plenty of sleep (Scott, 1973).

2. Provide a calm environment (Scott, 1973).

3. Have the student avoid flashing lights, as this may initiate a seizure (Anspaugh, Gilliland, and Anspaugh, 1980).

4. Be aware of signs that a seizure may be imminent. These include daydreaming, forgetfulness, comprehension difficulties, and shorter than usual attention span (Scott, 1973).

5. Maintain limits on the student's behavior if activity is known to initiate seizures (Freeman, 1979).

6. Provide quiet periods of rest (Freeman, 1979).

7. Alternate in-seat tasks with action-oriented ones (Freeman, 1979).

8. Present only a few tasks at a time (Freeman, 1979).

9. Provide structure that reinforces good behavior (Bagley, 1971).

During a Seizure:

1. Remain calm (Freeman, 1979).

2. Summon the school nurse (Freeman, 1979).

3. Remove any objects that are near the student (Freeman, 1979).

4. Don't restrain the student's movement (Anspaugh, Gilliland, and Anspaugh, 1980).

5. Do not force anything into the student's mouth (Anspaugh, Gilliland, and Anspaugh, 1980).

6. Loosen the top button of shirt or blouse (Freeman, 1979).

7. If the attack is short, allow a rest period and then allow the student to go home (Freeman, 1979).

8. If the seizure is violent or extended, call a physician (Freeman, 1979).

9. If the student appears confused or disoriented, offer help in a matter-of-fact way (Freeman, 1979).

10. Note what time seizure began and stopped (Anspaugh, Gilliland, and Anspaugh, 1980).

11. Arrange for someone to stay with the student until he is fully awake (Anspaugh, Gilliland, and Anspaugh, 1980).

12. Make arrangements for clean up if necessary (Anspaugh, Gilliland, and Anspaugh, 1980).

272
Flatulence; Passes Gas

1. Recommend an examination by a physician.

2. Reinforce the student when the behavior is not exhibited.

3. Provide negative consequences when the behavior is exhibited.

4. Ignore the inappropriate behavior (Keystone Area Education, 1983).

5. The behavior of passing gas may be an "attention getter." Help the student fit in better in the classroom to eliminate this behavior (J. Anderson, personal communication, 1985).

6. Have a discussion with the entire class. The discussion should center around the idea of ignoring the behavior of passing gas. The student exhibiting the behavior should also be a part of the discussion (J. Anderson, personal communication, 1985).

7. Insist that the student not interrupt the class with the undesirable behavior. Thus

the behavior is no longer an attention-getting factor (J. Anderson, personal communication, 1985).

8. Insist that the student excuse himself each time the behavior occurs (M. Baker, personal communication, 1985).

9. Work on modifying the student's present diet to include fewer gas-forming foods (M. Baker, personal communication, 1985).

10. Move around the classroom in order to combat attention-gaining factors (Keystone Area Education, 1983).

11. Utilize the "massed practice" technique. The student practices the inappropriate behavior as often as possible until he can no longer repeat it even once a minute (Miller, 1970; Sue, Sue, and Sue, 1981).

12. Recommend the use of over-the-counter anti-gas medication.

13. Allow the student to leave the room to expel gas.

14. If the student is unable to control the passing of gas, allow him to sit away from the others or near an open window or door.

273
Gets Hurt Easily in Physical Play

1. Send the student to the clinic or summon the nurse.

2. Have the student sit out if he is hurt (K. Alvis, personal communication, 1983).

3. Do not let the student have recess the next day if he pretends to be hurt (K. Alvis, personal communication, 1983).

4. Arrange for small groups of students with similar problems to work under the direction of a physical education teacher or a dance instructor.

5. Engage the student in gross motor activities to build coordination.

6. Engage the student in eye-hand coordination activities.

7. Privately talk good naturedly about the student's awkwardness.

8. Share moments when students have been hurt while playing. Have students talk about the reasons someone got hurt.

9. Show the student how to keep from getting hurt or how other students react in the same situation (Carberry, 1979).

10. Restructure the activity to prevent injury.

11. Suggest that the student engage in games or nonviolent sports.

12. Strictly enforce game rules to prevent dangerous behavior.

13. Engage students in more noncontact sports.

274
Hypersensitivity to Pain

1. Recommend a medical evaluation.

2. Recommend a psychological evaluation.

3. Praise the student when he is not overly demonstrative.

4. Ignore overreactions to pain.

5. Sternly tell the student to halt his excessive display of pain.

6. Distract the student from his pain with a pleasurable activity.

7. Have the student analyze upcoming activities to determine if they contain movements or conditions that would create pain.

8. Ask the parents to ask a physician whether pain-reducing drugs are appropriate for this student.

9. Devise a plan for the student to implement when he is in pain (e.g., leaving the room without permission to go to the nurse's office).

10. Call the student's parents to inquire about techniques or precautions to assist him in overcoming pain.

275
Has an Unusual Number of Accidents

1. Recommend a medical evaluation.

2. Recommend a perceptual-motor evaluation.

3. Recommend a vision examination.

4. Recommend a psychological evaluation.

5. Review proper procedures and actions prior to activities.

6. Encourage the student to "think through" his actions before engaging in an activity.

7. Encourage the student to review situations where he had an accident to determine if there was a way that it could have been prevented.

8. Arrange the environment to be less dangerous for the student.

9. Work on the student's fine motor coordination.

10. Work on the student's gross motor coordination.

11. Require the student to clean himself and the area after an accident.

276
Hypersensitivity to Sensory Stimulation

1. Recommend a medical evaluation.

2. Recommend a psychological evaluation.

3. Prepare the student for upcoming activities and changes.

4. Lower the sensory stimulation of the classroom by regulating temperature, lighting, and noise.

5. Wear bland clothing.

6. Place the student in a cubicle or carrel to work.

7. Seat the student away from windows, heaters, loud speakers, doors, and the like.

8. Seat the student away from others to avoid physical contact.

9. Instruct others not to yell at or touch the student.

10. Do not force the student to use materials that are known to cause adverse reactions (Sears, 1981).

11. Note the types of sensory stimulations that are acceptable to the student, and use materials that teach through that modality.

277

Hypochondria

1. Recommend professional counseling (Godenson, 1970).

2. Promote a classroom atmosphere in which students can develop a sense of belonging and ownership (Thompson, 1977).

3. Do not refer to symptoms as being entirely in the student's mind. Avoid making statements such as, "It's only your imagination" (Mead, 1975).

4. Find an understanding physician to explain that any symptoms the student may feel are real, but that there is not real cause for the pain (Mead, 1975).

5. Help the student avoid stressful situations. This will relieve the need to complain of aches and pains (Mead, 1975).

6. Lead the student to consider illness as being a reaction to stress. Once he realizes that the symptom is a result of stress, he can concentrate on finding other ways to deal with the stress (Mead, 1975).

7. Avoid extremes of reaction. Don't be overly or underly concerned. Try making statements like, "I'm sorry you're not feeling well," then change the subject (Mead, 1975).

8. Get the student involved in other activities that will give him less time to devote to thinking about illness (Mead, 1975).

9. Find out about the family background. Some parents may reinforce or actually cause the constant complaining. If so, work out a plan for change with the parents (Otto, Julian, Tether, and Madnick, 1976).

10. If the incident is isolated, ignore the complaint.

11. If complaining continues, in a private moment let the student know you understand that sometimes people don't feel their best. Remind him that the feelings may go away if he concentrates on something else (J. Mills, personal communication, 1984).

12. Remind the student that privileges are approaching (e.g., free time in class, recess, lunch, end of the school day) if he gets his work done (Stephens, 1975).

13. At the signs of possible sickness, send the student to the school nurse for evaluation (Mule, 1981).

14. Contact the parents to see if, in fact, the student has been stating similar complaints at home and what has been done about these complaints. Obtain information about any doctor's visits, any medications, and the conditions of the illness (J. Mills, personal communication, 1984).

15. Chart the student's complaints, including what time, where, and what activity was taking place. This chart may indicate that the student is avoiding a task or situation by feigning illness (Mule, 1981).

16. If possible, remove the obstacle that is causing illness for the student (Karlin and Berger, 1972).

17. Pull the student out of the anxious situation. After a period of time, gradually reintroduce him to it. For instance, simply for sitting in the group the student might earn something previously decided upon. Then the student must open a book, must contribute one idea a week, one idea a day, and so on until he takes a more complete and active role (Herbert, 1978).

18. Recommend that "flooding" be used. The student has to stay in the anxiety-provoking situation until he is no longer anxious. Observe cautions—flooding often causes emotional trauma (Herbert, 1978).

19. Hold a class meeting on the topic, "Stressful Situations and What Makes Me Upset" (J. Mills, personal communication, 1984).

278

Insensitive to Sensory Stimulation

1. Reinforce the student when he appropriately responds to or reports sensory stimulation.

2. Refer the student for a physical examination.

3. Refer the student to the school psychologist (M. C. Grothaus, personal communication, 1985).

4. Use physical contact such as a hug or touch with the student (M. C. Grothaus, personal communication, 1985).

5. Make your classroom visually stimulating by providing a colorful and attractive environment (M. C. Grothaus, personal communication, 1985).

6. Cook in the classroom. The student will be able to taste, smell, and see the food being cooked (M. C. Grothaus, personal communication, 1985).

7. Physically move the student's head or body part in the direction of a stimulus (M. C. Grothaus, personal communication, 1985).

8. Reposition yourself and the student so you are facing each other while interacting (McCollum, 1984).

9. Investigate the possible presence of autism (Wolman, 1965).

10. Use more vivid materials.

11. Combine sensory stimulants such as bright lights and loud noises.

12. Point out how others detect or respond to sensory stimulation in various situations (J. Steele, personal communication, 1985).

13. Make the student cognitively aware of the various degrees of stimulation by having him classify items from least to most bright,

colorful, loud, and so on (J. Steele, personal communication, 1985).

14. Determine if the student is taking prescribed or illicit drugs that would affect sensory perception.

279

Insensitive to Pain

1. Recommend a medical evaluation.

2. Accept, and perhaps even compliment, this student's way of coping.

3. Reinforce the student when he displays pain appropriately (J. Steele, personal communication, 1985).

4. Investigate the possibility that the student was brought up in a family that advocated a stoical approach to pain and discouraged "pain behavior" (Elton, Burrows, and Stanley, 1979).

5. Investigate the possibility that the student only appears to disregard pain due to a cultural background, such as American Indian or African, in which pain is often not displayed outwardly (Elton, Burrows, and Stanley, 1979).

6. Make use of situations in which peers display pain appropriately by indicating the circumstances surrounding others' pain (J. Steele, personal communication, 1985).

7. Make the student cognitively aware of varying degrees of pain by having him classify pictures of individuals experiencing pain into categories ranging from no pain at all to extreme pain (J. Steele, personal communication, 1985).

8. Investigate the possibility that the student is physically abused and, as a defense measure, has "turned-off" the experience of pain (J. Steele, personal communication, 1985).

9. Utilize art therapy. Create art activities through which the student can find an outlet for feelings, impulses, and tensions, and discover new ways to resolve the conflict

which prevents the expression of pain through catharsis and sublimation (Arieti and Brodie, 1981).

10. Use biofeedback to encourage the student to concentrate on and control various parts of the body (J. Steele, personal communication, 1985).

11. Have the student view the *Melbourne Pain Apperception Film (MPAF)* to measure his threshold to pain and pain tolerance (Elton, Burrows, and Stanley, 1979).

12. Suggest hypnotism to explore the possibility that pain is not experienced appropriately due to repression (J. Steele, personal communication, 1985).

13. To sensitize the student to pain in others, have him watch slides showing actors' facial expressions of pain for 10 seconds each and rate them on a 9-point scale ranging from "no-pain" to "excruciating pain." Inform the student that the individuals shown in the slides are expressing pain in response to electric shock (Von Baeyer, 1982).

14. Arouse the student's awareness of pain in others through the use of color videotapes of gruesome scenes excerpted from an automobile safety "scare film" borrowed from the local police force (Von Baeyer, 1982).

15. Recommend the presentation of painful stimuli in sessions when the student is exposed to so much stress that coping strategies do not work (Klepac, Hauge, Dowling, and McDonald, 1981).

16. Investigate the possibility of autism (Wolman, 1965).

17. Determine if the student is taking prescribed or illicit drugs that would affect pain perception.

280

Lacking in Muscle Tone

1. Develop an exercise program to strengthen the underdeveloped muscles (Logan, 1964).

2. Conduct stretching exercises to increase muscle tone caused by inactivity (Logan, 1964).

3. Recommend the use of a technique called "progressive resistance exercise" or building up muscle tolerance through exercise (DeLorme, 1951).

4. Use dance as a method to motivate the student to exercise.

5. Involve the student in running (N. Mulchrone, personal communication, 1985).

6. Involve the student in swimming (Logan, 1964).

7. Involve the student in a job-training program involving physical labor.

8. Enroll the student in an aerobics class (N. Mulchrone, personal communication, 1985).

9. Make exercise fun by using games to motivate the student.

10. Have the student chart his progress in strength, speed, or weight in order to provide motivation.

11. Recommend physical therapy involving weight bearing and patterning (N. Mulchrone, personal communication, 1985).

12. Encourage the student to walk or ride a bicycle to places where he would usually ride in a car.

13. Expose the student to numerous sports and games in an attempt to interest him in one.

14. Ask the student which sports he enjoys watching on television. Train him in skills and drills used in this sport.

281

Narcolepsy

1. Check with the parents about the student's sleeping habits (K. Alvis, personal communication, 1983).
2. Check with the parents about the student's use of medication (K. Alvis, personal communication, 1983).
3. Ask the parents and physician about a regular use of opiates, specifically codeine phosphate (Harper, 1981).
4. Consult the parents and physician about pharmacotherapy (Schneck, 1980).
5. Arrange activities so he will be outside whenever possible (Bain, 1979).
6. Include a great deal of physical exercise during the day (Alley, 1983).
7. Plan the day around periodic naps (Cavenar, Krishman, Miller, and Volow, 1984).
8. Plan exciting and interesting lessons (K. Alvis, personal communication, 1983).
9. Involve the student in the teaching of lessons (K. Alvis, personal communication, 1983).
10. Move the student to the front of the room so that your voice will sound louder (K. Alvis, personal communication, 1983).
11. Have another student tap the sleeping student on the shoulder to awaken him (K. Alvis, personal communication, 1983).
12. Refer the student for possible psychotherapy, specifically for depression (Krueger, 1979).
13. Refer the student for possible psychiatric care, possibly including electroconvulsive therapy (Cavenar, Krishman, Miller, and Volow, 1984; Hicks and Schrader, 1984).

282

Overweight

1. Praise the student for weight loss and proper eating habits (Lent, 1976).
2. Recommend a medical evaluation.
3. Recommend counseling.
4. Encourage enrollment in a Weight Watchers program for youth.
5. Encourage the student to eat smaller portions.
6. Encourage the student to exclude junk food from his diet.
7. Encourage the student to substitute low-calorie food and drink for higher calorie items.
8. Encourage the student to engage in more physical activity.
9. Encourage the parents to serve smaller portions.
10. Inform the parents that a lock on the refrigerator and cabinets will prevent snacking.
11. Make rewards and privileges contingent on weight loss.
12. Have the student chart his daily weight on a chart to provide motivation (Michaelis, 1980).
13. Implement self-monitoring of caloric intake (Michaelis, 1980).
14. Teach units on proper nutrition and caloric intake.
15. Encourage parents to avoid buying junk foods.
16. Teach a unit on the hazards of excess weight (e.g., heart disease, diabetes).
17. Inform the student that a loss of weight will make him appear more physically attractive to others.
18. Teach new eating behaviors (Fox, 1981).
19. Recommend a protein diet consisting of nibbling on foods high in protein six to eight times daily, to help maintain the blood sugar at levels that will not trigger sugar cravings (Smith, 1977).

20. Encourage parents to reward their child with rewards other than food (Smith, 1977).

21. Implement breaks during dining. This allows the blood sugar level to rise and inhibit hunger.

22. Suggest that the parents investigate the possibility of having the student's digestive tract "stapled" to decrease the amount of food that can be ingested.

23. Suggest that the parents investigate the possibility of having the student's teeth "braced" together so that only nutritional liquids can be ingested.

24. Suggest that the parents investigate the possibility of "fat suctioning" to remove body fat in their child.

283

Physically Weak

1. Recommend a medical evaluation.

2. Encourage activity and exercise (Logan, 1964).

3. Encourage and teach proper nutrition and diet.

4. Encourage adequate sleep.

5. Restructure vigorous activities to allow for the student's weakened condition.

6. Conduct stretching exercises to strengthen muscles (Logan, 1964).

7. Chart the student's strength on a chart, using this to motivate the student to improve. Devices and weights can be used to measure hand grip, lifting ability, and the like.

8. Assign a peer to assist with various tasks.

9. Assign a peer to model behaviors and encourage the student in physical activities.

10. Recommend physical therapy (N. Mulchrone, personal communication, 1985).

284

Pregnant

1. Be sure that the student has seen a physician for examination, planning, and so on.

2. Have the student speak with the school nurse daily.

3. Prepare the class for the upcoming changes that the student will be experiencing (Hampton, 1979).

4. Ask the student to share her emotional feelings with the class (Hampton, 1979).

5. Ask the student to share her physical feelings and changes with the class.

6. Encourage the student to talk to a social worker or counselor (Cottman, 1980).

7. Encourage the student to visit Planned Parenthood and similar agencies to discuss options.

8. Strengthen the student against exploitation (Klermant and Jekel, 1978).

9. Suggest counseling in the areas of prenatal care, birth procedures, and parenting (Hampton, 1979).

10. Discuss birth control to prepare this student and others for the future (Cottman, 1980).

11. Make available information on special programs, schools, and agencies (Hampton, 1979).

12. Foster good health care (Klermant and Jekel, 1978).

13. Help the student develop positive long-range goals (Cottman, 1980).

285

Smokes

1. Praise the student when he refrains from smoking (Rogers, 1977).

2. Obtain antismoking material for reading in class.

3. Have a discussion on the cosmetic draw-

backs of smoking (e.g., clothes smell of smoke, bad breath, yellow teeth).

4. Discuss the rights of others that are violated when they must breathe in smoke.

5. Have the student chain smoke cigarettes until he becomes ill.

6. Discuss the price of cigarettes and other ways in which that money could be spent.

7. Encourage the student to refrain from smoking for progressively longer periods of time.

8. Enforce school smoking regulations.

9. Have someone who is seriously ill due to smoking speak to your class.

10. Discuss product marketing and how he is influenced by advertising campaigns.

11. Have the student imagine scenes where he is smoking. Then have the student imagine the same scene without smoking (Fisher, Green, and Lowe, 1979).

12. Use the smoking countdown approach. Let the student smoke a total of 10 minutes the first day. Cut a minute each consecutive day until the student is no longer smoking at all (Fisher, Green, and Lowe, 1979).

13. Implement a smoking education program into the classroom curriculum to make students aware of the hazards of smoking.

14. Have the student research and write a paper on the effects of smoking on health.

15. Get students to conduct a survey that studies public opinion on smoking in various situations.

16. Have the student compose a list of benefits gained by not smoking (Danager and Lichtenstein, 1978).

17. Encourage the student to chew gum whenever the urge to smoke occurs (Danager and Lichtenstein, 1978).

18. Have the student imagine himself as a nonsmoker (Rogers, 1977).

19. Have the student collect cigarette butts in a large container. This lets the student see the filth involved in smoking (Rogers, 1977).

20. Suggest hypnosis (B. Slifer, personal communication, 1984).

21. Suggest that the student smoke a brand of cigarette that he finds to be distasteful (B. Slifer, personal communication, 1984).

22. Tell the student that having yellow teeth and bad breath is not way to impress the opposite sex.

23. Have the student calculate the amount of money spent on smoking each year. Translate this into the price of a possession that he would desire.

24. Have the student cut off successively larger parts of a cigarette. This allows him to smoke the same number of cigarettes while quitting.

25. Suggest the use of cigarettes made from vegetable leaves which are marketed to provide low-nicotine alternatives.

286

Staring Spells

1. Recommend a medical evaluation.

2. Investigate the possibility of staring being symptomatic of a petit mal epileptic seizure.

3. Investigate the possibility of a vision problem.

4. Recommend psychological counseling if you believe the student is preoccupied with life's events.

5. Recommend a psychological evaluation if you believe the student has lost contact with reality.

6. Regain the student's attention by calling his name.

7. Regain the student's attention by touching him on the shoulder.

8. Use a predetermined word or signal (e.g., snapping fingers) to bring the student back to task without drawing attention to him.

9. Make your lessons more interesting by varying your voice tone, using humor, us-

ing different learning modalities, and using hands-on activities.

10. Make worksheets and assignments more interesting by using the student's interests.

11. If the student is daydreaming, offer reinforcement if work is completed before a set time limit.

12. Do not allow the student to go to recess, lunch, or home until all work is done correctly.

287

Tobacco Chewing

1. Reinforce the student when he refrains from chewing tobacco.

2. Enforce school rules regarding tobacco usage.

3. Encourage the student to substitute chewing gum for tobacco.

4. Discuss product marketing and how he is influenced by advertising campaigns.

5. Teach a unit on the hazards of tobacco chewing.

6. Discuss the cosmetic drawbacks of chewing tobacco (e.g., bad breath, stained teeth, spitting).

7. Obtain antichewing literature for your classroom.

8. Discuss the price of chewing tobacco and other ways in which that money could be spent.

9. Encourage the student to refrain from chewing tobacco for progressively longer periods of time.

10. Have the student continue to chew until he becomes ill.

11. Recommend to the student that he chew a brand of tobacco that he dislikes. This may assist him in quitting.

288

Tactually Defensive; Overreacts to Being Touched

1. Recommend a medical examination for the student (D. Parker, personal communication, 1983).

2. Investigate the possibility that this behavior is due to physical abuse.

3. Seat the student at the end of tables, in the back of rows of desks, and out of general traffic patterns. These locations minimize unintentional tactile stimulation from the other students, thereby allowing him to attend to his work.

4. When having the class line up, place this student at the beginning or ending of the line (Ayres, 1979).

5. Assign special tasks that do not require close physical contact (Ayres, 1979).

6. Approach the student from the front so as not to startle him (Ayres, 1979).

7. Position yourself at the student's eye level so that all movements can be observed by him (Ayres, 1979).

8. Explain what is to occur before touching the student (Sears, 1981).

9. Verbally direct the student through an activity rather than assisting by touch (Sears, 1981).

10. Be careful not to brush against the student with a skirt, trousers, or sleeves; this unexpected tactile stimulation could induce a fight-or-flight response (Sears, 1981).

11. Note the types of tactile stimulation that are acceptable to the student and use teaching materials constructed of the same or similar textures and surfaces (Sears, 1981).

12. Do not force the student to use those materials that are known or observed to set off adverse reactions (Sears, 1981).

13. Allow the student to watch your actions. Knowing what to expect from you may place him at ease (Bettelheim, 1950).

14. Play a game with another student. Slowly

increase proximity to the touch-sensitive student (Bettelheim, 1950).

15. Use small, friendly animals to promote touching in this student (D. Parker, personal communication, 1983).

16. If severe and seen in conjunction with other symptoms of environmental withdrawal, investigate the possibility of autism.

25

Self-Abuse

289

Bites Self

1. Reinforce the student for refraining from biting (Gaylord-Ross, Weeks, Lipner, and Gaylord-Ross, 1983; Neufeld and Fantuzzo, 1984).

2. Remove a specific positive consequence after biting occurs (Gaylord-Ross, Weeks, Lipner, and Gaylord-Ross, 1983).

3. Give verbal punishment such as "No!" when the student begins to bite (Dorsey, Iwata, Ong, and McSween, 1980).

4. Withdraw verbal or physical contact after the student bites (Tate and Baroff, 1966).

5. Use "contingent restraint" by holding the student's mouth in a rigid position for a fixed period of time after biting (Gaylord-Ross, Weeks, Lipner, and Gaylord-Ross, 1983).

6. Ignore biting until the behavior is extinguished.

7. Use a "bubble-apparatus," which is a clear plastic sphere that fastens over the stu-

dent's head, shielding the mouth from contact with hands and forearms (Neufeld and Fantuzzo, 1984).

8. Train alternate behaviors that allow the student to communicate his anger or frustration.

9. Spray a water mist on the student's face when he begins to bite (Dorsey, Iwata, Ong, and McSween, 1980).

10. Refer the student for medical evaluation (Durand, 1982).

11. Refer the student for a psychological evaluation or counseling.

12. Recommend the administration of an electrical shock when biting occurs (Lovass and Simmons, 1969).

13. Administer a mild aversive consequence such as a stream of cold water from a squirt gun, tobasco sauce in the mouth, or soapy water in eyes when the behavior occurs (M. Pierre, personal communication, 1985).

14. Coat the area usually bitten with a bad-tasting liquid, available in drugstores, that prevents nail biting (M. Pierre, personal communication, 1985).

15. Have the student wear a hockey helmet with a face cage to prevent the insertion of body parts into the mouth.

16. Use an aversive consequence such as slapping, which is less hurtful than biting, but shocks the student because it is imposed by an outside source.

17. Have the student wear arm pads, heavy or metallic gloves, or other protective devices.

290

Self-Abusive

1. Recommend a medical evaluation.

2. Recommend a psychological evaluation or counseling (Blackhan, 1967).

3. Reinforce appropriate behavior or reduction in the frequency or duration of abuse (Repp and Deitz, 1974; Lovitt, 1978).

4. Have the student wear restraints or protective devices such as helmets, hand pads, and face masks to prevent injury (Durand, 1983).

5. Institute a loss of privileges (Durand, 1982).

6. Verbally reprimand the student (Dorsey, Iwata, Reid, and Davis, 1982; Durand, 1982).

7. If the self-abuse is infrequent, mild, and used to gain attention, ignore the behavior (D. Kirby, personal communication, 1983).

8. Work on improving the student's self-concept (Blackham, 1967).

9. Provide access to sensory-stimulating toys for the student to manipulate (Dorsey, Iwata, Reid, and Davis, 1982).

10. Use differential reinforcement of other behaviors (Dorsey, Iwata, Reid, and Davis, 1982).

11. Use some sort of pain-inducing device (Woots, 1982).

12. Wrap the head or body part in cloth or elastic bandages to dull the feelings gained from self-injury (Woots, 1982).

13. Place the student in a padded time-out room (Woots, 1982).

14. Each time the student self-abuses, take away a ticket from those previously given him. If he has any at the end of the week, he may trade them for a different reward (Woots, 1982).

15. Have the student wear a padded football helmet at all times (Dorsey, Iwata, Reid, and Davis, 1982).

16. Recommend the use of medication (Durand, 1982).

17. Restrain the head or body part in a padded chair (J. Grant, personal communication, 1984).

18. Implement stimulus control. Teach the student to stop the target behavior anytime the lights are turned off, he hears someone whistle, or someone calls his name (Archer, 1976).

26

Self-Care

291

Careless About Appearance

1. Reinforce the student for improved appearance (Axelrod, 1977; Sprick, 1981).

2. Find out if the home situation is contributing to this situation. Do the parents encourage bathing? Do they buy toothpaste? Does the student own a comb? If not, supply some of these items (K. Maier, personal communication, 1983).

3. Have the student wash his hands and face before he enters the classroom. Also keep a comb available for the student's use. Do not let the student enter the classroom unless these things have been done (K. Maier, personal communication, 1983).

4. Show films or filmstrips on good grooming and how it can improve one's appearance (K. Maier, personal communication, 1983).

5. Dress neatly and practice good grooming habits to model this behavior for the students (K. Maier, personal communication, 1983).

6. Involve the parents in encouraging good grooming habits at home (Axelrod, 1977).

7. Promote peer pressure to help those students who are careless about their appearance maintain good grooming habits (Axelrod, 1977).

8. Hold realistic expectations for the student. Some families cannot afford clothes, and many times students may be wearing hand-me-downs that look old and worn. The clothes should be clean, however (Hallahan and Kauffman, 1978).

9. Spend five minutes a day talking to the student about good hygiene practices (D. Gerdes, personal communication, 1984).

10. Pantomime a shower and other grooming and hygiene practices (D. Gerdes, personal communication, 1984).

11. Develop a training program for the student on how to develop good personal hygiene (Sprick, 1981).

12. Set aside some time for the student to practice personal hygiene (Sprick, 1981).

13. Plan and develop health lessons that can be

taught interestingly to the students (Averill, 1926).

14. Have the class work together to make a hygiene scrapbook that includes personal and community health and sanitation (Averill, 1926).

15. Ask the students to bring in pictures to make a bath or hygiene poster (Dansdill, 1924).

16. Hold morning inspections (Taylor and Sherrill, 1969).

17. Stress the importance of being clean to prevent sickness and to make and maintain friendships (Taylor and Sherrill, 1969).

18. Use soap carvings with plastic knives so students can make their favorite animal. While carving, they should discuss the clean smell, and so on (Taylor and Sherrill, 1969).

19. Teach poems and jingles to the students to help them remember how to look nice for school (Taylor and Sherrill, 1969).

20. Take a photograph of the student. Have him determine how he could improve his appearance.

21. Teach students that it's all right to get dirty sometimes. Discuss appropriate times (Taylor and Sherrill, 1969).

292
Careless About Belongings

1. Reinforce the student when items are returned to the proper place (Stumphauzer, 1973).

2. Put a checklist on student's desk. Everytime he picks up belongings or has those belongings, he puts a check after the object (N. Hammerschmidt, personal communication, 1984).

3. Sarcastically thank the student for wanting to share his belongings with the rest of the class. This will help him realize that his belongings are in the open and accessible to other students and will promote being

more careful with his belongings (J. Horsman, personal communication, 1984).

4. Have the student write a paper on which personal belongings are important and valuable in his life (C. Mattox, personal communication, 1984).

5. Have the student write about how he would feel if he were needy and without extra personal belongings (C. Mattox, personal communication, 1984).

6. Inform the student you will keep his belongings for a period of time if you find them lying around (D. Brown, personal communication, 1984).

7. Provide the student with his own drawer or closet and have him inventory the belongings at the end of each day (T. Marlier and K. Christensen, personal communication, 1984).

8. Number belongings and places where belongings should be at the end of each day. Have the student check in the morning and evening to see if the belongings are in their place (J. Camp, personal communication, 1984).

9. Collect belongings found out of place and make the student answer problems, read a section of an academic book, and so on in order to have possessions returned (L. Pfeiffer, personal communication, 1984).

10. Check belongings each morning and reward him if *all* the belongings are with him at the end of the day (C. Rodriquez, personal communication, 1984).

11. Assign the student to be a helper to pick up toys and clean up the room (C. Poteet, personal communication, 1984).

12. Set up a point system for treating belongings correctly and properly returning them (D. Gerdes, personal communication, 1984).

13. Start a system whereby the student who finds the belongings of another receives a reward from the student who lost it (L. Bevins, personal communication, 1984).

14. Keep the student's desk by yours and give him the materials he needs. After he is

done using them, he must return them to you (B. Yakos, personal communication, 1984).

15. Make a big chart for the classroom. When the students pick up their materials, they receive a star (L. Lienhart, personal communication, 1984).

16. Have the student pick up belongings at recess (P. Lammon, personal communication, 1984).

17. Give the student a checklist of duties or requirements regarding his belongings to assist in organizing and remembering (Stumphauzer, 1973).

18. Have a group discussion about putting things back where they belong and what will happen if they are not put away properly (Stumphauzer, 1973).

19. Have the student list things that must be remembered during a specific class period (Stumphauzer, 1973).

20. When the student leaves belongings unattended, take away one of his privileges (Stumphauzer, 1973).

21. If a belonging is left, lost, or handled inappropriately, ask the student if he is forgetting to do something (Stumphauzer, 1973).

22. Divide the class into groups of two or three. Devise a contest whereby the group that remembers their belongings best during the week gets a reward. In this way, the students will remind each other (Donaldson, 1980).

23. Use a sign-out sheet for materials (J. Hoffner, personal communication, 1984).

293
Finicky and Very Selective in What Is Eaten

1. Praise the student for ingesting new foods.
2. List all the foods that the student likes. Rank them to ascertain favorites (V. Croll and D. Wolfson, personal communication, 1983).

3. Think of other foods similar in appearance, taste, consistency to those preferred. Present these to the student to determine if they will be liked by him (V. Croll, personal communication, 1984).

4. Prepare foods, disguising new ingredients as the preferred foods. Discuss the taste of these after the student has eaten them (V. Croll, personal communication, 1984).

5. Implement a meal-time behavior management program or point system. Give one point for touching the food, two points for eating part of the meal, three points for eating most of the meal, and four points for eating the whole meal. Use a favorite food as a reinforcer. This food is not used at any other time. Replace the daily reinforcer with a larger weekly reinforcer (Blackman and Silberman, 1980).

6. Embed new food in preferred food. Make a game of this by having the student try to identify it. Emphasize the pleasant taste. Reward the student for eating the food (V. Croll and D. Wolfson, personal communication, 1983).

7. Include the student in grocery shopping. Have him choose a favorite food and an unknown or nonpreferred food (e.g., breakfast cereal plus a vegetable) (D. Wolfson, personal communication, 1983).

8. Designate that certain foods must be eaten before a desired activity can begin (V. Croll, personal communication, 1983).

9. Have the student participate in the preparation of food. Begin with favorites, then proceed to unknown foods (Walker and Shea, 1980).

10. Take the student to a restaurant periodically. The student must eat at least one food never eaten before in exchange for choosing his favorite. Extend this idea gradually to the choosing of unfamiliar main courses (V. Croll, personal communication, 1983).

11. Find out the student's occupational interests and tell him that you'll find out what kind of foods a person in his field of inter-

est eats. Then serve a sandwich that might be in a mechanic's lunch, or a casserole that you call "cowboy supper," or fruit or nut mix for "astronauts' snack" (K. Cowell, personal communication, 1986).

12. Do "blind" taste testing. Have the student rank the foods by taste.

294

Liable to Overeat if Not Watched Closely

1. Reinforce the student when he does not overeat. Do not use food as a reinforcer.
2. Use planned ignoring of inappropriate eating patterns (M. Burns, personal communication, 1983).
3. Identify something else that the student likes and use this activity to occupy time otherwise spent eating (M. Burns, personal communication, 1983).
4. If the student seems to be under a great deal of physical and emotional stress, recommend counseling (M. Burns, personal communication, 1983).
5. Have the student sit next to students who have good eating habits.
6. Limit the time or types of food available for lunch.
7. Do not allow second helpings of food.
8. Have the student chew his food slower.
9. Present units on good nutrition and calorie intake (M. Burns, personal communication, 1983).
10. Have the student keep a daily food intake record.
11. Enroll the student in a group for overweight youths (Schlechter, 1981).
12. Implement a weight control program, including dietary management, physical activity, and behavior modification. Classes should emphasize peer group involvement.
13. Recommend behavioral counseling that fo-

cuses on changing eating habits (Gormally and Rardin, 1981).

14. Have the student set weight-loss goals (Epstein, 1981).
15. Involve the student in daily observation and recording of calorie intake, exercise, and weight (Epstein, 1981).
16. Train friends and family to model, monitor, and reinforce appropriate eating and exercise behavior to refrain from punishing or criticizing the student's efforts (Pearce, 1981).
17. Provide breaks during the dining time. This allows the blood sugar to rise, thus bringing on a "full" feeling and inhibiting more eating.
18. Have the student's parents investigate the possibility of having his digestive tract stapled to allow for less ingestion of food.
19. Have the student's guardians investigate the possibility of having his teeth "braced" so that only nutritional liquids can be ingested.

295

Messy

1. Reinforce the student when he is neat.
2. Provide negative consequences for being messy.
3. Have the student think about his actions and behavior before engaging in an upcoming situation.
4. Review the recently completed activity or situation with the student to analyze his behavior and whether he could have been neater.
5. Videotape the student for later review and analysis.
6. Have the student clean up after himself.
7. Have the student wash his own clothes.
8. Have the student use a checklist to prevent or correct messiness in situations (e.g., put trash in can, wash hands and face, etc.).

9. Have the student wear a cape, old shirt, or bib to prevent getting clothes messy.

10. Teach neatness skills.

11. Assign a friendly peer assistant to remind the student to display neat behavior.

296
Messy or Sloppy Eating Habits

1. When the student eats without being messy, verbally praise that behavior (Stumphauzer, 1973).

2. Seat the student near others who have proper eating habits.

3. Stand close to the student when he is becoming messy. The student might not engage in this behavior when a teacher is present.

4. Have the student eat alone instead of with others if obtaining the attention of others is the goal (Whaly and Mallott, 1970).

5. When the student eats in a sloppy fashion, have him clean the table and other tables in the room (Alberto and Troutman, 1982).

6. When the student's eating habits become sloppy, deprive the student of recess, free time, or any other privileges that he might have otherwise been entitled to.

7. When the student begins eating in an inappropriate manner, take the food away for 10 seconds. Then return the food to the student. Repeat if necessary.

8. Teach proper eating behavior.

9. Review proper eating habits before each meal.

10. Present the meal in small parts. The student must eat the first portion neatly to earn the second portion.

11. Videotape the student for later replay and analysis.

12. Have the student wear an old white shirt while eating. Implement a point system in which the student loses one point of ten

previously given to him for each food spot on the shirt. A reward is earned for a designated number of points.

297
Pica; Puts Inedible or Unhealthy Things in Mouth

1. Reinforce the student when he chooses edible objects (Woody, 1971).

2. Use correspondence training. In phase one, reinforce the student with praise for an accurate report on his behavior whether or not pica occurred. During phase two, give additional food reinforcers for an accurate report of no pica (Madden, Russo, and Cataldo, 1980).

3. Present a variety of foods and inedible objects to the student in random order. Ask him, ''Is this something you should put in your mouth?'' Reinforce him for correct responses with food and specific verbal praise. Correct wrong responses (Madden, Russo, and Cataldo, 1980).

4. Employ modeling via videotaped episodes or admired peers (Woody, 1971).

5. Overcorrection techniques can be used each time pica is observed. Have the student brush his teeth for one minute with a toothbrush that has been dipped in mouthwash (Madden, Russo, and Cataldo, 1980).

6. Have the student conjure up an image of himself eating inedible objects. The student is then induced to visualize himself being witnessed by friends who laugh at and ridicule him. Then, as he visualizes discarding the inedible object with finality in mind, friends are seen as responding positively to him (Woody, 1971).

7. Recommend clinical suggestion and hypnosis by a professional therapist (Woody, 1971).

8. Suggest aversive therapy in which the student is presented with his choice inedible

object. As he begins to mouth it, a mild electric shock is administered. A less distasteful stimulus, such as an unpleasant noise or a squirt from a water gun, might work as well. After the student has been conditioned to expect the aversive stimulus if he mouths the object, the shock or noise is administered whenever he picks up the object and starts to bring it toward the mouth (Woody, 1971).

9. When the student begins to mouth an inedible object, place him in a time-out helmet that prevents eating (Ausman, Ball, and Alexander, 1974).

10. Recommend a medical evaluation.

11. Recommend a psychological evaluation.

12. If the pica behavior is due to a delusional system, recommend the possible use of medication. Trilafon has been successful in eliminating delusional systems, and consequently, the ingestion of foreign bodies (Fishbain and Rotondo, 1983).

13. Coat inedible items with the distasteful liquid often painted on fingernails to inhibit biting. This liquid is available in drugstores.

14. Remove small objects from the immediate area.

298

Prone to Get Dirty and Untidy Easily

1. Have the student practice washing and combing hair, and brushing teeth daily (Sprick, 1981).

2. Set aside a time for a training session for personal hygiene (Sprick, 1981).

3. Positively reinforce the student when he arrives at school properly groomed (Sprick, 1981).

4. Reinforce the student periodically throughout the day for remaining clean and tidy.

5. Give the student time to clean himself before reentering the classroom from outside.

6. Provide protective clothing for the student when working with art supplies, playing on the playground, and so on.

7. Talk to the student about staying clean before he leaves the room (S. Stidham, personal communication, 1981).

8. Designate a certain area of the playground that the student may occupy (S. Stidham, personal communication, 1981).

9. Provide the student with an incentive for staying clean, such as extra reading time or being your helper.

10. Stress the importance of being clean to prevent illness and acquire friends.

11. Prepare a unit on personal health care and cleanliness, using posters, bulletin boards, stories, and so on (D. Parker, personal communication, 1981).

12. Have morning inspections. Let the students know your expectations for a clean, well-groomed class. For those who are not presenting themselves appropriately, provide a few minutes to comb, brush, or wash up while the class is having morning discussion and preparing for the day (D. Parker, personal communication, 1981).

13. Teach your students this poem to help them remember how to look nice for school (Taylor and Sherrill, 1969).

Checking for School

Look at your face
Is it clean and bright?
Look at your teeth
Are they gleaming white?

Look at your hair
Is it brushed to a sheen?
Look at your nails
Are you sure they're clean?

Look at your hands
Would they damage a book?
Look at yourself
And see how you look!

14. Involve the student in soap carving using plastic knives. The student may make soap

carvings of his favorite animals. While carving, the student should be guided into a discussion about the clean smell of the soap and the importance of a daily bath. The student can use his soap "creatures" to make bathing or washing hands fun (Taylor and Sherrill, 1969).

15. Dress nicely in order to serve as a role model (D. Parker, personal communication, 1981).

16. Have students bring their favorite health-care products to class and try to persuade others, in the form of a commercial advertisement, that their product is the best (D. Parker, personal communication, 1981).

17. Let the student know that it's all right to get dirty sometimes. Talk about these times (Taylor and Sherrill, 1969).

299
Spends Too Much Time on Grooming

1. Reinforce the student for quick grooming.

2. Set a time limit on bathroom trips.

3. Set a time limit on grooming sessions. Provide a "countdown" for the student.

4. Do not allow grooming materials to be used during instructional time.

5. Encourage the student to purchase higher quality grooming aids which can be applied more quickly and produce longer lasting results.

6. Impose negative consequences for late arrival to class after physical education classes or hallway passing.

7. Ask a hallway monitor to rush students out of the lavatories as the hallway passing time nears an end.

8. Allow the student to earn extra grooming time.

9. Time the student's grooming sessions and determine the average time. Reward the student for grooming within a time limit set

by you that is lower than this average. Periodically reduce the allowed time.

10. Teach short cuts and proper grooming techniques to avoid the need for extra time.

11. Have the student end activities early in order to allow for more grooming time.

12. Take a photograph before and after grooming. Show the student that there is no noticeable difference.

300
Unable to Bathe Self without Supervision

1. Set a routine for bathing (Goldimond, 1965).

2. Teach bathing skills.

3. Reinforce appropriate bathing skills (S. Kennedy, personal correspondence, 1984).

4. Bring in a hand shower and start class by demonstrating a shower. Have the students role play this also (D. Gerdes, personal correspondence, 1984).

5. Task analyze bathing procedures and post a laminated checklist of steps in the student's shower or tub. The student must check off each step as completed.

6. Set up a program that utilizes the small steps in bathing that are necessary to complete the act. Small steps should be taught one at a time over a long period so the student can master each step. For example, start the process by having the student hold the washcloth until he can hold it for a period of time long enough to constitute bath time. Then steps should be added slowly until the student has mastered bathing on his own (K. Christensen, personal correspondence, 1984).

7. While assisting the student, plan an "interruption" so you will have to leave the bathroom. Hopefully, the student will continue bathing without someone present (K. Monty, personal correspondence, 1984).

8. If the student is in danger when bathing alone, put only a small amount of water in the bath tub (J. Mette, personal correspondence, 1984).

9. If behavior in the tub is the problem, allow no toys. Undress the youth, place him in the tub, and wash and rinse him without speaking. After the student is dressed, tell him that he may have one toy the next night if the bath is finished in 10 minutes. If the student fulfills this promise, keep adding toys and increase the time to an upper limit of 15 minutes (S. Stidham, personal correspondence, 1984).

10. If the student is not able to bathe without messing the bathroom, use systematic punishment. For example, if there is an excessive amount of water on the floor, or if he writes on walls or the floor with soap or shaving cream, a favorite activity could be removed from the schedule. The worse the mess, the stricter the consequences (K. Monte, personal correspondence, 1984).

11. In one day, at the same bath time:
    a. Fill the bath tub and help the person bathe from start to finish. Empty the bath.
    b. Immediately fill the bath again and help the student with most of the bath. Instruct the student to complete the bath by himself. Empty the bath tub.
    c. Immediately fill the tub again. This time, stop assisting after the washing is halfway finished. Instruct the student to finish on his own as in (b) above.
    d. Immediately fill the bath tub again. Leave before the bath is half-way finished. Instruct the student to finish as in (b) above.
    e. Immediately fill the tub again. Remove assistance after getting the student started.
    f. Immediately fill the bath tub again and leave immediately. Have the student finish on his own.
    g. Have the student take a bath on his own from start to finish (D. Brown, personal correspondence, 1984).

12. If the student refuses to bathe without supervision, positive expectations could be used. For example, the adult could leave after the bath is started, saying, "I expect you to be done and dried off when I return in 15 minutes." If the student has not complied, negative consequences are implemented (K. Monte, personal correspondence, 1984).

13. Have the student assist in bathing a pet.

14. Have the student assist in bathing a very young child.

15. Have the student bathe a doll (C. Walters, personal correspondence, 1984).

16. Use food coloring and bubble bath to make bathing more pleasurable.

17. Introduce toys into the bathing situation to make it more pleasurable (C. Walters, personal correspondence, 1984).

301

Unable to Dress Self without Supervision

1. Help the student put on articles of clothing. He is then to do it by himself as you gradually decrease the help given (J. Kitchner, personal communication, 1985).

2. Use verbal prompting and praise to encourage the student to dress himself (J. Kitchner, personal communication, 1985).

3. Help put a piece of clothing almost all the way on, then allow the student to finish that item. The student is encouraged to do more of the ending each time (K. Webster, personal communication, 1985).

4. Divide the process of dressing into several steps. Work on one step until the student can complete it himself. Then work on the next step.

5. Make use of dolls, puppets, and other manipulatives that the student can dress and undress to master zipping, buttoning, front/back concepts, and other basic dress-

ing skills (K. Webster, personal communication, 1985).

6. Make use of cloth books containing buttons, zippers, ties, and laces to increase independent dressing skills (K. Webster, personal communication, 1985).

7. Do not allow the student to go for recess unless he dresses himself to a degree expected by you.

8. Assign a peer assistant to help.

9. Use a stopwatch and set limits of how long the student can take to get dressed with supervision. Gradually move to dressing without supervision (N. Worstell, personal communication, 1985).

10. Have the student keep a chart of how long it took him to get dressed.

11. Give the student one point for each item that is partially or fully placed on the body correctly. The points are saved to be used in the purchasing of an item or privilege.

302

Urination into Clothing During Class

1. If the student does this to escape class work, have him remain in class until work is completed.

2. Encourage peer ignoring of this behavior.

3. Provide opportunity for success in class.

4. Allow the student to leave the room without permission if necessary.

5. Have the student sit near the door so that he may leave the room without drawing attention.

6. Allow frequent trips to the bathroom.

7. Ask the student to limit intake of fluids before class.

8. If the accident is a first occurrence, either allow the student to go home to clean up or ask the parent to bring a change of clothing (Sprick, 1981).

9. If the problem has occurred more than once, discuss the problem with the school nurse to determine if the student should receive a medical exam (Sprick, 1981).

10. If the problem has happened more than once and there is no physical problem, prepare a consequence for the next time the behavior occurs (Sprick, 1981).

11. When the problem has not occurred for a length of time, be very positive and supportive (D. Gerdes, personal correspondence, 1984).

12. After the incident, discuss the problem with the student to seek a solution (D. Gerdes, personal correspondence, 1984).

13. Encourage the student to wear plastic pants to keep the urine from showing through his clothing.

14. Have the student use a signal to let you know that he wishes to leave the room due to urination. Distract the class's attention to an area away from the door to allow the student to leave unnoticed.

15. Suggest a medical examination.

16. Suggest that the student meet with the school psychologist.

27

Self-Concept

303

Believes Nobody Loves Him

1. Have students say positive things to others in a group setting (Wagner, 1974; Jones, 1980).

2. Have those who love and care for this student show it in a way that the student will notice.

3. Promote positive interaction with others.

4. Have the student pick a classmate to get to know better. The two can talk about interests, ideas, hobbies, and so on (Dinkmeyer, McKay, and Dinkmeyer, 1980).

5. Focus the student's attention on his strengths and assets (Dinkmeyer, McKay, and Dinkmeyer, 1980).

6. Role play on the issue of "nobody loves me." After the performance, discuss character feelings and motivation (Dinkmeyer, McKay, and Dinkmeyer, 1980).

7. Use puppetry to act out appropriate sequences (Dinkmeyer, McKay, and Dinkmeyer, 1980).

8. Be gentle, supportive, and caring (Clarke, 1978).

9. Share something important with the student (Clarke, 1978).

10. Use the student's name frequently (Clarke, 1978).

11. Use reassuring statements, such as, "It's good to see you," "Glad you came today," "I enjoy being with you," and so on (Clarke, 1977).

12. Write positive self-thoughts on index cards. Every time the student says nobody loves him, he has to read a positive card (Newcomer, 1980).

13. If the student's statement has some truth to it, emphasize the need to gain strength from one's own personal deeds. Teach the student many different skills for self-sufficiency and solitary recreation.

14. Teach skills that will be helpful in assisting this student to become likable or lovable to others.

15. Help the student channel his pent-up emotions into sports, hobbies, or activities.

16. If this is done for attention or sympathy, ignore the behavior.

304
Blames Self When Things Go Wrong

1. Reinforce the student when things go well.
2. Teach the student to praise himself when things go well.
3. Have students say something positive to each other (Jones, 1980; Wagner, 1974).
4. Praise the student for taking the blame, but encourage him to forget it quickly.
5. Set small goals for the person to reach. If something goes wrong, seek another way to reach the goal (Watson and Tharp, 1981).
6. Give two students situations to role play in which either student could be at fault. Discuss the many times we think we have done something wrong when we have not (Jones, 1980).
7. Demand only that students do their best. Emphasize that complete success is not always necessary. Ask the student if he did his best. If this is the case, praise the student.
8. Have the student identify things that were done correctly even though the task, as a whole, failed. Praise the student for parts done correctly.
9. Have the student evaluate the situation and determine what could be done to make the task a success next time.
10. Hold a group meeting to discuss guilty feelings and how to handle them. You may also want to include what to expect as a consequence of the action (W. Chisholm, personal communication, 1985).
11. When in doubt as to whether or not the student's statement is true or untrue, ask him in a nonthreatening way to tell you which it is (Stephens, 1978).
12. Tell the student that mistakes are legitimate

and that everyone makes them. Stress that it does not have to be anyone's fault if something goes wrong (M. D'Arcy, personal communication, 1985).

13. Have the student analyze why he feels that it was his fault. Design a plan of action to prevent that circumstance from happening again. Have the student learn from his experiences.

305
Depreciates and Distrusts Own Abilities

1. Praise the student for accomplishments.
2. Ignore the student's self-depreciation.
3. Help the student set and obtain realistic goals (Watson and Tharp, 1981).
4. Work with the student to devise a plan to achieve set goals.
5. Each time the student depreciates his abilities, have him name one thing he does well.
6. Focus the student's attention on his strengths and assets (Dinkmeyer, McKay, and Dinkmeyer, 1980).
7. Ask only that the student do his best. Decrease emphasis on correctness.
8. Have the student list things that he did correctly even though the task, as a whole, failed.
9. Have the student review the situation to determine how it could be done differently next time.
10. Task analyze requirements. Teach necessary skills.
11. Provide guidance and assistance. Fade out assistance over time.
12. Encourage the student to "give it a try" before seeking your assistance.
13. Have the student keep a written record of successful accomplishments. Be sure all are listed (e.g., line leader duties, homework done correctly, etc.).

306

Has Too High an Opinion of Self

1. Reinforce modest behavior.
2. Ignore the student when he acts in a narcissistic manner (N. Hammerschmidt, personal communication, 1984).
3. Have the entire class list five areas in which they each feel that they need improvement in their lives (C. Gingerich, personal communication, 1984).
4. Have the student self-record the number of times he talks about himself in one day and compare this with the average of other students (T. Marlier, personal communication, 1984).
5. A student who is self-centered may be in need of a humbling experience. Assignments could be made that are extremely difficult, forcing him to ask for help or risk failure.
6. Engage the student in activities that equalize everyone's ability or chances to succeed, so he would not have an opportunity to outshine the others.
7. Assign the student the more menial classroom tasks, such as washing the chalkboard or sweeping the room. This would show that everyone has responsibilities for the classroom, and he is not better than anyone else (Monty, personal communication, 1984).
8. Explain to the student how others feel about him (S. Stidham, personal communication, 1984).
9. Tell the student that everyone has faults and that no one is perfect. Help the student in listing his faults and thinking of ways to improve them (J. Mette and D. Brown, personal communication, 1984).
10. Sit with the student and ask him to assess his impact on others. Suggest ways in which he might change relationships for the better. The discussion should be on a private, personal basis, analytical in nature,

with the student providing the analysis (Delp and Martinson, 1977).
11. Provide insight by having the student read fictional books about characters similar to himself (Lipson and Bolkosky, 1982).
12. Channel exaggerations into writing, role playing, and creativity by creating superheros (Walker and Walker, 1981).
13. Provide experiences that bring ego enhancement to the student who exhibits the tendencies of exaggeration, story telling, boasting, and bragging (Cruickshank, 1977).
14. Encourage adults not to gush over this student to such an extent that he begins to believe that he is better than others (O'Donnell and Duncan, 1980).
15. Use role playing to practice more appropriate ways of presenting oneself (N. Hammerschmidt, personal communication, 1984).
16. In a controlled environment, set up the student for failure. Follow this controlled failure with discussion (J. Camp, personal communication, 1984).
17. Assign the student readings on the lives of great men or women who lead humble lives (J. Camp, personal communication, 1984).
18. Encourage the student to talk about his accomplishments in an objective manner without undue elaboration.

307

Low Self-Esteem

1. Recommend counseling (Dobson, Campbell, and Dobson, 1982; Myrick and Dixon, 1985).
2. Praise the student for his accomplishments (Raviv, Levit, and Bartal, 1983; Lay and Wakstein, 1985).
3. Structure the classroom social environment in less competitive ways. Those who lose

in competition may feel inadequate (Henderson, 1980; Ames, 1984).

4. Teach the student to set attainable goals. Attaining goals can be a source of pride (Henderson, 1980).

5. Include a "skills for living" course, including introspective topics such as self-concept, feelings, attitudes, friends, and families, which would be studied in detail over a semester to improve self-esteem (Ayers, 1981).

6. Encourage the student to direct his attention away from himself and onto the task. This will enhance performance. With improved performance comes improved self-esteem (Brockner and Hulton, 1978).

7. Have the student become a reading and writing "tutor" for the primary grades. At the end of the peer-teaching experience, give the older student an award certificate (Borbe, 1985).

8. Ask the principal to set aside an hour each week to meet with individual students. Teachers select students and send both outstanding and unmotivated students. The principal sends a thank you note to the participants after the meeting (Battle, 1981; Borbe, 1985).

9. When reprimanding a student, never say, "You were bad." Instead, offer more positive approaches such as, "It upsets me to see books being thrown" (Johnson, 1980).

10. Have the student recognize his accomplishments and verbalize them (Johnson, 1980).

11. Build success by breaking tasks into small sections and having the student concentrate on one section at a time (Johnson, 1980).

12. Help the student develop a "game plan" for handling prejudice regarding his handicap. He should also know when to confront this prejudice. These survival strategies put the disabled student in a position of being able to make a choice, and thus having control (Rousso, 1985).

13. Use a computer as a tool to enhance self-esteem. Have the student learn a program

of interest and share it with the class (Furst, 1983).

14. Teach parents to give positive praise and ignore undesired behavior (Washington, 1977).

15. After engaging the class in a discussion focusing on the positive side of one's personality, have the student complete a checklist whereby he has to choose and check the abilities he has (e.g., I'm better at playing ball __ or drawing a picture __. I'm better at climbing a tree __ or writing a letter __.) (Farnette, Forte, and Loss, 1977).

16. Discuss how wonderful it would be to have the power to change things in the school, country, and world. Give possibilities. Outline the student's silhouette and have him list the things that can be changed within himself (Farnette, Forte, and Loss, 1977).

17. Have an "I'm OK" day during which everyone is supposed to say something nice about themselves (Felker, 1974).

18. Have the low-achieving student keep a self-evaluation record. This will serve as a reminder of how he is doing in relation to how he has done in the immediate past. This gives up perfection as a standard and stops the comparison of one student's work to another (Felker, 1974).

19. Encourage the class or group to make statements of self-praise (e.g., "We did a good job in reading group today," "We're the best helping class in the whole building") (Felker, 1974).

20. After a class session in which friction has taken place between you and your class, and possible lowering of self-esteem has occurred, invite the class outside into the warm sunshine. Just sit quietly. Every so often a student may come up to you and talk for a while. By the following class period the atmosphere should be back to normal (Smuin, 1978).

21. Ask each student to bring in a magazine picture depicting his personality. With the class sitting in a circle, each student shows his personality (Smuin, 1978).

22. Have each student develop a positive commercial for himself and present it in front of the class. It could be on a poster board, audiotape, videotape, or camera (Canfield and Wells, 1976).

23. The discovery of the knowledge that one's fingerprints are unique and different is enhancing to self-concept. Display everyone's prints (Canfield and Wells, 1976).

24. Have the student make four drawings to answer the questions: Where am I? Where am I going? What obstacles will I face? What inner quality will I need to develop to overcome these obstacles? (Canfield and Wells, 1976).

25. When the student writes or verbalizes negative things about himself, record the negative comment in more realistic terms. For example, "Yesterday I was bad" can be reworded into, "Yesterday I hit someone." These rewritten or reworded phrases do not imply worthlessness or hopelessness (Canfield and Wells, 1976).

26. Add more value to the traditional cut-out of the student's traced body. Make a heart and have the student tell who he loves and paste that name in the tracing. On the feet, write two things he is good at doing with his feet. On the hands, do the same thing. On the stomach, have him cut pictures of what he likes to eat. In the head, the student should put several things he likes to dream or think about (J. O'Malley, personal communication, 1985).

27. Encourage involvement in school activities outside of academics so that the student can identify with a group (Dobson, Campbell, and Dobson, 1982).

28. Plan cooperative learning and social experiences into the curriculum (Dobson, Campbell, and Dobson, 1982; Mongate, 1984).

29. Provide fast, public, evaluative feedback to promote positive perceptions in the student, whether the feedback is positive or negative. The feedback serves to inform the student that you are aware of his performance (Stipek and Tannat, 1984).

30. Project an image of knowledgeability and trustworthiness. A person who appears confident and assured is more likely to be successful in changing attitudes than someone who appears unsure of himself (Koballa and Rice, 1978).

31. Assign the student a daily chore that would promote interaction with others (C. Frankiewicz, personal communication, 1985).

32. Provide the opportunity for the student to present a lesson or demonstration of his hobby (C. Frankiewicz, personal communication, 1985).

33. Have the student do a task repeatedly to show that luck is not involved in his successful completion of the assignment (Pearl, 1985).

34. Have the student participate in a game in which he acts out the role of a person who was or is successful in life (Handell and Robert, 1982).

35. Publish a pamphlet with the student's composition in it (Mongate, 1984).

36. Use the mastery learning approach to allow the student a chance for success at his own pace (Ames, 1984).

37. Make the student responsible for an aspect of a total assignment. Have him master it and teach it to others (Michener, 1984).

38. Use drill techniques with the student. Perfect practice promotes further and more successful participation (Ames, 1984).

39. Give the student options whenever possible. The choices should be structured to match his skills, emotional stability, and developmental level (Bruce and Bruce, 1983).

40. Design assignments around the areas in which the student excells or has high interest (Bruce and Bruce, 1983).

41. Initiate activities in which the student has the opportunity to share in the viewpoints and opinions of others, thus increasing his own self-identity (Brennan, 1985).

42. Teach the student about the outside world. This extension of self reduces the tendency

toward self-absorption, which deters development of self-esteem (Brennan, 1985).

43. Have the student participate in activities in which he learns about his strengths, weaknesses, abilities, and limitations (Brennan, 1985).

44. Ask the student to create a bulletin board on a personal area of interest (D. Fegatilli, personal communication, 1985).

45. Suppress biases. Avoid implying that some students are more acceptable than others (Robinson and Bowie, 1982).

46. Divide students into small groups of four to six people. Stress cooperation in the groups and arrange assignments in the groups so that students have to cooperate in order to succeed. Give each student a piece of information that is vital for the completion of an assignment. All members of the group have to work together and rely on each other in order to complete the assignment. Therefore, the slowest member of the group is as important as the brightest (Battle, 1981).

47. Challenge the students' academic abilities in a way that the required learning is relevent to their lives (Curtis and Shaver, 1981).

48. Start out the school year with an emphasis on each student's individuality. Gear everything to their importance as a person. Don't allow the students to experience failure. Install confidence in each student (Walsh, 1973).

49. Select books for the student to read or have read to him, in which people like himself are portrayed favorably (Harvey and Denby, 1970).

50. Encourage the student to do what he can for himself, but help with tasks that are too difficult before frustration sets in (Hamilton, Flemming, and Hicks, 1976).

51. If corrective action is needed, do it quietly, firmly, and in such a manner as to avoid shaming the student in front of his peers (Hamilton, Flemming, and Hicks, 1976).

52. Celebrate the students' birthdays. For the students having birthdays in July and August, have "unbirthday" parties (Horn, 1976; Dial, 1977).

53. When a student encounters difficulty in answering a question and you know he is feeling "dumb," help him by giving hints or cues (Horn, 1976).

54. Devote a day to each student. Everything said about the student should be positive. Invite the parents into class to share the student's baby book and positive stories about him (L. Sahle, personal communication, 1985).

55. Allow students to use hand puppets to act out feelings of low self-esteem. Discuss these feelings with the class (L. Sahle, personal communication, 1985).

56. Have each student write about the person who has the most influence in his life. These stories can be shared with the class or kept private (L. Sahle, personal communication, 1985).

57. Express faith in the student's ability to solve problems (Dinkmeyer, McKay, and Dinkmeyer, 1980).

58. Encourage any sign of progress. Give immediate feedback (Dinkmeyer, McKay, and Dinkmeyer, 1980).

59. Keep spontaneous anecdotal records focusing on the positive observations made of this particular student. At the end of the day, share these observations with the student (Samuels, 1977).

60. Frequently communicate to the student that he is unique and there is nobody in the world like him (Horn, 1976).

61. Have the student look in the mirror and say something positive.

62. Delegate lots of classroom responsibilities to the student such as setting up visual aids or passing out papers (Dial, 1977).

63. Use one-to-one tutorial sessions to enrich academics and promote a positive self-concept (Battle, 1981).

64. Ask the student specific questions that you know he can answer. Frequently ask ques-

tions that have no right or wrong answer (Dial, 1977).

65. Physically demonstrate affection toward the student if that is acceptable to him (Samuels, 1977).

66. Encourage the student to draw pictures of a happy experience (Samuels, 1977).

67. Give the student frequent opportunities to give and receive applause (Horn, 1976).

68. When you correct the student, always tell him specifically what not to do and why. Then give an alternative (Clarke, 1978).

69. Create a "safe" classroom environment, free from ridicule by others (Newman, 1981).

70. Encourage self-reward or self-praise, which may lead to a self-fulfilling prophesy (Crosby, 1982).

71. Solicit the student's suggestions and use them (Survant, 1972).

72. Adopt a positive grading system by writing the number of correct answers on the student's paper rather than the number wrong. Always write encouraging comments (Vankoughnet and Smith, 1969).

73. Set up a bragging session in which students tell how wonderful they are.

74. Use a green pen, rather than red one, and underscore the good things in an assignment (Dial, 1977).

75. Use dance to improve self-esteem. Ethnic dances are particularly helpful, especially if they are from subcultures within the classroom (Trujillo, 1981).

76. Enroll the student in high-adventure activities that help one to overcome fears and personal limitations (e.g., "Outward Bound" programs, scuba diving, cliff climbing).

77. Guide the student through positive imagery activities. Ask him to imagine himself exhibiting desirable personality characteristics (Patrizi, 1982).

78. Give the student a scrapbook in which Polaroid pictures of the student doing some-thing positive are placed (Vankoughnet, 1969).

79. Have the student keep a personal journal in which he may record how he did in various activities in and out of school (Beane, Lipka, and Ludwig, 1980).

80. After each school progress report, ask the student to write a statement about what he has learned, what problems have been encountered and overcome, and what plan of action is next (Beane, Lipka, and Ludwig, 1980).

81. Have a "very important persons" bulletin board. Ask the student to put his life before others by allowing him to design and display past achievements and future aspirations (Campbell, 1981).

82. Put the student's picture on the bulletin board and have each class member write three good things about him under the picture (Dial, 1977).

83. Have the student make a collage about himself. Ask him to cut out pictures, symbols, and words that represent himself (T. Marlier, personal communication, 1984).

84. Expose the student to novels that are oriented toward the development of self-concept. *The Loner* by Ester Wier, for example, enables the reader to identify and relate to the character (Fennimore, 1970).

85. Send a "good news note" home to the student's parents when he is successful (Dial, 1977).

86. Send a "smile-o-gram" to the student which contains compliments (Dial, 1977).

87. Emphasize to the student that he should not be afraid to fail as long as he has given his best effort (K. Westray, personal communication, 1983).

308

Makes Self-Derogatory Remarks

1. Reinforce self-complimenting by the student (J. Bonwell, personal communication, 1984).

2. Ignore self-derogatory remarks (J. Bonwell, personal communication, 1984).

3. Don't require the student to perform in front of others, as it may be promoting the self-depreciating remarks (Biehler, 1974).

4. Whenever possible, point out the learner's success (e.g., "What you've done here is interesting. I like the words you used, and how you did it") (Spivak and Swift, 1975).

5. Assign group projects to insure success (J. Bonwell, personal communication, 1984).

6. Reinforce the student for attempting the task as well as for completing the task (Spivak and Swift, 1975).

7. Use self-instructional materials that provide immediate feedback. This allows the student to correct the work himself without negative evaluation from others (M. Burns, personal communication, 1983).

8. Have the student restate his remark into objective, nondemeaning terms.

9. In a group, have students say positive things about each other. Tell the student to respond by saying, "Thank you."

10. Have the student follow a self-depreciating remark with a remark about something he does well.

11. Provide successful experiences and let the student know that he has succeeded (Biehler, 1974).

12. Convey to the student that school is a place where questions and explorations are encouraged and he doesn't always have to be "right." Model curious and open approaches to problems yourself and let the student know that being willing to ask and seek out assistance is more important than knowing the right answer (Spivak and Swift, 1975).

13. Break assignments into smaller steps so that the student can gain confidence during the ongoing task as the smaller steps are achieved (Reinhart, 1980).

14. Give nongraded pretests before giving the real test so that the student can see progress (Melvin, 1983).

15. A few times each day, ask the student to tell you what he has done well today (Melvin, 1983).

16. Videotape a successful experience for this student and play it back for him. Teach the student to observe and record successes (Spivak and Swift, 1975).

28

Sexual Behavior

309

Boy Acts More Like Girl

1. Recommend counseling.
2. Reinforce behavior typical of a male (Lambley, 1974).
3. Encourage activities appropriate for both sexes in which all students take part (K. Webster, personal communication, 1985).
4. Investigate the possibility of homosexuality or transvestism (Kleinmuntz, 1974).
5. Require participation in activities enjoyed by boys.
6. Accept the behavior.
7. Make the student aware that he may face discrimination in the future.
8. Devise strategies to help the student handle discrimination and negative comments by others.
9. Discuss with the student the reasons for being able to be a "chameleon," who can demonstrate masculine behavior when necessary (e.g., job interviews, dinner parties, etc.).
10. Encourage the student to enroll and participate in groups and activities geared toward the interest of boys.
11. Promote tolerance and acceptance of others within your classroom.
12. If a male role model is not available in the home, encourage enrollment in a Big Brother program.
13. Incorporate male interests into the curriculum (K. Webster, personal communication, 1985).
14. Have the student interview older males to find out what their interests were while in school (N. Mulchrome, personal communication, 1985).
15. Recommend that the student attend a behavioral, emotional, and attitudinal development program that involves obtaining and discussing accurate sex information, and inquiring into and clarifying attitudes about sexual feelings and behavior (Brecher, 1978; Giarretto, 1982).

310

Boy or Girl Crazy

1. Reinforce appropriate interaction with the opposite sex (J. Monge, personal communication, 1983).
2. Isolate the individual and explain why (J. Monge, personal communication, 1983).
3. As the individual interacts appropriately with the opposite sex, allow him or her to have more time to interact with them (J. Monge, personal communication, 1983).
4. Hold a discussion on appropriate interaction with the opposite sex.
5. Teach proper interaction skills and use role playing to practice them.
6. Hold supervised activities to practice newly acquired skills.
7. Have the student sit in front of the room to avoid interaction with other students (B. Merrick, personal communication, 1984).
8. Say something such as, "I personally do not care for this sort of behavior in my room. Please reserve it for elsewhere" (Haas, Kasper, Kryst, and Young, 1982).
9. When this student is not present in class, inform the other students that his or her antics are not appropriate and that their assistance is needed to help control the behavior (Bellafiore and Salend, 1983).
10. Have the student participate in more activities with the same sex (C. Walters, personal communication, 1984).
11. Tell the student that you can appreciate his or her interests but he or she must not interfere with learning or the classroom routine.
12. Recommend that the student attend a behavioral, emotional, and attitudinal development program that involves obtaining and discussing accurate sex information, and inquiring into and clarifying attitudes about sexual feelings and behavior (Brecher, 1978; Giarretto, 1982).

311

Boy Has Gotten Girl Pregnant

1. Encourage the student to continue interacting with the girl to provide support, if both wish this.
2. Teach the student about contraception.
3. Teach the student about fetal development.
4. Teach the student about the female body and its functioning.
5. Teach the student about the male body and its functioning.
6. Discuss implications for the single girl during pregnancy and after birth.
7. Promote responsible sexual behavior through instruction, discussion, and counseling.
8. Have the student talk with never-married females who have given birth to a child.
9. Have the student talk with males who have gotten a girl pregnant. Include those who married the girl and those who did not.
10. Bring in speakers from agencies that deal with teen-age sex and pregnancy.
11. Offer the male adolescent the opportunity for reasoning about sexual issues in non-threatening situations, in particular, community agencies and youth-serving health groups (Chilman, 1980; Foster and Echard, 1978; Scales and Beckstein, 1982).
12. Present a positive attitude toward contraceptives (Scales and Beckstein, 1982).
13. Obtain permission to give formal classroom instruction in sex education (Chilman, 1980).
14. Recommend peer counseling. Appoint peers as leaders in group discussions on sexuality (Scales and Beckstein, 1982).
15. A technique for teaching risk to the "concrete operational" adolescent is the adaptation of games of chance to focus on risk taking on sexual or reproductive issues. Such a strategy uses familiar entertainment with high interest, and is often at a low reading

level (Smith, Wenney, Weinman, and Mumford, 1982).

16. Make the telephone number of the special hotline easily available to the students if they want to ask questions concerning sex (Scales and Beckstein, 1982).

17. Include male participants in rap sessions and counseling sessions that explore feelings concerning abortion. This allows for more responsible decision making concerning pregnancy and abortion (Scales and Beckstein, 1982).

18. Use educational materials such as books, films, newsletters, tapes, and posters that encourage family planning (Scales and Beckstein, 1982).

19. Use role play to have students act as another's antagonist, coach, and feedback source as they practice communicating contraceptive decisions (Schinke, 1981; Schinke, Blythe, and Gilchrist 1981; Schinke, Gilchrist, Smith, and Wong, 1979).

20. Non-macho behaviors should be modeled by adult male staff members (Scales and Beckstein, 1982).

21. Use problem-solving sessions led by an adult leader. During the course of the session the group should come up with ways to deal with the problems, judge the worth and payoff of these options, and plan how to apply selected options in demand situations (Goldfried and Goldfried, 1980; Schinke, Blythe, and Gilchrist, 1981).

22. Encourage the student to become active in a "Community Condom Promotion" (e.g., "Condom Couplet Contest," "Condom Six Pack"). These activities were developed by Planned Parenthood and are held yearly during "National Condom Week" (Scales and Beckstein, 1982).

23. Efforts should be made to conduct father-son workshops, because the father is the most important model of male appropriate behavior. During these workshops, discussions are held about male sexuality, sex roles, and relationships with women (Scales and Beckstein, 1982).

24. Recommend that the student attend a behavioral, emotional, and attitudinal development program that involves obtaining and discussing accurate sex information, and inquiring into and clarifying attitudes about sexual feelings and behavior (Brecher, 1978; Giarretto, 1982).

312
Employs Sexual Talk

1. Increase the amount of attention given to the student when he is using acceptable language (Lawrence and Steed, 1983).

2. Train the student's peers to ignore inappropriate behavior and reinforce appropriate behavior (Bellafiore and Salend, 1983).

3. Ask the student why he feels it necessary to employ sexual talk (Lawrence and Steed, 1983).

4. Point out others who are behaving well (Lawrence and Steed, 1983).

5. Place the student in time-out (Engelhardt, 1983).

6. Wash the student's mouth with soap.

7. Request that the student talk quietly with friends so that others are not offended.

8. Have the student attend counseling sessions with a teacher he prefers (Lawrence and Steed, 1983).

9. Contact the parents to discuss the problem (Lawrence and Steed, 1983).

10. Have the student repeat his statement using appropriate language.

11. Have the student tally the number of sexual remarks made each day. Give a reward if the student decreases this amount.

12. Teach acceptable terminology for nonappropriate sexual terminology.

13. Before class starts, remind the student to monitor his language.

14. Recommend that the student attend a behavioral, emotional, and attitudinal development program that involves obtaining

and discussing accurate sex information, and inquiring into and clarifying attitudes about sexual feelings and behavior (Brecher, 1978; Giarretto, 1982).

which legs, arms, and possibly the torso are exposed when properly attired.

15. Promote weight lifting or other muscle-developing sports.

313
Excessively Modest Regarding One's Body

1. Respect this behavior, especially if it reflects religious values.
2. Praise the student for approximations to the desired behavior.
3. Recommend counseling.
4. Develop a warm, easy-going, accepting climate in the classroom (Friedman, 1980).
5. Promote the development of friendly and positive relationships so that the student feels more comfortable around others (Friedman, 1980).
6. Develop a fitness program for the entire class. Help the students develop a body of which to be proud (Heyn, 1982).
7. Include the student in activities with others who are less modest in hopes that he will model the classmates' behavior.
8. Have boys and girls work in separate groups, as students often feel more at ease with members of their own sex (Friedman, 1980).
9. Pair the student with a close friend. Have them take turns complimenting each other's appearance (Franzoi, 1982).
10. Use drama and role play as often as possible. Allow the student to take on another personality that is less modest.
11. Have the student describe what he wants to be and how he wants to look (Franzoi, 1982).
12. Involve the student in activities that require rolling up one's shirtsleeves or trouser legs.
13. Have the class go "barefoot" for various reasons.
14. Encourage swimming or other sports in

314
Girl Acts More Like Boy

1. Reinforce behavior typical of a female (Lambley, 1974).
2. Recommend counseling.
3. Design activities that segregate the girls from the boys (N. Mulchrone, personal communication, 1985).
4. Seat the student next to feminine girls (N. Mulchrone, personal communication, 1985).
5. Find ways to compliment the student on her appearance regularly (N. Mulchrone, personal communication, 1985).
6. Encourage the student to participate in games such as jacks, jump rope, and hopscotch (N. Mulchrone, personal communication, 1985).
7. Incorporate cooking, sewing, and other activities into the student's curriculum (N. Mulchrone, personal communication. 1985).
8. Have the class conduct parent interviews to find out what their parents enjoyed as youngsters (N. Mulchrone, personal communication, 1985).
9. Encourage group conversation during free time in which other girls will model feminine behavior (N. Mulchrone, personal communication, 1985).
10. Have pupils bring their favorite possessions to school so the student will see what classmates enjoy (N. Mulchrone, personal communication, 1985).
11. Investigate the possibility of homosexuality or transvestism (Kleinmuntz, 1974).
12. Accept the fact that our society is becoming more unisex in orientation.

13. Discuss with the student the reasons for being able to be a "chameleon" who can demonstrate feminine behavior when necessary (e.g., dinner parties, proms, etc.).
14. Recommend that the student attend a behavioral, emotional, and attitudinal development program that involves obtaining and discussing accurate sex information, and inquiring into and clarifying attitudes about sexual feelings and behavior (Brecher, 1978; Giarretto, 1982).

315

Heterosexual Advances on Others

1. Make limitations in your situation clear to the student.
2. Reinforce appropriate heterosexual interaction.
3. Promote modeling by praising other students for appropriate behavior.
4. Provide negative consequences for inappropriate behavior.
5. Increase supervision of this student.
6. Direct the student's attention to more socially accepted behavior (Graubard, 1977).
7. Warn the student when his behavior is becoming inappropriate (E. Smith, personal communication, 1984).
8. Teach proper heterosexual interaction skills.
9. Teach other students how to decline advances in an assertive, polite manner.
10. Prevent in-school interaction with the opposite sex as much as possible.
11. Make continued interaction with the opposite sex dependent on appropriate behavior.
12. Enroll the student in a school that serves students of only one sex.
13. Contact the student's parents to obtain their support (E. Smith, personal communication, 1984).

14. Recommend that the student attend a behavioral, emotional, and attitudinal development program that involves obtaining and discussing accurate sex information, and inquiring into and clarifying attitudes about sexual feelings and behavior (Brecher, 1978; Giarretto, 1982).

316

Homosexual Advances on Others

1. Make limitations for your situation clear to the student.
2. Punish behavior that does not conform to set limits.
3. Reinforce heterosexual interaction.
4. Reinforce typical same-sex interaction behavior (Lambley, 1974).
5. Recommend counseling.
6. Promote modeling by praising other students for appropriate behavior.
7. Warn the student when his behavior is becoming inappropriate (E. Smith, personal communication, 1984).
8. Increase supervision of the student.
9. Direct the student's attention to more socially accepted behavior (Graubard, 1977).
10. Teach other students to decline advances in an assertive, polite manner.
11. Contact the student's parents to obtain their support (E. Smith, personal communication, 1984).
12. Make the student aware that discrimination may be faced in the future due to this behavior.
13. Have the student meet with adult homosexuals to discuss sexuality, lifestyles, proper interaction with others, and so on.
14. Recommend that the student attend a behavioral, emotional, and attitudinal development program that involves obtaining and discussing accurate sex information, and inquiring into and clarifying attitudes

about sexual feelings and behavior (Brecher, 1978; Giarretto, 1982).

317
Masturbates in Public

1. Reinforce appropriate behavior (D. Kirby, personal communication, 1983).
2. Reinforce the student when the target behavior is lower in frequency or duration than previously (Lovitt, 1978).
3. Discuss with the student the proper place to masturbate (D. Kirby, personal communication, 1983).
4. Plan activities that emphasize social skills (D. Kirby, personal communication, 1983).
5. Set up a self-monitoring system in which the student keeps track of how often he masturbates. If the student is aware of the frequency of masturbation, it may decrease the behavior (Murphy and Ross, 1983).
6. Use nonverbal signals to indicate that the behavior must stop (D. Kirby, personal communication, 1983).
7. Determine if clothing is too tight or uncomfortable, or if there might be a rash or physical problem (Worth, 1972).
8. Consider whether the work being given to the student is too difficult. Try to avoid anxiety-producing and tension-causing activities for a period of time (Worth, 1972).
9. Offer the student something, such as paper, pencil, or a book, that must be taken by his preoccupied hand (Worth, 1972).
10. Provide two-handed activities (Worth, 1972).
11. An agreed upon nonverbal signal could be used to remind the student that the behavior is unacceptable at that particular time or place. He can also signal back to you to indicate understanding (D. Kirby and D. Griesemyer, personal communication, 1983).
12. Ask the student to use a less obvious form of masturbation, such as a hand in the lap

or squeezing the thighs together. Continue to decrease the obviousness of the masturbation until the behavior becomes nonexistent.
13. Use projective techniques to elicit expression through visual symbols. For example, art therapy can involve the student in some type of art activity relating to sex, thus illustrating to him that the various parts of the body are related. This gives him an opportunity to channel the energy into some type of art form or activity (Horowitz, 1981).
14. Recommend that the student attend a behavioral, emotional, and attitudinal development program that involves obtaining and discussing accurate sex information, and inquiring into and clarifying attitudes about sexual feelings and behavior (Brecher, 1978; Giarretto, 1982).

318
Overly Interested in Sexual Matters

1. Make the student aware of limitations regarding this behavior in your classroom (R. Schwab, personal communication, 1986).
2. Reinforce adherence to limits set by you (R. Schwab, personal communication, 1986).
3. Administer negative consequences for violation of limits (G. Boudreau, personal communication, 1986).
4. Investigate the possibility of sexual abuse by adults.
5. Teach units on sexuality, reproduction, bodily changes, sex, and so on to inform the student in these areas (B. DiLoretto, personal communication, 1986).
6. Enroll the student in a sex education course (Onyehalu, 1983).
7. Discuss issues of interest to the student (L. DiLoretto, personal communication, 1986).
8. Provide tasteful educational materials on sexual matters for the student to read or

view (V. Condino, personal communication, 1986).

9. Encourage the student to read good literature in which the main characters are involved in developing sexuality (J. Cannon, personal communication, 1986).

10. Encourage the student's parents to speak with their child about sex and sexuality (B. Borsari, personal communication, 1986).

11. Recommend that the student attend a behavioral, emotional, and attitudinal development program that involves obtaining and discussing accurate sex information, and inquiring into and clarifying attitudes about sexual feelings and behavior (Brecher, 1978; Giarretto, 1982).

319

Reads Questionable Sexual Materials

1. Set limitations on materials that may enter your classroom (R. Schwab, personal communication, 1986).

2. Reinforce the student for adhering to the limitations (R. Schwab, personal communication, 1986).

3. Impose negative consequences for violating the classroom limitations (G. Boudreau, personal communication, 1980).

4. Appeal to the student's sense of moral reasoning. The student must learn to judge actions to be good, right, or moral, and others to be bad, wrong, or immoral according to his values or beliefs (Locke, 1983).

5. Calmly mention the discovery of the material, wondering why you had not seen it before. This situation could then provide an excellent opportunity for discussions on sexual function, sexual privacy, growing up and away from the nuclear family, and extra-familial emotional relationships (Paddock, 1981).

6. Investigate whether local stores are selling

these materials to minors. Encourage the stores not to sell questionable literature to minors (P. Gailey, personal communication, 1986).

7. Speak with the student's parents to enlist their assistance (D. Sajdak, personal communication, 1986).

8. Provide tasteful educational materials on sexual matters for the student to read or review (V. Condino, personal communication, 1986).

9. Ask the student why he feels it necessary to read sexual material (Lawrence and Steed, 1983).

10. Contact the parents to discuss the problem (Lawrence and Steed, 1983).

11. Use this material as a motivator for reading assignments (homework only).

12. Teach units on sexuality, reproduction, bodily changes, sex, and so on to inform the student and satisfy curiosity (B. DiLoretto, personal communication, 1986).

13. Use the materials to teach anatomy, sexuality, and so on (B. Covert, personal communication, 1986).

14. Calmly discuss issues of concern to the student (L. DiLoretto, personal communication, 1986).

15. Recommend that the student attend a behavioral, emotional, and attitudinal development program that involves obtaining and discussing accurate sex information, and inquiring into and clarifying attitudes about sexual feelings and behavior (Brecher, 1978; Giarretto, 1982).

320

Sexual Acting-Out (Fondling, Kissing Classmates, Exhibitionism, Sexual Inuendos)

1. Set limitations on sexual behavior in the classroom (R. Schwab, personal communication, 1986).

2. Reinforce adherence to set limits (R. Schwab, personal communication, 1986).

3. Impose negative consequences for violating set limits (G. Boudreau, personal communication, 1986).

4. Ignore the behavior.

5. Draw attention from sexual interests to more appropriate behavior (Behr, Pomeray, and Stewart, 1981).

6. Discuss proper times and places for the acting-out sexual behavior.

7. In a group, discuss whether this behavior is appropriate and what constrictions, if any, should be implemented.

8. Refer the student for counseling (Behr, Pomeray, and Stewart, 1981).

9. Encourage counseling and the teaching of parenting skills for the parents (Behr, Pomeray, and Stewart, 1981).

10. Directly confront the student and ask what should be done about the inappropriate behavior.

11. Discuss with the student how others view this behavior.

12. Recommend that the student attend a behavioral, emotional, and attitudinal development program that involves obtaining and discussing accurate sex information, and inquiring into and clarifying attitudes about sexual feelings and behavior (Brecher, 1978; Giarretto, 1982).

321

Shuns or Avoids Heterosexual Activities

1. Reinforce the student for interacting with members of the opposite sex.

2. Teach interaction skills and topics of conversation (Kilmann, Sabalis, Gearing, Bukstel, and Scavern, 1982).

3. Use role playing to practice skills in heterosexual interaction.

4. Have a socially competent student introduce this student to others and provide support.

5. Design nonthreatening activities that promote interaction with members of the opposite sex (M. Snider, personal communication, 1986).

6. Ask a co-ed group of students to invite this student to join them for an activity.

7. Investigate the possibility that the student is homosexual (Kleinmutz, 1974).

8. Talk with the student to determine the reasons why heterosexual activities are shunned. Devise a plan to overcome these difficulties.

9. If the student possesses a high-level skill, ask that he teach others in a heterosexual group.

10. Require that the student attend a heterosexual event and write a report on it. Try to arrange for positive interaction with others at the event.

11. Evaluate the student's sociosexual history. This history can clarify the reasons for the behavior and how they might affect future sexual relationships (Hartman, MacIntosh, and Engelhart, 1983).

12. Recommend that the student attend a behavioral, emotional, and attitudinal development program that involves obtaining and discussing accurate sex information, and inquiring into and clarifying attitudes about sexual feelings and behavior (Brecher, 1978; Giarretto, 1982).

322

Stares at Pornographic Pictures

1. Inform the student that these pictures are not allowed in school.

2. Reinforce the student for adhering to set limits.

3. Impose negative consequences for failing to obey set limits.

4. Calmly mention the discovery of the material, wondering why you have not seen it before. This situation could then provide an excellent opportunity for discussions on sexual function, sexual privacy, growing up and away from the nuclear family, and extra-familial emotional relationships (Paddock, 1981).

5. Appeal to the student's sense of moral reasoning. He must learn to judge actions to be good, right, moral, bad, wrong or immoral according to his values or beliefs (Locke, 1983).

6. Provide a comprehensive scheme for honest sex education and counseling for students (Onyehalu, 1983).

7. Teach interpersonal and social skills (Kilmann, Sabalis, Gearing, Bukstel, and Scavern, 1982).

8. Inform the class that there will be a notebook or desk check after the next recess. Look directly at the student in question to let him know that he is suspected of having this material and better remove it from the classroom.

9. Confiscate the materials.

10. Have the student place materials in his locker.

11. Recommend desensitization to pornographic pictures with minor electrical shock (Kilmann, Sabalis, Gearing, Bukstel, and Scavern, 1982).

12. Recommend that the student attend a behavioral, emotional, and attitudinal development program that involves obtaining and discussing accurate sex information, and inquiring into and clarifying attitudes about sexual feelings and behavior (Brecher, 1978; Giarretto, 1982).

13. Investigate whether local stores are selling these materials to minors and discourage them from doing so (P. Gailey, personal communication, 1986).

14. Speak with the student's parents to enlist their assistance (D. Sajdak, personal communication, 1986).

15. Provide tasteful educational materials on sexual matters for the student to read or review (V. Condino, personal communication, 1986).

16. Teach units on sexuality, reproduction, bodily changes, sex, and so on to inform the student and satisfy curiosity (B. DiLoretto, personal communication, 1986).

17. Use these materials to teach anatomy, sexuality, and so on (B. Covert, personal communication, 1986).

18. Calmly discuss issues of concern to the student (L. DiLoretto, personal communication, 1986).

323

Too "Touchy"; Likes to Touch Others and Be Hugged

1. Set limits on this behavior for your classroom (R. Schwab, personal communication, 1986).

2. Reinforce adherence to set limits (R. Schwab, personal communication, 1986).

3. Promote good modeling by others by reinforcing their appropriate behavior (Bartz, 1978).

4. Impose negative consequences for failure to obey set limits (G. Boudreau, personal communication, 1986).

5. Interrupt the behavior immediately upon its occurrence (Johnson, 1975).

6. Allow the student to come close to another individual without touching. If touching is necessary, allow the student to touch the other person on their hands or shoulder (V. Serd, personal communication, 1983).

7. Let the student show affection, but supervise it (Heshusuis, 1982).

8. Teach acceptable ways of greeting people, depending on their familiarity (V. Serd, personal communication, 1986).

9. Have the student earn hugs by completing tasks or displaying appropriate behavior

(K. Cowell, personal communication, 1986).

10. Teach others to decline this student's advances by assertively and politely saying, "No."

11. Investigate whether this student feels unloved or has limited affectionate contact at home.

12. If the student feels unloved, assist him in developing relationships and a good self-concept. Be warm and accepting.

13. Obtain a large stuffed animal for the student to hug (K. Cowell, personal communication, 1986).

14. Encourage the parents to purchase a mild-mannered, friendly pet.

15. Recommend that the student attend a behavioral, emotional, and attitudinal development program that involves obtaining and discussing accurate sex information, and inquiring into and clarifying attitudes about sexual feelings and behavior (Brecher, 1978; Giarretto, 1982).

324

Wears Revealing or Provocative Clothing

1. Set limitations on clothing that is worn to school.

2. Reinforce adherence to set limits.

3. Impose negative consequences for failure to obey set limits.

4. Seat the student in an area of the room where he or she is least likely to draw the attention of others.

5. Modify inappropriate dress through a peer-confrontation system. Train the student's peers to ignore inappropriate dress and reinforce appropriate clothing (Bellafiore and Salend, 1983).

6. Ask the student why he or she feels it necessary to wear sexually revealing clothes (Lawrence and Steed, 1983).

7. Have the student meet with the home economics teacher to devise ways to modify the provocative clothing so that it meets school standards.

8. Discuss the appropriateness of various styles of clothing in different types of social situations.

9. Talk with the student's parents to enlist their support in controlling the type of clothing worn to school.

10. Discuss future careers of choice and the type of clothing worn for each.

11. Have the student read *Dress for Success* or *Dress for Success for Women* (P. Barnett, personal communication, 1987).

12. Discuss the image presented to others when wearing sexually provocative clothing.

13. Recommend that the student attend a behavioral, emotional, and attitudinal development program that involves obtaining and discussing accurate sex information, and inquiring into and clarifying attitudes about sexual feelings and behavior (Brecher, 1978; Giarretto, 1982).

29

Unusual or Bizarre Actions and Thoughts

325

Acts as a Nonconformist

1. Reinforce the student for conformist behavior (T. Keeley, personal communication, 1984).

2. Give positive reinforcement to others who display appropriate behavior (J. Camp, personal communication, 1984).

3. When the student is not conforming to school or class policies, remove privileges (T. Keeley, personal communication, 1984).

4. Hold a puppet show that deals with a person who acts as a nonconformist. Make sure the good and bad points are brought out (N. Hammerschmidt, personal communication, 1984).

5. Provide an appropriate peer model and have the two students work together as much as possible (D. Brown, personal communication, 1984).

6. Role play a situation in which one student plays in a disturbing and unusual way.

Then discuss feelings and attitudes (T. Marlier, personal communication, 1984).

7. Have the student present his ideas and views to the class (C. Gingerich, personal communication, 1984).

8. Have the student write an essay on his different ideas (S. LeSage, personal communication, 1984).

9. Explain to the student that this is a positive characteristic, but he must get along with others in school and society, and some conformity is necessary (T. Roth, personal communication, 1984).

10. Respect his individuality, but don't encourage obnoxious behavior (B. Yakos, personal communication, 1984).

11. Compromise with the student on regulations (T. Keeley, personal communication, 1984).

12. Provide specific guidelines for each activity that must be followed (T. Keeley, personal communication, 1984).

13. Allow the student to continue this behavior if it does not violate the rights of others (T. Keeley, personal communication, 1984).

14. Recommend counseling.
15. Accept the behavior as an adolescent search for identity, as long as the rights of others are not violated.
16. Explain to the class how people are different and why that's a good thing.
17. Discuss with your class what would happen if we all had the same physical appearance and interests.
18. Plan units on populations and tribes that have beliefs that are unusual to our culture.
19. Discuss with the student the need to be a "chameleon," so that he can act as a conformist in situations such as job interviews, dinner parties, weddings, and the like.

still hear, and continue to give the direction and demand compliance.
13. Hold up a written sign in front of the student.
14. Tell the class that you will be doing something special in just a minute and that they must fold their hands and listen if they are going to participate. Anyone not listening cannot be allowed to participate because they wouldn't know what to do.
15. Teach about different loud, surprising sounds, such as construction noise, sirens, and the like, so that the student will be less frightened.

326
Covers Ears to Shut Out Sounds

1. Recommend a psychological evaluation.
2. Recommend counseling.
3. Gently assist in lowering the hands and speak calmly and firmly to the student.
4. Reinforce the student when he does not display this behavior.
5. Ignore the behavior.
6. Try humor such as, "Let's all take a break. Everybody cover your ears and rest." Participate also.
7. Give a nonverbal signal to remind him to put his hands down.
8. Give a direct appeal for the student to remove his hands from his ears.
9. Distract the student's attention from the sounds.
10. Touch the student gently to reassure him that you care that something is not right (Byrnes, 1984).
11. Tickle the student to lower the shoulders, arms, or hands.
12. Tell the student that you know that he can

327
Covers or Shuts Eyes or Turns Away to Avoid Seeing

1. Reinforce the student when he does not cover his eyes or turn away (S. Blaha, personal communication, 1985).
2. Ignore the behavior.
3. Praise the other students who do not shut their eyes or turn away (L. Abernethy, personal communication, 1985).
4. Show the student pictures of others engaged with the objects or activities that frighten him (J. Born, personal communication, 1985).
5. Discuss the student's fears with him (S. Blaha, personal communication, 1985).
6. Recommend counseling.
7. Role play situations that the student is afraid in order to show him that it is all right to look (S. Blaha, personal communication, 1985).
8. Prepare the student before the item or activity is presented.
9. Encourage the student to peek periodically.
10. Ask the student to look for at least a count of three.
11. Follow this procedure over a period of time

to desensitize the student: (a) talk about the object/activity, (b) show a black-and-white drawing, (c) show a black-and-white photograph, (d) show a color photograph, (e) show the object from a distance, and (f) have the student move progressively closer.

328

Delusions

1. Reinforce the student when his claims are accurate.
2. Ignore delusional claims.
3. Assist the student in trying to relax (Kleinmuntz, 1974).
4. Confront the student with the absurdity of the present situation (Kleinmuntz, 1974).
5. Provide information to the contrary of the delusion.
6. Ask the student to provide support for his claims.
7. Allow the student to act out his thoughts (Kleinmuntz, 1974).
8. Encourage the student to replace the present thought with another (J. Anderson, personal communication, 1985).
9. Utilize art therapy.
10. Utilize group "theraplay" (Jernberg, 1979).
11. Advise the parents to seek psychiatric treatment for the student (Kleinmuntz, 1974; Slavson, 1952).
12. Advise the parents to seek therapy in order to understand the behavior (Slavson, 1952).
13. Advise the parents to consult a physician for information concerning drug therapy (Kleinmuntz, 1974; Layton, 1982).

329

Does Not Respond When Spoken To; Plays Deaf

1. Recommend hearing testing to be sure that this is not a cause.
2. Reinforce the student when he responds to your verbal statements (Schloss, 1983; McGinnis, Sauerbry, and Nichols, 1985).
3. Impose negative consequences for ignoring you.
4. Provide constant feedback. This helps the student associate personal performance with resulting consequences (Schloss, 1983).
5. Teach small component behaviors, providing frequent opportunities for the student to display these prosocial behaviors (Schloss, Schloss, and Harris, 1984; McGinnis, Sauerbry, and Nichols, 1985).
6. Allow the student to play an active role in generating his own solutions to the problem (Fleming, Ritchie, and Fleming, 1983).
7. Teach the student how to meet people and carry on conversations with others by role playing and interviewing people (Lucas, 1984).
8. Have the student pick a topic about which he knows much, and make a button that invites others to ask about the subject. He must wear the button for one day, around school, at home, and in his neighborhood. Ask him to report on the kinds of questions that were asked and how he answered them (Suid, 1984).
9. Give each member of a group a list of 20 statements about communication. Have each student respond to the questions individually by rating them along a continuum of strongly agree to strongly disagree. Once each student has completed the list, the group must reach a consensus about each statement (McKinney, 1981).
10. Have a friend of the student interpret your words or convey your message to him.

11. Use a friend of the student to act as a translator for both parties if he will not speak to you directly.

12. Use a token system to reward the desired behavior of responding when spoken to (Heward and Orlansky, 1980).

13. Ask the class to withhold attention from that student until he decides to respond (Heward and Orlansky, 1980).

14. If the student does not respond when spoken to, quickly walk away and ignore him until he is ready to communicate (Heward and Orlansky, 1980).

15. Use stories during oral reading periods that require the student to consider behavior. Have him decide how he would respond in the same situation (Payne, Palloway, Smith, and Payne, 1981).

16. Talk to the student and ask him how he would feel if he was faced by others who did not respond to him. Use this as a stimulant for a discussion (C. Rivera, personal communication, 1986).

330

Explosive Unpredictable Behavior

1. Refer the student for psychological testing.

2. Recommend counseling for the student.

3. Reinforce appropriate behavior (L. DiMarzio, personal communication, 1985).

4. Impose negative consequences for exhibiting this behavior.

5. Set clear, firm, consistently enforced rules that are to be followed in the classroom (D. Randall, personal communication, 1985).

6. Relate to the student in a low-key, but resolute manner (Reinhart, 1980).

7. Enroll in a course on physical restraint and interventions for aggressive behavior.

8. Develop a cooperative assistance plan that involves other staff members when this student exhibits the behavior.

9. Empty the classroom of other students if the behavior is dangerous.

10. Be aware of any cues, hints, or signs that indicate that the student is about to "explode." Intervene before the explosive behavior.

11. Teach the student to be aware of signs that indicate that he is about to "explode." Teach him another way of "letting off steam."

12. Play soothing music when the student displays this behavior (Love, 1953; Lindecker, 1954).

13. Use role playing to teach new ways to react to frustration.

14. Remove the student from the situation by placing him in a small and quiet environment without toys or other activities (Johnson and Myklebust, 1967).

15. Give only moderate praise and encouragement to the student. Some students are overstimulated by excessive praise. They may become excited and disintegrate (Johnson and Myklebust, 1967).

16. Recommend family counseling to help the parents and siblings to understand the student's problems and strengths so that they can refocus their relationship (Johnson and Myklebust, 1967).

17. Allow the student to have controlled aggressive activity in play, sports, and therapy sessions. This may permit him to purge the aggressive impulses from his system, thus reducing the aggression in other areas.

18. Provide the student with structure and clearly set limits for classroom behavior and assignments (Turnbull and Schulz, 1979).

19. Tell the student that the behavior is not to be exhibited in your classroom.

20. Identify the problems that are causing this behavior (Nagel and Clement, 1984).

21. Give the student a choice of regaining control by himself or having it imposed by you (Nagel and Clement, 1984).

22. Use the strategies of distraction, redirec-

tion, and humor, either verbally or physically (Nagel and Clement, 1984).

23. Allow the student to release aggression through talking, writing, drawing pictures, puppeting, or other acceptable channels (Nagel and Clement, 1984).

24. Do not attempt to suppress the student's activity by harshness and corporal punishment, as it is not only irrational, but generally futile. The student may be responding to forces outside his control (Kronich, 1969).

25. Give the student direct instruction in social skills (Deshler, Schumaker, and Lenz, 1983).

26. Give the student emotional first aid on the spot. Provide the student with sympathetic understanding, interest, communication, and referee services (Ysseldyke and Algozzine, 1984).

331
Hallucinations

1. Refer the student for a psychological evaluation.

2. Recommend counseling.

3. Ask the psychologist for strategies in dealing with the student when he hallucinates.

4. Allow the student to hug you or a friend for comfort until the hallucinations subside.

5. Check the student's records to determine if this is a reaction to medication. Recommend a medication evaluation if this is suspected.

6. Restrain the student until the hallucinations subside.

7. When the student is not hallucinating, pretend that you see, hear, or sense something. Discuss this reversal of roles and hallucinations (K. Elliott, personal communication, 1983).

8. Give the student a tape recorder and ask him to record the voices he hears. Play the recording back to him later. Discuss the absence of voices (K. Elliott, personal communication, 1983).

9. Ask the student to come to you when hearing, seeing, or smelling imaginary things. Ask him where the stimulation is coming from. If this happens often, he may realize that the stimulation is imaginary (K. Elliott, personal communication, 1983).

10. Ask the student to write about what is heard, seen, or otherwise sensed. A counselor can then analyze the information and look for meanings as to why the student hears the imaginary voices (K. Elliott, personal communication, 1983).

11. Sit with the student until the imaginary voices, sights, or smells are sensed. Discuss the stimulation with him to help him realize that they do not exist (K. Elliott, personal communication, 1983).

12. Record the names of those people heard by the student within a certain episode. Ask the student to point to each individual on the list. Obviously, the student will not be able to find the imaginary people (K. Elliott, personal communication, 1983).

13. Find out if the student is abusing drugs. If so, recommend some type of rehabilitation program (K. Elliott, personal communication, 1983).

14. Give the student earplugs or a blindfold to help him avoid seeing or hearing the hallucinations.

15. Allow the student to work while listening to music through headphones so that hallucinations cannot be "heard."

16. Teach the student a magic word that will make the voices, visions, or smells go away. If the first few attempts don't work, inform the student that it is a matter of finding the correct word. Try again with a different one.

17. Help the student "escape" the hallucinations by leading him to a "safe" corner or room where the hallucinations cannot enter.

332

Laughs or Talks to Self

1. Reinforce quiet behavior.
2. Impose negative consequences for talking out.
3. Ignore the behavior if it is nondisruptive and seems to assist the student in attending to task.
4. Recommend a psychological evaluation.
5. Ask the psychologist or psychiatrist for strategies for dealing with this behavior.
6. Tape record the talking or laughing to make the student aware of the behavior.
7. Check the student's records to determine if this might be a reaction to medication. If this is a possibility, recommend a medication reevaluation.
8. Count the number of episodes daily. Reinforce the student for lowering the daily count.
9. Use role playing to teach quiet behavior (Kerr and Nelson, 1983).
10. Give an agreed upon nonverbal signal to remind the student to be quiet.
11. Have a friendly peer remind the student to be quiet.
12. Place the student in a cubicle off to one side of the room so that his laughing and talking will not be disruptive to the rest of the class (C. Walters, personal communication, 1985).
13. Implement the daily report card program. The behavior is written on a card and each day the student is rated by you on his behavior. At the end of each day, the card is sent home to the parents. The parents are asked to compliment for good behavior and address areas needing improvement. If a card is lost, all ratings are considered poor (Cohen, Millman, and Schaefer, 1981).
14. With permission from all necessary parties and the student's cooperation, place tape over his mouth.

333

Reality Distortion

1. Reinforce the student for accurate perceptions of the environment.
2. Recommend a psychological evaluation.
3. Recommend counseling.
4. Recommend the use of medication to control the distortion.
5. Recommend a reevaluation of the student's medication.
6. Determine if the student is abusing drugs.
7. Inform the student that his perceptions are incorrect.
8. Confront the student with the absurdity of the present situation (Kleinmuntz, 1974).
9. Provide evidence to the contrary of the distortion.
10. Recommend art therapy.
11. Recommend group "theraplay" (Jernberg, 1979).
12. Have someone the student trusts tell him that he is incorrect.

334

Recent Sudden Change in General Behavior

1. Reinforce the student when he acts appropriately (Dinkmeyer, McKay, and Dinkmeyer, 1980).
2. Provide negative consequences for undesirable behavior.
3. Show compassion and avoid seeking revenge for a displayed behavior (Dinkmeyer, McKay, and Dinkmeyer, 1980).
4. Accept this as a typical adolescent behavior indicating a search for identity.
5. Warn the student when actions are about to get out of bounds (Reinhart, 1980).
6. Recommend a psychological evaluation.
7. Recommend counseling.

8. Place the student in time-out if the behavior becomes too aggressive or disruptive (Reinhart, 1980).

9. Contact the student's parents to determine if a recent event or circumstance may be responsible for this behavior.

10. Observe and record the behavior and have a conference with the student about this behavior (Redl, 1954).

11. Have a morning conference with the student before he starts classes to discuss and diffuse any problems.

12. Investigate the possibility of drug abuse.

335

Ritualistic Behavior

1. Reinforce the student when he avoids going through his "routine" or compulsive behavior.

2. Impose negative consequences for the demonstration of ritualistic behavior.

3. Accept the ritual as an anxiety-relieving device (Kessler, 1972).

4. Recommend a psychological evaluation.

5. Recommend counseling (Biehler, 1974).

6. Discuss the behavior with the student. Ask why it is needed and whether it can be eliminated.

7. Ask the student to omit one part of his ritual. Periodically encourage him to eliminate another step.

8. Have another person perform the ritual for him to remove his presence from the behavior.

9. Have a friend encourage and provide support for the student as he avoids the ritualistic behavior.

10. List situations that produce ritualistic behaviors and grade them according to stimulus value. Present the mildest situation first and prevent the student's ritualistic behavior. Later, focus on more severe situations (Stanley, 1980).

11. After having the student refrain from the ritualistic behavior, discuss whether anything undesirable happened.

12. Ask the student to use a less involved ritual in place of the present one.

13. Use overcorrection to reduce the ritualistic behavior. The student is required to display the behavior until he tires of it and begins to dislike it (Luiselli and Michaud, 1983).

336

Rocking

1. Reinforce the student for refraining from rocking.

2. Administer nonphysical negative consequences for rocking (Watters and Watters, 1980).

3. Use physical punishment to reduce rocking (Harris and Wolchick, 1979).

4. Require the student to practice proper sitting when he displays rocking (Martin, Matson, and Ollendick, 1979).

5. Reinforce an incompatible behavior to eliminate body rocking by substituting the new behavior for the undesired one (Watters and Watters, 1980).

6. Immediately following the onset of an episode of body rocking, sternly say, "No body rocking," and then turn away from the student for 10 seconds. After the 10 seconds, turn back toward him to continue the task. If he is sitting quietly, give him reinforcement. If he is engaged in self-stimulatory behavior, repeat the time-out (Harris and Wolchik, 1979).

7. Hold exercise sessions. There is often a decrease in body rocking following exercise (Watters and Watters, 1980).

8. Arrange for trips. There is often a decrease in self-stimulatory behavior following field trips and outside excursions (Watters and Watters, 1980).

9. Recommend medication. Haloperidol administered in conservative doses is effec-

tive in reducing body rocking (Anderson, Campbell, Caplan, Perry, and Small, 1982).

10. Use differential reinforcement of other behaviors.

11. Decrease the magnitude of the rocking by attaching a "leash" which prevents an extended forward lean.

12. Startle the student, causing him to stop rocking. After a few seconds, reinforce him for not rocking.

13. Hold the shoulder of the student and say, "No rocking." Release the shoulders after one or two seconds. Restart the activity if rocking has stopped. If not, repeat the procedure.

337
Tells Untrue or Exaggerated Stories

1. Reinforce accurate or believable story telling (Blackman and Silberman, 1980).

2. Impose negative consequences for lying (Blackman and Silberman, 1980).

3. Ignore the student's claims (Blackman and Silberman, 1980).

4. Place the student in time-out.

5. Ask the student to prove the truthfulness of his story (S. Coad, personal communication, 1984).

6. Disprove the student's story (S. Coad, personal communication, 1984).

7. Say, "No, that's not true. Case closed." (L. Fearington, personal communication, 1984).

8. Read and discuss *The Boy Who Cried "Wolf"* or *Pinnochio*.

9. Channel the student's imagination to writing a creative story, drawing a picture, or building something out of clay (S. Coad, personal communication, 1984).

10. Discuss lying and the deception of others.

11. If the student's story is creative, tell him so, but explain that now is not the time for stories (L. Fearington, personal communication, 1984).

12. Have others tell stories. Have the student identify those that are exaggerated.

13. Record the student's story. Replay it. Have him raise one finger when he hears a fact and two fingers when he hears fiction (V. Croll, personal communication, 1983).

14. Devise class activities for fact-opinion and fact-fantasy discrimination (V. Croll, personal communication, 1983).

15. With the student, analyze "tall tales" as to what constitutes deviation from the truth (V. Croll, personal communication, 1983).

16. Introduce and discuss examples of literature that use fantasy (V. Croll, personal communication, 1983).

17. Have the student keep a log of his thoughts. At the end of the day, review the log with the student. Indicate which thoughts are fantasy and which are fact (V. Croll, personal communication, 1983).

18. During creative writing sessions, encourage the student to write stories using fantasy. When the story is read aloud, hold a class discussion about fiction, fantasy, nonfiction, and fact (V. Croll, personal communication, 1983).

19. Have a news program activity with a daily feature story entitled "Truth Is Stranger Than Fiction" (V. Croll, personal communication, 1983).

338
Unusual or Bizarre Behaviors

1. Warn the student when his behavior does not meet your standards (Williams, 1983).

2. Reinforce the student when he shows appropriate behavior (K. Schmitt, personal communication, 1985).

3. Impose negative consequences for the behavior.

4. Recommend a psychological evaluation.

5. Recommend counseling.

6. Place the student in a time-out (French, 1985).

7. Talk with the student and let him know that you are concerned about his behavior and want to help (K. Schmitt, personal communication, 1985).

8. Ignore temporary behaviors and work on the permanent odd or bizarre behaviors (Williams, 1983).

9. Determine if the student is falling behind in school or in any academic area. This may cause a change in behavior (K. Schmitt, personal communication, 1985).

10. Talk with the parents of the student to determine if he exhibits this behavior at home. An inappropriate behavior may be caused by poor family relationships or a change in the family structure (e.g., death, divorce, or moving) (McGee, 1984).

339

Unusual or Bizarre Thoughts or Fantasies

1. Reinforce the student for reality-based thoughts (S. Winkler, personal communication, 1984).

2. Ignore the student when he fantasizes (S. Winkler, personal communication, 1984).

3. Remove the activity when the student fantasizes (S. Winkler, personal communication, 1984).

4. Increase your positive interactions with the student (Sprick, 1982).

5. Recommend a psychological evaluation.

6. Recommend counseling (Sprick, 1982).

7. Interrupt the fantasy by calling the student's name (Blanco, 1972).

8. Stand near the student and touch him often to regain his attention (Blanco, 1972).

9. Ask the student to recite or contribute often (Blanco, 1972).

10. Change the topic when the student starts to fantasize.

11. Use a noncommittal response. Do not sound like you believe the fantasy, but do not criticize his thought patterns either (Sprick, 1982).

12. Allow an outlet for fantasy and creativity. Keeping a journal, drawing pictures, or making tape recordings might be good releases (Sprick, 1982).

13. Channel fantasies into constructive work such as creative writing (Blanco, 1972).

14. Plan more active participation activities such as group discussions, art, music, and physical education (Blanco, 1972).

15. Talk to the student to determine something about the theme of the fantasy (Blanco, 1972).

16. Discuss the fantasies with the student and compare them with reality.

17. Have the student tell the most unusual story possible. Then have him make it as realistic as possible.

18. Appoint an easy-going, friendly peer to be a partner to the student and to draw him into classroom reality (Blanco, 1972).

19. Provide tasks that require keen attention such as puzzles, speed tests, memorizing riddles and poems, taking notes, and correcting tests (Blanco, 1972).

20. Talk to the family to determine if there are any situations at home that may be causing the difficulty (Blanco, 1972).

340

Wears Unusual Clothing Styles

1. Reinforce the student on days when he is not dressed in an unusual manner (L. DiMarzio, personal communication, 1985).

2. Conduct a personal health and grooming unit (B. Tankersley, personal communication, 1985).

3. Have a fashion-knowledgeable person speak to your class (B. Tankersley, personal communication, 1985).

4. Talk to the student about times when this type of clothing would be improper (e.g., job interviews, dinner parties) (D. Randall, personal communication, 1985).

5. Talk to the parents to gain their assistance in sending the student to school in more acceptable clothing (D. Randall, personal communication, 1985).

6. Investigate the possibility that the family is poor and cannot afford other clothing.

7. Allow the student to continue the undesirable dress until he tires of it (Krumboltz and Krumboltz, 1972).

8. If the clothing is violating the school dress code, talk to your administrators (D. Randall, personal communication, 1985).

9. Set limits on the type of clothing that is acceptable in school.

10. If the unusual clothing is a reflection of a search for identity or identification with a certain lifestyle, be more accepting or work out a compromise with the student.

11. If the dress is reflective of the student's cultural background, conduct class discussions on the derivation of the dress and pride in one's culture.

12. Hold special days when students and teachers dress in a certain manner (e.g., semi-formal, sloppy, etc.).

13. Assist the student in differentiating between fad, fashion, and style.

14. Review the book *Dress for Success* with the student.

15. Have the student meet with the home economics teacher to devise ways to restyle the clothing.

341
Weird Drawings

1. Reinforce the student for drawings that meet stated expectations.

2. Have the student revise unacceptable artwork.

3. Have the student participate in a small group that draws one drawing (Fucigna, Ives, and Ives, 1982).

4. Sit with the student and draw with him (Fucigna, Ives, and Ives, 1982).

5. Talk with the student about his drawings. Find out what they represent (S. Blaha, personal communication, 1985).

6. Ask the student to draw about something he enjoys or loves (S. Blaha, personal communication, 1985).

7. Ask the student to write a short paragraph about his drawing (S. Blaha, personal communication, 1985).

8. Ignore the drawings. They might be a phase the student is going through (L. Abernethy, personal communication, 1985).

9. Compare the student's drawings to see if they have a similar theme (J. Born, personal communication, 1985).

10. Have each of the students go to the front of the class and tell about their drawings (R. Jones, personal communication, 1985).

11. Display student drawings around the room (R. Jones, personal communication, 1985).

12. Ask classmates to rate drawings in a number of categories, such as realism, precision, use of color, originality, and so on.

13. Require the student periodically to draw everyday fixtures, such as staircases, boxes, and chairs. Rate the student on accuracy.

14. Ask the student to draw the same concept in two different ways—his preferred way and your preferred way.

15. If the drawings appear to be a reflection of emotional difficulties, refer the student for psychological testing.

16. Teach the student about various types of art. Have him practice drawing each type.

30

Withdrawn or Overinhibited Behavior

342

Avoids Eye Contact

1. Reinforce the student for eye contact (Hartman, Lucas, and Stephens, 1982).

2. Accept the behavior if avoidance of eye contact is a cultural trait showing respect for a superior. This trait is evident in some Black and Hispanic cultures.

3. Teach the student to be a "chameleon" so that he gives eye contact while in school, but maintains this cultural trait at home.

4. Remind the student to give you eye contact (M. Burns, personal communication, 1983).

5. Have the student practice by talking to a poster of a famous face.

6. Encourage the student to maintain eye contact with others.

7. Use positive facial expressions when the student looks at you (Spivak and Swift, 1975).

8. Whenever the student looks at your face, smile or wink for reinforcement (J. Bonwell, personal communication, 1985).

9. Establish a stronger relationship with the student (Spivak and Swift, 1975).

10. Tell the student about a "secret" upcoming activity. Tell him that you will notify him with a wink to do the part that he was trained to present. The student will have to watch your eyes to detect the signal (Spivak and Swift, 1975).

11. Model eye contact by looking at others during direction giving or conversation (M. Burns, personal communication, 1983).

12. Bend down or move into the student's line of sight to gain eye contact (G. Heleine, personal communication, 1983).

13. Physically lift the student's chin with a light touch (G. Heleine, personal communication, 1983).

14. Provide the student with a visually stimulating sight to view by pasting a star to your nose or wearing a mask (G. Heleine, personal communication, 1983).

15. Write a word on each eyelid. Have the student read them before you open your eyes.

16. Compliment the student's eyes (G. Heleine, personal communication, 1983).

17. Play games that encourage eye contact (Hass, Kasper, and Kryst, 1979).

18. Play "Owl." In this game, two players look at each other. The first to avert their gaze from the eyes of the other loses.

19. Have the student look at a puppet while talking to it. Bring the puppet progressively closer to your face.

20. Have the student use a stopwatch to record the total amount of time that your eyes or the eyes of a peer are open. To do this, he must watch the eyes.

21. In a group of three, have the student call out the name of the person who has just opened his eyes that were closed. He must continually scan the other two faces, watching for eyes to open.

343

Difficult to Get to Know

1. Reinforce the student for interacting with others (C. Ritz, personal communication, 1985).

2. Observe the student during interaction with others to find out if it is the student or the others that inhibit friendship building (B. Yakos, personal communication, 1985).

3. Give the student an interest inventory to complete. Use these interests as topics of conversation (C. Ritz, personal communication, 1985).

4. Have others and yourself study an area of the student's interest. Discuss this topic.

5. Display the student's work for others to see (Fuller, 1984).

6. Talk with the student for five minutes each day and really listen to what he has to say (Fuller, 1984).

7. Hold a show-and-tell session. Have the student bring something to tell about so that he will start to interact with other students and you can find out more about him (C. Ritz, personal communication, 1985).

8. Ask the student for his opinion about subjects or issues (Fuller, 1984).

9. Have each student give a report about himself (C. Ritz, personal communication, 1985).

10. Have the class write autobiographies to share with others.

11. Assign many cooperative tasks.

12. Give multiple-choice questions on food preferences, play preferences, world views, and so on. Have the students compare and discuss their answers.

344

Does Not Engage in Group Activities

1. Encourage parallel activities. From parallel play, the student can often be involved slowly in a more active role in group activities (Reinhart, 1980).

2. Recommend counseling (J. Steele, personal communication, 1985).

3. Reinforce the student anytime he participates in group activities (Harris and Brown, 1981).

4. Allow the withdrawn student to care for pets in the classroom. Often students can relate to pets before relationships with people are possible (Reinhart, 1980).

5. Discuss unity and group importance. Focus on the concepts of working as a group to accomplish a goal (Kasda, 1980).

6. Allow physical involvement to replace verbal involvement in the beginning. For example, the student might hold the chart for the group in order to be involved at least peripherally (Reinhart, 1980).

7. In group assignments decide what work needs to be done by each member. Make certain that every member and his work are needed to complete the assignment (Kasda, 1980).

8. Encourage open, understanding, and

friendly classmates to approach the student with an offer of friendship (J. Steele, personal communication, 1985).

9. Arrange the physical environment in such a way that the student feels as comfortable as possible. Seat the student by a favorite friend (J. Steele, personal communication, 1985).

10. Read stories of accomplishments done by people who worked together (Kasda, 1980).

11. Encourage puppetry. Insure that at first only the puppet is visible. When appropriate, increase group size, visibility of student, length of puppet show, and so on (J. Steele, personal communication, 1985).

12. Use drama therapy in which the timid student is given an especially extroverted and assertive part in contrast to his normal introverted or nonassertive demeanor (Lowenstein, 1982).

13. Enroll the student in an assertiveness training class (J. Steele, personal communication, 1985).

14. Use cue-controlled relaxation. Progressive relaxation training techniques are taught first. The next step involves repeated pairings of an imaginal cue word, such as *calm*, with the relaxed muscular state. Use this cue word as the student interacts with an assigned group (McGlynn, Bichajian, Giesen, and Rose, 1981).

15. Require the student to participate in group activities (Lowenstein, 1982).

16. Ask the student to befriend others who could use a friend.

17. Stand near the student to provide support and security during group activities. Gradually distance yourself from the group.

345

Overly Pliant; Does Not Stand Up for Rights

1. Reinforce the student when he does support his views and rights (J. Mette, personal communication, 1984).

2. Tell the student that his opinion does matter to you (J. Mette, personal communication, 1984).

3. Assign the student to a panel that has to defend its position on an issue to other members of the class (J. Mette, personal communication, 1984).

4. Institute sharing times to make the student feel comfortable in speaking to others (J. Mette, personal communication, 1984).

5. Assign each class member to give a persuasive speech to influence the opinions of the audience (J. Mette, personal communication, 1984).

6. Use role playing to develop assertiveness skills.

7. Modify activities from adult books on being assertive.

8. Teach debating skills and hold a debate.

9. Have the student play a part in a trial reenactment or play, such as *To Kill a Mockingbird*, where he can be an influential, assertive lawyer.

10. After an incident in which the student was overly pliant, have him role play or write a more assertive response.

11. Have the student give his more assertive response later in a discussion of the event.

12. Serve as an intermediary in situations where the student is being pliant. Ask him for his opinions and feelings.

13. Have the student prepare his views for an upcoming confrontation or discussion.

346

Shyness

1. Praise the student for interaction with others.

2. If nonthreatening, call on the student as much as possible to involve him in class discussions.

3. Discuss this student with peers. Emphasize the importance of making him feel accepted

(K. Szumlas, personal correspondence, 1983).

4. Have the student practice initial social encounters that deal with the proper ways of meeting adults during initial social encounters (Newcomb and Meister, 1985).

5. Encourage adults and peers to say hello and include the shy student in activities.

6. Have the student tutor a student in a lower grade (Stipek and Tannat, 1984; Mercer, 1985).

7. Pair the student with another and send them on a treasure hunt (Upton, 1980).

8. Divide the class into pairs. Provide each group with a situation that does not have a conclusion. Require each group to come up with a conclusion. This may develop decision-making skills and decrease shyness (Evers-Pasquale and Sherman, 1975).

9. Provide the student with an objective description of any progress he has made, such as the ability to do something he was not able to do before (Johnson, 1956).

10. Help the student when you feel he needs help. This may avoid traumatic failure experiences and decrease the shyness (Johnson, 1956).

11. Point out how much fun the student will have if he joined others and played with them.

12. Place the student with others who are eager to play with him.

13. Encourage parallel play, having the student play beside others, to encourage later group play (Cammer, 1969).

14. Form study groups of two students to encourage working with others (Lancoini, 1982; Mercer and Mercer, 1985).

15. Encourage the student to view videotapes consisting of social interactions among students his age. Include a sound track that describes the thoughts of the student model moving from solitary play to active participation with his peers (e.g., "My name is Dave. I'm sitting here by myself, but I'd love to play with those kids. I'm afraid to," etc.) (Jakibchuk and Smeriglio, 1976).

16. Place the student's desk near others. Physical isolation should be avoided (Blanco, 1972).

17. Use music to motivate the student to participate with others. This might include group choral reading, clapping echo games, or group singing (Upton, 1980).

18. Assign students to work in groups to develop interview questions for a guest speaker (Petty, Petty, and Becking, 1981).

19. Assist the students in your class in forming a club based on their interests. Teach them the basic elements of parliamentary procedure. Involve all the students in the planning and process of creating the group and development of club activities (Petty, Petty, and Becking, 1981).

20. Hold a debate. Groups conduct research for the debate. Students are then chosen from each group to represent various positions on an issue (Petty, Petty, and Becking, 1981).

21. Give the student some type of special activity on which to work, such as a plant to nurture and share with others (Lancoini, 1982).

22. Give the student responsibility such as taking the attendance (Johnson, 1956).

23. Send the student on errands that require verbal communication.

24. Encourage all students to participate in show and tell. Provide a specific time for this and encourage students to bring in unique items to discuss (Petty, Petty, and Becking, 1981).

25. Give the student particular jobs in the classroom that involve association with all students (J. Bonwell, personal communication, 1985).

26. Have the student take a turn as leader for charades or captain for a team.

27. Promote interaction with pets (Reinhart, 1980).

28. Train peers in interaction overtures. En-

courage them to "try to get the other student to play with you" (Kerr and Strain, 1978).

29. Have the student set interaction goals. Monitor progress (Orr, 1981).

30. Arrange the environment to encourage the student to have contact with his peers (Johnson, 1956).

31. Hold a class discussion on a topic in which the student is interested (Newcomb and Meister, 1985).

32. Form a small "assertiveness training" group with shy and withdrawn students. Practice with them regarding how to get their ideas across to other students. Stress looking at others.

347

Tries Not to Call Attention to Self

1. Compliment the student regularly (N. Mulchrone, personal communication, 1985).

2. Encourage and reward contributions to discussions (Bornstein, Bellack, and Hersen, 1977).

3. Reinforce the student for talking to classmates at recess (Harris and Brown, 1981).

4. Reinforce the student for playing a group game (Harris and Brown, 1981).

5. Encourage the student to talk to his parents (Harris and Brown, 1981).

6. Encourage the student to talk to you (Harris and Brown, 1981).

7. Prepare the student to answer an upcoming question.

8. Reinforce the student for attempting to answer a question in class (N. Mulcrone, personal communication, 1985).

9. Design a group activity involving videotaping (Conger and Keane, 1981).

10. Prepare the student for an upcoming event that is mildly threatening (e.g., line leader, team captain).

11. Design activities that require all to participate.

12. Nonverbally reinforce eye contact with the student in situations where he used to avoid your glance for fear of being called upon.

13. Use the "round-robin" method of choosing students during oral reading.

14. Have the student participate in puppetry. Gradually expose him more to others during lengthier parts.

15. Allow the student to wear a mask during a play presentation.

348

Unemotional; Does Not Show Strong Feelings

1. Reinforce the student when he displays emotionality.

2. Encourage the student to identify with a sports team to cheer their victories and sorrow their losses.

3. Provide an accepting, secure environment. Let the student know that the environment is safe and that he can be open with his feelings (Wagner, 1974; Jones, 1980).

4. Bring students into the outdoors. The outdoors is a place to begin inquiry. Perhaps this involvement will bring out emotion in the student (Bain, 1979).

5. Incorporate the student's interest to help make activities more interesting, therefore increasing his input (D. Otto, personal communication, 1983).

6. Animals have a tendency to bring out the sentimentality of people. A science project involving animals might be useful (C. Young and D. Otto, personal communication, 1983).

7. Have the student portray the part of an emotional person in a play (C. Young and D. Otto, personal communication, 1983).

8. Teach methods of expression. Give exam-

ples of and model different types of expression (e.g., verbal, nonverbal, written, and body language) (Dittman, 1972).

9. Stress the importance of expressing feelings in an appropriate manner (Wagner, 1974).

10. Have the student act out different emotions. Have him act out both acceptable and not so acceptable ways of expression. This gives him a chance to see how others feel (Strayhorn, 1977; Wagner, 1979; Spence, 1983).

11. Have different hats or badges with emotions written or symbolized with faces on them. Students wear these hats or badges to identify how they feel.

12. Give hypothetical situations in which a person is involved (e.g., being hit by another, receiving a gift). Ask the student how that person would feel in that situation.

13. Practice "I messages." Some examples are, "I can see that : . . ," "I feel that . . . ," and "I like it when . . . ." These give the student an opportunity to state exact feelings (T. Keeley, personal communication, 1984).

14. Discuss real issues. Bring in topics that the student finds interesting. Discuss them indepth and talk about the feelings that are being brought out (Strayhorn, 1977).

15. For projects, pair the individual who is more reserved with a peer who is more outgoing (Spencer, 1983).

16. After having given a situation, have the student identify a variety of responses, predict the outcomes of each, and select the best response (Spence, 1983).

17. Identify emotions for the student (e.g., "You sound sad").

18. Identify appropriate emotions for each situation (e.g., "That would have made me very angry").

19. Discuss appropriate as well as inappropriate ways to show one's specific emotions. Talk about why one way is more appropriate than the other (Strayhorn, 1977).

349

Unimaginative Play

1. Reinforce the student when he uses his imagination.

2. Use Viola Brody's Developmental Play process, which introduces the use of physical contact, physical control, and singing in small groups. The environment is structured and predictable. Materials are made available and understandable to the student (Knoblock, 1983).

3. Use outdoor play situations to help lessen the pressures on students, which often result from living under crowded conditions. Outdoor play also offers many opportunities for physical activity, exploring, discovering, and learning (Leeper, Dales, Skipper, and Witherspoon, 1974).

4. Incorporate imitative activities into play. These include the imitations of actions or movements of another, an animal, or a machine. Initiate the activity by saying something like, "Show me how you would fly if you were a bird" (Leeper, Dales, Skipper, and Witherspoon, 1974).

5. Use puppetry to allow the student to be creative (Hyde, 1971).

6. Supply open-ended toys that can be used in many ways, allowing for more creative play. These include dress-up clothes, blocks of assorted sizes and shapes, sand, and water (Phi Delta Kappa, 1982).

7. Recommend or implement play therapy.

8. Be a model for playfulness (Phi Delta Kappa, 1982).

9. Play with your students. By playing with students, you are better able to help select appropriate props or play materials for them (Phi Delta Kappa, 1982).

10. Support the student's play. Praise the way he uses materials and comment on the roles he has assumed (Phi Delta Kappa, 1982).

11. Encourage students to pretend (Phi Delta Kappa, 1982).

12. Encourage students to talk about their play (Phi Delta Kappa, 1982).
13. Have a game with only a few rules. For example, form two teams. One point is scored when the bean bag is entered into the can, and no physical contact with others. Have teams plan their strategies before the start of each game.
14. Have the student try to catch a frisbee or ball in different ways.
15. Encourage students to cheat in a game.
16. Have a group of students brainstorm on a play problem (e.g., how to get all of their team from one line to another with the fewest number of total team footsteps).
17. Have the student change some rules for a popular recess game and teach others how to play the new version.

350

Withdrawn

1. When the student does well, mention that fact, but group his name with the names of others (C. Young, personal correspondence, 1983).
2. Reinforce any responsive behavior (Blanco, 1972; Lancioni, 1982).
3. Recommend counseling (Kaczmarek, 1980).
4. Provide as much individual attention as possible to the student (Swap, 1974).
5. Place the student's desk near others. Physical isolation should be avoided (Blanco, 1972).
6. Give the student a token for each question to which he verbally responds. Tokens can be traded for objects of the student's choice (Durlak and Mannarino, 1977).
7. Arrange the environment to encourage the student to have contact with his peers (Johnson, 1956).
8. Seat the student in the center of classroom (Freberg, 1982).
9. Look at the classroom seating chart and seek situations that afford the withdrawn student better interpersonal relationships (Seif and Atkin, 1979).
10. Surround the withdrawn student with students who have pleasant personalities (Gerson and Perlma, 1979).
11. In group activities allow the student to sit where he feels most comfortable (Freberg, 1982).
12. Ignore the withdrawn student when he is alone. Give him immediate attention when he initiates interaction with peers (Allen, Hart, Buell, Harris, and Wolf, 1964).
13. Seat the withdrawn student near others of similar interest, as this will allow him to work within a small group. Then add more loquacious students to the group from time to time to "liven it up" (DeVillis, McEvoy, and McCauley, 1978).
14. Try to have the withdrawn student seated near the lower population density or within subgroups, which will temper larger groups (Baum and Aiello, 1978).
15. Let the student practice his answers at home prior to school and give you his list of "ready" answers (Blanco, 1972).
16. Have the student express himself in writing and drawings (Blanco, 1972).
17. Encourage all students to participate in show-and-tell. Provide a specific time for this and encourage students to bring in unique items to discuss (Petty, Petty, and Becking, 1981).
18. Give the student particular jobs in the classroom that involve association with other students in the classroom (J. Bonwell, personal communication, 1985).
19. Have the student take a turn as leader for charades or captain for a team.
20. Give the student some type of special activity on which to work, such as nurturing a plant and sharing with others (Lancioni, 1982).
21. Allow the student to be the teacher's helper in order to involve him (Bertilson, Wonderlich, and Blum, 1983).

22. Give the student responsibility, such as taking the attendance (Johnson, 1956).

23. Send the student on an errand that requires verbal communication.

24. Encourage the withdrawn student to use a tape recorder when he feels like talking. Tell him that if he would like to share it with you, you will be glad to listen. Respond on tape if the student prefers (Mercer and Mercer, 1985).

25. Be sure that the student is not placed in a social situation where the effort required is very high and the chance of failure is very great (Lancioni, 1982).

26. Find areas or activities in which the student feels secure enough to participate (Johnson, 1956).

27. Hold a class discussion on a topic in which the student is interested (Newcomb and Meister, 1985).

28. In discussions, call on the student by name to participate. If he does not respond, help him along by starting to express the answer. Ask him to finish (Myer, 1980).

29. If nonthreatening, call on the student as much as possible to involve him in class discussions.

30. Have each student list activities that he enjoys. Ask them to list things that they would like to learn. Pair the students according to their interests and have them discuss these lists and share them with the class (Smuin, 1978).

31. Involve the student in a puppet show. This may make it easier for the student to express himself (Hammill and Bartel, 1975).

32. Get the student involved in extracurricular activities.

33. When playing a game, assign players into teams. Avoid having the student who is withdrawn being placed last.

34. Form a small "assertiveness training" group with withdrawn students. Practice with them how to get their ideas across to others. Stress looking at others when talking to them. Encourage talking in a loud firm voice and making gestures when appropriate. Have the group role play with each other such behaviors as greeting others and carrying on conversations. Record on a cumulative chart the times they made suggestions and the times their suggestions were accepted. As soon as all the students reach a certain point on the chart, reward the whole group (Hartman, Lucas, and Stephens, 1982).

35. Pair the withdrawn student with one who engages in frequent peer contact (Hendrickson, Strain, and Tremblay, 1980).

36. Team the withdrawn student with a partner to work in a one-on-one relationship (Newcomb and Meister, 1985).

37. Discuss this student with peers. Emphasize the importance of making him feel accepted (K. Szumlas, personal correspondence, 1983).

38. Have the student practice initial social encounters that deal with the proper ways of meeting adults (Newcomb and Meister, 1985).

39. Have the withdrawn student participate in scripted activities that strengthen weak social skills (Newcomb and Meister, 1985).

40. Have students take turns recording relevant oral contributions. Each time a student contributes, he earns points. No contribution would equal a grade of C. One point would bring up the grade to a C+, and more points would raise the grade accordingly (Smith, Schumaker, Schaeffer, and Sherman, 1982).

41. Make the student's grade contingent on participation (Smith, Schumaker, Schaeffer, and Sherman, 1982).

42. Have a socially outgoing peer tutor the withdrawn student (Lazerson, 1978; Gleissner, Nietupski, and Stainback, 1983; Mercer and Mercer, 1985).

43. Have the student tutor a pupil in a lower grade (Stipek and Tannat, 1984; Mercer and Mercer, 1985).

44. Pair the student with another and send them on a treasure hunt (Upton, 1980).

45. Divide the class into pairs. Provide each group with a situation that does not have a conclusion. Require each group to come up with a conclusion. This may develop decision-making skills and decrease shyness (Evers-Pasquale and Sherman, 1975).

46. Pair the withdrawn student with another who has learned appropriate social responses for classroom situations (Lancioni, 1982).

47. Involve the student in small group activities (Blanco, 1972; Gottman, Gonso, and Schuler, 1976; Kasda, 1980; Bertilsan, Wonderlich, and Blum, 1983; Newcomb and Meister, 1985).

48. Involve the student in less threatening small group activities and gradually build up to larger group activities.

49. In group assignments decide what work needs to be done by each member. Make certain that every member and his work are needed to complete the assignment (Kasda, 1980).

50. Discuss unity and group importance. Focus on the concepts of working as a group to accomplish a goal (Kasda, 1980).

51. Provide the student with an objective description of any progress he has made, such as the ability to do something he was not able to do before (Johnson, 1956).

52. Help the student when you feel he needs help. This may avoid traumatic failure experiences and decrease the shyness (Johnson, 1956).

53. Point out how much fun the student will have if he would join others and play with them.

54. Place the student with others who are eager to play with him.

55. Construct a "compliment meter." The meter looks like a thermometer and can be drawn on the chalkboard or a chart. Students write compliments to other members of the class and put them in a gaily decorated container. At the end of each day, the number of compliments are counted and the notes passed out. Each student must re-

ceive at least one compliment from someone else. The total is added to the meter. When the class reaches a predetermined goal, they may go on a picnic, have a popcorn party, have an extra 20 minutes for games, or some such treat. If the class is difficult to motivate, the teacher may give small rewards at increments along the way to the final goal (Azaroff and Mayer, 1977).

56. Do some self-awareness activities such as listing all of the student's positive traits or have some other classmate list the withdrawn student's traits of a positive nature. Have others in the class compliment him (Feningstein, 1979).

57. Use modeling techniques to teach various social skills. Praise the model for appropriate social behavior in the presence of the withdrawn student (Mercer and Mercer, 1985).

58. Videotape students modeling appropriate behavior and subsequently replay this tape to the withdrawn student (Dowrick, 1979).

59. Ask mothers of withdrawn students to provide participant modeling. Mothers provide a sufficient amount of physical and verbal prompts to ensure that an acceptable greeting to adults is made. Prompts gradually fade out as the student progresses (Gillet, 1981).

60. Suggest that the student participate in individual and group therapy with the parents and yourself. This will foster a warm and comfortable student-teacher relationship (Kirchenbaum, 1979).

61. Talk to the student after school. Ask him why he dislikes group activities (Myer, 1980).

62. Encourage parallel play by having the student play beside others to encourage later group play (Cammer, 1969).

63. Form study groups of two students to encourage working with others (Lancoini, 1982; Mercer and Mercer, 1985).

64. Have the student role play many different mature reactions to certain problems. Provide a choice of solutions from which he

may choose (A. Courtney, personal communication, 1985).

65. Have students role play personal problem-solving situations, such as a job interview, getting fired from a job, breaking up with a girlfriend or boyfriend, or a conflict with a parent or teacher. Give as many parts as possible to the students. Encourage those who didn't act in the role play to express their opinions about possible resolutions for each situation (Smuin, 1978).

66. Provide opportunities for role playing in small groups. Tape this activity, and allow the students to view the videotape, thus providing feedback.

67. Videotape the students in the classroom. Take the withdrawn student aside and have him view the tape and comment on all of the social interactions (Legingham and Schuailyma, 1984).

68. Encourage the student to view videotapes consisting of social interactions among students his age. Include a sound track that describes the thoughts of the student model moving from solitary play to active participation with his peers (e.g., "My name is Dave. I'm sitting here by myself, but I'd love to play with those kids. I'm afraid to," etc.) (Jakibchuk and Smeriglio, 1976).

69. Use music to motivate the student to participate with others. This might include group choral reading, clapping echo games, or group singing (Upton, 1980).

70. Assign students to work in groups to develop interview questions for a guest speaker (Petty, Petty, and Becking, 1981).

71. Assist the students in your class in forming a club based on their interests. Teach them the basic elements of parliamentary procedure. Involve all the students in the planning and process of creating the group and development of club activities (Petty, Petty, and Becking, 1981).

72. Hold a debate. Groups conduct research for the debate. Students are then chosen from each group to represent various positions on an issue (Petty, Petty, and Becking, 1981).

73. Promote interaction with pets (Reinhart, 1980).

74. Train peers in interaction overtures. Encourage them to "try to get the other student to play with you" (Kerr, 1978).

75. Have the student set interaction goals. Monitor progress (Orr, 1981).

Appendix:
Behavior Checksheet

Student's name _____   Today's date _____

Age _____   Person completing form _____

Teacher _____   Position _____

Directions

Make transparent overlays from these forms. Place them over the corresponding part in the main index for the strategy sheets. Rate all behaviors on a zero to five scale, with zero indicating average or better performance, and five indicating a very severe problem. Compare ratings over time to determine if your interventions have been effective.

Academic Products

___ 1   Messy Pictures and Drawings

___ 2   Poor Penmanship

___ 3   Poorly Organized Work

___ 4   Poor Test Performance

Activity Level

___ 5   Hyperactive

___ 6   Inactive, Lethargic, Lacks Energy, Fatigues Easily

Aggressive Behavior

___ 7   Bites Others

___ 8   Bossy

___ 9   Bullies Others

___ 10   Criticizes the Work or Ideas of Others

___ 11   Fighting

___ 12   Flares Up at Classmates if Teased or Pushed

___ 13   Picks on Others

___ 14 Rejects Classmates in a Hostile Manner

___ 15 Sarcastic

___ 16 Spits at Others

___ 17 Throws Objects

___ 18 Verbally Abusive

Attentional Problems

___ 19 Attention Span Not Increased by Punishment or Reward

___ 20 Distractible

___ 21 Jumpy; Easily Startled

___ 22 Oblivious to What Is Happening in Class

___ 23 Perseveration; Attention Becomes Fixated

___ 24 Quickly Loses Attention When Teacher Is Explaining Something

Authority Conflicts

___ 25 Argumentative

___ 26 Becomes Angry if Asked to Do Something

___ 27 Deliberately Tries to Get into Trouble

___ 28 Disrespectful of Authority

___ 29 Does the Opposite of What Is Asked

___ 30 Does Things in His Own Way

___ 31 Does Not Conform to Limits

___ 32 Impertinence or Sauciness

___ 33 Rebellious if Disciplined

___ 34 Lack of Respect for Rules

___ 35 Overly Obedient

___ 36 Overly Sensitive to Criticism

___ 37 Passive-Aggressive

___ 38 Pesters, Nags, or Persists When Told He Cannot Have Something

___ 39 Refuses to Do Assigned Work

___ 40 Resists Adult Assistance

___ 41 Satisfied with Negative Attention

___ 42 Uncooperative and Stubborn

___ 43 Welcomes Punishment

Classroom/School Behavior (Academic)

___ 44 Acts as if Work Is Done Correctly When It Is Not

___ 45 Always Asking for Help

___ 46 Cheats on Tests and Assignments

___ 47 Copies Other's Work

___ 48 Curses While Working

___ 49 Destroys Something He Has Made Rather than Take It Apart

___ 50 Disinterested in the Classwork of Others

___ 51 Does More Work than Assigned

___ 52 Does Not Bring Correct Materials to Class

___ 53 Does Not Complete Homework

___ 54 Does Not Complete Tasks

___ 55 Does Not Show Imagination

___ 56 Does Not Study

___ 57 Easily Frustrated; Gives Up Passively

___ 58 Easily Frustrated; Loses Emotional Control

___ 59 Fails to Finish Things that He Starts

___ 60 Gives Inappropriate Responses or Answers

___ 61 Hands in Assignments Late

___ 62 Has Trouble Starting a Task

___ 63 Looks to See What Others Are Doing Before Starting

___ 64 Raises Hand But Doesn't Know the Answer

___ 65 Satisfied with Inferior Performance

___ 66 Says He Is Not Capable of Doing Something

___ 67 Says School Work is Too Difficult

___ 68 Will Not Review Work

___ 69 Works Below Potential

Classroom/School Behavior (Nonacademic)

___ 70 Attempts to Run Away from Classroom or School Grounds

___ 71 Behaves in Ways Dangerous or Frightening to Self or Others

___ 72 Daydreaming

___ 73 Does Not Ask Questions

___ 74 Dogmatic and Opinionated

___ 75 Fails to Return Promptly from Bathroom or Errands

___ 76 Indecisive; Difficulty Choosing

___ 77 Offers to Help the Teacher Too Often

___ 78 Out of Seat

___ 79 Says Too Much Work Has Been Assigned

___ 80 Show-Off Behavior

___ 81 Skips Classes; Refuses to Attend Certain Classes

___ 82 Sneaky

___ 83 Swears

___ 84 Tardy for School or Class

Delinquency/Rule Breaking

___ 85 Belongs to a Gang

___ 86 Destroys Property

___ 87 Graffiti; Writes on Walls and Stalls

___ 88 Has Bad Companions

___ 89 Has Forbidden Objects in Possession

___ 90 Has Sexually Assaulted Another Person

___ 91 Loyal to Delinquent Friends

___ 92 Poor Sense of Right and Wrong

___ 93 Steals

___ 94 Truant; Skips School

___ 95 Uses Illegal Drugs

___ 96 Vandalism

Depression

___ 97 Depressed

___ 98 Suicidal

Disruption of Classroom Routine

___ 99 Belittles Subject Being Taught

___ 100 Class Clown

___ 101 Disruptive Behavior

___ 102 Disturbs Others While They Work

___ 103 Excessive Talking

___ 104 Interrupts Others

___ 105 Makes Noises in Class

___ 106 Talks Out; Speaks Without Raising Hand

Empathy/Concern for Others

___ 107 Cruel to Animals

___ 108 Exploits Others for Own Advantage

___ 109 Laughs When Others Are in Trouble

___ 110 Overremorse for Wrong Doing

___ 111 Shows No Shame or Guilt in Being Caught

Home Behavior

___ 112 Approaches Strangers Who Come to Visit the Unit or Home

___ 113 Comes Home Late at Night

___ 114 Demands Parents Do What He Wants

___ 115 Has Bad Dreams and Nightmares

___ 116 Resists Going to Bed; Stays Up as Late as Possible

___ 117 Runs Away from Home

___ 118 Sibling Rivalry; Complains That Siblings Are Favored

___ 119 Video Game Fanatic

___ 120 Watches Too Much Television

Immaturity

___ 121 Acts Silly

___ 122 Attention-Seeking Behavior

___ 123 Becomes Hysterical, Upset, or Angry When Things Do Not Go His Way

___ 124 Blushes Easily

___ 125 Complains About Other's Unfairness or Discrimination Toward Him

___ 126 Complains That He Never Has Fair Share of Things

___ 127 Denies Responsibility for Own Actions

___ 128 Dependent on Others

___ 129 Does Not Have Age-Appropriate Interests

___ 130 Gets Upset When Not the Center of Attention

___ 131 Gives Picture of "Poor Me"

___ 132 Immature

___ 133 Irresponsible

___ 134 Jealous of Adult Attention Given to Others

___ 135 Lies

___ 136 Reliant; Likes to Be Close to Teacher

___ 137 Says Teacher Doesn't Help Him Enough

___ 138 Seeks Constant Praise

___ 139 Self-Conscious; Easily Embarrassed

___ 140 Sulks

___ 141 Tattles

___ 142 Temper Tantrums

___ 143 Uses Others as Scapegoats; Blames Others

___ 144 Weeps or Cries with Little Provocation

___ 145 Whines or Complains

Impulse Control

___ 146 Acts Before Thinking

___ 147 Easily Overexcited

___ 148 Impatient; Impulsive; Unable to Wait

___ 149 Jumps to New Activity Before Finishing Previous One

___ 150 Rushes Through Work and Makes Many Mistakes

___ 151 Unable to Predict Consequences of Personal Behavior

___ 152 Unable to Refrain from Talking

___ 153 Writes Down Answers Without Thinking

Interaction

___ 154 Acts Like a Little Adult; Doesn't Know How to Have Fun

___ 155 Afraid to Be Different

___ 156 Aloof; Socially Reserved

___ 157 Annoys or Provokes Others into Hitting

___ 158 Associates with Loners

___ 159 Attempts to Monopolize

___ 160 Comments That No One Understands Him

___ 161 Gullible; Easily Led by Others

___ 162 Holds a Grudge

___ 163 Not Receptive to Opinions of Others

___ 164 Plays Tricks or Pranks on Others

___ 165 Rejected by Peers

___ 166 Rude; Unmannered

___ 167 Style of Behavior Is Deliberately Different from Others

Learning Difficulties

Confusion/Disorganization

___ 168 Confused About Directions and How to Get Around the School Building or Grounds

___ 169 Disorganized

___ 170 Does Not Seem to Understand Materials or Directions Given

___ 171 Easily Confused; Problem-Solving Difficulties

___ 172 Never Seems to Understand

___ 173 Poor Deductive Reasoning

___ 174 Poor Inductive Reasoning

___ 175 Poor Thinking and Reasoning Skills

Math

___ 176 Lacks Basic Arithmetic Processes

___ 177 Poor Arithmetic Reasoning

___ 178 Poor Math Concepts

___ 179 Poor Math Skills

Memory

___ 180   Forgets Learned Material

___ 181   Forgets Names of Classmates, Teachers, and School Personnel

___ 182   Forgets What to Do

___ 183   Has Difficulty Drawing Designs and Symbols from Memory

___ 184   Has Difficulty Remembering the Sequence of the Alphabet

___ 185   Has Difficulty Remembering the Sequence of Numbers

___ 186   Has Difficulty Remembering the Sequence of Sounds

___ 187   Has Difficulty Remembering Verbal Directions

___ 188   Unable to Retell a Simple Story in Sequential Order

Reading

___ 189   Has Difficulty Finding Smaller Words in Larger Words

___ 190   Misinterprets Written Directions

___ 191   Poor Comprehension of Reading Passages

___ 192   Poor Word Attack Skills

Visual Perception/Visual Motor

___ 193   Cannot Discriminate Between Shapes

___ 194   Cannot Match Pictures or Symbols

___ 195   Depth Perception Difficulties

___ 196   Has Difficulty Finding Hidden Pictures in the Background (Figure-Ground Problems)

___ 197   Has Difficulty Imitating Body Movements, Positions, or Patterns

___ 198   Has Difficulty Tracing, Drawing, and Forming Letters

Written Expression

___ 199   Can't Take Notes Properly

___ 200   Difficulties in Written Expression

___ 201   Poor Spelling

Other Problems

___ 202   Cannot Imitate Sound Patterns or Noises

___ 203   Has Difficulty Identifying Objects by Feel and Touch

___ 204   Has Difficulty Judging Time and Punctuality

___ 205   Has Difficulty Telling Time

___ 206   Has Difficulty Locating and Naming Body Parts

___ 207   Has Difficulty Understanding Spatial Concepts

___ 208   Performance Below Potential

___ 209   Poor Vocabulary

___ 210   Reversals

Motivation

___ 211   Bored with Schoolwork

___ 212   Bright But Doesn't Apply Self

___ 213   Dislike for School

___ 214   Has "I Don't Care" Attitude When Faced with Failure

___ 215   Lacks Motivation

___ 216   Planning to Drop Out of School

Movement

___ 217   Constricted Flexibility

___ 218   Difficulty with Balance

___ 219   Difficulty in Moving

___ 220   Poor Eye-Hand Coordination

___ 221   Poor Fine Motor Coordination

___ 222   Poor Gross Motor Coordination

___ 223   Poor Rhythm

___ 224   Tics

Neuroticism

___ 225   Achievement Anxiety

___ 226   Afraid of Being Hurt in Physical Play

___ 227   Afraid of Dirt and Germs

___ 228   Afraid of Doctors

___ 229   Afraid of Social Events and Crowds (Agorophobia)

___ 230   Afraid of Unfamiliar People

___ 231   Appears Tense or Nervous

___ 232   Avoids Competition

___ 233   Becomes Flustered or Ill When Asked to Express Self Verbally

___ 234   Compulsive Behavior

___ 235   Fearful of New Situations

___ 236   Fingernail Biting

___ 237   Firesetting (Pyromania)

___ 238   Moody

___ 239   Obsessed with Persistent Ideas That Occupy the Mind

___ 240   Overly Concerned About Right Directions

___ 241   Overly Religious

___ 242   Paranoia

___ 243   Perfectionist; Meticulous

___ 244   Phobic

___ 245   Preoccupied with Thoughts of Death

___ 246   Questions Indicate a Worry About the Future

___ 247   School Phobia

___ 248   Steals (Kleptomania)

___ 249   Suspicious; Distrustful of Others

___ 250   Test Anxiety

___ 251   Worries About Knowing the Correct Answer

___ 252   Worries Excessively

Oral Expression

___ 253   Echolalia

___ 254   Elective Mutism

___ 255   Incorrect Articulation

___ 256   Jumps from One Topic to Another When Talking

___ 257   Non-English Speaking

___ 258   Poor Oral Grammar

___ 259   Speaks in Incoherent or Meaningless Way

___ 260   Speaks Rapidly

___ 261   Stutters or Speaks Words or Phrases in a Repetitive Manner

___ 262   Uses Name Instead of "I" When Referring to Self

Physical Health Concerns

___ 263   Alcoholic

___ 264   Anorexic

___ 265   Asthma

___ 266   Becomes Physically Ill from Stress

___ 267   Bulimic

___ 268   Complains of Illness to Avoid Work

___ 269   Encopresis (Fecal Incontinence)

___ 270   Enuresis (Bedwetting)

___ 271   Epilepsy

___ 272   Flatulence; Passes Gas

___ 273   Gets Hurt Easily in Physical Play

___ 274   Hypersensitivity to Pain

___ 275   Has an Unusual Number of Accidents

___ 276   Hypersensitivity to Sensory Stimulation

___ 277   Hypochondria

___ 278   Insensitive to Sensory Stimulation

___ 279   Insensitive to Pain

___ 280   Lacking in Muscle Tone

___ 281   Narcolepsy

___ 282   Overweight

___ 283   Physically Weak

___ 284   Pregnant

___ 285   Smokes

___ 286   Staring Spells

___ 287   Tobacco Chewing

___ 288   Tactually Defensive; Overreacts to Being Touched

Self-Abuse

___ 289   Bites Self

___ 290   Self-Abusive

Self-Care

___ 291   Careless About Appearance

___ 292   Careless About Belongings

___ 293   Finicky and Very Selective in What Is Eaten

___ 294   Liable to Overeat if Not Watched Closely

___ 295   Messy

___ 296   Messy or Sloppy Eating Habits

___ 297   Pica; Puts Inedible or Unhealthy Things in Mouth

___ 298   Prone to Get Dirty and Untidy Easily

___ 299   Spends Too Much Time on Grooming

___ 300   Unable to Bathe Self without Supervision

___ 301   Unable to Dress Self without Supervision

___ 302   Urination into Clothing During Class

Self-Concept

___ 303   Believes Nobody Loves Him

___ 304   Blames Self When Things Go Wrong

___ 305   Depreciates and Distrusts Own Abilities

___ 306   Has Too High an Opinion of Self

___ 307   Low Self-Esteem

___ 308   Makes Self-Derogatory Remarks

Sexual Behavior

___ 309   Boy Acts More Like Girl

___ 310   Boy or Girl Crazy

___ 311   Boy Has Gotten Girl Pregnant

___ 312   Employs Sexual Talk

___ 313   Excessively Modest Regarding One's Body

___ 314   Girl Acts More Like Boy

___ 315   Heterosexual Advances on Others

___ 316   Homosexual Advances on Others

___ 317   Masturbates in Public

___ 318   Overly Interested in Sexual Matters

___ 319   Reads Questionable Sexual Materials

___ 320   Sexual Acting-Out (Fondling, Kissing Classmates, Exhibitionism, Sexual Inuendos)

___ 321   Shuns or Avoids Heterosexual Activities

___ 322   Stares at Pornographic Pictures

___ 323   Too "Touchy"; Likes to Touch Others and Be Hugged

___ 324   Wears Revealing or Provocative Clothing

Unusual or Bizarre Actions and Thoughts

___ 325   Acts as a Nonconformist

___ 326   Covers Ears to Shut Out Sounds

___ 327   Covers or Shuts Eyes, or Turns Away to Avoid Seeing

___ 328   Delusions

___ 329   Does Not Respond When Spoken To; Plays Deaf

___ 330   Explosive Unpredictable Behavior

___ 331   Hallucinations

___ 332   Laughs or Talks to Self

___ 333   Reality Distortion

___ 334   Recent Sudden Change in General Behavior

___ 335   Ritualistic Behavior

___ 336   Rocking

___ 337   Tells Untrue or Exaggerated Stories

___ 338   Unusual or Bizarre Behaviors

___ 339   Unusual or Bizarre Thoughts or Fantasies

___ 340   Wears Unusual Clothing Styles

___ 341   Weird Drawings

Withdrawn or Overinhibited Behavior

___ 342   Avoids Eye Contact

___ 343   Difficult to Get to Know

___ 344   Does Not Engage in Group Activities

___ 345   Overly Pliant; Does Not Stand Up for Rights

___ 346   Shyness

___ 347   Tries Not to Call Attention to Self

___ 348   Unemotional; Does Not Show Strong Feelings

___ 349   Unimaginitive Play

___ 350   Withdrawn

Note

If you have an idea or technique that has been effective in controlling a specific behavior, please let me know. If I use your suggestion, you'll be listed as a contributor in future editions of this book. Please use the format below when submitting ideas. Send your suggestions to Dr. Thomas McIntyre, 151 77th Street, Niagara Falls, New York 14304.

Behavior: (please use the wording from the strategy sheet section of this book)
Your suggestion:

I will allow Dr. Thomas McIntyre to list my idea(s) in a future book solely in exchange for being listed as a contributor.

Signed _____

Address _____

_____

Phone Number _____

Bibliography

AAMD (1981). *AAMD Adaptive Behavior Scale (School Edition)*. Monterey, CA: CTB/McGraw-Hill.

Aaron, T., and Beck, A. (1967). *Depression*. Philadelphia: University of Pennsylvania Press.

Abel, E. (1983). Marijuana and memory: Acquisition or retrieval? In *Behavior and social effects of Marijuana*. New York: MSS Information Corp.

Abrahamsen, D. (1980). *The psychology of crime*. New York: Columbia University Press.

Academic Therapy (1981). 65 ways to say good for you. *16*, 474.

Ackerman, A. M., and Shapiro, E. S. (1984). Self-monitoring and work productivity with mentally retarded adults. *Journal of Applied Behavior Analysis, 17* (3), 403–407.

Ackerman, P. B. (1984). Developmental differences in the use of retrieval cues to describe episodic information in memory. *Journal of Experimental Child Psychology. 38*, 147–173.

Ackerman, D., and Rathburn, A. (1984). Semantic and visual memory codes in learning disordered readers. *Journal of Experimental Child Psychology. 37* (1), 124–40.

Acredolo, L. P., and Boulter, L. T. (1984). Effects of hierarchical organization on children's judgments of distance and direction. *Journal of Experimental Child Psychology, 37*, 409–425.

Adams, J. (1982). *Classroom learning activities for social studies*. Oklahoma City: Oklahoma State Department of Education. (ERIC Document Reproduction Service No. ED 223 495).

Adams, P. (1973). *Obsessive children: A sociopsychiatric study*. New York: Brunner Mazel, Inc.

Adamson, D. R. (1978). Developing effective discussion skills. *Instructor, 88*, 172–178.

Adelman, H. S., and Taylor, L. (1983). Enhancing motivation for overcoming learning and behavior problems. *Journal of Learning Disabilities, 16* (7), 384–393.

Adler, S. (1964). *The non-verbal child*. Springfield, IL: Charles C. Thomas.

Advani, K., and Beaumaster, E. (1973). *The use of behavior modification techniques in a class of slow learners: A research report*. Kingston, Ontario: Educational Services, Frontenac County Board of Education. (ERIC Document Reproduction No. ED 077 161).

Ajchenbaum, M., and Reynolds, C. (1981). A brief case study using behavioral consultation for behavior reduction. *School Psychology Review, 10*, 407–408.

Alabiso, F. P. (1977). *The hyperactive child in the classroom*. Springfield, IL: Charles C. Thomas.

403

Al-Anon Family Group (1966). *Living with an alcoholic.* New York: Cornwall Press.

Alberto, P. A., and Troutman, A. C. (1982). *Applied behavior analysis for teaching.* Columbus, OH: Charles E. Merrill.

Alcoholics Anonymous (1983). *Alcoholics anonymous.* USA Alcoholics Anonymous World Services, Inc.

Alexander, C., and Campbell, E. (1964). Peer influence or adolescent educational aspirations and attainments. *American Sociological Review, 29* (4), 568–576.

Alford, N., and Brown, R. T. (1984). Ameliorating attentional deficits and comcomitant academic deficiencies in learning disabled children through cognitive training. *Journal of Learning Disabilities, 17* (1), 20–26.

Algozzine, B. (1982a). *The influence of teachers' tolerance for specific kinds of behavior on their ratings of a third grade student.* Minnesota University: Institute for Research on Learning Disabilities. (ERIC Document Reproduction No. ED 224 190).

Algozzine, B. (1982b). *Problem behavior management.* London: Aspen Systems Corp.

Algozzine, B. (1982c). *Teacher intervention for children exhibiting different behaviors in school.* Minnesota University: Institute for Research on Learning Disabilities. (ERIC Document Reproduction No. ED 224 192).

Algozzine, R.; Schmid, R.; and Mercer, C. (1981). *Childhood behavior disorders.* Rockville, MD: Aspen Systems Corp.

Ali, Y. (1980). *Development of pre-reading skills: A theoretical perspective. Manual I. Promising practices in the pre-elementary right-to-read programs.* (ERIC Document Reproduction No. 197 336).

Ali, Y. (1980). *Ideas for parents in pre-elementary right-to-read programs. Manual II. Promising practices in pre-elementary right-to-read programs.* (Eric Document Reproduction No. 197 337).

Ali, Y. (1980). *Promising practices for teachers in pre-elementary right-to-read programs. Manual III. Promising practices in pre-elementary right-to-read programs.* (ERIC Document Reproduction Service No. 197 338).

Allan, J. (1981). Resolution of scapegoating through classroom discussion. *Elementary School Guidance and Counseling, 16,* 121–132.

Allan, J., and Thompson, C. (1983). Scapegoating: Help for the whole class. *Elementary School Guidance and Counseling, 18* (2), 147–151.

Allen, J. T. (1980). Jogging can modify disruptive behaviors. *Teaching Exceptional Children, 72,* (2), 66–70.

Allen, K. E.; Hart, B. M.; Buell, J. S.; Harris, F. R.; and Wolf, M. M. (1964). Effects of social reinforcement of isolate behavior of a nursery school child. *Child Development, 35,* 511–518.

Allen, V. L., and Greenberger, D. B. (1978). An aesthetic theory of vandalism. *Crime and Delinquency, 24,* 309–321.

Alley, P. M. (1983). Helping individuals with sleep disturbances: Some behavior therapy techniques. *Personnel and Guidance Journal, 12,* 606–608.

Allington, R. (1975). Attention and application: The oft forgotten steps in teaching reading. *Journal of Learning Disabilities, 8* (4), 210–213.

Allred, R. A. (1977). *Spelling: The application of research findings.* Washington, D.C.: National Education Association.

Allyon, T.; Layman, D. N.; and Kandel, J. H. (1975). A behavioral-educational alternative to drug control of hyperactive children. *Journal of Applied Behavior Analysis, 8,* 137–146.

Allyon, T.; Smith, D.; and Rogers, M. (1970). Behavioral management of school phobia. *Journal of Behavior Therapy and Experimental Psychiatry, 1,* 125–138.

Altman, H., and Grose, K. (1982). *The teacher and the troublemaker.* Toronto: Detselig.

Alton, E. V. (1982). Using the bulletin board to teach. *The Arithmetic Teacher, 30,* 14–20.

Altrocchi, J. (1980). *Abnormal behavior.* New York: Harcourt Brace Jovanovich.

Alvino, J. (1984). Nurturing children's creativity and critical thinking skills. *Educational Digest, 49,* 48–49.

Aman, R. (1980). *Newsweek, 96,* 103.

Aman, R. (1985). Linguists proposed having national no-cuss day. *Jet, 68,* 31.

American Association for Health, Physical Education and Recreation (1968). *A multi-disciplinary concern.* Perceptual-Motor Symposium.

American Association of Suicidology (1977). *Suicide and how to prevent it.* West Point, PA: Merck Sharp & Dohme.

American Educational Coalition (1983). *A blueprint for classroom discipline. Action kit #3.* Washington, D.C.: American Education Coalition. (ERIC Document Reproduction Service No. ED 250 784).

American School and University (1980). Taming campus vandals. *53*, 44–48.

Amerikaner, M., and Summerlin, M. L. (1982). Effects of social skills and relaxation training on self-concept and classroom behavior. *Journal of Learning Disabilities, 15,* 340–343.

Ames, C., and Ames, R. (1984). Goal structures and motivation. *The Elementary School Journal, 85* (1), 39–52.

Ames, D. (1984). The self-worth theory of achievement motivation findings and implications. *The Elementary School Journal, 8,* 15–19.

Ames L. B., and Ilig, F. L. (1955). *Child behavior.* New York: Harper and Brothers.

Anderson, C. (1974). *Classroom activities for modifying misbehavior in children.* Denver: The Center for Applied Research in Education.

Anderson, H. (1984). Short term memory encoding and memory search in the word recognition of learning disabled children. *The Journal of Learning Disability, 17,* 321–342.

Anderson, L. T.; Campbell, M.; Caplan, R.; Perry, R.; and Small, A. M. (1982). The effect of haloperidol on learning and behavior in autistic children. *Journal of Autism and Developmental Disorders, 12,* 167–175.

Anderson, L., and Greeves, A. (1981). *101 activities for exceptional children.* Palo Alto, CA: Peek Publications.

Anderson, L. M., and Prawat, R. S. (1983). *Highlights from research on teaching self-control.* Alexandria, VA. (ERIC Document Reproduction Service No. ED 015 931).

Anderson, L., and Scott, C. (1978). The relationship among teaching methods, and student involvement in learning. *Journal of Teacher Education, 29* (3), 52–57.

Anderson, M. A. (1985). Cooperative group tasks and their relationship to peer acceptance and cooperation. *Journal of Learning Disabilities, 18* (2), 102–104.

Anderson, T. H. (1980). "Study strategies and adjunct aids." In R. J. Spiro, B. C. Bruce, and W. F. Brewer (Eds.), *Theoretical issues in reading comprehension.* Hillsdale, NJ: Lawrence Erlbaum Associates.

Andrews, M. M.; Davis, K.; Nash, R. T.; and Thorpe, H. W. (1979). A management program for elective mutism. *Psychology in the Schools, 16,* 246–253.

Andrews, S. K. (1985). The use of capsule ´paper in producing tactile maps. *The Journal of Visual Impairments and Blindness, 79,* 396–399.

Anspaugh, D., Gilliland, M., and Anspaugh, S. (1980). The student with epilepsy. *Today's Education, 79,* 79–86.

Antonelli, C. J. (1982). *Medical/behavioral treatment approaches within the interdisciplinary process.* Grand Rapids: Michigan Council for Exceptional Children Conference. (ERIC Document Reproduction Service No. ED 217 682).

Apolloni, T., and Cooke, T. P. (1977). Socially withdrawn children: The role of mental health practitioners. *Social Behavior, 5,* 337–343.

Apollini, T., and Cooke, T. P. (1978). Integrated programming at the infant, toddler, and preschool levels. *Journal of Applied Behavior Analysis, 9,* 22–26.

Aptic, J., and Conoley, J. (1973). *Childhood behavior disorders and emotional disturbance.* Englewood Cliffs, NJ: Prentice-Hall.

Archer, D. K. (1976). *Humane atmosphere within the school.* Dubuque, IA: Kendall/Hunt Publishing Co.

Argulewicz, E. N. (1982). Effects of an instructional program designed to improve attending behavior of learning disabled students. *Journal of Learning Disabilities, 15* (4), 23–27.

Arieti, S., and Brodie, K. H. (Eds.) (1981). *American handbook of psychiatry* (2nd ed.). New York: Basic books.

Armfield, M. (1977). *Getting a head start on prewriting skills.* (ERIC Document Reproduction No. ED 235 920).

Armstrong, D. K. (1978). All-consuming crime. *Saturday Evening Post, 250,* 22–24.

Arnheim, D. (1979). *The clumsy child.* St. Louis: Mosby.

Arnsdorf, E. (1979). Focusing: A teaching strategy to improve the learning of mathematics. *School Science and Mathematics, 79* (5), 431–433.

Ashmore, J., et al. (1984). A manual of instructional strategies (Project M.E.D.I.A.). Louisville, KY: Louisville University. (ERIC Document Reproduction Service No. ED 253 031).

Atlanta Teacher Corps Consortium, GA. (1978). Classroom management: Teaching techniques and strategies for dealing with discipline problems. (ERIC Document Reproduction Service No. ED 182 023).

Aukerman, R. C., and Aukerman, L. R. (1981). *How*

do I teach reading? New York: John Wiley and Sons.

Aulls, M. W. (1982). *Developing readers in today's elementary school.* Boston: Allyn and Bacon.

Ausman, J.; Ball, T. S.; and Alexander, D. (1974) Behavior therapy of pica with a profoundly retarded adolescent. *Mental Retardation, 12,* 16–18.

Averill, J.; DeWitt, G.; and Zimmer, M. (1978). The self attribution of emotion as a function of success and failure. *The Journal of Personality, 46,* 323–329.

Averill, L. A. (1926). *Educational hygiene.* Boston: Houghton Mifflin.

Avery, A. (1981). Teaching shy students: The role of the family life educater. *Family Relations, 1,* 39–43.

Awake (1983). Warning on video games, 30.

Axelrod, S. (1977). *Behavior modification for the classroom teacher.* New York: McGraw-Hill.

Ayers, R. (1981). A curriculum model to help students have more effective lives. *NASSP Bulletin, 65* (446), 90–95.

Ayllon, T.; Layman, D.; and Kandel, J. (1974). A behavioral-educational alternative to drug control of hyperactive children. *Journal of Applied Behavior Analysis, 7* (1), 71–76.

Ayres, B. (1979). *Sensory integration of the child.* Los Angeles: WPS.

Ayres, A. (1977). Tactile functions: Their relation to hyperactivity and perceptual-motor behavior. *American Journal of Occupational Therapy, 18,* 6–11.

Azaroff, B., and Mayer, G. R. (1977). Applying behavior-analysis procedures with children in youth. New York: Holt, Rinehart and Winston.

Azrin, N. H.; Besalel, V. A.; Hall, V. R.; and Hall, M. C. (Eds.) (1980). *How to use time out.* New York: H & H Enterprises.

Backman, J., and Fuqua, R. (1983). Management of unappropriate behavior of trainable mentally impaired students using antecedent exercise. *Journal of Applied Behavior Analysis, 16* (4), 477–484.

Baenninger, L., and Ulmer, L. (1976). School homework as a focus of intervention between parents children. *Journal of Learning Disabilities, 12* (2), 2–25.

Bagley, C. (1971). *The social psychology of the epileptic child.* Coral Gables: University of Miami Press.

Bailey, G. (1979). Student self-assessment: Helping students help themselves. *Kappa Delta Pi Record, 15* (3), 86–88.

Bain, R. (1979). *Teacher education: Learning to use the outdoors.* Ontario: Canada: University of Western Ontario. (ERIC Document Reproduction Service No. ED 212 419).

Baine, D. (1982). Using pictures to teach concepts to handicapped learners. *Special Education in Canada, 56* (3), 19–21.

Baker, D. (1982). What happened when? Activities for teaching sequencing skills. *Reading Teacher, 36* (2), 216–218.

Baker, H., and Bayner, A. (1984). *Not just a skinny kid.* Highland Park, IL: National Association of Anorexia Nervosa.

Baksh, E. J., and Martin, W. B. (1984). Teacher expectation and the student perspective. *The Clearing House, 10* (2), 341–343.

Bakwin, M., and Bakwin, R. (1972). *Clinical management of behavior disorders in children.* Philadelphia: Saunders Co.

Balk, D. (1983). Learned helplessness: A model to understand and overcome a child's extreme reaction to failure. *Journal of School Health, 53* (6), 365–370.

Baller, W. R. (1975). *Bed-wetting.* New York: Pergamon Press.

Banas, N., and Wills, I. (1977). *Prescriptive teaching.* Springfield, IL: Charles C. Thomas.

Bander, R. S. (1982). A comparison of cue-controlled relaxation and study skills counseling in the treatment of mathematics anxiety. *Journal of Educational Psychology, 74* (1), 96–103.

Bandler, L. C. (1978). *They lived happily ever after.* Cupertino, CA: Meta Publications.

Bandura, A. (1969). *Principles of behavior modification.* New York: Holt, Rinehart, and Winston.

Bandura, A. (1977). *Social learning theory.* Englewood Cliffs, NJ: Prentice-Hall.

Bandura, A., and Kupers, C. (1984). Transmission of patterns of self-reinforcement through modeling. *Journal of Abnormal and Social Psychology, 69,* 1–9.

Bandura, A., and McDonald, F. J. (1963). The influence of social reinforcement and the behavior of models in shaping children's moral judgements. *Journal of Abnormal and Social Psychology, 67,* 274–281.

Bandura, A., and Perloff, B. (1967). Relative efficacy self-monitored and imposed reinforcement system. *Journal of Personality and Social Psychology, 7,* 111–116.

Bandura, A., and Walters, C. (1963). *Social learning and personality development.* New York: Holt, Rinehart and Winston.

Bangs, T. (1968). *Language and learning disorders of the pre-academic child.* New York: Appleton, Century, & Crofts.

Bank, B. P., and Kahn, M. D. (1982). *The sibling bond.* New York: Basic Books.

Bankman, A. J., and Knickerbocker L. (1983). *Anorexia nervosa: More than just a teenager's disease.* Available from Counciling Center, Eastern Illinois University, Charleston, IL.

Banks, L. M., and Goggin, W. C. (1983). *The relationship of locus control and attribution of depression.* Atlanta: Annual Meeting of the Southeastern Psychological Association. (ERIC Document Reproduction Service No. ED 236 461).

Barabasz, A. F., and Barabasz, M. (1981). Effects of rational-emotive therapy on psychophysiological and reported measures of test anxiety arousal. *Journal of Clinical Psychology, 37* (3), 511–514.

Barasch, F. (1974). *A strategy for open admissions: Memory, imagination, form.* Binghamtom, NY: Annual Meeting of the New York State English Council. (ERIC Document Reproduction Service No. ED 096 651).

Barger, G. W. (1983). Classroom testing procedures and student anxiety. *Improving College and University Teaching, 31,* 25–26.

Barkley, R. A. (1982). *Hyperactive children: A handbook for diagnosis and treatment.* New York: Guilford Press.

Barkley, R. A.; Copeland, A. P.; and Sivage, C. (1980). A self-control classroom for hyperactive children. *Journal of Autism and Developmental Disorders, 10,* 75–89.

Barklin, B. (1981). *Learning disabilities: A book of resources for the classroom teacher.* (ERIC Document Reproduction No. ED 214 358).

Barklin, B.; Cross, R.; Frankel, D.; Ferrare, J.; Gardner, E.; Jaskiewicz, C; Kass, L.; Kerr, S.; Krigsmen, N.; Kropf, J.; Landau, C.; Perlman, B.; Polo, M.; Robinson, C.; Rosen, B.; Russotti, L.; Smith, J.; Trattner, J.; and Tylerlloyd, P. (1981). *Activities, ideas, definitions, strategies (AIDS) learning disabilities. A book of resources for the classroom teachers.* (ERIC Document Reproduction Service No. ED 214 358).

Baron, Jason D. (1983). *Kids and drugs: A parent's handbook of drug abuse prevention and treatment.* New York: Putnam Publishing.

Baroody, A. (1984). Children's difficulties in subtraction: Some causes and cures. *Arithmetic Teacher, 32* (3), 14–19.

Barrett, T. C. (1965). The relationship between measures of pre-reading visual discrimination and first grade reading achievement: A review of literature. *Reading Research Quarterly, 1,* 51–75.

Barrow, J. (1980). The student counseling center program in social anxiety management. *Journal of College Student Personnel, 20,* 552–553.

Bartel, N. R., and Hammill, D. D. (1984). *Teaching children with learning and behavior problems.*

Bartlett, F. (1964). *Remembering: A study in experimental and social psychology.* Cambridge: Cambridge University Press.

Bartol, C. R. (1980). *Criminal behavior: A psychological approach.* Englewood Cliffs, NJ: Prentice Hall.

Bartz, W. (1978). *Surviving with kids.* New York: Ballantine Books.

Baruch, D. W. (1949). *New ways in discipline.* New York: McGraw-Hill.

Basic Skills Curriculum Guide. Teaching Resources (1977). Teaching Resources Corp.

Basmajian, R. (1978). *Therapeutic exercise.* Baltimore, MD: Williams Wilkins Co.

Bass, C. (1985). Running can modify classroom behavior. *Medicine and Science in Sports, 10* (2). 41–42.

Bassoff, E. S. (1983). The pregnant client: Understanding and counseling her. *The Personnel and Guidance Journal, 62,* 20–23.

Battle, J. (1981). Enhancing self-esteem: A new challenge to teachers. *Academic Therapy, 16,* 541–550.

Bauer, B. (1983). *Bulemia: A model for group therapy.* Columbia: University of Missouri. (ERIC Document Reproduction Service No. ED 236 467).

Bauknight, S. T. (1978). *Psychotherapeutic treatment of a gastrointestinal disorder: Individual and family systems perspectives.* Denver, CO. (ERIC Document Reproduction Service No. ED 174 912).

Baum, A., and Aiello, J. (1978). Crowding and personal control: Social density and the development of learned helplessness. *The Journal of Personality, 36,* 1000–1011.

Baumeister, A. (1984). Processing of information in iconic memory: Differences between non-retarded and retarded subjects. *The Journal of Abnormal Psychology, 93,* 433–447.

Bayh, B. (1979). Battered schools: Violence and vandalism in public education. *Viewpoints in Teaching and Learning, 55,* 1–17.

Bayliss, J., and Livesey, P. (1985). Cognition strategies of children with reading disabilities and normal readers in visual sequential memory. *The Journal of Learning Disabilities, 18,* 326–332.

Beall, M. (1983). An experiment in teaching behavioral skills. *Music Educators Journal, 4,* 11–16.

Bean, A. (1980). A long term program for visual perception, concept formation and language. *Academic Therapy, 16* (1), 73–82.

Beane, J. A.; Lipka, P. P.; and Ludwig, J. W. (1980). Synthesis of research on self-concept. *Educational Leadership, 38,* 84–89.

Bear, G., and Richards, H. (1981). Moral reasoning and conduct problems in the classroom. *Journal of Educational Psychology, 73,* 664–670.

Beck, A. (1967). *Depression: Causes and treatment.* Philadelphia: University of Pennsylvania Press.

Beck, A. T.; Ruch, J. A.; Shaw, B. F.; and Emery, G. (1979). *Cognitive therapy of depression.* New York: Guilford Press.

Beck, C.; McCoy, N.; and Bradley-Cameron, J. (1982). Values education. *Curriculum Review, 21* (1), 20–25.

Beck, M. A.; Roblee, K.; and Johns, C. (1982). Psychoeducational management of disturbed children. *Education, 102* (3), 232–235.

Beck, T. (1981). Classroom attitudes: What are the warnings? *Elementary School Journal, 36,* 42–53.

Becker, L. D. (1976). Conceptual tempo and the early detection of learning problems. *Journal of Learning Disabilities, 9* (7), 433–442.

Becker, L., and Morrison, G. (1980). *The effects of levels of organization on clustering and recall in normal, learning disabled, and educable mentally retarded children. Final report.* Washington, D.C.: Bureau of Education for the Handicapped. (ERIC Document Reproduction Service No. ED 180 147).

Becker, W. C. (1971). *Parents are teachers: A child management program.* Eugene, OR: Research Press Comp.

Becker, W. C.; Engelmann, S.; and Thomas, D. R. (1975). *Teaching 1: Classroom management.* New York: Science Research Associates.

Beech, J. R., and Harding, L. M. (1984). Phonemic processing and the poor reader from a developmental lag viewpoint. *Reading Research Quarterly, 19* (3), 357–366.

Beers, C. S., and Beers, J. W. (1981). Three assumptions about learning to spell. *Language of Psychiatry, 138,* 119–125.

Behr, D.; Pomeray, J. C.; and Stewart, M. S. (1981). Abnormal sexual behavior in prepubescent children. *Journal of Psychiatry, 138,* 119–125.

Beimer, D. J. (1983). Shyness control: A systematic approach to social anxiety management in children. *School Counselor, 31,* 53–59.

Beisler, J. M., and Tsai, L. Y. (1983). A pragmatic approach to increase expressive language skills in young autistic children. *Journal of Autism and Developmental Disorders, 13,* 287–303.

Belensee, E. L., and Smyth, W. D. (1983). The success program and the A.D.D. child. *Reading Improvement, 20* (4), 274–277.

Bell and Howell Co. (1971). *Sensory education—A learning interpretation.* Columbus, OH: author.

Bell, T. (1979). Performance anxiety. *Coach Woman's Athletics,* (5), 48–49.

Bellafiore, L. A., and Salend, S. J. (1983). Modifying inappropriate behaviors through a peer-confrontation system. *Journal of Behavior Disorders, 8,* 274–279.

Beloit Public Schools (1980). *Handwriting ideas manual.* (ERIC Document Reproduction Service No. ED 222 893).

Bender, B., and Levin, J. (1978). *Strategies in reading comprehension: VIII. Pictures, imagery, and retarded children's story recall. Working paper No. 214.* Washington, D.C.: National Institute of Education. (ERIC Document Reproduction Service No. ED 152 031).

Bender, N. N. (1976). Self-verbalization in modifying impulsivity. *Journal of Educational Psychology, 68* (3), 347–354.

Benner, P. A., and Law, V. L. (1969). *Word attack.* Boston: Houghton Mifflin.

Bentley, E. J. (1980). *A stretch: Value clarification.* Northbrook, IL: S & R Publishers, Inc.

Bergman, B. L. (1981). *Dealing with test anxiety.* New York: Columbia University. (Great Studies Microfilm BF408 B46).

Berkowitz, N. (1983). Memory sharpening. *Vogue, 173,* 284.

Berler, E. S.; Gross, A. M.; and Drabner, R. S. (1982). Social skills training with children: Proceed with caution. *Journal of Applied Behavior Analysis, 15* (1), 41–53.

Bernard, S., and Rizzo, J. (1979). *Special children: An*

integrative approach. Glenview, IL: Scott, Foresman, and Company.

Berndt, D. J., and Kaiser, C. F. (1983). *The lonely and gifted adolescent: Stress, depression, and anger.* Chicago: Annual Meeting of the Midwestern Psychological Association. (ERIC Document Reproduction Service No. ED 236 495).

Berne, P. (1985). Seven secrets for building kid's self-esteem. *Instructor, 95,* 4.

Bernhardt, A. J., and Forehand, R. (1975). The effects of labeled and unlabeled praise upon lower and middle class children. *Journal of Experimental Child Psychology, 19,* 536–543.

Bernstein, A. C. (1982). Feeling great about myself. *Parents, 57,* 51–54.

Bernstein, G. B. (1979). Integration of visual stimulation in the classroom. *Journal of the Visually Handicapped, 11,* 14–18.

Berres, M. (1979). The passive aggressive child. *The Pointer, 24* (1), 27–31.

Berry M. (1969). *Language disorders of children: The bases and diagnoses.* Englewood Cliffs, NJ: Prentice Hall.

Berryman, C., and Perry, B. (1974). *A manual for teachers of learning disabled children.* Tenn: Bristol City Board of Education. (ERIC Document Reproduction Service No. ED 085 958).

Bers, S. A., and Rodin, J. (1984). Social-comparison jealousy: A developmental and motivational study. *Journal of Personality and Social Psychology, 47* (4), 766–779.

Bertilson, H. S.; Wonderlich, S. A.; and Blum, M. W. (1983). Withdrawal, matching, withdrawal-matching, and variable-matching strategies in reducing attack-instigated aggression. *Official Journal of the Society for Research on Aggression, 9,* 1–11.

Best, T. (1985). Central Junior High School, Monmouth, Illinois, Idea Place. *Instructor Magazine, 13* (5), 86.

Bettelheim, B. (1950). *Love is not enough.* New York: Avon Books.

Bettelheim, B. (1979). *Surviving: And other essays.* New York: Alfred A. Knopf.

Beyer, B. (1984). Improving thinking skills—practical approaches. *Phi Delta Kappan, 65* (8), 556–560.

Biehler, R. F. (1974). *Psychology applied to teaching.* Boston: Houghton Mifflin.

Bielawski, J. G., and Pomerleau, L. (1973). *Reading games make reading fun.* Ridgefield, CN: R. D. Communications.

Biemer, D. J. (1983). Shyness control: A systematic approach to social anxiety management in children. *School Counselor, 31,* 53–60.

Bigge, J. (1982). *Teaching individuals with physical and multiple disabilities.* Columbus, OH: Merrill Publishing Co.

Biggens, G., and Sayre, P. A. (1980). Teaching reading to slow learners: A new perspective. *Journal of reading improvement, 17* (4), 234–236.

Bigler, M. (1979). *Reading and the language arts.* Colorado: Educational Consulting Associates.

Billings, K. (1983). Developing mathematical concepts with microcomputer activities. *Arithmetic Teacher, 30,* (6), 18–19, 57–58.

Bitter, G. (1979). Count on the calculator! *Teacher, 96* (6), 67–76.

Bixenstine, V., and Abascal, J. (1985). Another test of the effect of group composition on member behavior change. *Journal of Clinical Psychology, 41* (5), 620–628.

Blackham, G. J. (1967). *The deviant child in the classroom.* Belmont, CA: Wadsworth Publishing.

Blackman, G. J., and Silberman, A. (1980). *Modification of child and adolescent behavior* (3rd ed.). Belmont, CA: Wadsworth Publishing.

Blackwell, S. L.; Cronin, C. M.; and McIntyre, C. W. (1978). Span of apprehension in learning disabled boys. *Journal of Learning Disabilities, 11* (8), 468–475.

Blair, T. (1984). Reading and the underachiever. *Reading Teacher, 38,* 138–42.

Blanchard, B. (1984). Think! *Vital Speeches Day, 50,* 593–596.

Blanck, P., and Rosenthal, R. (1984). Tone of voice used by teachers is different for talking to low social expectancy and high social expectancy students. *The Journal of Educational Psychology, 76,* 418–426.

Blanco, R. (1977). *Prescriptions for children with learning and adjustment problems.* Springfield, IL: Charles C. Thomas.

Blane, H. T. (1968). *The personality of the alcoholic.* New York: Harper & Row.

Blankenship, C. S., and Lovitt, T. C. (1976). Story problems: Merely confusing or downright befuddling? *Journal for Research in Mathematics Education, 7* (4), 290–298.

Blauvelt, P. D. (1981). *Effective strategies for school security.* Virginia: National Association of Secondary School Principals.

Block, G. H. (1977). Hyperactivity: A cultural perspective. *Journal of Learning Disabilities, 10* (4), 48–52.

Blodstein, O. (1969). *A handbook on stuttering.* Illinois: National Eastern Seal Society for Crippled Children & Adults.

Bloomer, R. H. (1961). *Skill games to teach reading.* USA: F. A. Owen Publishing Company.

Blotcky, M. J., and Looney, J. G. (1980). A psychotherapeutic approach to silent children. *American Journal of Psychotherapy, 24,* 487–495.

Blotnick, S. (1984). From Pac-man to GI Joe. *Forbes, 134,* 138–139.

Bluma, S. M.; Sherer, M. S.; Frohman, A. H.; and Hilliard, J. M. (1976). *Portage guide to early education.* Portage, WI: Cooperative Educational Service Agency.

Blumenfeld, P. C.; Pintrich, P. R.; Meece, J.; and Wessels, K. (1982). Self-perceptions of ability in the elementary classroom. *Education Digest, 48,* 43–46.

Bobowski, R. C. (1978). The care and feeding of talent. *American Education* (Talents unlimited project).

Boersma, F. J., and Chapman, J. W. (1977). *The student perception of ability scale.* Unpublished instrument. Edmonton: University of Alberta.

Bolles, E. B. (1982). *So much to say.* New York: St. Martin's Press Inc.

Bolstad, O., and Johnson, S. (1972). Self-regulations in the modification of disruptive classroom behavior. *Journal of Applied Behavior Analysis, 5,* 443–454.

Bolstad, O. D.; Johnson, S. M.; Broden M.; Bruce, C.; Mitchell, M. A.; Carter, V.; and Hall, R. V. (1972). Effects of teacher attention of attending behavior of two boys at adjacent desks. *Journal of Applied Behavior Analysis, 3,* 199–203.

Bond, G. L., and Tinker, M. A. (1967). *Reading difficulties: Their diagnosis and correction.* New York: Meredith Publishing Company.

Bond, G.; Tinker, M; and Wasson, B. (1979). *Reading difficulties.* Englewood Cliffs, NJ: Prentice-Hall.

Bondy, E. (1984). Thinking about thinking: Encouraging children's use of metacognitive processes. *Childhood Education, 60* (4), 234–238.

Book, R. (1983). *Management of the child with an attention disorder in the school.* Anaheim, CA: American Psychological Association. (ERIC Document Reproduction No. ED 243 005).

Bookman, J. M. (1983). Relationships of cognitive components of test anxiety to test performance: Implications for assessment and treatment. *Journal of Counseling Psychology, 30* (4), 527–536.

Booream, C.; Flowers, J.; and Schwartz, B. (1978). *Help your children be self-confident.* Englewood Cliffs, NJ: Prentice-Hall.

Booth, S. R., and Fairbanks, D. W. (1983). Video tape feedback as a behavior managemet technique. *Behavioral Disorders, 9,* 55–59.

Borba, C., and Borba M. (1978). *Self-esteem: A classroom affair.* Minneapolis: Winston Press.

Borbe, D. (1985). Improving student's self-image: 10 different ways. *Learning 85, 14* (3), 66–67.

Bornstein, J. (1980). *Outline for remediation of problem areas for children with learning disabilities.* Chicago: National Easter Seal Society for Crippled Children and Adults. (ERIC Document Reproduction Service No. ED 229 922).

Bornstein, M. (1977). Social skills training for unassertive children: A multiple baseline analysis. *Journal of Applied Behavior Analysis, 10,* 185–195.

Bornstein, M.; Bellack, A. S.; and Hersen, M. (1977). Social skills training for unassertive children: A multiple-baseline analysis. *Journal of Applied Behavior Analysis, 10,* 183–195.

Bornstein, M., and Stiles-Davis, J. (1984). Discrimination and memory for symmetry in young children. *Developmental Psychology, 20* (4), 637–649.

Bos, C. S., and Filip, D. (1984). Comprehensive monitoring in learning disabled and average students. *Journal of Learning Disabilities, 17* (4), 229–233.

Bostow, D., and Bailey, J. (1969). Modification of severe disruptive and aggressive behavior using brief time out and reinforcement procedures. *Journal of Applied Behavioral Analysis, 2,* 31–37.

Bourgeois, D. (1979). Positive discipline: A practical approach to disruptive student behavior. *NASSP Bulletin, 63,* 68–71.

Bousfield, W. (1953). The occurrence of clustering in the recall of randomly arranged associates. *Journal of General Psychology, 49,* 229–240.

Bovilsky, D. (1982). Up against the ivy wall. *Independent School, 41* (3), 51–55.

Bower, B. (1985). Caution: Emotions at play. *Science News, 127* (17), 266–267.

Bower, E., and Lambert, N. (1982). *Bower-Lambert scales.* Princeton, NJ: Educational Testing Service.

Bowman, R. (1983). Effective classroom management: A primer for practicing professionals. *Clearing House, 57* (3) 116–118.

Boyd, J. W., and Strunk, R. C. (1980). The student with asthma. *Today's Education, 4,* 70–72.

Boyd, L. (1980). Emotive imagery in the behavioral management of adolescent school phobia: A case approach. *School Psychology Review, 9,* 186–189.

Boyd, R. D. (1974). *Boyd Developmental Progress Scale.* USA: Robert W. Boyd.

Bozigar, J., and Hansen, R. (1984). Group treatment for electively mute children. *Social Work, 29* (5), 478–480.

Bransford, J. D. (1979). *Human cognition.* Belmont, CA: Wadsworth Pubishing.

Braun, C. (1976). Teacher expectation: Sociopsychological dynamics. *Review of Educational Research, 46,* 185–189.

Braun, J. A., and Slobodzian, K. A. (1982). Can computers teach values? *Educational Leadership, 39* (7), 508–510.

Bray, S. W. (1981). Benefits of syllabication: Tools instead of rules. *Reading Improvement, 18* (3), 218–221.

Brecher, E. (1978). *Treatment programs for sex offenders: A prescriptive package* (Grant No. 75-NI-99-0125). Washington, D.C.: National Institute of Law Enforcement and Criminal Justice.

Breitrose, H., and Nixon, S. (1970). *Production and evaluation of a film about behavioral techniques to increase task-oriented behavior.* Stanford, CA: Stanford University. (ERIC Document Reproduction Service ED 041 342).

Brennan, E. C. (1974). Meeting the affective needs of young children. *Children Today* in *Readings in Early Childhood Education,* 78/79. Guilford, CN: Dushkin Publishing Group.

Brennan, T. (1985). Participation and self-esteem: A test of six alternative explanations. *Adolescence, 2,* 443–450.

Bricklin, B., and Bricklin, P. (1976). *Bright child-poor grades.* Chicago: Delacorte Press.

Brinbauer, J.; Hopkins, N.; and Kauffman, J. (1981). The effects of vicarious prompting on attentive behavior of children with behavior disorders. *Child Behavior Therapy, 42,* 27–41.

Brinkley, G.; Goldberg, L.,; and Kukar, J. (1982). *Your child's first journey.* New Jersey: Avery Publishing Group.

Broadbent, D. E. (1977). The hidden preattentive processes. *American Psychologist, 32* (2), 109–118.

Broaden, M.; Beasley, A.; and Hall, R. V. (1969). Cited in D. Smith (1981). *Teaching the learning disabled.* Englewood Cliffs, NJ: Prentice-Hall.

Broadhurst, D.; Edmunds, M.; and MacDicken, R. (1979). Recognizing child abuse and neglect in the early childhood program setting. *Early Childhood Programs, 13,* 19.

Brockner, J., and Hulton, A. (1978). How to reverse the vicious cycle of low self-esteem: The importance of attentional focus. *Journal of Experimental Social Psychology, 14* (6), 564–578.

Broden, M.; Bruce, C.; Mitchell, M. A.; Carter, V.; and Hall, R. V. (1970). Effects of teacher attention on attending behavior or two boys at adjacent desks. *Journal of Applied Behavioral Analysis, 3,* 199–204.

Broening, E. (1983). *Fostering positive readers and thinkers from negative students.* Kiamesha Lake, NY: Annual meeting of New York State Reading Association Statewide Conference. (ERIC Document Reproduction Service No. ED 240 514).

Bromberg, W. (1972). *Crime and the mind.* Westport, CN: Greenwood Press.

Brookover, W. B.; Sailor, T.; and Paterson, A. (1964). Self-concept of ability and school achievement. *Sociology of Education, 37,* 277–278.

Brooks, J.; Lukoff, I.; and Whiteman, M. (1980). Initiation into adolescent marijuana use. *Journal of Genetic Psychology, 137,* 133–142.

Brookshire, S. (1978). *An introduction to aphasia.* Minneapolis, MN: BRK Publishers.

Brophy, J. E. (1983). Classroom organization and management. *The Elementary School Journal, 83* (4), 272–273.

Brophy, J. (1981). On praising effectively. *Elementary School Journal, 81,* 268–278.

Brophy, J. E. (1982). *Motivational factors in teacher's handling of problem students.* New York: National Institute of Education. (ERIC Document Reproduction Service No. ED 218 258).

Brophy J. E., and Evertson, C. M. (1981). *Student characteristics and teaching.* New York: Longman.

Brown, B. (1973). *Language skills development.* Boston: Teaching Resources Corporation.

Brown, A. L. (1972). A rehearsal deficit in retardates' continuous short-term memory: Keeping track of variables that have few or many states. *Psychonomic Science, 29,* 373–376.

Brown, A. R., and Avery, C. (1974). *Modifying children's behavior.* Springfield, IL: Charles C. Thomas.

Brown, D. (1971). *Changing student behavior: A new approach to discipline.* Dubuque, IA: William C. Brown.

Brown, G., and Carroll, D. (1984). *The effect of anxiety and boredom on cognitive test performance.* New Orleans: The Annual Conference of the Council of Exceptional Children. (ERIC Document Reproduction Service No. ED 244 968).

Brown, J. (1984). Affective consequences of ability versus effort ascriptions: controversies, resolutions, and quandaries. *Journals of Educational Psychology, 76,* 146–158.

Brown, J. L. (1983). On teaching thinking skills in the elementary and middle school. *Phi Delta Kappan, 64,* 10, 709–714.

Brown, K.; Hirshoren, A.; and Walters, S. (1978). The failure of a successful intervention—A case study. *Exceptional Child, 25* (1), 26–35.

Brown, L., and Hammill, D. (1978). *Behavior rating profile.* Austin, TX: Pro-Ed.

Brown, R. T. (1978). *A comparison of differential treatment approaches for impulsive responding of hyperactive children at two age levels.* Washington, D.C.: The Annual Conference of the Council for Exceptional Children. National Institue of Education. (ERIC Document Reproduction Service No. ED 244 496).

Brown, R. T. (1980). Impulsivity and modeling in hyperactivity and normal children. *Exceptional Child, 27* (2), 79–87.

Brown, R. T., and Conrad, K. J. (1982). Impulse control or selective attention: Remedial programs for hyperactivity. *Psychology in the Schools, 19* (1), 92–97.

Brown, W. E., and Payne, T. (1979). *Strategies for learning.* Novato, CA: Academic Therapy Publications.

Bruce, L., and Bruce, N. (1983). Adolescent care techniques altering self-esteem and world views. *Child Care Quarterly, 4,* 279–284.

Bruch, H. (1973). *Eating disorders.* New York: Basic Books.

Bruch, H. (1978). *The golden cage.* Cambridge, MA: Harvard University Press.

Bruch, M. A. (1979). Client fear of negative evaluation and type of couselor response style. *Journal of Counseling Psychology, 26,* 37–44.

Brulle, A., and McIntyre, T. C. (1984). School phobia: Its educational implications. *Elementary School Guidance and Counseling, 19* (3), 22–28.

Bruner, J., and Hall, E. (1982). Schooling children in a nasty climate. *Psychology Today, 15,* 134–140.

Brussel, J. A., and Irwin, T. (1975). *Understanding and overcoming depression.* New York: Hawthorn Brooks.

Bryan, T., and Bryan, J. (1975). *Understanding learning disabilities.* New York: Alfred Publishing Co.

Buckholtz, M. (1981). Heading off trouble. *American Education, 17,* 8–12.

Buckley, P. A., and Ribordy, S. C. (1982). Mathematics anxiety and the effects of evaluative instructions on math performance. (ERIC Document Reproduction Service No. 222 334).

Bucky, S. F. (1978). *The impact of alcoholism.* Center City, MN: Hazelden.

Budoff, M., and Conant, S. (1982). *A language training curriculum for severely language-delayed preschool and primary-grade children.* Cambridge, MA: Research Institute for Educational Problems. (ERIC Document Reproduction Service No. ED 240 762).

Buhler, C. (1952). *Childhood problems and the teacher.* New York: Henry Hild and Company.

Building students' self-esteem. *Today's Education.* 1982–83 Annual, 60.

Buktenica, N. (1968). *Visual learning.* San Rafael. CA: Dimensions Publishing Co.

Bullock, L. (1979). Promoting time in the classroom: Tips for teachers. *Pointer, 24,* 69–73.

Bumpass, E. R.; Fagelman, F. D.; and Brix, R. J. (1983). Intervention with children who set fires. *American Journal of Psychotherapy, 37,* 328–345.

Burgio, L., and Whitman, T. (1980). A self instructional package for increasing attending behavior. *Journal of Applied Behavior Analysis, 13,* 443–449.

Burke, B., and Reiter, I. (1977). *Reading improvement.* Cambridge: Cambridge University Press.

Burkholder, L. D. (1983). *A affective management strategies for behavior disorder students.* Sacramento, CA: Sacramento University. (ERIC Document Reproduction Service No. ED 229 993).

Burks, H. (1977). *Burks Behavior Rating Scales.* Los Angeles: Western Psychological Services.

Burnham, L. D. (1981). To hear or not to hear. *Teacher, 98,* 68–69.

Burton, G. (1982a). Learning the facts: It need not be

frustrating. *The Elementary School Journal, 83* (2), 149–154.

Burton, G. (1982b). Writing numerals: Suggestions for helping children. *Academic Therapy, 17,* 415–424.

Burton, G., and Edge, D. (1985). Helping children develop a concept of time. *School Science and Mathematics, 85* (2), 109–120.

Burton, R. L., and Daly, M. J. (1983). Self-esteem and irrational beliefs: An exploratory investigation with implications for counseling. *Journal of Counseling Psychology, 30* (3), 361–366.

Buser, R. L.; Long, R., and Tweedy, H. (1975). The who, what, why, and why not of student activity participation. *Phi Delta Kappan, 57,* 124–125.

Bush, R. (1980). *When a child needs help.* New York: Dell.

Bush, W., and Giles, M. (1977). *Aids to psycholinguistic teaching* (2nd ed.). Columbus, OH: Bell and Howell.

Bush, W., and Waugh, K. (1976). *Diagnosing learning disabilities.* Columbus, OH: Merrill.

Bussard, E., and Green, A. C. (1981). *Planning for declining enrollment: Single high school districts.* Education Facilities Laboratories: U.S. Dept of Education.

Butler, R. A., and Whipple, J. (1983). *The relationship of self-esteem to depressive cognition.* Anaheim: Annual Convention of the American Psychological Association. (ERIC Document Reproduction Service No. ED 240 469).

Buttery, T. J., and Anderson, P. J. (1980). Listen and learn. *Curriculum Review, 19* (4), 319–322.

Buxbaum, E. (1970). *Troubled children in a troubled world.* New York: International Universities Press.

Byrne, J., and Horowitz, F. (1984). The perception of stimulus movement. *Child Development, 55* (4), 1625–1629.

Byrne, S. (1977). *Introduction to communication disorders.* New York: Harper & Row Publishers.

Byrnes, D. A. (1984). Forgotten children in classrooms: Development and characteristics. *The Elementary School Journal, 3,* 10–15.

Caciari, E.; Laron, Z.; and Raiti, S. (1978). *Obesity in childhood.* San Francisco: Academic Press.

Cahalcon, D. (1970). *Problem drinkers.* San Francisco: Jossey Bass.

Caldwell, B. (1976). *I used to spell Wedn-Wenes-Wensday: A resource of teacher and student made materials.* Cushing, OK. (ERIC Document Reproduction Service No. ED 229 895).

Caldwell, B. M. (1977). Aggression and hostility in young children. *Young Children, 32* (2), 4–13.

Caldwell, J. (1979). Basic techniques for early classroom intervention. *Pointer, 24* (1), 53–60.

Calhoun, M., and Hawisher, M. (1979). *Teaching and learning strategies for physically handicapped students.* Baltimore: University Park Press.

Caliste, E. R. (1984). The effects of a twelve week dropout intervention program. *Adolescence, 19* (75), 649–657.

Callahan, C. (1982). Gifted girls: A neglected minority. *Gifted Children Newsletter, 3,* 5.

Callahan, L. (1979). *Screening withdrawn and depressed students in public schools.* Sacramento, CA: Sacramento Public Schools. (ERIC Document Reproduction Service No. ED 233 523).

Camarigg, N. (1980). Dictionary for the future. *Instructor, 89* (10), 56.

Cameron, J. R. (1980). Promoting talk through film. *Journal of English, 69,* 14–19.

Cammer, L. (1969). *Up from depression.* New York: Simon & Schuster.

Camp, B. (1980). Psychoeducational training with aggressive boys. In R. M. Knight and D. J. Bakkar (eds.), *Treatment of hyperactive and learning disordered children.* Baltimore: University Park Press.

Camp, B.; Blom, G.; Herbert, F.; and Van Doornick, W. (1977). ''Think aloud'': A program for developing self-control in young aggressive boys. *Journal of Abnormal Child Psychology, 5* (2), 157–169.

Campbell, A.; Scaturro, J.; and Lickson, J. (1983). Peer tutors help autistic students enter the mainstream. *Teaching Exceptional Children, 15,* 64–69.

Campbell, D. (1983). *Adolescent impulsivity and self instruction training: A pilot study.* Toronto: Ministry of Colleges and Universities. (ERIC Document Reproduction Service No. ED 240 156).

Campbell, L. (1981). Every student a success: Improving self-image to increase learning potential. *National Association of Secondary Principles Bulletin, 65,* 76–78.

Campbell, N., Dobson, J., and Bost, J. (1985). Educator perceptions of behavior problems of mainstreamed students. *Exceptional Children, 51* (4), 298–303.

Campione, J., et al., (1980). *Improving memory skills in mentally retarded children: Empirical research and strategies for intervention. Technical report No. 196.* Bethesda, MD: National Institute of Child Health and Human Development. (ERIC Document Reproduction Service No. ED 199 667).

Candler, A., and Goodman, G. (1979). SPACE for students to manage behaviors. *Academic Therapy, 15,* 87–90.

Canfield, J., and Wells, H. (1976). *100 ways to enhance self-concept in the classroom.* Englewood Cliffs, NJ: Prentice-Hall.

Cangelosia, J. S. (1984). *Cooperation in the classroom: Students and teachers together.* National Education Association of the United States.

Cannon, M. W. (1981). What educators can do to help prevent crime: Teach values. *Business Education Forum, 36,* 3–7.

Canter, L. (1974). *The whys and hows of working with behavior problems in the classroom.* San Rafael, CA: Academic Therapy Publications.

Canter, L. (1982). Assertive discipline for parents. Santa Monica, CA: Canter and Associates.

Canter, L., and Canter, L. (1976). *Assertive discipline.* Santa Monica, CA: Canter and Associates.

Cantrell (1974). Cited in P. George (1982). *Promoting attention in children with learning disabilities.* Houston. (ERIC Document Reproduction Service No. ED 218 912).

Capon, J. (1977a). *Approaches to programs of motor development and activities for young children.* Alameda, CA: Alameda University. (ERIC Document Reproduction Service No. ED 154 924).

Capon, J. (1977b). *Perceptual motor lessons plans* (vol. 2). Alameda, CA: Front Row Experiences.

Carberry, H. (1976). How can this child be helped? In *Instructor, Readings in Early Childhood Education 78/79.* Guilford, CN: Dushkin Publishing Group.

Carberry, H. (1978). Behavior blockbusters. *Instructor, 88,* 73–78.

Carberry, H. (1980). Behavioral blockbusters. *Reading in special education,* Boston: Special Learning Corporation.

Carnegie, D. (1936). *How to win friends and influence people.* New York: Simon and Schuster.

Carnine, D. (1976). The effects of teacher presentation rates on off-task behavior, answering correctly, and participation. *The Journal of Applied Behavioral Analysis, 9,* 199–206.

Carnine, L.; Carnine, D.; and Gersten, R. (1984). Analysis of oral reading errors made by econom-

ically disadvantaged students taught with a synthetic-phonics approach. *Reading Research Quarterly, 19* (3), 343–356.

Carr, E. M. (1985). The vocabulary overview guide: A metacognitive strategy to improve vocabulary comprehension and retention. *Journal of Reading, 28* (8), 684–689.

Carroll, C. (1970). *Alcohol: Use, nonuse and abuse.* Dubuque, IA: Wm. C. Brown.

Carroll, M. (1981). Behavior in the classroom. *Learning Magazine, 3,* 82–89.

Carter, R. (1972). *Help! These kids are driving me crazy.* Champaign, IL: Research Press.

Casale, U. P. (1985). Teach vocabulary with hand motions and imagery. *The Reading Teacher, 38* (8), 818.

Casey, M. B. (1984). Individual differences in use of left-right visual cues: A reexamination of mirror-image confusions in preschoolers. *Developmental Psychology, 20,* 551–559.

Castagna, S. A., and Codd, J. M. (1984). High school study skills: Reasons and techniques for counselor involvement. *School Counselor, 32* (1), 37–42.

Castenell, L. A. (1983). Achievement motivation: An investigation of adolescents' achievement patterns. *American Educational Research Journal, 20,* 503–510.

Catterall, C. D., and Gazda, G. M. (1978). *Strategies for helping students.* Springfield, IL: Charles C. Thomas.

Cavenar, J.; Krishnan, R.; Miller, P.; and Volow, M. (1984). Dreams of flying in narcoleptic patients. *Psychosomatics, 20,* 629–633.

Cawile, S. M.; Krishman, R. M.; Miller, P.; and Volow, M. (1984). Narcolepsy: Preliminary retrospective study of psychiatric and psychosocial aspects. *American Journal of Psychiatry, 20,* 629–633.

Ceci, S. J., and Bronfenbrenner, U. (1985). "Don't forget to take out the cupcakes from the oven": Prospective memory, strategic monitorings, and context. *Child Development, 56* (1), 152–164.

Cejka, J., and Needham, F. (1977). *Teaching resources' basic skills curriculum guides.* USA: Teaching Resources Corporation.

Center, D., and Wascom, A. (1984). Transfer of reinforcers: A procedure to enhance response cost. *Educational and Psychological Research, 4,* 19–27.

Cervantes, L. F. (1965). *The drop out—Causes and cures.* Ann Arbor, MI: University of Michigan Press.

Chafetz, M. E. (1978). *A very potent drug ethyl alcohol.* Narcotic Educational Foundation of America (NEFA).

Chance, P. (1982). Your child's self esteem. *Parent's, 57,* 54–59.

Chaney, C. M., and Kephart, C. N. (1968). *Motoric aids to perceptual training.* Columbus, OH: Charles E. Merrill.

Chang, C. (1983). Anorexia nervosa: Why do some people starve themselves? *Journal of School Health, 53,* 22–25.

Chapman, J. W.; Silva, P. A.; and Williams, S. M. (1982). Academic self-concept: Some developmental and emotional correlates in nine year old children. *British Educational Journal, 54,* 284–292.

Charm, R. (1977). Pawn or origin? Enhancing motivation in disaffected youth. *Educational Leadership, 34,* 444–448.

Chase, L. (1975). *The other side of the report card.* Pacific Palisades, CA: Goodyear Publishing Company.

Check, J., and Zeibell, D. (1980). Home work: A dirty word. *The Clearing House, 53* (9), 439–441.

Cheek, P. (1981). Comments that count. *School and Community, 67,* 11–15.

Chen, A. (1982). Ask the experts. *Gifted Children Newsletter, 3,* 17–18.

Chen, A. (1983). Strategies to help students make ethical decisions. *Early Years, 13,* 29–31.

Chernin, K. (1981). *The obsession: Reflections of the tyranny of slenderness.* New York: Harper Colophon Books.

Chernow, F., and Chernow, C. (1981). *Classroom discipline and control.* New York: Parker Publishing Company.

Cherry, C. (1983). *Please don't sit on the kids.* Belmont, CA: Pitman Learning.

Chess, S., and Massibi, M. (1978). *Principles and practices of child psychiatry.* New York: Plenum Press.

Child abuse and neglect: The problem and its management. (vol 1). (1975). U.S. Department of Health, Education, and Welfare Publication No. 7530073.

Chilman, C. (1980). *Adolescents, pregnancy and childbearing: Finding from research.* Public Health Service, National Institute of Health: U.S. Department of Health and Human Services.

Chittenden, M. (1984). Teaching spelling by syllables. *Clearing House, 57* (7), 309–312.

Choate, J. S., and Young, L. S. (1982). *Practical educational prescriptions for students in the mainstream.* Monroe: Northeast Louisiana University. (ERIC Document Reproduction Service No. ED 218 857).

Christensen, D. (1975). Effects of combining methylphenidate and a classroom token system in modifying hyperactive behavior. *American Journal of Mental Deficiency, 80* (3), 266–276.

Church, J.; Christie, D.; and Edwards, B. (1984). Helping pupils who refuse school. *Special Education: Forward Trends, 11,* (2), 28–32.

Chvany, C. (1972). *The uses of the language laboratory in teaching intermediate and advanced Russian.* New York: Annual Meeting of the American Association of Teachers of Slavic and East European Languages. (ERIC Document Reproduction Service No. ED 085 996).

Ciani, A. (1981). *Motivating reluctant readers.* Newark: International Reading Association.

Cieslicki, V. (1980). Working with children with handwriting problems. *Academic Therapy, 15* (5), 591–596.

Clarizio, H. (1980). *Toward positive classroom discipline* (3rd ed.). New York: John Wiley & sons.

Clarizio, H., and McCoy, G. (1970). *Behavior disorders in school-aged children.* Scranton, PA: Changler Publishing Co.

Clarizio, H., and McCoy, G. (1983). *Behavior disorders in children.* New York: Harper & Row.

Clark, D., and Teasdale, J. (1982). Diurnal variation in clinical depression and accessibility of memories of positive and negative experiences. *The Journal of Abnormal Psychology, 91,* 87–95.

Clark, F.; Deshler, D.; Schumaker, J.; Alley, G.; and Warner, M. (1984). Visual imagery and self-questioning: Strategies to improve comprehension of written material. *Journal of Learning Disabilities, 17* (3), 146.

Clark, L.; Hughes, R.; and Nakashima, E. N. (1973). Behavior effects of marijuana: Experimental studies. In *Behavior and Social Effects of Marijuana.* New York: MSS Information Corp.

Clarke, J. (1978). *Self-esteem: A family afair.* Minneapolis, MN: Winston Press.

Clement, S. (1975). School vandalism—Causes and cures. *National Association of Secondary School Principals Bulletin, 59,* 17–21.

Clements, J., and Tracy, D. (1977). Effects of touch and verbal reinforcement on the classroom behavior of emotionally disturbed boys. *Exceptional Children, 43,* 453–454.

Click, D., and Davis, W. (1982). *Moving right along.* Phoenix, AZ: Ed Corp.

Clinard, M. (1957). *Sociology of deviant behavior*. New York: Rinehart & Co.

Cline, S. (1979). A teaching strategy for the gifted. *The Gifted Child Quarterly, 23*, 269–287.

Clinebell, H. (1968). *Understanding and counseling the alcoholic*. New York: Abingdon Press.

Clubok, A. (1983). Teaching the slow learner: A holistic perspective. *American Secondary Education, 12*, 28–30.

Coca-Cola Bottle Company (1985). *Coca-cola hispanic education fund: Los Angeles program description*. Los Angeles: Coca-Cola Bottle Company. (ERIC Document Reproduction Service No. ED 254 353).

Coffey, C. (1971). *Up and down road*. Omaha, NB: Pacific Press.

Coffey, H., and Widner, L. (1967). *Group treatment of autistic children*. Englewood Cliffs, NJ: Prentice-Hall.

Cohen, A. (1966). *Deviance & control*. Englewood Cliffs, NJ: Prentice-Hall.

Cohen, J.; Millman, H.; and Schaefer, C. (1981). *Therapies for school behavior problems*. San Francisco: Jossey-Bass.

Cohen, M. (1974). *Bets wishs doc, a dynamic approach to learning disabilities*. New York: Arthur Fields Books.

Cohen, M., and Beattie, J. (1984). What works with LD adolescents? *Academic Therapy, 19* (4), 397–402.

Cohen, R. (1984). On the generality of the short term memory/reading ability relaitonship. *The Journal of Learning Disabilities, 17*, 193–218.

Cole, C. (1979). A group guidance approach to improving students study skills. *School Counselor, 27* (1), 29–33.

Cole, N. (1940). *The arts in the classroom*. New York: The John Day Company.

Coleman, J. (1964). *Abnormal psychology and modern life* (3rd ed.). Glenview, IL: Scott, Foresman and Company.

Coleman, J. (1979). *Contemporary psychology and effective behavior*. Glenview, IL: Scott Foresman and Company.

Collins, K. (1981). Control of concentration during academic tasks. *Journal of Educational Psychology, 13*, 122–128.

Columbia Department of Education (1981). Handwriting resources book: Grades 1–7. (ERIC Document Reproduction Service No. ED 209 686).

Combs, A.; Aspy, D.; Brown, D.; Clute, M.; and Hicks, L. (1978). *Humanistic education: Objectives and assessments*. Washington, D.C.: Association for Supervision and Curriculum Development.

Commonwealth, V., and Gootnick, D. M. (1974). Electrifying the classroom with the overhead projector. *Business Education Forum, 28*, 3–4.

Conger, J., and Keane, S. (1981). Social skills intervention in the treatment of isolated or withdrawn children. *Psychological Bulletin, 90* (3), 478–495.

Connecticut State Board of Education (1979). Working together for safe schools: A practical guide for reducing violence and vandalism in our schools. *Report of the Interagency Task Force on School Security*. Hartford, CN.

Connell, H. M. (1972). Depression in childhood. *Child Psychiatry and Human Development, 4*, 71–85.

Connor, J. (1974). *Classroom activities for helping hyperactive children*. New York: The Center for Applied Research in Education, Inc.

Conrad, P. (1976). *Identifying hyperactive children*. Lexington, MA: Heath and Company.

Cook, R. (1983). Why Jimmy doesn't try. *Academic Therapy, 19* (2), 155–163.

Coons, W., and McEachern, D. (1967). Verbal conditioning and acceptance of others. *Psychological Reports, 20*, 715–722.

Cooper, A. (1981). Learning centers: What they are and aren't. *Academic Therapy, 16*, 527–537.

Cooper, B. (1981). *Popular music in the social studies classroom: Audio resources for teachers, How to do it Series, Series 2, No. 13*. Washington, D.C.: National Council for the Social Studies. (ERIC Document Reproduction Service No. ED 209 163).

Cooper, H. (1982). Motivating the low achiever. *Journal of Education Psychology, 74*, 577–579.

Cooper, J. (1973). Application of the consultant role to parent-teacher management of school avoidance behavior. *Psychology in the Schools, 10* (2), 259–262.

Cooper, M. (1984). Self-identity in adolescent school refusers and truants. *Education Review, 36* (3), 229–237.

Copeland, A., and Weissbrod, C. (1983). The effects of modeling on behavior related to hyperactivity. *Journal of Educational Psychology, 72* (6), 875–883.

Costello, J. (1984). The last word. *Parents, 59* (3), 89.

Cotterell, J. (1982). Instructional approaches in relation to the student behavior: A matter of adaptiveness. *Journal of Educational Research, 75* (6), 333–338.

Cottman, G. (1980). Baby dolls. *Journal of School Health, 171,* 7–16.

Covington, M. V. (1984). The self-worth theory of achievement motivation: Findings and implications. *The Elementary School Journal, 85,* 5–20.

Cowen, E. (1982). Physical contact in helping interactions with young children. *Journal of Consulting and Clinical Psychology, 50,* 219–225.

Cox, C. M. (1976). Early mental traits of geniuses. In W. Dennis and M. Dennis (Eds.), *The intellectually gifted.* New York: Grune and Stratton.

Cox, T. (1985). Burn out and what to do about it. *Scholastic Coach, 54,* 22–23.

Craik, F., and Lockhart, R. (1972). Levels of processing: A framework of memory research. *Journal of Verbal Learning and Verbal Behavior, 11,* 671–84.

Cratty, B. (1969a). *Motor activity and the education of retardates.* Philadelphia: Lea and Febiger.

Cratty, B. (1969b). *Movement, perception and thought.* Palo Alto, CA: Peek Publications.

Cratty, B. (1970). *Some educational implications of movement.* Seattle, WA: Special Child Publications.

Cratty, B. (1971). *Active learning: Games to enhance academic abilities.* Englewood Cliffs, NJ: Prentice-Hall.

Cratty, B. (1973a). *Physical development for children: Selected perceptual motor activities to enhance movement attributes and sports skills.* Freeport, NY: Activity Boards.

Cratty, B. (1973b). *Physical development (activity cards) for children.* Freeport, NY: Activity Records.

Cratty, B. (1975). *Remedial motor activity for children.* Philadelphia: Lea and Febiger.

Cratty, B., and Hutton, R. (1969). *Experiments in movement behavior and motor learning.* Philadelphia: Lea and Febiger.

Cratty, B., and Martin, S. (1969). *Perceptual motor efficiency in children.* Philadelphia: Lea and Febiger.

Creekmore, N., and Madan, A. (1981). The use of sociodrama as a therapeutic technique with behavior disordered children. *Behavioral Disorders, 7,* 39–45.

Crisp, A., and Stonehill, E. (1976). *Sleep, nutrition, and mood.* New York: John Wiley & Sons.

Crisuola, N. (1981). Creative homework with the newspaper. *The Reading Teacher, 34,* 921–922.

Croll, V. *Picture reading.* Unpublished master's thesis. Charleston, IL: Eastern Illinois University.

Crook, W. (1983). Let's look at what they eat. *Academic Therapy, 18,* 629–631.

Crosby, R. (1982). Self-concept development. *The Journal of School Health, 52,* 432–436.

Crow, P. (1984). Waking up to the right lobe. *Vital Speeches Day, 50,* 600–601.

Crowley, R. F. (1969). Teaching the slow learner. *Today's Education, 58,* 48–49.

Cruickshank, W. M. (1977). *Learning disabilities in the home, school, and community.* Syracuse, NY: Syracuse University Press.

Cruickshank, W. M.; Bentzen, F. A.; Ratzburg, F. H.; and Tannhauser, M. T. (1961). *A teaching method for brain-injured and hyperactive children.* Syracuse, NY: Syracuse University Press.

Cruickshank, W., and Hallahan, D. (1975). *Perceptual and learning disabilities in children.* Syracuse, NY: Syracuse University Press.

Cunningham, P. (1979). Scratch and scribble. *Teacher, 96,* 183–187.

Cultice, W. (1969). *Positive discipline for a more productive educational climate.* Englewood Cliffs, NJ: Prentice-Hall.

Curtis, C., and Shaver, J. (1981). Improving slow learners' self-esteem in secondary social studies classes. *Journal of Educational Research, 74.*

Curtis, J. (1982). Emotional elements of mental illness: Psychological concomitants of stress. *Psychological Reports, 50* (3), 1207–1213.

Curwin, R. (1980). Are your students addicted to praise? *Instructor, 90,* 60–62.

Cushenbery, D. C. (1972). *Remedial reading in the secondary school.* New York: Parker Publishing Co.

Dabul, B. (1976). Therapeutic approaches to apraxia. *Journal of Speech and Hearing Disorders, 41.*

Daczmarek, M., and Levine, E. (1980). Expansion training: A counseling stance for the withdrawn rigid child. *Elementary School Guidance and Counseling, 5,* 31–38.

D'Alelio, W. A. (1976). A strategy for teaching remedial language arts: Creative Writing. In M. J. Long, W. C. Morse, and R. G. Newman (eds.), *Conflict in the classroom.* Belmont, CA: Wadsworth.

Daley, W. T. (1962). *Speech and language therapy with the brain damaged child.* Washington, D.C.: Catholic University of American Press.

Dalton, R., and Lynch, W. (1976). *The effects of an*

"episodic" style of teacher questioning on EMR *pupils lesson performance and learning of orally presented material. Final Report 29.31.* Washington, D.C.: Bureau of Education for the Handicapped. (ERIC Document Reproduction Service No. ED 111 148).

Daly, J., and Friedrich, G. (1981). The development of communications apprehension: A retrospective analysis of contributory correlates. *Communications Quarterly, 29* (4), 243–255.

D'Amico, J. (1980). Reviving student participation. *Educational Leadership, 38* (1), 44–46.

Dampf, P. III (1977). The elimination of inappropriate responses to adult direction. *Education and Treatment of Children,* (1), 19–22.

Danager, B., and Lichtenstein, E. (1978). *Become an ex-smoker.* Englewood Cliffs, NJ: Prentice-Hall.

Danforth, M. (1978). Aids for learning mathematics. *Arithmetic Teacher, 26,* 26–27.

Daniels, L. (1974). *The management of childhood behavior problems in the classroom.* Springfield, IL: Charles C. Thomas.

Dansdill, T. (1924). *Helath training in schools.* Boston: National Tuberculosis Association.

Dansereau, D. F. (1985). *Learning strategies: Meeting the cognitive and affective needs of learners.* Presented at conference at Hilton Inn, Rochester, NY, September 27, 1985.

Darley, C.; Aronson, T.; and Brown, K. (1975). *Motor speech disorder.* PA: W. B. Saunders Company.

Darley, C., and Tinklenberg, J. (1974). Marijuana and memory. In L. Miller (ed.), *Marijuana: Effects on human behavior.* New York: Academic Press.

Davey, B., and Porter, S. M. (1982). Comprehension rating: A procedure to assist poor comprehenders. *Journal of Reading, 26* (3), 197–202.

David, K. (1985). Motor sequencing strategies in school-aged children. *Physical Therapy, 65* (6).

Davids, A. (1974). *Children in conflict: A casebook.* New York: John Wiley & Sons.

Davidson, H. H., and Lang, G. (1960). Children's perceptions of their teacher's feelings toward them related to self-perception, school achievement, and behavior. *Journal of Experimental Education, 29,* 107–118.

Davis, D. (1982). Miracle motivators that inspire good conduct. *Instructor and Teacher, 91* (9), 23.

Davis, E. (1981). Teaching the slow learner in the secondary school. *Educational Forum, 45,* 333–336.

Dechant, E. (1969). *Diagnosis and remediation of reading disability.* New York: Parker Publishing Co.

Deffenbacher, J. L., and Deitz, S. R. (1978). Effects of test anxiety on performance, worry, and emotionality in naturally occurring exams. *Psychology in the Schools, 15* (3), 446–449.

Deffenbacher, J. L., and Kemper, C. C. (1974). Counseling test-anxious sixth graders. *Elementary School Guidance and Counseling, 9,* 22–29.

Deffenbacher, J. L., and Michaels, A. C. (1980). Two self control procedures in reduction of targeted and nontargeted anxieties a year later. *Journal of Counseling Psychology, 27,* 9–15.

DeGaetano, L. (1970). *Speech improvemnt duplicating masters.* Danville, IL: Interstate Publishers.

DeHirsch, K. (1984). *Language and the developing child.* Maryland: Monography No. 4, The Orton Dyslexia Society.

Deibert, A. N., and Harmon, A. J. (1977). *New tools for changing behavior.* Champaign, IL: Research Press.

Delattre, D. (1983). The liberal arts. *The Educational Digest, 14,* 2–5.

Delfasse. (1984). *Auditory processing in action.* Moline, IL: Lingui Systems.

Della-Piana, G. M. (1968). *Reading diagnosis and prescription: An introduction.* New York: Holt, Rinehart and Winston.

DeLorme, T. (1951). *Progressive resistance exercise.* New York: Appleton Century Crofts.

Delp, J., and Martinson, R. (1977). *A handbook for parents of gifted and talented.* Ventura, CA: Ventura County Superintendent of Schools Office.

Delquadri, J.; Greenwood, C.; Stretton, K.; and Hall, V. (1983). The peer tutoring spelling game: A classroom procedure for increasing opportunity to respond & spelling performance. *Education & Treatment of Children, 6* (3), 225–239.

DeMyer, M. (1979). *Parents and children in autism.* Washington, D.C.: V. H. Winston & Sons.

Department of Instruction and Support Services (1984). *Manual of instructional strategies.* Materials Production.

Derdeyn, A. (1983). Depression in childhood. *Child Psychiatry and Human Development, 14,* 16–29.

Deshler, D.; Schumaker, J.; and Lenz, B. (1984). Academic and cognitive interventions of learning disabled adolescents. *Journal of Learning Disabilities, 17* (2), 108–119.

Developmental Learning Materials (1969). *Body concept template.* Miles, IL: author.

DeVillis, R.; McEvoy, B.; and McCauley, C. (1978).

Vicarious acquisitions of learned helplessness. *The Journal of Personality, 36,* 894–899.

Devine, V. T., and Tomlinson, J. R. (1976). An alternative to token economies in the management of classroom behaviors. *Psychology in the Schools, 13,* 163–170.

Devinne, T. G. (1981). *Teaching study skills.* Boston: Allyn and Bacon.

Deykin, E. (1984). Assessing suicidal intent and lethality. *Eductional Horizons, 62,* 134–137.

Dial, D. (1977). Heightening the student's self image. *School and Community, 63,* 23.

Diamond, S. C. (1974). A school designed for self-esteem. *Clearing House, 48,* 342–346.

Dickerman, W. (1971). *Toward an efficient technique for teacher conducted behavior modification programs for disruptive classroom behavior.* Madison: Wisconsin University. (ERIC Document Reproduction Service No. ED 043 328).

Diem, R. (1984). Disruptive behavior in schools: A response model. *The High School Journal, 67,* 141–145.

Diers, C., et al. (1983). *Learning for the fun of it.* (ERIC Document Reproduction Service No. ED 240 401).

Dinkmeyer, D.; McKay, G.; and Dinkmeyer, D. (1980). *Systematic training for effective teaching.* Circle Plains, MN: American Guidance Service.

DiSibio, R., and Savitz, F. (1983). *But teacher, I don't like to read, or how to make reading alluring.* Kiamesha Lake, NY: Annual Meeting of the New York State Reading Association. (ERIC Document Service No. ED 237 971).

DiStegano, P., and Hagerty, P. (1985). Teaching spelling at the elementary level: A realistic perspective. *The Reading Journal, 38* (4), 373.

Dittman, A. L. (1972). *Interpersonal messages of emotion.* New York: Spring Publishing Co.

Doane, M. (1983). *Famine at the feast: A therapist's guide to working with the eating disordered.* Washington, D.C.: National Institute of Education. (ERIC Document Reproduction Service No. ED 239 191).

Dobson, J. E.; Campbell, N. J.; and Dobson, R. L. (1982). Relationship between children's self-concept, perceptions of school and life change. *Elementary School Guidance Counsel, 17,* 100–107.

Doleys, D. M., and Williams, S. C. (1977). The use of natural consequence and a make-up period to eliminate school phobic behaviors: A case study. *Journal of School Psychology, 15* (1), 44–50.

Dolgins, M.; Myers, M.; Flynn, P.; and Moore, J. (1984). How do we help the learning disabled? *Instructor, 93,* 30–36.

Doll, R. C., and Fleming, R. S. (1966). *Children under pressure.* Columbus, OH: Charles E. Merrill.

Dolly, J. P., and Page, P. (1981). The effects of behavior modification and reality therapy on the behavior emotionally disturbed institutionalized adolescents. *The Exceptional Child, 28* (3), 191–198.

Dolphin, J. E., and Cruickshank, W. M. (1951). The figure-background relationship in children with cerebral palsy. *Journal of Clinical Psychology, 7* (2), 228–231.

Donalds, S. (1973). About handwriting: Academic therapy. *Journal of Education, 19* (2), 139–146.

Donaldson, L. (1980). *Behavioral supervision: Practical ways to change unsatisfactory behavior and increase productivity.* Reading. MA: Addison-Wesley.

Donnellan, A. (1984) Analyzing the communicative function of aberrant behavior. *Journal of the Association for Persons with Severe Handicaps, 9,* 202–212.

Doray, M. (1982). *J is for jump!* California: Pitman Learning, Inc.

Dornbush, R.; Fink, M.; and Freedman, A. (1973). Marijuana, memory and perception. In *Behavior and Social Effects of Marijuana.* New York: MSS Information Corp.

Dorsey, M.; Iwata, B.; Ong, P.; and McSween, T. (1980). Treatment of self-injurious behavior using a water mist: Initial response suppression and generalization. *Journal of Applied Behavioral Analysis, 13,* 343–353.

Dorsey, M.; Iwata, B.; Reid, D.; and Davis, P. (1982). Protective equipment: Continuous and contingent application in the treatment of self-injurious behavior. *Journal of Applied Behavioral Analysis, 15,* 217–230.

Dougherty, E., and Dougherty, A. (1977). The daily report card: A simplified and flexible package for classroom behavior management. *Psychology in the Schools, 14* (2), 191–195.

Dougherty, J., and Davies, C. (1984). The psychological effects of unemployment on a group of adolescents. *Educational Review, 36* (3), 223–228.

Douglas, V. (1972). Stop, look and listen: The problem of sustained attention and impulse control in hyperactive and normal children. *Canadian Journal of Behavioral Science, 72* (4), 259–282.

Douglas, V. (1980). High mental processes in hyperactive children. In R. M. Knights, and D. J. Bakker, (eds). *Treatment of hyperactive and learning disordered children*. Baltimore: University Park Press.

Douglas, V. (1974). Cited in. T. George (1982). *Prompting attention in children with learning disabilities*. Houston, TX: The Annual Conference of the Council for Exceptional Children. (ERIC Document Reproduction Service No. ED 218 912).

Douglass, B. (1984). Variation on a theme: Writing with the LD adolescent. *Academic Therapy, 19* (3), 361–363.

Dowdall, C., and Colangelo, N. (1982). Underachieving gifted students: Review and implications. *Gifted Child Quarterly, 26*, 179–183.

Dowell, L. (1974). *Handbook of teaching and coaching points for basic physical education*. USA: Thomas Books.

Downing, C. (1977). Teaching children behavior change techniques. *Elementary School Guidance and Counseling, 11* (4), 277–282.

Downing, J. (1983). A positive way to help families. *Elementary School Guidance and Counseling, 17*, 208–213.

Dowrick, P. (1979). Single dose medication to create a self model film. *Child Behavior Therapy, 1* (2), 193–198.

Doyle, W. (1982). The effectiveness of color-coded cues in remediating reversals. *Journal of Learning Disabilities, 15*, 227–230.

Dreher, B. (1978). Selective reading can modify attitudes. *The Pointer for Special Educators, 23* (1), 40–43.

Dreikurs, R. (1972). *Coping with children's misbehaviors*. New York: Hawthorn Brooks.

Dreikurs, R., and Grey, L. (1970). *Guide to child discipline*. New York: Hawthorne.

Drew, B.; Evans, J.; Bostow, D.; Geiger, G.; and Drash, P. (1982). Increasing assignment completion and accuracy using a daily report card precedure. *Psychology in the Schools, 19* (4), 540–547.

Drucker, S., and Hexter, M. B. (1923). *Children astray*. Cambridge; MA: Harvard University Press.

Drummie, M. A. (1970). *A research report on New Brunswick school dropout in the academic year 1963-64*. New Brunswick: Department of Youth & Welfare (ERIC Document Reproduction Service No. ED 029 939).

Duanne, E. J. (1980). *Individualized instruction: Programs and materials*. New Jersey: Educational Technology Publications.

Duffin, B.; Kroll, B.; and Winkworth, J. (1977). *A study of writing problems in a remedial writing program for EOP students*. Davis, CA: University of California. (ERIC Document Reproduction Service No. ED 153 473).

Dugan, S. P. (1976). *The behaviorally disordered child*. Handout. Special Education Institute.

Dugle, J.; Browne, J.; and Cook, J. (1982). Sharing teaching ideas. *Mathematics Teacher, 75* (9), 755–758.

Duhl, L. (1983). *Technology and learning disabilities*. Washingon, D.C.: Office of Technology Assessment.

Dukar, S. (1971). *Teaching listening in the elementary school*. New Jersey: Scarecrow Press.

Duke, D., and Meckel, A. (1980). Student attendance problems. *Urban Education, 15*, 325–357.

Dumas, E. (1960). *Arithmetic games*. California: Fearon.

Dumas, E.; Howard, C.; and Dumas, J. (1960). *Arithmetic charts handbook*. California: Fearon.

Dunkleberger, G., and Knight, C. (1979). Cognitive consequences of mastery learning via computer-generated repeatable tests. *The Journal of Educational Research, 72*, 270–272.

Dunn, L. (1963). *Exceptional children in the schools*. New York: Holt, Rinehart and Winston.

Dunworth, J. (1982). *Handbook for alternatives to corporal punishment*. St. Louis Public Schools. (ERIC Document Reproduction Service No. ED 217 521).

Dupont, H. (1969). *Educating emotionally disturbed children*. New York: Holt, Rinehart, & Winston.

Durand, V. (1982). A behavioral/pharmacological intervention treatment of severe self-injurious behavior. *Journal of Autism and Developmental Disorders, 12*, 243–251.

Durkin, D. (1978). *Teaching them to read*. Boston: Allyn and Bacon.

Durlak, J. A., and Mannarino, A. P. (1977). The social development program: Description of a school-based preventive mental health program for high risk children. *Journal of Clinical Child Psychology, 6*, 43–52.

Ebersole, M.; Kephart, N.; and Ebersole, J. (1968). *Steps to achievement for the slow learner*. Columbus, OH: Charles E. Merrill.

Edelman, G. N. (1984). Getting kids to listen. *Parents, 59*, 52–56.

Eeds, M., and Cockrum, W. A. (1985). Teaching word meanings by expanding schemata vs. dictionary work vs. reading in context. *Journal of Reading, 28* (6), 492–497.

Effects of relaxation training on pulmonary mechanics in children with asthma (1979). *Journal of Applied Behavioral Analysis, 12,* 27–33.

Egeland, B. (1974). Training impulsive children in the use of more efficient scanning techniques. *Child Development, 45,* 165–171.

Ehri, L. C., and Wilce, L. S. (1982). The salience of silent letters in children's memory for word spelling. *Memory & Cognition, 10,* 155–166.

Ehri, L. C., and Wilce, L. S. (1985). Movement into reading: Is the first stage of printed word learning visual or phonetic? *Reading Research Quarterly, 20* (2), 163–179.

Ehrlich, V. Z. (1982). *Gifted children.* Englewood Cliffs, NJ: Prentice-Hall.

Eidelberg, J. (1968). *Encyclopedia of psychoanalysis.* New York: Free Press.

Ekwall, E. E. (1985). *Locating and correcting reading difficulties.* Columbus, OH: Charles E. Merrill.

Elliott, E. (1982). Building self esteem. *Journal of Youth and Adolescence, 11* (2), 135–153.

Elliott, S., and Carrol, J. (1980). Strategies to help children remember what they read. *Reading Improvement, 17* (4), 272–277.

Elkind, D. (1969). *Studies in cognitive development.* New York: Oxford University Press.

Elkins, R. (1981) Too much praise in abuse. *Educational Leadership, 38,* 482.

Ellingson, C. (1967). *The shadow children.* Chicago: Topaz Books.

Elson, E. F.; Peck, A.; Willey, G.; Hirsch, S.; Moore, T.; and Wynn, E. (1966). *The art of speaking.* Boston: Ginn and Company.

Elton, D.; Burrows, G. D.; and Stanley, G. V. (1979). The relationship between psychophysical and perceptual variables and chronic pain. *British Journal of Social and Clinical Psychology, 18* (4), 425–430.

Elwell, W. C. (1985). Data processing: Memories are made of this. *Clearing House, 58* (7), 315–317.

Emmer, E. T. (1984). *Management and instruction strategies for heterogeneous elementary school classrooms.* Austin: Texas University. (ERIC Document Reproduction Service No. ED 251 431).

Empey, L., and Hubeck, S. (1971). *Explaining delinquency.* Lexington, MA: D.C. Heath Company.

Encyclopedia of Educational Research (5th Ed). (1982). New York: Macmillan, pp. 195–199.

Englehardt, L. (1983). This system called for time out on student discipline problems. *American School Board Journal, 170* (6), 21–24.

Enright, B. E., and Roit, M. L. (1979). *Contingency contracting: A technique for developing responsibility and self-control.* Dallas, TX. (ERIC Document Reproduction Service No. ED 216 289).

Epstein, L. H. (1981). Child and parent weight loss in family-based behavior modification programs. *Journal of Consulting and Clinical Psychology, 49,* 674–685.

Epstein, N. and Maragos, N. (1983). Treating delinquent-prone adolescents and preadolescents. *Social Work, 28,* 66–68.

Epstein, N. (1982). What is self-esteem and how can it be measured? Washington: DC: The Symposium on *Functioning and measurement of self-esteem.* August 27.

Espenschade, T., and Eckert, B. (1967). *Motor development.* Columbus, OH: Charles E. Merrill.

Esveldt, K. C., Patrick, D. C., and Forness, S. R. (1974). Effect of videotape feedback on children's classroom behavior. *The Journal of Educational Research, 67,*453–456.

Evans, I., and Meyer, L. H. (1985). *An educative approach to behavior problems.* Maryland: Paul H. Brookes.

Evers-Pasquale, W., and Sherman, M. (1975). The reward value of peers: A variable influencing the efficacy of filmed modeling in modifying social isolation in preschoolers. *Journal of Abnormal Child Psychology, 3,* 179–189.

Eyde, B., and Fink, A. (1983). *Don't do that and other counseling strategies for the chronically disruptive.* Washington, D.C.: National Institute of Education. (ERIC Document Reproduction Service No. ED 226 308).

Faas, L. A. (1972). *Learning disabilities: A book of readings.* Springfield, IL: Charles C. Thomas.

Fagan, J. (1984). Long Island dropouts are dropping back in. *NYSSBA Journal, 11,* 18–19.

Faily, A., and Roundtree, G. A. (1979). Combating violence and vandalism in schools. *The National Association of Secondary School Principals, 63,* 100–104.

Fairchild, T. (1983a). Effects of daily report card system on an eighth grader exhibiting behavioral and motivation problems. *School Counselor, 31,* 83–86.

Fairchild, T. (1983b). Things that work. *School Counselor, 31* (1), 83–86.

Fallen, N. H. (1978). *Young children with special needs.* Columbus, OH: Charles E. Merrill.

Faller, K. (1981). *Social work with abused and neglected children.* New York: Free Press.

Fallone, P. (1985). Memory may not slip when mood dips. *Science News, 127,* 186.

Farrell, B. (1984). Attention in the processing of complex visual displays: Detecting features and their combinations. *Journal of Experimental Psychology, Human Perception and Performance, 10* (1), 40–64.

Farnette, C.; Forte, I.; and Loss, B. (1977). *I've got me and I'm glad.* Nashville, TN: Incentive Publications.

Farrald, R., and Schamber, R. (1973). *Handbook I: A mainstreamed approach to identification, assessment and amelioration of learning disabilities.* South Dakota: ADAPT Press.

Farrell, J. (1984). Tricks that help you remember. *Good Housekeeping, 198,* 298.

Fatis, M., and Konewko, P. J. (1983). Written contracts as adjuncts in family therapy. *Social Work, 28,* 161–163.

Fay, C. (1981). The function of immediate echolalia in autistic children. *Journal of Speech and Hearing Disorders, 50,* 20–33.

Feingold, B. (1975). *Why is your child hyperactive?* New York: Random House.

Feldman, R. S.; Salelsky, R.; and Sulivan, J. (1983). Child's actions are dependent on the child's perception of the teacher's competance. *The Journal of Educational Psychology, 75,* 27–32.

Feldsher, S. (1977). *Do it for early learners.* New York: Instructor Publications.

Felker, D. W. (1974). *Building positive self-concepts.* Minneapolis, MN: Burgess Publishing Co.

Fenichel, C. (1968). Psycho-educational approaches for seriously disturbed children in the classroom. In P. Knoblock (ed.)., *Intervention approaches in educating emotionally disturbed children.* Syracuse, NY: Syracuse University Press.

Feningstein, A. (1979). Self-conscious, self attention, and social interaction. *The Journal of Personality, 31,* 75–84.

Fenlon, A.; McPherson, E.; and Dorchak, L. (1979). *Getting ready for childbirth.* Englewood Cliffs, NJ: Prentice-Hall.

Fenner, S. W. (1984). *Reading in student teaching and special education.* Bridgeport, CT: Special Learning Corp.

Fennimore, F. (1970). Developing the adolescent's self concept with literature. *English Journal, 59,* 1272–1278.

Fensterheim, H. (1977). *Stop running scared: How to conquer your fears, phobias and anxieties.* New York: Rawson Associates Publishers.

Fentress, J. (1984). The development of coordination. *Journal of Motor Behavior, 16* (2), 99–134.

Fern, L., and Foster, K. (1977). *Writing workshops and reading.* San Diego, CA: San Diego State University. (ERIC Document Reproduction Service No. ED 159 681).

Fernald, G. M. (1943). *Remedial techniques in basic school subjects.* New York: McGraw-Hill Book Co.

Ferreday, M. (1980). *Classroom management.* New York: McDowell & Co.

Fidel, R. (1981). Toxic substances and you. *Alcohol, Tobacco, Marijuana, and Hard Drugs.*

Finch, A. J., and Kendall, P. C. (1979). *Clinical treatment and research in child psychopathology.* New York: SP Medical and Scientific Books.

Finch, A. J., and Weinberg, W. M. (1976). Reflection-impulsivity and behavior patterns in emotionally disturbed boys. *Journal of Genetic Psychology, 128,* 271–274.

Fine, M. J. (1977). *Principles and techniques of intervention with hyperactive children.* Springfield, IL: Charles C. Thomas.

Fine, R. (1983). Amnesia: A case of a fragmented past. *Science Digest, 91,* 73–76.

Fine, S., and Louie, D. (1979). Juvenile firesetters: Do the agencies help? *American Journal of Psychotherapy, 136,* 433–435.

Fischer, A. (1982). Do you stuff yourself one moment and starve yourself the next? *Seventeen, 41,* 106–107.

Fischer, I. (1985). Word recognition, use of context, and reading skill among deaf college students. *Reading Research Quarterly, 20* (2), 203–218.

Fischer, N. A. (1981). Good children, bad children. *Principal, 61,* 20.

Fish, M. C., and Pervan, R. (1985). Self instruction: A potential tool for school psychologists. *Journal of Experimental Child psychology, 6,* 297–301.

Fishbain, D. A., and Rotondo, D. J. (1983). Foreign body ingestion associated with delusional beliefs. *The Journal of Nervous and Mental Disease, 171* (5), 321–322.

Fisher, C. J. (1980). Individualized spelling. *Instructor, 39* (8), 164–170.

Fisher, E. B.; Green, L.; and Lowe, M. R. (1979). *Self-control with and without covert sensitization in smoking cessation.* (ERIC Document Reproduction Series No. ED 181 362).

Fisher, E. L.; White, J. M.; and Fisher, J. H. (1985). Using context and relationships to teach math. *Academic Therapy, 21* (1), 23–27.

Fisher, F. (1983). Spelling by speech synthesis: A new technology for an old problem. *Journal of Learning Disabilities, 16* (6), 368–369.

Fitzmaurice, P., et al. (1974). *Language development activities through the auditory channel.* Louisville, OH: Stark County Dept. of Education. (ERIC Document Reproduction Service No. ED 107 031).

Fitzsimmons, N., and Loomer, D. (1984). Best ways to teach spelling. *The Classroom Reading Teacher, 37* (7), 679.

Fleming, D.; Ritchie, B.; and Fleming, E. (1983). Fostering the social adjustment of disturbed students. *Teaching Exceptional Children, 16* (2), 172–175.

Flexer, B., and Borun, M. (1984). The impact of a class visit to a participatory science museum exhibit and a classroom science lesson. *Journal of Research in Science Teaching, 21* (9), 863–873.

Flick, L. (1979). Violence and vandalism in the classroom. *Forecast for Home Economics, 24,* 44.

Flindt, M. (1985). Seven ways to put some snap into your school's science fair. *Learning, 13* (7), 28–30.

Flowers, B. (1972). *The big book of language through sounds.* Dansville, IL: International Printer & Publishers.

Flowers, B. (1974). *The big book of sounds.* New York: Lingui Systems.

Floyd, W. III, and Hughes, H. (1980). A systems intervention procedure for the management of aggressive behavior. *The Exceptional Child, 27* (2), 99–105.

Foa, E. (1981). Phobias: How to keep your fears under control. *U.S. News and World Report, 91,* 69–70.

Fogelman, K. (1978). School attendance, attainment and behavior. *British Journal of Educational Psychology, 48* (2), 148–158.

Fogg, R. (1976). Discouraging cheating. *The Clearing House, 49,* 329–331.

Fontaine, E. (1981). The directed spelling thinking activity. *The Reading Teacher, 35* (2), 213.

Ford, J., and Veltri-Ford, A. (1980). Effects of time-out from auditory reinforcement on two problem behaviors. *Mental Retardation, 18* (6), 299–303.

Ford, P. (1983). *Learning through play: A guide for the parents of 3, 4 or 5-year olds.* (ERIC Document Reproduction Service No. ED 256 486).

Forish, B., and Forish, B. (1976). *Moral development and education.* Lincoln, NE: Professional Educators Publicators.

Forness, S., and Dvorak, R. (1982). Effects of test time-limits on achievement scores of behaviorally disordered adolescents. *Behavior Disorders, 7,* 207–212.

Forrest, D. (1983). Depression: Information and interventions for school counselors. *The School Counselor, 30,* 269–279.

Forrest, E. (1981). Visual imagery as an information processing strategy. *Journal of Learning Disabilities, 14* (10), 584–586.

Foster, D. (1982). Saving our children from alcoholism. *Momentum, 13,* 15–17.

Foster, J., and Echard, E. (1978). *Family planning visits by teenagers: USA: DHHS-PHS-81 1719.* National Center for Health Statistics. (ERIC Document Reproduction Service No. ED 232 084).

Foster, S. L. (1980). Bronco Junction prove asthmatic kids can live active lives. *Parks and Recreation, 6,* 31–33.

Foster, S. L.; Prinz, R. J.; and O'Leary, K. D. (1983). Impact of problem-solving communication training and generalization procedures on family conflict. *Child and Family Behavior Therapy, 5,* 1–23.

Fox, B. (1980). *Secondary special education. Part I: The "stepping stone model" designed for secondary learning disabled students. Part II: Adapting materials and curriculum.* Philadelphia, PA. (ERIC Document Reproduction Service No. ED 188 389).

Fox, R. (1981). Behavioral weight reduction procedures for obese mentally retarded individuals. *Mental Retardation, 19,* 157–161.

Foss, R. M., and Shapiro, S. T. (1978). The time out ribbon: A nonexclusionary time out procedure. *Journal of Applied Behavior Analysis, 2,* 125–136.

Frager, A., and Thompson, L. (1985). Teaching college study skills with a news magazine. *Journal of Reading, 28* (5), 404–407.

Frame, C., and Oltmann, T. (1982). Serial recall by schizophrenic and affective patients during and after psychotic episodes. *The Journal of Abnormal Psychology, 91,* 311–318.

Frances, L.; Pearson, P.; Carter, M.; and Kay, W. (1981). The relationship between neuroticism and religiosity among English 15 and 16 year olds. *The Journal of Social Psychology, 114,* 99–102.

Francis, J. (1982). A case for open-book examinations. *Educational Review, 34* (1), 13–26.

Frank, A. (1978). Teaching money skills with a numberline. *Teaching Exceptional Children, 11* (2), 13–16.

Franzoi, S. L. (1982). Private self-consciousness as an adaptation strategy. (ERIC Document Reproduction Series No. ED 220 779).

Frease, R. (1973). Delinquency, social class, and the schools. *Sociology and Social Research, 56,* 445–446.

Freberg, G. (1982). The classroom loner. *Learning Magazine, 3,* 45–48.

Fredericks, A. D. (1982). Developing positive reading attitudes. *Reading Teacher, 36,* 38–40.

Freeman, S. (1979). *The epileptic in home, school, and society.* Springfield, IL: Charles C. Thomas.

Freischlag, J. (1973). Motor activities to teach handwriting to the poorly coordinated. *School and Community, 59,* 28–94.

French, D. (1985). Behavior problems of peer-neglected and peer rejected elementary age children. *Child Development, 56* (1), 246–252.

French, R. W., and Jansma, P. (1982). *Special physical education.* Columbus, OH: Charles E. Merrill.

Frey, D., and Young, J. (1979). Self-concept continuum for understanding student behavior. *NASSAP Bulletin, 63* (428), 27–33.

Frick, S. (1985). Diagnosing boredom, confusion, and adaptation in school children. *Journal of School Health, 55* (7), 254–257.

Friebel, A. C. (1974). Mathways. *Elementary Teachers Ideas and Materials Workshop, 8* (4), 11–12.

Fried, H. (ed.). (1978). *Plain talk about dealing with the angry child.* Available from National Institute of Mental Health, Plain talk series. Division of Scientific and Public Information, 5600 Fishers Lane, Rockville, MD.

Friedling, C., and O'Leary, S. G. (1979). Effects of self-instructional training on second and third grade hyperactive children: A failure to replicate. *Journal of Applied Behavior Analysis, 12* (2), 211–219.

Friedman, P. (1980). *Shyness and reticence in students.* Washington, D.C.: National Education Association. (ERIC Document Reproduction Service No. ED 181 520).

Frierson, E. C., and Barbe, W. B. (1967). *Educating children with learning disabilities.* New York: Meridith Publishing Co.

Frostig, M., and Horne, D. (1964). *Teacher's guide, Frostig program for the development of visual perception.* Chicago: Follett.

Frostig, M., and Maslow, P. (1973). *Learning problems in the classroom.* New York: Grune & Stratton.

Frumkes, L. (1982). The neurotic personality: Are you screwed up? *Bazaar, 115,* 148–152.

Fucigna, Ives K., and Ives W. (1982). *American Artist, 48,* 14–16.

Fulkerson, F., and Martin, G. (1981). Effects of exam frequency on student performance, evaluations of instructor and test anxiety. *Teaching of Psychology, 8* (2), 90–93.

Fuller, G., and Fuller, D. (1982). Reality therapy: Helping learning disabled children make better choices. *Academic Therapy, 17,* 269–277.

Fuller, M. (1984). *Increasing self concept: An educational perspective.* Grand Forks: North Dakota University, Grand Forks Center for Teaching and Learning. (ERIC Document Reproduction Service No. ED 243 602).

Fundudis, T., and Kolvin, I. (1981). Elective mute children: Psychological development and background factors. *Journal of Child Psychology and Psychiatry and Allied Disciplines, 22,* 219–232.

Funkabiki, D. (1981). *An investigation of precipitating events and susceptibility factors in depression.* Pullman: Washington State University. (ERIC Document Reproduction Service No. ED 214 071).

Furst, M. (1983). Building self-esteem. *Academic Therapy, 19,* 11–15.

Gable, R. A., and Strain, P. S. (1981). Individualizing a token reinforcement system for the treatment of children's behavior disorders. *Behavioral Disorders, 7,* 39–45.

Gadow, K. (1980). Children on medication: A primer for school personnel. Reston, VA: Council for Exceptional Children.

Gadow, K. (1982). School involvement in pharmacotherapy for behavior disorders. *Journal of Special Education, 16,* 397.

Galassi, J. P.; Frierson, H. T.; and Sharer, R. (1981). Concurrent versus retrospective assessment in test anxiety research. *Journal of Consulting and Clinical Psychology, 49* (4), 614–615.

Gallagher, D. (1985). Employing adolescents. *Supervisory Management, 30* (7), 10–14.

Gallagher, P. (1971). *Positive classroom performance techniques for changing behavior.* Denver: Love.

Gallagher, P. (1979). *Teaching students with behavioral disorders: Techniques for classroom instruction.* Denver: Love.

Gallant, D., and Simpson, D. (1976). *Depression.* New York: Spectrum Publications.

Galloway, D. (1976). *Case studies in classroom management.* New York: Longman Group.

Ganger, S., et al. (1980). *Bibliographies of selected articles in reading comprehension.* Washington, D.C.: Bureau of Education for the Handicapped. (ERIC Document Reproduction Service No. ED 209 643).

Ganschow, L (1983). Teaching strategies for spelling success. *Academic Therapy, 19* (2), 185–193.

Ganschow, L (1984). Analyze error patterns to remediate severe spelling difficulties. *The Reading Teacher, 38* (3), 288.

Gappa, S., and Glynn, D. (1981). *Room to grow.* Los Angeles: Pitman Learning.

Gardner, L. R. (1985). Low vision enhancement: The use of figure-ground reversals with visually impaired children. *Journal of Visual Impairment and Blindness, 79,* 64–66.

Garfield, E. F., and Gibbs, J. (1982). Fostering parent involvement for drug prevention. *Journal of Drug Education, 12,* 87–96.

Garfinkel, P., and Moldofsky, H. (1980). The heterogeneity of anorexia nervosa. *Archives of General Psychiatry, 37,* 1036–1040.

Garza, R. T., and Lipton, J. (1978). Personality and reactions to praise and criticism. *The Journal of Personality, 46,* 9–12.

Gaudry, E., and Spielberger, C. D. (1971). *Anxiety and educational achievement.* New York: John Wiley & Sons.

Gavain, R. (1954). *Understanding juvenile delinquency.* New York: Oxford Book Co.

Gaylin, W. (1968). *The meaning of despair: Psychoanalytic contributions to the understanding of depression.* New York: Holt, Rinehart & Winston.

Gaylord-Ross, R. J.; Weeks, M.; Lipner, C.; and Gaylord-Ross, C. (1983). The differential effectiveness of four treatment procedures in suppressing self-injurious behavior among severely handicapped students. *Education and Training of the Mentally Retarded, 18,* 38–44.

Gearheart, B. R. (1976). *Teaching the learning disabled: A combined task-process approach.* St. Louis: C. V. Mosby.

Gearheart, B. R. (1981). *Learning disabilities educational strategies.* St. Louis: C. V. Mosby.

Geedy, P. S. (1981). What research tells us about spelling. *Academic Therapy, 15,* 448–450.

Gelder, M. (1979). Behavior therapy for neurotic disorders. *Behavior Modification, 3,* 469–495.

Gelzheiser, L. M.; Solar, R. A.; Shepherd, M.; and Wozniak, R. H. (1983). Teaching learning disabled children to memorize: A rationale for plans and practice. *Journal of Learning Disabilities, 16* (7), 421–425.

Gemake, J. (1984). Interactive reading: How to make children active readers. *The Reading Teacher, 37* (6), 462–466.

Gennaro, E. (1981). The effectiveness of using previsit instructional materials on learning from a museum field trip experience. *Journal of Research in Science Teaching, 18,* 275–279.

Gentile, J. R. (1984). *Motions, emotions, and commotions: Social learning at home and in the classroom.* Dubuque, IA: Kendall/Hunt.

Gentile, J. R.; Frazier, T. M.; and Morris, M. C. (1973). *Instructional applications of behavior principles.* California: Wadsworth Publishing Co.

Gentile, L. M. (1983). *Using sports and physical education to strengthen reading skills.* Delaware: International Reading Association.

George, P. (1982). *Promoting attention in children with learning disabilities: Techniques from a research, clinical and classroom perspective.* Houston, TX: Annual International Convention of the Council of Exceptional Children. (ERIC Document Reproduction Service No. ED 218 912).

George-Nichols, N., et al. (1982). *Special education handbook for secondary significant identifiable emotional or behavioral disorders.* Denver: Denver Public Schools, Department of Special Education. (ERIC Document Reproduction Service No. ED 252 019).

Gerber, M. M. (1983). Learning disabilities and cognitive strategies: A case for training or constraining problem solving. *Journal of Learning Disabilities, 16* (5), 255–257.

Gerson, A., and Perlma, D. (1979). Lonliness and expressive communications. *The Journal of Abnormal Psychology, 88,* 258–261.

Gersten, R. (1985). *Journal for Special Educators, 19* (1), 41–58.

Gervais, M.; Harvey, L.; and Roberts, J. (1984). Identification confusions among letters of the alphabet. *Journal of Experimental Psychology: Human Perception and Performance, 10* (5), 655–666.

Gervais, R. L., and Dittburner, D. A. (1979). *A handbook for classroom discipline problems with practical and positive solutions.* Wyoming: Wyoming University. (ERIC Document Reproduction Service No. ED 234 013).

Gervais, R., and Dittburner, D. (1981) *What do you do when..? A handbook for classroom discipline problems with practical and positive solutions.* Laramie, WY: Center for Research, Service, and Publication. (ERIC Document Reproduction Service No. ED 234 013).

Getman, G. N. (1983). About handwriting. *Academic Therapy, 19* (2), 139–146.

Getman, G. N. (1985). Hand-eye co-ordinations. *Academic Therapy, 20* (3), 261–275.

Gettinger, M. (1984). Applying learning principles to remedial spelling instruction. *Academic Therapy, 20* (2), 41–48.

Gettinger, M. (1985). Effects of teacher-directed vs. student directed instruction and cues vs. no cues for improving spelling performance. *Journal of Applied Behavioral Analysis, 18* (2), 102.

Ghent, L., and Bernstein, L. (1963). Effect of orientation of recognition of geometric forms by retarded children. *Child Development, 35,* 1127–1136.

Gholson, R., and Buser, R. (1981). Student activities: A guide for who is participating in what. *NASSP Bulletin, 65,* 43–47.

Giarretto, H. (1982). *Integrated treatment of child sexual abuse.* California: Science & Behavior Books.

Gibbs, G., et al (1979). *Understanding why students don't learn.* England: Open University Institute of Educational Technology. (ERIC Document Reproduction Service No. ED 189 982).

Gibson, E. (1969). *Principles of perceptual learning and development.* New York: Meredith Corp.

Gibson, E.; Gibson, J.; Pick, A.; and Osler, H. (1962). A developmental study of the discrimination of letter-life forms. *Journal of Comparative Physical Psychology, 55,* 897–907.

Giffin, P. (1980). *Social problems.* Boston: Allyn and Bacon.

Gifford, C. S., and Fluitt, J. L. (1980). How to make your students testwise. *American School Board Jounal, 167,* 29.

Gillespie, C. (1977). *Your pregnancy month by month.* New York: Harper & Row.

Gillet, P. (1977). Pointers for parents. *Pointer, 22* (1), 74–77.

Gillet, T. (1981). Assessment and treatment of clinical fears in mentally retarded children. *Journal of Applied Behavior Analysis, 14,* (3), 287–294.

Gillet, P. J., and Hornbeck, M. (1973). *Depression: A layman's guide to the symptoms and cures.* New York: E. P. Dutton.

Giordano, G. (1983). Integrating remedial writing into reading programs. *Academic Therapy, 18,* 599–607.

Givner, A., and Graubard, P. S. (1974). *A handbook of behavior modification for the classroom.* New York: Holt, Rinehart, and Winston.

Glaser, K. (1974). *Learning difficulties: Causes and psychological implications.* Springfield, IL: Charles C. Thomas.

Glaser, S. (1981). Oral communication apprehension and avoidance: The current status of treatment research. *Communication Education, 30* (4), 321–341.

Glasser, W. (1965). *Reality therapy.* New York: Harper & Row.

Glasser, W. (1979). A humanistic approach to behavior with preadolescent inner-city hearing disabled children. *Journal of Learning Disabilities, 12* (6), 31–34.

Glazzard, P. (1981). Training students to work independently in the classroom. *Teaching Exceptional Children, 13* (2), 66–70.

Gleason, B. (1982). Writing: A way out of the LD dilemma. *Academic Therapy, 17,* 573–579.

Gleason, J. J. (1983). ABCD's of motivating adolescent LD students. *Academic Therapy, 19* (1), 52–55.

Gleissner, L.; Nietupski, J.; and Stainback, W. (1983). Effects of socially outgoing versus withdrawn nonhandicapped peer partners on nonhandicapped/handicapped student interactions. *Behavior Disorders, 8* (4), 244–250.

Glendale Heights Community Hospital, Inc. Eating disorder program.

Glenn, E.C.; Glenn, P. J.; and Forman, S. H. (1984). *Your voice and articulation.* New York: Macmillian.

Glenwick, D. (1979). Training impulsive children in verbal self control by use of natural change agents. *Journal of Special Education, 13,* 387–398.

Gliner, C. (1985). A developmental investigation of visual and haptic preferences for shape and texture. *Society for Research in Child Development, 34,* 3–29.

Gluek, S., and Glueck, E. (1951). *Unraveling juvenile delinquency.* Cambridge, MA: Harvard University Press.

Glueck, S., and Glueck, E. (1970). *Towards a typology of juvenile offenders.* New York: Grune & Stratton.

Gnagey, W. J. (1968). *The psychology of discipline in the classroom.* New York: MacMillian.

Godenson, R. M. (1970). *The encyclopedia of human behavior psychology, psychiatry, and mental health, 1,* 583–585.

Goetz, E. M.; Thomson, C. L.; and Etzel, B. C. (1975). An analysis of direct and indirect teacher attention and primes in the modification of child social behavior: A case study. *Merrial-Palmer Quarterly, 21,* 55–65.

Goetze, H., and Heinz, N. (1978). *A structured student-centered approach for teaching hyperactive, emotionally disturbed children.* Washington, D. C.: World Congress on Future Special Education, U.S. Dept. HEW National Institute of Education. (ERIC Document Reproduction No. ED 157 366).

Gold, P. C. (1981). Two strategies for reinforcing sight vocabulary of language experience stories. *The Reading Teacher, 35* (2), 141.

Gold, Y. (1981). Teaching attentive listening. *Reading Improvement, 18* (4), 319–320.

Gold, Y. (1983). Reading detective stories can motivate students toward improved oral and written communication skills. *Reading Improvement, 20* (4), 259–262.

Golden, J. M. (1981). Depression in middle and late childhood: Implications for intervention. *Child Welfare, 60,* 457–465.

Goldenson, R. M. (1970). *The encyclopedia of human behavior: Psychology, psychiatry, and mental health* (Vol. 1). Garden City, NY: Doubleday.

Goldfried, M. R. (1976). *Behavioral management of anxiety: A clinician's guide and self-modification of anxiety. (Client instructions).* New York: Biomonitoring Applications.

Goldfried, M. R., and Goldfried, A. P. (1980). Cognitive change methods. In F. H. Kanfer and A. P. Goldstein (eds.), *Helping people change* (2nd ed.). New York: Pergamon Press.

Goldimond, P. (1965). Self-control procedures in personal behavior problems. *Psychological Reports, 17,* 851–868.

Golding-Mather, J. M., and Singer, J. L. (1981). *Phenomenological patterns of depressive moods.* Los An-

geles; University of California. (ERIC Document Reproduction Service No. ED 214 052).

Goldner, R. H. (1973). Changing children's behavior. *Instructor, 82* (9), 14–16.

Goldstein, A. P. and Rusenbaum, A. (1983). Aggress-Less. *Aggressive Behavior, 9,* 57–59.

Goldstein, A. P.; Sprafkin, P. R.; Gershaw, J.; and Klein, P. (1983). Structured learning: A psycho-educational approach for teaching social competencies. *Behavioral Disorders, 8* (3), 161–170.

Goldston, R. (1975). Coping with behavior problems. *Parent's Magazine,* May, 12.

Good Housekeeping (1982). Bulimia: The secret dieter's disease. *194,* 239.

Good Housekeeping (1984a). Tricks that help you remember. *198.*

Good Housekeeping (1984b). What makes you remember—And forget! *195, 317.*

Good, T., and Grouws, D. (1979). Teaching and mathematics learning. *Educational Leadership, 37* (1), 39–45.

Goode, E. (1970). *The marijuana smokers.* New York: Basic Books.

Goode E. (1980). Marijuana. *Journal of Sociology, 3,* 124–133.

Goodman, G., and Timko, M. G. (1976). Hot seats and aggressive behavior. *Academic Therapy, 11,* 447–448.

Goodson, J. (1984). The effects of word cueing. *The Journal of Abnormal Psychology, 93,* 98–105.

Goodwin, D. L., and Coates, T. J. (1976). *Helping students help themselves.* Englewood Cliffs, NJ: Prentice-Hall.

Goodwin, D. W. (1977) *Phobia: The facts.* Oxford: Oxford University Press.

Gordon, J. S. (1981). Reaching troubled youth. (ERIC Document Reproduction Service No. ED 217 333).

Gordon, S. R. (1979). *Science news of controversy: The case of marijuana.* (ERIC Document Reproduction Service No. ED 176 282).

Gormally, J., and Rardin, D. (1981). Weight loss and maintenance and changes in diet and exercise for behavioral counseling and nutrition education. *Journal of Counseling Psychology, 28,* 295–304.

Gorman, C. (1978). Sheltered workshop prepares potential dropouts for on-the-job training. *American Vocational Journal, 53* (3), 42–44.

Goss, S., and Ingersoll, G. (1981). *Management of dis-*

ruptive and off-task behavior: Selected resources, bibliographies. Washington, D. C.: National Institute of Education. (ERIC Document Reproduction Service No. ED 200 520).

Gottfried, A. E. (1983). Intrinsic motivation in young children. *Young Children, 39* (1), 64–71.

Gottman, J.; Gonso, J.; and Schuler, P. (1976). Teaching social skills to isolated children. *Journal of Abnormal Child Psychology, 4,* 179–197.

Gourley, T. J., and Micklus, C. S. (1982). *Olympics of the mind, coaches manual.* Glassforo, NJ: Creative Competition.

Gourney, C. (1981). Do nice girls swear? *Seventeen, 40,* 96–97.

Gowan J.; Khatena, J.; and Torrance, E. (1979). *Educating the ablest.* New York: Holt, Rinehart & Winston.

Guerney, B. G. and Flumen, A. B. (1970). Teachers as psychotherapeutic agents for withdrawn children. *Journal of School Psychology, 8,* 107–114.

Guerney, L. F. (1983). Play therapy with learning disabled children. In C. E. Schaefer and K. J. O'Connor (eds.), *Handbook of play therapy.* New York: John Wiley & Sons.

Guidance Associates (1972). *The trouble with truth.* 2 Filmstrips (102 fr.), color, 35mm, and 1 sound cassette, 1-7/8 ips., for manual or automatic operation. Approximate playing time: 12 minutes. Includes teacher's guide with script sources. Guidance Associates, Inc., Communications Park, Box 300, White Plains, New York, 10602.

Guthrie, J. T. (1981). Managing problem students. *Reading Teacher, 35,* 380–382.

Grabow, B. (1981). Using visual imagery in the classroom. *Academic Therapy, 16* (5), 615–619.

Graham, S. (1984). Teacher feelings and student thoughts: An attributional approach to affect in the classroom. *The Elementary School Journal, 85,* 91–104.

Graham, S., and Hudson F. (1979). Presenting instruction. *The Pointer for Special Educators,23* (3), 31–32.

Graham, S., and Maden, A. (1981). Teaching letter formation. *Academic Therapy, 16* (4), 389–396.

Grahm, T. L., and Knight, M. E. (1983). How to promote a positive self-concept. *Early Years, 14* (1), 40–50.

Grant, M. (1985). The kinesthetic approach to teaching: Building a foundation of learning. *Journal of Learning Disabilities, 18* (8), 455–461.

Graubard, P. S. (1977). *Positive parenthood.* Indianapolis, IN: Bobbs-Merrill Co.

Gray, J. M. (1981). Motivating today's students. Enjoy yourself and be flexible. *Today's Education, 70* (4), 34–35.

Graybill, D.; Jamison, M.; and Swerdlik, M. E. (1984). Remediation of impulsivity in learning disabled children by special education resource teachers using verbal self instruction. *Psychology in the Schools, 21,* 252–254.

Graziano, A. (1974). *Child without tomorrow.* New York: Pergamon Press.

Green, E. (1984). From the files of Ellie Green, Frederick, Maryland, 21701, *Arithmetic Teacher, 31* (8), 54.

Green, L. (1985). *Verge: Alcohol effects nastier than hangover.* Illinois: Eastern News, February 1.

Greenes, C. (1976). *Learning disabilities in the classroom.* State University of New York.

Greenstein, A., and O'Brien, C. P. (1981). Naltrexone: A short-term treatment of opiate dependence. *The American Journal of Drug and Alcohol Abuse, 8,* 291–300.

Greenstein, R. (1970). Can we lessen vandalism? *Instructor, 79,* 90–91.

Greenwood, A. (1981). Critique of differences between vowel and consonant sounds. *Journal of reading improvement, 18* (3), 224–225.

Greenwood, C. R. (1984). Teacher-versus peer-mediated instruction: An eco-behavioral analysis of achievement outcomes. *Journal of Applied Behavior Analysis, 17* (4), 521–538.

Gresham, F. M., and Nagle, R. (1981). Treating school phobia using behavioral consultation: A case study. *School Psychology Review, 10,* 104–107.

Greshan, F. A. (1984). Social Skills and self-efficacy for exceptional children. *Exceptional Children, 51* (3), 253–261.

Greiger, T.; Kauffman, J. M.; and Grieger, R. M. (1976). Effects of peer reporting on cooperative play and aggression of kindergarten children. *Journal of School Psychology, 14,* 307–313.

Groff, P. G. (1984). Word familiarity & spelling difficulty. *Education Resource, 26,* 33–35.

Groten, G., and Cautela, J. R. (1981). Behavior therapy: A survey of procedures for counselor. *Personnel and Guidance Journal, 60,* 175–180.

Gruber, A. R.; Heck, E. T.; and Mintzer, E. (1981). Children who set fires: Some background and behavioral characteristics. *American Journal of Othopsychiatry, 51,* 484–487.

Grzynkowicz, W. (1979). *Basic education for children with learning disabilities.* Springfield, IL: Charles C. Thomas.

Haas, K.; Kasper, K.; and Kryst, D. (1979) *Common solutions for the uncommon child.* Chicago: Illinois Council for Exceptional Children. (ERIC Document Reproduction Service No. ED 199 941).

Hagin, R. A. (1983). Write right-or left: A practical approach to handwriting. *Journal of Learning Disabilities, 16* (5), 268.

Hagtvet, K. A. (1982). *A construct validation study of test anxiety: A discriminant validation of fear of failure, worry, and emotionality.* (ERIC Document Reproduction Series. ED 222 535).

Halikas, J. A.; Goodwin, D. W.; and Guze, S. B. (1973). Marijuana effects: A survey of regular users. In *Behavior and social effects of marijuana.* New York: MSS Information Corp.

Hall, N. A. (1969). *Rescue: A handbook of classroom ideas to motivate the teaching of remedial reading.* Stevensville, IN: Educational Services.

Hall, R. V. (1968). Instructing beginning teachers in reinforcement procedures which improve classroom control. *Journal of Applied Behavior Analysis, 1,* 315–322.

Hall, R. T. (1979). *Moral education: A handbook for teachers.* Minneapolis, MN: Winston Press.

Hallahan, D. P., and Kauffman, J. M. (1975). Research on the education of distractible and hyperactive children. In W. M. Cruickshank and D. P. Hallahan (eds.), *Perceptual and learning disabilities in children. Vol. 2: Research and theory.* Syracuse, NY: Syracuse University Press.

Hallahan, D. P., and Kauffman, J. M. (1976). *Introduction to learning disabilities.* Englewood Cliffs, NJ: Prentice-Hall.

Hallahan, D. P., and Kauffman, J. M. (1978). *Exceptional children.* Englewood Cliffs, NJ: Prentice-Hall.

Hallahan, D. P.; Lloyd, J.; Koseiwicz, M. M.; Kauffman, J. M.; and Graves, A. W. (1979). Self-monitoring of attention as a treatment for a learning disabled boy's off-task behavior. *Learning Disabilities Quarterly, 2,* 24–32.

Hallahan, D. P.; Lloyd, J. W.; and Rooney, K. (1984). Self recording of attention by learning disabled students in the regular classroom. *Journal of Learning Disabilities, 17* (6), 360–364.

Hallahan, D. P., and Sapona, R. (1983). Self monitor-

ing of attention with learning disabled children: Past research and current issues. *Journal of Learning Disabilities, 16* (10), 618.

Hamachek, D. (1968). *Motivation and learning.* Washington, D.C.: NEA Pub.

Hamblin, R. L.; Buckholdt, D.; Bushnell, D.; Ellis, D.; and Ferritor, D. (1969). Changing the game from 'get the teacher' to 'learn.' *Transaction, 1,* 20–31.

Hamburg, D.; Pribram, K.; and Stunkard, A. *Perception and its disorders.* Baltimore: Waverly Press.

Hamilton, D. T.; Flemming, B. J.; and Hicks, J. D. (1976). I'm me! I'm special! A guide to teaching self-concept. *Instructor, 86,* 77–82.

Hamilton, J. (1983). Development of interest and enjoyment in adolescence: Boredom psychopathology. *Journal of Yourth Adolesence, 10* (3), 44–50.

Hamilton, J. (1984). How to beat reliance frustration. *Thrust, 13,* 15.

Hammill, D., and Meyers, P. (1969). *Methods for learning disorders.* New York: Wiley and Sons.

Hammill, D. B., and Bartel, N. R. (1975). *Teaching children with learning and behavioral disorders.* Boston: Allyn and Bacon.

Hammill, D. D., and Bartel, N. R. (1982). *Teaching children with learning and behavior problems,* 2nd ed. Boston: Allyn and Bacon.

Hampton, C. H. (1979). *Schoolgirl pregnancy: Old problems: new solutions.* New York: Springer Publishing Co.

Hampton, P. (1977). Training inreferral counseling of potential and actual dropout students. *College Student Journal, 11* (4), 324–328.

Handel, R., and Robert. S. (1982). *A positive self-image. It's your choice. A classroom program for the development of self-esteem.* New York. (ERIC Document Reproduction No. ED 242 600).

Hanford, G. (1984). Only connect—Critical thinking skills. *Vital Speeches Day, 50,* 211–214.

Hanna, R.; Hodges, E.; and Hanna, J. (1971). *Spelling: Structure and strategies.* Boston: Houghton Mifflin.

Hansen, J. J. (1976). *A didactic group therapy program for the treatment of depression.* Masters thesis, Department of Psychology, Eastern Illinois University, Charleston.

Hansen, J. M. (1981). Citizenship education: Decision making as a rediscovered fundamental. *Clearing House, 54* (9), 410–412.

Hanson, J., and Hoeft, D. (1983). One school district fights the battle of truancy with some success. *Phi Delta Kappan, 64,* 436–437.

Hansteen, R.; Miller, R; Loneero, L.; Reid, L.; and Jones, B. (1976). Effect of cannabis and alcohol on automobile driving and psychomotor tracking. *Annals of the New York Academy of Science, 282,* 240–255.

Hardin, B., and Bernstein, B. (1976). What about reversals? *Teacher, 94,* 104–108.

Hardy, R. E., and Cull, J. G. (1974). *Problems of adolescents.* Springfield, IL: Charles C. Thomas.

Haring, N. G. (1982). *Exceptional children and youth.* Columbus, OH: Charles E. Merrill.

Haring, N. G., and Phillips, E. L. (1962). *Educating emotionally disturbed children.* New York: McGraw-Hill.

Harnden, G. M. (1984). *The power of positive self-reporting.* Los Angeles. (ERIC Document Reproduction Service No. ED 217 344).

Harper, J. M. (1981). Gelineau's narcolepsy relieved by opiates. *The Lancet, 1,* 92.

Harris, A. (1980). Children with short fuses. *Instructor, 90,* 52–54.

Harris, A., and Brown, B., (1981). Cognitive behavior modification and ways to inform teachers on treatments of shy children. *Journal of Experimental Education, 50* (2), 139–144.

Harris, A., and Sipay, R. (1972). *Readings on reading instruction.* New York: David McKay.

Harris, F., and Mayhew, G. (1979). Decreasing self-injurious behavior: Punishment with citric acid and reinforcement of alternate behavior. *Behavior Modification, 3,* 322–336.

Harris, J. R. (1983). Parent-aided homework: A working model for school personnel. *School Counselor, 31* (2), 171–176.

Harris, L. P. (1976). Attention and learning disabled children: A review of the theory and remediation. *Journal of Learning Disabilities, 9* (2), 100–110.

Harris, L. S., and Wolchik, S. A. (1979). Suppression of self-stimulation: Three alternative strategies. *Journal of Applied Behavioral Analysis, 12,* 185–198.

Harris, M. (1982). Children with short fuses. *Instructor, 92,* 53–59.

Harris, M. B., and Merrill, C. E. (1972). *Classroom uses of behavior modification.* Columbus, OH: Charles C. Thomas.

Harris, S. (1980). School phobic children and adolescents: A challenge to counselors. *School Counselor, 27,* 263–268.

Harris, T., and Brown, S. (1981). Cognitive behavior modification and ways to inform teachers on treatment for shy children. *Journal of Experimental Education, 50* (2), 139–144.

Harrison, S. (1981). Open letter from a lefthanded teacher: Some sinistral ideas on the teaching of handwriting. *Teaching Exceptional Children, 13* (3), 116–120.

Harrow, A. J. (1977). *A taxonomy of the psychomotor domain.* New York: David McKay Co.

Hartford, E. F. (1958). *Moral values in public education: Lessons from the Kentucky experience.* New York: Harper & Brother.

Hartman, A. C.; Lucas, V. H.; and Stepens, T. M. (1982). *Teaching children basic skills.* Columbus, OH: Charles E Merrill.

Hartman C.; MacIntosh, B.; and Engelhart, B. (1983). The neglected and forgotten sexual partner of the physically disabled. *Social Work, 28* (5), 370–374.

Hartman, T. M.; Lucas, V. H.; and Stephens, T. M. (1982). *Teaching children basic skills.* Columbus, OH: Charles E. Merrill.

Harvat, W. H. (1971). *Physical education for children with perceptual motor learning disabilities.* Columbus, OH: Charles E. Merrill.

Harvey, P. E.; Weintraub, S.; and Neale, J. M. (1984). Distractibility in learning-disabled children: The role of measurement artifact. *Journal of Learning Disabilities, 17,* 4.

Harvey, R., and Denby, R. (1970). Life at an early age: Nourishing self-concept in the classroom. *Elementary English, 47,* 993–1001.

Haskell, L. L. (1979). *Art in the early childhood years.* Columbus, OH: Charles E. Merrill.

Haslett, J. (1982). *The art of movement and latter learning.* (ERIC Document Reproduction Service No. ED 214 912).

Haswell, K. L.; Hock, E.; and Wenar, C. (1982). Techniques for dealing with oppositional behavior in preschool children. *Young Children, 37,* 12–17.

Haswell, R. (1981). Oppositional behavior of preschool children: Theory and intervention. *Family Relations, 3,* 440–446.

Hawaii State Dept. of Education (1982). *Social skills: Alternatives to aggression.* Hawaii State Department of Education, Honolulu, Office of Instructional Services.

Hayden, A. H.; Smith, R.; Saaz, T.; and von Hipple, B. (1982) *Mainstreaming preschoolers: Children with learning disabilities.* U.S. Department of Health, Education and Welfare.

Hayes, M. L. (1974). *The tuned-in turned-on book about learning problems.* New York: Academic Therapy Publications.

Hayes, M. L. (1975). *Somebody said learning disabilities.* New York: Academic Therapy Publications.

Hayes, M. L. (1984). Materials for the resource room. *Academic Therapy, 20* (2), 289–297.

Hayward, H. (1982). The irrational beliefs which cause test anxiety.

Hazen, N.; Black, B.; and Johnson, F. (1984). Social acceptance. *Young Children, 39,* 11–14.

Heeting, K. (1978). *When your child is hyperactive.* Meinrad, IN: Abbey Press.

Hegeman, K. T. (1981). *Gifted children in the regular classroom.* New York: Trillium Press.

Heidmann, M. (1973). *The slow learner in the primary grades.* Columbus, OH: Charles E. Merrill.

Heitzman, A. J. (1983). Discipline and the use of punishment. *Education, 104,* 17–22.

Held, D., and Hein, R. (1963). Movement-produced stimulation in the development of visually guided behavior. *Journal of Comparative and Physiological Psychology, 56,* 872–876.

Helge, D. (1983). *Personal development skills and strategies for effective survival as a rural special educator. Student text for the curriculum module.* Laramie, WY: Center for Research, Service, and Publications.

Hellmuth, J. (1966). *Educational therapy.* Seattle, WA: Special Child Publication of the Seattle Seguin School.

Henderson, R. (1980). Social and emotional needs of culturally diverse children. *Exceptional Children, 46* (8), 598–605.

Hendricks, G., and Roberts, T. (1977). *The second centering book.* Englewood Cliffs, NJ: Prentice-Hall.

Hendricks, G., and Wills, R. (1975). *The centering book, awareness activities for children, parents, and teachers.* Englewood Cliffs, NJ: Prentice-Hall.

Hendrickson, E. (1980). *Checkbook education: A motivating classroom idea!* (ERIC Document Reproducting Service No. ED 239 965).

Hendrickson, J. M.; Strain, P. S.; and Tremblay, A. (1980). The activity context of preschool children's social interactions: A comparison of high and low social interactors. *Psychology in the Schools, 17* (3), 380–385.

Henson, K. (1977). A new concept of discipline. *Clearing House, 51* (10), 89–91.

Henson, K. (1980). What's the use of lecturing? *High School Journal, 64* (3), 115–119.

Herbert, M. (1978). *Conduct disorders of childhood and adolescence.* New York: John Wiley and Sons.

Herr, S. E. (1961). *Learning activities for reading.* Dubuque, IA: William C. Brown.

Hersen, M.; Eisler, R. M.; and Miller, P. M. (1981). *Progress in behavior modification.* New York: Academic Press.

Hersey, J. (1977). *Partnership in pleasure.* In D. R. Gallo (ed.), *Teaching writing: Advice from the professionals.* (ERIC Document Reproduction Service No. ED 151 846).

Hershey, M. (1983). Warm fingers, cool behavior. *Academic Therapy, 18* (5), 593–597.

Hershey, M., and Kearns, P. (1979). The effect of guided fantasy on the creative thinking and writing ability of gifted students. *Gifted Child Quarterly, 23,* 71–78.

Heshusuis, L. (1982). Sexuality, intimacy, and persons we label mentally retarded: What they think—what we think. *Mental Retardation, 4,* 164–168.

Heuchert, C. (1983). Can teachers change behavior? Try interviews! *Academic Therapy, 18* (3), 321–328.

Heward, W. L., and Orlansky, M. D. (1980). *Exceptional children: An introductory survey to special education.* Columbus, OH: Bell & Howell.

Hewett, F. (1964). A hierarchy of educational tasks for children with learning disorders. *Exceptional Children, 3* (14), 207–216.

Hewett, F. M. (1967). Educational engineering with emotionally disturbed children. *Exceptional Children, 33,* 459–467.

Hewett, F. M. *The emotionally disturbed child in the classroom: A developmental strategy for educating children with maladaptive behavior.* Boston: Allyn and Bacon.

Hewett, F. M., and Forness, S. R. (1977). *Education of exceptional learners.* Boston: Allyn and Bacon.

Heydorn, B. (1984). Reducing reversals in reading and writing. *Academic Therapy, 19,* 305–308.

Heyn, D. (1982). Why we're never satisfied with our bodies. *McCalls.*

Hickey, N. (1975). Does America want family viewing time? *TV Guide,* 8.

Hicks, E. P., and Schrader, G. (1984). Narcolepsy,

paranoid psychosis, major depression, and tardive dyskinesia. *Journal of Nervous and Mental Disease, 172,* 439–441.

Hiebert, J. (1984). Children's mathematics learning: The struggle to link form and understanding. *The Elementary School Journal, 84* (5), 111–116.

Higa, W. R.; Tharp, R. G.; and Calkins, R. P. (1978). Developmental verbal control of behavior: Implications for self-instructional training. *Journal of Experimental Child Psychology, 26,* 489–497.

Higginbotham, D .D., and Davis, M. (1981). A new look at show-and-tell. *Learning, 9,* 10–14.

Highbee, K. L. (1977). *Your memory: How it works and how to improve it.* Englewood Cliffs, NJ: Prentice-Hall.

Highland, A. (1984). When some kids get picked on. *Instructor, 93* (7), 66–68.

Hill, B. R. (1983). *Effective child guidance: An educator's guidebook.* Nova University. (ERIC Document Reproduction No. ED 258 702).

Hill, C. H. (1983). Round robin reading as a teaching method. *Reading Improvement, 2* (4), 263–266.

Hill, K. T. (1982). Interfering effects of test anxiety on test performance: A growing educational problem and solution to it. *Illinois School Research and Development, 20,* 8–19.

Hill, K. T., and Wigfield, A. (1984). Test anxiety: A major educational problem and what can be done about it. *The Elementary School Journal, 85,* 105–126.

Hill, P. L. (1973). *Solving behavior problems.* Dansville, NY: Instructor Publications.

Hillerich, R. L. (1982). That's teaching spelling? *Educational Leadership, 39* (8), 615–617.

Hillerich, R. L., and Gould, S. (1981). *Spelling for writing.* Columbus, OH: Charles E. Merrill.

Hindeland, M. (1973). Causes of delinquency: A partial replication and extension. *Social Problems, 20,* 471–487.

Hinsie, L. E., and Campbell, R. J. (1970). *Psychiatric dictionary* (4th ed.). New York: Oxford University Press.

Hipple, M. (1978). Classroom discipline problems? 15 humane solutions. *Childhood Education, 54* (3), 183–187.

Hirschi, T. (1969). *Causes of delinquency.* Berkeley, CA: University of California Press.

Hoberman, G. (1951). *Functional exercises.* Dayton, OH: William Davis Publishers.

Hoch, L. L., and Olszowy, J. (1981). What do teachers say? Another look at drug education. *Journal of Alcohol and Drug Education, 26,* 10–12.

Hodges, D. (1982). *A teachers guide to memory techniques.* (ERIC Document Reproduction Service No. ED 220 155).

Hofler, D. B. (1981). Word lines: An approach to vocabulary development. *The Reading Teacher, 35* (2), 216–217.

Holbrook, H. T. (1983). Invented spelling. *Language Arts, 60* (6), 800–804. (ERIC/RCS Report).

Holbrook, H. T. (1985). *A content for vocabulary.* (ERIC Document Reproduction Service No. ED 315 121).

Holden, M. (1973). *Fun with language arts.* New York: Instructor Publications.

Holland, E. (1968). The physiology of flexibility. *Kenesiology Review, 11,* 49–62.

Holland, E., and McLaughlin, T. (1982). Using public posting and group consequences to manage student behavior during supervision. *Journal of Educational Research, 76* (1), 29–34.

Hollingsworth, C. R. (1985). ERIC/RCS *Journal of Reading, 28* (6), 556–559.

Hollingworth, L. S. (1920). *The psychology of subnormal children.* New York: Macmillan.

Hollister, L. E. (1973). Hunger and appetite after single doses of marijuana, alcohol, and dextroamphetamine. In *Behavior and social effects of marijuana.* New York: MSS Information.

Holt, J. (1969). *The underachieving school.* New York: Dell Publishing.

Hood, J. M. (1979). A solution to discipline problems in schools. *Education, 99,* 375–377.

Horak, V., and Horak, W. (1983). Let's do it: Teaching time with slit clocks. *Arithmetic Teacher, 30* (5), 8–12.

Horn, D. (1976). Self-image boosters. *Instructors, 86,* 170.

Horn, E. (1967). *Teaching spelling.* National Education Association, Department of Classroom Teachers.

Horowitz, E. G. (1981). Developing the body image of visually handicapped child. *American Journal of Art Therapy, 20,* 19–24.

Houghton Mifflin. (1984). Creative problem solving in school mathematics, idea place. *Learning Magazine, 12* (9), 6–8.

House, E. R., and Lapan, S. D. (1978). *Survival in the classroom.* Boston: Allyn and Bacon.

How schools combat vandalism. (1980). *Nation Schools, 81,* 58–67.

Howard, M., and Anderson, R. (1978). Early identification of potential school dropouts: A literature review. *Child Welfare, 57* (4), 221–231.

Howarth, L., and Wagner, J. (1983). *An invitational approach to reducing anxiety in the learning and response behavior of children.* Montreal, Canada. (ERIC Document Reproduction Service No. ED 229 167).

Howe, F. W. (1971). Educating to make a difference. *Phi Delta Kappan, 52,* 547–549.

Hudesman, J.; Wiesner, E.; and Abramson, T. (1981). Student participation in the test-anxiety desensitization workshops as a function of the sex of the student and counselor. *Journal of College Student Personnel, 22* (2), 129–132.

Humes, A. E. (1984). Putting writing research into practice. *The Elementary School Journal, 74,* 3–17.

Hurn, H. (1962). *Drugs, medicines and man.* New York: Charles Schribner's Son.

Hurwitz, A. B., and Goddard, A. (1972). *Language arts games.* New York: Scholastic Magazines.

Hutton, J. B. (1983). How to decrease problem behavior at school by rewarding desirable behavior at home. *Pointer, 27,* 25–28.

Hutton, J. B. (1985). What reasons are given by teachers who refer problem students? *Psychology in the Schools, 22* (1), 79–82.

Hyde, N. (1971). Play therapy the troubled child's self-encounter. *American Journal of Nursing, 2,* 15–18.

Ianfolla, B.; Sonnschien, S.; and Whitehurst, G. (1981). Learning to communicate from models: Children confuse length with information. *Child Development, 52,* 507–513.

Indiana State Department of Public Education (1981). *Methods for motivation, grades 7–9.* Indianapolis Division of Reading Effectiveness. (ERIC Document Reproduction Services No. ED 210 647).

Indrisano, R. (1976). *Resource activity book.* Lexington, MA: Ginn.

Ingalls, Z. (1983). Alcohol on college campuses: Patterns and problems. *Chronicle of Higher Education, 25,* 9.

Instructo Corporation (1973). *My face and body.* Paoli, Pa: author.

Irwin, G. (1976). How to reduce school theft and vandalism. *Educational Digest, 41,* 9–11.

Isbistin, C. (1978). *Birth of a family.* New York: Hawthorn Books.

Isenstein, V. R., and Krasners, W. (1978). *Training foster parents to serve dependent children.* Maryland: National Institute of Mental Health. (ERIC Document Reproduction Services No. ED 169 424).

Ivancevich, J. M. (1982). Subordinates' reactions to performance appraisal interviews: A test of feedback and goal setting techniques. *Journal of Applied Psychology, 67,* 581–587.

Jablonsky, A. (1970). *School dropout: A review of the literature.* New York: Horace Mann-Lincoln Institute Teachers College. (ERIC Document Reproduction Service No. ED 035 778).

Jackson, A., and Randell, J. (1971). *Activities for elementary physical education.* West Nyack, NY: Parker Publishing Co.

Jackson, N. F.; Jackson, D. A.; and Monroe, C. (1983). *Getting along with others.* Champaign, IL: Research Press.

Jakibchuk, Z., and Smeriglio, V. L. (1976). The influence of symbolic modeling on the social behavior of preschool children with low levels of social responsiveness. *Child Development, 47,* 838–841.

James, B. (1976). *Suggestopedia: A teaching strategy for the severely disabled reader.* South Plains College. (ERIC Reproduction Service No. ED 158 242).

Janes, I. L., and Mann, L. (1977). *Decision making: A psychological analysis of conflict, choice, and commitment.* New York: Free Press.

Jaremko, M. E., and Lindsey, R. (1979). Stress coping abilities of individuals high and low in jealousy. *Psychological Reports, 44* (2), 547–553.

Jelinek, J. (1979). *A curriculum proposal for the development of maturity in students.* Tuscon: Arizona State University. (ERIC Document Reproduction Service No. ED 183 428).

Jellis, T., and Grainger, S. (1974). The back projection of kaleidoscopic patterns as a technique for eliciting verbalization in an autistic child. *British Journal of Disorders of Communication, 4,* 65–68.

Jensen, G. (1976). Race, achievement, and delinquence: A further look at delinquency in a birth cohort. *American Journal of Sociology, 82,* 379–387.

Jensen, G.; Erickson, M; and Gibbs, J. (1978). Perceived risk of punishment and self-reporting delinquency. *Social Forces, 57,* 57–78.

Jensen, G., and Rojeck, D. (1980). *Delinquency: A sociological view.* Lexington, MA: D. C. Heath.

Jensen, J. V. (1980). Oral skills enhance learning. *Improving College and University Teaching, 28,* 78–80.

Jernberg, A. M. (1979). *Theraplay.* San Francisco: Jossey-Bass.

Jersild, A. T. (1963). *The psychology of adolescence* (2nd. ed.). New York: Macmillan.

Jersild, A. T., and Tasch, R. J. (1949). *Children's interests and what they suggest for education.* New York: Columbia University Publications.

Jesness, C. (1963). *Redevelopment and revalidation of the Jesness Inventory.* Research Report No. 35. Sacramento, CA: California Youth Authority.

Job Corps Amendments (1984). *Job corps amendments of 1984. Hearing before the committee on labor and human resources, United States Senate. Ninety-Eight Congress, second session on s. 2111 to amend part b of title IV of the job training partnership act, to strengthen the job corps program.* Washington, D.C.: Congress of the United States. (ERIC Document Reproduction Service No. ED 253 744).

Jocquot, B.; Shelquist, J.; and Breeze, B. (1973). *Resource handbook for development of learning skills.* Eugene, OR: Educational Programmers.

Johns, E. (1985). Effects of list organization on HEM recognition. *Journal of Experimental Psychology, 11* (4), 605–619.

Johnson, D. J., and Myklebust, H. R. (1967). *Learning disabilities.* New York: Greene & Stratton.

Johnson, J. R. (1977). *Procedures for teachers of severely handicapped to follow in controlling serious behavior.* California: La Verne College. (ERIC Document Reproduction Service No. ED 165 396).

Johnson, M., and Bailey, J. S. (1974). Cross-age tutoring: Fifth graders as arithmetic tutors for kindergarten children. *Journal of Applied Behavior Analysis, 7* (2), 223–232.

Johnson, M. R.; Turner, P. F.; and Konarski, E. A. (1978). The "Good Behavior Game": A systematic replication two unruly transitional classrooms. *Education and Treatment of Children, 1* (3), 25–33.

Johnson, O. G. (1956). The teacher and the withdrawn child. *Mental Hygiene, 40,* 529–534.

Johnson, R. (1980). Helping children like themselves. *Day Care and Early Education, 7,* 14–16.

Johnson, S. B. (1978). Children's fears in the classroom setting. *School Psychology Digest, 8,* 382–396.

Johnson, T. D.; Langford, K. G.; and Quorn, K. C. (1981). Characteristics of an effective spelling program. *Language Arts, 58* (5), 581–588.

Johnson, V. (1975). *A step by step learning guide for retarded infants and children.* Syracuse, NY: Syracuse University Press.

Johnston, P. (1984). Instruction and student independence. *Elementary School Journal, 3,* 338–343.

Jolles, I. (1958). A teaching sequence for the training of visual and motor perception. *Journal of Mental Deficiency, 63,* 252–255.

Jones, B. M. (1983). Put your students in the picture for better problem solving. *The Arithmetic Teacher, 30,* 30–33.

Jones, K. L.; Shainber, L. W.; and Byer, C. O. (1969). *Drugs and alcohol.* New York: Harper and Row.

Jones, V. F. (1980). *Adolescents with behavior problems: Strategies for teaching, counseling, and parent involvement.* Boston: Allyn and Bacon.

Jones, V. (1981). School discipline: Problems and solutions. *Principal, 61* (1), 14–17.

Jongsma, E. (1985). Homework: Is it worthwhile? *The Reading Teacher, 28,* 702–704.

Jung, L. W. (1983). *Brain builders.* New York: Instructor Publications.

Kaczmarek, N. A. (1980). Expansion training: A counseling stance for the withdrawn child. *Elementary School Guidance and Counseling, 16,* 31–38.

Kaercher, D. (1980). Easier breathing for asthmatic victims. *Better Homes and Garden, 58,* 48.

Kahn, S. (1977). *Anxieties, phobias and fears.* New York: Philosophical Library.

Kaminsky, S., and Powers, R. (1981). Remediation of handwriting difficulties: A practical approach. *Academic Therapy, 17,* 19–25.

Kampwirth, T. (1983). Reducing reversal tendencies: 25 useful tips. *Academic Therapy, 18,* 469–474.

Kaplan, B. (1981). Attentional abilities and performance on conservation tasks. *Journal of Psychology, 109* (1), 35–41.

Kaplan, C. H., and White, M. A. (1980). Children's direction following behavior in grades K-5. *Journal of Educational Research, 74* (1), 43–48.

Kaplan, J., and Luck, E. (1977). The dropout phenomenon as a social problem. *Educational Forum, 42* (1), 41–56.

Kaplan, P. (1970). *Drug abuse perspectives on drugs.* Dubuque, IA: Wm. C. Brown.

Kaplan, S. P., and Thomas, K. R. (1981). Rehabilitative counseling student perceptions of obese clients. *Rehabilitative Counseling Bulletin, 25,* 106–109.

Karlin, M. S., and Berger, R. (1972). *Discipline and the disruptive child: A practical guide for elementary teachers.* West Nyack, NY: Parker Publishing Co.

Karmos, J., and Karmos, A. (1983). A closer look at classroom boredom. *Action Teacher Education, 14,* (2), 49–55.

Karstadt, R. (1976). Writing aids to reading. *The Reading Teacher, 30* (3), 297–298.

Kasda, P. (1980). *Behavior in the classroom.* New York: Wiley & Sons.

Kashani, J. H., and Ray, J. S. (1983). Depressive related symptoms among preschool age children. *Child Psychiatry and Human Development, 13,* 233–238.

Kasner, J. F. (1985). Theoretical support for and use of original drawings and associative cues in vocabulary acquisition by children with severe reading disorders. *Journal of Learning Disabilities, 18* (7), 390–397.

Katz, L. G. (1983). Neighborhood bullies. *Parents,* Sept., 104.

Katzman, M., and Wolchik, S. (1983). *Bulimics with and without prior anorexia nervosa: A comparison of personality characteristics.* Tempe: Arizona State University. (ERIC Document Reproduction Service No. ED 236 463).

Kauffman, J. M. (1985). *Characteristics of children's behavior disorders.* Columbus, OH: Charles E. Merrill.

Kauffman, J. M., (1985). Educating children with behavior disorders. In *Perspectives in special education Vol. 2: State of the art.* Glenview II: Scott, Foresman.

Kauffman, L. E. (1983). Make every word count! Word search puzzles. *Mother Earth News, 84,* 78–79.

Kaufman, I.; Heims, L. W.; and Reiser, D. E. (1961). A reevaluation of the psychodynamics of firesetting. *American Journal of Orthopsychiatry, 31,* 123.

Kaufman, J. J., and Lewis, M. V. (1968) *School environment and programs for dropouts.* University Park, PA: Institute for Human Resources. Penn State.

Kaye, E. (1974). *The family guide to children's television.* New York: Pantheon Books.

Kazarinoff, S. (1981). Playing to learn with collector's cards, *Academic Therapy, 17* (1), 63.

Kazdin, A. E. (1977). Vicarious reinforcement and direction of behavior change in the classroom. *Behavior Therapy, 8,* 57–63.

Kazdin, A. E. (1980). *Behavior modification in applied settings.* Homewood, IL: Dorsey Press.

Kazdin, A., and Forsberg, S. (1974). Effects of group reinforcement and punishment on classroom behavior. *Education and Training of the Mentally Retarded, 9* (2), 50–55.

Kazdin, A. E. and Klock, J. (1973). The effect of nonverbal teacher approval on student attentive behavior. *Journal of Applied Behavior Analysis, 6.*

Keat, D. (1981). Helping children with anger. *Elementary School Guidance Counseling, 16,* 152–156.

Keeler, M. H.; Ewing, J. A.; and Rouse, B. A. (1973). Hallucinogenic effects of marijuana as currently used. In *Behavior and social effects of marijuana.* New York: MSS Information.

Keith, C. R. (1981). A paradoxical effect of guilt in the psychotherapy of children. *American Journal of Psychotherapy, 25* (1), 16–26.

Kellam, S.; Hendricks, C.; and Fleming, J. (1982). Social adaptation to first grade and teenage drug, alcohol, and cigarette use. *Journal of School Health, 52,* 301–306.

Kellerman, J. (1981). *Helping the fearful child.* New York: W. W. Norton & Co.

Kelly, E. W. (1973). School phobia: A review of theory and treatment. *Psychology in the Schools, 10.*

Kelly L. M., and Lahey, B. (1983). *Irrational beliefs as moderators of the life stress-depression relationship.* Atlanta: Annual Meeting of the Southeastern Psychological Association. (ERIC Document Reproduction Service No. ED 234 335).

Kelly, M., and Stokes, T. F. (1982). Contingency contracting with disadvantaged youths: Improving classroom discipline. *Journal of School Applied Behavior Analysis, 15,* 447–454.

Kelly, S. R., and McLaughlin, T. F. (1983). Written practice with soft praise. *Journal of Special Education, 19,* 44–50.

Kelly, W. (1983). *Everything you always wanted to know about using humor in education but were afraid to laugh.* Detroit: MI: Annual International Convention of the Council for Exceptional Children. (ERIC Document Reproduction Service No. ED 232 381).

Kendal, P. (1984). Cognitive behavior self-control therapy for children. *Journal of Child Psychiatry and Allied Disciplines, 25,* 173–179.

Kendall, P., and Braswell, L. (1985). *Cognitive behavioral therapy for impulsive children.* New York: Guilford Press.

Kennedy, L., and Michon, R., (1973). *Games for individualizing mathematics learning.* Columbus, OH: Charles E. Merrill.

Keogh, B. (1976). Learn to labor and wait: Attentional

problems of children with learning disorders. *Journal of Learning Disabilities, 9* (5), 18–28.

Keogh, B., and Keogh, J. (1967). Pattern copying and pattern walking performance of normal and educationally subnormal boys. *American Journal of Mental Deficiency, 71,* 1009–1013.

Keon, T. L., and Willoughby, F. G. (1981). Developing structure to motivate in the classroom. *Journal of Business Education, 56,* 283–286.

Kephart, N. C. (1960). *The slow learner in the classroom.* Columbus, OH: Charles E. Merrill.

Kephart, N. C. (1975). *Learning disabilities—Last lectures of Newell C. Kephart.* Wineva Grzynkowicz and Martha Kephart (eds.). Romeoville, IL: WGMK Publishers.

Kern, L.; Koegel, R.; Dyer, D.; Blew, P. A.; and Fenton, L. R. (1982). The effects of physical exercise on self-stimulation and appropriate responding in autistic children. *Journal of Autism and Developmental Disorders, 12,* 399–394.

Kerr, D. (1985). Class management teaches social responsibilities. *School Safety, 3,* 14–16.

Kerr, M., and Nelson, C. (1983). *Strategies for managing behavior problems in the classroom.* Columbus, OH: Charles E. Merrill.

Kerr, M., and Strain, P. S. (1978). *The use of peer social initiation strategies to improve the social skills of withdrawn children.* Nashville, TN: Presented at World Congress on Future Special Education. (ERIC Document Reproduction No. ED 158 551).

Kerry, T. (1981). Teachers class management problems with bright pupils. *The Exceptional Child, 28* (3), 199–204.

Kessel, N., and Walton, H. (1967). *Alcoholism.* Great Britian: Penguin Books.

Kessler, J. W. (1972). Neurosis in childhood. In B. B. Wolman (ed.), *Manual of child psychopathology.* New York: McGraw-Hill.

Ketterman, G. H. (1983). *You and your child's problems.* Old Tappen, NJ: Fleming H. Revell.

Keutzer, C. S. (1972). Kleptomania: A direct approach to treatment. *British Journal of Medical Psychology, 45,* 159–163.

Keystone Area Education (1983). *Resource guide for emotional disabilities.* Elkdor, IA: Keystone Area Eduction. (ERIC Document Reproduction Service No. ED 243 266).

Kidder, J. (1984). I don't understand. Can you tell me again? *Academic Therapy, 19,* 357–360.

Kiechel, W. (1982). Looking out for the executive alcoholic. *Fortune, 105,* 117–118.

Kiefer, M. (1984). Art of control. *Esquire, 101,* June.

Kiernan, C. (1983). The use of nonvocal communication techniques with autistic individuals. *Journal of Childpsychology and Psychiatry and Allied Disciplines, 24,* 17–23.

Kiester, E. (1978). TV violence and the telly. *Better Homes and Gardens,* 13–21.

Kilmann, P.; Stabalis, R.; Gearing, M.; Bukstel, L; and Scavern, A. (1982). The treatment of sexual paraphilias: A review of the outcome research. *The Journal of Sex Research, 18* (3), 193–252.

Kirchenbaum, D. S. (1979). Social competence intervention and evaluation in the inner city: Cincinnati's social skills development program. *Journal of Consulting and Clinical Psychology, 47,* 778–780.

Kirchner, J.; Cunningham, K; and Warrell, T. (1979). *Introduction to movement education.* Dubuque, IA: Wm. C. Brown.

Kirk, S. A., and Gallagher, J. J. (1983). *Educating exceptional children.* Cambridge, MA: Houghton Mifflin.

Kirk, S. A., and Johnson, G. O. (1951). *Educating the retarded child.* Cambridge, MA: Houghton Mifflin.

Kirk, U. (1981). The development and use of rules in the acquisition of perceptual motor skills. *Child Development, 52* (1), 299–305.

Kirkland, K. and Hollandsworth, J. G. (1979). Text anxiety, study skills, and academic performance. *Journal of College Student Personnel, 20* (5).

Kirley, J. (1981). *Variety of procedures and its effects in skills-oriented fifth grade classrooms.* Los Angeles: Annual Meeting of the American Educational Research Association. (ERIC Document Reproduction Service No. ED 204 294).

Kirschner, N., and Levin, L. (1975). A direct school intervention program. *Psychology in the Schools, 12.*

Kisker, G. W. (1972). *The disorganized personality.* New York: McGraw-Hill.

Kistner, J. (1985). Attention deficits of learning disabled children. *Journal of Applied Behavior Analysis, 10* (3), 220–238.

Kiyoth, J. S. (1970). *The teacher and school discipline.* Metuchen, NJ: Scarecrow Press.

Klein, B. (1977). *Old starts—new beginnings.* In D. R. Gallo (ed.), Teaching writing: Advice from the professionals. *Connecticut English Journal, 12* (2), 5–6. (ERIC Document Reproduction Service No. ED 151 846).

Kleinmuntz, B. (1974). *Esentials of abnormal psychology.* New York: Harper & Row.

Klepac, R. K.; Hauge, G.; Dowling, J.; and McDonald, M. M. (1981). Direct and generalized effects of three components of stress inoculation for increased pain tolerance. *Behavior Therapy, 12* (3), 417–424.

Klermant, S., and Jekel, L. (1978). *School-age mothers.* Hamden, CT: Shoe String Press.

Klesius, J. P., and Homon, S. D. (1985). A validity and reliability update on the informal reading inventory with suggestions for improvement. *Journal of Learning Disabilities, 18* (2), 71–75.

Kline, T. (1977). *Children move to learn.* Columbus: Ohio State University Research Foundation.

Knickerbocker, L (1978). *A central approach to the development of spatial and temporal concepts.* Seattle: Special Child Pubs.

Knickerbocker, L. (1980). *A holistic approach to the treatment of learning disorders.* Thorofare, NJ: Slack.

Knickerbocker, L. (1983). *Anorexia Nervosa: More than just a teen-age disease.* Teaneck, NJ: The American Anorexia Nervosa Association.

Knoblock, P. (1983). *Intervention approaches in education emotionally disturbed children.* Boston: Houghton Mifflin.

Koballa, T. R., and Rice, D. R. (1978). What research says: Six strategies for improving attitudes toward science. *Science and Children, 22,* 32–34.

Koegel, R.; Lovaas, O.; and Schreibman, L. (1977). The autistic child language development through behavior modification. *Journal of Autism and Developmental Disorders, 14,* 16–21.

Koegel, R. L., and Rincover, A. (1974). Treatment of psychotic children in a classroom environment: Learning in a large group. *Journal of Applied Behavior Analysis, 7* (1), 45–59.

Kohl, H. (1985). Respecting the serious thinking that children do. *Education Digest, 50,* 28–31.

Kohut, S., and Range, D. G. (1979). *Classroom discipline: Case studies and viewpoints.* Washington, D.C.: National Education Association.

Kolansky, H., and Moore, W. (1978). Sufficient for alarm. In J. Brady and H. Brody (eds.), *Controversy in psychiatry.* Philadelphia: Saunders.

Kolvin, I.; MacKeith, R.; and Meadow, S. R. (1973). *Bladder control & enuresis.* Philadelphia: Spastice International Medical Publications.

Konczak, L., and Johnson, C. (1983). Reducing inappropriate verbalizations in a sheltered workshop through differential reinforcement of other behavior. *Education and Training of the Mentally Retarded, 18* (2), 120–124.

Konstantareas, M. (1984). Aggressive and prosocial behaviors before and after treatment in conduct-disordered children and in matched controls. *Journal of Child Psychology and Psychiatry and Applied Disciplines, 25* (4), 607–620.

Kopecky, G. (1980). Why women steal. *Mademoiselle,* 156–157.

Koppel, M. A. (1982). Anxiety: The school environment. Boston: Harvard University. (Great Studies microfilm BF 575 A6 K6).

Kops, C., and Belmont, I. (1985). Planning and attention of low achievers. *Journal of Learning Disabilities, 18* (1), 8–14.

Kornswiet, D. K., and Yarnell, G. D. (1981). Increasing attending to tasks and completion of tasks with an easily distracted, visually impaired 11 year old. *Education of the Visually Handicapped, 13,* 84–90.

Kounin, J. S. (1970). *Discipline and group management in classrooms.* New York: Holt, Rinehart, & Winston.

Kozloff, M. A. (1973). *Reaching the autistic child: A parent training program.* Champaign, IL: Research Press.

Kozloff, M. A. (1974). *Educating children with learning and behavior problems.* New York: John Wiley & Sons.

Kraft, A. (1970). Discipline as curriculum. *Instructor, 80* (1), 55–58.

Kratcoski, P. C., Kratcoski, L. D., and Washburn, D. P. (1979). The crisis of vandalism in our schools. *Education Digest, 44* (5), 12–14.

Kratochwill, T., and Morriss, R. (1983). *Treating children's fears and phobias.* New York: Pergamon Press.

Kretschmer, E. (1970). *Physique and character* (2nd ed.). New York: Cooper Square Publishers.

Kristine, F. A. (1985). Developing study skills: More than a handout. *College Teaching, 33* (2), 84–87.

Kronich, D. (1969). *Learning disabilities.* Chicago: Developmental Learning Materials.

Krout, M. (1932). *Psychology of children's lies.* Boston: Gorham Press.

Krueger, D. W. (1979). Psychodynamic and physiologic interactions in narcolepsy. *Psychosomatics, 20,* 629–633.

Krumboltz, J. D., and Duckham-Shoor, L. (1979). Reward direction, not perfection. *Learning, 8,* 154–159.

Krumboltz, J. D., and Krumboltz, H. D. (1972). *Changing children's behavior.* Englewood Cliffs, NJ: Prentice-Hall.

Kubany, E.S.; Weiss, L. E.; and Sloggett, B. B. (1971). The good behavior clock: A reinforcement/time-out procedure for reducing disruptive classroom behavior. *Journal of Behavior Therapy and Experimental Psychiatry, 2,* 173–179.

Kuczen, B. (1984). Even kids suffer from stress . . . and help begins at home. *Early Years, 15* (4), 26–27.

Kujoth, J. S. (1970). *The teacher and school discipline.* New Jersey: Scarecrow Press.

Kupietz, S. S., and Schwartz, I. L. (1982). Elective mutism. *New York State Journal of Medicine, 82,* 1073–1076.

Kvaraceus, W. C. (1966). *Anxious youths: Dynamics of delinquency.* Columbus, OH: Charles E. Merrill.

L'Abate, L., and Curtis, T. L. (1975). *Teaching the exceptional child.* Philadelphia: W. B. Saunders.

LaBerge, D., and Samuels, S. J. (1974). Toward a theory of automatic information processing in reading. *Cognitive Psychology, 6* (2), 293–323.

Labrie, (1973). *Learning disabilities activity guide for the elementary classroom.* (ERIC Document Reproduction Service No. ED 117 907).

LaGreca, A. M., and Mesibov, G. B. (1979). *Social skills intervention with learning disabled children.* Chicago. (ERIC Document Reproduction Service No. ED 179 884).

Lahey, B. (1979). *Behavior therapy with hyperactive and learning disabled children.* New York: Oxford University Press.

Lahey, B., and Ciminero, A. R. (1980). *Maladaptive behavior: An introduction to abnormal psychology.* Glenview, IL: Scott, Foresman & Company.

Laird, A. (1980). A comprehensive and innovative attack of action program for delinquency prevention and classroom success. *Education, 101* (2), 118–122.

Lake, A. (1983). The effect of alcoholism. *Chronicle of Higher Education, 25,* 9.

Lake, S. (1984). Study habits of the underachiever. *Thrust, 14,* 1–4.

Lall, G., and Lall, B. (1979). School phobia: It's real. . . . and growing. *Instructor, 89,* 96–98.

LaMancusa, K. C. (1966). *We do not throw rocks at the teacher.* Pennsylvania: Haddon Craftsmen.

Lamanna, M. (1981). Marijuana: Implications of use by young people. *Journal of Drug Education, 11,* 281–310.

Lamberg, L. (1984). New findings about hyperactive children. *PTA Today, 9* (3), 20–21.

Lamberts, F.; Ericksen, N.; Blickhan, J.; and Hollister, S. (1980). Listening and language activities for pre-school children. *Language, Speech and Hearing Services in the Schools, 46* (1), 3–9.

Lambley, P. (1974). *Journal of Behavior Therapy & Experimental Psychiatry, 1,* 101–102.

Lancioni, G. (1982). Normal children as tutors to teach social responses to withdrawn mentally retarded schoolmates: Training, maintenance, and generalization. *The Journal of Applied Behavior Analysis, 15,* 17–40.

Landau, E. (1983). *Why are they starving themselves? Understanding anorexia nervosa bulimia.* New York: Julian Messner.

Landers, D. M., and Landers, D. M. (1978). Socialization via interscholastic athletics: its effects on delinquency. *Sociology of Education, 5,* 299–303.

Landers, M. F. (1984). Helping the L.D. child with homework: Ten tips. *Academic Therapy, 20* (2), 209–215.

Lane, M. (1984). *Readings in microcomputers and emotional and behavioral disorders.* Connecticut: Special Learning Corp.

Lang, D. (1980). *Stress management and anxiety reduction through EMG biofeedback/relaxation training upon junior high school students.* Emporia, KS; Emporia State University. (ERIC Document Reproduction Service No. ED 217 017).

Larrabee, M. (1982). Working with reluctant clients through affirmation techniques. *Personnel and Guidance Journal, 61,* 105–109.

Larson, K. A., and Gerber, M. M. (1984). *Social metacognition: The efficacy of cognitive training for social adjustment of learning disabled delinquents.* Washington, D.C.: Special Education Programs. (ERIC Document Reproduction Service No. ED 253 034).

Lasley, T. J. (1981). Classroom misbehavior: Some field observations. *The High School Journal, 64,* 142–149.

Lasley, T. J. (1981). Discipline—A model and instrument. *NASSP Bulletin 65* (441).

Lawhon, T. (1984). Work and stress in the home: How do you help in the family? *Journal of Home Economics, 76,* 2–5.

Lawrence, J., Steed, D., and Young, C. (1983). Coping

with disruptive behavior. *Special Education: Forward Trends, 10* (1), 9–12.

Lay, B., and Wakstein, D. (1985). Race, academic achievement and self concept of ability. *Researching Higher Education, 1,* 53–64.

Layton, J. (1982). *Affective illnesses and their causes and treatment.* University of Illinois: The Board of Trustees of the University of Illinois.

Lazerson, D. B. (1978). *I must be good if I can teach!— Peer tutoring with aggressive and withdrawn children.* Washington, D.C.: Presented at World Congress on Future Special Education. U.S. Dept. HEW National Institute of Education. (ERIC Document Reproduction Service No. ED 158 515).

Learning (1984). 101 ideas to keep learning exciting. *13* (4), 87.

Learning (1984). Montessori: on a limited budget. *13* (4), 86.

Leary, B., and von Schneden, M. (1982). *"Simon says" is not the only game.* New York: American Foundation for the blind.

Lee, J. F., and Pruitt, K. W. (1979). Homework assignments: Classroom games or teaching tools? *The Clearing House, 53* (1), 31–35.

Lee, M. K. (1984). Debunking the Cinderella myth. *The Educational Forum, 48,* 327–334.

Lee, R. E. and Klopfer, C. (1978). Counselors and juvenile delinquents: Toward a comprehensive treatment approach. *Personal and Guidance Journal, 57,* 194–197.

Leeper, J.; Dales, R.; Skipper, M.; and Witherspoon, B. (1974). *Good schools for young children.* New York: Macmillan.

LeGall, S. N., and Jones, D. S. (1985). Teachers' and young children's perceptions of appropriate work strategies. *Child Study Journal, 15,* 29–42.

Legingham, J., and Schuailyma, A. (1984). A three-year follow up of aggression and withdrawn behavior in children: Preliminary findings. *The Journal of Abnormal Psychology, 12,* 157–168.

Lehman, J. (1982). *Three approaches to classroom management.* University Press of America.

Lent, J. (1976). More daily living skills programs. Belleview, WA: Edmark Association.

Lerch, H.; Becker, J.; Ward, B.; and Nelson, J. (1974). *Perceptual motor learning—Theory & practice.* California: Peek Publication.

Lerman, S. (1980). *Parent awareness: Positive parenting for the 1980's.* Minneapolis: Winston Press.

Lerner, J. (1976). *Children with learning disabilities* (2nd ed.). Boston: Houghton Mifflin.

Lerner, J. (1985). *Learning disabilities: Theories, diagnosis, and teaching strategies.* Boston: Houghton Mifflin.

Lessen, E. I. (1980). Scoring procedures for the evaluation of spelling performance. *Academic Therapy, 15* (3), 347–350.

Levin, J.; Nolan, J.; and Hoffman, N. (1985). A strategy for classroom resolution of chronic discipline problems. *NASSP Bulletin, 69,* 10–17.

Levine, H. (1978). *Vocabulary and composition through pleasurable reading.* New York: Amsco.

Levine, M.; Brooks, R.; and Shonkoff, J. P. (1980). *A pediatric approach to learning disorders.* New York: Wiley & Sons.

Levine, M., and Seligmann, J. H. (1973). *The parents encyclopedia.* New York: Thomas Y. Crowell.

Lewis, B. L., and Strain, P. S. (1978). Effects of feedback timing and motivational content on teachers' delivery of contigent social praise. *Psychology in the Schools, 15,* 423–430.

Lewis, J. C. (1978). A comprehensive approach to delinquency prevention and treatment. *Child Welfare, 57,* 675–684.

Lewis, R. B., and Kass, C. (1982). Labelling and recall in learning disabled students. *The Journal of Learning Disabilities, 15,* 238–241.

Licht, B. G. (1983). Cognitive-motivational factors that contribute to the achievement of learning-disabled children. *Journal of Learning Disabilities, 16,* 145–483.

Liebergott, J.; Favors, A.; Saaz; vonHippel, C.; and Needleman, H. L. (1980). *Children with speech and language impairments.* Massachusetts: U.S. Department of Health and Human Services.

Lieberman, L. M. (1983). The homework solution. *Journal of Learning Disabilities, 16* (7), 435.

Liebert, M. (1983). Cognitive and emotional components of anxiety. *Journal of Educational Psychology, 20,* 35–46.

Liepmann, L. (1973). *Your child's sensory world.* Maryland: Penguin Books.

Lin, A.; Blackman, L. S.; Clark, H. T.; and Gordon, R. (1983). Far generalization of visual analogies strategies by impulsive and reflective EMR students. *American Journal of Mental Deficiency, 88* (3), 297–306.

Lindberg, L., and Swedlow, R. (1976). *Early childhood education.* Boston: Allyn and Bacon.

Lindecker, I. M. (1954). Music therapy in a juvenile detention home. In E. T. Gaston (ed.), *Music therapy*. Lawrence, KS: Allen Press.

Lindgren, G. (1982). Achievemnt and mental ability of physically late and early maturing school children related to their social background. *Journal of Child Psychiatry and Allied Disciplines, 23*, 407–420.

Lindo, P. S. (1984). *Positive approach to self-discipline.* California: Lakeside Union School District. (ERIC Document Reproduction Service No. ED 015 985).

Lindon, J. (1985). Teaching poor readers to cope with maladaptive cognitive styles: A training program. *Journal of Learning Disabilities, 18* (7), 391–392.

Lindsay, D. (1977). Project real. *Pointer, 22* (1), 52–56.

Lindsay, J. D., and Frith, G. H. (1981). The learning disabled. *Clearing House, 54* (7), 322–325.

Liorens, L. A., and Bernstein, S. P. (1963). Fingerpainting with an obsessive-compulsive organically damaged child. *American Journal of Occupational Therapy, 17* (3), 120–121.

Lipson, G. B., and Bolkosky, S. M. (1982). *Mighty myth.* Carthage, IL: Good Apple.

Liselort, D. (1974). *Children learn physical skills,* Boston: Northeastern University. (ERIC Document Reproduction Service No. ED 169 029).

Liu, A. (1979). *Solitaire: A young woman's triumph over anorexia nervosa.* New York: Harper and Row.

Livingstone, I. J. (1971). Word building. *Instructor, 80* (5), 93–94.

Lobitz, W. C., and Burns, W. J. (1977). The "least intrusive intervention" strategy for behavior change procedures: The use of public and private feedback in school classrooms. *Psychology in the Schools, 14* (1), 89–94.

Locke, D. (1983). Doing what comes morally. *Human Development, 26*, 11–25.

Loffredo, D. (1984). Group relaxation training and parental involvement with hyperactive boys. *Journal of Learning Disabilities, 17*, 210–213.

Logan, G. (1964). *Adaptions of muscular activity.* Belmont, CA: Wadsworth.

Lolli, G. (1960). *Social drinking.* New York: World Publishing.

Long, B. H., and Henderson, E. H. (1968). Self-social concept of disadvantaged school beginners. *Journal of Genetics Psychology, 113*, 41–51.

Long, J., and Madsen, C. H. (1973). Five-year-olds as behavioral engineers for younger students in a day care center. In E. Ramp and G. Semb (eds.)., *Behavior analysis: Areas of research and application.* Englewood Cliffs, NJ: Prentice-Hall.

Long, J. D., and Frye, V. H. (1977). *Making it till Friday.* Princeton, NJ: Princeton Book Company.

Long, N. (1979). The conflict cycle. *The Pointer, 24* (1), 6–11.

Long, N. (1984). Teaching self control and pro-social behavior by using signs and sayings in classrooms for emotionally disturbed pupils. *Pointer, 28*, 36–39.

Long, N.; Morse, W.; and Newman, R. *Conflict in the classroom: The education of children with problems.* Belmont, CA: Wadsworth.

Lorayne, H. (1973). *Good memory—successful student.* New York: Thomas Nelson.

Lord, J. R. (1971). *Marijuana and personality change.* London: Lexington Books.

Lord, T. R. (1985). Enhancing the visual-spatial aptitude of students. *The Journal of Research in Science Teaching, 22*, 395–405.

Lovaas, O. I., and Bucher, B. D. (1974). *Perspectives in behavior modification with deviant children.* Englewood Cliffs, NJ: Prentice-Hall.

Lovaas, O. I., and Simmons, J. Q. (1969). Manipulation of self-destruction in three retarded children. *Journal of Applied Behavior Analysis, 2*, 143–157.

Love, H. (1978). *Teaching physically handicapped children.* New York: Thomas Publisher.

Love, R. E. (1953). The use of music with disturbed children. In E. G. Gilliland (ed.), *Music therapy 1952.* Lawrence, KS: Allen Press.

Lovitt, T. (1978). *Managing inappropriate behavior in the classroom.* Reston, VA: The Council for Exceptional Children.

Lovitt, T. C. (1973). Self-management projects with children with behavioral disabilities. *Journal of Learning Disabilities, 6*, 138–150.

Lovitt, T. C., and Curtiss, K. A. (1969). Academic response rate as a function of teacher and self-imposed contingencies. *Journal of Applied Behavior Analysis, 2* (1), 49–53.

Lovitt, T. C.; Guppy, T. E.; and Blattner, J. E. (1969). In D. Smith (ed.), *Teaching the learning disabled.* (1981). Englewood Cliffs, NJ: Prentice-Hall.

Lowenstein, L. F. (1982). The treatment of extreme shyness in maladjusted children by implosive, counselling, and conditioning approaches. *Acta Psychiatrica Scandinavica, 66* (3), 173–189.

Lowenthal, B. (1983). Gross motor activities: Movement for fun and learning. *Academic therapy, 18,* 555–560.

Lower, D. (1964). *Dropouts and their relation to guidance.* Unpublished master's thesis, Eastern Illinois University: Department of Educational Psychology, Charleston, IL.

Lucas, J. (1984). Communication apprehension in the classroom: Getting our students to talk. *Foreign Language Annals, 17* (6), 593–598.

Lucas, V., and Barbe, W. (1974). *Classroom activities for helping slower learning children.* New York: The Center for Applied Research in Education.

Luce, S. (1980). Predicting academic behavior from classroom behavior. *Review of Educational Research, 49* (3), 479–496.

Luce, S. C.; Delquadri, J.; and Hall, R. V. (1980). Contingent exercise: A mild but powerful procedure for suppressing inappropriate verbal and aggressive behavior. *Journal of Applied Behavior Analysis, 13,* 583–594.

Luchow, J. P.; Crawl, T. K.; and Kahn, J. P. (1985). Learned helplessness: Perceived effects of ability and effort on academic performance among EH and LD/EH children. *Journal of Learning Disabilities, 18* (8), 470–474.

Luiselli, J. (1985). Effects of brief overcorrection on stereotypic behavior of mentally retarded students. *Education and Treatment of Children, 7,* 125–138.

Luiselli, J. K., and Michaud, R. L. (1983). Behavioral treatment of aggression and self-injury in developmentally disabled, visually handicpped students. *Journal of Impairment and Blindness, 77,* 388–392.

Lukeman, J., and Sorensen, K. (1984). *Medical-surgical nursing psycho-physiological approach.* Philadelphia: Saunders.

Lyle, M. R. (1983). *Teaching listening skills for parents.* Florida: Annual Meeting of the Southern Speech Communication Association. (ERIC Document Reproduction No. ED 234 438).

Lynch, J. M. (1967). *The coming revolution against classroom boredom.* Clearing House Journal, *41,* 346–349.

Mabee, W. S.; Neimann, J.; and Lipton, P. (1979). The effects of self-pacing and use of study guide questions within behavioral instruction. *The Journal of Educational Research, 72,* 273–276.

Maccoby, E., and Bee, H. (1965). Some speculation concerning the lag between perceiving and performing. *Child Development, 36,* 367–378.

MacDonald, J. (1920). *Bombers and firesetters.* Springfield, IL: Charles Thomas.

Macht, L. B., and Mack, J. E. (1968). The firesetter syndrome. *Psychiatry, 31,* 123–126.

Mack, J. E. (1970). *Nightmares and human conflict.* London: J & A Churchhill.

MacLeod, S. (1981). *The art of starvation.* New York: Schocken Books.

MacMillan, D. L. (1975). *Behavior modification in education.* New York: MacMillan.

Macnab, F. A. (1968). *Estrangement and relationship: Experience with schizophrenics.* New York: Dell.

Madden, N. A.; Russo, D. C.; and Cataldo, M. F. (1980). Behavioral treatment of pica in children with lead poisoning. *Child Behavior Therapy, 2* (4), 67–81.

Madison, A. (1979). *Runaway teens.* New York: Elsevier/Nelson Publishing.

Madsen, C. H. (1968). Rules, praise and ignoring. *Journal of Applied Behavior Analysis, 1,* 139–151.

Madsen, C. H., and Madsen, C. K. (1981). *Teaching/discipline: A positive approach for educational development.* Boston: Allyn and Bacon.

Maggiore, R. P. (1983). Helping the impulsive pupil use self-control techniques in the classroom. *Pointer, 27* (14), 38–40.

Mahlberg, M. (1973). Music therapy in the treatment of an autistic child. *Journal of Music Therapy, 10,* 189–193.

Maher, C. (1981). Effects of involving conduct problem adolescents in goal setting—an exploratory investigation. *Psychology in the Schools, 18,* 471–474.

Mallet, J. J. (1975). *Classroom reading games activity kit.* New York: The Center of Applied Research in Education.

Mallick, J. (1984). Anorexia nervosa and bulimia: Questions and answers for school personnel. *Journal of School Health,* 299–301.

Mallon, B., and Berglund, R. (1984). The language experience approach to reading: Recurring questions and their answers. *The Reading Teacher, 37* (9), 68–72.

Maloney, D. M. (1982). Crisis intervention: A model youth program. Rockville, MD. (Eric Document Reproduction Service No. ED 218 549).

Maloy, R. W. and Seldin, C. A. (1983). The fallout of cutback: The invalidation of an educational model for school drop-outs. *High School Journal,* *66,* 261–266.

Mandell, J. (1984). *Teaching handicapped students.* St. Paul: West Publishing Company.

Mann, M. (1950). *Primer on alcoholism.* New York: Rinehart.

Mann, V. A., and Liberman, I. (1984). Phonological awareness and verbal short, term memory. *The Journal of Learning Disabilities, 17,* 592–600.

Manning, P. C. (1980). Getting it all together with math learning centers. *School Science and Mathematics, 80,* 703–705.

Maples, M. (1985). Three valuable constructs for classroom management. *The Education Digest, 50,* 50–52.

Marchbacks, G. (1965). Cues by which children recognize words. *Journal of Educational Psychology, 56,* 57–61.

Margolis, R., and Popkin, N. (1980). A review of medical research with implications for adolescents. *Personnel and Guidance Journal, 59,* 7–14.

Marino, J. L. (1981). Spelling errors: From analysis to instruction. *Language Arts, 58* (5), 567–572.

Markel, G. (1981). Improving test-taking skills of LD adolescents. *Academic Therapy, 16,* 333–342.

Markle, S. (1983). Time out for measuring time. *Instructor, 93* (3), 142–44.

Markman, E. M., and Siebert, J. (1976). Classes and collections: Internal organization and resulting holistic properties. *Cognitive Psychology, 8* (4), 561–577.

Marks, I. M. (1969). *Living with fear.* New York: McGraw-Hill.

Marks, J. (1983). My husband was an alcoholic. *Ladies Home Journal, 100,* May, 10–12.

Marlin, K. (1977). Dealing with disobedience and rebellion in *Children.* Available from Practical Parenting Publications, Box 18, Columbia, MO 65201.

Marsh, G. E., and Price, B. J. (1980). *Methods of teaching the mildly handicapped adolescent.* St. Louis, MO: C. V. Mosby Co.

Marshall, H. (1972). *Positive discipline and classroom interaction.* Springfield, IL: Charles C. Thomas.

Marshall, R. C. (1983). Communication styles of fluent aphasic clients. In H. Winitz (ed.), *Treating language disorders: For clinicians by clinicians.* Baltimore MD: University Park Press.

Martin, B., and Quilling, J. (1981). *Positive approaches to classroom discipline.* Washington: Home Economics Education Association. (ERIC Document Reproduction Service NO. ED 228 707).

Martin, D. L., Jr. (1981). *Identifying potential dropouts: A research report.* Frankfort: Kentucky State Department of Education. (ERIC Document Reproduction Service No. ED 216 304).

Martin, J. E.; Matson, J. L.; and Ollendick, T. H. (1979). Over-correction revisited: A long-term follow-up. *Journal of Behavioral Therapy and Experimental Psychiatry, 10,* 11–13.

Martin, L., and Martin, S. (1984). *Hyperactivity—Characteristics, possible causes and intervention strategies.* Washington, D.C.: Annual Convention for the Council of Exceptional Children. (ERIC Document Reproduction Service No. ED 245 483).

Martin, L. J., and DeGruchy, C. (1938). *The home in a democracy.* CA: Harr Wagner Publishing Co.

Martin, R., and Lauridsen, D. (1974). *Developing student discipline and motivation.* Illinois: Research Press Company.

Massong, S. R.; Dickinson, A. L.; Ritzler, B. A.; and Layne, C. C. (1982). Assertion and defense mechanism preference. *Journal of Counseling Psychology, 29,* 591–596.

Mastropieri, M. A. (1985). Mnemonic strategy instruction with learning disabled students. *The Journal of Learning Disabilities, 18,* 94–101.

Mastropieri, M. A. and Scruggs, T. E. (1984). *Memory strategies for learning disabled students.* Washington, D.C. (ERIC Document Reproduction Service No. ED 246 620).

Mastropieri, M. A.; Scruggs, T. E.; Levin, J. R.; Gaffney, J.; and McLoone, B. (1985). Mnemonic vocabulary instruction for learning disabled students. *Learning Disability Quarterly, 8* (1), 57–63.

Matson, J. (1982). Prevention of contracture deformities. *Clinical Management in Physical Therapy, 2* (3), 37–40.

Matson, J. L., and McCartney, J. R. (1981). *Handbook of behavior modification with the mentally retarded.* New York: Plenum Publishing.

Maurer, A. (1977). *Corporal punishment handbook.* Washington, D.C. National Education Association. (ERIC Document Reproduction No. ED 236 770).

Mayer, A. (1982). The gorge-purge syndrome. *Health, 14,* 50–52.

McAuley, R., and McAuley, P. (1977). *Child behavior problems.* New York: Free Press.

McCabe, D. (1982). The LD high school student. *Academic Therapy, 18,* 197–201.

McCall R. B. (1983). Turned off and tuned out. *Parents*, November, 104–109.

McCarthy, J. J., and McCarthy, J. F. (1969). *Learning disabilities*. Boston: Allyn and Bacon.

McCollum, J. (1984) Parenting an infant with a disability a practical guide for interaction. *The Exceptional Parent*, 14, (7), 45–50.

McCulloch, L. (1971). *Promoting learning readiness skills through perceptual motor training in physical education*. Washington, D.C.: National Education Foundation.

McDaniel, C., et al. (1982). *Motivational strategies for teaching language arts: A resource, K-12*. Atlanta: Georgia State Department of Education. (ERIC Document Reproduction Service No. ED 236 595).

McDaniel, T. R. (1977). Principles of classroom discipline: Toward a pragmatic synthesis. *Clearing House*, 51 (12), 149–152.

McDaniel, T. R. (1985). The Ten Commandments of motivation. *Clearing House*, 59, 19–23.

McDermott, P. A. and Watkins, M. W. (1983). Computerized vs. conventional remedial instruction for learning disabled pupils. *Journal of Special Education*, 17, 81–88.

McDowell, R.; Adamson, G.; and Wood, F. (1982). *Teaching emotionally disturbed children*. Boston: Little, Brown and Co.

McGee, G. (1984). Conventional skills for autistic adolescents: Teaching assertiveness in naturalistic game settings. *Journal of Autism and Developmental Disorders*, 14 (3), 319–329.

McGinnis, E.; Sauerbry, L.; and Nichols, P. (1985). Skill-streaming: Teaching social skills to children with behavioral disorders. *Teaching Exceptional Children*, 17 (3), 160–167.

McGinnis, K. (1983). An interview with a church leader. *U.S. Catholic*, 48 (11), 19–23.

McGlynn, F. D.; Bichajian, C.; Giesen, J. M.; and Rose, R. L. (1981). Effects of cue-controlled relaxation: A credible placebo treatment and no treatment on shyness among college males. *Journal of Behavior Therapy and Experimental Psychiatry*, 12 (4), 299–306.

McIntyre, T. (1982). The teachers role in the detection of child abuse. *Eastern Education Journal*, 15 (2), 15–17.

McKenry, P. C.; Tishler, C. I.; and Christman, K. L. (1980). Adolescent suicide and the classroom teacher. *Journal of School Health*, 50, 130–132.

McKinney, B. C. (1981). The effects of reticence on group interaction. *Communication Quarterly*, 30 (4), 321–341.

McKown, H. C. (1935). *Character education*. New York: McGraw-Hill.

McLaughlin, T. F. (1983). Effects of self-recording for on-task and academic responding: A life long term analysis. *Journal of Special Education Technology*, 6 (3), 5–12.

McLaughlin, T. F., and Malaby, J. (1972). Intrinsic reinforcers in a classroom token economy. *Journal of Applied Behavior Analysis*, 5, 263–270.

McLean, J.; Yoder, D.; and Schiefelbusch, R. (1972). *Language intervention with the retarded*. Baltimore MD: University Park Press.

McLoed, P. H. (1973). *Readiness for learning*. New York: J. B. Lippincott.

McLoughlin, J. A., and Lewis, R. B. (1981). *Assessing special students*. Columbus, OH: Charles E. Merrill.

McNinch, G. H. (1981). A method for teaching sight words to disabled readers. *The Reading Teacher*, 35 (3), 269.

McWhirter, J. J.; McWhirter, R. J.; and McWhirter, M. C. (1985). The learning disabled child: A retrospect view. *Journal of Learning Disabilities*, 18 (6), 308–310.

Meacham, J. A., and Colombo, J. A. (1980). External retrieval cues facilitate prospective remembering in children. *Journal of Educational Research*, 73 (5), 299–301.

Mead, B. T. (Speaker) (1975). *Living with a hypochondriac*. Cassette Recording No. 7520. Health Insights Cassette Library.

Medick, J. (1982). The loving teacher's guide to discipline. *Instructor*, 92, 66–70.

Meichenbaum, D. (1978). *Cognitive behavior modification*. New York: Plenum.

Meihofer, S. (1974). *The student and the learning environment*. Washington: National Education Association.

Melcer, D. (1981). *Family therapy and the school system*. Milwaukee, WI: National Council on Family Relations. (ERIC Document Reproduction Service No. ED 217 354).

Melear, J. (1973). *The cola manual: A guide to conceptual oral language activities*. California: Academic Therapy Publications.

Melvin, O. B. (1983). The impact of positive self-image on students. *Balance Sheet*, 64 (3), 149–152.

Mendez, R. (1984). Extracurricular activities in to-day's schools—Have we gone too far? *NASSP Bulletin, 68,* 60–64.

Menkin, N. (1976). The social validation and training of conversational skills. *Journal of Applied Behavioral Analysis, 9,* 127–139.

Mercer, C. D. (1985). *Students with learning disabilities* (2nd ed.). Columbus, OH: Charles E. Merrill.

Mercer, C. D., and Mercer, A. R. (1981). *Teaching students with learning problems.* Columbus, OH: Charles E. Merrill.

Merriam-Webster Dictionary. New York: G. & C. Merriam Co.

Merrill, N. A. (1947). *Problem of child delinquency.* Cambridge, MA: Riverside Press.

Messerer, J. (1984). Feuerstein's instrumental enrichment: A new approach for activating intellectual potential in learning disabled youth. *Journal of Education, 17* (6), 324–326.

Metler, M., and Robe, E. (1980). Verbal mediation for perceptual deficitsin learning disabilities: A review and suggestions. *Journal of Learning Disabilities, 13* (6), 319–321.

Meyer, C. E.; Dingman, H. F.; Orpet, R. E.; Sitkei, E. G.; and Watts, C. A. (1964). *Monographs of the society for research in child development.* Yellow Springs Antioch Press.

Meyer, L. E. (1972). *Developing units of instruction.* Iowa: C. Brown.

Meyer, R. G., and Osborne, Y. V. (1982). *Case studies in abnormal behavior.* Boston: Allyn and Bacon.

Meyers, L. F. (1984). Use of microprocessors to initiate language use in young non-oral children. *The Exceptional Parent, 14* (4), 19–24.

Michaelis, C. (1980). Why can't Johnny look nice too? *Exceptional Parent,* 114–118.

Michener, S. (1984). *Achievement and self-esteem implication of self presentation.* Chicago. (ERIC Document Reproduction No. ED 250 621).

Middleton, H. T. (1978). Lowdown doggone dirty shame. *Saturday Review 5,* 13.

Middleton, J. L. (1985). I just can't take tests!! *The Science Teacher, 52* (2), 34–35.

Milburn, J. F., and Lemke, J. A. (1977). The ticking teacher's aide. *Teaching Exceptional Children, 10* (1), 9–12.

Miles, C. (1954). Gifted children. *Manual of child psychology.* New York: Wiley.

Miles, M. R., and Killingsworth, L. (1984). *World of work—Education and jobs, Kit no. 705. Instructor's manual revised.* Columbia, SC: Dept. of Education. (ERIC Document Reproduction Service No. ED 253 686).

Millar, T. P. (1980). The reluctant learner: A strategy for intervention. *Children Today, 9,* 13–15.

Millar, T. P. (1985). What cherry tree? Training children not to lie. *Children Today, 14,* 28–29.

Miller, A. L. (1970). Behavior modification techniques. *Journal of Behavior Therapy and Experimental Psychiatry, 1,* 317–321.

Miller, A. P., and Linefsky, R. (1984). Operation success. *NYSSBA Journal, 11,* 8–10.

Miller, C. (1984). Building self-control: Discipline for young children. *Young Children, 40,* 15–19.

Miller, G. A.; Galanter, E.; and Pribram, K. H. (1960). *Plans and the structure of behavior.* New York: Hold and Company.

Miller, H. (1982). Children's and adult's integration of information about noise and interest levels in their judgement about learning. *Journal of Experimental Child Psychology, 33,* 536–546.

Miller, J. (1973). *Helping your learning disabled child at home.* California: Academic Therapy.

Miller, L. (1978). *Television and its effect on children.* Toronto, Canada: Ontario Educational Communications Authorities. (ERIC Document Reproduction Service No. ED 164 138).

Miller, L. (1981). *Louisville behavior checklist.* Los Angeles: Western Psychological Services.

Miller, L. L. (1974). *Marijuana: Effects on human behavior.* New York: Academic Press.

Miller, M. (1984). *Training workshop manual.* San Diego, CA: Suicide Information Center.

Miller, T. P. (1983). How do you give a child self-esteem? *Children Today, 12,* 2–3.

Millman, H. L.; Schaefer, C. E.; and Cohen, J. F. (1981). *Therapies for school behavior problems.* California: Jossey-Bass.

Millon, M. (1969). *Modern psychopathology.* Philadelphia: W. B. Saunders Co.

Milone, M., and Wasylk, T. (1982). Handwriting in special education. *Teaching Exceptional Children, 14,* (2), 58–61.

Milton, C. (1984). *Assist one to three.* Tuscon, AZ: Communication Skill Builders.

Minuchin, S.; Chamberlain, P.; and Graubard, P. (1967). A project to teach learning skills to disturbed, delinquent children. *American Journal of Orthopsychiatry, 37,* 558–567.

Mischel, W., and Patterson, C. J. (1976). Substantive and structural elements of effective plans for self-control. *Journal of Personality and Social Psychology, 34,* 942–950.

Mitchell, B. (1980). Program in reducing social anxieties. *Journal of School Psychology, 18,* 17–24.

Mitchell, R. M., and Klein, T. (1969). *Nine months to go.* U.S.A.: Ace Printing Co.

Mithaug, D. (1976). Employing task arrangements and verbal contingencies to promote verbalizations between retarded children. *Journal of Applied Behavioral Analysis, 9,* 301–314.

Mittenthal, S. (1983). I won't let alcohol destroy another innocent child. *Family Circle,* June, 22–23.

Molnar, G., and Reighard, C. (1984). *Kindergarten screening: A tool for early intervention of learning problems.* (ERIC Document Reproduction Service No. ED 253 319).

Moncure, B. J. (1982). Values education. *Curriculum Review, 21* (1), 20–25.

Money, J., and Schiffman, G. (1966). *The disabled reader.* Baltimore: Johns Hopkins Press.

Mongate, L. (1984). *Building self-esteem through the writing process: Writing teacher at work.* Washington, D.C: National Education Association (ERIC Document Reproduction No. ED 250 716).

Monroe, E. R., and Hicks, R. D. (1985). 44 ways to teach word meanings. *Clearing House, 58* (5), 218–219.

Montgomery, J. (1982). Puppets: The matter of motivation. *Early Years, 12,* 18–22.

Moracco, J. C., and Camilleri, J. (1983). A study of fears in elementary school children. *Elementary School Guidance and Counseling, 2,* 82–87.

Morgan, R. T. (1972). The conditioning treatment of childhood enuresis. *British Journal of Social Work, 2,* 503–509.

Morris, A. (1981). Keys to successful motor skill performance. *Journal of Physical Education and Recreation, 52* (3), 49–50.

Morris, L. W.; Davis, M. A.; and Hutchings, C. H. (1981). Cognitive and emotional components of anxiety: Literary review and a revised Worry-Emotionality Scale. *Journal of Educational Psychology, 73,* 541–555.

Morris, P. R., and Whiting, H. T. A. (1971). *Motor impairment and compensatory education.* London: G. Bell & Sons.

Morris, R., and Kratochwill, T. (1983). *Treating children's fears and phobias.* New York: Pergamon Press.

Morris, R. J., and Kratochwill, T. R. (eds.) (1983). *The practice of child therapy.* New York: Pergamon Press.

Morrison, D. (1978). *Sensory-motor dysfunction and therapy and early childhood.* Springfield, IL: Charles C. Thomas.

Morrissey, W. J., and Delgado, N. (1978). *A review of literature pertaining to fine motor control.* Las Cruces: New Mexico State University. (ERIC Document Reproduction Service No. ED 180 575).

Morse, W. C. (1975). Disturbed youngsters in the classroom. In J. M. Palardy (ed.), *Teaching today.* New York: Macmillan.

Morsink, C. V. (1984). *Teaching special needs students in the regular classroom.* Boston: Little Brown and Company.

Mosse, H. L. (1982). *the complete handbook of children's reading disorders.* New York: Human Services Press.

Mott, M. (1974). *Teaching the pre-academic child.* Springfield, IL: Charles C. Thomas.

Moyer, B. (1976). *Music for children with learning disabilities.* Montreal, Canada: International Scientific Conference of IFLD. (ERIC Document Service No. ED 135 134).

Moyer, M. (1983). Let's teach "time-using" as well as "time-telling." *Academic Therapy, 18* (4), 453–456.

Moyer, S., and Newcomer, P. (1977). Reversals in reading: Diagnosis and remediation. *Exceptional Children, 43,* 424–429.

Mueller, M. (1985). *Verge: Alcoholism: Fatal disease if not treated.* Charleston, IL: Eastern News.

Mulder, T., and Hulstijn, W. (1985). Sensory feedback in the learning of a novel motor task. *Journal of Motor Behavior, 17* (1), 110–128.

Mule, J. (1981). *Behavior in excess: An examination of the volitioncal disorders.* New York: Free Press.

Mullen, J. K. (1983). Understanding and managing the temper tantrum. *Child Care Quarterly, 12,* 59–70.

Munson, H. L.; Miller, J. K.; and Berman, J. J. (1981). Helping handicapped students learn to work in a mainstream environment. *The Exceptional Child, 28* (1), 19–29.

Muranaka, Y. (1986). Use of the simplified color video magnifier by young children with severely impaired vision. *The Journal of Visual Impairment and Blindness, 79,* 64–66.

Murphy, A. T.; and Fitzsimons, R. M. (1960). *Stuttering and personality dynamics.* New York: The Ronald Press Company.

Murphy, B. L., and Hirschberg (1968). *Learning disorders, Vol. 3.* Seattle, WA: Special Child Publication.

Murphy, L., and Ross, S. M. (1983). Student self-control as a basis for instructional adaptation with behaviorally disordered children. *Behavioral Disorders, 4,* 237–243.

Murray, F. S. (1983). *Judgment of intentionality by nursery school children.* Georgia: Annual Meeting of the South-Eastern Psychological Association. (ERIC Document Reproduction No. ED 230 284).

Murray, J., and Whittenberger, D. (1983). The aggressive, severely behavior disordered child. *Journal of Learning Disabilities, 16,* (2), 76–80.

Muson, H. (1978). Television violence: What parents can do. *Psychology Today, 50,* 54.

Mussen, P. (1973). *The psychological development of the child.* Englewood Cliffs, NJ: Prentice-Hall.

Myer, T. S. (1980). *The reluctant learner.* St. Louis: Finch & Baker.

Myers, G., and Hammill, D. D. (1976). *Methods for learning disorders.* New York: John Wiley & Sons.

Myers, R. E. (1961). *An experimental training program in creative thinking.* Minneapolis: University of Minnesota, Bureau of Educational research.

Myrick, R. D., and Dixon, R. W. (1985). Changing student attitudes and behavior through group counseling. *School Counselor, 32,* 325–330.

Myrick, R. D., and Kelly, F. D. (1971). Group counseling with primary school-age children. *Journal of School Psychology, 9,* 137–143.

Nagel, C., and Moore, F. (1968). *Skill development through games and rhythmic activities.* New York: National Press Publication.

Nagel, V., and Clement (1984). *The art of managing verbal aggression in the classroom.* (ERIC Document Reproduction Service No. ED 245 485).

Nagy, W. E.; Herman, P. A.; and Anderson, R. C. (1985). Learning words from context. *Reading Research Quarterly, 20* (2), 233–253.

Naiman, A. (1985). Higher-order thinking skills. *Personal Computing, 9,* 39.

National Association of Anorexia Nervosa and Associated Disorders (ANAD). Pamphlet produced by Boys Town Center.

National Education Association of the U.S. (1969). *Discipline in the classroom.* Washington, D.C.

National Education Association of the U.S. (1984). *Cooperation in the classroom: Students and teachers together.* Washington, D.C.

National Institute of Mental Health (NIMH) (1969). *Alcohol and alcoholism.* Maryland: National Center for Prevention and Control of Alcoholism.

National School Boards Association (1979). *Student discipline: Practical approaches.* Washington, D.C. (ERIC Document Reproduction Series No. ED 177 691).

Negley, H. H. (1981). *Methods for motivation, grades 7–9.* Indianapolis: Indiana State Department of Public Instruction. (ERIC Document Reproduction Service No. ED 210 647).

Neilans, T. H.; Irael, A. C.; and Pravder, M. D (1981). The effectiveness of transition to a self-control program in maintaining changes in children's behavior. *Child Care Quarterly, 10,* 297–306.

Neisworth, J. T., and Smith, R. M. (1973). *Modifying retarded behavior.* Boston: Houghton Mifflin.

Nelson, P. (1974). Take cursewords out of kids books. *Wilson Library Bulletin, 49,* 13–23.

Neufeld, A., and Fantuzzo, J. W. (1984). Contingent application of a protective device to treat the severe self-biting behavior of a disturbed autistic child. *Journal of Behavior Therapy and Experimental Psychiatry, 15,* 79–83.

Newcomb, A., and Meister, J. (1985). The initial social encounters of high and low social effectiveness school aged children. *The Journal of Abnormal Child Psychology, 13,* 45–48.

Newcomer, P. (1980). *Understanding and teaching emotionally disturbed children.* Boston: Allyn and Bacon.

Newell, K., and Hancock, P. (1984). Forgotten moments: A note of skewness and kurtosis as influential factors in interference extrapolated from response distributions. *Journal of Motor Behavior, 16* (3), 320–335.

Newman, R. (1981). *God bless the grass: Studies in helping children grow in self-esteem.* Palo Alto, CA: R. & E. Research Associates.

Newson (1979). *Toys and playthings.* New York: Pantheon Books.

Newton, R. J., and Matthews, P. V. (1985). The study skills paradox: "You can bring a horse to water but you cannot make it drink." *The Vocational Aspect of Education, 37* (96), 23–31.

Nicholas, R. (1957). *Are you listening?* New York: McGraw-Hill.

Nicholi, A. M. (ed.) (1978). *The Harvard guide to modern psychiatry.* Cambridge, MA: The Belknap Press of Harvard University Press.

Nicholls, J. G. (1976). When a scale measures more than its name denotes: The case of the test anxiety scale for children. *Journal of Consulting and Clinical Psychology, 44,* 976–985.

Nicholls, J. G. (1984). Achievement motivation: Conceptions of ability, subjective experience, task choice, and performance. *Psychological Review, 91* (3), 328–346.

Nielsen, L. (1983). Teaching adolescents self-management. *Clearing House, 57,* 76–81.

Niles, T. R., and Mustachio, J. A. (1978). Self-concept, learning styles, and grade achievement. *Community College Frontiers, 7,* 44–47.

Nixon, S. B. (1969). *Behavioral counseling cases and techniques.* New York: Holt, Rinehart and Winston.

Noah-Cooper, C. L., and Richards, R. G. (1983). Art therapy for an angry child: A case study. *Academic Therapy, 18* (1), 575–581.

Norris, R. V., and Sullivan, C. (1983). *PMS/Premenstrual syndrome.* New York: Berkley Books/Rawson Associates.

Norton, G. R.; Austen, S.; Allen, G. E.; and Hilton, J. (1983). Acceptability of time-out from reinforcement procedures for descriptive child behavior: A further analysis. *Child and Family Behavior Therapy, 5,* 31–42.

Noshpitz, J. D. (1971). The quiet ones. The noisy ones. *Today's Education, 60,* 24–27.

Novak, J. M., and Bennett, A. C. (1983). *Informing inviting moral development: Teacher perception and behavior regarding the handling of moral transgressions.* Paper presented at the Annual meeting of the American Education Research Association, Montreal, Quebec, Canada. (ERIC Document Reproduction Service No. ED 230 519).

Novakovich, D.; Smith, T.; and Teegarden, E. (1977). *Target on language.* Bethesda, MD: Christ Church Child Center Publications.

Novakovich, H., and Zoslow, S. (1973). *Target on language.* Bethesda, MD: Christ Church Child Center. (ERIC Document Reproduction Service No. ED 084 724).

Nurco, D. N. (1981). The self-help movement and narcotic addicts. *The American Journal of Drug and Alcohol Abuse, 8,* 139–151.

Nurcombe, B. (1964). Children who set fires. *Medical Journal of Australia, 1,* 579–584.

Oaklander, V. (1978). *Windows to our children.* Maob, UT: Real People Press.

O'Brien, T. P.; Riner, L. S.; and Budd, K. S. (1983). The effects of a child's self-evaluation program on compliance with parental instructions in the home. *Journal of Applied Behavior Analysis, 16,* 69–79.

Obstfeld, L. (1984). Adolescent sex education. *Journal of School Health, 54* (2), 68–70.

Oden, S., and Asher, S. R. (1977). Coaching children in social skills for friendship making. *Child Development, 48,* 495–506.

O'Donnell, M., and Duncan, R. (1980). *Gifted and talented children packet.* Washington D.C.: Office of the Gifted and Talented.

O'Leary, K. D., and O'Leary, S. G. (1977). *Classroom management* (92nd ed.). New York: Pergamon Press.

O'Leary, K. D., and Wilson, G. T. (1975). *Behavior therapy: Application and outcome.* Englewood Cliffs, NJ: Prentice-Hall.

Oliver, P. R.; Acker, L. E; and Oliver, D. D. (1977). Effect of reinforcement histories of compliance and noncompliance on nonreinforced imitation. *Journal of Experimental Child Psycology, 23* (2), 180–190.

O'Neil, C. (1982). *Starving for attention.* New York: Continum Publishing Co.

O'Neill, C. B. (1982). Starving for attention. *McCall's, 110,* 118–119.

O'Neill, K. K. (1978). Parent involvement: A key to the education of gifted children. *Gifted Child Quarterly, 22* (2), 235–242.

Onyehalu, A. (1983). Inadequacy of sex knowledge of adolescents: Implications for counselling and sex education. *Adolescence, 18* (71), 627–630.

Orbach, I.; Gross, Y.; and Glaubman, H. (1981). Some common characteristics of latency-age suicidal children. *Suicide and Life Threatening Behavior, 2,* 180–189.

Orbach, S. (1982). *Fat is a feminist issue II.* New York: Berkley Book.

Orlich, D. (1980). *Teaching strategies: A guide to better instruction.* Toronto: D. C. Heath.

Ornstein, A. C. (1975). Who are the disadvantaged? In J. M. Palardy (ed.), *Teaching today.* New York: Macmillan.

Orr, F. (1981). *Adolescent shyness and self-esteem.*

Kesington, Australia: New South Wales University. (ERIC Document Reproduction Service No. ED 212 388).

Orton, S. (1966). *Word-blindness in school children and other papers on strephosymbolia.* CN: Orton Society.

Osborn, L. (1980). Painless math drill. *Instructor, 90,* 124–129.

Osborn, S. (1985). Effect of teacher experience and selected temperment variables on coping strategies used with distractible children. *American Educational Research Journal, 22,* 79–89.

Ottens, G. (1982). A guaranteed scheduling technique to manage student's procrastination. *College Students Journal, 16* (4), 371–376.

Otto, J. H.; Julian, C. J.; Tether, J. E.; and Madnick, M. E. (1976). *Modern Health.* New York: Holt, Rinehart, & Winston.

Oursler, W. (1968). *Marijuana the Facts—The Truth,* New York: Paul Erikson.

Paddock, C. (1981). Children's possession of pornography. *Instructor Magazine, 15* (7), 19.

Padus, E. (1981). *The women's encyclopedia of health and natural healing.* New York: Rodale Press.

Palewicz, P., and Madaras, L. (1979). *The alphabet connection.* New York: Shocken Books.

Palmer, E., et al. (1968). *A comparative study of current educational television programs for preschool children. Final report.* Washington D.C.: Bureau of Research. (ERIC Document Reproduction Service No. ED 032 123).

Papalia, D. E., and Olds, S. W. (1979). *A child's world.* New York: McGraw-Hill.

Paquin, M. J. (1978). The effects of self graphing on academic performance. *Education and Treatment of Children, 1* (2), 5–15.

Park, C. C. (1972). Use of self instructional materials with gifted primary aged students. *Gifted Child Quarterly, 27,* 34.

Park, C. C. (1972). *The siege: The first eight years of an autistic child.* Boston: Little, Brown and Company.

Parker, J. E., and Johnson, C. E. (1981). *Affecting achievement motivation.* Washington, D.C. (ERIC Document Reproduction Service No. ED 226 833).

Parker Publishing Co. (1974). *Elementary Teaching Ideas and Materials, 8* (3), 1–3.

Parks, R. F. (1985). The mystery of memory. *Science,* 72–74.

Patrizi, F. M. (1982). *Self-attitude enchancement through positive mental imagery.* Ada, OK: East Central University. (ERIC Document Reproduction Service No. ED 230 878).

Patsey, R. L. (1981). Curbing violence and vandalism in our schools: A judicial view of what must be done. *Thrust, 11,* 11–36.

Patterson, G. R. (1965). *An application of conditioning techniques to the control of a hyperactive child.* New York: Holt.

Patton, J. E.; Stinard, T. A.; and Routh, D. K. (1984). Where do children study? *Educational Digest, 49,* 58–60.

Payne, J.; Palloway, E.; Smith, J.; and Payne, R. (1977). *Strategies for teaching the mentally retarded.* Columbus, OH: Charles E. Merrill.

Payne, J.; Palloway, E.; Smith, J.; and Payne, R. (1981). *Strategies for teaching the mentally retarded.* Columbus, OH: Bell & Howell.

Pearce, J. W. (1981). Role of spouse involvement in the behavioral treatment of overweight women. *Journal of Consultation and Clinician, 49,* 236–244.

Pearl, T. (1985). *Learning disabled children's self-esteem and desire for approval.* Chicago. (ERIC Document Reproduction No. ED 222 022).

Pearson, C. (1974). *Resolving classroom conflict.* Palo Alto, CA: Education Today Co.

Peck, R. N. (1977). In D. R. Gallo (ed.), Teaching writing: Advice from the professionals. *Connecticut English Journal, 12* (2), 20. (ERIC Document Reproduction Service No. ED 151 846).

Pelham, W. E., and Milich, R. (1984). Peer relations in children with hyperactivity/attention deficit disorder. *The Journal of Learning Disabilities, 17,* 560–567.

Pelow, R. (1981). *Motivational use of adaptable design in reinforcing geographic-social studies content.* Pittsburg, PA: Annual Meeting of the National Council for Geographic Education. (ERIC Document Reproduction Service No. ED 214 816).

Pennington, C. P., and James, E. (1967). *The stuttering child—In the school and in the home.* Illinois: The Interstate Printers & Publishers.

Pennsylvania Materials Center (1980). *Focus on individual programming for the visually handicapped.*

Penticuff, J. (1976). Development of the concept of self: Implications for the teachers role in promotion of mental health. *Educational Horizons, 55,* 15–18.

Peppard, H. M. (1925). *The correction of speech defects.* New York: MacMillan.

Peretti, P. O.; Clark, D.; and Johnson, P. (1984). Affect of parental rejection on negative attention-seeking classroom behavior. *Education, 104,* 313–317.

Perine, M. H. (1978). Growth in moral judgment through reading selected literature. *The Delta Kappa Gamma Bulletin, 45,* 11–17.

Perkins, W. H. (1978). *Human perspectives in speech and language disorders.* St. Louis: C. V. Mosby.

Perner, J.; Kohlmann, R.; and Wimmer, H. (1984). Young children's recognition and use of the vertical and horizontal in drawings: *Child Development, 55,* 1637–1645.

Perry, C.; Butterfield, P.; Swassing, D.; and McKay, G. (1984). Assessment and treatment of anorexia nervosa and bulimia in school age children. *School Psychology Review, 13,* 183–191.

Perry, L. A. (1984). Use commercial logos to teach basic sight words. *The Reading Teacher, 38* (1), 122.

Perry, R. H. (1980). Strategies for working with problem students. *Urban Education, 14,* 471–488.

Petersen, C. (1982). Test without trauma fearlessly uncovers the quiz whiz in all of us. *Chicago Tribune,* 10.

Peterson, D., and Quay, H. (1979). *Behavior problem checklist.* Unpublished. Available from D. Peterson, 39 North Fifth Ave., Highland Park, NJ 08904.

Petty, W.; Petty, D; and Becking, M. (1981). *Experiences in language: Tools and techniques for language arts development* (3rd ed.). Boston: Allyn and Bacon.

Pfeffer, C. (1981). Suicidal behavior of children. *Exceptional Children, 48,* 170–172.

Pfeffer, C. R.; Conte, H. R.; Plutchik, R.; and Jerrett, I. (1979). Suicidal behavior in latency age children: An empirical study. *Journal of the American Academy of Child Psychiatry, 18,* 679–692.

Phi Delta Kappa (1982). Practical applications of research. *Newsletter of Phi Delta Kappa's Center on Evaluation, Development, and Research, 5.*

Phillips, B. N. (1981). *Anxiety and school related interventions.* Albany: S.U.N.Y. of New York.

Piazza, R. (1979). *Motor disorders.* Guilford, CN: Special Learning Corp.

Piazza, R. (1979). *Perception and memory.* Guilford, CN: Special Learning Corp.

Pickett, C., and Clum, G. A. (1982). Relaxation instruction and attention redirection approach. *Journal of Consulting and Clinical Psychology, 50,* 439–441.

Pihl, R. (1980). Hyperactivity in children. Is there a treatment of choice? *Psychology in the Schools, 17* (4), 500–508.

Pimm, J., and McClure, G. (1978). *Ottawa school behavior checklist.* Ottawa, Canada: Pimm Consultants.

Pine, M. (1985). What makes children psychologically resilient? *The Education Digest, 50,* 32–35.

Pittman, D. J. Society (1970). *Culture and drinking problems.* New York: John Wiley and Sons.

Plake, B. S.; Ansorge, C. J.; Parker, C. S.; and Lowry, S. R. (1982). Effects of item arrangement, knowledge of arrangement, test anxiety and sex on test performance. *Journal of Educational Measurement, 19* (1), 13–26.

Platts, M. E. (1972). *Launch: A handbook of early learning techniques for the preschool and kindergarten teacher.* Stevensville, MI: Educational Services.

Platts, M. E.; Shumaker, E.; and Marguerite, R. (1960). *Spice: Activities to motivate teaching of the language arts.* Stevensville, MI: Educational Services.

Podolsky, E. (ed.) (1953). *Encyclopedia of aberrations.* New York: Philosophical Library.

Polk, K., and Schaefer, W. (1972). *Schools and delinquency.* Englewood Cliffs, NJ: Prentice-Hall.

Polon, L., and Pollitt, W. (1974). *Creative teaching games.* Minneapolis, MN: T. S. Denison and Co.

Polsgrove, L. (1982). Return to baseline: Some comments on Smith's reinterpretation of seclusionary timeout. *Behavioral Disorders, 8,* 50–52.

Pomerantz, V., and Schultz, D. (1983). How active is hyperactive? *Parents, 83* (58), 129.

Pope, L.; Edle, D.; and Haklay, A. (1979). *Special needs: Special answers.* Brooklyn: Booklab.

Poteet, J. A. (1973). *Behavior modification: A practical guide for teachers.* Minneapolis: Burgess Publishing Co.

Precision Teaching Materials. Montana State Board of Education.

Preston, F. (1984). A behavior management plan for middle level students. *NASSP Bulletin, 68* (473), 39–41.

Prout, H. T., and Harvey, J. R. (1978). Applications of desensitization procedures for school-related problems: A review. *Psychology in the Schools, 15* (4).

Prout, T. H. (1978). Behavioral intervention with hyperactive children: A review. *Journal of Learning Disabilities, 11* (17), 20–24.

Provence, S. (1985). Wham! Pow! Coping with kids' aggression. *Parents*, March, 72–76.

Pulido, J. (1981). ACABA: An alternative for underachieving chicano youth. *Bilingual education technology: Ethnoperspectives in psilanti*. Eastern Michigan University.

Purcell, V. (1985). From the files of Verona Purcell, Chicago Illinois 60660. *Arithmetic Teacher, 32* (5), 45.

Purvis, J., and Leonard, R. (1985). Strategies for preventing behavioral incidents in the nation's secondary schools. *Clearing House, 58* (8), 349–353.

Putnam, J. (1984). Idea place. *Learning, 12* (9), 93.

Quasius, E. L.; Koppman, P. S.; Goldman, S.; McQueen, T.; and Little, B. (1984). Homework sweet homework. *Instructor, 94* (3), 38–44.

Quimby, J. M. (1984). Dansville "connection" helps troubled youth. *NYSSBA Journal, 11*, 14–15.

Quinn, C. E. (1980). Spelling tricks for sight words. *Academic Therapy, 15*, 443–446.

Radler, D. H., and Kephart, N. C. (1960). *Success through play: How to prepare your child for school achievement and enjoy it*. New York: Harper.

Ramelli, E., and Mapelli, G. (1979). Melancholia and kleptomania. *Acta Psychiatrica Belgica, 79*, 56–74.

Ramsey, A. (1974). Marijuana and health. *Third Annual Report to the U.S. Congress*.

Ramsey, R. P. (1981). *Educator's discipline handbook*. West Nyack, NY: Parker Publishing Co.

Raschlos, D. (1981). Designing reinforcement surveys. Let the student choose the reward. *Teaching Exceptional Children, 14*, 92–96.

Ralsinski, T. (1983). *Using Jackdaws to build background and interest for reading*. Anaheim, CA: Annual Meeting of the International Reading Association. (ERIC Document Reproduction Service No. ED 234 351).

Raviv, A.; Levit, R.; and Bartal, D. (1983). Student reactions to attributes of ability and effort. *British Journal of Educational Psychology, 53*, 1–13.

Reasons, C. E., and Seem, J. (1978). Drug education: A case study of legislative intent and perceived effect. *Drug Forum, 7*, 181–195.

Redd, W. H.; Porterfield, A. L.; and Andersen, B. L. (1979). *Behavior modification: Behavioral approaches to human problems*. New York: Random House.

Redl, F. (1954). Old study in a new setting. *Children, 1*, 15–20.

Redl, F., and Wineman, D. (1957). *The aggressive child*. Glencoe, IL: Free Press.

Reducing violence and vandalism in the Newark Public Schools: A program for school administrators (1979). (ERIC Document Reproduction Service No. ED 195 594).

Reed, K. (1977). *On learning to write*. In D. R. Gallo (ed.), Teaching writing: Advice from the professionals. *Connecticut English Journal, 12* (2), 3. (ERIC Document Reproduction Service No. ED 151 846).

Reese, E. P. (1978). *Human behavior analysis & application*. Dubuque, IA: Wm. C. Brown.

Reese, S. C.; Murphy, R. J.; and Filipczak, J. (1981). Assessment of multiple behavioral procedures on academic and social classroom behavior. *Psychology in the Schools, 18* (3), 349–355.

Rehm, L. P. (1981). *Behavior therapy for depression*. New York: Academic Press.

Reid, L. N. (1978). *Regulating parental responsibility*. Seattle: Association for Education in Journalism. (ERIC Document Reproduction Service No. ED 159 679).

Reinhart, H. R. (1980). *Children in conflict*. St. Louis: C. V. Mosby Co.

Reis, S. M., and Cellerino, M. (1983). Guiding gifted students through independent study. *Teaching Exceptional Children, 15*, 139.

Reisman, F., and Kauffman, S. (1980). *Teaching mathematics to children with special needs*. Columbus, OH: Bell and Howell.

Reister, B. W.; Stockton, R. A.; and Maulsby, M. C. (1977). Counseling the test anxious: An alternative. *Journal of College Student Personnel, 18* (6), 506–510.

Reith, H.; Axelrod, S.; Anderson, R.; Hathaway, R.; Wood, K.; and Fitzgerald, C. (1974). Cited in D. Smith (ed.) (1981). *Teaching the learning disabled*. Englewood Cliffs, NJ: Prentice-Hall.

Renshaw, D. (1976). *The hyperactive child*. Chicago: Nelson-Hall.

Renwright, B., et al. (1982). Values education. *Curriculum Review, 21* (1), 20–25.

Renzulli, J. S. (1971). Scale for rating behavioral characteristics of superior students. *Exceptional Children, 38*, 243–248.

Repp, A. C., and Deitz, S. M. (1974). Reducing aggressive and self-injurious behavior through reinforcement of other behaviors. *Journal of Applied Behavioral Analysis, 1*, 313–325.

Resnik, H. L., and Hawthorne, B. C. (1974). *Teaching outlines in suicide studies and crisis intervention*. Bowie, MD: Charles Press Publishing.

Resource, A. L. (1969). Some implications for the classroom. *Teaching Exceptional Children, 11* (14), 42–45.

Rey, M., and Rey, H. A. (1966). *Curious George goes to the hospital.* Boston: Houghton Mifflin.

Reyes, D. (1981). Selecting reinforcers for positive classroom projects in inner city schools. *Illinois School Journal, 61,* 61–66.

Rhode, G.; Morgan, D.; and Young, R. (1983). Generalization and maintenance of treatment gains of behaviorally handicapped students from resource rooms to regular classrooms using self-evaluation procedures. *Journal of Applied Behavioral Analysis, 16* (2), 171–188.

Richard, H. (1984). Academically unpredictable school children: Their attitudes toward school subjects. *Journal of Educational Research, 77,* 273–276.

Richardson, G. E. (1976). Combating vandalism in the schools. *National Association of Secondary School Principals Bulletin, 60,* 60–65.

Richardson, G. E. (1981). Educational imagery: A missing link in decision making. *The Journal of School Health, 51* (8), 560–564.

Rieberg, E. H.; Parke, R. D.; and Hetherington, E. M. (1971). Modification of impulsive and reflective cognitive styles through observation of film-mediated models. *Developmental Psychology, 5,* 369–377.

Riess, P. (1968). Concepts of autism: A review of research. *Journal of Child Psychiatry and Psychology, 9,* 1–25.

Rimland, B. (1974). *Infant autism: Status and research.* New York: John Wiley & Sons.

Rimm, D. C., and Masters, J. C. (1979). *Behavior therapy: Techniques and empirical findings:* New York: Academic Press.

Rimm, S. (1984). Underachievement. *G/C/T, 31,* 26–29.

Rinne, C. (1982). Low profile classroom controls. *Phi Delta Kappan, 64* (1), 52–54.

Riper, C. V. (1961). *Your child's speech problems.* New York: Harper & Row.

Riper, C. V. (1963). *Speech correction: Principles and methods.* Englewood Cliffs, NJ: Prentice-Hall.

Ritvo, E. (1981). Autism: It may be a genetic defect. *Newsweek, 98,* 63.

Rivers, W. L. (1977). *The disruptive student and the teacher.* Washington D.C.: National Education Association. (ERIC Document Reproduction No. ED 144 931).

Robbins, P. R. (1976). *Marijuana: A short course.* Boston: Brandon Press.

Roberson, S.; Lewandowski, R.; Potts, M.; and Michell, A. (1982). Building students' self esteem. *Todays Education, 71* (3), 60–64.

Roberts, S. (1975). Helping the emotionally disturbed child feel secure in the classroom. *Journal for Special Education of the Mentally Retarded, 6* (2), 136–139.

Robin, A.; Schneider, M.; and Dolnick, M. (1976). The turtle technique: An extended case of self-control in the classroom. *Psychology in the Schools, 13,* 449–453.

Robinson, H. A. (1975). *Teaching reading and study strategies.* Boston: Allyn and Bacon.

Robinson, P. W.; Newby, T. J.; and Ganzell, S. L. (1981). A token system for a class of underachieving hyperactive children. *Journal of Applied Behavior Analysis, 14,* 307–314.

Robinson, S., and Bowie, C. (1982). Building student's self-esteem. *Today's Education, 70,* 60–64.

Rocks, T. G. (1985). The low achiever. *School Counselor, 32,* 213–238.

Rogers, D. M. (1972). *Classroom discipline: an idea handbook for elementary school teachers.* New York: The Center for Applied Research in Education.

Rogers, G. W. (1977). *Rationally dealing with test anxiety.* KY: Northern Kentucky University. (ERIC Document Reproduction Service No. ED 177 200).

Rogers, H., and Scklofske, D. H. (1985). Self-concepts, locus of control and performance expectations of L.D. children. *Journal of Learning Disability, 18* (5), 273–278.

Rogers, J. (1977) *You can stop.* New York: Simon and Schuster.

Rogers, T., and Mann, K. (1980). Present with past. *The American Journal of Occupational Therapy, 34* (6), 375–379.

Rogers, W. A., and Baer, D. M. (1976). Correspondence between saying and doing: Teaching children to share and praise. *Journal of Applied Behavior Analysis, 9,* 335–354.

Rohrkemper, M. (1984). Elementary school students: Reports of the cause and effects of problem difficulty in mathematics. *The Elementary School Journal, 85,* 127–147.

Romney, D. M., and Stevenson, D. T. (1984). Depression in learning disabled children. *Journal of Learning Disabilities, 17* (10), 579–582.

Rooney, K. J.; Hallahan, D. P.; and Lloyd, J. W. (1984). Self-recording of attention by learning disabled students in the regular classroom. *The Journal of Learning Disabilities, 17,* 360–364.

Rorschler, D. (1981). Designing reinforcement surveys: Let the student choose the reward. *Teaching Exceptional Children, 14,* 92–96.

Rose, M., and Cundick, B. (1983). Verbal rehearsal and visual imagery: Mnemonic aids for learning disabled children. *The Journal of Learning Disabilities, 16,* 352–355.

Rosenbaum, C. P. (1970). *The meaning of madness: Symptomatology, sociology, biology, and therapy of the schizophrenias.* New York: Science House.

Rosenbek, K. (1973). Treatment of developmental apraxia of speech: A case study. *Journal of Speech & Hearing Disorder, 38,* 462–472.

Rosenblatt, J. (1981). Shoplifting. Editorial Research Report, Vol. 2, No. 20. Washington D.C.: Congressional Quarterly.

Rosenfield, P. (1985). Desk arrangement effects on pupil classroom behavior. *Journal of Educational Psychology, 77* (1), 101–108.

Rosengrant, T. (1985). Using the microcomputer as a tool for learning to read and write. *Journal of Learning Disabilities, 18* (2), 113–115.

Rosenthal, M. S., and Mothner, I. (1972). *Drugs, parents and children.* Boston: Houghton Mifflin.

Rosner, J. (1973). *Perceptual skills curriculum program II. Auditory motor skills.* New York: Walker Educational Book Corp.

Rosner, J. (1973). *Perceptual skills curriculum program III. General—Motor skills.* New York: Walker Educational Book Corp.

Ross, A. O. (1976). *Psychological aspects of learning disabilities and reading disorders.* New York: McGraw-Hill.

Ross, A. O. (1977). *Learning disability the unrealized potential.* New York: McGraw-Hill.

Ross, A. O.; Lacey, H. M.; and Parlor, D. A. (1965). The development of a behavior checklist for boys and girls. *Child Development, 36,* 1013–1027.

Ross, C. P. (1980). Mobilizing schools for suicide prevention. *Suicide and Life-Threatening Behavior, 4,* 139–243.

Ross, D. D. (1980). The basic skills list: An influence on curriculum? *Peabody Journal of Education, 57,* 101–105.

Rothstein, L. (1983). Accountability for professional misconduct in providing education to handicapped children, *Journal of Law & Education, 14* (3), 349.

Rousso, H. (1985). Fostering healthy self-esteem. *Exceptional Parent, 14,* 9–10.

Rowe, A. R. (1982). Perceived religiosity and perceived sanctioned threat. *Perceptual and Motor Skills, 54,* 1225–1226.

Rowe, P., and Sugai, G. (1984). The effect of self-recording on out-of-seat behavior of an EMR Student. *Education and Training of the Mentally Retarded, 19* (1), 23–28.

Royce, D. (1981). Health in the classroom. *Child Welfare, 141,* 361–364.

Royce, J. E. (1981). *Alcohol problems and alcoholism.* New York: The Free Press.

Rubel, R. J. (1980). Vandalism in public schools: Combining new theories providing new insights. *National Association of Secondary School Principles Bulletin, 64,* 67–75.

Rubin, D. (1980). *Teaching elementary language arts.* New York: Holt Rinehart and Winston.

Ruble, D. N.; Feldman, N. S.; and Boggiano, A. K. (1976). Social comparison between young children in achievement situations. *Developmental Psychology, 12* (3), 192–197.

Rublowsky, J. (1983). The stoned age. *Family Circle, 159,* 35–42.

Russell, K. P. (1977). *Eastman's expectant motherhood.* Boston: Little, Brown and Co.

Rutter, M. (1978). Diagnosis and definition of childhood autism. *Journal of Autism and Childhood Schizophrenia, 8,* 139–161.

Safer, D. J., and Allen, R. P. (1976). *Hyperactive children: Diagnosis and management.* Baltimore: University Park Press.

Safran, S., and Safran, J. (1983). Classroom context and teachers perceptions of problem behaviors. *Journal of Educational Psychology. 73,* 122–128.

Safran, S., and Safran, J. (1984). The self-monitoring mood chart: Measuring affect in the classroom. *Teaching Exceptional Children, 16* (3), 172–175.

St. John, J. (1984). A hands-on (literally) approach to stress reduction: What's new in schools? *Trust, 13* (7), 12–14.

Salend, S. (1983). Guidelines for explaining targeted behaviors to students. *Elementary School Guidance and Counseling, 18,* 2.

Salend, S. J.; Esquivel, L.; and Pine, P. B. (1984). Regular and special education teachers' estimates of use of aversive contingencies. *Behavioral Disorders, 9* (2), 89–95.

Sallis, J. F. (1983). Aggressive behaviors of children: A review of behavioral interventions and future directions. *Education and Treatment of Children, 6,* 29–35.

Salovey, P., and Rodin, J. (1984). Some antecedents and consequences of social-comparison jealousy. *Journal of Personality and Social Psychology, 47* (4), 780–792.

Sampson, C., and Velten, E. (1978). *Rx for learning disabilities.* Chicago: Nelson-Hall.

Samuels, S. C. (1977). *Enhancing self-concept in early childhood: Theory and practice.* New York: Human Science Press.

SanAndres, L. (1979). The natural mathematician. *Teacher, 96* (7), 115.

Sandford, J. (1983). *management and organization in science classrooms.* Texas: Research and Development Center for Teacher education. (ERIC Document Reproduction Service No. ED 233 881).

Sants, D. (1980). Dancing: An important step toward self-esteem. *Voc Ed, 55* (6), 36–37.

Sarason, I. G.; Glasser, E. M.; and Rargo, A. G. (1972). *Reinforcing productive classroom behavior.* New York: Behavioral Publications.

Sarason, I. G., and Stoops, R. (1978). Test anxiety and the passage of time. *Journal of Consulting and Clinical Psychology, 46* (1), 102–109.

Saunders, K. (1984). Three number games. *MT: Mathematics Teacher,* 8–9.

Scales, P., and Beckstein, D. (1982). From macho to matuality: Helping young men make effective decisions about sex contraception, and pregnancy. In I. Stuart and C. Wells (eds.), *Pregnancy in adolescence: Needs, problems, and management.* New York: Van Nostrand Reinhold Co.

Scarrozzo, M. L. (1982). Let's dictate spelling success. *Academic Therapy, 18,* 213–215.

Schaefer, C. E., and Millman, H. L. (1977). *Therapies for children: A handbook of effective treatments for problem behaviors.* San Francisco: Jossey-Bass.

Schaefer, W.; Olexa, C.; and Polk, K. (1972). Programmed for social class tracking in high school. In K. Polk and W. Schaefer (eds.), *School and delinquency.* Englewood Cliffs, NJ: Prentice-Hall.

Scharf, P.; McCoy, W.; and Ross, D. (1979). *Growing up moral: Dilemmas for the intermediate grades.* Minneapolis, MN: Winston Press.

Schasre, J. M. (1978). *Helping children with problems.* New York: Walker and Company.

Schattner, R. (1971). *An early childhood curriculum for multiply handicapped children.* New York: The John Day Company.

Schell, R. E., and Hall, E. (1979). *Development and psychology today.* New York: Random House.

Schemp, P. G. (1984). Influence of decision making on attitudes, creativity, motor skills and self-concept in elementary children. *Research Quarterly for Exercise and Sports, 54,* 183–189.

Schilling, F. (1984). Sorting syllables. *Instructor, 43* (8), 126.

Schinke, S. P. (1981). Interpersonal skills training with adolescents. In M. Hersen, R. M. Eisler, and P. J. Miller (eds.), *Progress in behavior modification.* New York: Academic Press.

Schinke, S. P.; Blythe, B. J.; and Gilchrist, L. D. (1981). Cognitive behavioral prevention of adolescent pregnancy. *Journal of Counseling Psychology, 28* (5), 451–454.

Schinke, S. P.; Gilchrist, L. D.; Smith, T. E.; and Wong, S. E. (1979). Group interpersonal skills training in a natural setting: An experimental study. *Behaviour Research and Therapy, 17,* 149–154.

Schlechter, R. (1981). An experiment in group adolescent weight loss guidance. *The Journal of School Health, 51,* 123–124.

Schloss, P. J. (1983). Classroom based intervention for students exhibiting depressive reactions. *Behavioral Disorders, 8* (4), 231–235.

Schloss, P. J. (1983). An integrated social learning approach to the treatment of aggressive reactions. *Education, 104,* 104–112.

Schloss, P. J.; Schloss, C. N.; and Harris, L. (1984). A multiple baseline analysis of an interpersonal skills training program for depressed youth. *Behavioral Disorders, 9* (3), 182–188.

Schloss, P.; Schloss, C.; and Segraves, G. (1985). Professional settings on expectations of behaviorally disordered youth. *Journal for Special Educators, 20* (1), 27–63.

Schloss, P. J. and Sedlak, R. A. (1982). Behavioral features of the mentally retarded adolescent: Implications for mainstream educators. *Psychology in the Schools, 19* (1), 98–105.

Schneck, J. M. (1980). Hypnotherapy for narcolepsy. *International Journal of Clinical and Experimental Hypnosis, 28,* 95–100.

Schoknect, C., and Jorm, A. F. (1981). Role of visual work-recognition checking in children's spelling. *Australian Journal of Psychology, 33* (3), 393–403.

Schramm, W. (1961). *Television in the lives of our children.* Stanford, CA: Stanford University Press.

Schuler, A. L. (1979). Echolalia: Issues and clinical applications. *Journal of Speech and Hearing Disorders, 44,* 411–434.

Schultz, E. W., and Heuchert, C. M. (1983). *Child stress and the school experience.* New York: Human Sciences Press.

Schumaker, J., and Deshler, D. (1983). In J. Lerner (ed.) (1985). *Learning disabilities.* Boston: Houghton Mifflin.

Schumaker, J. B., and Hazel, S. (1984). Social skills assessment and training for the learning disabled: Who's on first and what's on second? Part II *Journal of Learning Disabilities, 17* (8), 492–499.

Schuman, M. (1980). Most of my students feel pressure from home: An elementary school teacher speaks. *Today's Education, 69,* 33–34.

Schunk, D. H. (1983). How children process attributional information and its effects on achievement outcomes. *Journal of Educational Psychology, 14,* 848–851.

Schunk, P. H. (1982). Effects of effort attributional feedback on children's perceived self-efficancy and achievement. *Journal of Educational Psychology, 74,* 548–566.

Schuster, R. (1978). Evaluation of a reality therapy stratification system in a residential drug rehabilitation center. *Drug Forum, 7,* 59–67.

Schwartz, S., and Johnson, J. H. (1981). *Psychopathology of childhood: A clinical experimental approach.* New York: Pergamon Press.

Schwarzer, R., and Schwarzer, C. (1982.) Achievement anxiety with respect to reference groups in schools. *Journal of Education Research, 75* (5), 305–308.

Schwarzrocks, L. (1984). *Coping with teenage problems.* Minnesota: American Guidance Service.

Schwitzgebel, R. K., and Kolb, D. A. (1974). *Changing human behavior: Principals of planned intervention.* New York: McGraw-Hill.

Scott, D. (1973). *About epilepsy.* New York: International University Press.

Scott, K. G. (1970). Learning and intelligence. *Psychometric intelligence.* New York: Appleton Century Crofts.

Scruggs, T., and Mastropieri, M. (1984). Improving memory facts: The "keyword" method. *Academic Therapy, 20* (2), 159–166.

Searls, E. F., and Klesius, J. P. (1984). 99 multiple meaning words for primary students and ways to teach them. *Reading Psychology, 5* (2), 55–63.

Sears, C. J. (1981). The tactile defense child. *Academic Therapy, 16,* 563–569.

Segraves, T. (1978). Controlling phobias through behavior modification. *USA Today, 107,* 8–9.

Seif, M., and Atkin, A. (1979). Some defensive and cognitive aspects of phobias. *The Journal of Abnormal Psychology, 88,* 42–51.

Seigel, E. (1961). *Helping the brain-damaged child.* Albany: New York Association for the Learning Disabled.

Seigel, E., and Gold, R. (1982). *Educating the learning disabled.* New York: Macmillan.

Self, M. R. (1982). *The conflict resolution curriculum for children in emotional conflict.* Springfield, IL: Charles C. Thomas.

Seligman, J., and Zabarsky, M. (1983). A deadly feast and famine. *Newsweek,* March, 59–60.

Senn, M. J. E., and Solnit, A. J. (1968). *Problems in child behavior and development.* Philadelphia: Lea & Febiger.

Sepie, A. C., and Keeling, B. (1978). The relationship between types of anxiety and underachievement in mathematics. *The Journal of Education Research, 72,* 15–19.

Serio, M. (1984). Can't spell cat. *Academic Therapy, 20* (2), 235–239.

Serrano, R. (1981–82). Networks and friendships in a high school class. *High School Journal, 65* (8), 254–258.

Setal, R. (1972). *No time to fool around.* Philadelphia: Westminster.

Sewell, T. E. (1981). High school dropout: Psychological, academic and vocational factors. *Urban Education, 16,* 65–76..

Sexton, M. J., and Hamilton, J. G. (1979). If your schools aren't using the procedures listed here, you're vulnerable to vandalism. *American School Board Journal, 166* (2), 38.

Sexton, M. J., and Killian, M. G. (1979). To combat vandalism: Do you build fences or bridges? *National Association of Secondary School Principals, 63* (424), 19–26.

Shainess, N. (1984). *Sweet suffering.* Indianapolis, IN: Bobbs-Merrill Co.

Shapiro, A. K.; Shapiro, E. S.; Brunn, R. D.; and Sweet, R. D. (1978). *Gilles de la Tourette syndrome.* New York: Raven Press.

Sharpley, A. M. (1983). Examination of the effectiveness of a cross age tutoring program in mathematics for elementary school children. *American Educational Research Journal, 20,* 103–111.

Shaver, P.; Lehauer, M.; and Sadd, S. (1980). Religiousness, conversion, and subjective well-being: The "healthy-minded" religion of modern American women. *American Journal of Psychiatry, 137* (12), 1563–1573.

Shaw, C. R., and Lucas, A. R. (1970). *The psychiatric disorders of childhood.* New York: Appleton Century Crofts Educational Division/Meredith Corp.

Shawsheen Valley Regional Vocational Technical High School (1979). *Finger dexterity work sample.* Boston: Massachusetts State Department of Education, Boston Division of Occupational Education. (ERIC Document Reproduction Service No. ED 236 430).

Shea, T. (1978). *Teaching children and youth with behavior disorders.* St. Louis: C. V. Mosby Co.

Shelby, A. (1985). Is your teaching style frustrating your students? *Learning, 85* (14), 3.

Shelquist, J.; Breeze, B.; and Jacquot, B. (1973). *Resource handbook for development of learning skills.* Oregon: Educational Programmers Co.

Shelton, T. L. Anastopoulos, A. D.; and Linden, J. D. (1985). An attribution training program with L.D. children. *Journal of Learning Disabilities, 18* (5), 265–268.

Shermis, S., and Barth, J. (1984). Problem solving & the social studies. *Education Digest, 50,* 33–35.

Shetterly, H. (1979). *Self and Social Perceptions and Personal Characteristics of a Group.* Michigan: University Microfilms.

Sheviakov, G. (1969). *Anger in children: Causes, characteristics, and consideration.* Washington D.C.: National Education Association.

Schneidman, E. S. (1981). Suicide thoughts and reflections. *Suicide and Life-Threatening Behavior, 4,* 197–363.

Shorr, J.; Sobel, G.; Robin, P.; and Conella, J. (1980). *Imagery: Its many dimensions and applications.* New York: Plenum Press.

Shrigley, R. L. (1979). Strategies in classroom management. *NASSP Bulletin, 63,* 1–9.

Shulman, S. (1979). *Nightmare.* New York: Mac-Millan.

Siedow, M. D., and Fox, B. J. (1983). Writing directions poor readers can understand. *Clearing House, 56,* 312–314.

Siegel, B. L. (1980). I can do it without cheating. *Today's Education, 69,* 32–33.

Siegel, L., and Peterson, L. (1980). Stress reduction in young dental patients through coping skills and sensory information. *Journal of Consulting and Clinical Psychology, 48,* 785–787.

Silberman, A. (1985). What's wrong with my child? *McCall's, 112* (7), 46–140.

Silberstein, R. M., and Blackman, S. (1965). Diagnosis and treatment of enuresis. *American Journal of Psychiatry, 12,* 120–124.

Silverman, M. (1980). *How to handle problem behaviors in school.* Lawrence, KS.: H & H Enterprises.

Simmons, J. S. (1980). Word study skills. *Perspectives in reading.* Delaware: International Reading Association.

Simmons, J. T., and Wasik, B. H. (1976). Grouping strategies, peer influence, and free time as classroom management techniques with first and third graders. *Journal of School Psychology, 14,* 322–332.

Simms, R. B. (1983). Feedback a key to effective writing. *Academic Therapy, 19* (1), 31–36.

Simon, D. J.; Velter-Zemitzch, A.; and Johnston, J. C. (1985). On campus: systemic behavioral interventions for behaviorally disordered adolescents. *Behavioral Disorders, 10,* 183–190.

Simon, J. B. (1980). *Teaching strategies.* New York: D.C. Heath and Co.

Simon, S. B.; Howe, L. W.; and Kirschenbaum, H. (1972). *Values clarification: A handbook of practical strategies for teachers and students.* New York: Hart Publishing Co.

Simons, R. L. (1982). Strategies for exercising influence. *Social Work, 27,* 268–273.

Simpson, D. D. (1974). Attention training through breathing control to modify hyperactivity. *Journal of Learning Disabilities,* 274–283.

Simpson, M. (1977). *Motor perceptual activities for the kindergarten child.* Wayne: NE: Wayne-Carroll Public Schools. (ERIC Document Reproduction Service No. ED 154 579).

Simpson, M. L. (1984). The status of study strategy instruction: Implications for classroom teachers. *Journal of Reading, 28* (2), 136–143.

Sinclair, E.; Guthrie, D.; and Forness, S. (1984). Establishing a connection between severity of learning disabilities and classroom attention problems. *Journal of Educational Research, 78,* 18–21.

Singer, R. N. (1972). *The psychomotor domain.* Philadelphia: Lea and Febeger.

Skinner, B. F..(1953). *Science and human behavior.* New York: Macmillan.

Slaby, R. G., and Crowley, C. G. (1977). Modification of cooperation and aggression through teacher attention to children's speech. *Journal of Experimental Child Psychology, 23,* 442–458.

Slater, E., and Roth (1969). *Clinical psychiatry* (3rd ed.). Baltimore: Williams and Wilkins Co.

Slavin, R. E. (1984). Students motivating students to excell: Cooperative incentives, cooperative tasks, and students achievement. *The Elementary School Journal, 85* (1), 53–63.

Slavson, S. R. (1952). *Child psychotherapy.* New York: Columbia University Press.

Sloane, H., and Jackson, D. (1974). *A guide to motivating learners.* Englewood Cliffs, NJ: Educational Technology.

Sloane, H. N. (1976). *Classroom management, remediation, and prevention.* New York: John Wiley & Sons.

Sloane, H. N., Jr. (1976). *Because I said so.* Fountain Valley, CA: Telesis, Ltd.

Smidt, I. (1984). Biomechanics and physical therapy. *Physical Therapy, 64* (12), 1809–1812.

Smith, B. (1969). *Perceptual training in the curriculum early.* Columbus, OH: Merrill Publishing Co.

Smith, B.; Schumaker, J.; Schaeffer, J.; and Sherman, J. (1982). Increasing participation and improving the quality of discussions in seventh grade social studies classes. *The Journal of Applied Behavioral Analysis, 15,* 97–110.

Smith, C. (1983). *Learning disabilities: The interaction of learner, task, and setting.* Toronto, Canada: Little, Brown & Company.

Smith, C. B., and Elliott, P. G. (1979). *Reading activities for middle and secondary schools.* New York: Holt, Rinehart and Winston.

Smith, D. D., and Lovitt, T. C. (1974). The influence of instructions and reinforcement contingencies on children's abilities to compute arithmetic problems. Kansas: University of Kansas. Paper presented at the Fifth Annual Conference on Behavior Analysis in Education.

Smith, D. L.; Hamrick, M. H.; and Anspaugh, D. J. (1981). Decision story strategy: A practical approach for teaching decision making. *The Journal of School Health, 51* (10), 637–640.

Smith, D. W. (1979). *Mothering your unborn baby.* London: W. B. Saunders Co.

Smith, J. (1981). Adolescent suicide: A growing problem for the school & family. *Urban Education, 16,* 279–296.

Smith, J. A. (1973). *Creative teaching of the language arts in the elementary school.* Boston: Allyn and Bacon.

Smith, L. (1977). *Improving your child's behavior chemistry.* New York: Guli and Western Corporation.

Smith, L., and Fowler, S. (1984). Positive peer pressure: The effects of peer monitoring on children's disruptive behavior. *Journal of Applied Behavior Analysis, 17* (2), 213–227.

Smith, P. B.; Wenney, S. W.; Weinman, M. L.; and Mumford, D. M. (1982). Factors affecting perception of pregnancy risk in adolescent. *Journal of Youth and Adolescence, 2* (3), 207–217.

Smith, P. J. (1983). Learning is fun. *Journal of Chemical Education, 60* (9), 741–43.

Smith, S. (1978). Some facts about asthma. *Journal of School Health, 48,* 311.

Smith, T. W.; Snyder, D. R.; and Perkins, S. C. (1983). The self-serving function of hypochondriacal complaints: Physical symptoms as self-handicapping strategies. *Journal of Personality and Social Psychology, 44* (4), 787–797.

Smith, W. (1981). A Christmas-theme test. *Mathematics Teacher, 74* (9), 718.

Smuin, C. (1978). *Turn-ons: 185 strategies for secondary classrooms* Belmont, CA: Fearon-Pitman.

Snell, M. E. (1973). *A modified language acquisition program for use by attendent-supervised, retarded trainer-student pairs.* (ERIC Document Reproduction Service No. ED 128 994).

Soderman, A. (1985). Dealing with difficult young children: Strategies for teachers and parents. *Young Children, 40* (5), 15–20.

Solomon, R. W., and Wahler, R. G. (1973). Peer reinforcement control or classroom problem behavior. *Journal of Applied Behavior Analysis, 6,* 49–56.

Sorell, H. (1978). *Innovative perceptual motor activities: Programming techniques that work.* (ERIC Document Reproduction Service No. ED 207 301).

Spadafore, G. (1979). A guide for the parent as tutor. *Exceptional Parent, 9* (4), 17–18.

Sparkmen, B., and Saul, J. (1977). *Preparing your preschooler for reading.* New York: Shocken Books.

Spaulding, R. (1983). A systematic approach to classroom discipline. Part 2. *Phi Delta Kappan, 65* (2).

Special Learning Corporation (1979). *Three models of learning disabilities.* Connecticut: Special Learning Corp.

Special Learning Corporation (1980). *Readings in spe-*

cial education. Connecticut: Special Learning Corp.

Spence, S. H. (1983). Teaching social skill to children. *Journal of Child Psychology and Psychiatry, 24,* 621.

Sperling, B. (1985). *Lively ideas for building reading readiness and language skills in extended day kindergartens.* (ERIC Document Reproduction Service No. ED 256 483).

Spielberger, C. D. (1966). *Anxiety and behavior.* New York: Academic Press.

Spivack, G., and Swift, S. (1975). *Aternative teaching strategies.* Champaign, IL: Research Press.

Spivak, G., and Spotts, J. (1966). *Devereux child behavior rating scale.* Devon, PA: Devereux Foundation.

Spivak, G.; Spotts, J.; and Haimes, P. (1967). *Devereux adolescent behavior rating scale.* Devon, PA: Devereux Foundation.

Spivak, G., and Swift, M. (1967). *Devereux elementary school behavior rating scale.* Devon, PA: Devereux Foundation.

Spivak, G., and Swift, M. (1971). *Hahnemann high school behavior rating scale.* Philadelphia: Hahnemann Medical College and Hospital.

Spivak, G., and Swift, M. (1975). *Hahnemann elementary school behavior rating scale.* Philadelphia: Hahnemann Medical College and Hospital.

Spock, B. (1976). *Baby and child care.* New York: Pocket Books.

Sprick, R. (1981). *The solution book: A guide to classroom discipline.* Chicago: Science Research Associates.

Staats, A. (1968). *Learning, language, and cognition.* New York: Holt, Rinehart and Winston.

Stahl, S. A. (1985). To teach a word well: A framework for vocabulary instruction. *Reading World,* 24 (3), 16–27.

Stamatelos, T., and Mott, D. (1983). *Writing as therapy.* New York: Teachers College Press.

Standish, R. (1983). *Creativity for kids through vocabulary development.* Illinois: Good Apple Publishing Company.

Stanley, L. (1980). Treatment of ritualistic behavior in an eight-year-old girl by response prevention: A case report. *Journal of Child Psychology and Psychiatry, 21,* 85–90.

Stanley, T.; Waglow, W.; and Alexander, P. (1973). *Physical education activities handbook.* Boston: Allyn and Bacon.

Staudacher, C. (1972). *Creative writing in the classroom.* New York: Scholastic Magazines.

Steere, A.; Peck, C. Z.; and Kahn, L. (1966). *Solving language difficulties.* Cambridge, MA: Educators Publishing Service.

Stefananich, G. P., and Bell, L. C. (1985). A dynamic model for classroom discipline. *NASSP Bulletin,* 69, 19–25.

Stein, M., and Davis, J. (1982). *Therapies for adolescents.* San Francisco: Jossey-Bass.

Stein, N., and Landis, R. (1978). Effects of age and collateral behavior on temporarily discriminated performance of children. *Perception and Motor Skills, 47,* 87–94.

Steinberg, F. (1980). *The immobilized patient.* New York: Plenum Medical Book.

Steinberg, R. (1985). How to teach intelligence. *Education Digest, 50,* 20–25.

Steindler, S. (1970). *Kinesiology of the human body.* Springfield, IL: Charles C. Thomas.

Stephens, J. (1981). *A practical guide to the use and implementation.* New York: Todd and Honeywell.

Stephens, T. (1975). *Implementation behavioral approaches in elementary and secondary schools.* Columbus, OH: Charles E. Merrill.

Stephens, T. (1978). *Social skills in the classroom.* Columbus, OH: Cedars Press.

Stephens, T.; Hartman, A.; and Lucas, V. (1978). *Teaching children basic skills.* Columbus, OH: Bell and Howell.

Stephens, T. M.; Hartman, S. C.; and Lucas, V. H. (1982). *Teaching children basic skills: A curriculum handbook.* Columbus, OH: Charles E. Merrill.

Stipek, D. J., and Tannat, L. (1984). Children's judgments of their own and their peers: Academic competence. *The Journal of Educational Psychology, 76,* 75–84.

Stivers, M. (1977). *The contract classroom.* Waukegan Behavior Analysis Follow Through Program. Washington D.C. (ERIC Document Reproduction Service No. ED 212 584).

Stock, C. (1970). *Learning activities.* Colorado: Learning Tasks.

Stokes, T. F., and Baer, D. M. (1977). An implicit technology of generalization. *Journal of Applied Behavior Analysis, 10,* 347–364.

Stoltz, M. (1977). *By going about it.* In D. R. Gallo (ed.), Teaching writing: Advice from the professionals. *Connecticut English Journal,* 12 (2), 8–9. (ERIC Document Reproduction Service No. ED 151 846).

Stone, M., and Sugarman, G. (1974). *Your hyperactive child.* Chicago: Henry Regnery Company.

Stoops, E. (1961). *Classroom personalities.* New York: The Economics Press.

Stoops, E., and King-Stoops, J. (1972). *Discipline or disaster?* Bloomington, IN: Phi Delta Kappa Educational Foundation.

Stowitschek, C. E., and Jobes, N. K. (1977). In D. Smith (ed.) (1981). *Teaching the learning disabled.* Englewood Cliffs, NJ: Prentice-Hall.

Stowitschek, J. (1984). *Direct teaching strategies for exceptional children.* Rockville, MD: Aspen Systems Corp.

Strachen, J. G. (1981). Conspicuous firesetting in children. *British Journal of Psychiatry, 138,* 26–29.

Strain, P. S.; Keer, M. M.; and Ragland, E. V. (1979). Effects of peer mediated social initiations in the treatment of social withdrawal. *Journal of School Psychology, 20,* 306–310.

Stratton, J. R., and Stratton, M. (1968). *Prevention of delinquency problems and programs.* London: Collier-Macmillian Limited.

Strauss, A., and Lehtinen, L. (1947). *Psychopathology and education of the brain-injured child, V.I.* New York: Grune & Stratton.

Straw, S. B. (1982). The effect of sentence manipulation on subsequent measures of reading and listening comprehension. *Reading Research Quarterly, 17,* 339–352.

Strayhorn, J. M., Jr. (1977). *Talking it out: Guide to effective communication and problem solving.* Champaign, IL: Research Press Co.

Strom, R. (1964). *The tragic migration.* Washington D.C.: Dept. of Home Economics, National Education Association.

Strothers, D. B. (1984). Homework: Too much, just right, not enough? *Phi Delta Kappan, 65* (6), 423–426.

Struthers, J. P.; Struthers, T. B.; and Williams, R. L. (1983). The effects of the add-a-word spelling program on spelling accuracy during creative writing. *Education & Treatment of Children, 6* (3), 277–283.

Stumphauzer, J. S. (1973). *Behavior therapy with delinquents.* Springfield, IL: Charles C. Thomas.

Stumphauzer, J. S. (1977). *Behavior modification principles.* Springfield, IL: Charles C. Thomas.

Sue, D.; Sue, D. W.; and Sue, S. (1981). *Understanding abnormal behavior.* Boston: Houghton-Mifflin.

Sugarman, M. D., and Stone, M. N. (1974). *Your hyperactive child.* Chicago: Henry Regnery Co.

Suicide prevention and crisis center of San Mateo County, CA. *Suicide in youth and what you can do about it: A guide for students.* West Point, PA: Merck Sharp & Dohme.

Suid, M. (1984). Speaking of speaking. *Instructor, 94* (9), 56–58.

Sulzer-Azaroff, B., and Mayer, R. (1977). *Applying behavior analysis procedures with children and youth.* New York: Holt, Rinehart and Winston.

Summers, E. G. (1980). Utilizing visual aids in reading materials for effective learning. *Perspectives in reading.* Delaware: International Reading Association.

Sunny, S.; Courington, T.; and Stephens, K. (1978). *A curriculum guide for early childhood.* Illinois: Developmental Learning Materials.

Survant, A. (1972). Building positive self-concepts. *Instructor, 81,* 94–95.

Sutherland, E., and Cressey, D. (1970). *Criminology.* Philadelphia: J. B. Lippincott.

Swanson, L. (1983). A study of nonstrategic linguistic coding on visual recall of learning disabled readers. *Journal of Learning Disabilities, 16,* 212–217.

Swap, S. (1974). Disturbing classroom behaviors: A developmental and ecological view. *Exceptional Children, 41* (3), 43–50.

Swartz, S. L.; Benjamin, C.; and Brown, D. J. (1981). *The use of time-out in a residential treatment program for emotionally disturbed children.* (ERIC Document Reproduction Service No. ED 212 111).

Swift, M. S., and Spivak, G. (1975). *Alternative teaching strategies.* Champaign, IL: Research Press.

Swisher, K. (1984). Increasing word power through spelling activities. *The Reading Teacher, 37,* 227–210.

Tahka, V. (1966). *The alcoholic personality.* Finland: Finnish Foundation for Alcohol Studies.

Tarvis, C. (1983). The furious feminist: Finding the line between blame and responsibility. *Ms, 11,* 81.

Tate, B. G., and Baroff, G. S. (1966). Aversive control of self-injurious behavior in a psychotic boy. *Behavior Research and Therapy, 4,* 281–287.

Tauber, R. (1981). Power struggles: Techniques to diffuse them. *NASSP Bulletin, 65* (448), 53–58.

Tauber, R. (1983). Utilizing overlooked sources of school discipline. *NASSP Bulletin, 57* (462), 52–57.

Taylor, A. (1977). In D. R. Gallo (ed.), Teaching writing: Advice from the professionals. *Connecticut*

English Journal, 12 (2), 11. (ERIC Document Reproduction Service No. ED 151 846).

Taylor, B., and Nosbush, L. (1983). Oral reading for meaning: A technique for improving word identification skills. *The reading teacher, 37* (3), 234–237.

Taylor, J. F. (1980). *The hyperactive child and the family.* New York: Everst House.

Taylor, L. B. (1979). *Shoplifting.* New York: Franklin Watts.

Taylor, L. B. (1982). When honest women steal. *Ladies Home Journal, 94* (1), 102.

Taylor, Z. A., and Sherrill, C. (1969). *A health-centered approach for educationally handicapped children.* Sunnyvale, CA: Peek Publications.

Teachman, G. (1979). In school truancy in urban schools: The problem and a solution. *Phi Delta Kappan, 61,* 203–205.

Teerney, C. C. (1985). Patterns in the multiplication tables. *Arithmetic Teacher, 32* (7), 36–40.

Terman, L. M., and Oden, M. H. (1976). The Terman study of intellectually gifted children. In W. Dennis and M. Dennis (eds.), *The intellectually gifted.* New York: Grune and Stratton.

Terrell, C. (1983). *The effects of a systematic study interval peer tutoring, and mutual behavioral contracting on unit spelling accuracy of adolescent learning disabled students.* Washington D.C.: (ERIC Document Reproduction Service No. ED 232 374).

Terry, B., et al. (1981). *Effects of environmental manipulation, curriculum changes and implementation of a token system on on-task behavior of second and third graders in a learning disabled classroom.* New Orleans: The council for Exceptional Children Conference on the Exceptional Black Child. (ERIC Document Reproduction Service No. ED 204 897).

Thoburn, T.; Schlatterbeck, R.; and Terry, A. (1983). *Macmillan English.* New York: Macmillan.

Thomas, E. L., and Robinson, H. A. (1972). *Improving reading in every class.* Boston: Allyn and Bacon.

Thompson, C., and Poppen, W. (1972). *For those who care: Ways of relating to youth.* Columbus, OH: Charles E. Merrill.

Thompson, L., and Shapiro, J. (1984). Differential recall as a function of mood disorder in clinically depressed patients: Between and within subject differences. *The Journal of Abnormal Psychology, 93,* 391–400.

Thompson, R. W.; Teare, J. F.; and Elliott, S. N.

(1983). Impulsivity from theoretical constructs to applied interventions. *Journal of Special Education, 17* (2), 157–169.

Thompson, V. M. (1977). The school nurse looks at psychogenic illness. *The Journal of School Health, 47,* 519–521.

Thornhill, M. (1976). *Motor enrichment.* Putnam City, OK: Putnam City Public Schools. (ERIC Document Reproduction Service No. ED 145 628).

Thorpe, H. W., and Borden, K. S. (1985). The effect of multisensory instruction upon the on-task behaviors and word reading accuracy of learning disabled children. *Journal of Learning Disabilities, 18* (5), 279–286.

Time (1980). Pilfering urges: Is shoplifting an illness? *116* (20), 94.

Tindel, C. (1983). 26 tips for building self-concept. *Academic Therapy, 19* (1), 103–105.

Tingey-Michaelis, C. (1985). Stress getting out from under. *Early Years, 15* (5), 35.

Tippelt, G. G. (1983). A process model of the pregnancy course. *Human Development, 26,* 134–147.

Titus, C. (1974). The use of the lecture. *Clearinghouse,* 383–384.

Tobias, S. (1980). Math anxiety: What you can do about it. *Today's Education, 69* (3), 26–29.

Today's Education (1982–83). Annual, 60.

Todt, E. (1983). *Evidence for an anorexic bulmic: MMPI profile.* Salt Lake City: University of Utah School of Medicine. (ERIC Document Reproduction Service No. ED 235 450).

Tollefson, N. (1981). *Implementing goal setting activities with learning disabled adolescents.* Kansas University. (ERIC Document Reproduction Service No. ED 217 653).

Tollesfson, N. (1982). *Parental strategies for reducing learned helplessness behavior among learning disabled students.* (ERIC Document Reproduction Service No. ED 226 547).

Toner, I. (1978). Effect of serving as a model of self-control on subsequent resistance to deviation in children. *Journal of Experimental Child Psychology, 26,* 85–91.

Torgesen, N. K. (1985). Memory processes in reading disabled children. *Journal of Learning Disabilities, 18* (6), 314–355.

Torrance, E. P. (1962). Curriculum frontiers for the elementary gifted pupil: Flying monkeys and silent lions. *Exceptional Child, 28,* 119–127.

Trabasso, A., and Bower, G. H. (1968). *Attention in learning.* New York: John Wiley & Sons.

Trabasso, A., and Bower, B. (1968). Cited in F. Geogre (1982). *Promoting attention in children with learning disabilities*. Houston, TX. (ERIC Document Reproduction Service No. ED 218 912).

Travers, K., et al. (1972) *Teaching resources for low achieving mathematics classes. Prep-30.* Washington D.C.: National Center for Education Communication. (ERIC Document Reproduction Service No. ED 059 413).

Treiber, F. A., and Lahey, B. B. (1983). Toward a behavioral model of academic remediation with learning disabled children. *Journal of Learning Disabilities, 16* (2), 111–115.

Treiman, R. (1985). Phonemic awareness & spelling: Children's judgements do not always agree with adults. *Journal of Experimental Child Psychology, 39* (1), 182–201.

Trentham, L. L. (1984). *Anxiety and stress.* Florida State University. (Great Studies microfilm BF 723 C7 T7).

Treslan, D. L. (1983). The mechanism for involving students in decision making. *Clearing House, 57* (3), 124–131.

Trice, A. D., and Parker, F. C. (1983). Decreasing adolescent swearing in an instructional setting. *Education and Treatment of Children, 6,* 29–35.

Trice, A. D.; Parker, F. C.; Furrow, F.; and Iwata, M. M. (1983). An analysis of home contingencies to improve school behavior with disruptive adolescents. *Education and Treatment of Children, 6,* 389–399.

Trojanowicz, R. (1978). *Juvenile delinquency concepts and control.* Englewood Cliffs, NJ: Prentice-Hall.

Trueman, D. (1984). The behavioral treatment of school phobia: A critical review. *Psychology in the Schools, 21* (2), 215–223.

Truhlicka, M. (1982). An investigation of the effects of behavior therapy vs drug therapy in the treatment of the hyperactive child. *Journal for Special Educators, 18* (4), 35–40.

Trujillo, L. A. (1981). *Enhancement of self-concept and academic achievement through ethnic dance.* (Report No. RC-013-775). Colorado University, Boulder: Center for Bilingual Multicultural Education Research and Service. (ERIC Document Reproduction Service No. ED 225 735).

Trombly, R. M. (1979). *Tobacco education: Substance abuse prevention.* (ERIC Document Reproduction Service No. ED 180 986).

Tunnell, G. (1981). *Variability in self-presentation to others: The effect of public self-consciousness.* Smith College. (ERIC Document Reproduction Service No. ED 211 893).

Turnbull, J., and Schulz, T. (1979). *Mainstreaming handicapped students.* Boston: Allyn and Bacon.

Turner, P. M. (1982). Cueing and anxiety in a visual concept learning task. (ERIC Document Reproduction Series No. ED 223 234).

Turner, R. K. (1973). *Conditioning treatment of noctural enuresis.* Philadelphia: Internal Medical Publication.

Turner, W. E. (1970). Individualizing spelling with 600 students. *Instructor, 80* (1), 123–126.

Tyne, F. (1979). The remediation of elementary students low social status through a teacher-centered program. *Journal of School Psychology, 17,* 244–245.

Tyrrell, R.; McCarty, F.; and Johns, F. (1977). The many faces of anger. *Teacher, 94,* 60–63.

Underwood, G. (1976). *Attention and memory.* New York: Pergamon Press.

Unger, K.; Douds, A.; and Pierce, R. (1978). Truancy prevention project. *Phi Delta Kappan, 60,* 317.

U.S. Department of Health and Human Services (1981). *Stuttering: hope through research.* Maryland: National Institute of Health.

University of Illinois, Board of Trustees (1984). *Suicide prevention.* Urbana-Champaign, Ill.

University of Illinois, Board of Trustees (1984). *Understanding depression.* Urbana-Champaign, Ill.

Upton, G. (1980). *Physical and creative activities for the mentally handicapped.* Cambridge, England: Cambridge University Press.

Usova, G. M. (1980). Reducing discipline problems in the elementary schools: Approaches and suggestions. *Education, 99,* 419–422.

Vacc, N. A., and Siegel, P. (1980). Children who are physically separated in the classroom. *Journal of Behavior Disorders, 5,* 235–239.

Valett, R. (1974). *The remediation of learning disabilities, a handbook of psychoeducational resource programs.* California: Fearon Pitman Publishers.

Valett, R. (1983). Developing linguistic auditory memory patterns. *The Journal of Learning Disabilities, 16,* 462–466.

Van Allen, A.; Roach, L.; Allen, N.; and Clalyce, M. (1976). *Language experience activities.* Boston: Houghton Mifflin.

Vandersall, T. A., and Wiener, J. M. (1970). Children who set fires. *Archives of General Psychiatry, 22,* 63–71.

Van Hauten, R.; Nau, P. A.; Mackenzie-Keating, S. E.; Sameoto, D.; and Cdaneichia, B. (1982). An analysis of some variables influencing the effectiveness of reprimands. *Journal of Applied Behavior Analysis, 15* (1), 65–83.

Vankoughnet, B. C., and Smith, M. E. (1969). Enhancing the self-concept in the school. *Educational Leadership, 27,* 253–254.

VanNagel, C., and Deering-Levin, S. (1984). *The art of managing verbal aggression in the classroom.* Washington, D.C.: (ERIC Document Reproduction Service No. ED 245 485).

Van Riper, C. (1971). *The nature of stuttering.* Englewood Cliffs, NJ: Prentice-Hall.

Van Riper, C. (1973). *The treatment of stuttering.* Englewood Cliffs, NJ: Prentice-Hall.

Van Riper, C. (1978). *Speech corrections: Principles and methods.* Englewood Cliffs, NJ: Prentice-Hall.

Van Witsen, B. (1979). *Perceptual training activities handbook.* New York: Teachers College Press.

Van Witsen, E. (1984). *Perceptual activities handbook.* Garden Grove, CA: CANHC Publication and Resources.

Vargas, J. S. (1977). *Behavioral psychology for teachers.* New York: Harper & Row.

Vernon, W. M. (1972). *Motivating children.* New York: Holt, Rinehart and Winston.

Verville, E. (1967). *Behavior problems of children.* Philadelphia: W. B. Saunders.

Vestermark, S. D., and Blauvelt, P. D. (1978). *Controlling crime in the school: A complete security handbook for administrators.* West Nyack, NY: Parker Publishing Co.

Vetter, A. (1979). The withdrawn child. *The Pointer, 24* (1), 21–23.

Vincent, J., and Glennon (1952). An interdisciplinary approach. *The Mathematical Education of Exceptional Children and Youth Professional Reference Series, 12* (2), 18–21.

Virden, T. (1984). *Supportive peer groups: A behavior management program for children.* (ERIC Document Reproduction Service No. ED 247 693).

Von Baeyer, C. (1982). Repression, sensitization, stress, and perception of pain in others. *Perceptual and Motor Skills, 55* (1), 315–320.

Wade, B., and Moore, R. (1984). Coping with disruption at school. *Special education, Forward trends, 11* (3), 27–30.

Wade, B. E. (1981). Highly anxious pupils in formal and informal primary classrooms: The relationship between inferred coping strategies and I-cognitive attainment. *British Journal of Educational Psychology, 51* (1), 50–57.

Wagberg, E. G.; Thompson, B.; and Levitov, J. E. (1984). First steps toward an adult basic word list. *Journal of Reading, 28* (3), 244–247.

Wagner, H. (1983). Discipline in the schools is inseparable from teaching. *Education, 103,* 390–394.

Wagner, M. E. (1974). *Put it all together.* Grand Rapids: Zondervan.

Wagner, R. (1971). *Dyslexia and your child.* New York: Harper & Row.

Wagoner, G. (1975). The trouble is in your set: The television as homonuculus. *Phi Delta Kappan, 3,* 179–184.

Walberg, H. (1984). Families as partners in educational productivity. *Phi Delta Kappan, 65,* 397–400.

Walch, M. W. and Gist, J. W. *Open token economy system.* Springfield, IL: Charles C. Thomas.

Walden, E., and Thompson, S. (1981). Review all alternate approaches to drug management of hyperactive children. *Journal of Learning Disabilities, 14* (4), 213–217.

Walker, H. (1979). *The acting-out child: Coping with classroom disruption.* Boston, Allyn and Bacon.

Walker, H. (1983). *Walker problem behavior identification checklist.* Los Angeles: Western Psychological Services.

Walker, H. M., and Buckley, N. K. (1968). The use of positive reinforcement in conditioning attending behavior. *Journal of Applied Behavior Analysis,* (1), 245–250.

Walker, H. M. and Shea, T. M. (1980). *Behavior modification* (2nd ed). St. Louis: C. V. Mosby.

Walker, J. J., and Walker, W. G. (1981). *Create a superhero.* Carthage, IL: Good Apple.

Walker, M. M. (1982). Phosphates and hyperactivity: Is there a connection? *Academic Therapy, 17* (4), 439–446.

Wallace, E. E. (1984). *The Riverside spelling program.* Illinois: Riverside Publishing Co.

Wallace, G., and Kauffman, J. M. (1973). *Teaching children with learning problems.* Columbus, OH: Bell and Howell.

Wallace, G., and McLoughlin, J. (1975). *Learning disabilities: Concepts and characteristics.* Columbus, OH: Charles Merrill.

Walsh, S. (1973). I'm me! *Teaching Exceptional Children, 5* (6), 78–83.

Walters, R. (1981). *Anger—yours and mine and what to do about it.* Grand Rapids: Zondervan.

Warner, J. (1973). *Learning disabilities: Activities for remediation.* Illinois: The Interstate Printers and Publishers.

Warner, J.; Byers-Brown, B.; and McCartney, E. (1984). *Speech therapy: A clinical companion.* Dover, NH: Manchester University Press.

Warner, M., and Alley, G. (1981). *Teaching learning disabled junior high students to use visual imagery as a strategy for facilitating recall for reading passages.* Washington D.C.: Bureau of Education for the Handicapped. (ERIC Document Reproduction Service No. ED 217 654).

Warren, S. (1977). The truth about children's lies. *The Education Digest, 42,* 51–53.

Warrenfeltz, R. B. (1981). Social skills training of behavior disordered adolescents with self-monitoring to promote generalization to a vocational setting. *Behavioral Disorders, 7,* 18–27.

Washington, R. (1977). Success: A parent effectiveness approach for developing urban children's self-concepts. *Young Child, 32,* 5–10.

Wasicko, M. M., and Ross, S. M. (1982). How to create discipline problems. *Clearing House, 56* (4), 149–152.

Wassermann, S. (1984). Promoting thinking in the classroom. *Education Digest, 50,* 49–51.

Wasson, A. (1980). Stimulus seeking perceived school environment and school misbehavior. *Adolescence, 15,* 603–608.

Waters, G. S.; Seidenberg, M. S.; and Bruck, M. (1984). Children's and adult's use of spelling sound information in three reading tasks. *Memory and Cognition, 12* (3), 293–305.

Waters, H. (1978). What TV does to kids. *Newsweek,* 63–65.

Watrin, R., and Furfey, P. H. (1978). *Learning activities for the young preschool child.* New York: VanNostrand.

Watson, A., and Dodd, C. (1984). Alleviating communication apprehension through rational emotive therapy: A comparative evaluation. *Communication Education, 33* (3), 257–266.

Watson, D. L., and Tharp, R. G. (1981). *Self directed behavior: Self-modification for personal adjustment.* New York: Brookes & Cole.

Watson, G. (1963). *No room at the botton.* Washington D.C.: NEA Publications.

Watson, J. (1982). Activities to help communication.

Special Education Forward Trends: British Journal of Special Education, 9, 35–36.

Watson, L. S. (1973). *Child behavior modification: A manual for teachers, nurses, or parents.* Elmsford, NY: Pergamon Press.

Watson, L. S., Jr. (1972). *How to use behavior modification with mentally retarded and autistic children.* IL: Behavior Modification Technology.

Watters, R. G., and Watters, W. E. (1980). Decreasing self-stimulatory behavior with physical exercixe in a group of autistic boys. *Journal of Autism and Developmental Disorders, 10,* 379–387.

Webb, C., and Baird, J. (1980). Three strategies for motivating pupils. *Clearing House, 54* (1), 27–29.

Webb, N. M. (1982). Group composition, group interaction, and achievement in cooperative small groups. *Journal of Educational Psychology, 74,* 475–484.

Webster, R. E. (1981). *A cognitive behavioral approach for dealing with emotionally disturbed adolescents in a public school setting.* Manchester, CT: Manchester Community College. (ERIC Document Reproduction Service No. ED 213 166).

Wedemeyer, A., and Cejka, B. (1975). *Creative ideas for teaching exceptional children.* Denver: Love Publishing Company.

Wegman, R., and Talent, B. (1982). *Todays Education, 71* (3), 44–45.

Weingartner, H. (1985). Tips to help remember what was it you forgot. *U.S. News & World Report, 98,* 72.

Weinhold, B. K., and Hilferty, J. (1983). The self esteem matrix: A tool for elementary counselors. *Elementary School Guidance and Counseling, 4,* 243–251.

Weisfeld, G., and Feldman, R. (1982). A former street gang leader reinterviewed eight years later. *Crime and Delinquency, 28,* 567–581.

Weiss, H. G., and Weiss, M. S. (1982). Training kids to be winners in the handling of writing skills. *Academic Therapy, 18,* 75–82.

Weissbourd, B. (1984). Understanding aggression. *Parents,* Nov., 168.

Weissenburger, F. E., and Loney, J. (1977). Hyperkinesis in the classroom: If cerebral stimulants are the last resort, what is the first resort? *Journal of Learning Disabilities, 10* (6), 18–26.

Wellington, C. B., and Wellington, J. (1979). The underachiever. *Challenges and Guidelines.* Chicago: Rand McNally & Co.

Wells, T., and Luttgens, N. (1976). *Kinesiology*. Philadelphia: W. B. Saunders.

Wender, P. H. (1973). *The hyperactive child*. New York: Crown Publishers.

Werner, H., and Strauss, A. A. (1941). Pathology of figure-background relation in the child. *Journal of Abnormal and Social Psychology, 36* (2), 336–348.

Werner, P. H., and Burton, E. C. (1979). *Learning through movement: Teaching cognitive content through physical activities*. St. Louis: C. V. Mosby Co.

Wesley, G. R. (1972). *A primer of misbehavior*. Chicago: Nelson Hall.

Wessel, D. (1982). *Reducing problems in fine motor development among primary children through the use of multi-sensory techniques*. A practium report submitted to the faculty of the center for the advancement of education at Nova University for the degree of master of science. (ERIC Document Reproduction Service No., ED 235 912).

Wessel, D., and Body, A., (1970). *Contouring and conditioning through movement*. Boston: Allyn and Bacon.

Wessman, A. E., and Ricks, D. F. (1966). *Mood and personality*. New York: Holt, Rinehart & Winston.

West, D. (1973). *Who becomes delinquent?* London: Heinemann.

Whaley, D. L., and Mallott, R. W. (1970). *Elementary principles of behavior*. Englewood Cliffs, NJ: Prentice-Hall.

Wheeler, K., and Wheeler, M. (1974). School phobia. *Instructor, 83*, 16.

Whitehurst, G. (1984). Developing referential communication a hierarchy of skills. *Child Development, 55*, 1936–1945.

Whong, P. L.; Fletcher, R. K.; and Fawcett, S. B. (1982). Training counseling skills: An experimental analysis and social validation. *Journal of Applied Behavior Analysis, 15*, (3), 325–334.

Wiens, J. W. (1983). Metacognition and the adolescent passive learner. *Journal of Learning Disabilities, 16* (3), 147.

Wiesen, A. E. (1974). *Changing classroom behavior*. New York: Intext Educational Publishers.

Wietig, P., and Elston, J. (1980). Structured learning: A curricular response. Paper presented to Amherst Junior High School Curriculum Awareness, Amherst, N.Y.

Wilcox, R. T. (1983). Discipline made gentle. *Clearing House, 57* (4), 30–35.

Wiley, W. (1974). *The series in clinical psychology*. Washington D.C.: Hemisphere Publishing Corp.

Wilkinson, A. (1976). Counting strategies and semantic analysis as applied to class inclusion. *Cognitive Psychology, 8* (1), 64–85.

Williams, J. D. (1952). Teaching technique in primary maths. *Exploring Education National Foundation for Educational Research in England and Wales, 10* (1), 19–24.

Williams, S. (1983). A comparison of objective classroom measures and teacher ratings of attention deficit disorder. *Journal of Abnormal Child Psychology, 13* (1), 155–169.

Williams, R., Sbaschnig, V. Polk, L., and Hleim, W. (1984). *99 easy to use speech and language activities*. Tuscon, AZ: Communication Skill Builders.

Williamson, B. L., and Crewell, R. M. (1984). Dropping the dropout rate in Guilderland. *NYSSBA Journal, 11*, 20–23.

Williamson, G. (1980). The ecological treatment of hyperkinesis. *Psychology in the Schools, 17* (2), 249–256.

Willings, D. (1983). Issues in career choices for gifted children. *Teaching Exceptional Children, 15*, 226–233.

Willoughby, H., and Plumton, D. (1983). Modern rythmic gymnastics: A supplement to K-12 physical education. *Curriculum Guide, Curriculum support Series*. (ERIC Document Reproduction Service No. ED 219 496).

Wilson, G., and O'Leary, K. (1980), *Priniciples of behavior therapy*. Englewood Cliffs, NJ: Prentice Hall.

Wilson, M. G., and Glynn, T. L. (1983). Increasing self-selection and self-location of words by mildly retarded children during story writing. *Exceptional Child, 30* (3), 210–220.

Wilson, R. (1984). A review of self control treatments for aggressive behavior. *Behavioral Disorders, 9*, 131–140.

Wilt, J., and Watson T. (1977). *Touch*. Texas: Creative Resources.

Windwer, C. (1980). An ascending music stimulus program and hyperactive children. *Journal of Research in Music Education, 29*, 176–181.

Winfield, E. (1984). Books for building self-esteem and understanding. *PTA Today, 9* (5), 22-23.

Winick, M. (1975). *Childhood obesity*. New York: Wiley & Sons.

Winn, M. (1977). *The plug-in drug*. New York: Viking Press.

Winston, S. (1979). How to get organized at work and home. *U.S. News and World Report, 86*, 76–79.

Winter, A., and Wright, E. N. (1983). *A follow up of pupils who entered learning disabilities, self contained in 1981–1982*. Ontario. (ERIC Document Reproduction Service No. ED 238 224).

Wirtanen, I. D. (1969). *Why and how young men drop out of high school: Some preliminary findings*. Ann Arbor, MI: Institute of Social Research (ERIC Document Reproduction Service No. ED 028 491).

Witt, J. (1968). *The life enrichment activity program: A brief history*. New Haven, CT: Leap.

Witt, J. (1985). Acceptability of reductive interventions for the control of inappropriate child behavior. *Journal of Abnormal Child Psychology, 13* (1), 59–67.

Witt, J. C., and Elliot, S. N. (1982). The response cost lottery: A time efficient and effective classroom intervention. *Journal of School Psychology, 20* (2), 155–161.

Wold, R. M. (1969). *Visual and perceptual aspects for the achieving and underachieving child*. Seattle, WA: Special Child Publications.

Wolf, E. (1982). *Handbook for special education teachers*. (ERIC Document Reproduction No. ED 255 006).

Wolf, S., and Berle, B. (1976). *The biology of the schizophrenic process*. New York: Plenum Press.

Wolfe, V. V.; Boyd, L. A.; and Wolfe, D. A. (1983). Teaching cooperative play to behavior problem preschool children. *Education and Treatment of Children, 6*, 1–9.

Wolff, J. M., and Lipe, D. (1978). *Help for the overweight child*. New York: Stein & Day Publishers.

Wolfgang, C. (1980). Many faces of praise. *Early Child Development and Care, 9*, 237–243.

Wolfgang, C. H., and Glickman, C. D. (1980). *Solving discipline problems: Strategies for classroom teachers*. Boston: Allyn and Bacon.

Wolfgang, M.; Figlio, R.; and Sellin, T. (1972). *Delinquency in birth cohort*. Chicago: University of Chicago Press.

Wollert, R. (1981). *Casual attributes and normal mood variations*. Portland State University. (ERIC Document Reproduction Service No. ED 214 043).

Wolman, B. (ed.). (1965). *Handbook of clinical psychology*. New York: McGraw-Hill.

Womack, S. T. (1983). How to stop kids from talking back. *Clearing House, 56* (5), 221–222.

Wood, J. (1984). Let's take a closer look. *Academic Therapy, 20*, 149–157.

Wooden, W. S. (1985). Little swamis. *Psychology Today, 19*, 16.

Woodworth, R. (1938). *Experimental psychology*. New York: Holt, Rinehart, and Winston.

Woody, R. H. (1971). Controlling pica via an environmental psychological behavioral strategy: With special reference to lead poisoning. *The Journal for School Health, 41* (10), 548–555.

Woolfolk, A. E., and Woolfolk, R. L. (1974). A contingency management technique for increasing student attention in a small group setting. *Journal of School Psychology, 12*, 204–212.

Woots, T. (1982). Reducing severe aggressive and self-injurious behaviors: A nonintrusive, home based approach. *Behavioral Disorders, 7*, 180–188.

Worden, P.; Malmgren, I.; and Gabourie, P. (1982). Memory stories for learning disabled adults. *The Journal of Learning Disabilities, 15*, 145–153.

Worden, P. E. (1975). Effects of sorting on subsequent recall of unrelated items. *Child Development, 46* (3), 687–695.

Worden, P. E. (1976). The effects of classification structure on organized free recall in children. *Journal of Experimental Child Psychology, 22* (3), 519–529.

World book encyclopedia, 11. Chicago.

Worth, M. (1972). *Deviations from sexual norms, H.E.L.P.* Champaign: University of Illinois.

Wriely, M. (1982). Student drop outs: When did the problem begin? *Elementary School Journal, 8*, 12–16.

Wright, D., and Wright, J. (1980) Handwriting: The effectiveness of copying from moving versus still models. *Journal of Educational Research. 74* (2), 95–98.

Wright, L. (1975). Handling the encopretic child. *Professional Psychology, 4*, 137–144.

Yamamoto, K. (1972). *The child and his image*. Boston: Houghton Mifflin.

Yass, F. (1973). Therapy in development apraxia of speech. *Journal of Speech & Hearing Disorder, 38*, 481–486.

Yinger, J., et al. (1976). *Organizing and managing the classroom: The responsive education program curriculum guide*. San Francisco, CA: Far West Lab for Education Research and Development. (ERIC Document Reproduction Service No. ED 244 905).

Young, M. (1967). *Teaching children with special learn-*